A Literal Translation of Those Satires of Juvenal and Persius Which Are Read in Trinity College, Dublin; With Copious Explanatory Notes

Juvenal & Persius.

R. BEERE AND CO. PRINTERS, 28, L. STRAND-ST.

Junius Decimus Juvenalis

A

LITERAL TRANSLATION

OF THOSE

SATIRES

OF

JUVENAL AND PERSIUS

WHICH ARE READ IN

Trinity College, Dublin;

WITH

COPIOUS EXPLANATORY

NOTES.

BY THE REVEREND M. MADAN.

In this Edition the exceptionable Passages are omitted, several inaccuracies corrected and deficiencies supplied.

" *Ardet...Instat...Aperte jugulat.*"   SCAL. in JUV.

DUBLIN:

PRINTED FOR A. WATSON, CAPEL-STREET.

1822.

PREFACE

TO

JUVENAL.

DECIMUS JUNIUS JUVENAL was born at Aqui-
num, a town of the Volsci, a people of Latium: hence,
from the place of his birth, he was called Aquinas. It is
not certain whether he was the *son*, or foster-child, of a
rich freedman. He had a learned education, and, in the
time of Claudius Nero, pleaded causes with great reputation. About his middle age he applied himself to the
study of *Poetry*; and, as he saw a daily increase of vice
and folly, he addicted himself to writing *Satire*: but having said something (sat. vii. l. 88—92.) which was deemed
a reflection on Paris the actor, a minion of Domitian's, he
was banished into Egypt, at * eighty years of age, under
pretence of sending him as *captain* of a company of soldiers. This was looked upon as a sort of humourous punishment for what he had said, in making Paris the bestower
of posts in the army.

However, Domitian dying soon after, Juvenal returned
to Rome, and is said to have lived there to the times † of
Nerva and Trajan. At last, worn out with old age, he ex-
pired in a fit of coughing.

* Quanquam Octogenarius. MARSHALL, in Vit. Juv.
† Ibique ad Nervæ et Trajani tempora supervixisse dicitur MARSHAL. Ib.

He was a man of excellent morals, of an elegant taste and judgment, a fast friend to Virtue, and an irreconcilable enemy to Vice in every shape.

The attentive reader of Juvenal may see, as in a glass, a true portraiture of the Roman manners in his time: here he may see, drawn to the life, a people sunk in sloth, luxury, and debauchery, and exhibiting to us the sad condition of human nature, when untaught by divine truth, and uninfluenced by a divine principle. However polite and refined this people was, with respect to the cultivation of letters, arts, and sciences, beyond the most barbarous nations, yet, as to the true knowledge of God, they were upon a footing with the most uninformed of their contemporaries, and consequently were, equally with them, sunk into all manner of wickedness and abomination. The description of the Gentiles in general, by St. Paul, Rom. i. 19—32. is fully verrified as to the Romans in particular.

Juvenal may be looked upon as one of those rare meteors, which shone forth even in the darkness of Heathenism. The mind and conscience of this great man were, though from * whence he knew not, so far enlightened, as to perceive the ugliness of vice, and so influenced with a desire to reform it, as to make him, according to the light he had, a severe and able reprover, a powerful and diligent witness against the vices and follies of the people among which he lived; and indeed, against all who, like them, give a loose to their depraved appetites, as if there were no other liberty to be sought after but the most unrestrained indulgence of vicious pleasures and gratifications.

As to the old objection, that translations of the Classics tend to make boys idle, this can never happen but through the fault of the master, in not properly watching over the method of their studies. A master should never suffer a

* Rom. ii. 15. Comp. Isaiah xlv. 5. See Sat. x. l. 332. and note.

boy to construe his lesson in the school, but from the Latin by itself, nor without making the boy parse, and give an account of every necessary word; this will drive him to his *grammar* and *dictionary*, nearly as much as if he had no translation at all: but in private, when the boy is preparing his lesson, a literal *translation*, and *explanatory notes*, so facilitate the right comprehension and understanding of the author's language, meaning, and design, as to imprint them with ease on the learner's mind, to form his taste, and to enable him not only to construe and explain, but to get those portions of the author by heart, which he is at certain periods to repeat at school, and which, if judiciously selected, he may find useful, as well as ornamental to him, all his life.

To this end I have considered that there are three purposes to be answered. First that, the reader should know *what* the author says; this can only be attained by literal translation: as for poetical versions, which are so often miscalled translations, paraphrases, and the like, they are but ill calculated for this fundamental and necessary purpose.

The next thing to be considered, after knowing *what* the author says, is *how* he says it: this can only be learnt from the original itself, to which I refer the reader, by printing the Latin, line for line, opposite to the English, and, as the lines are numbered, the eye will readily pass from the one to the other. The information which has been received from the translation, will readily assist in the grammatical construction.

The third particular, without which the reader would fall very short of understanding the author, is to know *what he means*; to explain this is the intention of the notes, for many of which I gratefully acknowledge myself chiefly indebted to various learned commentators, but who, having written in Latin, are almost out of the reach of those for whom this work is principally intended. Here and there I have selected some notes from English writers: this indeed the student might have done for himself; but I hope he will not take it amiss, that I have brought so many different commentators into one view, and saved much trouble to him, at the expence of my own labour. The rest of the notes, and those no inconsiderable number, perhaps the most, are my own, by which, if I have been happy enough to supply any deficiencies of others, I shall be glad.

The corrections of the present Edition are in general taken from that published for the use of the Students by Dr. Elrington, (now Bishop of Limerick). In some parts, Notes which appeared unnecessary have been omitted, and others of more consequence introduced. The Translation has been retained according to the original plan; except where the most approved commentators were not followed, or the sentiments of the Author were too obscurely expressed.—As this is professedly a *literal* Translation, and aspires not to elegance of style, objections should be directed not against the performance, but the principle on which it is formed; with respect to this, it may be sufficient to remark, that Translations, on the plan of the present, while they afford sufficient assistance to the industrious, are far from granting that pernicious aid, which disheartens the studious by placing the negligent on a level with them, and which by encouraging idleness, effectually prevents any solid classical acquirements.

DECIMI

JUNII JUVENALIS

AQUINATIS

SATIRÆ SELECTÆ.

SELECT SATIRES

OF

JUVENAL.

B

DECIMI
JUNII JUVENALIS
AQUINATIS
SATIRÆ SELECTÆ.

Satira Prima.

ARGUMENT.

JUVENAL begins this satire with giving some humourous reasons for his writing: such as hearing, so often, many ill poets rehearse their works, and intending to repay them in kind. Next he informs us, why he addicts himself to satire, rather than to other poetry, and gives a summary and general view of the reigning vices and follies of his time. He laments the restraints which the

SEMPER ego auditor tantum ? nunquamne reponam,
Vexatus toties rauci Theseïde Codri ?
Impune ergo mihi recitaverit ille togatas,

Satires] Or satyrs. Concerning this word, see CHAMBERS's Dictionary.

Line 1. Only a hearer.] Juvenal complains of the irksome recitals, which the scribbling poets were continually making of their vile compositions, and of which he was a hearer, at the public assemblies, where they read them over. It is to be observed, that, sometimes, the Romans made private recitals of their poetry, among their peculiar friends. They also had public recitals, either in the temple of Apollo, or in spacious houses, which were either hired, or lent, for the purpose, by some rich and great man, who was highly honoured for this, and who got his clients and dependents together on the occasion, in order to increase the audience, and to encourage the poet by their applauses. See sat. vii. 40—4. Persius prolog. l. 7. and note. HOR. lib. i. sat. iv. l. 73, 4.

—*Repay.*] Reponam here is used metaphorically ; it alludes to the borrowing and repayment of money. When a man had repaid money which he had borrowed, he was said to replace it—reponere. So our poet, looking upon himself as indebted to the reciters of their compositions for the trouble which they had given him, speaks as if he intended to repay them in kind, by writing and reciting his verses, as as they had done theirs. Sat. vi. l. 40, —4. PERSIUS, prolog. l. 7. HOR. lib. i. sat. iv. l. 73, 4.

2. *Theseis.*] A poem, of which Theseus was the subject.

SELECT

SATIRES

OF

JUVENAL.

First Satire.

satirists then lay under from a fear of punishment, and professes to treat of the dead, personating, in their names, certain living vicious characters. His great aim, in this, and in all his other satires, is to expose and reprove vice itself, however sanctified by custom, or dignified by the examples of the great.

SHALL I always be only a hearer?—shall I never repay,
Who am teaz'd so often with the Theseis of hoarse Codrus?
Shall one (poet) recite his comedies to me with impunity,

—— *Hoarse Codrus.*] A very mean poet; so poor, that he gave rise to the proverb, "Codro pauperior." He is here supposed to have made himself hoarse, with frequent and loud reading his poem.

3. *Comedies.*] Togatas—so called from the low and common people, who were the subjects of them. These wore gowns, by which they were distinguished from persons of rank.

There were three different sorts of comedy, each denominated from the dress of the person which they represented.

First, The Togata; which exhibited the actions of the low sort; and was a species of what we call low comedy.

Secondly, The Prætextata, so called from the prætexta, a white robe ornamented with purple, and worn by magistrates and nobles. Hence the comedies, which treated of the actions of such, were called prætextatæ. In our time we should say, genteel comedy.

Thirdly, The Palliata; from Pallium, a sort of upper garment worn by the Greeks, and in which the actors were habited, when the manners and actions of the Greeks were represented. This was also a species of the higher sort of comedy.

It is most probable that Terence's plays, which he took from Menander, was reckoned among the palliatæ, and represented in the pallium, or Grecian dress: more especially too, as the scene of every play lies at Athens.

Hic elegos ? impune diem consumpserit ingens
Telephus ? aut summi plenâ jam margine libri   5
Scriptus et in tergo necdum finitus Orestes ?
    Nota magis nulli domus est suæ; quam mihi lucus
Martis, et Æoliis vicinum rupibus antrum
Vulcani.   Quid agant venti ; quas torqueat umbras
Æacus ; unde alius furtivæ devehat aurum   10
Pelliculæ : quantas jaculetur Monychus ornos ;
Frontonis platani, convulsaque marmora clamant
Semper, et assiduo ruptæ lectore columnæ.
Expectes eadem a summo, minimoque poëtâ.

4. *Elegos*] These were little poems
on mournful subjects, and consisted
of hexameter and pentameter verses
alternately.   We must despair of
knowing the first elegiac poet, since
Horace says, Art. Poet. l. 77, 8.

  Quis tamen exiguos elegos emiserit
    auctor,
  Grammatici certant, et adhuc sub
    judice lis est.
  By whom invented critics yet contend,
  And of their vain disputing find no
    end.   FRANCIS.

Elegies were at first mournful, yet
afterwards they were composed on
cheerful subjects. Hor. Ib. l. 75, 76.

  Versibus impariter junctis querimo-
    nia primum,
  Post etiam inclusa est voti sententia
    compos.
  Unequal measures first were tun'd to
    flow,
  Sadly expressive of the lover's woe·
  But now to gayer subjects form'd
    they move,
  In sounds of pleasure, and the joys of
    love.   FRANCIS.

—*Bulky Telephus.*] Some prolix and
tedious play, written on the subject of
Telephus, king of Mysia, who was mor-
tally wounded by the spear of Achilles,
but afterwards healed by the rust of the
same spear.   OVID. Trist. v 2 15.

—*Waste a day*] In hearing it read
over, which took up a whole day.

5. *Or Orestes*] Another play on the
story of Orestes, the son of Agamemnon
and Clytemnestra.   He slew his own
mother, and Ægysthus, her adulterer,
who had murdered his father. This too,
by the description of it in this line and
the next, must have been a very long and
tedious performance.   It was usual to
leave a margin, but this was all filled
from top to bottom—it was unusual
to write on the outside, or back, of
the parchment; but this author had
filled the whole outside, as well as
the inside.

5. *Of the who'e bool.*] Or, of the
whole of the book.   Liber primarily
signifies the inward bark or rind of a
tree ; hence a book or work written,
at first made of barks of trees, afterwards of paper and parchment. Summus is derived from supremus; hence
summum-i, the top, the whole, the sum.

6. *The grove of Mars.*] The history of Romulus and Remus, whom
Ilia, otherwise called Rhea Sylvia,
brought forth in a grove sacred to
Mars at Alba: hence Romulus was
called Sylvius ; also the son of Mars.
This, and the other subjects mentioned, were so dinned perpetually into his
ears, that the places described were as
familiar to him as his own house.

—*The den of Vulcan*] The history
of the Cyclops and Vulcan, the scene
of which was laid in Vulcan's den.
See VIRG. Æn. viii l. 416—22.

9. *The Æolian rocks.*] On the north
of Sicily are seven rocky islands, which
were called Æolian, or Vulcanian ; one
of which was called Hiera, or sacred,
as dedicated to Vulcan. From the frequent breaking forth of fire and sulphur out of the earth of these islands,
particularly in Hiera, Vulcan was supposed to keep his shop and forge there.

Here also Æolus was supposed to
confine and preside over the winds.
Hence these islands are called Æolian.
See VIRG. Æn. i. l 55—67.

—*What the winds can do.*] This probably alludes to some tedious poetical

Another his elegies? shall bulky Telephus waste a day
With impunity? or Orestes—the margin of the whole book
    already full,   5
And written on the back too, nor as yet finished?
    No man's house is better known to him, than to me
The grove of Mars, and the den of Vulcan near
The Æolian rocks: what the winds can do: what ghosts
Æacus may be tormenting: from whence another could con-
    vey the gold   10
Of the stolen fleece: how great wild-ash trees Monychus
    could throw:
The plane-trees of Fronto, and the convuls'd marbles resound
Always, and the columns broken with the continual reader:
You may expect the same things from the highest and from
    the least poet.

treatises, on the nature and operations of the winds. Or, perhaps, to some play, or poem, on the amours of Boreas and Orithya, the daughter of Erectheus, King of Athens.

10. *Æacus may be tormenting.*] Æacus was one of the fabled judges of hell, who with his two assessors, Minos and Rhadamanthus, were supposed to torture the ghosts into a confession of their crimes. See VIRG. Æn. vi. l. 566—69.

—*From whence another, &c.*] Alluding to the story of Jason, who stole the golden fleece from Colchis.

11. *Monychus.*] This alludes to some play, or poem, which had been written on the battle of the Centaurs and Lapithæ.

The word Monychus is derived from the Greek μόνος, solus, and ονυξ, ungula, and is expressive of an horse's hoof, which is whole and entire, not cleft or divided.

The Centaurs were fabled to be half men and half horses; so that by the Monychus we are to understand one of the Centaurs, of such prodigious strength, as to make use of large trees as weapons, which he threw, or darted at his enemies.

12. *The palm-trees of Fronto.*] Julius Fronto, a noble and learned man, at whose house the poets recited their works, before they were read, or performed in public. His house was planted round with plane-trees, for the sake of their shade.

—*The convuls'd marbles.*] This may refer to the marble statues which were in Fronto's hall, and were almost shaken off their pedestals by the din and noise that were made; or to the marble with which the walls were built, or inlaid; or to the marble pavement; all which appeared as if likely to be shaken out of their places by the incessant noise of these bawling reciters of their works.

13. *The columns broken.*] The marble pillars too were in the same situation of danger, from the incessant noise of these people.

The poet means to express the wearisomeness of the continual repetition of the same thing over and over again, and to censure the manner, as well as the matter, of these irksome repetitions; which were attended with such loud and vehement vociferation, that even the trees about Fronto's house, as well as the marble within it, had reason to apprehend demolition. This hyperbole is humourous, and well applied to the subject.

14. *You may expect the same things, &c.*] i. e. The same subjects, treated by the worst poets, as by the best. Here he satirizes the impudence and presumption of these scribblers, who, without genius or abilities, had ventured to write, and expose their verses to the public ear; and this, on subjects which had been treated by men of a superior cast.

Et nos ergo manum ferulæ subduximus : et nos   15
Consilium dedimus Syllæ, privatus ut altum
Dormiret. Stulta est clementia, cum tot ubique
Vatibus occurras, perituræ parcere chartæ.
Cur tamen hoc libeat potius decurrere campo,
Per quem magnus equos Auruncæ flexit alumnus :   20
Si vacat, et placidi rationem admittitis, edam.
Patricios omnes opibus cum provocet unus,
Quo tondente gravis juveni mihi barba sonabat :
Cum pars Niliacæ plebis, cum verna Canopi
Crispinus, Tyrias humero revocante lacernas,   25
Ventilet æstivum digitis sudantibus aurum,
Nec sufferre queat majoris pondera gemmæ :
Difficile est Satiram non scribere. Nam quis iniquæ
Tam patiens urbis, tam ferreus, ut teneat se,
Causidici nova cum vehiat lectica Mathonis   30

15. *Therefore.*] *i. e.* In order to qualify myself as a writer and declaimer. His meaning seems to be, that as all, whether good or bad, wrote poems, why should not he, who had had an education in learning, write as well as they.

—*Have withdrawn my hand, &c.*] The ferule was an instrument of punishment, as at this day, with which schoolmasters corrected their scholars, by striking them with it over the palm of the hand : the boy watched the stroke, and, if possible, withdrew his hand from it.

Juvenal means to say, that he had been at school, to learn the art of poetry and oratory, and had made declamations, of one of which the subject was, " Whether Sylla should take the " dictatorship, or live in ease and " quiet' as a private man?" He maintained the latter proposition.

18. *Paper that will perish.*] *i. e.* That will be destroyed by others, who will write upon it if I do not; therefore there is no reason why I should forbear to make use of it.

19. *In the very field.*] A metaphor, taken from the chariot-races in the Campus Martius.

20. *The great pupil of Aurunca, &c.*] Lucilius, the first and most famous Roman satirist, born at Aurunca, an ancient city of Latium, in Italy.

He means perhaps, you will ask,

" how is it that I can think of taking " the same ground as that great satir- " ist Lucilius; and why I should ra- " ther choose this way of writing, " when he so excelled in it, as to be " before all others not only in point of " time, but of ability in that kind " of writing ?"

21. *Hearken to my reason.*] Literally, the verb admitto signifies to admit; but it is sometimes used with auribus understood, and then it denotes attending, or hearkening, to something : this I suppose to be the sense of it in this place, as it follows the si vacat.

22. *The patricians.*] The nobles of Rome. They were the desendants of such as were created censors in the time of Romulus. Of these there were, originally, only one hundred— afterwards more were added to them.

23. *Who clipping, &c.*] The person here meant is supposed to be Licinius, the freeman and barber of Augustus, or perhaps Cinnamus. See sat. x. l. 215, 6.

—*Sounded.*] Alluding to the sound of clipping the beard with scissars. Q. D. who with his scissars clipped my beard, when he was a young man, and first came under the barber's hands.

24. *Part of the commonality of the Nile.*] One of the lowest of the Egyptians who had come as slaves to Rome.

—*Canopus.*] A city in Egypt, addicted to all kind of effeminacy and

And I therefore have withdrawn my hand from the ferule :
   and I   15
Have given counsel to Sylla, that, a private man, soundly
He should sleep. It is a foolish clemency, when every where
   so many
Poets you may meet, to spare paper, that will perish.
But why it should please me rather to run along in the very
   field,   19
Through which the great pupil of Aurunca drave his horses,
I will tell you, if you have leisure, and kindly hearken to
   my reason.
When one can vie with all the patricians in riches,
Who clipping my beard troublesome to me a youth sounded :
When a part of the commonalty of the Nile, when a slave
   of Canopus,
Crispinus, his shoulder recalling the Tyrian cloaks,   25
Can ventilate the summer-gold on his sweating fingers,
Nor can he bear the weight of a larger gem ;
It is difficult not to write satire. For who can so endure
The wicked city—who is so insensible, as to contain himself,
When the new litter of lawyer Matho comes   30

debauchery ; famous for a temple of Serapis, a god of the Egyptians. This city was built by Menelaus, in memory of his pilot, Canopus, who died there, and was afterwards canonized. See sat xv. l. 46.

25. *Crispinus.*] He, from a slave, had been made master of the horse to Nero.

—*His shoulder recalling.*] Revocante—The Romans used to fasten their cloaks round the neck with a loop, but in hot weather, perhaps, usually went with them loose. As Juvenal is now speaking of the summer season, (as appears by the next line,) he describes the shoulder as recalling, or endeavouring to hoist up and replace the cloak, which, from not being fastened by a loop to the neck, was often slipping away, and sliding downwards from the shoulders.

—*Tyrian cloaks.*] i. e. Dyed with Tyrian purple, which was very expensive. By this he marks the extravagance and luxury of these upstarts.

27. *Ventilate the summer-gold, &c.*] The Romans were arrived at such an height of luxury, that they had rings for the winter, and others for the summer, which they wore according to the season. Ventilo signifies, to wave any thing to and fro in the air. Crispinus is described as wearing a summer-ring, and cooling it by, perhaps, taking it off, and by waving it to and fro in the air with his hand—which motion might likewise contribute to the slipping back of the cloak.

29. *So insensible.*] Ferreus literally signifies any thing made of iron, and is therefore used here, figuratively, to denote hardness or insensibility.

30. *The new litter.*] The lectica was a sort of sedan, with a bed or couch in it, wherein the grandees were carried by their servants : probably something like the palanquins in the East. This was a piece of luxury which the rich indulged in.

—*Lawyer Matho.*] He had been an advocate, but had amassed a large fortune by turning informer. The emperor Domitian gave so much encouragement to such people, that many made their fortunes by secret informations ; insomuch that nobody was safe, however innocent ; even one informer was afraid of another. See below, l. 33, 4, and notes.

Plena ipso? et post hunc magni delator amici,
Et cito rapturus de nobilitate comesâ
Quod superest: quem Massa timet: quem munere palpat
Carus; et a trepido Thymele summissa Latino.
· Quid referam? quântâ siccum jecur ardeat irâ,   35
Cum populum gregibus comitum premat hic spoliator
Pupilli plorantis? et hic damnatus inani
Judicio (quid enim salvis infamia nummis?)
Exul ab octavâ Marius bibit, et fruitur Dîs
Iratis? at tu victrix provincia ploras!   40
Hæc ego non credam Venusinâ digna lucernâ?
Hæc ego non agitem? sed quid magis Heracleas,
Aut Diomedeas, aut mugitum labyrinthi,

31. *Full of himself.*] Now grown
bulky and fat. By this expression, the
poet may hint at the self-importance of
this upstart fellow.

—*The secret accuser of a great friend.*]
This was probably Marcus Regulus,
(mentioned by Pliny in his Epistles,)
a most infamous informer, who occasioned, by his secret informations, the
deaths of many of the nobility in the
time of Domitian.

Some think that the great friend here
mentioned was some great man, an intimate of Domitian's; for this emperor
spared not even his greatest and most
intimate friends, on receiving secret
informations against them,

But, by the poet's manner of expression, it should rather seem, that
the person meant was some great man,
who had had been a friend to Regulus,
and whom Regulus had basely betrayed.

32. *From the devoured nobility.*] i. e.
Destroyed through secret accusations,
or pillaged by informers for hush-
money.

33. *Whom Massa fears.*] Babius
Massa, an eminent informer; but so
much more eminent was M. Regulus,
above mentioned, in this way, that he
was dreaded even by Massa, lest he
should inform against him.

34. *Carus sooths.*] This was another of the same infamous profession,
who bribed Regulus, to avoid some
secret accusation.

—*Thymele.*] The wife of Latinus
the famous mimic; she was sent privately by her husband and prostituted
to Regulus, in order to avoid some
information which Latinus dreaded,
and trembled under the apprehension
of.

35. *What shall I say?*] Q. D. How
shall I find words to express the indignation which I feel?

—*My dry liver burnt.*] The ancients
considered the liver as the seat of the
irascible affections. So Hor. lib. i. od.
xiii. l. 4. says,

Difficili bile tumet jecur—to express his resentment and jealousy, at
hearing his mistress commend a rival.

Again, lib. iv. od. i. l. 12. Si tor-
rere jecur quæris idoneum—by which
he means, kindling the passion of love
within the breast.

Our poet here means to express the
workings of anger and resentment
within him, at seeing so many examples of vice and folly all around him, and
particularly in those instances which
he is now going to mention.

36. *A spoiler of his pupil, &c.*] The
tutelage of young men, who had lost
their parents, was committed to guardians, who were to take care of their
estates and education. Here one is
represented as a spoliator—a spoiler—
i. e. a plunderer or pillager of his ward
as to his affairs.

—*Presses on the people.*] Grown
rich by the spoils of his ward, he is
supposed to be carried, in a litter,
along the streets, with such a crowd
of attendants, as to incommode other
passengers.

Full of himself? and after him the secret accuser of a great
    friend,
And who is soon about to seize from the devoured nobility
What remains: whom Massa fears: whom with a gift
Carus sooths, and Thymèle sent privately from trembling
    Latinus.   34
What shall I say?—With how great anger my dry liver burns,
When here a spoiler of his pupil lamenting presses on the
    people
With flocks of attendants? and here condemned by a frivolous
Judgment, (for what is infamy when money is safe?)
The exile Marius drinks from the eighth hour, and enjoys the
Angry gods? but thou vanquishing province, lamentest! 40
Shall I not believe these things worthy the Venusinian lamp?
Shall I not agitate these (subjects?)—but why rather Hera-
    cleans,
Or Diomedeans, or the lowing of the labyrinth,

37—8. *By a frivolous judgment.*]
Inani judicio—because, though inflicted on Marius, it was of no service
to the injured province; for, instead
of restoring to it the treasures of which
it had been plundered, part of these,
to a vast amount, were put into the
public treasury. As for Marius himself, he lived in as much festivity as
as if nothing had happened, as the
next two verses inform us.

39. *The exile Marius.*] Marius Priscus, proconsul of Africa, who, for pil-
laging the province of vast sums of
money, was condemned to be banished.
—*From the eighth hour.*] Began his
carousals from two o'clock in the afternoon, which was reckoned an instance
of dissoluteness and luxury, it being
an hour sooner than it was customary
to sit down to meals. See note on sat.
xi. l. 204. and on Persius, sat. iii. l. 4.

39—40. *He enjoys the angry Gods.*]
Though Marius had incurred the anger of the gods by his crimes, yet, re-
gardless of this, he enjoyed himself
in a state of the highest jollity and festivity.
—*Vanquishing province, &c.*] Victrix was used as a forensic term, to
denote one who had got the better in
a law-suit. The province of Africa
had sued Marius, and had carried the
cause against him, but had still reason to deplore her losses: for though

Marius was sentenced to pay an immense fine, which came out of what
he had pillaged, yet this was put into the public treasury, and no part of
it given to the Africans; and, besides
this, Marius had reserved sufficient to
maintain himself in a luxurious manner. See above, note on l. 39, 40.

41. *Worthy the Venusinian lamp.*]
i. e. The pen of Horace himself? This
charming writer was born at Venusi-
um, a city of Apulia. When the poets
wrote by night, they made use of a
lamp.

42. *Shall I not agitate, &c.*] Agitem
implies pursuing, as hunters do wild
beasts—hunting—chasing. So inveighing against by satire, driving
such vices as he mentions out of their
lurking places, and hunting them down,
as it were, in order to destroy them.
—*But why rather Heracleans?*] Juvenal here anticipates the supposed
objections of some, who might perhaps
advise him to employ his talents on
some fabulous and more poetical subjects—such as the labours of Hercules,
&c. " Why should I prefer these (as
" if he had said) when so many sub-
" jects in real life occur, to exercise
" my pen in a more useful way?"

43. *Or Diomedeans.*] i. e. Verses on
the exploits of Diomede, a king of
Thrace, who fed his horses with man's
flesh. Hercules slew him, and threw

Et mare percussum puero, fabrumque volantem ?
    Cum fas esse putet curam sperare cohortis,   45
Qui bona donavit præsepibus, et caret omni
Majorum censu, dum pervolat axe citato
Flaminiam : puer Automedon nam lora tenebat,
Ipse lacernatæ cum se jactaret amicæ.
    Nonne libet medio ceras implere capaces   50
Quadrivio — cum jam sextâ cervice feratur
(Hinc atque inde patens, ac nudâ penè cathedrâ,
Et multum referens de Mæcenate supino)
Signator falso, qui se lautum, atque beatum
Exiguis tabulis, et gemmâ fecerat udâ ?   55

43. *The lowing of the labyrinth.*] The story of the Minotaur, the monster kept in the labyrinth of Crete, who was half a bull, and slain by Theseus. See AINSW. *Minotaurus.*

44. *The sea stricken by a boy.*] The story of Icarus, who, flying too near the sun, melted the wax by which his wings were fastened together, and fell into the sea; from him called Icarian. See HOR. lib. iv. od. ii. l. 2—4.

—*The flying artificer.*] Dædalus, who invented and made wings for himself and his son Icarus, with which they fled from Crete. See AINSW. *Dædalus.*

45. *A cohort*] A company of foot in a regiment, or legion, which consisted of ten cohorts.

46 *Hath given his estate to stables.*] *i. e.* Has squandered away all his patrimony in breeding and keeping horses. Præsepe sometimes means, a cell, stew, or brothel. Perhaps this may be the sense here, and the poet may mean, that this spendthrift had lavished his fortune on the stews, in lewdness and debauchery.

46—7. *Lacks all the income,* &c.] Has spent the family estate.

47. *While he flies,* &c.] The person here meant is far from certain. Commentators differ much in their conjectures on the subject. Britannicus gives the matter up. "This passage," says he, " is one of those concerning which " we are yet to seek."

But whether Cornelius Fuscus be meant, who when a boy was charioteer to Nero, as Automedon was to Achilles,

and who, after wasting his substance in riotous living, was made commander of a regiment ; or Tigellinus, an infamous favourite of Nero's, be here designed, whose character is supposed to have answered to the description here given, is not certain ; one or other seems to be meant. The poet is mentioning various subjects as highly proper for satire ; and among others, some favourite at court, who, after spending all his paternal estate in riot, extravagance, and debauchery, was made a commander in the army, and exhibited his chariot, driving full speed over the Flaminian way, which led to the emperor's villa ; and all this, because when a boy, he had been Nero's charioteer, or, as the poet humourously calls him, his Automedon, and used to drive out Nero and his minion Sporus, whom Nero castrated, to make him, as much as he could, resemble a woman, and whom he used as a mistress, and afterwards took as a wife, and appeared publicly in his chariot with him, openly caressing, and making love, as he passed along.

The poet humourously speaks of Sporus in the feminine gender. As the lacerna was principally a man's garment, by lacernatæ amicæ, the poet may be understood as if he had called Sporus, Nero's male-mistress, being habited like a man, and caressed as a woman.

The above appears to me a probable explanation of this obscure and difficult passage. Holiday gives it a different turn, as may be seen by his annotation on this place. I do not pre-

And the sea stricken by a boy, and the flying artificer?
  When he can think it right to hope for the charge of a
    cohort,   45
Who hath given his estate to stables, and lacks all
The income of his ancestors, while he flies, with swift axle, over
The Flaminian way : for the boy Automedon was holding
  the reins,
When he boasted himself to his cloaked mistress.
  Doth it not like one to fill capacious waxen tablets in the
    middle of a   50
Cross-way—when now can be carried on a sixth neck
(Here and there exposed, and in almost a naked chair,
And much resembling the supine Mæcenas)
A signer to what is false ; who himself splendid and happy
Has made, with small tables, and with a wet gem ?   55

sume to be positive, but will say with Britannicus, " Sed quum in ambiguo " sit, de quo poeta potissimum intel- " ligat, unusquisque, si neutrum ho- " rum probabile visum fuerit, quod " ad loci explanationem faciat, exco- " gitet."

48. *The Flaminian way.*] A road made by Caius Flaminius, colleague of Lepidus, from Rome to Ariminum.

49. *When he boasted himself.*] Jactare se alicui signifies to recommend, to insinuate one's self into the favour or good graces of another ; as when a man is courting his mistress. By ipse, according to the above interpretation of this passage, we must understand the emperor Nero.

50. *Capacious waxen tablets.*] These are here called ceras ; sometimes they are called ceratæ tabellæ, because they were thin pieces of wood, covered over with wax, on which the ancients wrote with the point of a sharp instrument, called stylus, (see Hor. lib. i. sat. x. l. 72.) it had a blunt end to rub out with. They made pocket books with these.

51. *Cross-way*] Juvenal means, that a man might please himself by filling a large book with the objects of satire which he meets in passing along the street. Quadrivium properly means a place where four ways meet, and where there are usually most people passing—a proper stand for observation.

—*On a sixth neck.*] i. e. In a litter carried by six slaves, who bare the poles on the shoulder, and leaning against the side of the neck. These were called hexaphori, from Gr. ἓξ, six, and φέρω, to bear or carry. See Sat. vii. l. 141, n.

52. *Exposed, &c.*] Carried openly to and fro, here and there, through the public streets, having no shame for what he had done to enrich himself.

53. *The supine Mæcenas.*] By this it appears, that Mæcenas was given to laziness and effeminacy.

Horace calls him Malthinus, from μαλθακος, which denotes softness and effeminacy. See Hor. lib. i. sat. ii. l. 25.

54. *A signer, &c.*] Signator signifies a sealer or signer of contracts or wills. Here it means a species of cheat, who imposed false wills and testaments on the heirs of the deceased, supposed to be made in their own favour, or in favour of others : with whom they shared the spoil. See sat. x. l. 305, and note. Some suppose this to be particularly meant of Tigellinus, a favourite of Nero's, who poisoned three uncles, and, by forging their wills, made himself heir to all they had.

55. *By small tables.*] Short testaments, contained in a few words. Comp. note on l. 50.

—*A wet gem.*] i. e. A seal, which was cut on some precious stone, worn

Occurrit matrona potens, quæ molle Calenum
Porrectura viro miscet sitiente rubetam,
Instituitque rudes melior Locusta propinquas,
Per famam et populum, nigros efferre maritos.
Aude aliquid brevibus Gyaris, et carcere dignum,   60
Si vis esse aliquis : PROBITAS LAUDATUR, ET ALGET.
Criminibus debent hortos, prætoria, mensas,
Argentum vetus, et stantem extra pocula caprum.
Quem patitur dormire nurûs corruptor avaræ ?
Quem sponsæ turpes, et prætextatus adulter ?   65
Si natura negat, facit indignatio versum,
Qualemcunque potest : quales ego, vel Cluvienus.
Ex quo Deucalion, nimbis tollentibus æquor,
Navigio montem ascendit, sortesque poposcit,

in a ring on the finger, and occasion-
ally made use of to seal deeds or wills
—this they wetted to prevent the wax
sticking to it. This was formerly
known among our forefathers by the
name of a seal-ring.

56. *A potent matron occurs.*] Another
subject of satire the poet here adverts
to, namely, women who poison their
husbands, and this with impunity.
The particular person here alluded to,
under the description of matrona potens, was probably, Agrippina, the
wife of Claudius, who poisoned her
husband, that she might make her son
Nero emperor.

—*Occurs.*] Meets you in the public
street, and thus occurs to the observation of the satirist. Comp. l. 50, 51.

—*Calenian wine.*] Calenum was a
city in the kingdom of Naples, famous
for a soft kind of wine.

57. *About to reach forth.*] Porrectura
—The husband is supposed to be so
thirsty as not to examine the contents
of the draught; of this she avails
herself, by reaching to him some Calenian wine with poison in it, which
was extracted from a toad.

58. *A better Locusta.*] This Locusta
was a vile woman, skilful in preparing poisons. She helped Nero to poison Britannicus, the son of Claudius
and Messalina ; and Agrippina to dispatch Claudius. The woman alluded
to by Juvenal, l. 56. he here styles,
melior Locusta, a better Locusta, i. e.
more skilled in poisoning than even
Locusta herself.

—*Her rude neighbours.*] i. e. Unacquainted, and unskilled before, in
this diabolical art.

59. *Through fame and the people.*]
Setting all reputation and public report at defiance ; not caring what people should say.

—*To bring forth.*] For burial—
which efferre particularly means: See
TER. And. act. i. sc. i. l, 90.

—*Black husbands.*] Their corpses
turned putrid and black, with the effects of the poison.

60. *Dare.*] i. e. Attempt—presume
—be not afraid—to commit.

—*Something.*] Some atrocious crime,
worthy of exile, or imprisonment.

The narrow Gyaræ.] Gyaras was
an island in the Ægean sea, small, barren, and desolate, to which criminals
were banished.

61. *If you would be somebody.*] i. e.
If you would make yourself taken notice of, as a person of consequence, at
Rome. A severe reflection on certain
favourites of the emperor, who, by being informers, and by other scandalous actions, had enriched themselves.

—*Probity is praised, &c.*] This
seems a proverbial saying, and applies
to what goes before, as well as to
what follows, wherein the poet is
shewing, that vice was, in those days,
the only way to riches and honours.
Honesty and innocence will be commended, but those who possess them
be left to starve.

62. *Gardens.*] i. e. Pleasant and

A potent matron occurs, who soft Calenian wine
About to reach forth, her husband thirsting, mixes a toad,
And, a better Locusta, instructs her rude neighbours,
Through fame and the people, to bring forth their black
   husbands.
Dare something worthy the narrow Gyaræ, or a prison,   60
If you would be somebody. PROBITY IS PRAISED AND
   STARVES WITH COLD.
To crimes they owe gardens, palaces, tables,
Old silver, and a goat standing on the outside of cups.
Whom does the corrupter of a covetous daughter in-law
   suffer to sleep?
Whom base spouses, and the noble young adulterer?   65
If nature denies, indignation makes verse,
Such as it can; such as I, or Cluvienus.
From the time that Deucalion (the showers lifting up the sea)
Ascended the mountain with his bark, and asked for lots,

beautiful retreats, where they had gardens of great taste and expence.

—*Palaces.*] The word prætoria denotes noblemens seats in the country, as well as the palaces of great men in the city.

Tables.] Made of ivory, marble, and other expensive materials.

63. *Old silver.*—Ancient plate—very valuable on account of the workmanship.

—*A goat standing, &c.*] The figure of a goat in curious bas relief—which animal, as sacred to Bacchus, was very usually expressed on drinking cups.

64. *Whom.*] i. e. Which of the poets or writers of satire, can be at rest from writing, or withhold his satiric rage?

—*The corrupter.*] i. e. The father, who takes advantage of the love of money in his son's wife, to debauch her.

65. *Base spouses.*] Lewd and adulterous wives.

—*The noble young adulterer.*] Prætextatus, i. e. the youth, not having laid aside the prætexta, or gown worn by boys, sons of the nobility, till seventeen years of age—yet, in this early period of life, initiated into the practice of adultery.

66. *Indignation makes verse.*] Forces one to write, however naturally without talent for it.

67. *Such as I, or Cluvienus.*] i. e. Make or write. The poet names himself with Cluvienus, (some bad poet of his time,) that he might the more freely satirize him, which he at the same time does, the more severely, by the comparison.

68. *From the time that Deucalion.*] This and the three following lines relate to the history of the deluge, as described by Ovid. See Met. lib. i. l. 264—315.

69. *Ascended the mountain, &c.*] Alluding to Ovid:

  Mons ibi verticibus petit arduus astra duobus,
  Nomine Parnassus—
  Hic ubi Deucalion (nam cætera texerat æquor)
  Cum consorte tori parvâ rate vectus adhæsit.

—*Asked for lots.*] Sortes here means the oracles, or billets, on which the answers of the gods were written. Ovid. (ubi supra,) l. 367, 8. represents Deucalion, and his wife Pyrrha, resolving to go to the temple of the goddess Themis, to inquire in what manner mankind should be restored.

  ——*placuit cæleste præcari*
  Numen, et auxilium per sacras quærere sortes.

And, l. 381. Mota Dea est, sortemque dedit.

Again, l. 389. Verba datæ sortis.

To this Juvenal alludes in this line; wherein sortes may be rendered, oracular answers.

Paulatimque animâ caluerunt mollia saxa,   70
Quicquid agunt homines, votum, timor, ira, voluptas,
Gaudia, discursus, nostri est farrago libelli.
Et quando uberior vitiorum copia? quando
Major avaritiæ patuit sinus? alea quando
Hos animos? neque enim loculis comitantibus itur   75
Ad casum tabulæ, positâ sed luditur arcâ
Prælia quanta illic dispensatore videbes
Armigero! simplexne furor sestertia centum
Perdere, et horrenti tunicam non reddere servo?
Quis totidem erexit villas? quis fercula septem   80
Secreto cœnavit avus? nunc sportula primo
Limine parva sedet; turbæ rapienda togatæ.

70. *The soft stones, &c.*] When Deucalion and Pyrrha, having consulted the oracle how mankind might be repaired, were answered, that this might be done by their casting the bones of their great mother behind their backs, they picked stones from off the earth, and cast them behind their backs, and they became men and women.

Jussos lapides sua post vestigia mittunt:
Saxa ————
Ponere duritiem cœpere, suumque rigorem,
Mollirique morâ, mollitaque ducere formam, &c. ib. l. 399—402.
Hence Juvenal says—mollia saxa.

It is most likely that the whole account of the deluge, given by Ovid, is a corruption of the Mosaical history of that event.—Plutarch mentions the dove sent out of the ark.

73. *The composition &c.*] Farrago signifies a mixture, a hodge-podge—as we say, of various things mixed together. The poet means, that the various pursuits, inclinations, actions, and passions of men, and all those human follies and vices, which have existed, have been increasing, ever since the flood, are the subjects of his satires.

74. *Bosom of avarice.*] A metaphorical allusion to the sail of a ship when expanded to the wind—the centre whereof is called sinus—the bosom. The larger the sail, and the more open and spread it is, the greater the capacity of the bosom for receiving the wind, and the more powerfully is the ship driven on through the sea.

Thus avarice spreads itself far and wide; it catches the inclinations of men, as the sail the wind, and thus drives them on in a full course—when more than at present? says the poet.
—*The die.*] A chief instrument of gaming—put here for gaming itself. METON.

75. *These spirits.*] Animus signifies spirit of courage; and in this sense we are to understand it here. As if the poet said, when was gaming so encouraged? or when had games of hazard, which were forbidden by the law, (except only during the Saturnalia,) the courage to appear so open and frequently as they do now? The sentence is elliptical, and must be supplied with habuit, or some other verb of the kind, to govern—hos animos.

—*They do not go with purses, &c.*] Gaming has now gotten to such an extravagant height, that gamesters are not content to play for what can be carried in their purses, but stake a whole chest of money at a time—this seems to be implied by the word posita. Pono sometimes signifies—laying a wager—putting down as a stake. See an example of this sense, from Plautus. AINSW. pono, No. 5.

77. *How many battles, &c.*] i. e. How many attacks on one another at play.

—*The steward.*] Dispensator signifies a dispenser, a steward, one who lays out money, a manager.

78. *Armour-bearer.*] The armigeri

And the soft stones by little and little grew warm with life; 70
Whatever men do—desire, fear, anger, pleasure,
Joys, discourse—is the composition of my little book.
And when was there a more fruitful plenty of vices? when
Has a greater bosom of avarice lain open? when the die 74
These spirits?—they do not go, with purses accompanying,
To the chance of the table, but a chest being put down is
    played for.
How many battles will you see there; the steward
Armour-bearer! is it simple madness an hundred sestertia
To lose and not give a coat to a ragged servant?
Who has erected so many villas? What ancestor on seven
    dishes   80
Has supped in secret? Now a little basket at the first
Threshold is set, to be snatched by the gowned crowd.

were servants who followed their masters with their shields, and other arms, when they went to fight. The poet still carries on the metaphor of prælia in the preceding line. There gaming is compared to fighting; here he humourously calls the steward the armour-bearer, as supplying his master with money, a necessary weapon at a gaming table, to stake at play, instead of keeping and dispensing it, or laying it out for the usual and honest expenses of the family.

—*Simple madness, &c.*] All this is a species of madness, but not without mixture of injury and mischief; and therefore may be reckoned something more than mere madness, where such immense sums are thrown away at a gaming table, as that the servants of the family cannot be afforded common decent necessaries. The Romans had their sestertius and sestertium. The latter is here, meant, and contains 1000 of the former, which was worth about 1½d. See l. 92, n.

79. *And not give a coat, &c.*] The poet here puts one instance, for many, of the ruinous consequences of gaming.

Juvenal, by this, severely censures the gamesters, who had rather lose a large sum at the dice, than lay it out for the comfort, happiness, and decent maintenance of their families.

80. *So many villas.*] Houses of pleasure for the summer season. These

were usually built and furnished at a vast expense. The poet having inveighed against their squandering at the gaming table, now attacks their luxury, and prodigality in other respects; and then the excessive meanness into which they were sunk.

81. *Supped in secret, &c.*] The ancient Roman nobility, in order to shew their munificence and hospitality, used, at certain times, to make an handsome and splendid entertainment, to which they invited their clients and dependents. Now they shut out these, and provided a sumptuous entertainment for themselves only, which they sat down to in private. Which of our ancestors, says the poet, did this?

—*Now a little basket, &c.*] Sportula —a little basket or pannier, made of a kind of broom called sportum. KENNET, Antiq. p. 375. In this were put victuals, and some small sums of money, to be distributed to the poor clients and dependents at the outward door of the house, who were no longer invited, as formerly, to the entertainment within.

82. *To be snatched, &c.*] i. e. Eagerly received by the hungry poor clients, who crowded about the door.

—*The gowned crowd.*] The common sort of people were called turba togata, from the gowns they wore, by which they were distinguished from the higher sort. See note before on l. 3.

Ille tamen faciem prius inspicit, et trepidat ne
Suppositus venias, ac falso nomine poscas:
Agnitus accipies. Jubet a præcone vocari　　　85
Ipsos Trojugenas; nam vexant limen et ipsi
Nobiscum: da Prætori, da deinde Tribuno.
Sed libertinus prior est: prior, inquit, ego adsum:
Cur timeam, dubitemve, locum defendere? quamvis
Natus ad Euphraten molles quod in aure fenestræ　　90
Arguerint, licet ipse negem: sed quinque tabernæ
Quadringenta parant: quid confert purpura majus

83. *But he.*] *i. e.* The person who
distributes the dole.

—*First inspects the face.*] That he
may be certain of the person he gives to.

—*And trembles.*] At the apprehension of being severely reproved by
his master, the great man, if he
should make a mistake, by giving to
people who assume a false name, and
pretend themselves to be clients, when
they are not.

85. *Acknowledged, &c.*] Agnitus,
owned, acknowledged, as one for
whom the dole is provided.

Perhaps, in better days, when the
clients and dependents of great men
were invited to partake of an entertainment within doors, there was a
sportula, or dole basket, which was
distributed, at large to the poor, at
the doors of great men's houses. Now
times were altered; no invitation of
clients to feast within doors, and no
distribution of doles, to the poor at
large without: none now got any
thing here but the excluded clients,
and what they got was distributed
with the utmost caution, l. 83, 4.

—*He commands to be called.*] *i. e.*
Summoned, called together. The poet
is now about to inveigh against the
meanness of many of the nobles and
magistrates of Rome, who could suffer themselves to be summoned by the
common crier, in order to share in the
distribution of the dole-baskets.

86. *The very descendants of the
Trojans.*] Ipsos Trojugenas; from
Troja or Trojanus, and gigno. The
very people, says he, who boast of
their descent from Æneas and the ancient Trojans, who first came to settle in Italy; even these are so degenerate, as to come and scramble, as it

were, among the poor, for a part of
the sportula. The word ipsos makes
the sarcasm the stronger.

—*Molest the threshold.*] Crowd
about it, and are very troublesome.
So Hor. lib. i. sat. viii. l. 18.—hunc
vexare locum.

87. *With us.*] Avec nous autres,
as the French say.

—*Give to the Prætor.*] In Juvenal's
time this was a title of a chief magistrate, something like the lord-mayor
of London; he was called Prætor
Urbanus, and had power to judge
matters of law between citizen and
citizen. This seems to be the officer
here meant: but for a further account of the Prætor, see AINSW.
Prætor.

87. *The Tribune.*] A chief officer
in Rome. The tribunes, at their first
institution, were two, afterwards came
to be ten; they were keepers of the
liberties of the people, against the
encroachments of the senate. They
were called tribunes, because at first
set over the three tribes of the people.
See AINSW. *Tribunus* and *Tribus.*

Juvenal satirically represents some
of the chief magistrates and officers of
the city as bawling out to be first served out of the sportula.

88. *The libertine.*] An enfranchised
slave. There were many of these in
Rome, who were very rich, and very
insolent: of one of these we have an
example here.

—*Is first; &c.*] "Hold," says this
upstart, "a freedman, rich as I am,
"is before the prætor; besides I came
"first, and I'll be first served."

89. *Why should I fear, &c.*] *i. e.* I
am neither afraid nor ashamed to chal-
lenge the first place. I will not give

But he first inspects the face, and trembles, lest
Put in the place of another you come, and ask in a false name.
Acknowledged you will receive. He commands to be called
   by the crier   85
The very descendants of the Trojans: for even they molest
   the threshold
Together with us: " Give to the Prætor—then give to the
  " Tribune."
But the libertine is first: I the first, says he, am here present.
Why should I fear, or doubt to defend my place? altho'
Born at the Euphrates, which the soft holes in my ear   90
Prove, though I should deny it : but five houses
Procure 400 (sestertia), what does the purple confer more

it up to any body.

89—90. *Although born at the Euphrates.*] He owns that he was born of servile condition, and came from a part of the world from whence many were sold as slaves. The river Euphrates took its rise in Armenia, and ran through the city of Babylon, which it divided in the midst.

90. *The soft holes, &c.*] The ears of all slaves in the East were bored, as a mark of their servitude. They wore bits of gold by way of ear-rings ; which custom is still, in the East Indies, and in other parts, even for whole nations ; who bore prodigious holes in their ears, and wear vast weights at them. DRYDEN. PLIN. lib. xi. c. 37.

The epithet *molles* may, perhaps, intimate, that this custom was looked upon at Rome (as among us) as a mark of effeminacy. Or the poet, by Hypallage, says, Molles in aure fenestræ, for, fenestræ in molli aure.

91. *Five houses.*] Tabernæ here may be understood to mean shops or warehouses, which were in the forum, or market-place, and which by reason of their situation, were let to merchants and traders at a great rent.

92. *Procure 400.*] In reckoning by sesterces, the Romans, had an art which may be understood by these three rules :

First : If a numeral noun agree in number, case, and gender, with sestertius, then it denotes so many sestertii ; as decem sestertii.

Secondly : If a numeral noun of an-

other case be joined with the genitive plural of sestertius, it denotes so many thousand, as decem sestertium signifies 10,000 sestertii.

Thirdly : If the adverb numeral be joined, it denotes so many 100,000 : as decies sestertiûm signifies ten hundred thousand sestertii. Or if the numeral adverb be put by itself, the signification is the same : decies or vigesies stand for so many 100,000 sestertii, or, as they say, so many hundred sestertia.

The sestertium contains a thousand sestertii, and amounted to about £17. 16s. 3d. of our money. KENNET, Ant. 374, 5.

After 400, quadringenta, sestertia must be understood, according to the third rule above.

The freedman brags, that the rents of his houses brought him in 400 sestertia, which was a knight's estate.

—*What does the purple, &c.*] The robes of the nobility and magistrates were decorated with purple. He means that, though he cannot deny that he was born a slave, and came to Rome as such, (and if he were to deny it,) the holes in his ears would prove it,) yet he was now a free citizen of Rome, possessed of a larger private fortune than the prætor or the tribune. What can even a patrician wish for more ? Indeed, " when I see a noble-" man reduced to keep sheep for his " livelihood, I cannot perceive any " great advantage he derives from his " nobility ; what can it, at best, con-" fer, beyond what I possess ?"

D

Optandum, si Laurenti custodit in agro
Conductas Corvinus oves? Ego possideo plus
Pallante, et Licinis : expectent ergo Tribuni.   95
Vincant divitiæ ; sacro nec cedat honori
Nuper in hanc urbem pedibus qui venerat albis ;
Quandoquidem inter nos sanctissima divitiarum
Majestas : etsi, funesta Pecunia, templo
Nondum habitas, nullas nummorum ereximus aras,   100
Ut colitur Pax, atque Fides, Victoria, Virtus,
Quæque salutato crepitat Concordia nido.
   Sed cum summus honor finito computet anno,
Sportula quid referat, quantam rationibus addat :
Quid facient comites, quibus hinc toga, calceus hinc est, 105
Et panis, fumusque domi ? densissima centum
Quadrantes lectica petit, sequiturque maritum
Languida, vel prægnans, et circumducitur uxor.
Hic petit absenti, notâ jam callidus arte,
Ostendens vacuam, et clausam pro conjuge sellam :   110
Galla mea est, inquit ; citius dimitte : moraris ?
Profer, Galla, caput. Noli vexare, quiescit.

93. *Corvinus.*] One of the noble family of the Corvini, but so reduced, that he was obliged to keep sheep, as an hired shepherd, near Laurentum, in his own native country. Laurentum is a city of Italy, now called Santo Lorenzo.

95. *Pallas.*] A freedman of Claudius.

—*The Licini.*] The name of several rich men, particularly of a freedman of Augustus ; and of Licinius Crassus, who was surnamed Dives.

96. *Let riches prevail.*] Vincant, overcome, defeat all other pretensions.

—*Sacred honour.*] Meaning the tribunes, whose office was held so sacred, that if any one hurt a tribune, his life was devoted to Jupiter, and his family was to be sold at the temple of Ceres.

97. *With white feet.*] It was the custom, when foreign slaves were exposed to sale, to whiten over their naked feet with chalk. This was the token by which they were known.

98. *The majesty of riches.*] Intimating their great and universal sway among men, particularly at Rome, in its corrupt state, where every thing was venal, which made them reverenced, and almost adored. This intimates too the command and dominion which the rich assumed over others, and the self-importance which they assumed to themselves ; a notable instance of which appears in this impudent freedman.

99. *Baleful money.*] i. e. Destructive, the occasion of many cruel and ruinous deeds.

100. *Altars of Money.*] i. e. No temple dedicated, no altars called aræ nummorum, as having sacrifices offered on them to riches, as there were to peace, faith, concord, &c.

102. *Which chatters, &c.*] Crepito here signifies to chatter like a bird. The temple of Concord, at Rome, was erected by Tiberius, at the request of his mother Livia. About this birds, such as choughs, storks, and the like, used to build their nests. What the poet says alludes to the chattering noise made by these birds, particularly when the old ones revisited their nests, after having been out to seek food for their young. See AINSW. *Salutatus,* No. 2.

103. *The highest honour, &c.*] i. e. People of the first rank and dignity.

—*Can compute, &c.*] i. e. Can be so sunk into the most sordid and meanest avarice, as to be reckoning, at the

To be wished, for, if, in the field of Laurentum, Corvinus
Keeps hired sheep? I possess more   94
Than Pallas and the Licini: let the Tribunes, therefore, wait.
Let riches prevail: nor let him yield to the sacred honour,
Who lately came into this city with white feet:
Since among us the majesty of riches is
Most sacred: altho', O baleful money! in a temple   99
As yet thou dost not dwell, we have erected no altars of money,
As Peace is worshipp'd, and Faith, Victory, Virtue,
And Concord, which chatters with a visited nest.
   But when the highest honour can compute, the year being
      finished,
What the sportula brings in, how much it adds to its accounts,
What will the attendants do, to whom from hence is a gown,
   from hence a shoe,   105
And bread, and smoke of the house? A thick crowd of litters
An hundred farthings seek; and the wife follows the husband,
And, sick or pregnant, is led about.
This asks for the absent, cunning in a known art,   109
Shewing the empty and shut-up sedan instead of the wife,
" It is my Galla," says he, " dismiss her quickly: do you delay?"
" Galla put out your head"—" don't vex her—she is asleep."

year's end, what they have gained out
of these doles which were provided for
the poor.
   105. *The attendants, &c.*] The poor
clients and followers, who, by these
doles, are, or ought to be, supplied
with clothes, meat, and fire. What
will these do, when the means of their
support is taken from them by great
people?
   —*From hence.*] i. e. By what they
receive from the dole-basket.
   —*A shoe.*] Shoes to their feet, as
we say.
   106. *Smoke of the house.*] Wood or
other fuel for firing: or firing, as we
say. The effect, smoke, for the
cause, fire. METON.
   —*Crowd of litters.*] The word densissima here denotes a very great number, a thick crowd of people carried
in litters.
   107. *An hundred farthings.*] The
quadrans was a Roman coin, the fourth
part of an as, in value not quite an
halfpenny of our money. An hundred
of these were put into the sportula, or
dole-basket: and for a share in this

paltry sum, did the people of fashion
(for such were carried in litters) seek
in so eager a manner, as that they
crowded the very door up, to get at
the sportula.
   108. *Is led about.*] The husband
lugs about his sick or breeding wife
in a litter, and claims her dole.
   109. *This asks for the absent.*] Another brings an empty litter, pretending
his wife is in it.
   —*Cunning in a known art.*] t. e.
He had often practiced this trick with
success.
   110. *It is my Galla.*] The supposed
name of his wife.
   111. *Put out your head.*] i. e. Out
of the litter that I may see you are
there, says the dispenser of the dole.
   —*Don't vex her,*] " Don't disturb
" her," replies the husband: " don't
" disquiet her, she is not very well,
" and is taking a nap." By these
methods he imposes on the dispenser,
and gets a dole for his absent wife;
though, usually, none was given but
to those who came in person: and in
order to this, the greatest caution was
commonly used. See l. 83, 4.

Ipse dies pulchro distinguitur ordine rerum ;
Sportula, deinde forum, jurisque peritus Apollo,
Atque triumphales, inter quas ausus habere   115
Nescio quis titulos Ægyptius, atque Arabarches ;
Cujus ad effigiem non tantum mejere fas est.
Vestibulis abeunt veteres, lassique clientes,
Votaque deponunt, quanquam longissima cœnæ
Spes homini: caules miseris, atque ignis emendus.   120
Optima sylvarum interea, pelagique vorabit
Rex horum, vacuisque toris tantum ipse jacebit:
Nam de tot pulchris, et latis orbibus, et tam

The violent hurry which this impostor appears to be, in (l. 111.) was no doubt, occasioned by his fear of a discovery, if he staid too long.

Thus does our poet satirize not only the meanness of the rich in coming to the sportula, but the tricks and shifts which they made use of to get at the contents of it.

113. *The day itself, &c.*] The poet having satirized the mean avarice of the higher sort, now proceeds to ridicule their idle manner of spending time.

114. *The sportula.*] See before, l. 81. The day began with attending on this.

—*The forum.*] The common place where courts of justice were kept, and matters of judgment pleaded. Hither they next resorted to entertain themselves, with hearing the causes which were there debated.

—*Apollo learned in the law.*] Augustus built and dedicated a temple and library to Apollo, in his palace on mount Palatine ; in which were large collections of law-books, as well as the works of all the famous authors in Rome.

Hor. lib. i. epist. iii. 1, 16, 17. mentions this ;

Et tangere vitat
Scripta Palatinus quæcunqe recepit
Apollo.

But I should rather think, that the poet means here the forum which Augustus built, where, it is said, there was an ivory statue of Apollo, which Juvenal represents as learned in the law, from the constant pleadings of the lawyers in that place. Here idle people used to lounge away their time.

115. *The triumphals.*] The statues of heroes, and kings, and other great men who had triumphed over the enemies of the state. These were placed in great numbers in the forum of Augustus, and in other public parts of the city.

—*An Egyptian, &c.*] Some obscure low wretch, who for no desert, but only on account of his wealth, had his statue placed there.

116. *An Arabian præfect.*] Arabarches. So Pompey is called by Cic. epist. ad Attic. l. 2. epist. xvii. because he conquered a great part of Arabia, and made it tributary to Rome. But Juvenal means here some infamous character, who had probably been præfect, or vice-roy, over that country, and had, by rapine and extortion, returned to Rome with great riches, and thus got a statue erected to him, like the Egyptian above mentioned, whom some suppose to have been in a like occupation in Egypt, and therefore called Ægyptius. Arabarches from Αραψ or Αραβιος and αρχη.

117. *To make water.*] There was a very severe law on those who did this, at or near the images of great men. This our poet turns into a jest on the statues above mentioned. Some are for giving the line another turn, as if Juvenal meant, that it was right, or lawful, not only to do this, non tantum mejere, but something worse. But I take the first interpretation to be the sense of the author, by which he would intimate, that the statues of such vile people were not only erected among those of great men, but were actually protected, like them, from all marks of indignity. So PERS. sat.

The day itself is distinguished by a beautiful order of things:
The sportula, then the forum, and Apollo learned in the
   law,
And the triumphals: among which, an Egyptian, I know
   not who,   115
Has dared to have titles: and an Arabian præfect;
At whose image it is not right so much as to make water.
The old and tired clients go away from the vestibules,
And lay aside their wishes, altho' the man has had a very
   long
Expectation of a supper: pot-herbs for the wretches, and
   fire is to be bought.   120
Meanwhile their lord will devour the best things of the
   woods, and of the sea,
And he only will lie on the empty beds:
For from so many beautiful, and wide, and ancient dishes,

i. l. 110. Sacer est locus, ite prophani, extro mejite.

118. *The old and tired clients.*] The clients were retainers, or dependents, on great men, who became their patrons: to these the clients paid all reverence, honour, and observance. The patrons, on their part, afforded them their interest, protection, and defence. They also in better times, made entertainments, to which they invited their clients. See before, note on l. 81. Here the poor clients are represented as wearied out with waiting, in long expectation of a supper, and going away in despair, under their disappointment. Cliens is derived from Greek κλειω, celebro, celebrem reddo; for it was no small part of their business to flatter and praise their patrons.

—*Vestibules.*] The porches, or entries of great men's houses.

Vestibulum ante, ipsum primoque in limine. VIRG. Æn. ii. l. 469.

120. *Pot-herbs.*] Caulis properly denotes the stalk or stem of an herb, and by Synecdoche, any kind of pot-herb, especially coleworts, or cabbage. See AINSW. *Caulis*, No. 2.

—*To be bought.*] The hungry wretches go from the patron's door, in order to lay out the poor pittance which they may have received from the sportula in some kind of pot-herbs, and in buying a little fire-wood, in order to dress them for a scanty meal.

The poet seems to mention this by way of contrast to what follows.

121. *Their lord.*] i. e. The patron of these clients. Rex, not only signifies a king, but any great or rich man; so a patron. This from the power and dominion which he exercised over his clients. Hence, as well as from his protection and care over them, he was called patronus, from the Greek πατρων, ωνος, from πατηρ, a father.

—*Meanwhile.*] i. e. While the poor clients are forced to take up with a few boiled coleworts.

—*The best things of the woods, &c.*] The woods are to be ransacked for the choicest game, and the sea for the finest sorts of fish, to satisfy the patron's gluttony: these he will devour, without asking any body to partake with him.

122. *On the empty beds.*] The Romans lay along on beds, or couches, at their meals. Several of these beds are here supposed to be round the table which were formerly occupied by his friends and clients, but they are now vacant—not a single guest is invited to occupy them, or to partake of the entertainment with this selfish glutton.

123. *Dishes.*] Which were round, in an orbicular shape; hence called orbes.

—*Beautiful.*] Of a beautiful pattern —ancient—valuable for their antiquity; made probably, by some artists of old time.

Antiquis, unà comedunt patrimonia mensâ.
Nullus jam parasitus erit: sed quis feret istas   125
Luxuriæ sordes? quanta est gula, quæ sibi totos
Ponit apros, animal propter convivia natum?
Pœna tamen præsens, cum tu deponis amictus
Turgidus, et crudum pavonem in balnea portas:
Hinc subitæ mortes, atque intestata senectus.   130
It nova, nec tristis per cunctas fabula cœnas:
Ducitur iratis plaudendum funus amicis.
Nil erit ulterius, quod nostris moribus addat
Posteritas: eadem cupient, facientque minores.
OMNE IN PRÆCIPITI VITIUM STETIT: utere velis,   135
Totos pande sinus. Dicas hic forsitan, "unde
"Ingenium par materiæ? unde illa priorum
"Scribendi quodcunque animo flagrante liberet

---

124. *At one meal.*] Mensa.—lit. table—which (by Meton.) stands here for what is set upon it. Thus they waste and devour their estates in this abominable and selfish gluttony.

125. *No parasite.*] From παρα near, and σιτον food.

These were a kind of jesters, and flatterers, who were frequently invited to the tables of the great; and who, indeed, had this in view, when they flattered and paid their court to them. Terence, in his Eunuch, has given a most spirited and masterly specimen of parasites, in his inimitable character of Gnatho.

But so fallen were the great into the meanest avarice, and into the most sordid luxury, that they could gormandize by themselves, without even inviting a parasite, to flatter or divert them. But who, even though a parasite, would endure (feret) such a sight?

126. *Filthiness of luxury.*] Sordes, nastiness; a happy word to describe the beastliness of such gluttony with regard to the patron himself, and its stinginess and niggardliness, with respect to others,

—*How great is the gullet.*] The gluttonous appetite of these men.

—*Puts.*] Ponit, sets, places on the table.

127. *Whole boars, &c.*] A whole boar at a time, the wild boar, espe-

cially the Tuscan, was an high article of luxury at all grand entertainments. The word natum is here used as the word natis. Hon. lib. i. od. xxvii. l. 1. See also OVID, Met. lib. xv. l. 117.

Quid meruistis, oves, placidum pecus, inque tuendos

NATUM *homines?*

Juvenal speaks as if boars were made and produced for no other purpose than convivial entertainments.

128. *A present punishment.*] Of such horrid gluttony.

—*Put off your clothes.*] Strip yourself for bathing.

129. *Turgid.*] Turgidus, swoln; puffed up with a full stomach.

—*An indigested peacock.*] Which you have devoured, and which is crude and indigested within you.

—*To the baths.*] It was the custom to bathe before meals; the contrary was reckoned unwholesome. See PERS. sat. iii. l. 98—105. and HOR. Epist. lib. i. Ep. vi. l. 61.

130. *Sudden deaths.*] Apoplexies and the like, which arise from too great repletion. Bathing with a full stomach must be likely to occasion these, by forcing the blood with too great violence towards the brain.

—*Intestate old age.*] i. e. Old gluttons thus suddenly cut off, without time to make their wills.

131. *A new story, &c.*] A fresh piece of news which nobody is sorry for.

They devour patrimonies at one meal.
There will now be no parasite: but who will bear that   125
Filthiness of luxury? how great is the gullet, which, for
    itself, puts
Whole boars, an animal born for feasts?
Yet there is a present punishment when you put off your
    clothes,
Turgid, and carry an indigested peacock to the baths:
Hence sudden deaths, and intestate old age.   130
A new story, nor is it a sorrowful one, goes thro' all com-
    panies:
A funeral, to be applauded by angry friends, is carried forth.
There will be nothing farther, which posterity can add
To our morals: those born after us will desire and do the
    same things.
ALL VICE IS AT THE HEIGHT. Use sails,   135
Spread their whole bosoms open. Here, perhaps, you'll
    say—"Whence
" Is there genius equal to the matter? Whence that simplicity
" Of former (writers), of writing whatever they might like,
    with

132. *A funeral is carried forth.*]
The word ducitur is peculiarly used
to denote the carrying forth a corpse
to burial, or to the funeral pile. So
VIRG. Geor. iv. 256.
    Exportant tectis, et tristia funera
    DUCUNT.
Owing perhaps to the procession of
the friends, &c. of the deceased, which
went before the corpse, and led it to
the place of burning, or interment.
    —*Applauded by angry friends.*]
Who, disobliged by having nothing
left them, from the deceased's dying
suddenly, and without a will, express
their resentment by rejoicing at his
death instead of lamenting it. See
PERS. sat. vi. 33, 4.
    134. *To our morals.*] Our vices and
debaucheries, owing to the depravity
and corruption of our morals.
    —*Those born after us.*] Minores, i.e.
natu, our descendants; the opposite
of majores natu, our ancestors.
    135. *All vice is at the height.*] In
præcipiti stetit, hath stood, hath been
for some time at its highest pitch, at
its summit, so that our posterity can

carry it no higher. Compare the two
preceding lines.
    Vice is at stand, and at the highest
    flow.   DRYDEN.
On tip-toe. AINSW.
    135—6. *Use sails, Spread, &c.*] A
metaphor taken from sailors, who,
when they have a fair wind, spread
open their sails as much as they can.
The poet here insinuates, that there
is now a fair opportunity for satire to
display all its powers.
    136—7. *Whence is there genius, &c.*]
Here he is supposed to be interrupted
by some friend, who starts an objection, on his invocation to Satire to
spread all its sails, and use all its
powers against the vices of the times.
    Where shall we find genius equal
to the matter? equal to range so wide
a field? equal to the description and
due correction of so much vice?
    137. *Whence that simplicity, &c.*]
That simple and undisguised freedom
of reproof which former writers exercised. Alluding, perhaps, to Lucilius,
Horace, and other writers of former
times.

" Simplicitas, cujus non audeo dicere nomen ?
" Quid refert dictis ignoscat Mutius, an non?   140
" Pone Tigellinum, tædâ lucebis in illâ,
" Quâ stantes ardent, qui fixo gutture fumant,
" Et latum mediâ sulcum deducis arena.
" Qui dedit ergo tribus patruis aconita, vehetur
" Pensilibus plumis, atque illinc despiciet nos ?   145
" Cum veniet contra, digito compesce labellum :
" Accusator erit, qui verbum dixerit, hic est.
" Securus licet Æneam, Rutilumque ferocem

139. *A burning mind.*] Inflamed with zeal, and burning with satiric rage against the vices and abuses of their times.

—*Of which I dare not, &c.*] It is hardly safe now to name, or mention, the liberty of the old writers; it is so sunk and gone, that the very naming it is dangerous.

140. *Mutius.*] Titus Mutius Albutius, a very great and powerful man. He was satirized by Lucilius, and this most severely by name. See note on PERS. sat i l. 115.

Lucilius feared no bad consequences of this, in those days of liberty.

141. *Set down Tigellinus.*] i. e. Expose him as an object of satire—satirize this creature and infamous favourite of Nero's, and most terrible will be the consequence.

—*In that torch.*] This cruel punishment seems to have been proper to incendiaries, in which light the poet humourously supposes the satirizers of the emperor's favourites, and other great men, to be looked upon at that time.

After Nero had burnt Rome, to satisfy his curiosity with the prospect, he contrived to lay the odium on the Christians, and charged them with setting the city on fire. He caused them to be wrapped round with garments, which were bedaubed with pitch, and other combustible matters, and set on fire at night, by way of torches to enlighten the streets ; and thus they miserably perished. See KENNETT, Ant. p. 147.

142 *Standing.*] In an erect posture.
—*With fixed throat.*] Fastened by the neck to a stake.

143. *And you draw out a wide fur-*

row, &c.] After all the danger which a satirist runs of his life, for attacking Tigellinus, or any other minion of the emperor's, all his labour will be in vain ; there is no hope of doing any good. It would be like ploughing in the barren sand, and would yield nothing to reward your pains.

Commentators have given various explanations of this line, which is very difficult, and almost unintelligible where the copies read deducet, as if relating to the fumant in the preceding line; but this cannot well be, that the plural should be expressed by the third person singular. They talk of the sufferer's making a trench in the sand, by running round the post, to avoid the flames; but how can this be, when the person has the combustibles fastened round him, and must be in the midst of fire, go where he may ? Besides, this idea does not agree with fixo gutture, which implies being fastened, or fixed, so as not to be able to stir.

Instead of deducet, or deducit, I should think deducis the right reading, as others have thought before me. This agrees, in number and person, with lucebis, l. 141, and gives us an easy and natural solution of the observation ; viz. that, after all the dangers incurred by satirizing the emperor's favourites, no good was to be expected : they were too bad to be reformed.

The Greeks had a proverbial saying, much like what I contend for here, to express labouring in vain, viz. Αμμον μιτρεις—Arenam metiris, you measure the sand—i. e. of the sea.

Juvenal expresses the same thought, sat. vii. 48, 9. as I would suppose him to do in this line.

" A burning mind, of which I dare not tell the name.
" What signifies it, whether Mutius might forgive what
      they said or not?   140
" Set down Tigellinus, and you will shine in that torch,
" In which standing they burn, who with fixed throat
      smoke;
" And you draw out a wide furrow in the midst of sand.
" Shall he, therefore, who gave wolf's bane to three uncles,
      be carried   144
" With pensile feathers, and from thence look down on us?"
" When he shall come opposite, restrain your lip with your
      finger—
" There will be an accuser (of him) who shall say the word—
      " That's he."
" Though, secure, Æneas and the fierce Rutilian

Nos tamen hoc agimus, tenuique in pulvere sulcos. Ducimus, et littus sterili versamus aratro.

144. *Wolf's bane.*] Aconitum is the Latin for this poisonous herb; but it is used in the plural, as here, to denote other sorts of poison, or poison in general. See Ovid, Met. i. 147.
Lurida terribiles miscent ACONITA *novercæ.*
—*Three uncles.*] Tigellinus is here meant, who poisoned three uncles that he might possess himself of their estates. And, after their death, he forged wills for them, by which he became possessed of all they had. He likewise impeached several of the nobility, and got their estates. See more in AINSW. under *Tigellinus.*
—*Shall he, therefore, &c.*] " And because there may be danger in writing satire, as things now are, is such a character as this to triumph in his wickedness unmolested? Shall he be carried about in state, and look down with contempt upon other people, and shall I not dare to say a word?" This we may suppose Juvenal to mean, on hearing what is said about the danger of writing satire, and on being cautioned against it.
145. *With pensile feathers.*] Pensilis means, literally, hanging in the air. It was a piece of luxury to have a mattress and pillows stuffed with feathers; on which the great man repo-

sed himself in his litter. Hence the poet makes use of the term pensilibus to plumis, as being in the litter which hung in the air, as it was carried along by the bearers. See before, l. 30. and note; and l. 51, 2. and note.
—*From thence.*] From his easy litter.
—*Look down.*] With contempt and disdain.
146. *When he shall come opposite.*] The moment you meet him, carried along in his stately litter, (says Juvenal's supposed adviser,) instead of saying any thing, or taking any notice of him, let him pass quietly— lay your hand on your mouth—hold your tongue—be silent.
147. *There will be an accuser.*] An informer, who will lay an accusation before the emperor, if you do but so much as point with your finger, or utter with your lips, " That's he." Therefore, that neither of these may happen, lay your finger upon your lips, and make not the slightest remark.
—*(Of him) who.*] Illi or illius is here understood before qui, &c.
148. *Though, secure.*] Though you must not meddle with the living, you may securely write what you please about the dead.
—*Æneas and the fierce Rutilian.*] i. e. Æneas, and Turnus, a king of the Rutilians, the rival of Æneas, and slain by him. See VIRG. Æn. xii. 919, &c.

" Committas: nulli gravis est percussus Achilles :
" Aut multum quæsitus Hylas, urnamque secutus. 150
" Ense velut stricto quoties Lucilius ardens
" Infremuit, rubet auditor, cui frigida mens est
" Criminibus, tacitâ sudant præcordia culpâ :
" Inde iræ, et lachrymæ. Tecum prius ergo voluta
" Hæc animo ante tubas ; galeatum sero duelli 155
" Pœnitet." Experiar quid concedatur in illos,
Quorum Flaminiâ tegitur cinis, atque Latinâ.

149. *You may match.*] Committas is a metaphorical expression, taken from matching or pairing gladiators, or others, in single combat.

Martial says,

Cum JUVENALE *meo cur me committere tentas ?*

" Why do you endeavour to match " me with my friend Juvenal ?" *i. e.* in a poetical contest with him.

By committas we are therefore to understand, that one might very safely write the history of Æneas and Turnus, and match them together in fight, as Virgil has done.

—*Smitten Achilles.*] Killed by Paris in the temple of Apollo.

—*Is grievous to none.*] Nobody will get into danger, or trouble, by writing the history of this event.

150. *Hylas much sought.*] By Hercules when he had lost him. See VIRG. ecl. vi. 43, 44.

—*Followed his pitcher.*] with which he was sent by Hercules, to the river Ascanius to draw some water : where being seen, and fallen in love with by three river-nymphs, they pulled him into the stream.

On subjects like these, saith the adviser, you may say what you please, and nobody will take offence : but beware of attacking the vices of living characters, however infamous or obnoxious.

151. *Ardent.*] Inflamed with satiric rage against the vices of his day.

152. *Raged.*] Infremuit—roared aloud, in his writings, which were as terrible to the vicious, as the roaring of a lion, which the verb infremo signifies : hence Met. to rage [violently, or tumultuously.

—*Reddens.*] With anger and shame.

152–3. *Frigid with crimes.*] Chilled, as it were, with horror of conscience —their blood ran cold as we should say.

153. *The bosom.*] Præcordia—lit. the parts about the heart—supposed to be the seat of moral sensibility.

—*Sweats.*] Sweating is the effect of hard labour. Sudant is here used metaphorically, to denote the state of a

" You may match ; smitten Achilles is grievous to none :
" Or Hylas much sought, and having followed his pitcher.
" As with a drawn sword, as often as Lucilius ardent 151
" Raged—the hearer reddens, who has a mind frigid
" With crimes ; the bosom sweats with silent guilt :
" Hence anger and tears. Therefore first revolve, with thyself,
" These things in thy mind, before the trumpets : the hel-
    " meted late of a fight   ·155
" Repents." I'll try what may be allowed towards those,
Whose ashes are covered in the Flaminian and Latin way.

mind labouring, and toiling, under the grievous burden of a guilty conscience. This image is finely used, Mat. xi. 28.

154. *Anger and tears.*] Anger at the satirist—tears of vexation and sorrow at being exposed.

155. *Before the trumpets.*] A metaphor taken from the manner of giving the signal for battle, which was done with the sound of trumpets.

Think well, says the adviser, before you sound the alarm for your attack —weigh well all hazards before you begin.

—*The helmeted, &c.*] When once a man has gotten his helmet on, and advances to the combat, it is too late to change his mind. Once engaged in writing satire, you must go through; there is no retreating.

156. *I'll try, &c.*] Well, says Juvenal, since the writing satire on the living is so dangerous, I'll try how far it may be allowed me to satirize the dead.

Hence he writes against no great and powerful person, but under the feigned name of some vicious character that lived in past time.

157. *Whose ashes are covered.*] When the bodies were consumed on the funeral pile, the ashes were put into urns and buried.

—*The Flaminian and Latin way.*] These were two great roads, or ways, leading from Rome to other parts. In the via Flaminia and via Latina, urns and remains of the nobles were buried, and had monuments erected. Hence have been so often found in ancient Roman inscriptions on monuments, Siste viator.

It was ordered by the law of the Twelve Tables that nobody should be buried within the city; hence the urns of the great were buried, and their monuments were erected on those celebrated roads or ways. For the Flaminian way, see before, l. 48. note. The via Latina was of great extent, reaching from Rome, through many famous cities, to the farthest part of Latium.

Satira Tertia.

Juvenal introduces Umbritius, an old friend of his, tak-
ing his departure from Rome, and going to settle in a
country retirement at Cumæ. He accompanies Umbri-
tius out of town; and, before they take leave of each
other, Umbritius tells his friend Juvenal the reasons

QUAMVIS digressu veteris confusus amici,
Laudo tamen vacuis quod sedem figere Cumis
Destinet, atque unum civem donare Sibyllæ.
Janua Baiarum est, et gratum littus amœni
Secessûs   Ego vel Prochytam præpono Suburræ.   5
Nam quid tam miserum, tam solum vidimus, ut non
Deterius credas horrere incendia, lapsus
Tectorum assiduos, ac mille pericula sævæ
Urbis, et Augusto recitantes mense poëtas?
Sed dum tota domus rhedâ componitur unâ.   10

Line 2. Cumæ.] An ancient city of Campania near the sea. Some think it had its name from κυματα, waves: the waves, in rough weather, dashing against the walls of it. Others think it was so called from its being built by the Cumœi of Asia. PLIN. III. 4. Juvenal calls it empty in comparison with the populousness of Rome. it was now, probably, much decayed, and but thinly inhabited: on this account it might be looked upon as a place of leisure, quiet, and retirement; all which may be understood by the word vacuis.

3. The Sybil.] Quasi σιου βουλη, Dei consilium. AINSW. The Sibyls were women, supposed to be inspired with a spirit of prophecy. Authors are not agreed as to the number of them; but the most famous was the Cumæan, so called from having her residence at Cumæ Umbritius was now going to bestow, donare, one citizen on this abode of the Sybil, by

taking up his residence there. See VIRG. Æn. vi. l. 10. et seq.

4. The gate of Baiæ.] Passengers from Rome to Baiæ were to pass through Cumæ; they went in on one side, and came out on the other, as through a gate

—*Baiæ*] A delightful city of Campania, of which HOR. lib. I. epist. i. l. 83

Nullus in orbe sinus Baiis prælucet
amœnis.

Here were fine warm springs and baths, both pleasant and healthful: on which account it was much resorted to by the nobility and gentry of Rome, many of whom had villas there for their summer residence. It forms part of the bay of Naples.

—*A grateful shore.*] Gratum: grateful, here, must be understood in the sense of agreeable, pleasant. The whole shore, from Cumæ to Baiæ, was delightfully pleasant, and calculated for the most agreeable retire-

Third Satire.

---

which had induced him to retire from Rome: each of which is replete with the keenest satire on its vicious inhabitants. Thus the Poet carries on his design of inveighing against the vices and disorders which reigned in that city.

THOUGH troubled at the departure of an old friend,
I yet approve that to fix his abode at empty Cumæ
He purposes, and to give one citizen to the Sibyl.
It is the gate of Baiæ, and a grateful shore of pleasant
Retirement. I prefer even Prochyta to Suburra: 5
For what so wretched, so solitary do we see, that you
Would not think it worse to dread fires, the continual
Falling of houses, and a thousand perils of the fell
City, and poets reciting in the month of August?
But while his whole house is put together in one vehicle, 10

---

ment. See the latter part of the last note.

5. *Prochyta.*] A small rugged island in the Tyrrhenian sea, desert and barren.

—*Suburra.*] A street in Rome, much frequented, but chiefly by the vulgar, and by women of ill fame. Hence MART. vi. 66.

  Famæ non nimium bonæ puella,
  Quales in mediâ, sedent Suburrâ.

6. *For what so wretched &c.*] Solitary and miserable as any place may be, yet it is better to be there than at Rome, where you have so many dangers and inconveniences to apprehend.

7. *Fires.*] House-burnings, to which populous cities, from many various causes are continually liable.

8. *Falling of houses.*] Owing to the little care taken of old and ruinous buildings. Propertius speaks of the two foregoing dangers.

  Præterea domibus flammam, domi-
  busque ruinam.

8—9. *The fell city.*] That habitation of daily cruelty and mischief.

9. *And poets reciting.*] Juvenal very humourously introduces this circumstance among the calamities and inconveniences of living at Rome, that even in the month of August, the hottest season of the year, when most people had retired into the country, so that one might hope to enjoy some little quiet, even then you were to be teazed to death, by the constant din of the scribbling poets reciting their wretched compositions, and forcing you to hear them. Comp. sat. i. l. 1—14. where our poet expresses his peculiar aversion to this.

10. *His whole house, &c.*] While all his household furniture and goods were packing up together in one waggon, (as *rheda* may here signify,) Umbritius was moving all his bag and baggage, (as we say,) and, by its taking up no more room, it should seem to have been very moderate in quantity.

Substitit ad veteres arcus, madidamque Capenam:
Hîc, ubi nocturnæ Numa constituebat amicæ,
Nunc sacri fontis nemus, et delûbra locantur
Judæis: quorum cophinus, fœnumque supellex.
Omnis enim populo mercedem pendere jussa est   15
Arbor, et ejectis mendicat sylva Camœnis.
In vallem Ægeriæ descendimus, et speluncas
Dissimiles veris: quanto præstantius esset
Numen aquæ, viridi si margine clauderet undas

11. *He stood still.*] He may be sup-posed to have walked on out of the city, attended by his friend Juvenal, expecting the vehicle with the goods to overtake him, when loaded: he now stood still to wait for its coming up; and in this situation he was, when he began to tell his friend his various reasons for leaving Rome, which are just so many strokes of the keenest satire upon the vices and fol-lies of its inhabitants.

—*At the old arches.*] The ancient triumphal arches of Romulus, and of the Horatii, which were in that part. Or perhaps the old arches of the aqueducts might here be meant.

—*Wet Capena.*] One of the gates of Rome, which led towards Capua: it was sometimes called Triumphalis, because those who rode in triumph passed through it; it was also called Fontinalis, from the great number of springs that were near it, which occa-sioned building the aqueducts, by which the water was carried by pipes into the city: hence Juvenal calls it madidam Capenam. Here is the spot where Numa used to meet the goddess Ægeria.

12. *Numa.*] Pompilius, successor to Romulus.

—*Nocturnal mistress.*] The more strongly to recommend his laws, and the better to instil into the Romans a reverence for religion, he persuaded them, that every night he conversed with a goddess, or nymph, called Æge-ria, from whose mouth he received his whole form of government, both civil and religious; that their place of meeting was in a grove without the gate Capena, dedicated to the Muses, wherein was a temple consecrated to them and to the goddess Ægeria, whose fountain waters the grove; for she is

fabled to have wept herself into a fountain, for the death of Numa. This fountain, grove, and temple, were let out to the Jews, at a yearly rent, for habitation; they having been dri-ven out of the city by Domitian, and compelled to lodge in these places, heretofore sacred to the Muses. De-lubra is a general term for places of worship. See AINSW. By the phrase nocturnæ amicæ constituebat, Juve-nal speaks as if he were describing an intrigue, where a man meets his mistress by appointment at a particu-lar place: from this we can be at no loss to judge of our poet's very slight opinion of the reality of the transac-tion.

14. *A basket and hay, &c.*] These were all the furniture which these poor creatures had—the sum total of their goods and chattels.

This line has been looked upon as very difficult to expound. Some com-mentators have left it without any at-tempt to explain it. Others have ra-ther added to, than diminished from, whatever its difficulty may be. They tell us, that these were the marks not of their poverty, but, by an ancient custom, of their servitude in Egypt, where, in baskets, they carried hay, straw, and such things, for the mak-of brick, and in such like labours. See Exod. v. 7—18. This comment, with the reasons given to support it, we can only say, is very far fetched, and is not warranted by any account we have of the Jewish customs.

Others say, that the hay was to feed their cattle. But how could these poor Jews be able to purchase, or to maintain cattle, who were forced to beg in order to maintain themselves? Others, that the hay was for their bed on which they lay; but neither is this

He stood still at the old arches, and wet Capena:
Here, where Numa appointed his nocturnal mistress,
Now the grove of the sacred fountain, and the shrines are
        hired
To the Jews : of whom a basket and hay are the household
        stuff.   14
For every tree is commanded to pay a rent to the people :
And the wood begs, the muses being ejected.
We descend into the vale of Ægeria, and into caves
Unlike the true : how much better might have been
The deity of the water, if, with a green margin, the grass
        inclosed

likely ; for the poet, in another satire, describes a mendicant Jewess as coming into the city, and leaving her basket and hay behind her ; which implies, that the basket and hay were usually carried about with them when they went a begging elsewhere. Now it is not to be supposed that they should carry about so large a quantity of hay, as served them to lie upon when at home in the grove.

It is clear that the basket and hay are mentioned together here, and in the place before mentioned, from whence I infer, that they had little wicker baskets in which they put the money, provisions, or other small alms which they received of the passers by, and, in order to stow them the better, and to prevent their dropping through the interstices of the wicker, put wisps of hay, or dried grass, in the inside of the baskets. These Jew beggars were as well known by baskets with hay in them, as our beggars are by their wallets, or our soldiers by their knapsacks. Hence the Jewess, in the satire above alluded to, left her basket and hay behind her when she came into the city, for fear they should betray her, and subject her to punishment for infringing the emperor's order against the Jews coming into the city. Her manner of begging too, by a whisper in the ear, seems to confirm this supposition. The Latin cophinus is the same as Gr. κοφινος, which is used several times in the New Testament to denote a provision-basket, made use of among the Jews. See Matt. xiv. 20. Matt. xvi. 9, 10. Mark vi. 43. Mark viii.

19, 20. Luke ix. 17. John vi. 13.

15. To pay a rent.] The grove being let out to the Jews, every tree, as it were, might be said to bring in a rent to the people at Rome. The poet seems to mention this as a proof of the public avarice, created by the public extravagance, which led them to hire out these sacred places for what they could get, by letting them to the poor Jews, who could only pay for them out of what they got by begging.

16. The wood begs, &c.] i. e. The Jews, who were now the inhabitants of the wood, (meton.) were all beggars ; nothing else was to be seen in those once sacred abodes of the Muses, who were now banished.

17. We descend, &c.] Umbritius and Juvenal sauntered on, till they came to that part of the grove which was called the vale of Ægeria, so called, probably, from the fountain, into which she was changed, running there.

17-18. And into caves unlike the true.] These caves, in their primitive state, were as nature formed them, but had been profaned with artificial ornaments, which had destroyed their native beauty and simplicity.

18. How much better.] How much more suitably situated.

19. The deity of the water.] Each fountain was supposed to have a nymph, or naiad, belonging to it, who presided over it as the goddess of the water ; Ægeria may be supposed to be here meant.

—If, with a green margin, &c.] If, instead of ornamenting the banks

Herba, nec ingenuum violarent marmora tophum ?   20
Hic tunc Umbritius : quando artibus, inquit, honestis
Nullus in urbe locus, nulla emolumenta laborum,
Res hodie minor est, here quam fuit, atque eadem cras
Deteret exiguis aliquid ; proponimus illuc
Ire, fatigatas ubi Dædalus exuit alas :   25
Dum nova canities, dum prima, et recta senectus,
Dum superest Lachesi quod torqueat, et pedibus me
Porto meis, nullo dextram subeunte bacillo,
Cedamus patriâ : vivant Arturius istic,
Et Catulus : maneant qui nigra in candida vertunt,   30
Queis facile est ædem conducere, flumina, portus, ·

with artificial borders made of marble, they had been left in their natural state, simple and unadorned by human art, having no other margin but the native turf, and the rude stone (tophum) which was the genuine produce of the soil. These were once consecrated in honour of the fountain-nymph, but had now been violated and destroyed, in order to make way for artificial ornaments of marble, which Roman luxury and extravagance had put in their place.

21. *Here then Umbritius.*] Juvenal and his friend Umbritius being arrived at this spot, at the profanation of which they were both equally scandalized, Umbritius there began to inveigh against the city of Rome, from which he was now about to depart, and spake as follows.

—*Honest arts.*] Liberal arts and science, such as poetry, and other literary pursuits, which are honourable. Comp. sat. vii 1–6. Honestis artibus, in contradistinction to the dishonest and shameful methods of employment, which received countenance and encouragement from the great and opulent. Umbritius was himself a poet. See this sat. l. 310, 11.

22. *No emoluments of labour.*] Nothing to be gotten by all the pains of honest industry.

23. *One's substance, &c.*] Instead of increasing what I have, I find it daily decrease ; as I can get nothing to replace what I spend, by all the pains I can take.

—*And the same to-morrow, &c.*] This same poor pittance of mine will to-morrow be wearing away something from the little that is left of it to-day : and so I must find myself growing poorer from day to day. Deteret is a metaphorical expression, taken from the action of the file, which gradually wears away and diminishes the bodies to which it is applied. So the necessary expences of Umbritius and his family were wearing away his substance in that expensive place, which he determines to leave, for a more private and cheaper part of the country.

24. *We propose.*] i. e. I and my family propose—or proponimus for propono. Synec.

25–6. *Thither to go.*] i. e. To Cumæ, where Dædalus alighted after his flight from Crete.

26. *Greyness is new.*] While grey hairs, newly appearing, warn me that old age is coming upon me.

—*Fresh and upright.*] While old age in its first stage appears, and I am not yet so far advanced as to be bent double, but am able to hold myself upright. The ancients supposed old age first to commence about the 46th year. Cic. de Senectute. Philosophers (says Holyday) divide man's life according to its several stages. First, infantia to three or four years of age. Secondly, pueritia, thence to ten. From ten to eighteen, pubertas. Thence to twenty-five, adolescentia. Then juventus, from twenty-five to thirty-five or forty. Thence to fifty, ætas virilis. Then came senectus

The waters, nor had marbles violated the natural stone ? 20
Here then Umbritius :—Since for honest arts, says he,
There is no place in the city, no emoluments of labour,
One's substance is to-day less than it was yesterday, and the
　　same to-morrow,
Will diminish something from the little : we propose thither
To go, where Dædalus put off his weary wings,　　　25
While greyness is new, while old age is fresh and upright,
While there remains to Lachesis what she may spin, and
　　on my feet
Myself I carry, no staff sustaining my hand,
Let us leave our native soil : let Arturius live there,
And Catulus : let those stay who turn black into white. 30
To whom it is easy to hire a building, rivers, ports,

prima et recta till sixty-five ; and then
ultima et decrepita till death.

27. *While there remains to Lachesis, &c.*] One of the three destinies :
she was supposed to spin the thread
of human life.

The Parcæ, or poetical fates or destinies, were Clotho, Lachesis, and
Atropos. The first held the distaff ;
the second drew out, and spun the
thread ; which the last cut off when
finished.

—*And on my feet, &c.*] While I
can stand on my own legs, and walk
without the help of a staff.

29. *Let us leave, &c.*] Let me, and
all that belongs to me, take an ever-
lasting farewell of that detested city,
which, though my native place, I am
heartily tired of, as none but knaves
are fit to live there.

29–30. *Arturius and Catulus.*] Two
knaves, who, from very low life, had
raised themselves to large and affluent
circumstances. Umbritius seems to
introduce them as examples, to prove
that such people found more encouragement in Rome, than the professors of the liberal arts could hope for.
See before, l. 21. note 2.

30. *Let those stay, &c.*] He means
those, who by craft and subtlety
could utterly invert and change the
appearances of things, making virtue
appear as vice, and vice as virtue ;
falsehood as truth, and truth as falsehood. Such were Arturius and
Catulus.

31. *To hire a building.*] The word

ædem, here being joined with other
things of public concern, such as rivers, ports, &c. seems to imply their
hiring some public buildings, of which
they made money ; and it should
seem, from these lines, that the several branches of the public revenue
and expenditure were farmed out to
certain contractors, who were answerable to the ædiles, and to the other
magistrates, for the due execution of
their contracts. Juvenal here seems
to point at the temples, theatres, and
other public buildings, which were
thus farmed out to these people, who,
from the wealth which they had acquired, and of course from their re-
sponsibility, could easily procure such
contracts, by which they made an immense and exorbitant profit. Ædis is
signifies any kind of edifice. AINSW.
Omne ædeficium ædis dicitur.

—*Rivers.*] Fisheries perhaps, by
hiring which, they monopolized them,
so as to distress others, and enrich
themselves ; or the carriage of goods
upon the rivers, for which a toll was
paid ; or, by flumina, may here be
meant, the beds of the rivers, hired
out to be cleaned and cleared at the
public expence.

—*Ports.*] Where goods were export-
ed and imported ; the customs of these
ports they rented, and thus became
farmers of the public revenue, to the
great grievance of those who were to
pay the duties, and to the great emolument of themselves, who were sure
to make the most of their bargain.

F

Siccandam eluviem, portandum ad busta cadaver,
Et præbere caput dominâ venale sub hastâ
Quondam hi cornicines, et municipalis arenæ
Perpetui comites, notæque per oppida buccæ,   35
Munera nunc edunt, et verso pollice vulgi
Quemlibet occidunt populariter : inde reversi
Conducunt foricas : et cur non omnia ? cum sint
Quales ex humili magna ad fastigia rerum
Extollit, quoties voluit Fortuna jocari.   40
Quid Romæ faciam ? mentiri nescio : librum,
Si malus est, nequeo laudare, et poscere : motus

32. *A sewer to be dried.*] Eluvies signifies a sink or common-sewer; which is usual in great cities, to carry off the water and filth that would otherwise incommode the houses and streets. From cluo, to wash out, wash away.

These contractors undertook the opening and clearing these from the stoppages to which they were liable, and by which, if not cleansed, the city would have been in many parts overflowed. There was nothing so mean and filthy, that these two men would not have undertaken for the sake of gain. Here we find them scavengers.

—*A corpse, &c.*] Busta were places where dead bodies were burned; also graves and sepulchres. AINSW. Bustum from ustum. Sometimes these people hired or farmed funerals, contracting for the expence at such a price. In this too they found their account.

33. *And to expose, &c*] These fellows sometimes were mangones, sellers of slaves, which they purchased, and then sold by auction. See PERS. vi. 72, 3.

—*The mistress-spear.*] Domina hasta. It is difficult to render these two substantives literally into English, unless we join them, as we frequently do some of our own; as in master-key, queen-bee, &c.

We read of the hasta decemviralis which was fixed before the courts of justice. So of the hasta centumviralis, also fixed there. A spear was also fixed in the forum where there was an auction, and was a sign of it: all things sold there were placed near it, and were said to be sold *under the*

spear. Hence (by meton.) hasta is used, by Cicero and others, to signify an auction, or public sale of goods. The word domina seems to imply the power of disposal of the property in persons and things sold there, the possession and dominion over which were settled by this mode of sale, in the several purchasers. So that the spear, or auction, might properly be called domina, as ruling the disposal of persons and things.

34. *These, in time past, horn-blowers.*] Such was formerly the occupation of these people; they had travelled about the country, from town to town, with little paltry shows of gladiators, fencers, wrestlers, stage-players, and the like, sounding horns to call the people together, like our trumpeters to a puppet-show.

—*Municipal theatre*] Municipium signifies a city or town-corporate, which had the privileges and freedom of Rome, and at the same time governed by laws of its own, like our corporations. Municipalis denotes any thing belonging to such a town. Most of these had arenæ, or theatres, where strolling companies of gladiators, &c. (like our strolling players,) used to exhibit. They were attended by horn-blowers and trumpeters, who sounded during the performance.

35. *Cheeks known, &c.*] Blowers on the horn, or trumpet, were sometimes called buccinatores, from the great distension of the cheeks in the action of blowing. This, by constant use, left a swollen appearance on the cheeks, for which these fellows were well known in all the country towns. Perhaps buccæ is here put for buccinæ.

A sewer to be dried, a corpse to be carried to the pile,
And to expose a venal head under the mistress-spear.
These, in time past, horn blowers, and on a municipal
  theatre
Perpetual attendants, and cheeks known through the towns;
Now set forth public shows, and the people's thumb being
  turned   36
Kill whom they will, as the people please: thence returned
They hire jakes: and why not all things? since they are
Such, as, from low estate, to great heights of circumstances
Fortune raises up, as often as she has a mind to joke.   40
What can I do at Rome? I know not to lie: a book
If bad I cannot praise, and ask for: the motions

the horns, trumpets, and such wind instruments as these fellows strolled with about the country. See AINSW. *Bucca*, No. 3.

36. *Now set forth public shows.*] Munera, so called because given to the people at the expence of him who set them forth. These fellows, who had themselves been in the mean condition above described, now are so magnificent, as to treat the people with public shows of gladiators at the Roman theatre.

—*The people's thumb, &c.*] This alludes to a barbarous usage at fights of gladiators, where, if the people thought he that was overcome behaved like a coward, without courage or art, they made a sign for the vanquisher to put him to death, by clenching the hand, and holding or turning the thumb upward. If the thumb were turned downward, it was a signal to spare his life.

37. *Whom they will, &c.*] These fellows, by treating the people with shows, had grown so popular, and had such influence among the vulgar, that it was entirely in their power to direct the spectators, as to the signal for life or death, so that they either killed or saved, by directing the pleasure of the people. See AINSW. *Populariter*, No. 2.

—*Thence returned, &c.*] Their advancement to wealth did not alter their mean pursuits; after returning from the splendour of the theatre, they contract for emptying bog-houses of their soil and filth. Such

were called at Rome, foricarii and latrinarii; with us, night-men.

38. *Why not all things?*] Why hire they not the town, not every thing,

Since such as they have fortune in a string?   DRYDEN.

39. *Such, as, from low estate.*] The poet here reckons the advancement of such low people to the height of opulence, as the sport of fortune, as one of those frolics which she exercises out of mere caprice and wantonness, without any regard to desert. See HOR. lib. i. ode xxiv. l. 14–16. and lib. iii. ode xxix, l. 49–52.

40. *Fortune.*] Had a temple and was worshipped as a goddess. The higher she raised up such wretches, the more conspicuously contemptible she might be said to make them, and seemed to joke, or divert herself, at their expence. See sat. x. 335.

41. *I know not to lie.*] Dissemble, cant, flatter, say what I do not mean, seem to approve what I dislike, and praise what in my judgment I condemn. What then should I do at Rome, where this is one of the only means of advancement?

42. *Ask for.*] It was a common practice of low flatterers to commend the writings of rich authors, however bad, in order to ingratiate themselves with them, and be invited to their houses; they also asked, as the greatest favour, for the loan or gift of a copy, which highly flattered the composers. This may be meant by *poscere*, in this place. See HOR. Art.

Astrorum ignoro : funus promittere patris
Nec volo, nec possum : ranarum viscera nunquam
Inspexi : ferre ad nuptam quæ mittit adulter,   45
Quæ mandat, nôrint alii : me nemo ministro
Fur erit ; atque ideo nulli comes exeo, tanquam
Mancus, et extinctæ corpus non utile dextræ.
Quis nunc diligitur, nisi conscius, et cui fervens
Æstuat occultis animus, semperque tacendis ?   50
Nil tibi se debere putat, nil conferet unquam,
Participem qui te secreti fecit honesti.
Carus erit Verri, qui Verrem tempore, quo vult,
Accusare potest. Tanti tibi non sit opaci
Omnis arena Tagi, quodque in mare volvitur aurum,   55

Poet. l. 419–37. Martial has an epi-
gram on this subject. Epigr. xlviii.
lib. vi.

   Quod tam grande σοφῶς clamat tibi
    turba togata,
  Non, tu, Pomponi, cœna diserta
    tua est.
  Pomponius, thy wit is extoll'd by
   the rabble,
  'Tis not thee they commend—but the
   cheer at thy tables

42–3. *Motions of the stars, &c.*] I
have no pretensions to skill in astro-
logy.

43. *The funeral of a father, &c.*]
He hereby hints at the profligacy and
want of natural affection in the
young men who wished the death of
their fathers, and even consulted
astrologers about the time when it
might happen ; which said pretended
diviners cozened the youths out of
their money, by pretending to find out
the certainty of such events by the
motions or situations of the planets.

This, says Umbritius, I neither can
nor will do.

44. *The entrails of toads.*] Rana is
a general word for all kinds of frogs
and toads.

The language here is metaphorical,
and alludes to augurs inspecting the
entrails of the beasts slain in sacrifice, on the view of which, they drew
their good or ill omens.

Out of the bowels of toads, poisons,
charms, and spells, were supposed to
be extracted, sat. i. 57. Umbritius
seems to say, "I never foretold the
death of fathers, or of other rich re-

lations ; nor searched for poison,
"that my predictions might be made
"good by the secret administration
"of it."

45. *To carry to a married woman.*]
I never was pimp, or go-between, in
carrying on adulterous intrigues, by
secretly conveying love-letters, presents, or any of those matters which
gallants give in charge to their confi-
dants. I leave this to others.

46. *I assisting, &c*] No villainy
will ever be committed by my advice
or assistance.

47. *I go forth, &c.*] For these reasons I depart from Rome, quite
alone, for I know none to whom I can
attach myself as a companion, so uni-
versally corrupt are the people.

48. *Maimed.*] Like a maimed
limb, which can be of no service in
any employment : just as unfit am I
for any employment which is now
going forward in Rome.

—*The useless body, &c.*] As the body,
when the right-hand, or any other
limb that once belonged to it, is lost
and gone, is no longer able to maintain itself by laborious employment ;
so I, having no inclination or talent,
to undergo the drudgery of vice of
any kind, can never thrive at Rome.

Some copies read, extincta dextra ;
abl. abs the right hand being lost.
The sense amounts to the same.

49. *Unless conscious.*] Who now
has any favour, attention, or regard
shewn him, but he who is conscious,
privy to, acquainted with, the wicked
secrets of others ?

Of the stars I am ignorant of : the funeral of a father to
   promise
I neither will, nor can : the entrails of toads I never
Have inspected : to carry to a married -woman what an
   adulterer sends,   45
What he commits to charge, let others know : nobody, I
   assisting,
Shall be a thief ; and therefore I go forth a companion to
   none, as
Maimed, and the useless body of an extinct right-hand.
Who now is loved, unless conscious, and whose fervent
Mind boils with things hidden, and ever to remain in si-
   lence ?   50
He thinks he owes you nothing, nothing will he bestow,
Who hath made you partaker of an honest secret.
He will be dear to Verres, who Verres, at any time he will,
Can accuse.   Of so much value to you let not of shady
Tagus the whole sand be, and the gold which is rolled into
   the sea,   55

49—50. *Fervent mind boils, &c.*] Is
in a ferment, agitated between telling
and concealing what had been committed to its confidence.   The words
fervens and æstuat are, in this view,
metaphorical, and taken from the
raging and boiling of the sea, when
agitated by a stormy wind.   Fervet
vertigine pontus.   Ov. Met. xi. 549.
So, æstuare semper fretum.   CURT.
iv. 9.   AINSW. *Æstuo*, No. 4.

Hence æstuans signifies boiling
with any passion, when applied to the
mind.   Animo æstuante reditum ad
vada retulit.   CatulL   See AINSW.
See Isa. lvii. 20.

Or we may give the words another
turn, as descriptive of the torment
and uneasiness of mind which these
men must feel, in having become acquainted with the most flagitious
crimes in others, by assisting them,
or partaking with them in the commission of them, and which, for their
own sakes, they dare not reveal, as
well as from the fear of those by
whom they are intrusted.

*Who now is lov'd but he who loves
   the times,
Conscious of close intrigues, and
   dipp'd in crimes :*

*Lab'ring with secrets which his
   bosom burn,
Yet never must to public light
   return.*   DRYDEN.

51. *He thinks he owes you nothing,
&c.*] Nobody will think himself obliged
to you for concealing honest and fair
transactions, or think it incumbent on
him to buy your silence by conferring
favours on you.

53. *Verres.*] Juvenal mentions him
here as an example of what he has
been saying.   Most probably, under
the name of Verres, the poet means
some characters then living, who
made much of those who had them
in their power by being acquainted
with their secret villanies, and who, at
any time, could have ruined them by
a discovery.

54—5. *Shady Tagus.*] A river of
Spain, which discharges itself into
the ocean near Lisbon, in Portugal.
It was anciently said to have golden
sands.   It was called opacus, dark,
obscure, or shady, from the thick
shade of the trees on its banks.

*Æstus serenos aureo franges Tago
Obscurus umbris arborum.*
    MART. lib. i. epigr. 50.
Or opacus may denote a dusky turbid
appearance in the water.

Ut somno careas, ponendaque præmia sumas
Tristis, et a magno semper timearis amico.
    Quæ nunc divitibus gens acceptissima nostris,
Et quos præcipue fugiam, properabo fateri;
Nec pudor obstabit. Non possum ferre, Quirites,   60
Græcam urbem : quamvis quota portio fæcis Achææ?
Jampridem Syrus in Tiberim defluxit Orontes,
Et linguam, et mores, et cum tibicine chordas
Obliquas, necnon gentilia tympana secum

56. *That you should want sleep,
&c.*] O thou, whoe'er thou art, that
may be solicited to such criminal se-
cresy by the rich and great, reflect on
the misery of such flagitious confidence, and prefer the repose of a quiet
and easy conscience, to all the golden
sands of Tagus, to all the treasures
which it can roll into the sea ! These
would make you but ill amends for
sleepless nights, when kept awake by
guilt and fear.
    —*Accept rewards to be rejected.*]
i. e. Which ought to be rejected—by
way of hush-money, which, so far,
poor wretch, from making you happy,
will fill you with shame and sorrow,
and which, therefore, are to be looked
upon as abominable, and to be utterly
refused, and laid aside. Ponenda;
lit. to be laid down ; but here it has
the sense of abominanda—respuenda
—rejicienda—abneganda. See Hor.
lib. iii. od. ii. l. 19.
    57. *Feared, &c.*] The great man
who professes himself your friend,
and who has heaped his favours upon
you in order to bribe you to silence,
will be perpetually betraying a dread
of you, lest you should discover him.
The consequence of which, you may
have reason to apprehend, may be his
ridding himself of his fears by ridding the world of you, lest you should
prove like others — magni delator
amici. See sat. i. 31. But whether
the great man betrays this fear or not,
you may be certain he will be constantly possessed with it ; and a much
greater proof of this you cannot have,
than the pains he takes to buy your
silence. When he grows weary of
this method, you know what you may
expect. Alas ! can all the treasures
of the whole earth, make it worth
your while to be in such a situation !
Comp. l. 103.

58. *What nation, &c.*] Umbritius
proceeds in his reasons for retiring
from Rome. Having complained of
the sad state of the times, insomuch
that no honest man could thrive there,
he now attacks the introduction of
Grecians and other foreigners, the
fondness of the rich and great towards
them, and the sordid arts by which
they raised themselves.
    60. *Nor shall shame hinder.*] In
short, I'll speak my mind without re-
serve, my modesty shall not stand in
my way.
    —*O Romans*] Quirites—this an-
ciently was a name for the Sabines,
from the city Cures, or from quiris,
a sort of spear used by them : but after their union with the Romans, this
appellation was used for the Roman
people in general. The name Quirinus was first given to Romulus.
    Probably the poet used the word
Quirites here, as reminding them of
their ancient simplicity of manners
and dress, by way of contrast to their
present corruption and effeminacy in
both ; owing very much to their fondness of the Greeks and other foreigners, for some time past introduced
among them.
    61. *A Grecian city.*] Meaning
Rome—now so transformed from
what it once was, by the rage which
the great people had for the language,
manners, dress, &c. of those Greeks
whom they invited and entertained,
that, as the inferior people are fond of
imitating their superiors, it was not
unlikely that the transformation might
become general throughout the whole
city : no longer Roman, but Grecian.
Umbritius could not bear the thought.
    —*Tho' what is the portion, &c.*]
Though, by the way, if we consider
the multitudes of other foreigners,

That you should want sleep, and should accept rewards to
    be rejected,
Sorrowful, and be always feared by a great friend.
    What nation is now most acceptable to our rich men,
And whom I would particularly avoid, I will hasten to con-
    fess ;
Nor shall shame hinder. O Romans, I cannot bear   60
A Grecian city : tho' what is the portion of Achæan dregs :
Some while since Syrian Orontes has flow'd into the Tiber,
And its language, and manners, and, with the piper, harps
Oblique, also its national timbrels, with itself

with which the city now abounds, what, as to numbers, is the portion of the Greeks ? they are comparatively few. See sat. xiii. 157. Hæc quota pars scelerum, &c. What part is this (i. e. how small a part or portion) of the crimes, &c.

—*Achæan dregs.*] Achæ, or Achaia, signifies the whole country of Greece, anciently called Danaë, whence the Greeks are called Danaï. Aιναω. Dregs—metaph. taken from the foul, turbid, filthy sediment which wine deposits at the bottom of the cask. A fit emblem of these vile Greeks, as though they were the filth and refuse of all Greece.

Sometimes the word Achæa, or Achaia, is to be understood in a more confined sense, and denotes only some of that part of Greece called Peloponnesus, or Pelops' island, now the Morea, anciently divided into Arcadia, and Achaia, of which Corinth was the capital : the inhabitants of this city were proverbially lewd and wicked : κορινθιαζειν was a usual phrase to express doing acts of effeminacy, lewdness, and debauchery—what then must the dregs of Corinth and its environs have been ? See 1 Cor. vi. 9—11, former part.

62. *Syrian Orontes.*] Orontes was the greatest river of Syria, a large country of Asia. Umbritius had said (at l. 61.) that the portion of Grecians was small in comparison : he now proceeds to explain himself, by mentioning the inundation of Syrians, and other Asiatic strangers, who had for some time been flocking to Rome : these were in such numbers from Syria, and they had so introduced

their eastern manners, music, &c. that one would fancy one's self on the banks of the Orontes, instead of the Tiber. The river Orontes is here put for the people who inhabited the tract of country through which it ran. Menton. So the Tiber for the city of Rome, which stood on its banks.

62. *Has flow'd.*] Metaph. This well expresses the idea of the numbers, as well as the mischiefs they brought with them, which were now overwhelming the city of Rome, and utterly destroying the morals of the people.

63. *With the piper.*] Tibicen signifies a player on a flute, or pipe. A minstrel. They brought eastern musicians, as well as musical instruments. The flute was an instrument whose soft sound tended to mollify and enervate the mind.

63—4. *Harps oblique.*] Chordas, literally strings : here it signifies the instruments, which, being in a crooked form, the strings must of course be obliquely placed.

64. *National timbrels.*] Tabours, or little drums, in form of a hoop, with parchment distended over it, and bits of brass fixed to it to make a jingling noise ; which the eastern people made use of, as they do to this day, at their feasts and dancings, and which they beat with the fingers.

64—5. *With itself hath brought.*] As a river, when it breaks its bounds, carries along with it something from all the different soils through which it passes, and rolls along what it may meet with in its way ; so the torrent of Asiatics has brought with it from Syria to Rome, the language, morals,

Vexit, et ad Circum jussas prostare puellas.   65
Ite, quibus grata est pictâ lupa Barbara mitrâ
  Rusticus ille tuus sumit trechedipna, Quirine,
Et ceromatico fert niceteria collo.
  Hic altâ Sicyone, ast hic Amydone relictâ,
Hic Andro, ille Samo hic Trallibus, aut Alabandis,   70
Esquilias, dictumque petunt a vimine collem;
Viscera magnarum domuum, dominique futuri.
  Ingenium velox, audacia perdita, sermo
Promptus, et Isæo torrentior: ede quid illum

dress, music, and all the enervating and effeminate vices of the several eastern provinces from whence they came.

65. *Circus.*] There were several circi in Rome, which were places set apart for the celebration of several games: they were generally oblong, or almost in the shape of a bow, having a wall quite round, with ranges of seats for the convenience of spectators. The Circus maximus, which is probably meant here, was an immense building; it was first built by Tarquinius Priscus, but beautified and adorned by succeeding princes, and enlarged to such a prodigious extent, as to be able to contain, in their proper seats, two hundred and sixty thousand spectators. See KENNETT, Ant. part ii. book i. c. 4.

—Go ye, &c.] Umbritius may be supposed to have uttered this with no small indignation.

66. *Strumpet.*] Lupa literally signifies a she-wolf; but an appellation fitly bestowed on common whores or bawds, whose profession led them to support themselves by preying at large on all they could get into their clutches. Hence a brothel was called lupanar. The Romans called all foreigners barbarians.

—A painted mitre.] A sort of turban, worn by the Syrian women as a part of their head-dress, ornamented with painted linen.

67. *O Quirinus.*] O Romulus, thou great founder of this now degenerate city! See note on l. 60.

— That rustic of thine.] In the days of Romulus, and under his government, the Romans were a hardy race of shepherds and husbandmen. Sat. viii. l. 273, 4. rough in their

dress, and simple in their manners. But alas! how changed!

—A Grecian dress.] Trechedipna— from τρεχω, to run, and διιπνον, a supper. A kind of garment in which they ran to other people's suppers. AINSW. It was certainly of Greek extraction, and though the form and materials of it are not described, yet we must suppose it of the soft, effeminate or gaudy kind, very unlike the garb and dress of the ancient rustics of Romulus, and to speak a sad change in the manners of the people. Dryden renders the passage thus:

O Romulus, and father Mars, look down!
Your herdsman primitive, your homely clown,
Is turn'd a beau, in a loose tawdry gown.

68. *Grecian ornaments.*] Niceteria, —rewards for victories, as rings, collars of gold, &c. Prizes. From Gr. νικη, victory.

—On his perfumed neck.] Ceromatico collo. The ceroma (Gr. κηρωμα, from κηρος, cera) was an oil tempered with wax, wherewith wrestlers anointed themselves.

But what proofs of effeminacy, or depravation, doth the poet set forth in these instances.

Using wrestlers' oil, and wearing on the neck collars of gold, and other insignia of victory, if to be understood literally, seems but ill to agree with the poet's design, to charge the Romans with a loss of all former hardiness and manliness: therefore we are to understand this line in an ironical sense, meaning, that, instead of wearing collars of gold as tokens of victory, and rewards of courage and

Hath brought, and girls bidden to prostitute themselves at
the Circus.— 65
Go ye, who like a Barbarian strumpet with a painted mitre,
That rustic of thine, O Quirinus, assumes a Grecian dress,
And carries Grecian ornaments on his perfumed neck.
One leaving high Sicyon; but another Amydon,
He from Andros, another from Samos, another from Tralles,
or Alabanda; 70
Seek the Esquiliæ, and the hill named from an osier,
The bowels, and future lords, of great families.
A quick wit, desperate impudence, speech
Ready, and more rapid than Isæus. Say—what do you

activity, their niceteria were trinkets
and gewgaws, worn merely as ornaments suitable to the effeminacy and
luxury into which, after the example
of the Grecians, Syrians, &c. they
were sunk. By the ceroma he must
also be understood to mean, that, instead of wrestlers' oil, which was a
mere compound of oil and wax, their
ceroma was some curious perfumed
unguent with which they anointed
their persons, their hair particularly,
merely out of luxury. Thus, Mr,
Dryden :

His once unkem'd and horrid looks
    behold
Stilling sweet oil, his neck enchain'd
    with gold :
Aping the foreigners in every dress,
Which, bought at greater cost; be-
    comes him less.

69. High Sicyon.] An island in the
Ægean sea, where the ground was
very high. The Ægean was a part
of the Mediterranean sea, near Greece,
dividing Europe from Asia. It is now
called the Archipelago, and by the
Turks, the White sea.

—Amydon.] A city of Macedonia.

70. Andros.] An island and town
of Phrygia the Lesser, situate in the
Ægean sea.

—Samos.] An island in the Ionian
sea, west of the bay of Corinth, now
under the republic of Venice, now
Cephalonie.

—Tralles.] A city of Lesser Asia
between Caria and Lydia.

—Alabanda.] A city of Caria in the
Lesser Asia.

71. Esquiliæ.] The mons esquilinus,

one of the seven hills in Rome ; so
called from esculus, a beech-tree, of
which many grew upon it. See AINSW.

—The hill named, &c.] The collis
viminalis, another of the seven hills
on which Rome was built : so called
from a wood or grove of osiers which
grew upon it. There was an altar
there to Jupiter, under the title of
Jupiter Viminalis,

These two parts of Rome may
stand (by synec.) for Rome itself; or
perhaps these were parts of it where
these foreigners chiefly settled.

72. The bowels, &c.] Insinuating
themselves, by their art and subtlety,
into the intimacy of great and noble
families, so as to become their confi-
dants and favourites, their vitals as it
were, insomuch that, in time, they
govern the whole : and, in some instances, become their heirs, and thus
lords over the family possessions.—
The wheedling and flattering of rich
people, in order to become their heirs,
are often mentioned in Juvenal ; such
people were called captatores.

73. A quick wit.] Ingenium velox.
Ingenium is a word of many mean-
ings ; perhaps, here joined with velox, it might be rendered a ready invention.

—Desperate impudence.] That nothing can abash or dismay.

73-4. Speech ready.] Having words
at will.

74. Isæus.] A famous Athenian
orator; preceptor of Demosthenes.
Torrentior, more copious, flowing
with more precipitation and fullness,
more like a torrent.

Esse putes ?, quemvis hominem secum attulit ad nos :   75
Grammaticus, Rhetor, Geometres, Pictor, Aliptes,
Augur, Schœnobates, Medicus, Magus : omnia novit.
Græculus esuriens in cœlum, jusseris, ibit.
Ad summum non Maurus erat, nec Sarmata, nec Thrax,
Qui sumpsit pennas, mediis sed natus Athenis.   80
Horum ego non fugiam conchylia ? me prior ille
Signabit ? fultusque toro meliore recumbet,
Advectus Romam, quo pruna et coctona, vento ?
Usque adeo nihil est, quod nostra infantia cœlum
Hausit Aventini, baccâ nutrita Sabinâ   85
Quid !—quod adulandi gens prudentissima laudat
Sermonem indocti, faciem deformis amici,
Et longum invalidi collum cervicibus æquat
Herculis, Antæum procul a tellure tenentis—

74. *Say, &c.*] Now by the way, my friend, tell me what you imagine such a man to be ; I mean of what calling or profession, or what do you think him qualified for ?

75. *What man, &c.*] Well, I'll not puzzle you with guessing, but at once inform you, that, in his own single person, he has brought with him every character that you can imagine : in short, he is a jack of all trades. As the French say, C'est un valet à tout faire. Or, as is said of the Jesuits, Jesuitus est omnis homo.

76. *Anointer.*] Aliptes, (form Gr. αλειϕω, to anoint,) he that anointed the wrestlers, and took care of them. AINSW.

77. *He knows all things.*] Not only what I have mentioned, but so versatile is his genius, that nothing can come amiss to him. There is nothing that he does not pretend to the knowledge of.

78. *A hungry Greek.*] The diminutive Græculus is sarcastical. *q. d.* Let my little Grecian be pinched with hunger, he would undertake any thing you bade him, however impossible or improbable ; like another Dædalus, he would even attempt to fly into the air.

79. *In fine, &c.*] Ad summum ; upon the whole, be it observed, that the Greeks of old were a dexterous people at contrivance ; for the attempt at flying was schemed by Dædalus, a native of Athens. No man of any

other country has the honour of the invention.

81. *The splendid dress.*] Conchylia ; shell-fish ; the liquor thereof made purple, or scarlet colour ; called also murex. Conchylium, by meton. signifies the colour itself ; also garments dyed therewith, which were very expensive, and worn by the nobility and other great people.

Shall not I fly, fugiam, avoid the very sight of such garments, when worn by such fellows as these, who are only able to wear them by the wealth which they have gotten by their craft and imposition ?

81-2. *Sign before me.*] Set his name before mine, as a witness to any deed &c. which we may be called upon to sign.

82. *Supported by a better couch, &c.*] The Romans lay on couches at their convivial entertainments ; these couches were ornamented more or less, some finer and handsomer than others, which were occupied according to the quality of the guests. The middle couch was esteemed the most honourable place, and so in order from thence. Must this vagabond Greek take place of me at table, says Umbritius, as if he were above me in point of quality and consequence ? As we should say, Shall he sit above me at table ? Hor. lib. ii. sat. viii. l. 20-3. describes an arrangement of the company at table.

83. *Brought to Rome.*] Advectus ;

Think him to be? He has brought us with himself what
    man you please;   75
Grammarian, Rhetorician, Geometrician, Painter, Anointer,
Augur, Rope-dancer, Physician, Wizard : he knows all
    things.
A hungry Greek will go into heaven, if you command.
  In fine—he was not a Moor, nor Sarmatian, nor Thracian,
Who assumed wings, but born in the midst of Athens. 80
Shall I not avoid the splendid dress of these? before me
    shall he
Sign? and supported by a better couch shall he lie at table,
Brought to Rome by the same wind as plumbs and figs?
Is it even nothing that our infancy the air
Of Aventinus drew, nourished by the Sabine berry? 85
What!—because a nation, most expert in flattery, praises
The speech of an unlearned, the face of a deformed friend,
And equals the long neck of the feeble, to the neck of
Hercules, holding Antæus far from the earth—

imported from a foreign country, by the same wind, and in the same ship, with prunes, and little figs, from Syria. These were called coctona, or cottana as supposed, from Heb. ‪קטן‬ littlei MART. lib. xiii. 28. parva cottana. Syria peculiares habet arbores, in ficorum genere. Caricas, et minores ejus generis, quæ coctana vocant. PLIN. lib. xiii. c. 5.

  Juvenal means to set forth the low origin of these people ; that they, at first, were brought out of Syria to Rome, as dealers in small and contemptible articles. Or he may mean, that as slaves they made a part of the cargo, in one of these little trading vessels. See sat. i. 96. 97.

  85. *Aventinus, &c.*] One of the seven hills of Rome; so called from Avens, a river of the Sabines. AINSW. Umbritius here with a patriotic indignation at the preference given to foreigners, asks, What! is there no privilege in having drawn our first breath in Rome? no pre-eminence in being born a citizen of the first city, in the world, the conqueror and mistress of all those countries from whence these people came? Shall such fellows as these not only vie with Roman citizens, but be preferred before them.

  —*Sabine berry.*] A part of Italy on the banks of the Tiber, once belong-

ing to the Sabines, was famous for olives, here called bacca Sabina. But we are to understand all the nutritive fruits and produce of the country in general. Pro specie genus. Syn. In contradistinction to the pruna et coctona, l. 83.

  86. *What!*] As if he had said, What! is all the favour and preference which these Greeks meet with, owing to their talent for flattery? are they to be esteemed more than the citizens of Rome, because they are a nation of base sycophants?

  87, *The speech, &c.*] Or discourse, talk, conversation, of some ignorant, stupid, rich patron, whose favour is basely courted by the most barefaced adulation.

  —*Face of a deformed, &c.*] Persuading him that he is handsome; or that his very deformities are beauties.

  88. *The long neck, &c.*] Compares the long crane-neck of some puny wretch, to the brawney neck and shoulders (cervicibus) of Hercules.

  89. *Holding, &c.*] This relates to the story of Antæus, a giant of prodigious strength, who, when knocked down by Hercules, recovered himself by lying on his mother earth; Hercules therefore held him up in his left hand, between earth and heaven, and, with his right hand, dashed his brains out.

Hæc eadem licet et nobis laudare : sed illis   90
Creditur. An melior cum Thaïda sustinet, aut cum
Uxorem comædus agit, vel Dorida nullo
Cultam palliolo ? mulier nempe ipsa videtur,
Non persona loqui : nec erit mirabilis illic
Aut Stratocles, aut cum molli Demetrius Hæmo :   95
Natio comœda est : rides ? majore cachinno
Concutitur : flet, si lachrymas conspexit amici,
Nec dolet : igniculum brumæ si tempore poscas,
Accipit endromidem : si dixeris, æstuo, sudat.
Non sumus ergo pares : melior qui semper, et omni   100
Nocte dieque potest alienum sumere vultum ;
Scire volunt secreta domûs atque inde timeri.
. Et quoniam cœpit Græcorum mentio, transi

90. *We may praise also*] To be
sure we Romans' may flatter, but
without success ; we shall not be believed : the Greeks are the only people
in such credit as to have all they say
pass for truth.

91. *Whether is he better when he
plays, &c.*] Sustinet, sustains the part
of a Thais, or courtezan, or the more
decent character of a matron, or a
naked sea nymph : there is no saying
which a Grecian actor excels most in ;
he speaks so like a woman, that you'd
swear the very woman seems to speak,
and not the actor. Persona signifies
a false face, a mask, a vizor, in which
the Grecian and Roman actors played
their parts, and so by meton. became
to signify an actor.

This passage shews, that women's
parts were represented by men : for
which these Greeks had no occasion
for any alteration of voice : they differed from women in nothing but
their sex.

92. *Doris, &c.*] A sea nymph represented in some play. See AINSW.
Doris. Palliolum was a little upper
garment : the sea nymphs were usually represented naked, nullo palliolo,
without the least covering over their
bodies. Palliolum, dim. of pallium.

96. *Do you laugh ?*] The poet here
illustrates what he had said, by instances of Grecian adulation of the
most servile and meanest kind.

If one of their patrons happens to
laugh, or even to smile, for so rideo

also signifies, the parasite sets up a
loud horse-laugh, and laughs aloud,
or, as the word concutitur implies,
laughs ready to split his sides, as we
say.

97. *He weeps, &c.*] If he finds his
friend in tears, he can humour this
too ; and can squeeze out a lamentable appearance of sorrow, but without
a single grain of it.

98. *If in winter-time you ask, &c.*]
If the weather be cold enough for the
patron to order a little fire, the versatile Greek instantly improves on the
matter, and puts on a thick gown—
endromidem—a sort of thick rug,
used by wrestlers, and other gymnasi-
asts, to cover them after their exercise, lest they should cool too fast.

99. *I am hot, &c.*] If the patron
complains of heat, the other vows that
he is all over in a sweat.

Shakespeare has touched this sort
of character something in the way of
Juvenal, Hamlet, act v. sc. ii. where
he introduces the short but well-drawn
character of Osrick, whom he represents as a complete temporizer with
the humours of his superiors.

HAM. *Your bonnet to his right use—
'tis for the head.*

OSR. *I thank your lordship, 'tis
very hot.*

HAM. *No, believe me, 'tis very
cold ; the wind is northerly.*

OSR. *It is indifferent cold, my lord,
indeed.*

HAM. *But yet, methinks, it is very*

These same things we may praise also : but to them   90
Credit is given.   Whether is he better when he plays Thais,
    or when
The comedian acts a wife, or Doris with no
Cloak dressed ? truly a woman herself seems to speak,
Not the actor : nor admirable there will
Either Stratocles, or Demetrius, with soft Hæmus, be :   95
The nation is imitative. Do you laugh? with greater laughter
Is he shaken : he weeps, if he has seen the tears of a friend,
Not that he grieves : if in winter-time you ask for a little
    fire,
He puts on a great coat : if you should say, "1 am hot"—
    he sweats.
We are not therefore equals : better is he who always and all
Night and day, can assume another's countenance,   101
They will know the secrets of the family, and thence be
    feared.
And because mention of Greeks has begun, pass over

---

sultry, and hot, for my complexion.
    OSR. Exceedingly, my lord, it is
very sultry, as it were, I can't tell
how.——
    But Terence has a full length pic-
ture of one of these Grecian parasites,
which he copied from Menander.
See TER. Eun. the part of Gnatho
throughout : than which nothing can
be more exquisitely drawn, or more
highly finished.
    This, by the way, justifies Juvenal
in tracing the origin of such characters from Greece.   Menander lived
about 350 B. C.   Terence died about
159 B. C.
    100. We are not therefore equals.]
We Romans are no match for them—
they far exceed any thing we can attempt in the way of flattery.
    —Better is he, &c.] He who can
watch the countenance of another
perpetually, and, night and day, as it
were, practise an imitation of it, so
as to coincide, on all occasions, with
the particular look, humour, and disposition of others, is better calculated
for the office of a sycophant, than we
can pretend to be.
    102. And thence be feared.] Lest
they should reveal and publish the se-

crets which they become possessed of.
See before, l. 50–7.
    Farnaby, in his note on this place,
mentions an Italian proverb, which
is much to the purpose.
    Servo d'altrui si fa, chi dice il suo
secreto a chi no 'l sa.
    " He makes himself the servant of
" another, who tells his secret to one
" that knows it not."
    103. And because mention, &c.] q. d.
And, by the way, as I have begun to
mention the Greeks.
    —Pass over, &c.] Transi, imp. of
transeo, to pass over or through ; also
to omit, or say nothing of ; to pass a
thing by, or over.
    Each of these senses is espoused by
different commentators. Those who
are for the former sense, make the
passage mean thus : " Talking of
" Greeks, let us pass through their
" schools, so as to see and observe
" what is going forward there."
    The others make the sense to be,
" Omit saying any thing of the
" schools ; bad as they may be, they
" are not worth mentioning, in com-
" parison of certain other worse
" things."

Gymnasia, atque audi facinus majoris abollæ.
Stoïcus occidit Baream, delator amicum, 105
Discipulumque senex, ripâ nutritus in illâ
Ad quam Gorgonei delapsa est penna caballi.
Non est Romano cuiquam locus hic, ubi regnat
Protogenes aliquis, vel Diphilus, aut Erimanthus,
Qui gentis vitio nunquam partitur amicum; 110
Solus habet. Nam cum facilem stillavit in aurem
Exiguum de naturæ, patriæque veneno,
Limine summoveor: perierunt tempora longi
Servitii: nusquam minor est jactura clientis.
Quod porro officium, (ne nobis blandiar,) aut quod 115
Pauperis hic meritum, si curet nocte togatus

I rather think with the former, whose interpretation seems best to suit with the et audi in the next sentence. q. d. " As we are talking of " the Grecians, I would desire you " to pass from the common herd, go " to the schools, take a view of their " philosophers, and hear what one of " their chiefs was guilty of."

104. *The schools.*] Gymnasia here signifies those places of exercise, or schools, where the philosophers met for disputation, and for the instruction of their disciples. See AINSW. *Gymnasium.*

—A deed.] Facinus, in a bad sense, means a foul act, a villainous deed, a scandalous action.

—Greater abolla.] Abolla was a sort of cloak, worn by soldiers, and also by philosophers. The abolla of the soldiers was less than the other, and called minor abolla; that of the philosopher, being larger, was called major abolla.

Juvenal also uses the word abolla (sat. iv. 76.) for a senator's robe.

Here, by meton. it denotes the philosopher himself.

105. *Stoic.*] One of the straitest sects of philosophers among the Greeks. See AINSW. *Stoici-orum.*

—Killed, &c.] By accusing him of some crime for which he was put to death. This was a practice much encouraged by the emperors Nero and Domitian, and by which many made their fortunes. See note on sat. i. 31, 4.

—Bareas.] The fact is thus related by Tacitus, Ann. vi. " P. Ægnatius " (the Stoic above mentioned) circum- " vented by false testimony Bareas " Soranus, his friend and disciple, " under Nero."

106. *His disciple.*] To whom he owed protection.

—Nourished on that bank, &c.] By this periphrasis we are to understand, that this Stoic was originally bred at Tarsus, in Cilicia, a province of ancient Greece, which was built by Perseus, on the banks of the river Cydnus, on the spot where his horse Pegasus dropped a feather out of his wing. He called the city Ταρσος, which signifies a wing, from this event.

107. *Gorgonean.*] The winged horse Pegasus was so called; because he was supposed to have sprung from the blood of the gorgon Medusa, after Perseus had cut her head off.

108. *For any Roman.*] We Romans are so undermined and supplanted by the arts of these Greek sycophants, that we have no chance left us of succeeding with great men.

109. *Some Protogenes.*] The name of a famous and cruel persecutor of the people under Caligula. See ANT. Univ. Hist. vol. xiv. p. 302.

—Diphilus.] A filthy favourite and minion of Domitian.

—Erimánthus.] From εϱις, strife, and μαντις, a prophet, i. e. a foreteller of strife. This name denotes some notorious informer.

The schools, and hear a deed of the greater abolla.
A Stoic killed Bareas, an informer his friend,   105
And an old man his disciple, nourished on that bank,
At which a feather of the Gorgonean horse dropped down.
No place is here for any Roman, where reigns
Some Protogenes, or Diphilus, or Erimanthus,   109
Who, from the vice of his nation, never shares a friend;
He alone hath him: for, when he has dropp'd into his easy ear
A little of the poison of his nature, and of his country,
I am removed from the threshold :—times of long service
Are past and gone—no where is the loss of a client less.
Moreover, what is the office, (that I may not flatter our-
          selves,) or what   115
The merit of a poor man here, if a client takes care by night

The sense of this passage seems to be, "There is now no room for us Romans to hope for favour and preferment, where nothing but Greeks are in power and favour, and these such wretches as are the willing and obsequious instruments of cruelty, lust, and persecution."

110. Vice of his nation.] (See before, l. 86.) That mean and wicked art of engrossing all favour to themselves.

—Never shares a friend.] With any body else.

111. He alone hath him.] Engages and keeps him wholly to himself.

—He has dropped, &c.] Stillavit; hath insinuated by gentle and almost imperceptible degrees.

—Into his easy ear.] i. e. Into the ear of the great man, who easily listens to all he says.

112. The poison of his nature.] Born, as it were, with the malicious propensity of advancing themselves by injuring others.

—And of his country.] Greece, the very characteristic of which is this sort of selfishness.

113. I am removed, &c.] No longer admitted within my patron's or friend's doors.

114. Past and gone.] Perierunt: lit. have perished. My long and faithful services are all thrown away, forgotten, perished out of remembrance, and are as if they had never been.

—No where, &c.] There is no part

of the world where an old client and friend is more readily cast off, and more easily dismissed, than they are at Rome: or where this is done with less ceremony, or felt with less regret.

Look round the world, what country will appear,
Where friends are left with greater ease than here.   DRYDEN.

The word jactura signifies any loss or damage: but its proper meaning is, loss by shipwreck, casting goods overboard in a storm. The old friends and clients of great men, at Rome, were just as readily and effectually parted with.

115. What is the office.] Officium, business, employment, service.

—That I may not flatter, &c.] q. d. Not to speak too highly in our own commendation, or as over-rating ourselves and our services.

115-6. What the merit, &c.] What does the poor client deserve for the assiduous and punctual execution of his office towards his patron.

116. If a client.] So togatus signifies here. It was usual for great men, on these occasions, to have a number of their dependents and clients to attend them: those who went before were called anteambulones; those who followed, clientes togati, from the toga, or gown, worn by the common people.

—Takes care.] Makes it his constant business.

Currere, cum Prætor lictorem impellat, et ire
Præcipitem jubeat, dudum vigilantibus orbis,
Ne prior Albinam, aut Modiam collega salutet?
Divitis hic servi claudit latus ingenuorum   120
Filius; alter enim quantum in legione Tribuni
Accipiunt, donat Calvinæ, vel Catienæ,
Cum tibi vestiti facies scorti placet, hæres,
Et dubitas altâ Chionem deducere sellâ.

116–7. *By night to run.*] To post
away after his patron before day-
break to the early levees of the rich.

These early salutations or visits
were commonly made with a view to
get something from those to whom
they were paid; such as persons of
great fortune who had no children,
rich widows who were childless, and
the like. He who attended earliest,
was reckoned to shew the greatest
respect, and supposed himself to stand
fairest in the good graces, and, perhaps, as a legatee in the wills of such
persons as he visited and complimented.

The word currere implies the haste
which they made to get first.

117. *The Prætor drives on, &c.*]
The Prætor was the chief magistrate
of the city. He was preceded by officers called lictors, of which there
were twelve, who carried the insignia
of the Prætor's office, viz. an axe tied
up in a bundle of rods, as emblems
of the punishment of greater crimes
by the former, and of smaller crimes
by the latter. The lictors were so
called from the axe and rods bound or
tied (ligati) together. So lector, from
lego, to read.

So corrupt were the Romans, that
not only the nobles, and other great
men, but even their chief magistrates, attended with their state officers, went on these mercenary and
scandalous errands, and even hastened on the lictors (who on other occasions marched slowly and solemnly
before them) for fear of being too late.

117–8. *To go precipitate.*] Headlong, as it were, to get on as fast as
they could.

118. *The childless, &c.*] Orbus signifies a child that has lost its parents,
parents that are bereaved of their
children, women who have lost their

husbands without issue, &c. this last
(as appears from the next line) seems
to be the sense of it here.

These ladies were very fond of being addressed and complimented at
their levees by the flattering visitors
who attended there, and were ready
very soon in the morning, even up
before day-light, for their reception.
The Prætor drives on his attendants
as fast as he can, lest he should not
be there first, or should disoblige the
ladies by making them wait.

*The childless matrons are long since
    awake,*
*And for affronts the tardy visits
    take.*   DRYDEN.

120. *Lest first his colleague.*] Another reason for the Prætor's being in
such a hurry, was to prevent his colleague in office from being there before him.

It is to be observed, that, though
at first there was but one Prætor,
called Prætor Urbanus, yet, as many
foreigners and strangers settled at
Rome, another Prætor was appointed
to judge causes between them, and
called Prætor Peregrinus.

Juvenal gives us to understand,
that, on such occasions, both were
equally mean and mercenary.

—*Albina or Modia.*] Two rich and
childless old widows, to whom these
profligate fellows paid their court, in
hopes of inheriting their wealth.

This passage, from l. 116 to 120,
inclusive, relates to what Umbritius
had just said about the very easy manner in which the great men at Rome
got rid of their poor clients, notwithstanding their long and faithful services: q. d. " I don't mean to boast,
" or to rate our services too high;
" but yet, as in the instance here
" given, and in many others which
" might be mentioned, when what

To run, when the Prætor drives on the lictor, and to go
Precipitate commands him, (the childless long since awake,)
Lest first his colleague should salute Albina or Modia?
Here, the son of a rich slave closes the side of the   120
Free-born : but another, as much as in a legion Tribunes
Receive, presents to Calvina, or Catiena :
When the face of a well-dressed harlot pleases thee, thou
    hesitatest,
And doubtest to lead forth Chione from her high chair.

" we do, and what we deserve, are
" compared together, and both with
" the ungrateful return we meet
" with, in being turned off to make
" room for the Grecian parasites,
" surely this will be allowed me as
" another good reason for my depar-
" ture from Rome."

120. *Here.*] At Rome.
—*The son of a rich slave, &c.*] A
person of mean and servile extraction, whose father, originally a slave,
got his freedom, and by some means
or other acquired great wealth.
The sons of such were called li-
bertini.
—*Closes the side.*] Walks close to
his side in a familiar manner : perhaps, as we say, arm in arm ; thus
making himself his equal, and intimate.
120–1. *The free-born.*] Of good
extraction ; a gentleman of liberal
birth, of a good family ; such were
called ingenui.
The poet seems alike to blame the
insolence of these upstarts, who aimed
at a freedom and intimacy with their
betters ; and the meanness of young
men of family, who stooped to inti-
macies with such low people.
121. *Another.*] Of these low-born
people, inheriting riches from his
father.
—*Tribunes.*] He means the Tribuni Militum, of which there were
six to each legion, which consisted of
ten regiments or cohorts. See sat. i.
l. 45. n.
122. *Presents to Calvina, or Catiena.*] He scruples not to give as
much as the pay of a tribune amounts
to, to purchase the favours of these
women ; who probably were courte-
zans of notorious characters, but held
their price very high.

123. *Well-dressed.*] Vestitus means
not only apparelled, but decked and
ornamented. AINSW. Some are for
understanding vestiti, here, as syno-
nimous with togati, to express a low
strumpet, but I find no authority for
such a meaning of the word vestitus.
124. *Chione.*] Some stately courtezan of Rome, often spoken of by
Martial. See lib. i. epigr. 35–6, et
al. So called from Gr. χιων, snow.
—*Her high chair.*] Sella signifies a sedan chair, borne aloft on
men's shoulders : which from the epithet alta, I take to be meant in this
place—q. d. While these upstart fellows care not what sums they throw
away upon their whores, and refrain
from no expence, that they may carry
their point, their betters are more
prudent, and grudge to lavish away
so much expence upon their vices,
though the finest, best-dressed, and
most sumptuously attended woman
in Rome were the object in question.
—*To lead forth.*] Deducere ; to
hand her out of her sedan, and to attend her into her house.
Many other senses are given of this
passage, as may be seen in Holyday,
and in other commentators ; but the
above seems to me best to apply to the
poet's satire on the insolent extravagance of these low-born upstarts, by
putting it in opposition to the more
decent prudence and frugality of their
betters.
Dryden writes as follows :
*But you, poor sinner, tho' you love
    the vice,
And like the whore, demur upon the
    price :
And, frighted with the wicked sum,
    forbear
To lend an hand, and help her from
    the chair.*

H

Da testem Romæ tam sanctum, quam fuit hospes   125
Numinis Idæi : procedat vel Numa, vel qui
Servavit trepidam flagranti ex æde Minervam :
Protinus ad censum ; de moribus ultima fiet
Quæstio : quot pascit servos ? quot possidet agri
Jugera ? quam multa, magnaque paropside cænat ?   130
QUANTUM QUISQUE SUA NUMMORUM SERVAT IN ARCA,
TANTUM HABET ET FIDEI.   Jures licet et Samothracum,
Et nostrorum aras, contemnere fulmina pauper
Creditur, atque Deos, Dis ignoscentibus ipsis.
Quid, quod materiam præbet causasque jocorum   135
Omnibus hic idem, si fœda et scissa lacerna,
Si toga sordidula est, et ruptâ calceus alter
Pelle patet : vel si consuto vulnere crassum
Atque recens linum ostendit non una cicatrix ?
NIL HABET INFELIX PAUPERTAS DURIUS IN SE,   140
QUAM QUOD RIDICULOS HOMINES FACIT.   Exeat, inquit,

As to translating (as some have done) vestiti by the word masked, it is totally incongruous with the rest of the sentence ; for how can a face, with a mask on, be supposed to please, as it must be concealed from view ? Besides, it is not said vestita facies, but facies vestiti scorti.

However, it seems not very probable, that the poet only means to say, that the man hesitated, and doubted about coming up to the price of Chione, because he was so poor that he had it not to give her, as some would insinuate ; for a man can hardly hesitate, or doubt, whether he shall do a thing that is out of his power to do.

125. *Produce a witness.*] Umbritius here proceeds to fresh matter of complaint against the corruption of the times, insomuch that the truth of a man's testimony was estimated, not according to the goodness of his character, but according to the measure of his property.

125-6. *The host of the Idean deity.*] Scipio Nasica, adjudged by the senate to be one of the best of men. He received into his house an image of the goddess Cybele, where he kept it until a temple was built for it. She had various names from the various places where she was worshipped, as Phrygia, Ida, &c. Ida was a high hill in Phrygia, near Troy, sacred to Cybele.

See VIRG. Æn. x. 252.

126. *Numa.*] See before, notes on l. 12. He was a virtuous and religious prince.

127. *Preserved trembling Minerva.*] Lucius Metellus, the high priest, preserved the palladium, or sacred image of Minerva, out of the temple of Vesta, where it stood trembling, as it were, for its safety when that temple was on fire. Metellus lost his eyes by the flames.

128. *Immediately as to income, &c.*] q. d. Though a man had all their sanctity, yet would he not gain credit to his testimony on the score of his integrity, but in proportion to the largeness of his income ; this is the first and immediate object of inquiry. As to his moral character, that is the last thing they ask after.

129. *In how many, &c.*] What sort of a table he keeps. See AINSW. *Paropsis.*

132. *Swear by the altars.*] Jurare aras signifies to lay the hands on the altar, and to swear by the gods. See HOR. Epist. lib. ii. epist. i. 1. 16. AINSW. *Juro.* Or rather, as appears from HOR. to swear in or by the name of the god to whom the altar was dedicated.

133. *Samothracian.*] Samothrace was an island near Lemnos, not far from Thrace, very famous for religi-

Produce a witness at Rome, as just as was the host, 125
Of the Idean deity: let even Numa come forth, or he who
Preserved trembling Minerva from the burning temple:
Immediately as to income, concerning morals will be the last
Inquiry: how many servants he maintains? how many acres
    of land.
He possesses? in how many and great a dish he sups? 130
AS MUCH MONEY AS EVERY ONE KEEPS IN HIS CHEST,
SO MUCH CREDIT TOO HE HAS.   Tho' you should swear by
    the altars, both
Of the Samothracian, and of our gods, a poor man to con-
    temn thunder
Is believed, and the gods, the gods themselves forgiving him.
What, because this same affords matter and causes of jests
To all, if his garment be dirty and rent,   136
If his gown be soiled, and one of his shoes with torn
Leather be open: or if not one patch only shews the coarse
And recent thread in the stiched-up rupture?
UNHAPPY POVERTY HAS NOTHING HARDER IN ITSELF 140
THAN THAT IT MAKES MEN RIDICULOUS.   Let him go out,
    says he,

ous rites. From hence Dardanus, the founder of Troy, brought into Phrygia the worship of the DII MAJORES; such as Jupiter, Minerva, Mercury, &c. From Phrygia, Æneas brought them into Italy.

—*Our gods.*] Our tutelar deities, Mars and Romulus. *q. d.* Were you to swear ever so solemnly.

134. *The gods themselves, &c.*] Not punishing his perjury, but excusing him, on account of the temptations which he is under from his poverty and want.

135. *What.*] Quid is here elliptical, and the sense must be supplied.— *q. d.* What shall we say more? because it is to be considered, that, besides the discrediting such a poor man as to his testimony, all the symptoms of his poverty are constant subjects of jests and railery. See AINSW. *Quid,* No. 2.

—*This same.*] Hic idem; this same poor fellow.

136. *His garment.*] Lacerna, here, perhaps means what we call a surtout, a sort of cloak for the keeping off the weather. See AINSW. *Lacerna.*

137. *Gown.*] Toga; the ordinary dress for the poorer sort. See sat. i. 3.

—*Soiled.*] Sordidula, dim. of sordidus; and signifies somewhat dirty or nasty.

—*With torn leather, &c.*] One shoe gapes open with a rent in the upper leather.

138-9. The poet's language is here metaphorical; he humourously, by vulnere, the wound, means the rupture of the shoe; by cicatrix, (which is, literally, a scar, or seam in the flesh,) the aukward seam on the patch of the cobbled shoe, which exhibited to view the coarse thread in the new-made stitches.

141. *Says he.*] i. e. Says the person who has the care of placing the people in the theatre.

—*Let him go out, &c.*] Let the man who has not a knight's revenue go out of the knight's place or seat.

It is to be observed, that formerly, all persons placed themselves, as they came, in the theatre, promiscuously; now in contempt of the poor, that license was taken away. Lucius Ros-

Si pudor est, et de pulvino surgat equestri,
Cujus res legi non sufficit, et sedeant hic
Lenonum pueri, quocunque in fornice nati.
Hic plaudat nitidi præconis filius inter   145
Pinnirapi cultos juvenes, juvenesque lanistæ :
Sic libitum vano, qui nos distinxit, Othoni.
Quis gener hic placuit censu minor, atque puellæ
Sarcinulis impar ? quis pauper scribitur hæres ?
Quando in consilio est Ædilibus ? agmine facto 150
Debuerant olim tenues migrâsse Quirites.

cius Otho, a tribune of the people, instituted a law, that there should be fourteen rows of seats, covered with cushions, on which the knights were to be seated. If a poor man got into one of these, or any other, who had not 400 sestertia a year income, which made a knight's estate, he was turned out with the utmost contempt.

143. *Is not sufficient for the law.*] i. e. Who has not 400 sestertia a-year, according to Otho's law.

144. *The sons of pimps, &c.*] The lowest, the most base-born fellows, who happen to be rich enough to answer the conditions of Otho's law, are to be seated in the knights' seats ; and persons of the best family are turned out, to get a seat where they can, if they happen to be poor. See Hor. epod. iv. l. 15, 16.

145. *Crier.*] A low officer among the Romans, as among us, who proclaimed the edicts of magistrates, public sales of goods, &c. The poet says, nitidi præconis ; intimating that the criers got a good deal of money, lived well, were fat and sleek in their appearance, and affected great spruceness in their dress.

—*Applaud.*] Take the lead in applauding theatrical exhibitions. Applause was expressed, as among us, by clapping of hands.

146. *Of a sword-player.*] Pinnirapi denotes that sort of gladiator, called also Retiarius, who, with a net which he had in his hand, was to surprise his adversary, and catch hold on the crest of his helmet, which was adorned with peacock's plumes ; from pinna, a plume or feather, and rapio, to snatch. Where we shall find the figure of a fish on the helmet ; and as

pinna also means the fin of a fish, perhaps this kind of gladiator was called Pinnirapus, from his endeavouring to catch this in his net.

—*The youths.*] The sons—now grown young men—juvenes. Such people as these were entitled to seats in the fourteen rows of the equestrian order, on account of their estates : while sons of nobles, and gentlemen of rank, were turned out because their income did not come up to what was required, by Otho's law, to constitute a knight's estate.

—*A fencer.*] Lanista signifies a fencing-master, one that taught boys to fence.

147. *Thus it pleased vain Otho.*] q. d. No sound or good reason could be given for this ; it was the mere whim of a vain man, who established this distinction, from his own caprice and fancy, and to gratify his own pride and vanity.

However, Otho's law not only distinguished the knights from the plebeians, but the knights of birth from those who were advanced to that dignity by their fortunes or service ; giving to the former the first rows on the equestrian benches. Therefore Hor. epod. iv. where he treats in the severest manner Menas, the freedman of Cn. Pompeius, who had been advanced to a knight's estate, mentions it as one instance of his insolence and pride, that he sat himself in one of the first rows after he became possessed of a knight's estate.

Sedilibusque magnus in primis eques,
Othone contempto, sedet.

See Francis, notes in loc.

148. *What son-in-law.*] Umbritius still proceeds in shewing the miseries

If he has any shame, and let him rise from the equestrian
    cushion,
Whose estate is not sufficient for the law, and let there sit
    here
The sons of, pimps, in whatever brothel born.
Here let the son of a spruce crier applaud, among   145
The smart youths of a sword-player, and the youths of a
    fencer :
Thus it pleased vain Otho, who distinguished us.
What son-in-law, here, inferior in estate, hath pleased, and
    unequal
To the bags of the girl? what poor man is written down heir?
When is he in counsel with Ædiles ? In a formed body,
The mean Romans ought long ago to have migrated.   151

of being poor, and instances the dis-
advantages which men of small fortunes lie under with respect to marriage.

—*Inferior in estate.*] Census signifies a man's estate, wealth, or yearly
revenue. Also a tribute, tax, or sub-
sidy, to be paid according to men's
estates.

According to the first meaning of
census, censu minor may signify,
that a man's having but a small fortune, unequal to that of the girl
to whom he proposes himself in marriage, would occasion his being rejected, as by no means pleasing or
acceptable to her father for a son-in-
law.

According to the second interpretation of the word census, censu minor may imply the man's property to
be too small and inconsiderable for entry in the public register as an object
of taxation. The copulative atque
seems to favour the first interpretation, as it unites the two sentences ;
as if Umbritius had said, Another instance, to shew how poverty renders
men contemptible at Rome is, that
nobody will marry his daughter to
one whose fortune does not equal
hers; which proves, that in this, as
in all things else, money is the grand
and primary consideration.

Themistocles, the Athenian general, was of another mind, when he
said, " I had rather have a man for
" my daughter without money, than
" money without a man."

149. *Written down heir ?*] Who
ever remembered a poor man in his
will, so as to make him his heir ?

150. *Ædiles.*] Magistrates in Rome,
whose office it was to oversee the repairs of the public buildings and
temples; also the streets and con-
duits ; to look to weights and measures; to regulate the price of corn
and victuals ; also to provide for solemn funerals and plays.

This officer was sometimes a senator, who was called Curulis, a sellâ
curuli, a chair of state made of ivory,
carved, and placed in curru, in a
chariot, in which the head officers of
Rome were wont to be carried into
council.

But there were meaner officers
called Ædiles, with a similar jurisdiction in the country towns, to inspect and correct abuses in weights
and measures, and the like. See sat.
x. 101, 2.

When, says Umbritius, is a poor
man ever consulted by one of the
magistrates ? his advice is looked
upon as not worth having ; much less
can he ever hope to be a magistrate
himself, however deserving or fit
for it.

—*In a formed body.*] Agmine facto—i. e. collected together in one
body, as we say. So VIRG. Georg. iv.
167. of the bees flying out in a swarm
against the drones. And again, Æn.
i. 86. of the winds rushing forth together from the cave of Æolus.

151. *Long ago.*] Alluding to the

HAUD FACILE EMERGUNT, QUORUM VIRTUTIBUS OBSTAT
RES ANGUSTA DOMI; sed Romæ durior illis
Conatus : magno hospitium miserabile, magno
Servorum ventres, et frugi cœnula magno.   155
Fictilibus cœnare pudet, quod turpe negavit
Translatus subito ad Marsos, mensamque Sabellam,
Contentusque illic Veneto, duroque cucullo.
  Pars magna Italiæ est, si verum admittimus, in quâ
Nemo togam sumit, nisi mortuus. Ipsa dierum   160
Festorum herboso colitur si quando theatro
Majestas, tandemque redit ad pulpita notum

sedition and the defection of the plebeians, called here tenues Quirites; when oppressed by the nobles and senators, they gathered together, left Rome, and retired to the Mons Sacer, an hill near the city consecrated to Jupiter, and talked of going to settle elsewhere; but the famous apologue of Menenius Agrippa, of the belly and the members, prevailed on them to return. This happened about 500 years before Juvenal was born. See ANT. Un. Hist. vol. xi. 383-403.

—*Ought long ago to have migrated.*] To have persisted in their intention of leaving Rome, and of going to some other part, where they could have maintained their independency. See before, l. 60. Quirites.

152. *Easily emerge.*] Out of obscurity and contempt.

—*Whose virtues, &c.*] The exercise of whose faculties and good qualities is cramped and hindered by the narrowness of their circumstances: and, indeed, poverty will always prevent respect, and be an obstacle to merit, however great it may be. So Hor. sat. v. lib. ii. l. 8.

——*Atqui*
Et genus et virtus, nisi cum re,
  vilior algâ est,
But high descent and meritorious
  deeds,
Unblest with wealth, are viler than
  sea-weeds.   FRANCIS.

154. *The endeavour.*] But to them—illis—to those who have small incomes, the endeavouring to emerge from contempt is more difficult at Rome than in any other place; because their little is, as it were, made less, by the excessive dearness of even

common necessaries; a shabby lodging, for instance; maintenance of slaves, whose food is but coarse; a small meal for one's self, however frugal; all these are at an exorbitant price.

156. *It shameth, &c.*] Luxury and expence are now got to such an height, that a man would be ashamed to have earthen ware at his table.

—*Which he denied, &c.*] The poet is here supposed to allude to Curius Dentatus, who conquered the Samnites and the Marsi, and reduced the Sabellans (descendants of the Sabines) into obedience to the Romans. When the Samnite ambassadors came to him to treat about a league with the Romans, they found him among the Marsi, sitting on a wooden seat near the fire, dressing his own dinner, which consisted of a few roots, in an earthen vessel, and offered him large sums of money; but he dismissed them, saying, " I had rather com- " mand the rich, than be rich my- " self; tell your countrymen, that " they will find it as hard to corrupt " as to conquer me."

Curius Dentatus was at that time consul with P. Corn. Rufinus, and was a man of great probity, and who, without any vanity or ostentation, lived in that voluntary poverty, and unaffected contempt of riches, which the philosophers of those times were wont to recommend. He might, therefore, well be thought to deny that the use of earthen ware was disgraceful, any more than of the homely and coarse clothing of those people, which he was content to wear. See ANT. Univ. Hist. vol. xii. p. 139.

THEY DO NOT EASILY EMERGE, TO WHOSE VIRTUES NARROW
FORTUNE IS A HINDRANCE; but at Rome more hard to them is,
The endeavour; a miserable lodging at a great price, at a
    great price
The bellies of servants, and a little frugal supper at a great
    price.   155
It shameth to sup in earthen ware: which he denied to be
    disgraceful,
Who was translated suddenly to the Marsi, and to the Sa-
    bellan table,
And there was content with a Venetian and coarse hood.
There is a great part of Italy, if we admit the truth, in
    which   159
Nobody takes the gown, unless dead. The solemnity itself of
Festal days, if at any time it is celebrated in a grassy
Theatre, and at length a known farce returns to the stage,

But among commentators there are those, who, instead of negavit, are for reading negabit—not confining the sentiment to any particular person, but as to be understood in a general sense, as thus: However it may be reckoned disgraceful, at Rome, to use earthen ware at table, yet he who should suddenly be conveyed from thence to the Marsi, and behold their plain and frugal manner of living, as well as that of their neighbours the Sabellans, will deny that there is any shame or disgrace in the use of earthen ware at meals, or of wearing garments of coarse materials.

This is giving a good sense to the passage—but as Juvenal is so frequent in illustrating his meaning, from the examples of great and good men who lived in past times, and as negavit is the reading of the copies, I should rather think that the first interpretation is what the poet meant.

157. *Translated suddenly.*] On being chosen consul, he was immediately ordered into Samnium, where he and his colleague acted separately, each at the head of a consular army. The Marsi lay between the Sabelli and the Samnites.

158. *A Venetian and coarse hood.*] Venetus-a-um, of Venice—dyed in a Venice blue, as the garments worn by common soldiers and sailors were. AINSW. This colour is said to be first used by the Venetian fishermen,

The cucullus was a cowl, or hood, made of very harsh and coarse cloth, which was to pull over the head, in order to keep off the rain.

160. *Unless dead.*] It was a custom among the Romans to put a gown on the corpse when they carried it forth to burial. In many parts of Italy, where they lived in rustic simplicity, they went dressed in the tunica, or jacket, never wearing the toga, the ordinary habit of the men at Rome, all their lifetime. Umbritius means to prove what he had before asserted, (l. 153–5.) that one might live in other places at much less expence than at Rome. Here he is instancing in the article of dress.

—*The solemnity, &c.*] The dies festi were holidays, or festivals, observed on some joyful occasions; when people dressed in their best apparel, and assembled at plays and shows.

161–2. *A grassy theatre.*] He here gives an idea of the ancient simplicity which was still observed in many parts of Italy, where, on these occasions, they were not at the expence of theatres built with wood or stone, but with turfs dug from the soil, and heaped one upon another, by way of seats for the spectators. See VIRG. Æn. v. 286–90.

162. *A known farce.*] Exodium (from Gr. εξοδος, exitus,) was a farce or interlude, at the end of a tragedy

Exodium, cum personæ pallentis hiatum
In gremio matris formidat rusticus infans:
Æquales habitus illic, similemque videbis   165
Orchestram, et populum : clari velamen honoris,
Sufficiunt tunicæ summis Ædilibus albæ.
✓ Hic ultra vires habitûs nitor : hic aliquid plus
Quam satis est ; interdum alienâ sumitur arcâ.
Commune id vitium est : hic vivimus ambitiosâ 170
Paupertate omnes : quid te moror ? Omnia Romæ
Cum pretio. Quid das, ut Cossum aliquando salutes ?
Ut te respiciat clauso Veiento labello ?
Ille metit barbam, crinem hic deponit amati :
Plena domus libis venalibus : accipe et, illud 175

het to will

exhibited to make the people laugh.
Notum exodium signifies some well-
known, favourite piece of this sort,
which had been often represented.

162. *Stage.*] So pulpitum signifies,
i. e. that part of the theatre where the
actors recited their parts.

163. *The gaping of the pale-looking
mask.*] Persona, a false face, vizard,
or mask, which the actors wore over
the face : they were painted over with
a pale flesh-colour, and the mouth
was very wide open, that the perfor-
mer might speak through it the more
easily. Their appearance must have
been very hideous, and may well be
supposed to affright little children.
A figure, with one of these masks on,
may be seen in Holyday, p. 55. col. 2.
Also in the copperplate, facing the
title of the ingenious Mr. Colman's
translation of Terence. See also Juv.
edit. Casaubon, p. 73.

165. *Habits are equal there.*] All
dress alike there ; no finical distinctions of dress are to be found among
such simple people.

166. *The orchestra, &c.*] Among
the Greeks this was in the middle of
the theatre, where the Chorus danced ;
but among the Romans, it was the
space between the stage and the common seats, where the nobles and senators sat.

No distinction of this sort was
made, at those rustic theatres, between the gentry and the common
people.

—*The clothing of bright honour.*]
The chief magistrates of these country
places did not wear, as at Rome, fine

robes decked with purple ; but were
content to appear in tunics, or jack-
ets, white and plain, even when they
gave or presided at these assemblies.
See AINSW. *Tunica,* No. 1, letter *b,*
under which this passage is quoted.

167. *Ædiles.*] See before, l. 150,
and note.

168. *Here, &c.*] Here at Rome
people dress beyond what they can
afford.

168-9. *Something more than
enough.*] More than is sufficient for
the purpose of any man's station, be
it what it may ; in short, people seem
to aim at nothing but useless gaudy
show.

169. *Sometimes it is taken, &c.*]
This superfluity in dress is sometimes
at other people's expence : either
these fine people borrow money to pay
for their extravagant dress, which
they never repay ; or they never pay
for them at all—which, by the way,
is a vice very common among such
people.

170-1. *Ambitious poverty.*] Our
poverty, though very great, is not
lowly and humble, content with hus-
banding, and being frugal of the little
we have, and with appearing what
we really are—but it makes us ambitious of appearing what we are not,
of living like men of fortune, and thus
disguising our real situation from the
world. This is at the root of that dis-
honesty before mentioned, so common now-a-days, of borrowing money, or contracting debts, which we
never mean to pay. See l. 169.

171. *Why do I detain you ?*] Quid

When the gaping of the pale-looking mask
The rustic infant in its mother's bosom dreads:
Habits are equal there, and there alike you will see   165
The orchestra and people: the clothing of bright honour,
White tunics, suffice for the chief Ædiles.
Here is a finery of dress beyond ability: here is something
   more
Than enough: sometimes it is taken from another's chest:
That vice is common. Here we all live in ambitious   170
Poverty:—why do I detain you? All things at Rome
Are with a price. What give you that sometimes you may
   salute Cossus?
That Veiento may look on you with shut lip?
One shaves the beard, another deposits the hair of a favourite:
The house is full of venal cakes: take, and that   175

te moror? So Hor. sat. i. lib. i. l. 14, 15.

    ——Ne te morer audi
    Quo rem deducam——
This is a sort of a phrase like our "In short—not to keep you too long."

172. *With a price.*] Every thing is dear at Rome; nothing is to be had without paying for it; viz. extravagantly. See l. 154–5.

—*What give you, &c.*] What does it cost you to bribe the servants of Cossus, that you may get admittance? Cossus was some wealthy person, much courted for his riches. Here it seems to mean any such great and opulent person.

173. *Veiento.*] Some other proud nobleman, hard of access, who, though suitors were sometimes with difficulty admitted to him, seldom condescended to speak to them. Hence Umbritius describes him, clauso labello. Yet even to get at the favour of a look only, it cost money in bribes to the servants for admittance.

174. *One shaves the beard.*] On the day when they first shaved their beard, they were reckoned no longer youths, but men. A festival was observed on the occasion among the richer sort, on which presents were made; and the misery was, that the poor were expected to send some present, on pain of forfeiting the favour of the great man. But the poet has a meaning here, which may be gathered from the

next note, and from the word amati at the end of this line.

—*Another deposits the hair.*] It was usual for great men to cut off the hair of their minions, deposit it in a box, and consecrate it to some deity. On this occasion, too, presents were made. It was, indeed, customary for all the Romans to poll their heads at the age of puberty.

Umbritius still is carrying on his design of lashing the vices of the great, and of setting forth the wretchedness of the poor—q. d. "A great "man can't shave his minion for the "first time, or poll his head, but pre-"sents are expected on the occasion "from his poor clients, ill as they "can afford them, and presently "there's a houseful of cakes sent in, "as offerings to the favourite."

175. *Venal cakes.*] These were made of honey, meal, and oil, and sent, as presents or offerings, from the poorer to the richer sort of people, on their birth-days, (hence some read here libis genialibus,) and on other festal occasions. They came in such numbers as to be an object of profit, insomuch that the new trimmed favourite slave, to whom they were presented, sold them for some considerable sum. Hence the text says, libis venalibus.

—*Take, &c.*] The language here is metaphorical: cakes have just been mentioned, which were leavened, or

I

Fermentum tibi habe : præstare tributa clientes
Cogimur, et cultis augere peculia servis.
Quis timet, aut timuit gelidâ Præneste ruinam ;
Aut positis nemorosa inter juga Volsiniis, aut   180
Simplicibus Gabiis, aut proni Tiburis arce ?
Nos urbem colimus tenui tibicine fultam
Magna parte sui : nam sic labentibus obstat
Villicus, et veteris rimæ contexit hiatum :
Securos pendente jubet:dormire ruinâ.   185
Vivendum est illic, ubi nulla incendia, nulli
Nocte metus : jam poscit aquam, jam, frivola transfert
Ucalegon : tabulata tibi jam tertia.fumant :
Tu nescis ; nam si gradibus trepidatur ab imis,
Ultimus, ardebit, quem tegula sola tuetur

---

fermented, in order to make them light. Umbritius is supposed, from this, to use the word fermentum, as applicable to the ideas of anger and indignation, which ferment, or raise the mind into a state of fermentation.

Accipe—" there," says Umbritius, " take this matter of indignation, let " it work within your mind, as it " does in mine, that the poor clients " of great men are obliged, even on " the most trivial and most infamous " occasions, to pay a tribute towards " the emolument of their servants, " on pain and peril, if they do it not, " of incurring their displeasure, and " being shut out of their doors."

By cultis servis the poet means to mark those particular slaves of great men, whose spruce and gay apparel bespake their situation as favourites ; and, indeed, the word cultis may very principally allude to this last circumstance ; for the verb colo not only signifies to trim, deck, or adorn, but also to love, to favour, to be attached to. See AINSW.

Peculia seems here to imply what we call vails.

178. Cold Præneste.] A town in Italy, about twenty miles from Rome. It stood on a hill, and the waters near it were remarkably cold ; from which circumstance, as well as its high situation, it was called gelida Præneste. VIRG. Æn. vii. 68?.

179. Volsinium.] A town in Tuscany, the situation of which was pleasant and retired.

180. Simple Gabii.] A town of the Volscians, about ten miles from Rome ; it was called simple, because deceived into a surrender to Tarquin the proud, when he could not take it by force ; or perhaps from the simple and unornamented appearance of the houses.

—The tower of prone Tibur.] A pleasant city of Italy, situate about sixteen miles from Rome, on the river Anio : it stood on a precipice, and had the appearance of hanging over it. Arx signifies the top, summit, peak, or ridge of any thing, as of a rock, hill, &c. also a tower, or the like, built upon it.

181. We.] Who live at Rome.

—Supported, &c.] In many parts of it very ruinous, many of the houses only kept from falling, by shores or props set against them, to prevent their tumbling down.

182. The steward.] Villicus here seems to mean some officer, like a steward or bailiff, whose business it was to overlook these matters ; a sort of city surveyor, (see sat. iv. 76.) who, instead of a thorough repair, only propped the houses, and plastered up the cracks in their walls, which had been opened by their giving way ; so that, though they might to appearance be repaired and strong, yet they were still in the utmost danger of falling. Villicus may perhaps mean the steward, or bailiff, of the great man who was landlord of these houses : it was the steward's duty to

Leaven have to thyself : we clients to pay tributes
Are compelled, and to augment the wealth of spruce servants.
  Who fears, or hath feared the fall of a house in cold
    Præneste;
Or at Volsinium placed among shady hills, or at
Simple Gabii, or at the tower of prone Tibur ?   180
We inhabit a city supported by a slender prop
In a great part of itself ; for thus the steward hinders
What is falling, and has covered the gaping of an old chink :
He bids us to sleep secure, ruin impending.   184
There one should live, where there are no burnings, no fears
In the night.—Already Ucalegon asks for water, already
Removes his lumber : already thy third floors smoke :
Thou know'st it not : for if they are alarmed from the
    lowest steps,
The highest will burn, which the roof alone defends

see that repairs were timely and properly done.

184. *He bids us to sleep, &c.*] If we express any apprehension of danger, or appear uneasy at our situation, he bids us dismiss our fears, and tells us, that we may sleep in safety, though at the same time the houses are almost tumbling about our ears.

Umbritius urges the multitude of ruinous houses, which threaten the lives of the poor inhabitants, as another reason why he thinks it safest and best to retire from Rome.

185. *There one should live, &c.*] As a fresh motive for the removal of Umbritius from Rome, he mentions the continual danger of fire, especially to the poor, who being obliged to lodge in the uppermost parts of the houses in which they are inmates, sat. x. l.18. run the risk of being burned in their beds; for which reason he thought it best to live where there was no danger of house-burning, and nightly alarms arising from such a calamity.

186. *Already Ucalegon.*] He seems here to allude to Virg. Æn. ii. 310–12. where he is giving a description of the burning of the city of Troy :

—*Jam Deiphobi dedit ampla ruinam,*
'*Vulcano superante,' domus : jam*
proximus ardet
Ucalegon.—

Some unhappy Ucalegon, says Umbritius, who sees the ruin of his

neighbour's house, and his own on fire, is calling out for water, is removing his wretched furniture (frivola, trifling, frivolous, of little value) to save it from the flames.

187. *Thy third floors.*] Tabulatum, from tabula, a plank, signifies any thing on which planks are laid ; so the floors of a house.

188. *Thou know'st it not.*] You a poor inmate, lodged up in the garret, are, perhaps, fast asleep, and know nothing of the matter ; but you are not in the less danger, for if the fire begins below, it will certainly reach upwards to the top of the house.

—*If they are alarmed.*] Trepidatur, impers. (like concurritur, HOR. sat. i. L 7.) if they tremble, are in an uproar. (AINSW.) from the alarm of fire.

—*From the lowest steps.*] Gradus is a step or a stair of a house ; imis gradibus, then, must denote the bottom of the stairs, and signify what we call the ground-floor.

189. *The highest.*] Ultimus, i. e. gradus, the last stair from the ground, which ends at the garret, or cockloft, (as we call it,) the wretched abode of the poor. This will be reached by the ascending flames, when the lower part of the house is consumed.

—*The roof.*] Tegula, lit. signifies a tile ; a tego, quod tegat ædes ; hence it stands for the roof of a house.

A pluviâ; molles ubi reddunt ova columbæ.   190
Lectus érat Codro Proculâ minor : urceoli sex
Ornamentum abaci ; necnon et parvulus infra
Cantharus, et recubans sub eodem marmore Chiron ;
Jamque vetus Græcos servabat cista libellos,
Et divina Opici rodebant carmina mures.   195
Nil habuit Codrus : quis enim negat? et tamen illud
Perdidit infelix totum nil : ultimus autem
Ærumnæ cumulus, quod nudum, et frusta rogantem
Nemo cibo, nemo hospitio, tectoque juvabit.
Si magna Arturii cecidit domus : horrida mater,   200
Pullati proceres, differt vadimonia Prætor :
Tunc gemimus casus urbis, tunc odimus ignem :

190. *Where the soft pigeons.*] The plumage of doves and pigeons is remarkably soft. Perhaps molles here has the sense of gentle, tame ; for this sort love to lay their eggs and breed in the roofs of buildings.

191. *Codrus had a bed, &c.*] Umbritius still continues to set forth the calamities of the poor, and shews that, under such a calamity as is above mentioned, they have none to relieve or pity them,

Codrus, some poor poet : perhaps he that is mentioned sat. i. l. 2. which see, and the note,

The furniture of his house consisted of a wretched bed, which was less, or shorter, than his wife Procula, who is supposed to have been a very little woman. Minor signifies less in any kind, whether in length, breadth, or height.

—*Six little pitchers.*] Urceoli, (dim. of urceus,) little water pitchers made of clay, and formed on the potter's wheel.

       —*Amphora cæpit
Institui, currente rota cur urceus
    exit?*   Hor. ad Pis. l. 21, 2.

192-3. *A small jug.*] Cantharus, a sort of drinking vessel, with a handle to it ; Attritâ pendebat cantharus ansâ. Virg. ecl. vi. 17.

193. *A Chiron reclining, &c.*] A figure of Chiron the centaur in a reclining posture under the same marble, i. e. under the marble slab, of which the cupboard was formed, perhaps by way of support to it.

Some suppose Umbritius to mean by sub eôdem marmore, that this was a shabby figure of Chiron made of the same materials with the cantharus, viz. of clay, which he jeeringly expresses by marmore, for of this images were usually made.

194. *An old chest, &c.*] This is another instance of the poverty of Codrus—he had no book-case, or library, but only a few Greek books in an old worm-eaten wooden chest.

195. *Barbarous mice, &c.*] Opicus is a word taken from the Opici, an ancient, rude, and barbarous people of Italy, so called from Ops, i.e. Terra, as being the aborigines ; hence the adjective opicus signifies barbarous, rude unlearned. The poet, therefore, humourously calls the mice opici, as having so little respect for learning, that they gnawed the divine poems, perhaps even of Homer himself, which might have been treasured up, with others, in the chest of poor Codrus.

Some suppose opici to be applied to mice, from Gr. ὀπή, a cavern—alluding to the holes in which they hide themselves.

196. *Who forsooth denies it?*] By this it should appear, that the Codrus mentioned here, and in sat. i. l. 2. are the same person, whose poverty was so great, and so well known, as to be proverbial. See note, sat. i. l. 2.

197-8. *The utmost addition, &c.*] Ultimus cumulus—the utmost height —the top—of his unhappiness ; as the French say, Le comble de son malheur. The French word comble evidently comes from Lat. cumulus,

From the rain: where the soft pigeons lay their eggs, 190
    Codrus had a bed less than Procula: six little pitchers
The ornament of his cupboard; also, underneath, a small
    Jug, and a Chiron reclining under the same marble.
And now an old chest preserved his Greek books,
And barbarous mice were gnawing divine verses. 195
Nothing had Codrus—who forsooth denies it? and yet all that
Nothing unhappy he lost. But the utmost
Addition to his affliction was, that, naked, and begging
        scraps,
Nobody will help him with food, nobody with entertain-
        ment, and an house.
    If the great house of Arturius hath fallen; the mother
        is ghastly, 200
The nobles sadly clothed, the Prætor defers recognizances:
Then we lament the misfortunes of the city: then we hate fire:

which signifies, in this connexion, that
which it over and above measure—
the heaping of any measure—when
the measure is full to the brim, and
then more put on, till it stands on an
heap above, at last it comes to a point,
and will hold no more. BOYER explains comble to mean, Ce qui peut
tenir par dessus une mesure déja
pleine. We speak of accumulated
affliction, the height of sorrow, the
completion of misfortune, the finishing stroke, and the like, but are not
possessed of any English phrase, which
literally expresses the Latin ultimus
cumulus, or the French comble du
malheur.

198. *Naked.*] Having lost the few
clothes he had by the fire.
    —*Scraps.*] Frusta—broken victu-
als, as we say. In this sense the
word is used, sat. xiv. 128.
    199. *With entertainment.*] So hos-
pitium seems to mean here, and is to
be understood, in the sense of hospitality, friendly or charitable reception
and entertainment: some render it
lodging—but this is implied by the
next word.
    —*And an house.*] Nobody would
take him into their house, that he
might find a place where to lay his
head, secure from the inclemency of
the weather.
    Having shewn the miserable estate
of the poor, if burnt out of house and
home, as we say, Umbritius proceeds

to exhibit a strong contrast, by stating
the condition of a rich man under
such a calamity; by this he carries
on his main design of setting forth the
abominable partiality for the rich, and
the wicked contempt and neglect of
the poor.
    200. *Arturius.*] Perhaps this may
mean the same person as is spoken of,
l. 29. However, this name may stand
for any rich man, who, like Arturius,
was admired and courted for his riches.
    —*Hath fallen.*] A prey to flames;
hath been burnt down.
    —*The mother is ghastly.*] Mater
may here mean the city itself. All
Rome is in a state of disorder and la-
mentation, and puts on a ghastly appearance, as in some public calamity;
or, the matrons of Rome, with torn
garments and dishevelled hair, appear
in all the horrid signs of woe. See
VIRG. Æn. ii. l. 489.
    201. *The nobles sadly clothed.*]
Pullati; clad in sad-coloured apparel,
as if in mourning.
    —*The Prætor, &c.*] The judge ad-
journs his court, and respites the
pledges, or bonds, for the suitors' appearances to a future day.
    202. *Then we lament, &c.*] Then
we lament the accidents to which the
city is liable; particularly the loss of
so noble an edifice as the house of
Arturius, as if the whole city was in-
volved in the misfortune.
    —*We hate fire.*] We can't bear the

Ardet adhuc—et jam accurrit qui marmora donet,
Conferat impensas : hic nuda et candida signa ;
Hic aliquid præclarum Euphranoris, et Polycleti ;   205
Phæcasianorum vetera ornamenta deorum.
Hic libros dabit, et forulos, mediamque Minervam ;
Hic modium argenti : meliora, ac plura reponit
Persicus orborum lautissimus, et merito jam
Suspectus, tanquam ipse suas incenderet ædes.   210
   Si potes avelli Circensibus, optima Soræ,
Aut Fabrateriæ domus, aut Frusinone paratur,
Quanti nunc tenebras unum conducis in annum :
Hortulus hic, puteusque brevis, nec reste movendus,

very mention of fire. It was customary for mourners to have no fire in their houses. Perhaps this may be meant.

203. *It burns yet*] i. e. While the house is still on fire, before the flames have quite consumed it

—*And now runs o.ic, &c*] Some officious flatterer of Arturius loses no time to improve his own interest in the great man's favour, but hastens to offer his services before the fire has done smoking, and to let him know, that he has marble of various kinds, which he wishes to present him with, for the rebuilding of the house.

204. *Cun contribute expences*] i. e. Can contribute towards the expence of repairing the damage, by presenting a large quantity of this fine marble, which was a very expensive article.

—— *Another, &c*] Of the same stamp ; as one furnishes marble to rebuild the outside of the house, another presents ornaments for the inside ; such as Grecian statues, which were usually naked, and made of the finest white marble.

205. *Another something famous, &c.*] Some famous works of Euphranor and Polycletus, two eminent Grecian statuaries.

206. *Of Phæcasian gods*] The ancient images of the Grecian deities were called Phæcasian, from φαικασυς calceus albus ; because they were represented with white sandals ; probably the statues here mentioned had been ornaments of Grecian temples.

207. *Minerva down to the waist.*]

Probably this means a bust of Minerva, consisting of the head, and part of the body down to the middle.

—*Pallas to the breast.* DRYDEN.

Grangius observes, that they had their imagines aut integræ, aut dimidiatæ ; of which latter sort was this image of Minerva.

Britannicus expounds mediam Minervam, " Statuam Minervæ in me-" dio reponendam, ad exornandam " bibliothecam."—" A statue of Mi-" nerva to be placed in the middle, " by way of ornamenting his li-" brary."

208. *A bushel of silver*] A large quantity ; a definite for an indefinite ; as we say, " such a one is worth a " bushel of money."—So the French say, un boisseau d'écus. · Argenti, here, may either mean silver to be made into plate, or silver plate already made, or it may signify money. Either of these senses answers the poet's design, in setting forth the attention, kindness, and liberality shewn to the rich, and forms a striking contrast to the want of all these towards the poor.

209. *The Persian, &c.*] Meaning Arturius, who either was a Persian, and one of the foreigners who came and enriched himself at Rome, (see l. 72.) or so called, on account of his resembling the Persians in splendor and magnificence.

—*The most splendid of destitutes.*] Orbus means one that is deprived of any thing that is dear, necessary, or useful ; as children of their parents ;

It burns yet—and now runs one who can present marbles,
Can contribute expences: another naked and white statues;
Another something famous of Euphranor and Polycletus;
The ancient ornaments of Phæcasian gods.   206
This man will give books, and book-cases, and Minerva
    down to the waist;
Another a bushel of silver: better and more things doth
The Persian, the most splendid of destitutes lay up, and
    now deservedly
Suspected, as if he had himself set fire to his own house.
    Could you be plucked away from the Circenses, a most
    excellent house   211
At Sora, or Fabrateria, or Frusino, is gotten
At the price for which you now hire darkness for one year:
Here is a little garden, and a shallow well, not to be drawn
    by a rope,

men of their friends; or of their substance and property, as Arturius, who had lost his house, and every thing in it, by a fire. But, as the poet humourously styles him, he was the most splendid and sumptuous of all sufferers, for he replaced and repaired his loss, with very considerable gain and advantage, from the contributions which were made towards the rebuilding and furnishing his house, with more and better (meliora et plura) materials for both, than those which he had lost.

The contrast to the situation of poor Codrus is finely kept up, as well as the poet's design of exposing the monstrous partiality which was shewn to riches.

209–10. *Now deservedly suspected.*] See MARTIAL, epigr. 51. lib. iii.

The satire upon the venality, self-interestedness, and mercenary views of those who paid their court to the rich and great, is here greatly heightened, by supposing them so notorious, as to encourage Arturius to set his own house on fire, on the presumption that he should be a gainer by the presents which would be made him from those who expected, in their turn, to be richly repaid by the entertainments he would give them during his life, and, at his death, by the legacies he might leave them in his will. Such were called captatores. See sat. x. 202. HOR. lib. ii. sat. v. l. 57.

As for poor Codrus, he was left to starve; nobody could expect any thing from him, either living or dying, so he was forsaken of all—orborum miserrimus—whereas Arturius was, as the poet calls him, orborum lautissimus.

211. *The Circenses.*] The Circensian games; so called, because exhibited in the Circus. See KENNETT, Antiq. book v. part ii. chap. ii. These shows were favourite amusements, and therefore the Romans could hardly be prevailed on to absent themselves from them; hence he says, Si potes avelli.

212. *Sora, &c.*] These were pleasant towns in Campania, where, says Umbritius to Juvenal, a very good house and little garden is purchased (paratur) for the same price (quanti) as you now, in these dear times, hire (conducis) a wretched, dark, doghole (tenebras) at Rome for a single year.

214. *A shallow well, &c.*] The springs lying so high, that there is no occasion for a rope for letting down a bucket to fetch up the water; the garden may be watered with the greatest ease, by merely dipping, and thus, facili haustu, with an easy drawing up by the hand, your plants be refreshed. This was no small acquisition in Italy, where, in many parts, it seldom rains.

In tenues plantas facili diffunditur haustu.   215
Vive bidentis amans, et culti villicus horti,
Unde epulum possis centum dare Pythagoræis.
Est aliquid quocunque loco, quocunque recessu,
Unius sese dominum fecisse lacertæ.
Plurimus hic æger moritur vigilando; (sed illum   220
Languorem peperit cibus imperfectus, et hærens
Ardenti stomacho,) nam quæ meritoria somnum
Admittunt? Magnis opibus dormitur in urbe.
Inde caput morbi. Rhedarum transitus arcto
Vicorum inflexu, et stantis convicia mandræ   225
Eripiunt somnum Druso, vitulisque marinis.
Si vocat officium, turbâ cedente vehetur
Dives, et ingenti curret super ora Liburno,

216. *Live fond of the fork.*] i. e.
Pass your time in cultivating your
little spot of ground. The bidens, or
fork of two prongs, was used in husbandry; here, by met. it is put for
husbandry itself.

217. *An hundred Pythagoreans.*]
Pythagoras taught his disciples to abstain from flesh, and to live on vege-
tables.

219. *Of one lizard.*] The green
lizard is very plentiful in Italy, as
in all warm climates, and is very fond
of living in gardens, and among the
leaves of trees and shrubs.

——*Seu virides rubum
Dimovēre lacertæ*——

Hor. lib. i. od xxiii. l. 6, 7.
The poet means, that, wherever a
man may be placed, or wherever retired from the rest of the world, it is
no small privilege to be able to call
one's self master of a little spot of
ground of one's own, however small
it may be, though it were no bigger
than to contain one poor lizard. This
seems a proverbial or figurative kind
of expression.

220. *With watching.*] With being
kept awake. Another inconvenience
of living in Rome is, the perpetual
noise in the streets, which is occasioned by the carriages passing at all
hours, so as to prevent one's sleeping.
This, to people who are sick, is a
deadly evil.

220–1. *But that languor, &c.*] q. d.
Though, by the way, it must be admitted, that the weak, languishing,

and sleepless state, in which many of
these are, they first bring upon themselves by their own intemperance;
and therefore their deaths are not
wholly to be set down to the account
of the noise by which they are kept
awake, however this may help to
finish them.

221. *Food—imperfect.*] i. e. Im-
perfectly digested—indigested—and
lying hard at the stomach—hærens,
adhering, as it were, to the coats of
the stomach, so as not to pass, but to
ferment, and to occasion a burning or
scalding sensation. This seems to be
a description of what we call the
heart-burn, (Gr. καρδιαλγια,) which
arises from indigestion, and is so painful and troublesome as to prevent
sleep: it is attended with risings of
sour and sharp fumes from the stomach into the throat, which occasion
a sensation almost like that of scald
ing water.

222. *For what hired lodgings, &c.*]
The nam, here, seems to join this sentence to vigilando, l. 221. I therefore have ventured to put the inter-
mediate words in a parenthesis,
which, as they are rather digressive,
makes the sense of the passage more
easily understood.

Meritorium—a merendo—locus qui
mercede locatur, signifies any place
or house that is hired. Such, in the
city of Rome, were mostly, as we
may gather from this passage, in the
noisy part of the town, in apartments

Is poured with an easy draught on the small plants. 215
Live fond of the fork, and the farmer of a cultivated garden,
Whence you may give a feast to an hundred Pythagoreans.
It is something in any place, in any retirement,
To have made one's self master of one lizard.
 Here many a sick man dies with watching; (but that 220
Languor food hath produced, imperfect, and sticking
To the burning stomach,) for what hired lodgings admit
Sleep?—By great wealth one sleeps in the city.
Thence the source of the disease: the passing of carriages
 in the narrow
Turning of the streets, and the foul language of the
 standing team,   225
Take away sleep from Drusus, and from sea-calves.
If business calls, the crowd giving way, the rich man will be
Carried along, and will pass swiftly above their faces with a
 huge Liburnian,

next to the street, so not very friendly
to repose.
 223. *With great wealth.*] Dormitur is here used impersonally, like
trepidatur, l. 188. None but the rich
can afford to live in houses which are
spacious enough to have bed-cham-
bers remote from the noise in the
streets; those who, therefore, would
sleep in Rome, must be at a great expence, which none but the opulent
can afford.
 224. *Thence the source, &c.*] One
great cause of the malady complained
of (morbi, i. e. vigilandi, l. 220.) must
be attributed to the narrowness of the
streets and turnings, so that the carriages must not only pass very near
the houses, but occasion frequent
stoppages; the consequence of which
is, that there are perpetual noisy dis-
putes, quarrels, and abuse (convicia)
among the drivers. Rheda signifies
any carriage drawn by horses, &c.
 225. *Of the standing team.*] Man-
dra signifies, literally, a hovel for
cattle, but, by meton. a company or
team of horses, oxen, mules, or any
beasts of burden; these are here supposed standing still, and not able to
go on, by reason of meeting others in
a narrow pass; hence the bickerings,
scoldings, and abusive language which
the drivers bestow on each other for
stopping the way.

226. *Drusus.*] Some person remarkable for drowsiness.
 —*Sea-calves.*] These are remarkably sluggish and drowsy; they will
lay themselves on the shore to sleep,
in which situation they are found, and
thus easily taken.
 *Sternunt se somno diversæ in littore
 phocæ.* VIRG. Georg. iv. 432.
 227. *If business calls.*] Umbritius,
having shewn the advantages of the
rich, in being able to afford themselves quiet repose, notwitstanding the
constant noises in the city, which
break the rest of the poorer sort, now
proceeds to observe the advantage
with which the opulent can travel
along the crowded streets, where the
poorer sort are inconvenienced beyond
measure.
 Si vocat officium—if business, either
public or private, calls the rich man
forth, the crowd makes way for him
as he is carried along in his litter.
 228. *Pass swiftly, &c.*] Curret—
lit. will run: while the common passengers can hardly get along for the
crowds of people, the rich man passes
on without the least impediment,
being exalted above the heads of the
people, in his litter, which is elevated
on the shoulders of tall and stout
Liburnian bearers.
 The word ora properly means faces
or countenances; the super ora may

K

Atque obiter leget, aut scribet, aut dormiet intus ;

Namque facit somnum clausâ lectica fenestrâ.　　　　230

Ante tamen veniet : nobis properantibus obstat

Unda prior, magno populus premit agmine lumbos

Qui sequitur : ferit hic cubito, ferit assere duro

Alter ; at hic tignum capiti incutit, ille metretam;

Pinguia crura luto : plantâ mox undique magnâ　　　235

Calcor, et in digito clavus mihi militis hæret.

　　Nonne vides quanto celebretur sportula fumo ?

Centum convivæ ; sequitur sua quemque culina :

Corbulo vix ferret tot vasa ingentia, tot res

Impositas capiti, quot recto vertice portat　　　　240

---

denote his being carried above the faces of the crowd, which are turned upwards to look at him as he passes.

228. *A huge Liburnian.*] The chairmen at Rome commonly came from Liburnia, a part of Illyria, between Istria and Dalmatia. They were remarkably tall and stout.

229. *Read, or write, or sleep.*] He is carried on with so much ease to himself, that he can amuse himself with reading, employ himself in writing, or, if he has a mind to take a nap, has only to shut up the window of his litter, and he will be soon composed to sleep. All this he may do, obiter, in going along—En chemin faisant—en passant, as the French say.

231. *But he will come before us.*] He will lose no time by all this ; for, however he may employ himself in his way, he will be sure to arrive before us foot-passengers at the place he is going to.

—*Us hastening.*] Whatever hurry we may be in, or whatever haste we wish to make, we are sure to be obstructed ; the crowd that is before us, in multitude and turbulence, like waves, closes in upon us, as soon as the great man, whom they made way for, is passed, so that we can hardly get along at all.

232. *The people who follow, &c.*] As the crowd which is before us stops up our way, that which is behind presses upon our backs, so that we can hardly stir either backward or forward.

233. *One strikes with the elbow.*] To jostle us out of his way.

233-4. *Another—with a large joist.*] Which he is carrying along, and runs it against us. Asser signifies a pole, or piece of wood ; also the joist of an house ; which, from the next word, we may suppose to be meant here, at least some piece of timber for building, which, being carried along in the crowd, must strike those who are not aware of it, and who stand in the way.

Some understand asser in this place to mean a pole of some litter that is passing along ; a chair pole, as we should call it.

234. *Drives a beam, &c.*] Another is carrying tignum, a beam, or rafter, or some other large piece of wood used in building, which, being carried on the shoulder, has the end level with the heads of those it meets in its way, and must inflict a severe blow.

—*A tub.*] Metreta signifies a cask of a certain measure, which, in being carried through the crowd, will strike and hurt those who don't avoid it.

235. *Thick with mud.*] Bespattered with the mire of the streets, which is kicked up by such a number of people upon each other.

235-6. *On all sides—the nail, &c.*] I can hardly turn myself but some heavy, splay-footed fellow tramples upon my feet ; and at last some soldier's hob-nail runs into my toe. The soldiers wore a sort of harness on their feet and legs, called caliga, which was stuck full of large nails.

Such are the inconveniences which the common sort of people meet with in walking the streets of Rome.

And in the way he will read, or write, or sleep within ;
For a litter with the window shut causeth sleep.   230
But he will come before us : us hastening the crowd before
Obstructs : the people who follow press the loins with a large
Concourse : one strikes with the elbow, another strikes with a
    large
Joist, but another drives a beam against one's head, another
    a tub.
The legs thick with mud : presently, on all sides, with a
    great foot   235
I'm trodden on, and the nail of a soldier sticks in my toe.
    Do not you now see with how much smoke the sportula
      is frequented ?
An hundred guests : his own kitchen follows every one :
Corbulo could hardly bear so many immense vessels, so
    many things   239
Put on his head, as, with an upright top, an unhappy little

237. *Do not you see, &c.*] Umbritius proceeds to enumerate farther inconveniences and dangers which attend passengers in the streets of Rome.

Some understand fumo, here, in a figurative sense—*q. d.* With how much bustle, with what crowds of people, like clouds of smoke, is the sportula frequented ? Others think it alludes to the smoke of the chafing dishes of hot coals which were put under the victuals, to keep them warm as they were carried along the street : this, from the number, must have been very offensive.

—*The sportula.*] Of this, see sat. i. 81. note. But, from the circumstances which are spoken of in the next four lines of this passage, it should seem, that the sportula mentioned here was of another kind than the usual poor dole-basket. Here are an hundred guests invited to partake of it, and each has such a share distributed to him as to be very considerable.

238. *His own kitchen follows*] Each of the hundred sharers of this sportula had a slave, who, with a chafing-dish of coals on his head, on which the victuals were put, to keep them hot, followed his master along the street homewards : so that the whole made a very long procession.

Culina denotes a place where victuals are cooked ; and as the slaves followed their masters with vessels of fire placed under the dishes so as to keep them warm, and, in a manner, to dress them as they went along, each of these might be looked upon as a moveable or travelling kitchen : so that the masters might each be said to be followed by his own kitchen.

239. *Corbulo.*] A remarkably strong and valiant man in the time of Nero. Tacitus says of him, Corpore ingens erat, et supra experientiam sapientiamque erat validus.

240. *An upright top.*] The top of the head, on which the vessels of fire and provision were carried, must be quite upright, not bending or stooping, lest the soup, or sauce, which they contained, should be spilt as they went along, or vessels and all slide off. The tot vasa ingentia, and tot res, shew that the sportula abovementioned was of a magnificent kind, more like the splendor of a coena recta, a set and full supper, than the scanty distribution of a dole-basket.

240–1. *Unhappy little slave.*] Who was hardly equal to the burden which he was obliged to carry in so uneasy a situation, as not daring to stir his head.

Servulus infelix ; et cursu ventilat ignem.
Scinduntur tunicæ sartæ: modo longa coruscat
Sarraco veniénte abies, atque altera pinum
Plaustra vehunt, nutant alte, populoque minantur.
Nam si procubuit, qui saxa Ligustica portat   245
Axis, et eversum fudit super agminą montem,
Quid superest de corporibus? quis membra, quis ossa,
Invenit? obtritum vulgi perit omne cadaver
More animæ. Domus interea secura patellas
Jam lavat, et buccâ foculum excitat, et sonat unctis   250
Strigilibus, pleno et componit lintea gutto.
Hæc inter pueros varie properantur ; at ille
Jam sedet in ripâ, tetrumque novitius horret
Porthmea ; nec sperat cœnosi gurgitis alnum

241. *In running ventilates, &c.*]
He blew up, or fanned, the fire under
the provisions, by the current of air
which he excited in hastening on
with his load. These processions Umbritius seems to reckon among other
causes of the street being crowded,
and made disagreeable and inconvenient for passengers.

242. *Botched coats are torn.*] Some
refer this to the old botched clothes
of these poor slaves ; but I should
rather imagine, that Umbritius here
introduces a new circumstance, which
relates to the poor in general, whose
garments being old, and only hanging together by being botched and
mended, are rent and torn off their
backs, in getting through the crowd,
by the violence of the press, which is
increased by the number of masters
and servants, who are hurrying along
with the contents of the sportula.

—*A long fir-tree.*] Another inconvenience arises from the passing of
timber-carriages among the people in
the streets. SENECA, epist. xl. Longo vehiculorum ordine, pinus aut
abies deferebatur vicis intrementibus.

—*Brandishes.*] Corusco signifies
to brandish or shake ; also neut. to
be shaken, to wave to and fro ; which
must be the case of a long stick of
timber, of the ends especially, on a
carriage. This may be very dangerous if approached too near.

243. *The waggon coming.*] Moving on its way ; sarracum signifies a
waggon, or wain, for the purpose of
carrying timber.

244. *They nod on high.*] These
trees being placed high on the carriages, and lying out beyond them at
each end, tremble aloft, and threaten
the destruction of the people.

245. *But if the axle, &c.*] i. e. If
the stone-carriage has overturned by
the breaking of the axle-tree.

—*Ligustian stones.*] Which were
hewn, in vast masses, in Liguria,
from the quarries of the Appenine
mountains.

246. *The overturned mountain.*]
Hyperbole, denoting the immensity
of the block of stone.

—*Upon the crowd.*] Agmen denotes
a troop or company ; also a number
of people walking together, as in a
crowded street.

247. *What remains, &c.*] If such
an immense mass should, in its fall,
light upon any of the people, it must
grind them to atoms : no trace of a
human body, its limbs, or bones,
could be found.

249. *In the manner of the soul.*]
i. e. The particles which composed
the body could no more be found,
than could the soul which is immate-
rial ; both would seem to have vanished away, and disappeared together.

— *Meanwhile.*] Interea — q. d.
While the slave is gone to bring home
the provisions, and is crushed to
pieces, by the fall of a stone-carriage,
in his way. See l. 252-3.

—*The family.*] The servants of the
family (comp. l. 252.) safe at home,
and knowing nothing of what had

Slave carries; and in running ventilates the fire.—
Botched coats are torn.—Now a long fir-tree brandishes,
The waggon coming, and a pine other
Carts carry, they nod on high, and threaten the people,/
But if the axle, which carries the Ligustian stones,   245
Hath fallen down, and hath poured forth the overturned
    mountain upon the crowd,
What remains of their bodies? who finds members—who
Bones? every carcase of the vulgar, ground to powder,
    perishes
In the manner of the soul. Meanwhile, the family secure
    now washes
The dishes, and raises up a little fire with the cheek, and
    makes a sound with anointed   250
Scrapers, and puts together the napkins with a full cruse.
These things among the servants are variously hastened:
    but he
Now sits on the bank, and, a novice, dreads the black
Ferryman; nor does he hope for the boat of the muddy
    gulph,

happened, set about preparing for supper.

250. *The dishes.*] Patella signifies any sort of dish to hold meat. One washes and prepares the dishes which are to hold the meat when it arrives.

—*Raises up a little fire, &c.*] Another, in order to prepare the fire for warming the water for bathing before supper, blows it with his mouth. Hence it is said, buccâ foculum excitat; alluding to the distension of the cheeks in the act of blowing.

250-1. *With anointed scrapers.*] Strigil denotes an instrument for scraping the body after bathing; it had some oil put on it, to make it slide with less friction over the skin. Scrapers were made of gold, silver, iron, or the like, which, when gathered up, or thrown down together, made a clattering sound.

251. *Puts together the napkins.*] Lintea—linen napkins, or towels, made use of to dry the body after bathing: these he folds and lays in order.

—*A full cruse.*] Gutto—a sort of oil-cruet, with a long and narrow neck, which poured the oil, drop by drop, on the body after bathing, and

then it was rubbed all over it.

252. *These things among the servants, &c.*] Each servant, in his department, made all the haste he could, to get things ready against the supper should arrive.

—*But he.*] Ille—i. e. The servulus infelix, (which we read of, l. 241.) in his way home with his load of provisions, is killed by the fall of a block of stone upon him.

253. *Sits on the bank.*] Of the river Styx. By this account of the deceased, it is very clear that Juvenal was no Epicurean, believing the soul to perish with the body, which some have wrongly inferred, from what he says. l. 249. more animæ.

—*A novice.*] Just newly arrived, and now first beholding such a scene.

253-4. *The black ferryman.*] Porthmea—from Gr. πορθμευς, a ferryman, one who ferries people over the water. Charon, the fabled ferryman of hell, is here meant.

254. *Nor does he hope for the boat, &c.*] Alnus properly signifies an elder-tree; but as the wood of this tree was used in making boats, it therefore, by met. signifies a boat.

As the poor deceased had died a

Infelix, nec habet quem porrigat ore trientem.   255
   Respice nunc alia, ac diversa pericula noctis :
Quod spatium tectis sublimibus, unde cerebrum
Testa ferit, quoties rimosa et curta fenestris
Vasa cadunt, quanto percussum pondere signent,
Et lædant silicem : possis ignavus haberi,   260
Et subiti casûs improvidus, ad cœnam si
Intestatus eas ; adeo tot fata, quot illâ
Nocte patent vigiles, te prætereunte, fenestræ.
Ergo optes, votumque feras miserabile tecum,
Ut sint contentæ patulas effundere pelves.   265
   Ebrius, ac petulans, qui nullum forte cecidit,
Dat pœnas, noctem patitur lugentis amicum
Pelidæ ; cubat in faciem, mox deinde supinus :
Ergo non aliter poterit dormire : QUIBUSDAM
SOMNUM RIXA FACIT : sed quamvis improbus annis,   270

violent death, and such a one as dis-
sipated all the parts of his body, so as
that they could not be collected for
burial, he could not pass over the
river Styx, but must remain on its
banks an hundred years, which was
held to be the case of all unburied bodies. . See VIRG. Æn. vi. 325–29.
365–6. and HOR. lib. i. ode xxviii.
35–6. This situation was reckoned
to be very unhappy.
   255. *Nor hath he a farthing, &c.*]
The triens was a very small piece of
money, the third part of the AS,
which was about three farthings of
our money. It was a custom among
the Greeks to put a piece of money
into the mouth of a dead person,
which was supposed to be given to
Charon, as his fare, for the passage
in his boat over the river Styx. This
unhappy man, being killed in the
manner he was, could not have this
done for him.
   Though Juvenal certainly believed
a future state of rewards and punishments, yet he certainly means here,
as he does elsewhere, to ridicule the
idle and foolish superstitions, which
the Romans had adopted from the
Greeks, upon those subjects, as well
as on many others relative to their received mythology.
   256. *Now consider, &c.*] Umbritius still pursues his discourse, and
adds fresh reasons for his departure

from Rome : which, like the former
already given, arise from the dangers
which the inhabitants, the poorer sort
especially, are exposed to, in walking
the streets by night. These he sets
forth with much humour.
   —*Other, and different dangers.*]
Besides those already mentioned. l.
184–190.
   257. *What space from high roofs.*]
How high the houses are, and, consequently, what a long way any thing
has to fall, from the upper windows
into the street, upon people's heads
that are passing by ; and therefore
must come with the greater force ;
insomuch that pieces of broken
earthen ware, coming from such a
height, make a mark in the flint
pavement below, and, of course, must
dash out the brains of the unfortunate
passenger on whose head they may
happen to alight.
   260. *Idle.*] Ignavus—indolent—
negligent of your affairs. *q. d.* A man
who goes out to supper, and who has
to walk home through the streets at
night, may be reckoned very indolent,
and careless of his affairs, as well as
very improvident, if he does not make
his will before he sets out.
   262. *As many fates.*] As many
chances of being knocked on the head,
as there are open windows, and people watching to throw down their

Wretch [that he is]—nor hath he a farthing which he can.
   reach forth from his mouth.   -   255
  Now consider other, and different dangers of the night:
What space from high roofs, from whence the brain
A potsherd strikes, as often as from the windows cracked
   and broken
Vessels fall, with what weight they mark and wound
The stricken flint : you may be accounted idle,   260
And improvident of sudden accident, if to supper
You go intestate ; there are as many fates as, in that
Night, there are watchful windows open, while you pass by.
Therefore you should desire, and carry with you a miserable
   wish,
That they may be content to pour forth broad basons. 265
  One drunken and petulant, who haply hath killed nobody,
Is punished ; suffers the night of Pelides mourning
His friend ; he lies on his face, then presently on his back :
For otherwise he could not sleep : To SOME,
A QUARREL CAUSES SLEEP : but tho' wicked from years 270

broken crockery into the street, as you pass along.

264. *Therefore you should desire, &c.*] As the best thing which you can expect, that the people at the windows would content themselves with emptying the nastiness which is in their pots upon you, and not throw down the pots themselves.

Pelvis is a large bason, or vessel, wherein they washed their feet, or put to more filthy uses.

266. *One drunken, &c.*] Umbritius, among the nightly dangers of Rome, recounts that which arises from meeting drunken rakes in their cups.

—*Drunken and petulant.*] We may imagine him in his way from some tavern, very much in liquor, and very saucy and quarrelsome, hoping to pick a quarrel, that he may have the pleasure of beating somebody before he gets home ; to fail of this is a punishment to him.

267. *The night of Pelides.*] The poet humourously compares the uneasiness of one of these young fellows, on missing a quarrel, to the disquiet of Achilles (the son of Peleus) on the loss of his friend Patroclus ; and almost translates the description

which Homer gives of that hero's restlessness on the occasion. Iliad Ω. 10, 11.

Αλλοτ' επι πλευρας κατακειμενος,
  αλλοτε δ' αυτε
Υπτιος, αλλοτε δε πρηνης
Nunc lateri incumbens, iterum post.
  paulo supinus
Corpore, nunc pronus.
So the poet describes this rake-helly youth, as tossing and tumbling in his bed, first on his face, then on his back (supinus)—thus endeavouring to amuse the restlessness of his mind, under the disappointment of having met with nobody to quarrel with and beat—thus wearying himself, as it were, into sleep.

269–70. *To some a quarrel, &c.*] This reminds one of Prov. iv. 16. " For they (the wicked and evil men, " ver. 14.) sleep not, except they " have done mischief, and their sleep " is taken away unless they cause " some to fall."

270. *Wicked from years.*] Improbus also signifies lewd, rash, violent, presumptuous.—Though he be all these, owing to his young time of life, and heated also with liquor, yet he takes care whom he assaults.

Atque mero fervens, cavet hunc, quem coccina læna
Vitari jubet, et comitum longissimus ordo ;
Multum præterea flammarum, atque ænea lampas.
Me quem Luna solet deducere, vel breve lumen
Candelæ, cujus dispenso.et tempero filum,   275
Contemnit : miseræ cognosce prooemia rixæ,
Si rixa est, ubi tu pulsas ego vapulo tantum.
Stat contra, starique jubet ; parere necesse est ;
Nam quid agas, cum te furiosus cogat, et idem
Fortior ? unde venis ? exclamat : cujus aceto,   280
Cujus conche tumes ? quis tecum sectile porrum
Sutor, et elixi vervecis labra comedit ?
Nil mihi respondes ? aut dic, aut accipe calcem :
Ede ubi consistas : in quâ te quæro proseuchâ ?
Dicere si tentes aliquid, tacitusve recedas,   285
Tantundem est : feriunt pariter : vadimonia deinde
Irati faciunt.   Libertas pauperis hæc est :
Pulsatus rogat, et pugnis concisus adorat,
Ut liceat paucis cum dentibus inde reverti.

271. *A scarlet cloak.*] Instead of attacking, he will avoid any rich man or noble, whom he full well knows from his dress, as well as from the number of lights and attendants which accompany him.

The læna was a sort of cloak usu-ally worn by soldiers : but only the rich and noble could afford to wear those which were dyed in scarlet. Coccus signifies the shrub which pro-duced the scarlet grain, and coccinus implies what was dyed with it of a scarlet colour.

273. *Brazen lamp.*] This sort of lamp was made of Corinthian brass : it was very expensive, and could only fall to the share of the opulent.

274. *Me whom the moon,* &c.] Who walk by moon-light, or, at most, with a poor, solitary, short candle, which I snuff with my fin-gers—such a one he holds in the ut-most contempt.

276. *Know the preludes,* &c.] At-tend a little, and hear what the pre-ludes are of one of these quarrels, if that can properly be called a quarrel, where the beating is by the assailant only.

Rixa signifies a buffeting, and fight-ing, which last seems to be the best sense in this place, *viz.* if that can be called fighting, where the battle is all on one side.

278. *He stands opposite.*] Directly in your way, to hinder your passing, and orders you to stop.

279. *What can you do,* &c.] You must submit, there's no making any resistance ; you are no match for such a furious man.

280. *With whose vinegar,* &c.]— Then he begins his taunts, in hopes to pick a quarrel. Where have you been? with whose sour wine have you been filling yourself ?

281 *With whose bean,* &c.] Conchis means a bean in the shell, and thus boiled—a common food among the lower sort of people, and very filling, which is implied by tumes.

—*What cobler.*]—He now falls foul of your company, as well as your entertainment.

282. *Sliced leek.*] Sectilis signifies any thing that is or may be easily cut asunder. But see sat. xiv. 1. 133 note.

—*A boiled sheep's head.*] Vervex particularly signifies a wether sheep. Labra, the lips, put here, by synec. for all the flesh about the jaws.

283. *A kick.*] Calx properly signi-

And heated with wine, he is aware of him whom a scarlet
    cloak
Commands to avoid, and a very long train of attendants,
Besides a great number of lights, and a brazen lamp.
Me whom the moon is wont to attend, or the short light
Of a candle, the wick of which I dispose and regulate, 275
He despises; know the preludes of a wretched quarrel,
If it be a quarrel where you strike and I am beaten only.
He stands opposite, and bids you stand; it is necessary to
    obey;
For what can you do, when a madman compels, and he
The stronger? "Whence come you," he exclaims, "with
    "whose vinegar,   280
"With whose bean, swell you? What cobler with you
"Sliced leek, and a boiled sheep's head, hath eaten?
"Do you answer me nothing?—either tell, or take a kick;
"Tell where you abide—in what begging-place shall I seek
    "you?"—
If you should attempt to say any thing, or retire silent, 285
It amounts to the same: they equally strike: then, angry,
    they
Bind you over. This is the liberty of a poor man.
Beaten he asks, bruised with fists he entreats,
That he may return thence with a few of his teeth.

fies the heel—but by meton. a spurn
or kick with the heel.
284. *Where do you abide.*] Consisto
signifies to abide, stay, or keep in one
place—here I suppose it to allude to
taking a constant stand, as beggars
do, in order to beg: as if the assailant, in order to provoke the man
more, whom he is wanting to quarrel
with, meant to treat him as inso-
lently as possible, and should say,
"Pray let me know where you take
"your stand for begging?" This idea
seems countenanced by the rest of the
line. Sat. iv. 114. xiv. 134.
—*In what begging-place, &c.*]—
Proseucha properly signifies a place
of prayer, from the Gr. προσευχεσθαι
in the porches of which beggars used
to take their stand. Hence by met.
a place where beggars stand to ask
alms of them who pass by.
286. *They equally strike.*] After
having said every thing to insult and
provoke you, in the hope of your

giving the first blow, you get nothing
by not answering; for their determination is to beat you; therefore either
way, whether you answer, or whether you are silent, the event will be
just the same—it will be all one.
—*Then angry, &c.*] Then, in a
violent passion, as if they had been
beaten by you, instead of your being
beaten by them—away they go, swear
the peace against you, and make you
give bail, as the aggressor, for the
assault.
287. *This is the liberty, &c.*] So
that, after our boasted freedom, a
poor man at Rome is in a fine situation—all the liberty which he has is,
to ask, if beaten, and to supplicate
earnestly, if bruised unmercifully with
fisty-cuffs, that he may return home,
from the place where he was so used,
without having all his teeth beat out
of his head—and perhaps he is to be
prosecuted, and ruined at law, as the
aggressor.

L

Nec tamen hoc tantum metuas : nam qui spoliet te   290
Non deerit; clausis domibus, postquam omnis ubique
Fixa catenatæ siluit compago tabernæ.
Interdum et ferro subitus grassator agit rem,
Armato quoties tutæ custode tenentur
Et Pontina palus, et Gallinaria pinus.   295
Sic inde huc omnes tanquam ad vivaria currunt.
    Quâ fornace graves, quâ non incude catenæ ?
Maximus in vinclis ferri modus, ut timeas, ne
Vomer deficiat, ne marræ et sarcula desint.
Felices proavorum atavos, felicia dicas   300
Secula, quæ quondam sub regibus atque tribunis
Viderunt uno contentam carcere Romam.
    His alias poteram, et plures subnectere causas :
Sed jumenta vocant, et sol inclinat ; eundum est :
Nam mihi commotâ jamdudum mulio virgâ   305

290. *Yet neither, &c.*] Umbritius, as another reason for retiring from Rome, describes the perils which the inhabitants are in from house and street-robbers.

291. *The houses being shut up.*] The circumstance mentioned here, and in the next line, mark what he says to belong to the alia et diversa pericula noctis, l. 256.

292. *The chained shop.*] Taberna has many significations; it denotes any house made of boards, a tradesman's shop, or warehouse; also, an inn or tavern. By the preceding domibus he means private houses. Here, therefore, we may understand tabernæ to denote the shops and taverns, which last were probably kept open longer than private houses or shops; yet even these are supposed to be fastened up, and all silent and quiet within.—This marks the lateness of the hour, when the horrid burglar is awake and abroad, and when there is not wanting a robber to destroy the security of the sleeping inhabitants.

Compago signifies a joining, or closure, as of planks, or boards, with which the tabernæ were built—fixa compago denotes the fixed and firm manner in which they were compacted or fastened together— Inductâ etiam per singulos asseres grandi catenâ—Vet. Schol.—" with a great " chain introduced through every

" plank "—in order to keep them from being torn asunder, and thus the building broken open by robbers. The word siluit, here, shews that the building is put for the inhabitants within. Meton. The noise and hurry of the day was over, and they were all retired to rest.

293. *The sudden footpad.*] Grassator means an assailant of any kind, such as highwaymen, footpads, &c. One of these may leap on a sudden from his lurking-place upon you, and do your business by stabbing you. Or perhaps the poet may here allude to what is very common in Italy at this day, namely assassins, who suddenly attack and stab people in the streets late at night.

295. *Pontinian marsh.*] Strabo describes this as in Campania, a champain country of Italy, in the kingdom of Naples ; and Suet. says, that Julius Cæsar had determined to dry up this marsh ; it was a noted harbour for thieves.

—*Gallinarian pine.*] *i. e.* Wood, by synec. This was situated near the bay of Cumæ, and was another receptacle of robbers.

When these places were so infested with thieves, as to make the environs dangerous for the inhabitants, as well as for travellers, a guard was sent there to protect them, and to apprehend the offenders; when this was

Yet neither may you fear this only: for one who will rob
　you will not　　　　　　　　　　　　　　　　　290
Be wanting, the houses being shut up, after, every where,
　every
Fixed fastening of the chained shop hath been silent:
And sometimes the sudden footpad with a sword does your
　business,
As often as, with an armed guard, are kept safe
Both the Pontinian marsh, and the Gallinarian pine; 295
Thus from thence hither all run as to vivaries.

In what furnace, on what anvil are not heavy chains?
The greatest quantity of iron (is used) in fetters, so that
　you may fear, lest
The ploughshare may fail, lest hoes and spades may be
　wanting.
You may call our great-grandfathers happy, happy　300
The ages, which formerly under kings and tribunes,
Saw Rome content with one prison.

To these I could subjoin other and more causes,
But my cattle call, and the sun inclines, I must go:
For long since the muleteer, with his shaken whip,　305

the case, the rogues fled to Rome, where they thought themselves secure; and then these places were rendered safe.

296. *As to vivaries.*] Vivaria are places where wild creatures live, and are protected, as deer in a park, fish in a stew-pond, &c. The poet may mean here, that they are not only protected in Rome, but easily find subsistence, like creatures in vivaries. See sat. iv. l. 50.

What Rome was to the thieves, when driven out of their lurking places in the country, that London is to the thieves of our time. This must be the case of all great cities.

297. *In what furnace, &c.*] In this, and the two following lines, the poet, in a very humurous hyperbole, describes the numbers of thieves to be so great, and to threaten such a consumption of iron in making fetters for them, as to leave some apprehensions of there being none left to make ploughshares, and other implements of husbandry.

300. *Our great grandfathers, &c.*] *i. e.* Our ancestors of old time—pro-

avorum atavos—old grandsires, or ancestors indefinitely.

301. *Kings and tribunes.*] After the expulsion of the kings, tribunes, with consular authority, governed the republic.

302. *With one prison.*] Which was built in the forum, or market-place, at Rome, by Ancus Martius, the fourth king. Robberies, and the other offences above mentioned, were then so rare, that this one jail was sufficient to contain all the offenders.

303. *And more causes.*] *i. e.* For my leaving Rome.

304. *My cattle call.*] Summon me away. It is to be supposed, that the carriage, as soon as the loading was finished, (see l. 10.) had set forward, had overtaken Umbritius, and had been some time waiting for him to proceed.

—*The sun inclines.*] From the meridian towards its setting.

——*Inclinare merediem*

Sentis— Hor. lib. iii. od. xxviii. l. 5.

305. *The muleteer.*] Or driver of the mules, which drew the carriage containing the goods, (see l. 10.) had

Innuit : ergo vale nostri memor ; et quoties te
Roma tuo refici properantem reddet Aquino,
Me quoque ad Helvinam Cererem, vestramque Dianam
Convelle a Cumis : Satirarum ego (nî pudet illas)
Adjutor gelidos veniam caligatus in agros.   310

long since given a hint, by the motion of his whip,. that it was time to be gone. This Umbritius, being deeply engaged in his discourse, had not adverted to till now.

306. *Mindful of me.*] · An usual way of taking leave. See HOR. lib. iii. ode xxvii. l. 14.

Et memor nostri Galatea vivas.

307. *Hastening to be refreshed.*] The poets, and other studious persons, were very desirous of retiring into the country from the noise and hurry of Rome, in order to be refreshed with quiet and repose.

HOR. lib. i. epist. xviii. l. 104.

Me quoties refîcit gelidus Digentia rivus, &c.

See also that most beautiful passage, O Rus, &c. lib. ii. sat. vi. l. 60-2.

—*Your Aquinum.*] A town in the Latin way, famous for having been the birth-place of Juvenal, and to which, at times, he retired.

308. *Helvine Ceres.*] Helvinam Cererem—Helvinus is used by Pliny to denote a sort of flesh-colour. AINSW. Something perhaps approaching the yellowish colour of corn. Also a pale red-colour—*Helvus.* AINSW. But we may understand Ceres to be called Helvinus or Elvinus, which was near Aquinum. Near the fons Helvinus was a temple of Ceres and also of Di-

Hath hinted to me: therefore farewell mindful of me : and
    as often as
Rome shall restore you, hastening to be refreshed, to your
    Aquinum,
Me also to Helvine Ceres, and to your Diana,
Rend from Cumæ: I of your Satires (unless they are
    ashamed)
An helper, will come armed into your cold fields,   310

ana, the vestiges of which are said to remain till this day.

309. *Rend from Cumæ.*] Convelle —pluck me away ; by which expression Umbritius describes his great unwillingness to be taken from the place of his retreat, as if nothing but his friendship for Juvenal could force him (as it were) from it.

310. *Armed, &c.*] Caligatus—the caliga was a sort of harness for the leg, worn by soldiers, who hence were called caligati. It is used here metaphorically.

" I (says Umbritius,) unless your " Satires should be ashamed of my " assistance, will come, armed at all " points, to help you in your attacks " upon the people and manners of the " times." By this it appears that Umbritius was himself a poet.

—*Your cold fields.*] Aquinum was situated in a part of Campania much colder than where Cumæ stood.

Satira Quarta.

From the luxury and prodigality of Crispinus, whom he
lashes so severely, sat. i. 25—8, Juvenal takes occasion
to describe a ridiculous consultation, held by Domitian
over a large turbot; which was too big to be contained
in any dish that could be found. The Poet with great
wit and humour, describes the senators being summoned
in this exigency, and gives a particular account of their
characters, speeches, and advice. After long consulta-

ECCE iterum Crispinus ; et est mihi sæpe vocandus
Ad partes ; monstrum nullâ virtute redemptum
A vitiis, æger, solâque libidine fortis :
Quid refert igitur quantis jumenta fatiget
Porticibus, quantâ nemorum vectetur in umbrâ,   5
Jugera quot vicina foro, quas emerit ædes ?
NEMO MALUS FELIX ; minime corruptor, et idem
Incestus, cum quo nuper vittata jacebat
Sanguine adhuc vivo terram subitura sacerdos.

Line 1. Again Crispinus.] Juvenal
mentions him before, sat. i. 25. He
was an Egyptian by birth, and of very
low extraction ; but having the good
fortune to be a favourite of Domitian's
he came to great riches and preferment, and lived in the exercise of all
kinds of vice and debauchery.

2. *To his parts.*] A metaphor,
taken from the players, who, when
they had finished the scene they were
to act, retired, but were called again
to their parts, as they were successively to enter and carry on the piece.

Thus Juvenal calls Crispinus again,
to appear in the parts, or characters,
which he has allotted him in his
Satires.

—*By no virtue, &c.*] He must be
a monster indeed, who had not a single virtue to rescue him from the total dominion of his vices. Redemptum here is metaphorical, and alludes

to the state of a miserable captive,
who is enslaved to a tyrant master,
and has none to ransom him from
bondage.

3. *Sick.*] Diseased—perhaps full of
infirmities from his luxury and debauchery. Æger also signifies weak,
feeble. This sense too is to be here
included, as opposed to fortis.

—*And strong in lust, &c.*] Vigorous and strong in the gratification of
his sensuality only.

4. *In how large porches, &c.*] It
was a part of the Roman luxury to
build vast porticos in their gardens,
under which they rode in wet or hot
weather, that they might be sheltered
from the rain, and from the too great
heat of the sun. Jumentum signifies
any labouring beast, either for carriage
or draught. Sat. iii. 304.

5. *How a great shade, &c.*] Another piece of luxury was to be carried

Fourth Satire.

---

tion, it was proposed that the fish should be cut to pieces, and so dressed : at last they all came over to the opinion of the senator Montanus, that it should be dressed whole : and that a dish, big enough to contain it, should be made on purpose for it. The council is then dismissed, and the Satire concludes ; but not without a most severe censure on the emperor's injustice and cruelty towards some of the best and most worthy of the Romans.

BEHOLD again Crispinus ! and he is often to be called
    by me
To his parts : a monster by no virtue redeemed
From vices—sick, and strong in lust alone :
What signifies it, therefore, in how large porches he fatigues
His cattle, in how great a shade of groves he may be carried,
How many acres near the forum, what houses he may have
    bought ?   6
No bad man is happy : least of all a corrupter, and the same
Incestuous, with whom there lay, lately, a filletted
Priestess, about to go under ground with blood as yet alive.

in litters among the shady trees of their groves, in sultry weather.

6. *Acres near the forum.*] Where land was the most valuable, as being in the midst of the city.

—*What houses, &c.*] What purchases he may have made of houses in the same lucrative situation. Comp. sat. i. l. 91. and note.

7. *No bad man, &c.*] This is one of those passages, in which Juvenal speaks more like a Christian, than like an heathen. Comp. Isa. lvii. 20, 21.

—*A corrupter.*] A ruiner, a debaucher of women.

8. *Incestuous.*] Incestus—from in and castus—in general is used to denote that species of unchastity, which consists in defiling those who

are near of kin—but, in the best authors, it signifies unchaste ; also guilty, profane. As in Hor. lib. iii. ode ii. l. 29.

    ——*Sæpe Diespiter*
  Neglectus incesto addidit integrum.
In this place it may be taken in the sense of profane, as denoting that sort of unchastity which is mixed with profaneness, as in the instance which follows, of defiling a vestal virgin.

8-9. *A filletted priestess.*] The vestal virgins, as priestesses of Vesta, had fillets bound round their heads, made of ribbons, or the like.

9. *With blood as yet alive.*] The vestal virgins vowed chastity, and if any broke their vow, they were buried alive ; by a law of Numa Pompilius their founder.

Sed nunc de factis levioribus: et tamen alter   10
Si fecisset idem, caderet sub judice morum.
Nam quod turpe bonis, Titio, Seioque, decebat
Crispinum: quid agas, cum dira, et fœdior omni
Crimine persona est? mullum sex millibus emit,
Æquantem sane paribus sestertia libris,   15
Ut perhibent, qui de magnis majora loquuntur.
Consilium laudo artificis, si munere tanto
Præcipuam in tabulis ceram senis abstulit orbi.
Est ratio ulterior, magnæ si misit amicæ,
Quæ vehitur clauso latis specularibus antro.   20
Nil tale expectes: emit sibi: multa videmus,

10. *Lighter deeds.*] i. e. Such faults as, in comparison with the preceding, are trivial, yet justly reprehensible, and would be so deemed in a character less abandoned than that of Crispinus, in whom they are in a manner eclipsed by greater.

11. *Under the judge, &c.*] This seems to be a stroke at the partiality of Domitian, who punished Maximilla, a vestal, and those who had defiled her, with the greatest severity. SUET. Domit. ch. viii. See note 2. on l. 59.

Crispinus was a favourite, and so he was suffered to escape punishment, however much he deserved it, as was the vestal whom he had defiled, on the same account.

Suet. says, that Domitian, particularly—Morum correctionem exercuit in vestales.

12. *What would be base, &c.*] So partial was Domitian to his favourite Crispinus, that what would be reckoned shameful, and be punished as a crime, in good men, was esteemed very becoming in him.

—*Titius, or Seius.*] It does not appear who these were; but probably they were some valuable men, who had been persecuted by the emperor for some supposed offences. See this sat. l. 149–50.

13. *What can you do, &c.*] q. d. What can one do with such a fellow as Crispinus? what signifies satirizing his crimes, when his person is more odious and abominable than all that can be mentioned? What he IS, is so much worse than what he DOES, that one is at a loss how to treat him.

This is a most severe stroke, and introduces what follows on the gluttony and extravagance of Crispinus.

14. *A mullet.*] Mullus—a sea fish, of a red and purple colour, therefore called mullus, from mulleus, a kind of red or purple shoe, worn by senators and great persons. AINSW. I take this to be what is called the red mullet, or mullus barbatus; by some rendered barbel. Horace speaks of this fish as a great dainty:

Laudas insane, trilibrem
Mullum——

Hor. sat. ii. lib. ii. l. 33, 4.
So that about three pounds was their usual weight: that it was a rarity to find them larger, we may gather from his saying, l. 37. His breve pondus.

But Crispinus meets with one that weighed six pounds, and rather than not purchase it, he pays for it the enormous sum of six thousand sestertii, or six sestertia, making about 46l. 17s. 6d. of our money.

For the manner of reckoning sesterces, see before, sat. i. l. 92. and note.

This fish, whatever it strictly was, was in great request, as a dainty, among the Romans. Asinius Celer, a man of consular dignity under the emperor Claudius, is said to have given 8000 nummi (i. e. eight sestertia) for one. See SENEC. epist. xcv.

15. *Truly equalling, &c.*] That is, the number of sestertia were exactly equal to the number of pounds which the fish weighed, so that it cost him a sestertium per pound.

16. *As they report, &c.*] So Crispinus's flatterers give out, who, to

But now concerning lighter deeds: and yet another,   10
If he had done the same, would have fallen under the judge
    of manners:
For what would be base in good men, in Titius, or Seius,
    became
Crispinus: what can you do, since dire, and fouler than every
Crime, his person is ?—He bought a mullet for six sestertia,
Truly equalling the sestertia to a like number of pounds, 15
As they report, who of great things speak greater.
I praise the device of the contriver, if, with so large a gift,
He had obtained the chief wax on the will of a childless old
    man.
There is further reason, if he had sent it to a great mistress,
Who is carried in a close litter with broad windows.   20
Expect no such thing: he bought it for himself: we see
    many things

excuse his extravagance, probably re-present the fish bigger than it was, for it is not easily credible that this sort of fish ever grows so large. Pliny says, that a mullet is not to be found that weighs more than two pounds. Hor. ubi supr. goes so far as three pounds—so that probably these embellishers of Crispinus made the fish to be twice as big as it really was.

17. *I praise the device, &c.*] If this money had been laid out in buying such a rarity, in order to present it to some childless old man, and, by this, Crispinus had succeeded so well as to have become his chief heir, I should commend such an artifice, and say that the contriver of it deserved some credit.

18. *Had obtained the chief wax, &c.*] It was customary for wills to consist of two parts: the first named the primi hæredes, or chief heirs, and was therefore called cera præcipua, from the wax which was upon it, on which was the first seal. The other contained the secundi hæredes, or lesser heirs: this was also sealed with wax —this was called cera secunda. Hor. Lib. ii. Sat. v. 53.

19. *There is further reason, &c.*] There might have been a reason for his extravagance, even beyond the former; that is, if he had purchased it to have presented it to some rich woman of quality, in order to have

ingratiated himself with her as a mistress, or to induce her to leave him her fortune, or perhaps both. Comp. sat. iii. 119, 20, and ib. 123.

20. *Carried in a close litter.*] Antrum properly signifies a den, cave, or the like—but here it seems to be descriptive of the lectica, or litter, in which persons of condition were carried close shut up.

—*Broad windows.*] Latis specularibus. Specularis means any thing whereby one may see the better, belonging to windows or spectacles. The specularis lapis was a stone, clear like glass, cut into small thin panes, and in old times used for glass. This was made use of in the construction of the litters, as glass is with us in our coaches and sedan chairs, to admit the light, and to keep out the weather. The larger these windows were, the more expensive they must be, and the more denote the quality of the owner.

21. *Expect no such thing, &c.*] If you expect to hear that something of the kind above mentioned was a motive for what he did, or that he had any thing in view, which could in the least excuse it, you will be mistaken; for the truth is, he bought it only for himself, without any other end or view than to gratify his own selfishness and gluttony.

Quæ miser et frugi non fecit Apicius : hoc tu
Succinctus patriâ quondam, Crispine, papyro.
Hoc pretium squamæ ? potuit fortasse minoris
Piscator, quam piscis, emi. Provincia tanti   25
Vendit agros : sed majores Apulia vendit.
   Quales tunc epulas ipsum glutisse putemus
Induperatorem, cum tot sestertia, partem
Exiguam, et modicæ sumptam de margine cœnæ
Purpureus magni ructârit scurra palati,   30
Jam princeps equitum, magnâ qui voce solebat
Vendere municipes pactâ mercede siluros?
   Incipe Calliope, licet hic considere : non est
Cantandum, res vera agitur : narrate puellæ.

22. *Apicius.*] A noted epicure and
glutton in the days of Nero. He
wrote a volume concerning the ways
and means to provoke appetite, spent
a large estate on his guts, and, growing poor and despised, hanged himself.
   The poet means, that even Apicius,
glutton as he was, was yet a mortified
and frugal man in comparison of
Crispinus.
   *Thou, Crispinus, hast done, what
Apicius never did.*
23. *Formerly girt, &c.*] q. d. Who
wast, when thou first camest to
Rome, a poor Egyptian, and hadst
not a rag about thee better than what
was made of the flags that grow
about the river Nile. Of the papyrus,
ropes, mats, and, among other things,
a sort of clothing was made.
   This flag, and the leaves of it, were
equally called papyrus. See sat. i. l.
24-5. where Crispinus is spoken of
much in the same terms.
24. *The price of a scale.*] Squamæ,
here, by synec. put for the fish itself : but, by this manner of expression, the poet shews his contempt of
Crispinus, and means to make his
extravagance as contemptible as he
can.
25. *A province, &c.*] In some of
the provinces which had become subject to Rome, one might purchase an
estate for what was laid out on this
mullet.
26. *But Apulia, &c.*] A part of
Italy near the Adriatic gulph, where
land, it seems, was very cheap, either

from the barrenness and craggy height
of the mountains, or from the un-
wholesomeness of the air, and the
wind atabulus :
      Montes Apulia notos
      Quos torret atabulus.
            Hor. lib. i. sat. v. l. 77, 8.
q. d. The price of this fish would purchase an estate in some of the provinces ; but in Apulia a very extensive one.
   For less some provinces whole acres
      sell :
   Nay, in Apulia, if you bargain
      well,
   A manor would cost less than such a
      meal.   DUKE.
27. *The emperor, &c.*] Domitian.
q. d. What must we suppose to be
done by him in order to procure
dainties ? how much expence must
lie be at to gratify his appetite, if
Crispinus can swallow what cost so
many sestertia in one dish ; and that
not a principal one ; not taken from
the middle, but merely standing as a
side-dish at the edge of the table ;
not a part of some great supper,
given on an extraordinary occasion,
but of a common ordinary meal.
30. *A purple buffoon.*] No longer
clad with the papyrus of Egypt, (see
note on l. 23.) but decked in sumptuous apparel, ornamented with purple. So sat. i. 25.
   Crispinus, Tyrias humero revocante
      lacernas.
Though advanced to great dignity, by
the favour of the emperor, yet letting
himself down to the low servility

Which the wretched and frugal Apicius did not: this thou
     [didst]
Crispinus, formerly girt with your own country flag.
Is this the price of a scale? perhaps, at less might
The fisherman, than the fish, be bought. At so much a
     province   25
Sells fields: but Apulia sells greater.
     What dainties then can we think the emperor himself
To have swallowed, when so many sestertia, a small
Part, and taken from the margin of a moderate supper,
A purple buffoon of the great palace belched?   30
Now chief of knights, who used, with a loud voice,
To sell his own country shads for hire.
     Begin Calliope, here you may dwell: you must not
Sing, a real matter is treated: relate it ye Pierian

and meanness of a court-jester or
buffoon.
     —*Belched.*] The indigestions and
crudities, which are generated in the
stomachs of those who feed on various
rich and luscious dainties, occasion
flatulencies, and nauseous eructations.
The poet here, to express the more
strongly his abhorrence of Crispinus's
extravagant gluttony, uses the word
ructarit—the effect for the cause. See
sat. iii. 221. note.
     31. *Chief of knights.*] i. e. Chief
of the equestrian order.
     Horace hath a thought like this,
concerning a low-born slave, who, like
Crispinus, had been advanced to
equestrian dignity.
          Sedilibusque in primis eques
          Othone contempto sedet.
                         Epod. iv. l. 15, 16.
See before, sat. iii. 147. and note.
     31-2. *Who used—to sell. &c.*] Who
used formerly, in his flag-jacket, (l.
23.) to cry fish about the streets.
     22. *Shads.*] What the siluri were I
cannot find certainly defined; but
most agree that they were a small
and cheap kind of fish, taken in great
numbers out of the river Nile; hence
the poet jeeringly styles them municipes, q. d. Crispinus's own countrymen. AINSW.
     —*For hire.*] Various are the read-
ings of this place; as fracta de merce
—pacta de merce—pharia de merce;
but I think, with Casaubon, that

pacta mercede gives the easiest and
best sense; it still exaggerates the
wretchedness and poverty of Crispinus
at his outset in life, as it denotes, that
he not only got his living by bawling
fish about the streets, but that these
fish were not his own, and that he
sold them for the owners, who bar-
gained with him to pay him so much
for his pains.—pacta mercede—lit. for
agreed wages or hire.
     33. *Calliope.*] The mother of Or-
pheus, and chief of the nine muses:
said to be the inventress of heroic verse.
     To heighten the ridicule, Juvenal
prefaces his narrative with a burlesque invocation of Calliope, and then
of the rest of the muses.
     —*Here you may dwell.*] A subject
of such importance requires all your
attention, and is not lightly to be
passed over, therefore, here you may
sit down with me.
     33-4. *Not sing.*] Not consider it as
a matter of mere invention, and to
be treated, as poetical fictions are,
with flights of fancy: my theme is
real fact, therefore, non est cantandum, it is not a subject for heroic
song; or, tibi understood, you are
not to sing—
          Begin Calliope, but not to sing;
          Plain honest truth we for our
               subject bring.   DUKE.
     34. *Relate.*] Narrate corresponds
with the non est cantandum; q. d.
deliver it in simple narrative.

Pierides: prosit mihi vos dixisse puellas.   35
'Cum jam semianimum laceraret Flavius orbem
Ultimus, et calvo serviret Roma Neroni,
Incidit Adriaci spatium admirabile rhombi,
Ante domum Veneris, quam Dorica sustinet Ancon,
Implevitque sinus : neque enim minor hæserat illis.   40
Quos operit glacies Mæotica, ruptaque tandem
Solibus effundit torpentis ad ostia Ponti,
Desidiâ tardos, et longo frigore pingues.
    Destinat hoc monstrum cymbæ linique magister
Pontifici summo : quis enim proponere talem,   45
Aut emere auderet ? cum plena et littora multo
Delatore forent : dispersi protinus algæ

34–5. *Fierian maids.*] The muses were called Pierides, from Pieria, a district of Thessaly, where was a mountain, on which Jupiter, in the form of a shepherd, was fabled to have begotten them on Mnemosyne. See Ov. Met. vi. 114.

35. *Let it avail me, &c.*] He banters the poets who gave the appellations of nymphæ and puellæ to the muses, as if complimenting them on their youth and chastity. It is easily seen that the whole of this invocation is burlesque.

36. *When now.*] The poet begins his narrative, which he introduces with great sublimity, in this and the following line ; thus finely continuing his irony ; and at the same time dating the fact in such terms, as reflect a keen and due severity on the character of Domitian.

—*The last Flavius.*] The Flavian family, as it was imperial, began in Vespasian, and ended in Domitian, whose monstrous cruelties are here alluded to, not only as affecting the city of Rome, but as felt to the utmost extent of the Roman empire, tearing, as it were, the world to pieces. Semianimum, half dead under oppression. Metaph.

37. *Was in bondage to bald Nero.*] Was in bondage and slavery to the tyrant Domitian. This emperor was bald ; at which he was so displeased, that he would not suffer baldness to be mentioned in his presence. He was called Nero, as all the bad emperors were, from his cruelty. Servire,

implies the service which is paid to a tyrant : parere, that obedience which is paid to a good prince.

38. *There fell, &c.*] Having related the time when, he now mentions the place where, this large turbot was caught. It was in the Adriatic sea, near the city of Ancon, which was built by a people originally Greeks, who also built there a temple of Venus. This city stood on the shore, at the end of a bay which was formed by two promontories, and made a curve like that of the elbow when the arm is bent ; hence it was called αγκων, the elbow. The poet, by being thus particular, as if he were relating an event, every circumstance of which was of the utmost importance, enhances the irony.

The Syracusans, who fled to this part of Italy from the tyranny of Dionysius, were originally from the Dorians ; a people of Achaia : hence Ancon is called Dorica : it was the metropolis of Picenum. Ancona is now a considerable city in Italy, and belongs to the papacy.

39. *Sustains.*] Sustinet does not barely mean, that this temple of Venus stood at Ancon, but that it was upheld and maintained, in all its worship, rites, and ceremonies, by the inhabitants.

40. *Into a net.*] Sinus, lit. means the bosom or bow of the net, which the turbot was so large as entirely to fill.

—*Stuck.*] Hæserat, had entangled itself, so as to stick fast.

Maids—let it avail me to have called ye maids— 35
   When now the last Flavius had torn the half-dead
World, and Rome was in bondage to bald Nero,
There fell a wondrous size of an Adriatic turbot,
Before the house of Venus which Doric Ancon sustains, 39
Into a net and filled it, for a less had not stuck than those,
Which the Mæotic ice covers, and at length, broken
By the sun, pours forth at the entrance of the dull Pontic,
Slow by idleness, and, by long cold, fat.
   The master of the boat and net destines this monster
For the chief pontiff—for who to offer such a one to
   sale, 45
Or to buy it, would dare? since the shores too with many
An informer might be full: the dispersed inquisitors of
   sea-weed

41. *The Mæotic ice.*] The Mæotis was a vast lake, which in the winter was frozen over, and which, when thawed in summer, discharged itself into the Euxine sea, by the Cimmerian Bosphorus.

Here vast quantities of fine fish were detained while the frosts lasted, and then came with the flowing waters into the mouth of the Pontus Euxinus. These fish, by lying in a torpid state during the winter, grew fat and bulky.

42. *The dull Pontic.*] So called from the slowness of its tide. This might, in part, be occasioned by the vast quantities of broken ice, which came down from the lake Mæotis, and retarded its course.

The Euxine, or Pontic sea, is sometimes called Pontus only. See AINSW. *Euxinus* and *Pontus.*

44. *Net.*] Linum, lit. signifies flax, and, by meton. thread, which is made of flax; but as nets are made of thread, it frequently, as here, signifies a net. Meton. See VIRG. Georg. ii. l. 142.

45. *For the chief pontiff.*] Domitian, whose title, as emperor, was Pontifex Summus, or Maximus. Some think that the poet alludes to the gluttony of the pontiffs in general, which was so great as to be proverbial. The words glutton and priest were almost synonymous; Cœnæ pontificum, or the feasts which they made

on public occasions, surpassed all others in luxury. Hence HOR. lib. ii. ode xiii. ad fin.

Pontificum potiore cœnis.
Juvenal, therefore, may be understood to have selected this title of the emperor, by way of equivocally calling him what he durst not plainly have expressed, the chief of gluttons. He was particularly the Pontifex Summus of the college at Alba. See note on l. 59. ad fin.

The poor fisherman, who had caught this monstrous fish, knew full well the gluttony, as well as the cruelty of Domitian: he therefore determines to make a present of it to the emperor, not daring to offer it to sale elsewhere, and knowing that, if he did, nobody would dare to buy it; for both the buyer and seller would be in the utmost danger of Domitian's resentment, at being disappointed of such a rarity.

46. *Since the shores, &c.*] The reign of Domitian was famous for the encouragement of informers, who sat themselves in all places to get intelligence. These particular people, who are mentioned here, were officially placed on the shore to watch the landing of goods, and to take care that the revenue was not defrauded. They appear to have been like that species of revenue officers amongst us, which are called tide-waiters.

47. *Inquisitors of sea-weed.*] Alga

Inquisitores agerent cum remige nudo
Non dubitaturi fugitivum dicere piscem,
Depastumque diu vivaria Cæsaris, inde   50
Elapsum, veterem ad dominum debere reverti.
Si quid Palphurio, si credimus Armillato,
Quicquid conspicuum, pulchrumque est æquore toto,
Res fisci est, ubicunque natat. Donabitur ergo,
Ne pereat. Jam lethifero cedente pruinis   55
Autumno, jam quartanam sperantibus ægris,
Stridebat deformis hyems, prædamque recentem
Servabat : tamen hic properat, velut urgeat Auster :
Utque lacus suberant, ubi, quanquam diruta, servat

signifies a sort of weed, which the tides cast up and leave on the shore. The poet's calling these people algæ inquisitores, denotes their founding accusations on the merest trifles, and thus oppressing the public. They dispersed themselves in such a manner as not to be avoided.

48. *Would immediately contend,* &c.] They would immediately take advantage of the poor fisherman's forlorn and defenceless condition, to begin a dispute with him about the fish ; and would even have the impudence to say, that, though the man might have caught the fish, yet he had no right to it—that it was astray, and ought to return to the right owner.

50. *Long had fed,* &c.] Vivarium, as has been before observed, denotes a place where wild beasts or fishes are kept, a park, a warren, a stew or fishpond.

The monstrous absurdity of what the poet supposes these fellows to advance, in order to prove that this fish was the emperor's property, (notwithstanding the poor fisherman had caught it in the Adriatic sea,) may be considered as one of those means of oppression, which were made use of to distress the people, and to wrest their property from them, under the most frivolous and groundless pretences, and at the same time under colour of legal claim.

52. *Palphurius—Armillatus.*] Both men of consular dignity ; lawyers, and spies, and informers, and so favourites with Domitian.

Here is another plea against the poor fisherman, even granting that

the former should fail in the proof; namely, that the emperor has, by his royal prerogative, and as part of the royal revenue, a right to all fish which are remarkable in size or value, wheresoever caught in any part of the sea ; and as this turbot came within that description, the emperor must have it, and this on the authority of those great lawyers above mentioned. By the law of England, whale and sturgeon are called royal fish, because they belong to the king, on account of their excellence, as part of his ordinary revenue, in consideration of his protecting the seas from pirates and robbers. See BLACKS. Com. 4to. p. 290.

54. *Therefore it shall be presented.*] The poor fisherman, aware of all this, rather than incur the danger of a prosecution at the suit of the emperor, in which he could have no chance but to lose his fine turbot, and to be ruined into the bargain, makes a virtue of necessity, and therefore wisely determines to carry it as a present to Domitian, who was at that time at Alba.

55. *Lest it should be lost.*] Lest it should be seized, and taken from him by the informers.

The boatman then shall a wise present make,

And give the fish, before the seizers take.   DUKE.

Or, It shall be presented, and that immediately, lest it should grow stale and stink.

—*Deadly autumn,* &c.] By this we learn, that the autumn, in that part of Italy, was very unwholesome. Hor. Lib. ii. Sat. vi. 19.

Would immediately contend with the naked boatman,
Not doubting to say that the fish was a fugitive,
And long had fed in Cæsar's ponds, thence had   50
Escaped, and ought to return to its old master.
If we at all believe Palphurius, or Armillatus,
Whatever is remarkable, and excellent in the whole sea,
Is a matter of revenue, wherever it swims.—Therefore it
     shall be presented   54
Lest it should be lost. Deadly autumn was now yielding to
Hoar-frosts, the unhealthy now expecting a quartan,
Deformed winter howled, and the recent prey
Preserved : yet he hastens as if the south wind urged.
And as soon as they had got to the lakes, where, tho' de-
     molished, Alba

and that, at the beginning of the winter, quartan agues were expected by
persons of a weakly and sickly habit.
Spero signifies to expect either good
or evil. This periphrasis describes
the season in which this matter happened, that it was in the beginning of
winter, the weather cold, the heats of
autumn succeded by the hoar-frosts,
so that the fish was in no danger of
being soon corrupted.

58. *Yet he hastens, &c.*] Notwithstanding the weather was so favourable for preserving the fish from
tainting, the poor fisherman made as
much haste to get to the emperor's
palace, as if it had been now sum-
mer-time.

59. *They.*] *i. e.* The fisherman, and
his companions the informers, they
would not leave him.

—*Got to the lakes.*] The Albanian
lakes : these are spoken of by Hor.
lib. iv. od. i. l. 19, 20.

     Albanos prope te lacus
  Ponet marmoream sub trabe citrea.
The city of Alba was built between
these lakes and the hills, which, for
this reason, were called Colles Albani ; hence these lakes were also
called Lacus Albani. Alba was about
fifteen miles from Rome.

—*Tho' demolished, &c.*] Tullus
Hostilius, king of Rome, took away
all the treasure and relics which the
Trojans had placed there in the temple of Vesta ; only, out of a superstitious fear, the fire was left ; but he
overthrew the city. See ANT. Un.

Hist. vol. xi. p. 310. All the temples
were spared. LIV. l. i.

The Albans, on their misfortunes,
neglecting their worship, were commanded, by various prodigies, to restore their ancient rites, the chief of
which was, to keep perpetually burning the vestal fire which was brought
there by Æneas, and his Trojans, as
a fatal pledge of the perpetuity of the
Roman empire.

Alba Longa was built by Ascanius
the son of Æneas, and called Alba,
from the white sow which was found
on the spot. See VIRG. Æn. iii. 390-
3. Æn. viii. 43-8.

Domitian was at this time at Alba,
where he had instituted a college of
priests, hence called Sacerdotes, or
Pontifices Albani. As he was their
founder and chief, it might be one
reason of his being called Pontifex
Summus, l. 45. when at that place.
The occasion of his being there at that
time, may be gathered from what
Pliny says in his epist. to Corn. Mu-
natianus.

" Domitian was desirous to punish
" Corn. Maximilla, a vestal, by bu-
" rying her alive, she having been
" detected in unchastity ; he went to
" Alba, in order to convoke his col-
" lege of priests, and there, in abuse
" of his power as chief, he con-
" demned her in her absence, and
" unheard." See before, l. 11. and
note.

Suetonius says, that Domitian went
every year to Alba, to celebrate the

Ignem Trojanum, et Vestam colit Alba minorem,   60
Obstitit intranti miratrix turba parumper :
Ut cessit, facili patuerunt cardine valvæ :
Exclusi spectant admissa opsonia patres.
Itur ad Atridem : tum Picens, accipe, dixit,
Priyatis majora focis ; genialis agatur   65
Iste dies ; propera stomachum laxare saginis,
Et tua servatum consume in sæcula rhombum :
Ipse capi voluit. Quid apertius ? et tamen illi
Surgebant cristæ : nihil est, quod credere de se
Non possit, cum laudatur Dîs æqua potestas.   70
Sed deerat pisci patinæ mensura : vocantur
Ergo in concilium proceres, quos oderat ille :

Quinquatria, a feast so called, because it lasted five days, and was held in honour of Minerva, for whose service he had also instituted the Albanian priests ; this might have occasioned his being at Alba at this time.

60. *The lesser Vesta.*] So styled, with respect to her temple at Alba, which was far inferior to that at Rome built by Numa.

61. *Wondering crowd.*] A vast number of people assembled to view this fine fish, insomuch that, for a little while, parumper, they obstructed the fisherman in his way to the palace.

62. *As it gave way.*] i. e. As the crowd, having satisfied their curiosity, retired, and gave way for him to pass forward.

—*The gates, &c.*] Valvæ, the large folding doors of the palace are thrown open, and afford a ready and welcome entrance to one who brought such a delicious and acceptable present.— Comp. Hon. lib. i. od. xxv. l. 5, 6.

63. *The excluded fathers.*] Patres —i. e. patres conscripti, the senators, whom Domitian had commanded to attend him at Alba, either out of state, or in order to form his privy-council on state affairs.

There is an antithesis here between the admissa opsonia and the exclusi patres, intimating, that the senators were shut out of the palace, when the doors were thrown open to the fisherman and his turbot : these venerable personages had only the privilege of looking at it as it was carried through the crowd.

Many copies read expectant.—*q. d.* The senators are to wait, while the business of the turbot is settled, before they can be admitted : lit. they await the admitted victuals. See expectant used in this sense. VIRG. Æn. iv. l. 134.

Casaubon reads spectant, which seems to give the most natural and easy sense.

—*Dainties.*] Opsonium-ii, signifies any victuals eaten with bread, especially fish. AINSW. Gr. οψον, proprie, piscis. Hed. So likewise in Johnvi.9. δυο οψαρια, two little fishes. Here Juvenal uses opsonia for the rhombus.

64. *Atrides.*] So the poet here humourously calls Domitian, in allusion to Agamemnon, the son of Atreus, whose pride prompted him to be styled the commander over all the Grecian generals. Thus Domitian affected the titles of Dux ducum, Princeps principum, and even Deus.

—*The Picenian.*] i. e. The fisherman, who was an inhabitant of Picenum.

—*Accept.*] Thus begins the fisherman's abject and fulsome address to the emperor, on presenting the turbot.

65. *What is too great.*] Lit. greater than private fires. Focus is properly a fire-hearth, by met. fire. Focis, here, means the fires by which victuals are dressed, kitchen fires ; and so, by met. kitchens, q. d. The turbot which he presented to the emperor was too great and valuable to be dressed in any private kitchen.

Preserves the Trojan fire, and worships the lesser Vesta, 60
A wondering crowd, for a while, opposed him as he entered :
As it gave way, the gates opened with an easy hinge :
The excluded fathers behold the admitted dainties.
He comes to Atrides : then the Picenian said " Accept
" What is too great for private kitchens : let this day be
  "passed 65
" As a festival ; hasten to release your stomach from its
  " crammings,
" And consume a turbot reserved for your age :
" Itself it would be taken."—What could be plainer? and yet
His crest arose : there is nothing which of itself it may not
Believe, when a power equal to the gods is praised. 70
But there was wanting a size of pot for the fish : therefore
The nobles are called into council, whom he hated :

66. *As a festival.*] The adj. genialis signifies cheerful, merry, festival ; so genialis dies, a day of festivity, a festival ; such as was observed on marriage or on birth-days : on these latter, they held a yearly feast in honour of their genius, or tutelar deity, which was supposed to attend their birth, and to live and die with them. See Hor. lib. ii. Ep. ii. 187. and Pers. sat. ii. l. 3. and note. Probably the poet here means much the same as Horace, lib. iii. ode xvii. by genium curabis, you shall indulge yourself, make merry.

—*Hasten to release, &c.*] The poet here lashes Domitian's gluttony, by making the fisherman advise him to unload, and set his stomach at liberty from the dainties which it contained, (which was usually done by vomits,) in order to whet it, and to make room for this turbot. Sagina lit. means any meat wherewith things are crammed or fatted, and is well applied here to express the emperor's stuffing and cramming himself, by his daily gluttony, like a beast or a fowl that is put up to be fattened.

67. *Reserved for your age.*] As if Providence had purposely formed and preserved this fish for the time of Domitian.

68. *Itself it would be taken.*] The very fish itself was ambitious to be caught for the entertainment and gratification of your Majesty.

—*What could be plainer ?*] What flattery could be more open, more palpable than this ?- says Juvenal.

69. *His crest arose.*] This flattery, which one would have thought too gross to be received, yet pleased Domitian, he grew proud of it—surgebant cristæ. Metaph. taken from the appearance of a cock when he is pleased, and struts and sets up his comb.

—*There is nothing, &c.*] i. e. When a prince can believe himself equal in power to the gods, (which was the case with Domitian,) no flattery can be too gross, fulsome, or palpable to be received ; he will believe every thing that can be said in his praise, and grow still the vainer for it.

Mr. Dryden, in his ode called Alexander's Feast, has finely imagined an instance of this, where Alexander is almost mad with pride, at hearing himself celebrated as the son of Jupiter by Olympia.

> With ravish'd ears
> The monarch hears ;
>   Assumes the god,
>   Affects to nod,
> And seems to shake the spheres.

71. *But—a size, &c.*] They had no pot capacious enough, in its dimensions, to contain this large turbot, so as to dress it whole. Patina is a pot of earth or metal, in which things were boiled, and brought to table in their broth. Ainsw.

72. *The nobles.*] Proceres—the senators—called patres, l. 63.

—*Are called into council.*] To deliberate on what was to be done in this momentous business.

N

In quorum facie miseræ, magnæque sedebat
Pallor amicitiæ.   Primus, clamanté Liburno,
Currite, jam sedit, raptâ properabat abollâ   75
Pegasus, attonitæ positus modo villicus urbi :
Anne aliud tunc Præfecti ? quorum optimus, atque
Interpres legum sanctissimus ; omnia quanquam
Temporibus diris tractanda putabat inermi
Justitiâ. Venit et Crispi jucunda senectus,   80
Cujus erant mores, qualis facundia, mite
Ingenium.   Maria, ac terras, populosque regenti
Quis comes utilior, si clade et peste sub illa
Sævitiam damnare, et honestum afferre liceret
Consilium ? sed quid violentius aure tyranni,   85
Cum quo de nimbis, aut æstibus, aut pluvioso
Vere locuturi fatum pendebat amici ?
Ille igitur nunquam direxit brachia contra

72. *Whom he hated.*] From a con-
sciousness of his being dreaded and
hated by them.
73. *The paleness.*] We have here
a striking representation of a tyrant;
who, conscious that he must be hated
by all about him, hates them, and
they, knowing his capricious cruelty,
never approach him without horror
and dread, lest they should say or do
something, however undesignedly,
which may cost them their lives.
Comp. l. 85–87.
74. *A Liburnian.*] Some have observed that the Romans made criers
of the Liburnians, a remarkable lusty
and stout race of men, (sat. iii. l. 228.)
because their voices were very loud
and strong. Others take Liburnus
here for the proper name of some particular man who had the office of
crier.
75. *Run, &c.*] " Make haste, lose
" no time ; the emperor has already
" taken his seat at the council-table—
" don't make him wait."
—*With a snatched-up gown.*]—
Abolla here signifies a senator's robe.
In sat. iii. 104. it signifies a philosopher's gown. On hearing the summons, he caught up his robe in a violent hurry, and huddled it on, and
away he went.
This Pegasus was an eminent
lawyer, who had been appointed præfect or governor of the city of Rome.

Juvenal calls him villicus, or bailiff,
as if Rome, by Domitian's tyranny,
had so far lost its liberty and privileges,
that it was now no better than an insignificant village, and its officers had
no more power or dignity than a
country bailiff ; a little paltry officer
over a small district.
The præfectus urbis (says Kennett, Ant. lib. iii. part ii. c. 13.)
was a sort of mayor of the city,
created by Augustus, by the advice
of his favourite Mæcenas, upon whom
at first he conferred the new honour.
He was to precede all other city magistrates; having power to receive ap-
peals from the inferior courts, and to
decide almost all causes within the limits of Rome, or one hundred miles
round. Before this, there was sometimes a præfectus urbis created, when
the kings, or the greater officers,
were absent from the city, to admi-
nister justice in their room.
But there was an end of all this,
their hands were now tied up, their
power and consequence were no more ;
Domitian had taken every thing into
his own hands, and no officer of the
city could act farther than the emperor deigned to permit, who kept the
whole city in the utmost terror and
astonishment at his cruelty and oppression.
77. *Of whom, &c.*] This Pegasus
was an excellent magistrate, the best

In the face of whom was sitting the paleness of a miserable,
And great friendship;—First, (a Liburnian crying out—
" Run—he is already seated,")—with a snatched-up gown,
　hastened 　　　　　　　　　　　　　　　　　　　75
Pegasus, lately appointed bailiff to the astonished city—
Were the Præfects then any thing else ?—of whom [he
　　- was] the best, and
Most upright interpreter of laws ; tho' all things,
In direful times, he thought were to be managed with un-
　armed
Justice. The pleasant old age of Crispus also came,　　80
Whose manners were, as his eloquence, a gentle
Disposition : to one governing seas, and lands, and people,
Who a more useful companion, if, under that slaughter and
　pestilence,
It were permitted to condemn cruelty, and to give honest
Counsel ? But what is more violent than the ear of a tyrant,
With whom the fate of a friend, who should speak of
　showers, 　　　　　　　　　　　　　　　　　　86
Or heats, or of a rainy spring, depended ?
He therefore never directed his arms against

---

of, any that had filled that office ;
most conscientious and faithful in his
administration of justice; never straining the laws to oppress the people,
but expounding them fairly and honestly.

79—80. *With unarmed justice.*]—
Such was the cruelty and tyranny of
Domitian, that even Pegasus, that
good and upright magistrate, was de-
terred from the exact and punctual
administration of justice, every thing
being now governed as the emperor
pleased ; so that the laws had not
their force ; nor dared the judges execute them, but according to the will
of the emperor ; justice was disarmed
of its powers.

80. *Crispus.*] Vibius Crispus, who,
when one asked him if any body was
with Cæsar ? answered, " Not even
" a fly." Domitian, at the beginning of his reign, used to amuse himself with catching flies, and sticking
them through with a sharp pointed instrument. A sure presage of his future cruelties.

81-2. *A gentle disposition.*] He
was as remarkable for sweetness of
temper, as for his eloquence, plea-

santry, and good nature. Com. Hor.
lib. ii. sat. i. l. 72. Mitis sapientia
Læli.

83. *Who a more useful companion.*]
The meaning is, who could have been
a more salutary friend and companion,
as well as counsellor, to the emperor,
if he had dared to have spoken his
mind, to have reprobated the cruelty
of the emperor's proceedings, and to
have given his advice to a man, who,
like sword and pestilence, destroyed
all that he took a dislike to.

85. *What is more violent, &c.*]
More rebellious against the dictates
of honest truth—more impatient of
advice—more apt to imbibe the most
fatal prejudices.

86. *Speak of showers, &c.*] Such
was the capriciousness and cruelty of
Domitian, that it was unsafe for his
friends to converse with him, even on
the most indifferent subjects, such as
the weather, and the like : the least
word misunderstood, or taken ill,
might cost a man his life, though to
that moment he had been regarded as
a friend.

88. *Never directed, &c.*] Never
attempted to swim against the stream,

Torrentem : nec civis erat, qui libera posset
Verba animi proferre, et vitam impendere vero.   90
Sic multas hyemes, atque octogesima vidit
Solstitia : his armis, illâ quoque tutus in aulâ.
Proximus ejusdem properabat Acilius ævi
Cum juvene indigno, quem mors tam sæva maneret,
Et domini gladiis jam festinata : sed olim   95
Prodigio par est in nobilitate senectus :
Unde fit, ut malim fraterculus esse gigantum.
Profuit ergo nihil misero, quod cominus ursos
Figebat Numidas, Albanâ nudus arenâ
Venator : quis enim jam non intelligat artes   100
Patricias ? quis priscum illud miretur acumen,
Brute, tuum ? facile est barbato imponere regi ?
Nec melior vultu, quamvis ignobilis ibat
Rubrius, offensæ veteris reus, atque tacendæ ;

as we say. He knew the emperor too well ever to venture an opposition to his will and pleasure.

90. *Spend his life, &c.*] Crispus was not one of those citizens who dared to say what he thought ; or to hazard his life in the cause of truth, by speaking his mind.

91-2. *Eightieth solstices.*] Eighty solstices of winter and summer ; i. e. he was now eighty years of age.

92. *With these arms, &c.*] Thus armed with prudence and caution, he had lived to a good old age, even in the court of Domitian, where the least offence or prejudice would long since have taken him off.

93. *Acilius.*] Glabrio, a senator of singular prudence and fidelity.

94. *With a youth, &c.*] Domitius, the son of Acilius, came with his father ; but both of them were soon after charged with designs against the emperor, and were condemned to death. The father's sentence was changed into banishment, the more to grieve him with the remembrance of his son's death.

—*Unworthy.*] Not deserving that so cruel a death should await him.

This unhappy young man, to save his life, affected madness, and fought naked with wild beasts in the amphitheatre at Alba, where Domitian every year celebrated games in honour of Minerva : but he was not to be deceiv-

ed, and he put Domitius to death in a cruel manner. See L. 100, 101.

95. *The swords.*] Gladiis, in the plur. either by syn. for gladio, sing. or perhaps to signify the various methods of torture and death used by this emperor.

—*Of the tyrant.*] Domini, lit. of the lord, i. e. the emperor Domitian, who thus lorded it over the lives of his subjects.

96. *Old age in nobility.*] q. d. From the days of Nero, till this hour, it has been the practice to cut off the nobility, when the emperor's jealousy, fear, or hatred, inclined him so to do ; insomuch that to see a nobleman live to old age, is something like a prodigy ; and indeed this has long been the case.

97. *Of the giants.*] These fabulous beings were supposed to be the sons of Titan and Tellus. These sons of Earth were of a gigantic size, and said to rebel and fight against Jupiter. See Ov. Met. lib. i, fab. vi.

q. d. Since to be born noble is so very dangerous, I had much rather, like these Terræ filii, claim no higher kindred than my parent Earth, and, though not in size, yet as to origin, be a brother of theirs, than be descended from the highest families among our nobility.

100. *Who cannot now, &c.*] Who is ignorant of the arts of the nobility,

Prit. with great.

The torrent : nor was he a citizen, who could utter   89
The free words of his mind, and spend his life for the truth.
Thus he saw many winters, and the eightieth
Solstices : with these arms, safe also in that court.
Next, of the same age, hurried Acilius
With a youth unworthy, whom so cruel a death should await,
And now hastened by the swords of the tyrant : but long
    since.   95.
Old age in nobility is equal to a prodigy :
Hence it is, that I had rather be a little brother of the
    giants.
Therefore it nothing availed the wretch that he pierced
Numidian bears in close fight, a naked hunter in the Alban
Theatre : for who cannot now understand the arts   100
Of the nobles ? who can wonder at that old subtlety of thine,
O Brutus ? It is easy to impose on a bearded king.
Nor better in countenance, tho' ignoble, went
Rubrius, guilty of an old crime, and ever to be kept in
    silence :

either to win the emperor's favour, or to avoid his dislike, or to escape the effects of his displeasure ? these are known to every body, therefore it can hardly be supposed that they are unknown to the emperor ; hence poor Domitius miscarried in his stratagem. See note on l. 94.

Domitian could perceive, yet could swallow down the grossest flattery, and thus far deceived himself, (comp. l. 69.) yet no shift, or trick, to avoid his destructive purposes could ever deceive him.

101. *Who can wonder, &c.*] Lucius Junius Brutus saved his life by affecting to play the fool in the court of Tarquin the Proud, when many of the nobility were destroyed, and, among the rest, the brother of Brutus. Hence he took the surname of Brutus, which signifies senseless, void of reason.

q. d. This old piece of policy would not be surprising now ; it would be looked upon but as a shallow device : therefore, however it might succeed in those days of ancient simplicity, we find it would not do now, as the wretched Domitius sadly experienced.

102. *On a bearded king.*] Alluding

to the simplicity of ancient times, when Rome was governed by kings, who, as well as their people, wore their beards ; for shaving and cutting the beard were not in fashion till later times. Barbatus was a sort of proverbial term for simple, old-fashioned. See AINSW.

It is remarkable that, long before the days of Brutus, we have an instance of a like device, by which David saved himself at the court of Achish, king of Gath. 1 Sam. xxi. 10–15.

103. *Nor better in countenance.*] He looked as dismal as the rest. See l. 73.

—*Tho' ignoble.*] Though he was of plebian extraction, and therefore could not be set up as a mark for Domitian's envy and suspicions, as the nobles were, yet he well knew that no rank or degree was safe ; as none were above, so none were below his displeasure and resentment.

104. *Guilty, &c.*] What this offence was is not said particularly ; however, its not being to be named, must make us suppose it something very horrible ; or that it was some offence against the emperor, which was kept secret,

. Montani quoque venter adest, abdomine tardus :   105
Et matutino sudans Crispinus amomo ; \
Quantum vix redolent duo funera : sævior illo
Pompeius tenui jugulos aperire susurro :
Et, qui vulturibus servabat viscera Dacis,
Fuscus, marmoreâ meditatus prælia villâ :   110
Et cum mortifero prudens Veiento Catullo,
Qui nunquam visæ flagrabat amore puellæ,
Grande, et conspicuum nostro quoque tempore monstrum !
Cæcus adulator, dirusque a ponte satelles.
Dignus Aricinos qui mendicaret ad axes,   115
Blandaque devexæ jactaret basia rhedæ.
Nemo magis rhombum stupuit : nam plurima dixit
In lævum conversus : at illi dextra jacebat
Bellua : sic pugnas Cilicis laudabat, et ictus,

Some commentators have supposed it to have been debauching Julia, Domitian's wife.

105. *The belly, &c.*] As if his belly were the most important thing belonging to him, it, rather than himself, is said to be present. This Montanus was some corpulent glutton, fat and unwieldy.

106. *Crispinus, &c.*] Here we find Crispinus brought forward again, vocatus ad partes. See l. 1 and 2.

—*With morning perfume.*] The amomum was a shrub which the Easterns used in embalming. Of this a fine perfumed ointment was made, with which Crispinus is described as anointing himself early in a morning, and in such profusion, as that he seemed to sweat it out of his pores.

Some think that the word matutino here alludes to that part of the world from whence the amomum came, *i. e.* the East, where the sun first arises : but I find no example of such a use of the word.

107. *Two funerals, &c.*] Crispinus had as much perfume about him as would have served to anoint two corpses for burial. It was a custom among the ancients to anoint the bodies of persons who died with sweet ointments See Matt. xxvi. 12. This custom, among others, was derived from the Easterns to the Romans.

108. *Than him more cruel, &c*] Pompeius was another of this assem-

bly, more cruel than Crispinus, in getting people put to death, by the secret accusations which he whispered against them into the emperor's ear.

109. *Fuscus, who was preserving, &c*]. Cornelius Fuscus was sent by Domitian general against the Dacians, where his army and himself were lost, and became food for the birds of prey.

110. *Meditated wars, &c.*] An irony, alluding to his being sent to command, without having any other ideas of war, than he conceived amid the sloth and luxury of his sumptuous villa.

111. *Prudent Veiento.*] See sat. iii. 173. The poet gives Veiento the epithet of prudent, from his knowing how to conduct himself wisely, with regard to the emperor, so as not to risk his displeasure, and from his knowing when, and how, to flatter to the best advantage. See l. 121.

—*Deadly Catullus.*]. So called from his causing the death of many by secret accusations. He was raised by Domitian from begging at the foot of the Aricine hill, in the Via Appia, to be a minister of state.

112. *Who burn'd, &c*] Catullus was blind, but his lust was so great, that he could not hear a woman mentioned without raging with desire. Or perhaps this alludes to some particular mistress which he kept, and was very fond of.

The belly of Montanus too is present, slow from his
    paunch: 105
And Crispinus sweating with morning perfume:
Two funerals scarcely smell so much. Pompeius too,
Than him more cruel to cut throats with a gentle whisper.
And Fuscus, who was preserving his bowels for the
    Dacian
Vultures, having meditated wars in his marble villa.   110
And prudent Veiento, with deadly Catullus,
Who burn'd with the love of a girl never seen ;
A great, and also, in our times, a conspicuous monster !
A blind flatterer, a dire attendant from the bridge,
Worthy that he should beg at the Aricinian axles,   115
And throw kind kisses to the descending carriage.
Nobody more wonder'd at the turbot : for he said many
    things
Turned to the left, but on his right hand lay
The fish : thus he praised the battles and strokes of the
    Cilician,

113. *In our times, &c.*] He was so wicked, as, even in the most degenerate times, to appear a monster of iniquity.

114. *A blind flatterer.*] As he could admire a woman without seeing her, so he could flatter men whom he never saw ; rather than fail, he would flatter at a venture.

—*A dire attendant, &c.*] There was a bridge in the Appian way, which was a noted stand for beggars. From being a beggar at this bridge, he was taken to be an attendant on the emperor ; and a most direful one he was, for he ruined and destroyed many by secret accusations.

115. *Worthy that he should beg.*] This he might be allowed to deserve, as the only thing he was fit for. See note 111.

—*Aricinian axles.*] Axes—by syn. for currus or rhedas—i. e. the carriages which passed along towards or from Aricia, a town in the Appian way, about ten miles from Rome, a very public road, and much frequented ; so very opportune for beggars. See Hor. lib. i. sat. v. l. 1. Hor. la Ricca.

116. *Throw kind kisses.*] Kissing his hand, and throwing it from his mouth towards the passengers in the carriages, as if he threw them kisses, by way of soothing them into stopping, and giving him alms.

—*The descending carriage:*] Aricia was built on the top of an high hill, which the carriages descended in their way to Rome ; this seems to be the meaning of devexæ. See AINSW. Devexus-a-um. From de and veho, q. d. Deorsum vehitur.

117. *Nobody more wonder'd.*]— That is, nobody pretended more to do so, out of flattery to Domitian ; for as for the fish, which Juvenal here calls Bellua, (speaking of it as of a great beast,) he could not see it, but turned the wrong way from it, and was very loud in its praises : just as he used to flatter Domitian, by praising the fencers at the games he gave, and the machinery at the theatre, when it was not possible for him to see what was going forward. Juvenal might well call him, l. 114. cæcus adulator.

119. *The Cilician.*] Some famous gladiator, or fencer, from Cilicia, who probably, was a favourite of Domitian.

Et pegma, et pueros inde ad velaria raptos.   120
Non cedit Veiento, sed ut fanaticus œstro
Percussus, Bellona, tuo divinat; et ingens
Omen habes, inquit, magni clarique triumphi :
Regem aliquem capies, aut de temone Britanno
Excidet Arviragus : peregrina est bellua, cernis   125
Erectas in terga sudes ? hoc defuit unum
Fabricio, patriam ut rhombi memoraret, et annos.
Quidnam igitur censes ? conciditur ? absit ab illo
Dedecus hoc, Montanus ait ; testa alta paretur,
Quæ tenui muro spatiosum colligat orbem.   130
Debetur magnus patinæ subitusque Prometheus :
Argillam, atque rotam citius properate : sed ex hoc
Tempore jam, Cæsar, figuli tua castra sequantur.
Vicit digna viro sententia : noverat ille

120. *The machine.*] Pegma, (from Gr. πηγνυμι, figo) a sort of wooden machine used in scenical representations, which was so contrived, as to raise itself to a great height : boys were placed upon it, and on a sudden carried up to the top of the theatre.

—*The coverings.*] Velaria—were sail-cloths, extended over the top of the theatre, to keep out the weather. AINSW.

121. *Veiento.*] We read of him, sat. iii. l. 173. as observing great silence towards those who were his inferiors ; but here we find him very lavish of his tongue when he is flattering the emperor. See l. 111.

—*Does not yield.*] Is not behindhand to the others in flattery, not even to blind Catullus who spoke last.

122. *O Bellona.*] The supposed sister of Mars ; she was fabled to preside over war : VIRG. Æn. v. iii. l. 703. describes her with a bloody scourge. Her priests, in the celebration of her feasts, used to cut themselves, and dance about as if they were mad, pretending also to divine or prophesy future events.

Œstrus signifies a sort of fly, which we call a gad-fly ; in the summertime it bites or stings cattle, so as to make them run about as if they were mad. See VIRG. G. iii. l. 146—53. By meton. inspired fury of any kind. Hence our poet humourously calls the

spirit which inspired the priests of Bellona by this name.

—*Divines.*] In flattery to Domitian, he treats the event of the turbot as something ominous, as if the taking it predicted some signal and glorious victory, the taking some monarch prisoner—perhaps Arviragus, then king of the Britons, with whom Domitian was at war, might be prefigured, as falling wounded from his chariot into the hands of the emperor.

125. *Is foreign.*] Therefore denotes some foreign conquest.

126. *Spears, &c.*] Sudes properly signifies a stake, a pile driven into the ground in fortifications ; also a spear barbed with iron. Hence καταχριςκως, the fin of a fish. AINSW.

q. d. Do you perceive his sharp fins rising on his back ; they look like so many spears, and portend and signify the spears which you shall stick in the backs of vanquished foes.

127. *Fabricius.*] i. e. Fabricius Veiento. He was so diffuse in his harangue, that, in short, there wanted nothing but his telling where it was bred, and how old it was, to complete and establish his prophetic history of the fish.

128. *What thinkest thou then, &c.*] The words of Domitian, who puts the original question for which he assembled these senators, L. 71. *viz.* as no pot could be got large enough to dress the turbot in, that they should ad-

And the machine, and the boys snatched up to the co-
   verings.   120
Veiento does not yield: but as a fanatic stung with thy
   gad-fly,
O Bellona, divines, and says, " A great omen
 " You have, of a great and illustrious triumph ;
 " You will take some king, or from a British chariot
 " Arviragus will fall ; the fish is foreign ; do you perceive
 " The spears erect on his back ?" This one thing was
   wanting   126
To Fabricius, that he should tell the country of the turbot,
   and its age.
 " What thinkest thou then ?—Must it be cut ?" " Far
   " from it be
 " This disgrace," says Montanus : " let a deep pot be
   " prepared,
 " Which, with its thin wall, may collect the spacious
   " orb.   130
 " A great and sudden Prometheus is due to the dish :
 " Hasten quickly the clay, and the wheel : but now, from
   " this
 " Time, Cæsar, let potters follow your camps."
The opinion, worthy the man, prevailed : he had known

vise what was to be done ; this they
had said nothing about : therefore
Domitian asks, if it should be cut in
pieces.

129. *Montanus.*] The glutton—
See l. 105. He concludes the debate,
with expressing a dislike of disfigur-
ing this noble fish, by dividing it,
and, at the same time, by flattering
the emperor, and raising his vanity.

—*Let a deep pot.*] Testa signifies a
pot, or pan, made of clay. He advises that such a one be immediately
made, deep and wide enough to hold
the fish within its thin circumference,
(tenui muro :) by this means the fish
will be preserved entire, as in such
a pot it might be dressed whole.

131. *Prometheus, &c.*] The poets
feigned him to have formed men of
clay, and to have put life into them
by fire stolen from heaven. Juvenal
humorously represents Montanus as
calling for Prometheus himself, as it
were, instantly to fashion a pot on so
great an occasion, when so noble a

fish was to be dressed, and that for so
great a prince.

132. *Hasten.*] That the fish may
not be spoiled before it can be dressed.

—*The clay and the wheel.*] Clay is
the material, and a wheel, which is
solid, and turns horizontally, the engine on which the potter makes his
ware. This was very ancient. Jer.
xviii. 3.

133. *Let potters follow, &c.*] This
is a most ludicrous idea, and seems
to carry with it a very sharp irony on
Domitian, for having called his council together on such a subject as this ;
but, however, it might be meant, the
known gluttony of Montanus, which
is described, l. 134-41. made it pass
for serious advice, and as such Domitian understood it, as the next
words may inform us.

134. *The opinion, &c.*] What Montanus had said about dressing the fish
whole, was thoroughly worthy his
character ; just what might have been
expected from him, and as such prevailed.

o

Luxuriam imperii veterem, noctesque Neronis   135
Jam Medias, aliamque famem, cum pulmo Falerno
Arderet : nulli major fuit usus edendi
Tempestate meâ. Circæis nata forent, an
Lucrinum ad saxum; Rutupinove edita fundo
Ostrea, callebat primo deprendere morsu ;   140
Et semel aspecti littus dicebat echini.
  Surgitur, et misso proceres exire jubentur
Concilio, quos Albanam dux magnus in arcem
Traxerat attonitos, et fastinare coactos,
Tanquam de Cattis aliquid, torvisque Sicambris   145
Dicturus ; tanquam diversis partibus orbis
Anxia præcipiti venisset epistola pennâ.
  Atque utinam his potius nugis tota illa dedisset
Tempora sævitiæ, claras quibus abstulit urbi
Illustresque animas impune, et vindice nullo.   150
Sed periit, postquam cerdonibus esse timendus
Cœperat : hoc nocuit Lamiarum cæde madenti.

---

134. *He had known, &c.*] He was an
old court glutton, and was well acquainted with the luxury of former
emperors, here meant by luxuriam
imperii. No man understood eating,
both in theory and practice, better
than he did, that has lived in my
time, says Juvenal.

135. *Nero.*] As Suetonius observes, used to protract his feasts from
mid-day to mid-night.

136. *Another hunger, &c.*] i. e.
What could raise a new and fresh appetite, after a drunken debauch.

138. *Circæi.*] -orum. A town of
Campania, in Italy, at the foot of
mount Circello on the sea coast.

139. *The Lucrine rock.*] The Lucrine rocks were in the bay of Lucrinum, in Campania. All these places
were famous for different sorts of
oysters. Hor. Epod. ii. 49. & Sat. ii.
4, 43.

—*Rutupian bottom.*] Rutupæ-arum,
Richburrow in Kent——Rutupina
littora, the Foreland of Kent. The
luxury of the Romans must be very
great, to send for oysters at such a
distance, when so many places on the
shores of Italy afforded them.

141. *Sea-urchin.*] Echinus, a sort
of crab with prickles on its shell,

reckoned a great dainty. *q. d.* So
skilled in eating was Montanus, that
at the first bite of an oyster, or at the
first sight of a crab, he could tell
where they were taken.

142. *They rise.*] Surgitur, imp. the
council broke up. See l. 64. itur.

143. *The great general.*] Domitian,
who gave the word of command for
them to depart, as before to assemble.

—*Into the Alban tower.*] To the
palace at Alba, where the emperor
now was. The word traxerat is very
expressive, as if they had been dragged
thither sorely against their wills.

144. *Astonished—compelled, &c.*]—
Amazed at the sudden summons, but
dared not to delay a moment's obedience to it. Comp. l. 75.

145. *Catti.*] A people of Germany,
now subject to the Landgrave of
Hesse—Sicambri, inhabitants of Gu-
elderland. Both these people were
formidable enemies.

147. *An alarming epistle, &c.*]—
Some sorrowful news had been dis-
patched post-haste from various parts
of the empire.

Little could the senators imagine,
that all was to end in a consultation
upon a turbot.

The satire here is very fine, and re-

The old luxury of the empire, and the nights of Nero 135
Now half spent, and another hunger, when the lungs with
    Falernan
Burned : none had a greater experience in eating
In my time. Whether oysters were bred at Circæi, or
At the Lucrine rock, or sent forth from the Rutupian
    bottom,
He knew well to discover at the first bite ; 140
And told the shore of a sea-urchin once looked at.
    They rise—and the senators are commanded to depart
       from the dismissed
Council, whom the great general into the Alban tower
Had drawn astonished, and compelled to hasten, 144
As if something concerning the Catti and the fierce Si-
    cambri
He was about to say ; as if from different parts of the
    world
An alarming epistle had come with hasty wing.
    And I wish that rather to these trifles he had given all
    those
Times of cruelty, in which he took from the city renowned
And illustrious lives with impunity, and with no avenger.
But he perished, after that to be fear'd by coblers 151
He had begun ; this hurt him reeking with slaughter of the
    Lamiæ.

presents Domitian as anxious about a matter of gluttony, as he could have been in affairs of the utmost importance to the Roman empire.

148. *And I wish, &c.*] i. e. It were to be wished that he had spent that time in such trifles as this, which he passed in acts of cruelty and murder, which he practised with impunity, on numbers of the greatest and best men in Rome, nobody daring to avenge their sufferings.

151. *But he perished, &c.*] Cerdo signifies any low mechanics, such as coblers, and the like. Cerdonibus stands here for the rabble in general.

While Domitian only cut off, now and then, some of the nobles, the people were quiet, however amazed they might be, (comp. l. 76.) but when he extended his cruelties to the plebeians, means were devised to cut him off, which was done by a conspi-

racy formed against him. See Ant. Un. Hist. vol. xv. p. 87.

152. *The Lamiæ.*] The Lamian family was most noble. See Hor. lib. iii. ode xvii. Of this was Ælius Lama, whose wife, Domitia Longina, Domitian took away, and afterwards put the husband to death.

The Lamiæ here may stand for the nobles in general, (as before the cerdones for the rabble in general,) who had perished under the cruelty of Domitian, and with whose blood he might be said to be reeking, from the quantity of it which he had shed during his reign.

He died ninety-six years after Christ, aged forty-four years, ten months, and twenty-six days. He reigned fifteen years and five days, and was succeeded by Nerva ; a man very unlike him, being a good man, a good statesman, and a good soldier.

Satira Septima.

This Satire is addressed to Telesinus, a poet. Juvenal laments the neglect of encouraging learning. That Cæsar only is the patron of the fine arts. As for the rest of the great and noble Romans, they gave no heed to

ET spes, et ratio studiorum in Cæsare tantum :
Solus enim tristes hâc tempestate camœnas
Respexit; cum jam celebres, notique poëtæ
Balneolum Gabiis, Romæ conducere furnos
Tentarent: nec fœdum alii, nec turpe putarent   5
Præcones fieri; cum desertis Aganippes
Vallibus, esuriens migraret in atria Clio.
Nam si Pieriâ quadrans tibi nullus in umbrâ
Ostendatur, ames nomen, victumque Machæræ;
Et vendas potius, commissa quod auctio vendit   10

Line 1. *The hope and reason, &c.*] i. e. The single expectation of learned men, that they shall have a reward for their labours, and the only reason, therefore, for their employing themselves in liberal studies, are reposed in Cæsar only, Domitian seems to be meant : for though he was a monster of wickedness, yet Quintilian, Martial, and other learned men, tasted of his bounty. Quintilian says of him, " Quo nec præsentius aliquid " nec studiis magis propitium numen " est." See l. 20—1.

2. *The mournful muses.*] Who may be supposed to lament the sad condition of their deserted and distressed votaries.

4. *Bath at Gabii.*] To get a livelihood by. Gabii was a little city near Rome. Balneolum, a small bagnio.

—*Ovens.*] Public bakehouses, where people paid so much for baking their bread.

6. *Criers.*] Præcones—whose office at Rome was to proclaim public meetings, public sales, and the like—a very mean employment; but the poor starving poets disregarded this circumstance—" any thing rather " than starve"—and indeed, however meanly this occupation might be looked upon, it was very profitable. See sat. iii. l. 146. note.

—*Aganippe.*] A spring in the solitary part of Bœotia, consecrated to the nine Muses.

7. *Hungry Clio.*] One of the nine Muses, the patroness of heroic poetry: here, by meton. put for the starving poet, who is forced, by his poverty, to leave the regions of poetry, and would fain beg at great men's doors. Atrium signifies the court, or court-yard, before great men's houses, where these poor poets are supposed to stand, like other beggars, to ask alms.

Seventh Satire.

ARGUMENT.

the protection of poets, historians, rhetoricians, gram-
marians, &c. These last were not only ill paid, but
even forced to go to law, for the poor pittance which they
had earned, by the fatigue and labour of teaching school.

BOTH the hope, and reason of studies, is in Cæsar only:
For he only, at this time, hath regarded the mournful
   Muses,
When now our famous and noted poets would try
To hire a small bath at Gabii, or ovens at Rome :
Nor would others think it mean, nor base,   5
To become criers ; when, the vallies of Aganippe
Being deserted, hungry Clio would migrate to court-yards.
For if not a farthing is shewn to you in the Pierian shade,
You may love the name, and livelihood of Machæra ;
And rather sell what the intrusted auction sells   10

8. *In the Pierian shade.*] See sat. iv. 1. 34. note. *q. d.* If by passing your time, as it were, in the abodes of the Muses, no reward or recompence is likely to be obtained for all your poetical labours. Some read arca—but Pieria umbra seems best to carry on the humour of the metonymy in this and the preceding line.

9. *Love the name, &c.*] Machæra seems to denote the name of some famous crier of the time, whose business it was to notify sales by auction, and, at the time of sale, to set a price on the goods, on which the bidders were to increase ; hence such a sale was called auctio. See AINSW. *Præco,* No. 1.

q. d. If you find yourself penny-less, and so likely to continue by the exercise of poetry, then, instead of thinking it below you to be called a crier, you may cordially embrace it,

and be glad to get a livelihood by auctions, as Machæra does.

10. *Intrusted.*] So Holyday. Commissus signifies any thing committed to one's charge, or in trust.

Goods committed to sale by public auction are intrusted to the auctioneer in a twofold respect—first, that he sell them at the best price ; and, secondly, that he faithfully account with the owner for the produce of the sales.

Commissa may also allude to the commission, or license, of the magistrate, by which public sales in the forum were appointed.

Some understand commissa auctio in a metaphorical sense, alluding to the contention among the bidders, who, like gladiators matched in fight, (see sat. i. 149. note.) oppose and engage against each other in their several biddings.

Stantibus, œnophorum, tripodes, armaria, cistas,
Alcithoen Pacci, Thebas et Terea Fausti.
Hoc satius, quam si dicas sub judice, Vidi,
Quod non vidisti: faciant equites Asiani,
Quanquam et Cappadoces faciant, equitesque Bithyni,   15
Altera quos nudo traducit Gallia talo.
Nemo tamen studiis indignum ferre laborem
Cogetur posthac, nectit quicunque canoris
Eloquium vocale modis, laurumque momordit.
Hoc agite, ô Juvenes: circumspicit, et stimulat vos,   20
Materiamque sibi ducis indulgentia quærit.
Si qua aliunde putas rerum expectanda tuarum
Præsidia, atque ideo croceæ membrana tabellæ
Impletur; lignorum aliquid posce ocyus, et quæ
Componis, dona Veneris, Telesine, marito: 25
Aut claude, et positos tineâ pertunde libellos.

11. *To the standers by.*] i. e. The people who attend the auction as buyers.

12. *The Alcithoe—the Thebes, &c.*] Some editions read Alcyonem Bacchi, &c. These were tragedies written by wretched poets, which Juvenal supposes to be sold, with other lumber, at an auction.

13. *Than if you said, &c.*] This, mean as it may appear, is still getting your bread honestly, and far better than hiring yourself out as a false witness, and forswearing yourself for a bribe, in open court.

14. *The Asiatic knights.*] This satirizes those of the Roman nobility, who had favoured some of their Asiatic slaves so much, as to enrich them sufficiently to be admitted into the equestrian order. These people were, notwithstanding, false, and not to be trusted.

Minoris Asiæ populis nullam fidem esse adhibendam.
                              Cic. pro Flacco.

15. *The Cappadocians.*] Their country bordered on Armenia. They were, like the Cretans, (Tit. i. 12.) liars and dishonest to a proverb; yet many of these found means to make their fortunes at Rome.

—*The knights of Bithynia.*] Bithynia was another eastern province, a country of Asia Minor, from whence many such people, as are above described, came, and were in high favour, and shared in titles and honours.

16. *The other Gaul.*] Gallo Græcia, or Galatia, another country of Asia Minor: from hence came slaves, who, like others, were exposed to sale with naked feet. Or it may rather signify, that these wretches (however afterwards highly honoured) were so poor, when they first came to Rome, that they had not so much as a shoe to their feet.

The poet means, that getting honest bread, in however mean a way, was to be preferred to obtaining the greatest affluence, as these fellows did, by knavery.

—*Brings over.*] Traducit signifies to bring, or convey, from one place to another. It is used to denote transplanting trees, or plants, in gardens, &c. and is a very significant word here, to denote the transplanting, as it were, of these vile people from the east to Rome.

18. *That joins, &c.*] The perfection of heroic poetry, which seems here intended, is the uniting grand and lofty expression, eloquium vocale, with tuneful measures, modis canoris.

Vocalis signifies something loud, making a noise—therefore, when applied to poetry, lofty—high-sounding. q. d. No writer, hereafter, who ex-

To the standers by, a pot, tripods, book-cases, chests,
The Alcithoë of Paccius, the Thebes and Tereus of
    Faustus.
This is better than if you said before a judge, " I have
    " seen,"
What you have not seen : tho' the Asiatic knights
And the Cappadocians may do this, and the knights of
  - Bithynia,   15
Whom the other Gaul brings over barefoot.
But nobody to undergo a toil unworthy his studies
Hereafter shall be compelled, whoe'er he be that joins, to
    tuneful
Measures, melodious eloquence, and hath bitten the laurel.
Mind this, young men, the indulgence of the emperor 20
Has its eye upon, and encourages you, and seeks matter
    for itself.
If you think protectors of your affairs are to be expected
From elsewhere, and therefore the parchment of your
    saffron-colour'd tablet
Is filled, get some wood quickly, and what   24
You compose, Telesinus, give to the husband of Venus :
Or shut up, and bore thro' with the moth your books laid
    by,

cels in uniting loftiness of style with harmony of verse, shall be driven, through want, into employments which are below the dignity of his pursuits as a poet. Comp. l. 3–6.

19. *Bitten the laurel.*] Laurum momordit. It was a notion, that, when young poets were initiated into the service of the Muses, it was a great help to their genius to chew a piece of laurel, in honour of Apollo. Some think that the expression is figurative, and means those who have tasted of glory and honour by their compositions ; but the first sense seems to agree best with what follows.

20. *Mind this.*] Hoc agite—lit. do this—i. e. diligently apply yourselves to poetry.

—*Of the emperor.*] Ducis is here applied to the emperor, as the great patron and chief over the liberal arts.

21. *Seeks matter for itself.*] Carefully endeavours to find out its own gratification by rewarding merit.

23. *Therefore the parchment, &c.*]

They wrote on parchment, which sometimes was dyed of a saffron-colour ; sometimes it was white, and wrapped up in coloured parchment. The tabellæ were the books themselves —i. e. the pages on which their manuscripts were written.

If, says the poet, you take the pains to write volumes full, in hopes of finding any other than Cæsar to reward you, you had better prevent your disappointment, by burning them as fast as you can. Lignorum aliquid posce ocyus—lose no time in procuring wood for the purpose.

25. *Telesinus.*] The poet to whom this Satire is addressed.

  —*The husband of Venus.*] Vulcan, the fabled god of fire—here put for the fire itself. He was the husband of Venus.

  q. d. Put all your writings into the fire.

26. *Or shut up, and bore, &c.*]— Lay by your books, and let the moths eat them.

Frange miser calamos, vigilataque prælia dele,
Qui facis in parvâ sublimia carmina cellâ,
Ut dignus venias hederis, et imagine macrâ.
Spes nulla ulterior : didicit jam dives avarus   30
Tantum admirari, tantum laudare disertos,
Ut pueri Junonis ayem. Sed defluit ætas,
Et pelagi patiens, et cassidis, atque ligonis.
Tædia tunc subeunt animos, tunc seque suamque
Terpsichoren odit facunda et nuda senectus.   35
Accipe nunc artés, ne quid tibi conferat iste,
Quem colis : Musarum et Apollinis æde relictâ,
Ipse facit versus, atque uni cedit Homero,
Propter mille annos. At si dulcedine famæ
Succensus recites, Maculonus commodat ædes;   40
Ac longe ferrata domus servire jubetur,
In quâ sollicitas imitatur janua portas.
Scit dare libertos extremâ in parte sedentes
Ordinis, et magnas comitum disponere voces.
Nemo dabit regum, quanti subsellia constent,   45

27. *Your watched battles.*] Your writings upon battles, the descriptions of which have cost you many a watchful, sleepless night.

28. *A small cell.*] A wretched garret, as we say.

29. *Worthy of ivy, &c.*] That, after all the pains you have taken, you may have an image, *i. e.* a representation of your lean and starved person, with a little paltry ivy put round the head of it, in the temple of Apollo.

30. *There is no farther hope.*] You can expect nothing better, nothing beyond this.

32. *As boys the bird of Juno.*] As children admire, and are delighted with the beauty of a peacock, (see AINSW. tit. *Argus,*) which is of no service to the bird; so the patrons, which you think of getting, however rich and able to afford it they may be, will yet give you nothing but compliments on your performances; these will do you no more service, than the children's admiration does the peacock.

32–33. *Your age passes away.*] You little think that, while you are employing yourself to no purpose, as to your present subsistence, or provision

for the future, by spending your time in writing verses, your life is gliding away, and old age is stealing upon you; your youth, which is able to endure the toils and dangers of the sea, the fatigues of wars, or the labours of husbandry, is decaying.

34. *Then.*] When you grow old.

—*Weariness, &c.*] You'll be too feeble, in body and mind, to endure any labour, and become irksome even to yourself.

35. *Hates both itself and its Terpsichore.*] Your old age, however learned, clothed in rags, will curse itself, and the Muse that has been your undoing. Terpsichore was one of the nine Muses, who presided over dancing and music; she is fabled to have invented the harp; here, by meton. lyric poetry may be understood.

36. *His arts, &c.*] The artifices which your supposed patron will use, to have a fair excuse for doing nothing for you.

37. *The temple, &c.*] There was a temple of the Muses at Rome, which was built by Martius Philippus, where poets used to recite their works. Augustus built a library, and a temple to Apollo, on Mount Palatine, where the poets used also to recite their

Wretch, break your pens, and blot out your watched
    battles,
Who makest sublime verses in a small cell,
That you may become worthy of ivy, and a lean image.
There is no farther hope : a rich miser hath now learnt 30
As much to admire, as much to praise witty men,
As boys the bird of Juno. But your age, patient of the
    sea,
And of the helmet, and of the spade, passes away.
Then weariness comes upon the spirits ; then, eloquent 34
And naked old age hates both itself and its Terpsichore.
Hear now his arts, lest he whom you court should give you
Any thing : both the temple of the Muses, and of Apollo,
    being forsaken,
Himself makes verses, and yields to Homer alone,
Because a thousand years [before him.] But if, with the
    desire of fame   39
Inflamed, you repeat your verses, Maculonus lends a house;
And the house strongly barr'd is commanded to serve you,
In which the door imitates anxious gates.
He knows how to place his freedmen, sitting in the extreme
    part
Of the rows, and to dispose the loud voices of his attendants.
None of these great men will give as much as the benches
    may cost,   45

verses, and where they were deposited. See PERS. prol. l. 7. and HOR.
lib. i. epist. iii. l. 17.
    Among the tricks made use of by
these rich patrons, to avoid giving
any thing to their poor clients, the
poets, they affected to make verses
so well themselves, as not to stand in
need of the poetry of others ; therefore they deserted the public recitals,
and left the poor retainers on Apollo
and the Muses to shift as they could.
    38. *Yields to Homer alone.*] In his
own conceit : and this only upon account of Homer's antiquity, not as
thinking himself Homer's inferior in
any other respect.
    39. *If, with the desire of fame,
&c.*] If you don't want to get money
by your verses, and only wish to repeat them for the sake of applause.
    40. *Maculonus, &c.*] Some rich
man will lend you his house.
    41. *Strongly barr'd.*] Longe—lit.

exceedingly—very much—*q. d.* If
you are thought to want money of
him for your verses, the doors of his
house will be barred against you, and
resemble the gates of a city when besieged, and under the fear and anxiety
which the besiegers occasion ; but if
you profess only to write for fame, he
will open his house to you, it will be
at your service, that you may recite
your verses within it, and will procure you hearers, of his own freedmen and dependents, whom he will
order to applaud you.
    43. *He knows how to place, &c.*]
Dare, lit. to give.—*q. d.* He knows
how to dispose his freedmen on the
farthest seats behind the rest of the
audience, that they may begin a clap,
which will be followed by those who
are seated more forward. Ordo is a
rank or row of any thing, so of
benches or seats.
    44. *And to dispose, &c.*] How to

P

Et quæ conducto pendent anabathra tigillo,
Quæque reportandis posita est orchestra cathedris.
Nos tamen hoc agimus, tenuique m pulvere sulcos
Ducimus, et littus sterili versamus aratro.
Nam si discedas, laqueo tenet ambitiosi   50
Consuetudo mali : tenet insanabile multos
Scribendi cacoèthes, et ægro in corde senescit.
Sed vatem egregium, cui non sit publica vena,
Qui nihil expositum soleat deducere, nec qui
Communi feriat carmen triviale monetâ :   55
Hunc, qualem nequeo monstrare, et sentio tantum,
Anxietate carens animus facit, omnis acerbi
Impatiens, cupidus sylvarum, aptusque bibendis
Fontibus Aonidum : neque enim cantare sub antro
Picrio, thyrsumve potest contingere sana   60
Paupertas, atque æris inops, quo nocte dieque
Corpus eget.   Satur est, cum dicit Horatius, Euhoe !
Quis locus ingenio : nisi cum se carmine solo

dispose his clients and followers, so as best to raise a roar of applause—euge !—bene !—bravo ! as we say, among your hearers. All this he will do, for it costs him nothing.

46. *The stairs, &c.*] These were for the poet to ascend by into his rostium, and were fastened to a little beam, or piece of wood, which was hired for the purpose.

47. *The orchestra, &c*] The orchestra at the Greek theatres was the part where the chorus danced—the stage. Among the Romans it was the space between the stage and the common seats, where the senators and nobles sat to see plays acted. The poor poet is here supposed to make up such a place as this for the reception of the better sort, should any attend his recitals ; but this was made up of hired chairs, by way of seats, but which were to be returned as soon as the business was over.

48. *Yet we still go on.*] Hoc agimus—lit. we do this—we still pursue our poetical studies. Hoc agere is a phrase signifying to mind, attend to, what we are about. See TER. And. act i. sc. ii. l. 12. So before, l. 20. hoc agite, O Juvenes.

—*Draw furrows, &c.*] We take much pains to no purpose, like peo-

ple who should plough in the dust, or on the sea-shore. Comp. sat. i. 143. note.

50. *Would leave off.*] Discedas—if you would depart from the occupation of making verses.

—*Custom of ambitious evil.*] Evil ambition, which it is so customary for poets to be led away with.

51. *An incurable ill habit*] Cacoethes (from Gr. κακος, bad, and ηθος, a custom or habit) an evil habit. Many are got into such an itch of scribbling, that they cannot leave it off. Cacoethes also signifies a boil, an ulcer, and the like.

52. *Grows inveterate, &c.*] It grows old with the man, and roots itself, as it were, by time, in his very frame.

53. *No common vein*] Such talents as are not found among the generality.

54. *Nothing trifling*] Expositum—common, trifling, obvious—nothing in a common way.

55. *Trivial verse, &c.*] Trivialis comes from trivium, a place where three ways meet, a place of common resort : therefore I conceive the meaning of this line to be, that such a poet as Juvenal is describing writes nothing low or vulgar ; such verses as are usually sought after, and purchased by the common people in the street.

And the stairs which hang from the hired beam,
And the orchestra, which is set with chairs, which are to be
    carried back.
Yet we still go on, and draw furrows in the light
Dust, and turn up the shore with a barren plough.
For if you would leave off, custom of ambitious evil   50
Holds you in a snare: many an incurable ill habit of writing
Possesses, and grows inveterate in the distemper'd heart.
But the excellent poet, who has no common vein,
Who is wont to produce nothing trifling, nor who
Composes trivial verse in a common style,   55
Him (such a one I can't shew, and only conceive)
A mind free from anxiety makes; of every thing dis-
    pleasing
Impatient, desirous of woods, and disposed for drinking the
Fountains of the Muses; for neither to sing in the
Pierian cave, or to handle the thyrsus, is poverty,   60
Sober, and void of money, (which night and day the body
    wants,)
Able. Horace is satisfied, when he says—Euhoe!
What place is there for genius, unless when with verse alone

The word feriat is here metaphorical. Ferio literally signifies to strike, or hit; thus to coin or stamp money; hence to compose or make (hit off, as we say) verses; which, if done by a good poet, may be said to be of no common stamp. Moneta is the stamp, or impression, on money; hence, by meta. a style in writing. Hor. A. P. 59.

57. *A mind, &c.*] i. e. Such a poet is formed by a mind that is void of care and anxiety.

58. *Impatient.*] That hates all trouble, cannot bear vexation.

—*Desirous of woods.*] Of sylvan retirement. Hor. Epis. ii. 2, 77.

59. *Fountains of the Muses.*] Called Aonides, from their supposed habitation in Aonia, which was the hilly part of Bœotia, and where there were many springs and fountains sacred to the Muses. Of these fountains good poets were, in a figurative sense, said to drink, and by this to be assisted in their compositions,

59–60. *In the Pierian cave, &c.*] Pieria was a district of Macedon, where was a cave, or den, sacred to the Muses.

60. *Thyrsus.*] A spear wrapt about with ivy, which they carried about in their hands at the wild feasts of Bacchus, in imitation of Bacchus, who bore a thyrsus in his hand. The meaning of this passage is, that, for a poet to write well, he should be easy in his situation; and in his circumstances: for those who are harrassed with poverty and want cannot write well, either in the more sober style of poetry, or in the more enthusiastic and flighty strains of composition. By sana paupertas, the poet would insinuate, that no poor poet that had his senses would ever attempt it.

62. *Horace is satisfied, &c.*] It might be objected, that Horace was poor when he wrote, therefore Juvenal's rule will not hold, that a poor poet cannot write well. To this Juvenal would answer, "True, Horace was "poor, considered as to himself; but "then remember what a patron he "had in Mecænas, and how he was "enabled by him to avoid the cares "of poverty. When he wrote his "fine Ode to Bacchus, and uttered "his sprightly Evæ or Euhoe, he,

Vexant, et dominis Cirrhæ, Nisæque feruntur
Pectora nostra, duas non admittentia curas?   65
Magnæ mentis opus, nec de lodice parandâ
Attonitæ, currus et equos, faciesque Deorum
Aspicere, et qualis Rutulum confundit Erinnys.
Nam si Virgilio puer, et tolerabile desit
Hospitium, caderent omnes a crinibus hydri :   70
Surda nihil gemeret grave buccina.   Poscimus ut sit
Non minor antiquo Rubrenus Lappa cothurno,
Cujus et alveolos et lænam pignerat Atreus ?
Non habet infelix Numitor, quod mittat amico ;
Quintillæ quod donet, habet : nec defuit illi,   75
Unde emeret multâ pascendum carne leonem
Jam domitum.   Constat leviori bellua sumptu
Nimirum, et capiunt plus intestina poëtæ.
Contentus famâ jaceat Lucanus in hortis
Marmoreis : at Serrano, tenuique Saleio   80

" doubtless, was well sated with good " cheer."   See lib. ii. ode xix. l. 5–8.

64. *The lords of Cirrha and Nisa.*] Apollo and Bacchus, the tutelar gods of poets. Cirrha was a town of Phocis, near Delphos, where Apollo had an oracle.

Nisa, a den in Arabia, where Bacchus was educated by the nymphs, when sent thither by Mercury. From hence Bacchus was called Dionysius, ex Διος, and Nisa ; Gr. Διονυσιος.

65. *Carried on.*] *i. e.* Inspired, and assisted.

66. *Not of one, &c.*] *q. d.* It is the work of a great and powerful mind, above want, not of one that is distracted about getting a blanket for his bed, to fix the eye of the imagination, so as to conceive and describe horses and chariots, and godlike appearances, in such a manner as to do justice to these sublime subjects of heroic verse. See VIRG. Æn. xii. l. 326, 7.

68. *And what an Erinnys.*] How Alecto looked when she astonished the Rutulian king Turnus, when she filled him with terror, by throwing her torch at him. Æn. vii. l. 456, 7. Erinnys is a name common to the three furies of hell, of which Alecto was one.

70. *All the snakes would have fallen, &c.*] *q. d.* Had Virgil been poor, and

without his pleasures and conveniences, he never would have been able to describe, in the manner he has done, the snaky tresses of Alecto. See Æn. vii. l. 450. All this had been lost to us.

71. *The silent trumpet.*] Surdus not only means to express one who does not hear, but that also which gives no sound. See sat. xiii. l. 194. Juvenal alludes to Æn. vii. l. 519, 20, 1.

72. *Rubrenus Lappa, &c.*] An ingenious, but poor and miserable tragic poet, who lived in Juvenal's time.

—*Less than the ancient buskin.*] Not inferior to the old writers of tragedy. Cothurno, per metonym. put here for the tragic poets, as it often is for tragedy.

73. *Atreus had laid in pawn.*] It has been observed by Ainsworth, against Stephanus and other lexicographers, that pignero does not mean to take, or receive, a thing in pawn, but to send it into pawn. In this view we may understand Atreus to be the name of some tragedy, on the subject of Atreus, king of Mycenæ, which met with such bad success as to oblige poor Rubrenus to pawn his clothes and furniture. Stephanus and others understand pignerat in the sense of taking to pawn, and suppose Atreus to be the name of the pawn-

Our minds trouble themselves, and by the lords of Cirrha
    and Nisa
Are carried on, not admitting two cares at once ?   65
It is the work of a great mind, not of one that is amazed
    about
Getting a blanket, to behold chariots, and horses, and the
    faces
Of the gods, and what an Erinnys confounded the Rutulian:
For if a boy, and a tolerable lodging had been wanting to
    Virgil,
All the snakes would have fallen from her hairs :   70
The silent trumpet have groan'd nothing disastrous. Do
    we require
That Rubrenus Lappa should not be less than the ancient
    buskin,
Whose platters, and cloke, Atreus had laid in pawn ?
Unhappy Numitor has not what he can send to a friend ;
He has what he can give to Quintilla: nor was there
    wanting to him   75
Wherewithal he might buy a lion, to be fed with much flesh,
Already tamed. The beast stands him in less expence,
Doubtless, and the intestines of a poet hold more.
Lucan, content with fame, may lie in gardens adorn'd with
Marble: but to Serranus, and to thin Saleius,   80

broker, to whom Rubrenus had pawned his goods.

The first sense seems to have the best authority ; but with which ever we may agree, the thought amounts to the same thing in substance ; viz. Can it be expected that this poor poet should equal the fire and energy of the old tragic writers, while his clothes and furniture were pawned, in order to supply him with present necessaries to keep him from starving ? A man in such distress, whatever his genius might be, could not exert it.

74. *Numitor.*] The name Numitor may stand here for any rich man, who would let a poet starve for want of that money which he lays out upon his mistress, or in buying some useless curiosity, such as a tame lion. Infelix is here ironical.

78. *Doubtless, &c.*] Ironically said. No doubt it would cost more to maintain a poet than a lion.

79. *Lucan, &c.*] A learned and rich poet of Corduba in Spain, who, coming to Rome, was made a knight. He wrote, but lived not to finish, the civil wars between Cæsar and Pompey, in an heroic poem, called *Pharsalia.* He was put to death by Nero. See more, AINSW. *Lucanus.*

—*May lie in gardens, &c.*] Repose himself in ease and luxury, fame being sufficient for one who wants nothing else. Marmoreis—adorned with fine buildings of marble.

80. *Serranus, and to thin Saleius, &c.*] These were two poor poets in Juvenal's time. Of the latter Tacitus says, " Who takes any notice of, " or even attends or speaks to our " excellent poet Saleius ?"

These men may get fame by the excellence of their compositions ; but what signifies that, if they get nothing else ? fame wont feed them.

Perhaps the poet calls Saleius tenuis, thin, from his meagre appearance,

Gloria quantalibet, quid erit, si gloria tantum est?
Curritur ad vocem jucundam, et carmen amicæ
Thebaïdos, lætam fecit cum Statius urbem,
Promisitque diem : tantâ dulcedine captos
Afficit ille animos, tantâque libidine vulgi   85
Auditur : sed cum fregit subsellia versu,
Esurit, intactam Paridi nisi vendat Agaven.
Ille et militiæ multis largitur honorem ;
Semestri vatum digitos circumligat auro.
Quod non dant proceres, dabit histrio.   Tu Camerinos 90
Et Bareas, tu nobilium magna atria curas ?
Præfectos Pelopea facit, Philomela tribunos.
Haud tamen invideas vati, quem pulpita pascunt.
Quis tibi Mecænas ? quis nunc erit aut Proculeius,
Aut Fabius ? quis Cotta iterum ? quis Lentulus alter.? 95

82. *They run.*] Curritur, here used impersonally, like concurritur. Hor. sat. i. l. 7.

—*The pleasing voice.*] i. e. Of Statius, when he reads over his Thebais in public.

84. *Promised a day.*] i. e. Appointed a day for a public recital of his poem on the Theban war.

86. *Broken the benches, &c.*] By the numbers of his hearers, who flocked to attend him when he recited his Thebais. Notwithstanding this he must starve, for any thing the nobles will do for him.

87. *His untouched Agave.*] His new play called *Agave*, which has never been heard, or performed. This play was formed upon the story of Agave, the daughter of Cadmus, who was married to Echion king of Thebes, by whom she had Penthæus, whom she, and the rest of the Menades, in their mad revels, tore limb from limb, because he would drink no wine, and for this was supposed to slight the feasts of Bacchus. Answ. See Hor. Sat. lib. ii. sat. iii. l. 303 ; and Ovid. Met. iii. 725–8.

—*Paris.*] A stage-player, in high favour with Domitian ; insomuch that Domitian fell in love with him, and repudiated his wife Domitia for his sake.

What Juvenal says here, and in the three following lines, in a seeming complimentary way, was no more

than a sneer upon Paris the player, and, through him, upon the emperor, who so understood it, and turned our author's jest into his punishment ; for in his old age he sent him into Egypt, by the way of an honorary service, with a military command. This shews that this Satire was written in the time of Domitian, and he is meant by Cæsare, l. 1.

However, it is very evident, that Juvenal meant to rebuke the nobles for their parsimony towards men of genius, by shewing how generous Paris was to them, insomuch that they ought to be ashamed to be outdone by a stage-player.

89. *Semestrian gold.*] Semestris not only means a space of six months, (sex mensium), but the half or middle of a month. The moon is called semestris, when she is arrived at the middle of her month, and is quite round in form.

The aurum semestre here means gold in a round form, i. e. a ring ; such as was worn by knights, to which dignity some poets had been raised, through the interest of this stage-player with the emperor. But qu.— If there be not here an allusion to the winter and summer rings? See sat. i. l. 27.

91. *Camerini and Barcæ, &c.*]—Some rich nobles, whose levees the poor poets might attend in vain.

92. *Pelopea makes prefects.*] The

What will ever so much fame be, if it be only fame?
They run to the pleasing voice, and poem of the favourite
Thebaïs; when Statius has made the city glad,
And has promised a day: with so great sweetness does he
　　affect.
The captivated minds, and is heard with so much eager
　　desire　　　　　　　　　　　　　　　　　　85
Of the vulgar: but when he has broken the benches with
　　his verse,
He hungers, unless he should sell his untouched Agave to
　　Paris.
He also bestows military honour on many;
He binds round the fingers of poets with Semestrian gold.
What nobles do not give, an actor will. Dost thou trouble
　　thine　　　　　　　　　　　　　　　　　　90
Head about the Camerini and Bareæ, and the great courts
　　of nobles?
Pelopea makes prefects, Philomela tribunes.
Yet envy not the poet whom the stage maintains.
Who is your Mecænas? who will now be either a Proculeius,
Or a Fabius? who a second Cotta? who another Lentulus?

tragedy of Pelopea, the daughter of Thyestes, who was lain with by her own father, and produced Ægysthus, who killed Agamemnon and Atreus.

—*Philomela tribunes.*] The tragedy of Philomela, the daughter of Pandion king of Athens, ravished by Tereus, who had married her sister Progne. See more, AINSW. tit. *Philomela.*

The poet seems here to insinuate, that the performance of Paris, in these tragedies, so charmed the emperor, and gave the actor such an ascendancy over him, as to enable Paris to have the great offices of state at his disposal, so that they were conferred on whomsoever he pleased.

93. *Envy not, &c.*] q. d. Though, in some instances, great things have been done for some individuals, thro' the influence and interest of Paris, yet, in general, those who have nothing else to depend on but writing for the stage, are left to starve, and therefore are hardly (haud) to be envied. Pulpita—see sat. iii. l. 163. note.

94. *Mecænas.*] Who is the rich man that is such a patron to you, as

Mecænas was to Horace? who not only enriched him, but made him his friend and companion, and introduced him to the favour of the emperor Augustus.

—*Proculeius.*] A Roman knight, intimate with Augustus. He was so liberal to his two brothers, Scipio and Murena, that he shared his whole patrimony with them, when they had been ruined by the civil wars. See HOR. lib. ii. ode ii. l. 5–6.

95. *Fabius.*] The Fabius is, perhaps, here meant, to whom Ovid wrote four epistles in his banishment, as to a noble and generous patron of men of genius. Or it may relate to Fabius Maximus, who sold his estate, in order to redeem some Romans who had been taken prisoners by Hannibal.

—*Cotta.*] A great friend to Ovid, who wrote to him three times from Pontus, as to a constant patron. Ovid says to him,

*Cumque labent alii, jactataque vela
　　relinquant,
Tu laceræ remanes anchora sola
　　rati:*

Tunc par ingenio pretium : tunc utile multis
Pallere, et vinum toto nescire Decembri.
Vester porro labor fœcundior, historiarum
Scriptores : petit hic plus temporis, atque olei plus :
Namque oblita modi millesima pagina surgit   100
Omnibus, et crescit multâ damnosa papyro.
Sic ingens rerum numerus jubet, atque operum lex.
Quæ tamen inde seges ? terræ quis fructus apertæ ?
Quis dabit historico, quantum daret acta legenti ?
Sed genus ignavum, quod lecto gaudet et umbrâ.   105
Dic igitur, quid causidicis civilia præstent
Officia, et magno comites in fasce libelli ?
Ipsi magna sonant ; sed tunc cum creditor audit
Præcipue, vel si tetigit latus acrior illo,
Qui venit ad dubium grandi cum codice nomen :   110
Tunc immensa cavi spirant mendacia folles,

Grata tua est igitur pictas. Ignoscimus illis,
Qui, cum fortunâ, terga dedére fugæ.

95. *Lentulus.*] A man of great liberality, to whom Cic. epist. vii. lib. i. ad famil. thus writes : Magna est hominum opinio de te, magna commendatio liberalitatis.

96. *Reward was equal, &c.*] When there were such men as these to encourage genius, and to be the patrons of learning, then reward was equal to merit.

97. *To be pale.*] With constant study and application, which were then sure to be profitable. Comp. Hor. epist. iii. l. 10. Pers. sat. i. 124.

—*To know nothing of wine, &c.*]— The feast of the Saturnalia was observed in the month of December, with great festivity and jollity, with plenty of wine and good cheer: all this it was worth a poet's while to give up entirely for his study; and rather than not finish what he was about, not taste so much as a single drop of wine during the whole festival, knowing that he was certain to be well paid for his pains.

98. *Your labour, &c.*] He now speaks of the writers of history, whose labour and fatigue are beyond those of other writers, and yet they are equally neglected.

98-9. *Is more abundant, &c.*] The subject-matter more various and extensive.

99. *More oil.*] Alluding to the lamps which they used to write by, in which they consumed a great quantity of oil. See sat. i. l. 41. note.

100. *Forgetful of measure.*] The subjects are so various, and the incidents crowd in so fast upon the historian, that he passes all bounds, without attending to the size of his work, it rises to a thousand pages before you are aware.

101. *Ruinous with much paper.*]— So much paper is used, as to ruin the poor historian with the expence of it.

102. *The great number of things.*] i. e. Which are treated.

—*The law of such works.*] The rules of history, which oblige the historian to be particular in his relation of facts, and, of course, diffuse.

103. *What harvest.*] What profit do you reap.

—*The far-extended ground.*] The wide and boundless field of history. Comp. Virg. Geor. iii. 194-5. and Geor. ii. 280.

Some think that this expression of terræ apertæ, taken in connection with the seges, is, as that is, metaphorical, and alludes to the labour of the husbandman, in opening the ground by tillage, in order to prepare it for the seed. So the historian

Then reward was equal to genius: then 'twas useful to
      many   96
To be pale, and to know nothing of wine for a whole De-
      cember.
  Moreover your labour, ye writers of histories, is more
Abundant: this demands more time, and more oil ;
For the thousandth page, forgetful of measure, arises 100
To ye all, and increases ruinous with much paper:
Thus the great number of things ordains, and the law of
      (such) works.
What harvest is from thence? what fruit of the far-ex-
      tended ground?
Who will give an historian as much as he would give to a
      collector of the registers?
But they are an idle race, which rejoices in a couch or a
      shade.   105
Tell me then, what civil offices afford to the lawyers,
And the libels their attendants in a great bundle?
They make a great noise, but especially then, when the
      creditor
Hears, or if one, more keen than he, has touched his side,
Who comes with a great book to a doubtful debt :   110
Then his hollow bellows breathe out prodigious lies,

ploughs, and digs, and labours, as it
were, in the field of history, in hopes
of reaping profit thereby.
  104. *A collector of the registers.*]—
The acta were journals, registers, acts
of the senate, or the like records.
The clerk, who wrote or collected
them, was called actuarius. He was
a sort of historian in his way.
  105. *They are an idle race, &c.*]—
But perhaps it may be said, that,
though they write much, yet that
they write at their ease; that they, as
well as the poets, are a lazy set of fellows, who write lolling upon their
couches, or repose themselves in shady
places. Hence Hor. lib. i. ode xxxii. 1.
  *Poscimus. Si quid vacui sub umbra
    Lusimus tecum.*
Again :—*Somno gaudentis et umbra.*
Epist. ii. lib. ii. l. 78.
  106. *Civil offices, &c.*] What they
get by their pleading for their clients
in civil actions.
  107. *The libels, &c.*] Their bundles of briefs which they carry with
them into court.

108. *A great noise.*] Bawls aloud
—magna, adverbially, for magnopere.
Græcism.
  108-9. *Especially—when the creditor hears.*] Creditor signifies one that
lends, or trusts ; a creditor.
  The lawyer here spoken of must be
supposed to be of council with the
plaintiff, or creditor, who makes a
demand of money lent to another. If
the lawyer observes him to be within
hearing, he exerts himself the more.
  109. *One more keen.*] If another,
of a more eager disposition, and more
earnest about the event of his cause,
who sues for a book-debt of a doubtful nature, and brings his account-
books to prove it, thinks that the
lawyer does not exert himself sufficiently in his cause, and intimates this
to the pleader, by a jog on the side
with his elbow—then, &c. See AINSW.
Codex, No. 2 ; and *Nomen,* No. 5.
  111. *Hollow bellows.*] i.e. His lungs,
  —*Breathe out prodigious lies.*] In
order to deceive the court, and to
make the best of a bad cause.

Q

Conspuiturque sinus. Verum deprendere messem
Si libet ; hinc centum patrimonia causidicorum,
Parte aliâ solum russati pone Lacertæ.
Consedêre duces : surgis tu pallidus Ajax,   115
Dicturus dubiâ pro libertate, Bubulco
Judice. Rumpe miser tensum jecur, ut tibi lasso
Figantur virides, scalarum gloria, palmæ.
Quod vocis pretium ? siccus petasunculus, et vas
Pelamidum, aut veteres, Afrorum epimenia, bulbi ;   120
Aut vinum Tiberi devectum : quinque lagenæ,
Si quater egisti. Si contigit aureus unus,
Inde cadunt partes, ex fœdere pragmaticorum.
Æmilio dabitur, quantum petet, et melius nos

111. *Is spit upon.*] Is slavered all over with his foaming at the mouth.

—*If you would discover, &c.*] Were it possible to compute the gains of lawyers, you might put all they get in one scale, and in the other those of Domitian's coachman, and there would be no comparison, the latter would so far exceed.

As some understand by the russati Lacertæ, a charioteer belonging to Domitian, who was clad in a red livery, and was a great favourite of that emperor, so others understaud some soldier to be meant, who, as the custom then was, wore a red or russet apparel : in this view the meaning is, that the profits of one hundred lawyers, by pleading, do not amount in value to the plunder gotten by one soldier. So Mr. C. DRYDEN :

Ask what he gains by all this lying prate,
A captain's plunder trebles his estate.

So Joh. Britannicus.—*Russati Lacertæ.* Lacerta, nomen militis, fictum a poeta : nam milites Romani usi sunt in prælio vestibus russatis, &c.

115. *The chiefs, &c.*] Consedere duces. The beginning of Ovid's account of the dispute, between Ulysses and Ajax, for the armour of Achilles. OVID, Met. lib. xiii. l. i. here humourously introduced to describe the sitting of the judges on the bench in a court of justice.

—*Thou risest a pale Ajax.*] Alluding to OVID, lib. xiii. l. 2.

Surgit ad hos clypei dôminus septemplicis Ajax—

by way of ridicule on the eager and agitated lawyer, who is supposed to arise with as much fury and zeal in his client's cause, as Ajax did to assert his pretensions to the armour in dispute.

116. *Doubtful freedom.*] The question in the cause is supposed to be, whether such or such a one is entitled to the freedom of the city ; there were many causes on this subject.

116—17. *Bubulcus being judge.*]— This may mean C. Atilius Bubulcus, who was consul. Or, by Bubulcus, the poet may mean some stupid, ignorant fellow, who was fitter to be an herdsman, than to fill a seat of justice. And thus the poet might satirize the advancement of persons to judicial offices, who were totally unqualified and unfit for them.

117. *Break your stretched liver.*]— Which, with the other contents in the region of the diaphragm, must be distended by the violent exertions of the speaker : or it may mean the liver distended by anger. So Horace on another occasion, fervens difficili bile tumet jecur. HOR. ode xiii. lib. i. l. 4.

118. *Green palms, &c.*] It was the custom of the client, if he succeeded in his cause, to fix such a garland at the lawyer's door.

—*The glory of your stairs.*] By which the poor lawyer ascended to his miserable habitation.

119. *Of your voice.*] Of all your bawling—What do you get by all the noise which you have been making ?

120. *Of sprats.*] Pelamidum. It

And his bosom is spit upon. But if you would discover
the
Profit, put the patrimony of an hundred lawyers on one
side,
And on the other that of the red-clad Lacerta only.   114
The chiefs are set down together, thou risest a pale Ajax,
In order to plead about doubtful freedom, Bubulcus
Being judge : break, wretch, your stretched liver, that, to
you fatigued,
Green palms may be fixed up, the glory of your stairs.
What is the reward of your voice? a dry bit of salt bacon,
and a vessel
Of sprats, or old bulbous roots which come monthly from
Africa,
Or wine brought down the Tiber: five flagons,   121
If you have pleaded four times—If one piece of gold befalls,
From thence shares fall, according to the agreement of
pragmatics.
To Æmilius will be given as much as he will ask; and we
have

is not very certain what these fish were; but some small and cheap fish seem to be here meant. Ainsworth says they were called pelamides, à Gr. πηλος, lutum—clay, or mud. Most likely they were chiefly found in mud, like our grigs in the Thames, and were, like them, of little worth.

—Old bulbous roots, &c.] Perhaps onions are here meant, which might be among the small presents sent monthly from Africa to Rome. See AINSW. Epimenia. PLIN. xix. 5. calls a kind of onion, epimenidium, from Gr. επιμηνιδιον. AINSW. Epimenedium. Those sent to the lawyer were veteres—old and stale.

121. Wine brought down the Tiber.] Coming down the stream from Veiento, or some other place where bad wine was made.

—Five flagons.] Lagena was a sort of bottle in which wine was kept. The five lagenæ cannot be supposed to make up any great quantity. Five bottles of bad wine, for pleading four causes, was poor pay.

122. A piece of gold, &c.] If it should so happen, that you should get a piece of gold for a fee. The

Roman aureus was in value about 1l. 4s. 3d. according to Pliny, lib. xxxiii. c. 3. See post, l. 243.

123. Thence shares fall, &c.] This poor pittance must be divided into shares, and fall equally to the lot of others besides yourself.

—According to the agreement, &c.] Ainsworth says, that the pragmatici were prompters, who sat behind the lawyers while they were pleading, and instructed them, telling them what the law, and the meaning of the law, was. For this, it may be supposed, that the pragmatici agreed with the lawyers, whom they thus served, to share in the fees. We use the word pragmatical, to denote busily meddling and intruding into others' concerns; hence foolishly talkative, impertinent, saucy. PHILLIPS. Gr. πραγματικος—solers in negotiis agendis.

124. To Æmilius will be given, &c.] We may suppose that this Æmilius was a rich lawyer, who, though of inferior abilities to many poor pleaders, yet got a vast deal of money by the noble and splendid appearance which he made.

Egimus : hujus enim stat currus aheneus, alti   125
Quadrijuges in vestibulis, atque ipse feroci
Bellatore sedens curvatum hastile minatur
Eminus, et statuâ meditatur prælia luscâ.
Sic Pedo conturbat, Matho deficit : exitus hic est
Tongilli, magno cum rhinocerote lavari   130
Qui solet, et vexat lutulentâ balnea turbâ,
Perque forum juvenes longo premit assere Medos,
Empturus pueros, argentum, myrrhina, villas :
Spondet enim Tyrio stlataria purpura filo.
Et tamen hoc ipsis est utile : purpura vendit   135
Causidicum, vendunt amethystina : convenit illis
Et strepitu, et facie majoris vivere censûs.
Sed finem impensæ non servat prodiga Roma.
Ut redeant veteres, Ciceroni nemo ducentos

124—5. *We have pleaded better.*]— Though there be some among us who are abler lawyers.

125. *A brazen chariot, &c.*] He had a large brazen statue, a fine bronze, as we should call it, of a chariot, drawn by four horses, placed in his vestibule, or entrance to his house, which made a magnificent appearance. Quadrijugis signifies four horses harnessed together, and drawing in a chariot.

126—7. *Himself—sitting, &c.*]— There was also an equestrian statue of Æmilius himself, mounted on a war-horse, in the very action of bending back his arm, as if ready to throw a javelin.

128. *A blinking statue.*] The statue represents Æmilius as meditating some great stroke against an enemy, and having one eye shut, in order to take aim with the other. Or perhaps Æmilius had but one eye, which the statue represented. All these things, which can add no real worth or ability to the owner of them, yet strike the vulgar with high veneration for Æmilius, and engage them to employ him in preference to others, insomuch that he may have what fees he pleases. See l. 124.

129. *Thus Pedo breaks.*] Conturbat—ruins himself, by wanting to appear rich, in order to draw clients.

—*Matho fails.*] Becomes bankrupt, as it were, by the expence he puts himself to on the same account.

130. *Of Tongillus.*] This was some other lawyer, who ruined himself by wanting to seem rich and considerable.

—*With larger rhinoceros.*] The richer sort used to go to the baths, with their oil in a vessel made of the horn of a rhinoceros, which was very expensive. Tongillus did this in order to be thought rich. So ivory is called elephant. Geor. iii. 26. Meton.

131. *With a dirty crowd.*] Who followed him through the dirty streets, as his attendants, and therefore were themselves muddy and dirty, and, of course, very offensive to the gentry who resorted to the public baths.

132. *Presses the young Medes.*] He rides through the forum in a litter, set upon poles which rested on the shoulders of the bearers,

—*Young Medes.*] The Romans were furnished with slaves from Media and Persia, who were very tall and robust ; these were chiefly employed in carrying the lecticæ, or litters, in which the richer people were carried through the streets of Rome.

133. *Going to buy, &c.*] Appearing thus, as some great man who was going to lay out money in various articles of luxury. Pueros, here, means young slaves.

134. *His foreign purple.*] His dress was also very expensive, and was such as the nobles wore.

—*Promises for him.*] i. e. Gains

Pleaded better: for a brazen chariot stands, and four
  stately 125
Horses in his vestibules, and himself on a fierce
War-horse sitting, brandishes a bent spear,
Aloft, and meditates battles with a blinking statue.
Thus Pedo breaks—Matho fails: this is the end
Of Tongillus, who to bathe with large rhinoceros 130
Is wont, and vexes the baths with a dirty crowd;
And thro' the forum presses the young Medes with a long
  pole,
Going to buy boys, silver, vessels of myrrh, and villas;
For his foreign purple with Tyrian thread promises for him,
And yet this is useful to them: purple sells 135
The lawyer, violet-colour'd robes sell him: it suits them,
To live with the bustle and appearance of a greater income.
But prodigal Rome observes no bounds to expence.
Tho' the ancients should return, nobody would give Cicero

him credit. Spondeo properly signifies to undertake, to be surety for
another, and it is here used in a metaphorical sense; as if the expensive
dress of Tongillus was a surety for
him as being rich, because by this he
appeared to be so.
  —*Foreign purple.*] Stlatarius, (from
stlata, a ship or boat) signifies out-
landish, foreign, as imported by sea
from a foreign country.
  —*Tyrian thread.*] The thread, of
which the garment of Tongillus was
made, was dyed in the liquor of the
murex, a shell-fish, of which came
the finest purple dye, and the best of
which were found near Tyre; therefore we often read of the Tyrian purple. See Æn. iv. 262. Hor. epod.
xii. l. 21.
  135. *This is useful, &c.*] All this
parade of appearance is a means of re-
commending the lawyers to observation, and sometimes to employment,
therefore may be said to have its use
where it succeeds.
  135-6. *Purple sells the lawyer.*]—
His fine appearance is often the cause
of his getting employment, in which,
for the price of his fee, he may be
said to sell himself to his client.
  136. *Violet-coloured robes.*] Amethystina. The amethyst is a precious
stone of a violet-colour. This colour

also the gentry among the Romans
were fond of wearing; and this, therefore, also recommended the lawyers
to observation, and sometimes to employment.
  137. *With the bustle, &c.*] They
found it suitable to their views of re-
commending themselves, to live above
their fortunes, and, of course, to be
surrounded with numbers of attendants, &c. and, from this, and the
appearance of their dress, to seem
richer than they were: this, as the
next line imports, because nobody
was looked upon that was not supposed able to afford to be extravagant;
such was the monstrous prodigality
of the times, that the expences of
people were boundless.
  139. *Nobody would give Cicero,
&c.*] Such is the importance of fashi-
onable and expensive appearance, that
even Tully himself, (if he could return from the dead,) though the
greatest orator that Rome ever saw,
as well as the ablest advocate, nobody
would give him a fee, though ever
so small, unless he appeared with a
ring of great value glittering upon
his finger, ducentos nummos. The
nummus argenti was a sesterce, the
fourth part of a denarius, but seven
farthings of our money.

Nunc dederit nummos, nisi fulserit annulus ingens. 140.
Respicit hoc primum qui litigat, an tibi servi
Octo, decem comites, an post te sella, togati
Ante pedes. Ideo conductâ Paulus agebat
Sardonyche, atque ideo pluris, quam Cossus agebat,
Quam Basilus. Rara in tenui facundia panno. 145
Quando licet flentem Basilo producere matrem?
Quis bene dicentem Basilum ferat? accipiat te
Gallia, vel potius nutricula causidicorum
Africa, si placuit mercedem imponere linguæ.
Declamare doces? ô ferrea pectora Vectî! 150
Cum perimit sævos classis numerosa tyrannos;
Nam quæcunque sedens modo legerat, hæc eadem stans
Proferet, atque eadem cantabit versibus îsdem.

141. *He that litigates, &c.*] He
that wants to employ counsel, instead
of first inquiring into the abilities of
the man whom he employs, asks
how many servants he keeps; and in
what style he lives.

141–2. *Eight servants.*] i. e. Slaves
to carry your litter. The litters were
more or less respectable, as to their
appearance, from the number of bearers which carried them; some had
six. See sat. i. l. 51, and note 2.
These were called hexaphori, from
Gr. ἑξ, six, and φερω, to bear.

*Laxior hexaphoris tua sit lectica
licebit.* MART. lib. ii. ep. 81.
*Quum tibi non essent sex millia,
Cæciliane,
Ingenti late vectus es hexaphoro.*
MART. lib. iv. ep. 50.

Tranquillus writes, that Caligula
was carried on a litter borne by eight
—octophoro. This piece of state
might afterwards be affected by those
who wished to make a great and
splendid appearance.

142. *Ten attendants.*] Comites,
attendants upon him. It was the
custom, says Grangius, not only for
princes, but for others, who were carried in litters, to have a number of
people attending them, who were
called comites.

—*Whether a chair, &c.*] Whether,
though you may walk on foot, you
have a litter carried after you, that
you may get into when you please.

—*Gownsmen, &c.*] Poor clients,
called togati, from the gowns which

they wore. See sat. i. l. 3, and note;
and sat. iii. l. 117, note. Numbers
of these were seen walking before the
great, on whom they were dependent.

—*Therefore Paulus, &c.*] Some
poor lawyer, who, though he could
not afford to buy a ring set with a
sardonyx, yet hired one to make his
appearance with at the bar; and by
this means got greater fees than those
who appeared without some such ornament.

145. *Cossus or Basilus.*] Two poor,
but, probably, learned lawyers of the
time.

—*Eloquence is rare, &c.*] Nobody
will give a man credit for being eloquent, if he appears in rags, at least
very rarely.

146. *When can Basilus produce,
&c.*] When will Basilus, or any man
with a mean appearance, be employed
in a cause of great consequence, as
Cicero for Fonteius, where a mother
was produced in court, weeping and
supplicating for the life of her son.

147. *Who will bear Basilus, &c.*]
i. e. Let a lawyer be ever so able, or
speak ever so well, nobody will pay
him the least attention, if his appearance be poor and shabby.

—*Let Gallia, &c.*] France and
Africa were remarkable, at that time,
for encouraging eloquence, and had
great lawyers who got large fees. See
Mr. C. Dryden's note.

Comp. sat. xv. l. 111. Ainsw. explains nutricula, a breeder, a bringer-
up.

Now-a-days two hundred sesterces, unless a great ring
    shone.   140
He that litigates regards this first, whether you have eight
Servants, ten attendants, whether a chair is after you,
Gownsmen before your steps. Therefore Paulus pleaded
    with an hired
Sardonyx, and therefore pleaded at an higher fee than
Cossus or than Basilus. Eloquence is rare in a mean
    clothing.
When can Basilus produce a weeping mother?   145
Who will bear Basilus (tho') speaking well? let Gallia
Receive you, or rather, that nurse of lawyers,
Africa, if it has pleased you to set a reward upon your
    tongue.
Do you teach to declaim? O the iron heart of Vectius!
When a numerous class hath destroy'd cruel tyrants: 151
For whatever, sitting it has just read, these same things
    standing,
It will utter, and rehearse the same, over and over, in the
    same verses.

149. *If it has pleased you, &c.*] i. e.
If you make a point of getting money
by your eloquence at the bar.

150. *Do you teach, &c.*] Having
shewn how badly the lawyers were
off, in this dearth of encouragement
given to liberal sciences, and of rewarding real merit and abilities, he
now proceeds to shew, that the teachers of rhetoric, who opened schools
for the laborious employment of instructing youth in the knowledge and
art of declamation, were, if possible,
still worse off.

—O the iron heart, &c.] q. d. O the
patience of Vectius! One would think
that his mind was insensible of fatigue, quite steeled, as it were, against
the assaults of impatience or weariness. See sat. i. l. 31.

—Vectius.] The name of some
teacher of rhetoric, or perhaps put
here, for any person of that profession.

151. *When a numerous class, &c.*]
Classis here signifies a number of boys
in the same form, or class, every one
of which was to repeat over a long
declamation to the master, on some
particular subject which was given
put to them as a thesis.

—Destroyed cruel tyrants.] Alluding to the subject of the declamation, as, "Whether tyrants should
" not be destroyed by their subjects?"
The declaimers are supposed to hold
the affirmative. Comp. sat. i. 15–17,
and note on l. 15.

Some refer this to Dionysius, the
tyrant of Sicily, who, after he was
deposed, went to Corinth and set up
a school, where Juvenal humourously
supposes him to be killed by the fatigue of his employment; but the
first sense, which is given above,
seems to be the most natural.

152. *For whatever, sitting, &c.*] It
is probable, that the rhetoricians first
taught their scholars the manner of
pronounciation and utterance, which
they might do, when their scholars
read over their declamations sitting;
but when they instructed them in
gesture and action, then they were
made to stand up, still repeating the
same things over and over again, and
the master exerting himself, to shew
them the best method of speaking and
action.

153. *Rehearse over, &c.*] Canto—
lit. signifies to sing or chant. Perhaps the ancients, in their declama-

Occîdit miseros crambe repetita magistros.
Quis color, et quod sit causæ genus, atque ubi summa 155
Quæstio, quæ veniant diversâ parte sagittæ,
Scire volunt omnes, mercedem solvere nemo.
Mercedem appellas ? quid enim scio ? culpa docentis
Scilicet arguitur, quod lævâ in parte mamillæ
Nil salit Arcadico juveni, cujus mihi sextâ   160
Quâque die miserum dirus caput Hannibal implet.
Quicquid id est, de quo deliberat ; an petat urbem
A Cannis ; an post nimbos et fulmina cautus
Circumagat madidas a tempestate cohortes.
Quantum vis stipulare, et protinus accipe quod do,   165
Ut toties illum pater audiat. Ast alii sex
Et plures uno conclamant ore sophistæ,

tion, used a kind of singing, or chanting, to mark the cadences of their periods. Canto also signifies to repeat the same thing over and over again, in the same letters and syllables ; nothing more than this seems to be meant here. Versus, as well as a verse, signifies a line, even in prose. AINSW. Versus, No. 5.

. 154. The cabbage, &c.] Crambe—a kind of colewort, or cabbage. The poet means (in allusion to the Greek saying, Δις κραμβη θανατος) that the hearing the same things for ever (like cabbage warmed up, and served at table many times to the same persons) must be nauseous and surfeiting, enough to tire and weary the masters to death.

Others read Cambre, a town near mount Gaurus, in Campania, where a battle had been fought between the Campanians and the people of Cumæ. This had been made the subject of a declamation, which the scholars repeated so often in the schools, for their exercises, as to tire their masters almost to death.

155. What the colour.] That which the ancients called the colour, was that part of the declamation which was introduced by way of cause, or reason, for the thing supposed to be done, and by way of plea or excuse for the action. As Orestes, when he confessed killing his mother, " I did " it," says he, " because she killed " my father.".

—What the kind of cause.] Deliberative, demonstrative, or judicial —or whether defensible or not.

156. The chief question.] That on which the whole cause must turn.

—What arrows, &c.] What arguments may come from the other side. Metaph. from shooting arrows at a mark.

157. All would know, &c.] Every body is willing enough to be taught these things, but very few choose to pay the master for his pains in teaching them.

158. Do you call for your reward ?] i. e. What do you mean by asking for payment ? (says the scholar.) What do I know more than before ? This is supposed to be the language of the scholar, when the master demands payment for his trouble. The dull and inapprehensive scholar, who gets no benefit from the pains of the master, lays his ignorance upon the master, and not upon his own inattention or stupidity ; and therefore is supposed to blame the master, and to think that he deserves nothing for all the pains he has taken.

159. In the left part of the breast, &c.] The heart is supposed to be in the left part of the breast, and to be the seat of understanding and wisdom ; in both which the youth here spoken of seems to be as deficient, as if his heart were almost without motion, without that lively palpitation which is found in others. Lit. no-

The cabbage repeated kills the miserable masters.   154
What the colour, and what the kind of cause, and where
The chief question, what arrows may come from the con-
    trary party.
All would know, nobody pay the reward!
Do you call for your reward?—what, forsooth, do I know?
    The fault of the teacher
You may be sure is blamed, because in the left part of the
    breast
The Arcadian youth has nothing that leaps, whose dire
    Hannibal,   160
Every sixth day, fills my miserable head:
Whatever it be concerning which he deliberates, whether
    he should go to the city
From Cannæ, or after showers and thunder cautious,
He should wheel about his troops wet with the tempest.
Bargain for as much as you please, and immediately take
    what I give,   165
That his father should hear him as often. But six other
Sophists, and more, cry together with one mouth,

thing leaps to the Arcadian youth in the left part of the breast.

169. *Arcadian youth.*] Arcadia was famous for its breed of asses, to which, by the appellation Arcadico, this young man is compared, whose dulness had prevented his profiting under the pains which his master took with him. (See PERS. sat. iii. l. 9.)

—*Whose dire Hannibal, &c.*]. No theme was more common, in the Roman schools, than the adventures of Hannibal. "Every week," says the master, does the story of Hannibal torment my poor head upon a de- claiming day.

162. *Go to the city.*] March directly to Rome, after the battle of Cannæ.

164. *Wheel about his troops wet, &c.*] Hannibal, when within about three miles from Rome, was assault- ed by a dreadful tempest. Maherbal, his general of horse, persuaded him to go on, and promised him that he should, that night, sup in the capitol; but Hannibal deliberated, whether he should not lead his troops back into Apulia, as they were so assaulted and dismayed by the violence of the tempest.

These circumstances are supposed to be the constant subjects of decla- mations in the schools.

165. *Bargain for, &c.*] Ask what you please, I will give it you, if you can get this stupid boy's father to hear him as often as I do: then I think he would be persuaded of his son's dulness, and think also that I deserve to be handsomely paid for what I have gone through in hearing him. See AINSW. *Stipulor.*

166-7. *Six other sophists, &c.*]— Sophistæ meant at first learned men (from Gr. σοφος, wise); afterwards it meant pretenders to learning, prat- ing cavillers. It also signifies orators: in this last sense it seems used here, where the poet means to say, that many of these teachers of rhetoric had left the schools, where fictitious matters only were declaimed upon, for the bar, where real causes were agitated.

167. *Cry together with one mouth.*] i. e. All agree with one consent to take this step, *viz.* to have done with teaching school, and to go to the bar.

R

Et veras agitant lites, raptore relicto:
Fusa venena silent, malus ingratusque maritus,
Et quæ jam veteres sanant mortaria cæcos.   170
Ergo sibi dabit ipse rudem, si nostra movebunt
Consilia, et vitæ diversum iter ingredietur,
Ad pugnam qui rhetoricâ descendit ab umbrâ,
Summula 'ne pereat, quâ vilis tessera venit
Frumenti: quippe hæc merces lautissima.   Tenta   175
Chrysogonus quanti doceat, vel Pollio 'quanti
Lautorum pueros, artem scindens Theodori.
Balnea sexcentis, et pluris porticus, in quâ
Gestetur dominus quoties pluit: anne serenum
Exspectet, spargatve luto jumenta recenti?   180
Hic potius: namque hic mundæ nitet ungula mulæ.
    Parte aliâ longis Numidarum fulta columnis
Surgat, et algentem rapiat cœnatio solem.
Quanticunque domus, veniet qui fercula docte

---

168. *The ravisher being left.*] i. e. Leaving the fictitious subjects of declamation, such as some supposed ravisher, or perhaps the rape of Helen, Proserpine, &c.

169. *The mixed poisons are silent.*] Nothing more is said about the poisons of Medea. Fusa—poured and mixed together.

—*Ungrateful husband.*] Jason, who having married Medea, left her, and married another.

170. *What medicines now heal, &c.*] Mortaria—mortars. Per met. medicines brayed in a mortar. What medicines recovered old Æson to his youth and sight again. Ov. Met. lib. vii. l. 287–93.

Grangius thinks that this alludes to the story of a son, who made up some medicines to cure his father's eyes, and who was accused by his mother-in-law of having mixed up poison, which the father believing, disinherited him. So Farnaby.

171. *Therefore.*] Ergo—q. d. As the profession of teaching school is so miserable, and without profit, I would therefore advise those who have left the shadowy declamation of the school for the real contention of the bar, to follow a new course of life, and never think of returning to teaching rhetoric again, lest they should have no-

thing left to buy bread with; this seems to be the sense of the passage.

—*Discharge himself.*] Sibi dabit ipse rudem—literally, he will give himself the wand.

The rudis was a rod, or wand, given to sword-players, in token of a discharge, or release, from that exercise. Hence the phrase, dare rudem, to give a discharge, to dismiss. See Hor. ep. i. l. 2. donatum jam rude—dismissed. Francis.

He will discharge himself from keeping school.

173. *The rhetorical shadow.*] From the poor empty declamations in the schools, which at best are but a shadow of reality, and are but shadows in point of profit.

—*Real engagement.*] To engage in pleading causes at the bar, which have reality for their subject, and which, he hopes, will produce real profit. Descendit ad pugnam—a military phrase.

174–5. *A vile wheat-ticket.*] In any dole made by the emperor, or by one of the city magistrates for distributing corn, the poor citizens had each a tally, or ticket, given them, which they first shewed, and then received their proportion, according to the money they brought to buy wheat from the public magazines, at a lower

And agitate real causes, the ravisher being left :
The mixed poisons are silent, the bad and ungrateful
   husband,
And what medicines now heal old blind men.   170
Therefore he will discharge himself, if my counsels will
Move ; and he will enter upon a different walk in life,
Who has descended from the rhetorical shadow to real en-
   gagement,
Lest the small sum should perish, from which cometh a vile
Wheat-ticket : for this is a most splendid reward. Try 175
For how much Chrysogonus teaches, or Pollio the children
Of the quality, dividing the art of Theodorus.
Baths are at six hundred sestertia, and a portico at more,
   in which
The lord is carried when it rains : can he wait for
Fair weather, or dash his cattle with fresh mud ?   180
Here rather, for here the hoof of the clean mule shines.
  In another part, propp'd with tall Numidian pillars,
A supper-room arises, and will snatch the cool sun.
Whatever the house cost, one will come who composes
   skilfully

than the market price. This tally, or ticket, was called tessera, it being four-square : it was made of a piece of wood, or of lead—hence Juvenal calls it vilis.

*175. *A most splendid reward.*]— Though they should get only a wheat-ticket for a fee, yet this is noble, in comparison of what they get by teaching rhetoric.

176. *Chrysogonus—Pollio.*] Rhetoric-masters, who read to their pupils the works of Theodorus Gadareus, an excellent orator, born at Gadara, a city of Syria, not far from Ascalon.

177. *The quality.*] The nobility, the rich fathers of the poor rhetorician's pupils.

—*Dividing.*] Scindens—dividing, taking to pieces, and thus opening and explaining the several parts.

—*Baths are at six hundred sestertia.*] Which they built for themselves, and maintained at a great expence. See Sat. i. l. 92. note.

—*A portico at more.*] They were still more expensive in their porticos, or covered ways, where they used to ride in rainy or dirty weather.

179. *Can he wait, &c.*] Should

these great people be forced to stay at home till fine weather, came, or else go out and splash themselves, and their fine horses with dirt ?

181. *Here rather, &c.*] To be sure he will use the portico, where not only he, but his very mules, are protected from having their feet soiled.

182. *Tall Numidian pillars.*] The room raised high on pillars of marble from Numidia, which was very elegant and expensive.

183. *A supper-room.*] A dining-room we should call it ; but cœnatio, among the Romans, signified a room to sup in, for their entertainments were always at supper.

—*Snatch the cool sun.*] The windows so contrived as to catch the sun in winter-time. The Romans were very curious in their contrivances of this sort. They had rooms toward the north-east, to avoid the summer sun ; and toward the south-west, to receive the sun in winter.

184. *Whatever the house cost.*]— They little regarded the expence they were at in building.

—*One will come, &c.*] They will be sure to have their tables sumptuously

Componit, veniet qui pulmentaria condit.   185
Hos inter sumptu, sestertia Quintiliano,
Ut multum, duo sufficient ; res nulla minoris
Constabit patri, quam filius.   Unde igitur tot
Quintilianus habet saltus ? exempla novorum
Fatorum transi : felix et pulcher et acer,   190
Felix et sapiens et nobilis et generosus,
Appositam nigræ lunam subtexit alutæ :
Felix, orator quoque maximus, et jaculator,
Et si prefixit, cantat bene.   Distat enim, quæ
Sidera te excipiant, modo primos incipientem   195
Edere vagitus, et adhuc a matre rubentem.
Si Fortuna volet, fies de rhetore consul.
Si volet hæc eadem, fies de consule rhetor.
Ventidius quid enim ? quid Tullius ? anne aliud quam
Sidus, et occulti miranda potentia fati ?   200
Servis regna dabunt, captivis fata triumphos.
Felix ille tamen, corvo quoque rarior albo.
Pœnituit multos vanæ sterilisque cathedræ,
Sicut Thrasymachi probat exitus, atque Secundi
Carrinatis ; et hunc inopem vidistis, Athenæ,   205

furnished by cooks, confectioners, &c.
Pulmentaria seems used here for victuals in general. ATNSW.
    186. *Amidst these expences, &c.*]—
Which they squander away in buildings, eating, and drinking, they
think two poor sestertia (about 15*l.*)
enough to pay Quintilian (the great
rhetorician) for teaching their children.
    187–8. *Will cost, a father less, &c.*]
They laid out their money with cheerfulness on their gluttony, &c. but
grudged ever so little expence for the
education of their children : therefore
nothing costs them so little.
    188–9. *Hath Quintilian, &c.*] If
these things be so, how comes Quintilian to have so large an estate, and to
be the owner of such a tract of country?
    189. *Examples of new fates, &c.*]
There is nothing to be said of men,
whose fortunes are so new and singular as this : they must not be mentioned as examples for others. As if
he had said, Who but Quintilian ever
grew rich by the cultivation of the
liberal arts ? It is quite a novelty.
The Romans called an unusual good
fortune, nova fata,

    190. *The fortunate is handsome,
&c.*] In these lines the poet is saying,
that, " luck is all ;" let a man be but
fortunate, and he will be reckoned
every thing else.
    —*Witty.*] Acer—sharp, as we say,
—acer ingenio.
    192. *The moon, &c.*] The hundred
patricians, first established by Romulus, were distinguished by the numeral letter C fixed on their shoes,
which, from its resemblance to an
half moon, was called luna. This
was continued down to later times, as
a mark of distinction among the patricians : they wore a sort of buskin
made of black leather. HOR. lib. i.
sat. vi. 27. By this line the poet
means to say, that the fortunate may
become senators and nobles. Aluta—
lit. tanned leather : by meton. any
thing made thereof ; hence a leather
shoe, or buskin. Mart. xii. 26. 9.
    193. *A dart-thrower.*] This is the
literal sense of jaculator : but we must
here suppose it to mean, one skilful in
throwing out, or darting, arguments—
i. e. a great disputant—l. 156.
    194. *There is a difference, &c.*]—

Dishes of meat, and one who seasons soups. 185
Amidst these expences, two sestertiums, as a great deal,
Will suffice for a Quintilian, No thing will cost a father
Less than a son. Whence, therefore, hath
Quintilian so many forests?—The examples of new fates
Pass over : the fortunate is handsome, and witty, 190
The fortunate is wise, and noble, and generous,
And subjoins the moon set upon his black shoe.
The fortunate is also a great orator, a dart-thrower,
And, if he be hoarse, sings well : for there is a difference what
Stars receive you, when you first begin 195
To send forth crying, and are yet red from your mother.
If Fortune please, you will from a rhetorician become a
　　consul :
If this same please, you will from a consul become a
　　rhetorician.
For what was Ventidius ? what Tullius ? was it other than
A star, and the wonderful power of hidden fate ? 200
The fates will give kingdoms to slaves, triumphs to captives.
Yet that fortunate person is also more rare than a white crow.
Many have repented the vain and barren chair,
As the exit of Thrasymachus proves, and of Secundus
Carrinas, and him whom poor you saw, O Athens, 205

The Romans were very superstitious, and thought that the fortune of their future life mainly depended on the stars, or constellations, which presided over their natal hour.

196. *Red from your mother.*] The skin of infants just born, is red, on account of its delicacy.

197. *From a rhetorician, &c.*] For instance, Cicero.

198. *This same.*] Fortune.

—*From a consul, &c.*] Valerius Licianus, who from being a senator, and consul, was obliged to turn rhetorician. PLIN. Ep. l. iv. ep. 11.

199. *Ventidius.*] Bassus, son of a bondwoman at Ascalon. He was first a carman, then a muleteer; afterwards, in one year, he was created prætor and consul.

—*Tullius.*] The sixth king of Rome, born of a captive.

199–200. *Other than a star.*] i. e. To what did these men owe their greatness, but to the stars which presided at their birth, and to the mysterious power of destiny ?

202. *More rare, &c.*] However, that same fortunate and happy man is rare to be met with.

203. *Many have repented, &c.*] Of the barren and beggarly employment of teaching rhetoric—which they did, sitting in a chair, desk, or pulpit.

204. *Thrasymachus.*] Who hanged himself. He was a rhetorician of Athens, born at Carthage.

204–5. *Secundus Carrinas.*] He came from Athens to Rome, and, declaiming against tyrants, was banished by Caligula.

205. *Him whom poor you saw, &c.*] Socrates, whom you saw, ungrateful Athenians! almost starving, and paid him nothing for his lectures, but the barbarous reward of cold hemlock, with which he was poisoned by the sentence of his judges. Hemlock has such a refrigerating power over the blood and juices, as to cause them to stagnate, and thus occasion death ; it is therefore reckoned among the cold poisons. The word *ausæ*, here, is very significant, to intimate the dar-

Nil præter gelidas ausæ conferre cicutas.
Di majorum umbris tenuem, et sine pondere terram,
Spirantesque crocos, et in urnâ perpetuum ver,
Qui præceptorem sancti voluere parentis
Esse loco.   Metuens virgæ jam grandis Achilles   210
Cantabat patriis in montibus: et cui non tunc
Eliceret risum citharœdi cauda magistri?
Sed Ruffum, atque alios cædit sua quæque juventus:
Ruffum, qui toties Ciceronem Allobroga dixit.
Quis gremio Enceladi, doctique Palæmonis affert   215
Quantum grammaticus meruit labor? et tamen ex hoc,
Quodcunque est, (minus est autem, quam rhetoris æra,)
Distipuli custos præmordet Acœnitus ipse,
Et qui dispensat, frangit sibi.   Cede, Palæmon,
Et patere inde aliquid decrescere, non aliter, quam   220
Institor hybernæ tegetis, niveique cadurci:

ing insolence and cruelty of the Athe-nians, who, to their own eternal in-famy, could reward such a man in such a manner.

207. *Grant, &c.*] This sentence is elliptical, and must be supplied with some verb to precede umbris, as give, grant, or the like.

—*Thin earth, &c.*] It was usual with the Romans to express their good wishes for the dead in the man-ner here mentioned, that the earth might lie light upon them.

Sit tibi terra levis, mollique tegaris arenâ. MARTIAL.

208. *Breathing crocuses.*] Breath-ing forth sweets. Crocus, lit. saffron; also the yellow chives in the midst of flowers. What we call a crocus blows early in the spring.

—*Perpetual spring, &c.*] May flow-ers be perpetually growing and bloom-ing, as in the spring of the year. They were fond of depositing the urns of their deceased friends among banks of flowers.

209. *Who would have a preceptor, &c.*] Who venerated their masters and teachers as if they were their parents; and esteemed them, as standing in the place of parents.

210. *Achilles, &c.*] The famous son of Thetis, when almost a man, was in great awe of his tutor Chiron the Centaur.

211. *Sang.*] Practised lessons in vocal and instrumental music under his tutor.

—*In his paternal mountains.*] The mountains of Thessaly, from whence came Peleus the father of Achilles.

212. *Would not the tail, &c.*] The upper part of Chiron was like a man, the lower like an horse. His figure must be ridiculous enough, with a man's head and an horse's tail, and would have been laughed at by most people; but Achilles had too much reverence for his master to make a joke of his figure, as more modern scholars would have done.

212. *Harper his master.*] Chiron is said to have taught music, as well as medicine and astronomy.

213. *But Ruffus, &c.*] Now, so far from the masters receiving veneration from their scholars, it is a common practice for the scholar to beat the master, as had been the case of Ruf-fus and others. So PLAUTUS, Bacch. iii. 3. 37. Puer septuennis pædagogo tabula dirumpit caput.

214. *Ruffus, &c.*] This Ruffus charged Cicero with writing barbarous Latin, like an Allobrogian, or Savoy-ard. Even this great grammarian could not obtain respect from his scholars.

215. *Who brings, &c.*] Who pays Enceladus a reward equal to his la-bours? He was a famous grammarian. Gremio here denotes a loose cavity, or hollow, formed by the doubling of the robe or garment.—*q. d.* A lap, into which things were put. Gr. κολπος. Comp. Luke vi. 38.

Daring to bestow nothing but cold hemlock.
Grant, ye gods, to the shades of our ancestors thin earth,
  and without weight,
And breathing crocuses, and perpetual spring upon their
  urn,
Who would have a preceptor to be in the place of a sacred
Parent. Achilles, now grown up, fearing the rod,   210
Sang in his paternal mountains; and from whom then,
Would not the tail of the harper his master have drawn
  forth laughter?
But Ruffus, and others, each of their own young men
  strike,
Ruffus, who so often called Cicero an Allobrogian.
Who brings to the lap of Enceladus, or of the learned
  Palæmon,   215
As much as grammatical labour has deserved? and yet
  from this,
Whatever it be, (but it is less than the money of the
  rhetorician,)
Accenitus himself, the keeper of the scholar, snips,
And he who manages, breaks off some for himself. Yield,
  Palæmon,
And suffer something to decrease from thence, not other-
  wise than   220
A dealer in winter-rug, and white blanket.

—*The learned Palæmon,*] Rhemnius Palæmon, a very learned and distinguished grammarian, but who was so conceited, as to say, that learning would live and die with him. See SUET. de Gramm. 23.

217. *Whatever it be, &c.*] After all, small as the pay of a grammarian may be, (which at the most is even smaller than that of a rhetorician) there are sad defalcations from it.

218. *Accenitus—the keeper, &c.*]— The Accenitus is a feigned name for some pedagogue, (Gr. παις, a boy, and αγω, to lead,) who was a sort of servant, that followed his young master, took care of his behaviour, and particularly attended him to his exercise, and to school.

He is properly called here, disci-puli custos. He insisted on having part of the poor grammarian's pay, as a perquisite. The word præmor-det is here peculiarly happy, and in-

timates that the pedagogue, who, perhaps, carried the pay, took a part of it before he delivered it to the master: like a person who is to give a piece of bread to another, and bites a piece off first for himself.

219. *He who manages, &c.*] Qui dispensat, i. e. dispensator, the steward, or housekeeper; either the one belonging to the grammarian, into whose hands the money is paid, and who retains some part of it for his wages, or the steward of the gentleman who pays it, retains a part of it by way of poundage, or perquisite, to him-self. Frangit.—metaph. from breaking something that was entire.

—*Yield, Falæmon, &c.*] Sub-mit to these abatements, and be glad to have something, though less than your due, as it fares with tradesmen who are willing to abate something in their price, rather than not sell their goods. See AINSW. *Institor.*

Dummodo non pereat, mediæ quod noctis ab horâ
Sedisti, quâ nemo faber, quâ nemo sederet,
Qui docet obliquo lanam deducere ferro:
Dummodo non pereat totidem olfecisse lucernas,   225
Quot stabant pueri, cum totus decolor esset
Flaccus, et hæreret nigro fuligo Maroni.
Rara tamen merces, quæ cognitione Tribuni
Non egeat.   Sed vos sævas imponite leges,
Ut præceptori verborum regula constet;   230
Ut legat historias, auctores noverit omnes,
Tanquam ungues digitosque suos ; ut forte rogatus
Dum petit aut thermas, aut Phœbi balnea, dicat
Nutricem Anchisæ, nomen, patriamque novercæ
Archemori : dicat quot Acestes vixerit annos,   235
Quot Siculus Phrygibus vini donaverit urnas.
Exigite, ut mores teneros ceu pollice ducat,
Ut si quis cerâ vultum facit : exigite, ut sit
Et pater ipsius cœtûs, ne turpia ludant,

222. *Let it not be lost, &c.*] Only take care to have something for your trouble; let not all your pains, which you have taken, be thrown away, in rising at midnight to teach your boys; a fatigue that no common mechanic would undergo.

224. *To draw out wool, &c.*] To comb wool, which they did, as we find by this passage, with a card having crooked teeth made of iron, like those now in use.

225. *To have smelt, &c.*] Let it not be for nothing that you have been half poisoned with the stink of as many lamps as you have boys standing round you to say their lessons before it is light, and therefore are each of them with a lamp in his hand to read by.

226-7. *Horace all discolour'd.*]—With the oil of the lamps, which the boys, through carelessness, let drop on their books.

227. *Black Virgil.*] Made black with the smoke of the lamps, which the boys held close to their books, when they were reading their lessons.

228. *Yet pay is rare, which, &c.*] Though little is left of the pay to the grammarian, after all the deductions above-mentioned; yet it is very rare

that they get any thing at all, unless they go to law for it. The tribune here means the judge who tried civil causes.

229. *But impose ye, &c.*] Though the poor grammarian labours under all these difficulties, be sure, you that send your sons to them, to impose all the task upon them that ye can: make no abatement in his qualifications : expect that he knows every rule of grammar.

231. *Read histories, &c.*] That he should be a good historian : that he should know all authors at his fingers' ends, ad unguem, as the saying is.

233. *The hot baths.*] There were thermæ, hot baths, in Rome, as well as cold baths, balnea ; to the former they went to sweat, in the other they washed. Now this poor grammarian was expected to be ready to answer any questions which were asked him, by people whom he met with, when he went either to the one or the other.

233. *Phœbus.*] The name of some bath-keeper.

234. *The nurse of Anchises.*] The poet here, perhaps, means to ridicule the absurd curiosity of Tiberius, who used to be often teasing the grammarians with silly and unedifying ques-

Only let it not be lost, that from the midnight hour
You have sat, in which no smith, in which nobody would
   sit,
Who teaches to draw out wool with the crooked iron :
Only let it not be lost to have smelt as many lamps   225
As boys were standing, when all discolour'd was
Horace, and soot stuck to black Virgil.
Yet pay is rare which may not want the cognizance
Of the Tribune.—But impose ye cruel laws,   229
That the rule of words should be clear to the preceptor :
That he should read histories, should know all authors
As well as his own nails and fingers ; that, by chance, being
   ask'd
While he is going to the hot baths, or the baths of Phœbus,
   he should tell
The nurse of Anchises, the name and country of the step-
   mother
Of Archemorus : should tell how many years Acestes lived :
How many urns of wine the Sicilian presented to the
   Phrygians.   236
Require, that he should form the tender manners as with
   his thumb,
As if one makes a face with wax : require, that he should
   be
Even a father of his flock, lest they should play base
   tricks ;

tions ; as, Who was Hecuba's mother ? What was the name of Achilles
when dressed in woman's clothes ?
What the Sirens sung ? and the like.
See Suet. in TIBERIO, cap. lxx.

Such foolish questions might be
asked the grammarian, when he met
with people at the baths ; and he was
bound to answer them, under peril of
being counted an ignoramus.

Caieta, the nurse of Æneas, is
mentioned, Æn. vii, 1–2 ; but there
is no mention of the nurse of Anchises : perhaps Juvenal means to ridicule the ignorance of the querist, as
mistaking Anchises for Æneas.

234–5. Of the step-mother of Archemorus.] For Anchemolus, (see
Æn. x. l. 389.) who seems here
meant ; but perhaps the querist may
be supposed to call it Archemorus.

235. Acestes.] Æn. i. 199 ; and
Æn. v. 73.

236. The Sicilian.] Meaning Acestes,
who was king of Sicily, of his giving
wine to the Trojans. See Æn. i. 199–
200.

237. Require.] Exigite, exact—
that, beside his teaching your children, (and, in order to that, he be
perfectly learned,) he also should
watch over their morals, and form
them with as much nicety, care, and
exactness, as if he were moulding a
face in wax with his fingers. Ducat
—metaph. taken from statuaries.
Comp. Virg. Æn. vi. l. 848.

239. A father of his flock.] Require also, that he should be as anxious, and as careful of his scholars, as
if he were their father.

Hæc, inquit, cures; sed cum se verterit annus,　　240
Accipe, victori populus quod postulat, aurum.

240. *When the year, &c.*] When the year comes round—at the end of the year.

241. *Accept a piece of gold.*] Aurum. The Roman aureus (according to Ainsw. Val. and Proportion of Roman coins) was about 1l. 0s. 9d. of our money: but, whatever the precise value of the aurum mentioned here might be, the poet evidently means to say, that the grammarian does not get more for a whole year's labour in teaching, and watching over a boy's morals, than a victorious fencer, or sword-player, gets by a single battle won upon the stage, viz. about 4l. (or rather about 5l.) of our money, which Marshal, after Vet. Schol. says, was the stated sum, and which was not to be exceeded.

241. *Which the people require.*]— When a fencer, or gladiator, came off victorious, the Roman people required the quinque aurei to be given to him by the prætor, tribune, or other person, who gave and presided at the show. This passage is, by some, referred to MART. lib. x. epigr.

These things, says he, take care of—but when the year turns
    itself,   240
Accept a piece of gold, which the people require for a
    conqueror.

74. where he mentions one Scorpus, a famous charioteer, who, by being victor in a chariot-race, carried off, in one hour's time, fifteen sacks full of gold. But this does not seem to agree with what Juvenal says of the gains of the poor grammarian, which the poet evidently supposes to be no more than the perquisite of a common gladiator that had come off conqueror: even this was five times as much as a lawyer got by a cause. Comp. l. 122.

Thus Juvenal concludes this Satire, having fully accomplished his purpose; which was to shew, by many instances, the shameful neglect of learning and science, as well as of the professors of them, which then prevailed among the nobility of Rome.

Satira Octava.

ARGUMENT.

In this Satire the Poet proves, that true nobility does not consist in statues and pedigrees, but in honourable and good actions. And, in opposition to persons nobly born,

STEMMATA quid faciunt? quid prodest, Pontice, longo
Sanguine censeri, pictosque ostendere vultus
Majorum, et stantes in curribus Æmilianos,
Et Curios jam dimidios, humeroque minorem
Corvinum, et Galbam auriculis nasoque carentem?   5
Quis fructus generis tabulâ jactare capaci
Corvinum, et post hunc multâ deducere virgâ
Fumosos equitum cum Dictatore Magistros,
Si coram Lepidis male vivitur? effigies quo
Tot bellatorum, si luditur alea pernox   10
Ante Numantinos? si dormire incipis ortu

Line 1. *What do pedigrees?*] i. e. Of what use or service are they, merely considered in themselves?

—*Ponticus.*] There was a famous heroic poet of this name, much acquainted with Propertius and Ovid: but the person here mentioned, to whom this Satire is addressed, was probably some man of quality, highly elevated by family pride, but whose manners disgraced his birth.

2. *By a long descent.*] Longo sanguine, a descent through a long train of ancestors of noble blood.

—*Painted countenances, &c.*] It was customary among the Romans to have their houses furnished with family pictures, images, &c. and it was no small part of the pride of the nobility.

3–4–5. *The Æmilii—Curii—Corvinus.*] Were noble Romans, the founders of illustrious families, and an honour to their country.

3. *Standing in chariots.*] Triumphal cars, as expressed in the triumphal statues.

4. *Now half.*] i. e. Half demolished by length of time.

4–5. *Less by a shoulder Corvinus.*] His statue thus mutilated by time and accident.

5. *Galba.*] The statue of Sergius Galba, a man of consular dignity, and who founded an illustrious family, was also defaced and mutilated by time.

6. *What fruit.*] i. e. Of what real, solid use can it be.

—*The capacious table.*] viz. A large genealogical table.

7. *By many a branch.*] The genealogical tables were described in the form of trees: the first founder of

Eighth Satire.

ARGUMENT.

who are a disgrace to their family, he displays the worth
of many who were meanly born, as Cicero, Marius, Serv.
Tullius, and the Decii.

WHAT do pedigrees? what avails it, Ponticus, to be
    valued
By a long descent, and to shew the painted countenances
Of ancestors, and Æmilii standing in chariots,
And Curii now half, and less by a shoulder
Corvinus, and Galba wanting ears and nose?   5
What fruit to boast of Corvinus in the capacious table
Of kindred, and after him to deduce, by many a branch,
Smoky masters of the knights, with a Dictator,
If before the Lepidi you live ill? whither (tend) the
    effigies
Of so many warriors, if the nightly die be played with   10
Before the Numantii? if you begin to sleep at the rising of

---

the family was the root, his immediate descendants the stem, and all the
collaterals from them were the
branches. So among us.

8. *Smoky masters of the knights.*]
Images of those who had been magistri equitum, masters or chiefs of
the order of knights, now tarnished,
and grown black, by the smoke of
the city.

—*With a dictator.*] An image of
some of the family who had filled that
office. He was chief magistrate a-
mong the Romans, vested with absolute power, and from whom lay no
appeal. Twenty-four axes were carried before him. He was never
chosen but in some great danger or
trouble of the state; and commonly

at the end of six months was to re-
sign his office.

9. *If before the Lepidi, &c.*] *i. e.*
If before the images of those great
men you exhibit scenes of vileness and
infamy?

10. *The nightly die, &c.*] Pernox
signifies that which lasts through the
night. What avails it, that your
room is furnished with busts, pictures, &c. of your noble ancestors,
if, in that very room, before their
faces, as it were, you are gambling
and playing all night at dice?

11. *If you begin to sleep, &c.*] If
you, after a night's debauch, are going to bed at day-break, the very time
when those great generals were setting forth on their march to attack
an enemy.

Luciferi, quo signa Duces et castra movebant?
Cur Allobrogicis, et magnâ gaudeat arâ,
Natus in Herculeo Fabius lare, si cupidus, si
Vanus, et Euganeâ quantumvis mollior agnâ?   15
Si tenerum attritus Catinensi pumice lumbum
Squallentes traducit avos: emptorque veneni
Frangendâ miseram funestat imagine gentem?
Tota licet veteres exornent undique ceræ
Atria, NOBILITAS SOLA EST ATQUE UNICA VIRTUS.   20
Paulus, vel Cossus, vel Drusus moribus esto:
Hos ante effigies majorum pone tuorum:
Præcedant ipsas illi, te consule, virgas.
Prima mihi debes animi bona.   Sanctus haberi,
Justitiæque tenax factis dictisque mereris?   25
Agnosco procerem: salve, Getulice, seu tu
Silanus, quocunque alio de sanguine rarus
Civis, et egregius patriæ contingis ovanti.
Exclamare libet, populus quod clamat Osiri

13. *Fabius, &c.*] Why should Fabius, the son of Qu. Fab. Maximus, who overcame the Allobroges, boast in his father's achievements, and in the origin of his family's descent from Hercules, the care of whose altar was hereditary in that family, if he be covetous and vain, and unworthy of the honour which he claims? This altar was built by Evander.

15. *Softer than an Euganean lamb.*] The sheep bred upon the Euganean downs had the finest and softest fleeces in all Italy. To have a very soft and delicate skin was a mark of great effeminacy; but more especially if, as the following line supposes, it was made so by art.

16. *Catinensian pumice.*] The best pumice stones were gathered in Sicily, at the foot of Mount Ætna; with these the effeminate Italians used to smooth their skins. Catina (now Catania) was a city near Mount Ætna, almost ruined by an earthquake, in 1693. Here were the finest pumice stones.

17. *He shames, &c.*] He dishonours the old and venerable pictures, or images, of his rough and hardy ancestors; now dirty with the rust of time, and thus disgraces the memory of those great men. Traduco signifies to expose to public shame. AINSW. No. 5.

18. *An image to be broken.*] If he should cast a sadness over the whole family, as it were, by having his own image placed among those of his ancestors, when he does such things as to deserve to have his image broken. If any one, who had an image of himself, was convicted of a grievous crime, his image was to be broken to pieces, and his name erased from the calendar, either by the sentence of the judge, or by the fury of the people. Comp. sat. x. l. 58. Such must, most likely, be the case of a man who dealt in poisons to destroy people.

19. *Old waxen figures.*] Images and likenesses of ancestors, made in wax, and set up as ornaments and memorials of the great persons from whom they were taken.

20. *Virtue, &c.*] All the ensigns of grandeur and nobility are nothing without this—it is this alone which stamps a real greatness upon all who possess it.

21. *Paulus.*] Æmilius, who conquered Perses king of Macedonia, and led him and his children in triumph: he was a man of great frugality and modesty.

—*Cossus.*] He conquered the Getulians, under Augustus Cæsar, hence was called Getulicus. See l. 26.

Lucifer, at which those generals were moving their standards
    and camps?
Why should Fabius, born in a Herculean family, rejoice
In the Allobroges, and the great altar, if covetous, if
Vain, and never so much softer than an Euganean lamb?
If, having rubb'd his tender loins with a Catinensian
    pumice,   16
He shames his dirty ancestors—and, a buyer of poison,
He saddens the miserable family with an image to be
    broken?
Tho' the old waxen figures should adorn the courts on all
    sides,
VIRTUE IS THE ONLY AND SINGLE NOBILITY.   20
Be thou in morals Paulus, or Cossus, or Drusus;
Put these before the effigies of your ancestors:
Let them, you being consul, precede the fasces themselves.
You owe me first the virtues of the mind—do you deserve
To be accounted honest, and tenacious of justice, in word
    and deed?   25
I acknowledge the nobleman:—Hail, Getulian!—or thou
Silanus, from whatever other blood, a rare, and
Choice citizen, thou befallest thy triumphing country.
We may exclaim, what the people call out to Osiris

—Drusus.] There were three of
this name, all of which deserved well
of the republic.
22. Put these before, &c.] Prefer
the examples of those good men before the statues of your family.
23. Let them, &c.] If ever you
should be consul, esteem them before
the fasces, and all the ensigns of your
high office.
24. You owe me, &c.] The ornaments—bona, the good qualities—
of the mind, are what I first insist
upon; these I expect to find in you,
before I allow you to be indeed noble.
25. Honest.] Sanctus is an extensive word, and here may include
piety to the gods, as well as justice,
honesty, and truth towards men. See
sat. iii. 126.
26. I acknowledge, &c.] I then acknowledge you as a man of quality.
—Hail, Getulian!] I salute you as
if you were Cossus, the conqueror of
Getulia—hence called Getulicus, l.
21. note.
—Or thou, &c.] Silanus was a no-

ble Roman, who conquered Magon
the Carthaginian general, took Han-
non, another commander, prisoner,
and did other great services to his
country.
q. d. If, besides your personal private virtues; (l. 24-5.) you shew
yourself a rare and choice citizen,
eminently serviceable and useful to
your country, like Silanus of old,
from whatever blood you may derive
your pedigree, however mean it may
be, yet your country will rejoice that
such a man has fallen to its lot—and
exclaim, as the Egyptians did, when
they found Osiris.
29. Osiris, &c.] The chief deity of
Egypt, which the Egyptians worshipped under the form of a bull, or
ox. This said bull was supposed to
be inhabited by Osiris: but they used,
once in a few years, to put this bull
to death, and then go, with their
priests, howling, and making lamentations, in search of another Osiris,
or Apis, with the same exact marks
as the former had; which, when they

Invento: quis enim generosum dixerit hunc, qui　　　30
Indignus genere, et præclaro nomine tantum
Insignis? nanum cujusdam Atlanta vocamus:
Æthiopem cygnum: parvam extortamque puellam,
Europen : canibus pigris, scabieque vetustâ
Lævibus, et siccæ lambentibus ora lucernæ,　　　35
Nomen erit pardus, tigris, leo; si quid adhuc est,
Quod fremat in terris violentius.　Ergo cavebis,
Et metues, ne tu sic Creticus, aut Camerinus.
　His ego quem monui? tecum est mihi sermo, Rubelli
Plaute : tumes alto Drusorum sanguine, tanquam　　　40
Feceris ipse aliquid, propter quod nobilis esses ;
Ut te conciperet, quæ sanguine fulget Iüli,
Non quæ ventoso conducta sub aggere texit.
Vos humiles, inquis, vulgi pars ultima nostri,
Quorum nemo queat patriam monstrare parentis :　　　45.
Ast ego Cecropides.　Vivas, et originis hujus
Gaudia longa feras: tamen imâ ex plebe Quiritem

—Licking the mouths, &c.] So hungry and starved as to lick the stinking oil off the edges of lamps. Giving the titles of nobility, and calling those noble who are, by their evil manners, and bad actions, a disgrace to their families, is calling a dwarf, a giant; a blackmoor, a fine white swan; a crooked deformed wench, Europa : we may as well call a pack of mangy, worthless hounds, tigers, leopards, and lions ; or by the name of nobler beasts, if nobler can be found.

37. *Beware, &c.*] Cavebis—metues —lit. you will be cautious, and will fear, lest the world flatter you with the mock titles of Creticus and Camerinus in the same way.

Publ. Sulpitius Camerinus was an illustrious and virtuous Roman, who was sent by the senate, with Posthumius and Manlius, to Athens, to copy the laws of Solon, as well as those of other cities. See sat. vii. l. 90.

39. *By these things.*] By what I have been saying.

40. *Rubellius Plautus.*] Some read Plancus, others Blandus; but Plautus seems to be right. Rubellius Blandus was his father, who married Julia the daughter of Drusus, son of Livia, wife of Augustus.

Ευρηκαμεν ! Ευρηκαμεν ! we have found him ! we have found him ! Συγχαιρωμεν ! let us rejoice together!

31. *An illustrious name.*] Or title, derived from some great and illustrious ancestor.

32. *The dwarf of some one.*] The people of quality used to keep dwarfs for their amusement.

—Atlas.] A high hill in Mauritania, so high that the poets make a person of it, and feign that he was the brother of Prometheus, and turned into this mountain by Perseus, at the sight of the gorgon's head. From its height it was fabled to support the celestial globe. See VIRG. Æn. iv. l. 481–2.

33. *An Ethiopian—a swan.*] i. e. Black white.

34. *Europa.*] The beautiful daughter of Agenor, king of the Phœnicians, whom Jupiter in the form of a bull carried into Crete. From her the quarter of the globe, called Europe, is said to take its name. See HOR. lib. iii. od. xxvii. l. 75–6.

—Slow dogs.] Slow hounds that are unfit for the chace.

35. *Smooth.*] Having all their hair eaten off by the mange.

When found.—But who would call him noble, who is   30
Unworthy his race, and for an illustrious name only
Remarkable? We call the dwarf of some one, Atlas:
An Ethiopian, a swan: a little and deformed wench,
Europa: to slow dogs, and with an old mange
Smooth, and licking the mouths of a dry lamp,   35
The name of lion, leopard, tiger shall belong; and if there
    be yet
Any thing on earth that rages more violently. Therefore
    beware,
And dread, lest thou should'st thus be Creticus, or Came-
    rinus.
    Whom have I admonished by these things? with thee is
    my discourse,
Rubellius Plautus: you swell with the high blood of the
    Drusi, as if   40
You yourself had done something, for which you should be
    noble;
That she should have conceived you, who shines with the
    blood of Iülus,
Not she who, being hired, has woven under the windy mount.
"Ye are low," say you, "the last part of our common
    "people;
"Of whom none can shew the country of his parent: 45
"But I am a Cecropian."—May you live—and long enjoy
    the happiness
Of this origin: yet, from the lowest of the people, an elo-
    quent Roman

—Of the Drusi.] You are very
proud of your descent on your mother's
side. Compare the preceding note.
41. Done something, &c.] As if
you yourself had done something to
make you illustrious, and deserving
the honour of a mother of the Julian
line.
43. Not she, &c.] Instead of being
the son of some poor creature who
knitted stockings for her bread under
the town wall. The agger, here mentioned, is the mount raised by Tarquin, for the defence of the city, a
place much resorted to by low people. Ventoso merely signifies lofty,
thus Homer says " the windy Ilion."
Il. iii. l. 305.
Some read sub acre, i. e. sub dio—
in the open air.

44. The last part, &c.] The very
dregs of our plebeians.
45. Of whom none, &c.] Of such
obscure parentage, as to be unable to
trace out the birth-place of your
parents.
46. I am a Cecropian.] Descended
from Cecrops, the first king of Athens.
This is an insolent speech, which
some proud noble is supposed to make
in scorn and derision of those whom
he thought his inferiors.
—May you live, &c.]. Sir, I wish
you much joy of your noble descent.
Ironically spoken. Viva! as the Italians say.
47. Yet, from the lowest, &c.]—
Much as you despise them, there
have been men of the highest talents
and abilities from among them, some

T

Facundum invenies : solet hic defendere causas
Nobilis indocti : veniet de plebe togatâ, .
Qui juris nodos, et legum ænigmata, solvat.   50
Hic petit Euphraten juvenis, domitique Batavi
Custodes aquilas, armis industrius : at tu
Nil nisi Cecropides, truncoque simillimus Hermæ :
Nullo quippe alio vincis discrimine, quam quod
Illi marmoreum caput est, tua vivit imago.   55
Dic mihi, Teucrorum proles, animalia muta
Quis generosa putet, nisi fortia ?´ nempe volucrem
Sic laudamus equum, facilis cui plurima palma
Fervet, et exultat rauco victoria circo.
Nobilis hic, quocunque venit de gramine, cujus   60
Clara fuga ante alios, et primus in æquore pulvis.
Sed venale pecus Corythæ, posteritas et.—
Hirpini, si rara jugo victoria sedit.
Nil ibi majorum respectus, gratia nulla
Umbrarum ; dominos pretiis mutare jubentur   65
Exiguis, tritoque trahunt epirhedia collo

who have defended the causes of ignorant nobles, when they themselves
could not have defended them.

49. *The gowned people.*] i. e. The
common people, called togati, from
the gowns which they wore. See. sat.
i. l. 3, and note.

50. *Who can untie, &c.*] Some
great and eminent lawyer, able to
solve all the difficulties, and unfold
all the perplexities of jurisprudence.

51. *Seeks the Euphrates, &c.*] Another goes into the East, and distin-
guishes himself as a soldier.

—*Conquer'd Batavus.*] The Batavi,
or Hollanders, conquered by Domitian when a youth.

52. *The guardian eagles.*] The eagles mean the Roman troops, which
had the figures of eagles on their
standards, and were set to keep the
newly conquered Batavi from re-
volting.

Another of the common people dis-
tinguishes himself as a useful person
to his country, by joining the troops
that were sent on this occasion.

53. *But a Cecropian.*] As for you,
when you have called yourself a Cecropian, you have no more to say ;
and this most properly belongs to
you, from your resemblance to one

of the Hermæ at Athens, that is
made of marble ; so, in point of insensibility, are you : that has neither
hands nor feet ; no more have you,
in point of usefulness, to your country, yourself, or to any body else.

—*A mutilated Herma.*] Herma-æ
signifies a statue of Hermes, or Mercury. Mercury was called Hermes,
from Gr. ερμηνευω, to interpret ; because he was the supposed inventor
of speech, by which men interpret
their thoughts to each other. See
Hor. lib. i. ode x. l. 1–3.

It was a piece of religion at Athens,
to have a figure of Mercury fixed up
against their houses, of a cubic form,
without hands or feet ; this was called
Herma. The poet, therefore, humourously compares this Rubellius Plautus, who boasted of his descent from
Cecrops, and therefore called himself
a Cecropian, to the useless figures of
Mercury, which were set up at
Athens, or, perhaps, to the posts on
which they stood. In this sense he
might call himself Cecropian.

54. *You excel.*] You have no preference before him in point of utility
to your country, or in any thing else,
than that you are a living statue, and
he a dead one.

You will find : this is used to defend the cause of an
Unlearned nobleman : there will come from the gowned
    people
Another, who can untie the knots of right, and the riddles
    of the laws.   50
This youth seeks the Euphrates, and of conquer'd Batavus
The guardian eagles, industrious in arms ; but thou
Art nothing but a Cecropian, and most like to a mutilated
    Herma ;
For you excel by no other difference, than that
He has a marble head, your image lives.   55
Tell me, thou offspring of the Trojans, who thinks dumb
    animals
Noble, unless strong ? for thus a swift
Horse we praise, for whom many a kind hand
Glows, and victory exults in the hoarse circus.
He is noble, from whatever pasture he comes, whose flight
Is famous before the others, and whose dust is first on the
    plain.   61
But the cattle of Corytha are set to sale, and the posterity of
Hirpinus, if victory seldom sits on their yoke.
There is no respect of ancestors, no favour
Of shades; they are commanded to change their masters 65
For small prices, and draw waggons with a worn neck,

56. *Thou offspring of the Trojans.*]
Meaning Rub. Plautus, who, though
he boasted himself of being descended from Cecrops the first king of
Athens, and who is supposed to have
lived before Deucalion's flood, yet
likewise might boast, that he was
also descended from ancestors, who
derived their blood, in later times,
from the Trojans who first settled in
Italy.

Some think that we may read this,
Ye Trojans, meaning the chief people of Rome in general, who prided
themselves on their descent from the
Trojans, and to whom he may be
supposed to address himself. Comp.
sat. i. 86. where he calls them Trojugenas. But see l. 71. post.

57. *Strong.*] Fortia—vigorous, cou-
rageous; fit for the purposes for which
they are wanted.

58. *Many a kind hand, &c.*] They
used to clap their hands, in token of
applause, at the public shows and
sports.

59. *The hoarse circus.*] i. e. The
people in the circus, hoarse with their
applauding acclamations.

60. *From whatever pasture.*] Lit.
grass—q. d. wherever bred.

61. *Whose dust is first, &c.*] Who
keeps before the others, so that the
first dust must be raised by him.

62. *The cattle of Corytha.*] The
breed, or stock, of a famous mare,
so called, are sold.

63. *Hirpinus.*] A famous horse, so
called from the place where he was
bred, being a hill in the country of
the Sabines.

—*If victory, &c.*] If they seldom win in the chariot race.

65. *Of shades.*] No regard to the
ghosts of their departed ancestors.

—*To change their masters, &c.*]—
Their present master disposes of
them very cheaply to others.

66. *With a worn neck.*] They are
put into teams, and the hair is all
worn off their necks, which are
galled with the harness with which

Segnipedes, dignique molani versare Nepotis.
Ergo ut miremur te, non tua, primum aliquid da,
Quod possim titulis incidere præter honores,
Quos illis damus, et dedimus, quibus omnia debes.   70
   Hæc satis ad juvenem, quem nobis fama superbum
Tradit, et inflatum, plenumque Nerone propinquo.
Rarus enim ferme sensus communis in illâ
Fortunâ. Sed te censeri laude tuorum,
Pontice, noluerim, sic ut nihil ipse futuræ   75
Laudis agas: MISERUM EST ALIENÆ INCUMBERE FAMÆ,
Ne collapsa ruant subductis tecta columnis.
Stratus humi palmes viduas desiderat ulmos.
Esto bonus miles, tutor bonus, arbiter idem
Integer: ambiguæ si quando citabere testis   80
Incertæque rei, Phalaris licet imperet ut sis
Falsus, et admoto dictet perjuria tauro,
SUMMUM CREDE NEFAS ANIMAM PRÆFERRE PUDORI,
Et propter vitam vivendi perdere causas.

---

they are fastened to the carriage. See *Epirhedium.* AINSW.

67. *Of Nepos.*] The name of some miller) who ground corn in horse-mills.

68. *Admire you, not yours, &c.*]— That we may admire you personally for your own sake, and not merely for your family, or fortune, or title.

—*Shew something, &c.*] Give us some proof, by some noble and worthy actions, of true nobility, which, besides your high titles, may be recorded with honour to yourself.

70. *Which we give, &c.*] i. e. To your ancestors, to whom, as things are at present, you stand solely indebted for every mark of respect that is bestowed upon you.

71. *To the youth, &c.*] q. d. So much for Rubellius Plautus, a youth (as fame represents him, &c.)

72. *His kinsman Nero.*] His relationship to Nero. Comp. note on l. 40.

73. *Rare, &c.*] Very seldom found in such a situation of life.

75: *Ponticus, &c.*] See l. 1. of this Sat. and note.

The poet tells the person to whom he addresses this Satire, that he should be sorry to have him esteemed merely on account of his ancestors.

76. *Nothing of future praise.*]— That he should do nothing himself, in order to raise his own character in times to come.

77. *Lest the house fallen, &c.*]— Metaph. i. e. lest, like a building which tumbles into ruins, when the pillars which support it are removed, so you, if you have no other support to your character, than what your ancestors have done, if this be once put out of the question, should fall into contempt.

78. *The vine, &c.*] If you owe the support of your fame entirely to that of others, let that be removed, and you will be like a vine which wants the support of an elm to keep it from crawling along the ground.

They used to fasten up their vines, by tying them to the trunks of elm-trees. See VIRG. Georg. l. l. 2.

If by any accident the vines broke from the trees, and lay upon the ground, they called the trees *viduas ulmos,* alluding to their having lost the embraces of the vine, as a widow those of her husband when he dies.

79. *A good soldier.*] Serve your country in the army.

—*A faithful tutor.*] Quasi tuitor —a trusty guardian to some minor, having the charge of his person and

Slow of foot, and worthy to turn the mill of Nepos.
Therefore that we may admire you, not yours, first shew
    something,
Which I may inscribe among your titles besides your
    honours,
Which we give, and have given, to them to whom you owe
    all.   70
    These things are enough to the youth, whom fame de-
      livers to us
Proud, and puffed up, and full of his kinsman Nero.
For common sense is, for the most part, rare in that
Condition. But to have thee esteemed from the praise of
    your ancestors,
Ponticus, I should be unwilling, so as that yourself should
    do   75
Nothing of future praise: 'TIS MISERABLE TO REST ON
    ANOTHER'S FAME,
Lest the house fallen, by the pillars being taken away,
    should tumble into ruins.
The vine strow'd on the ground wants the widow'd elms.
Be you a good soldier, a faithful tutor, an uncorrupted
Umpire also: if you are summoned as a witness in a doubt-
    ful   80
And uncertain thing, though Phalaris should command that
    you
Should be false, and should dictate perjuries with the bull
    brought to you,
BELIEVE IT THE HIGHEST IMPIETY TO PREFER LIFE TO
    REPUTATION,
And, for the sake of life, to lose the causes of living.

affairs, till he comes of age to manage for himself.

79-80. *An uncorrupted umpire.*]—When called upon to decide a cause by your arbitration, distinguish yourself by the utmost impartiality.

80. *A witness, &c.*] If called upon as a witness in some dark and difficult matter, let your testimony be true, fair, and unbiassed.

81. *Phalaris, &c.*] One of the most cruel of all the Sicilian tyrants; he had a brazen bull, in which he enclosed people, and burnt them to death.

Though this tyrant were to bring his bull, and threaten to put you to death, by burning you alive, if you would not speak falsely, yet let not even this make you deviate from the truth.

83. *The highest impiety, &c.*]—Esteem it a crime of the deepest dye to value your life, so as to preserve it in a dishonourable way, at the expence of your reputation and honour. *Pudor*—fame, reputation.—AINSW.

84. *To lose, &c.*] i. e. The only causes which make life valuable, the purposes for which it was ordained, and for which it should be desirable, honour, truth, and surviving fame.

Dignus morte perit, cœnet licet ostrea centum   85
Gaurana, et Cosmi toto mergatur aheno.
    Expectata diu tandem provincia cum te
Rectorem accipiet, pone iræ frœna, modumque
Pone et avaritiæ : miserere inopum sociorum.
Ossa vides regum vacuis exhausta medullis.   90
Respice, quid moneant leges, quid curia mandet ;
Præmia quanta bonos maneant ; quam fulmine justo
Et Capito et Tutor ruerint, damnante senatu,
Piratæ Cilicum : sed quid damnatio confert,
Cum Pansa eripiat quicquid tibi Natta reliquit ?   95
Præconem, Chærippe, tuis circumspice pannis,
Jamque tace : furor est post omnia perdere naulum.
Non idem gemitus olim, nec vulnus erat par
Damnorum, sociis florentibus, et modo victis.
Plena domus tunc omnis, et ingens stabat acervus   100

---

85. *He perishes, &c.*] Such a wretch, who would prefer his safety to his innocence, deserves to perish utterly, and, when he dies, to have his memory perish with him, however sumptuously he may have lived.

86. *Gaurane oysters.*] Lucrine oysters, taken about the port at Baiæ, near the mountain Gaurus, in Campania.

—*Immersed, &c.*] The Romans gave particular names to particular perfumed ointments ; sometimes they named them after the country from whence they came, sometimes (as probably here) after the name of the confectioner, or perfumer, who prepared them. They had an ungentum Cosmianum, so called from one Cosmus, who, by boiling various aromatics together, produced his famous ointment. The poet here means, that, if the person spoken of were not to anoint himself, as others, but could afford to purchase, and dip himself in a whole kettle full at once of this rare perfume, yet his name would deservedly rot with his carcase. It is not living sumptuously, but living well, that gives reputation after death.

87. *The province, &c.*] He now advises Ponticus as to his behaviour towards the people he is to govern, when in possession of the government of one of the conquered provinces, which he had long expected.

88. *Put checks, &c.*] Frœna—literally, bridles. *q. d.* Bridle your anger, keep your passion within proper bounds.

89. *Put to covetousness.*] Restrain your avarice, set bounds to your desires.

—*The poor associates.*] The poor people who have been reduced by conquest, and now become the allies of the Romans.

90. *The bones of kings, &c.*] *i. e.* You see some of the kings, which we conquered, unmercifully squeezed, and the very marrow, as it were, sucked out of their bones. Ossa vacuis medullis—*i. e.* ossa vacua a medullis, Hypallage.

91. *The state.*] Curia literally signifies a court, more especially where the senate or council assembled : here (by metonym.) it may stand for the senate itself—Curia pro senatu—Campus pro comitiis—Toga pro pace, &c. appellatur. Cic. de Orat. iii. 42. It was usual for the senate to give a charge to new governors, on their departure to the provinces over which they were appointed.

92. *How just a stroke.*] How justly they were punished by a decree of the senate, which fell on them like a thunderbolt.

He perishes worthy of death, though he should sup on an
 hundred   85
Gaurane oysters, and should be immersed in the whole cal-
 dron of Cosmus.
 When at length the province, long expected, shall receive
  you
Governor, put checks to anger, and measure also
Put to covetousness: pity the poor associates.   89
You see the bones of kings exhausted, with empty marrow:
Regard what the laws may admonish, what the state com-
 mand;
How great rewards may await the good; with how just a
 stroke
Both Capito and Tutor fell; the senate condemning,
The robbers of the Cilicians: but what does condemnation
 avail,
When Pansa can seize whatever Natta left you? 95
Look about for a crier, Chærippus, for your rags,
And now be silent: it is madness, after all, to lose your
 freight.
There were not the same complaints formerly, nor was the
 wound of
Losses equal, when our associates flourished, and were just
 conquer'd.
Then every house was full, and there was standing a great
 heap   100

94. *Robbers of the Cilicians.*] Cos-sutianus Capito, and Julius Tutor, had been successively prefects, or governors, of Cilicia, and both recalled and condemned by the senate for peculation and extortion.

95. *Pansa can seize, &c.*] Where is the use of making examples of wicked governors, when, if you punish one, his successor will still seize on all he left behind him, and thus complete the ruin which he began.

96. *Chærippus.*] He introduces Chærippus, a subject of this plundered province, whom he advises to make a sale of his clothes, and the rest of his poor rags, which he had left, before the successor comes with a fresh appetite, and devours all, supposing that if he turned what he had into money, it might be better concealed.

97. *Be silent.*] Say nothing of the money, for fear the new governor should seize it.

—*Your freight.*] Naulum signifies the freight, or fare, paid for a passage over the sea in a ship. The poet seems here to mean, that it would be no better than madness, to let the governor know of the money which the goods sold for; for, by these means, even this would be seized, and the poor sufferer not have enough left to pay his passage to Rome, in order to lodge his complaint before the senate, against the oppressor.

98–9. *The wound of losses, &c.*]— The hurt or damage received by the rapine of governors, with respect to the property of individuals.

99. *Associates.*] Sociis. The conquered provinces were allied with the Romans, and called socii.

100. *Every house was full.*] i. e. Of valuable things, as well as of large

Nummorum, Spartana chlamys, conchylia Coa,
Et cum Parrhasii tabulis, signisque Myronis,
Phidiacum vivebat ebur, nec non Polycleti.
Multus ubique labor : raræ sine Mentore mensæ.
Inde Dolabella est, atque hinc Antonius, inde   105
Sacrilegus Verres. Referebant navibus altis
Occulta spolia, et plures de pace triumphos.
Nunc sociis juga pauca boum, et grex parvus equarum ;
Et pater armenti capto eripietur agello :
Ipsi deinde Lares, si quod spectabile signum,   110
Si quis in ædiculâ Deus unicus : hæc etenim sunt
Pro summis : nam sunt hæc maxima. Despicias tu
Forsitan imbelles Rhodios, unctamque Corinthum :
Despicias merito : quid resinata juventus,
Cruraque totius facient tibi lævia gentis ?   115

sums of money, which the conquerers left untouched.

101. *A Spartan cloak.*] A garment richly dyed with the purple of the murex taken on the shore of Laconia, a country of Peloponnesus, the chief city of which was Sparta.

101. *Purples of Cos.*] Cos, or Coos, was an island of the Ægean sea, near which the fish, from whence the purple dye was taken, was also found. Sat. iii. l. 81, note.

102. *Parrhasius.*] A famous painter of Greece, who contended with Zeuxis, and gained the prize. See Hor. ode viii. lib. iv, l. 6.

—*Myron.*] An excellent statuary, whose works were in high esteem, especially his brazen cow, which exercised the pens both of the Greek and Roman poets. Ut similis veræ vacca Myronis opus. Ov. è Pont. iv. l. 34.

103. *Phidias.*] A famous painter and statuary : he is here said to have wrought so curiously in ivory, that his figures seemed to be alive. See also AINSW. *Phidias.*

104. *Polycletus.*] A Sicyonian, a famous statuary and sculptor. There were many of his works among this collection.

—*Mentor.*] A noble artist in chasing and embossing plate. We are to understand here, that there were few tables, *i. e.* entertainments, where, in the courses and services of the table, there were not some cups,

dishes, plates, &c. of Mentor's workmanship.

All these fine ornaments were permitted to remain in the houses of the owners by their first conquerors ; but the avarice and rapine of the governors who succeeded, stripped them of all.

105. *Thence.*] These things left by the conquerors proved a source of rapine and plunder to the prefects who succeeded.

—*Dolabella.*] A proconsul of Asia, accused by Scaurus, and condemned, for plundering the province over which he presided.

—*Antony.*] C. Antonius, a proconsul of Achaia, likewise condemned for plundering the province.

106. *Sacrilegious Verres.*] The plunderer of Sicily, who spared not even sacred things. The province prosecuted him, and, Tully undertaking the cause, he was condemned and banished. Vid. Cic. in Verrem.

107. *Hidden spoils.*] Which they kept, as much as they could, from public view ; not daring to expose them, as was usual by fair conquerors in their triumphs.

—*More triumphs, &c.*] Than others did from war. *q. d.* They got a greater booty, by stripping the poor associates, now at peace, and in amity with Rome, than the conquerors of them did, when they subdued them by open war.

Of money, a Spartan cloak, purples of Cos,
And with pictures of Parrhasius, statues of Myron,
The ivory of Phidias was living, also every where
Much of the labour of Polycletus: few tables without
   Mentor.
Thence is Dolabella, and thence Antony, thence   105
The sacrilegious Verres: they brought in lofty ships
Hidden spoils, and more triumphs from peace.
Now the associates have a few yokes of oxen, and a small
   herd of mares.
And the father of the herd will be taken away from the
   captured field.
Then the very household gods, if any remarkable image,
If any one single god be in the small shrine. But these
   (crimes) are   111
For chiefs, for these are the greatest.—You may despise,
Perhaps, the weak Rhodians, and anointed Corinth:
You may deservedly despise them: what can an effeminated
   youth
And the smooth legs of a whole nation do to you?   115

109. *The father of the herd, &c.*]
Mr. Stepney, in his poetical translation of this passage, has well expressed the sense of it; viz.

   ——*our confederates, now,*
Have nothing left but oxen for the
   plough,
Or some few mares reserv'd alone
   for breed;
Yet, lest this provident design
   succeed,
They drive the father of the herd
   away,
Making both stallion and his pas-
   ture prey.

110. *The very household gods, &c.*]
These plunderers of the provinces
are so merciless and rapacious, that
they refrain not even from the lares,
or little images, of those tutelar deities which were placed in people's
houses; and, particularly, if any of
these struck their fancy, as a handsome, well-wrought image—spectabile signum. Nay, though there were
but one single image, they would
take even that. See AINSW. *Lar.*

112. *For chiefs.*] Pro summis, i. e.
viris. q. d. These sacrilegious depre-
dations are for Roman chiefs to commit, because they are the most enor-

mous (maxima, the greatest) crimes
of all—(scelera understood)—such as
no others would be guilty of.

   Other senses are given to this passage; but the above seems best to
agree with the poet's satire on the
Roman chiefs, who plundered the
conquered provinces after their alliance with Rome.

113. *The weak Rhodians.*] A people infected with sloth and effeminacy.

   —*Anointed Corinth.*] So called
from its luxury and use of perfumed
ointments, a sure sign of great effeminacy.

   You may safely, and indeed with
good reason, despise such people as
these; for you have nothing to fear,
either from their resistance, or from
their revenge.

114. *An effeminated youth.*] A race
of youth, or young men, wholly sunk
into effeminacy. Resinata juventus
—literally, the youth (of Corinth)
who are resined—i. e. bedaubed all
over with perfumes and essences of
aromatic resins or gums. See AINSW.
Resinatus.

115. *Smooth legs, &c.*] It was customary for the delicate young men to

U

Horrida vitanda est Hispania, Gallicus axis,
Illyricumque latus.   Parce et messoribus illis,
Qui saturant urbem, circo, scenæque vacantem.
Quanta autem inde feres tam diræ præmia culpæ,
Cum tenues nuper Marius discinxerit Afros ?   120
Curandum imprimis, ne magna injuria fiat
Fortibus et miseris, tollas licet omne quod usquam est
Auri atque argenti ; scutum gladiumque relinques,
Et jacula, et galeam ; spoliatis arma supersunt.
Quod modo proposui, non est sententia ; verum   125
Credite me vobis folium recitare Sibyllæ,
    Si tibi sancta cohors comitum ; si nemo tribunal
Vendit acersecomes ; si nullum in conjuge crimen ;
Nec per conventus, et cuncta per oppida curvis
Unguibus ire parat nummos raptura Celæno ;   130
Tunc licet a Pico numeres genus ; altaque si te
Nomina delectent, omnem Titanida pugnam

remove, as much as possible, the
hair which grew on their limbs. The
poet here means, that an oppressive
governor could have nothing to fear
from such people as these, who could
not have spirit, or courage enough,
to attempt any resistance.

116. *Rough Spain.*] Then a hardy
and brave people, who would not
tamely submit to injuries done them
by the Roman prefects. ·

—*Gallic axis.*] The Gauls fought
from chariots.

117. *The coast of Illyria,*] Latus—
lit. the side. The Illyrians inhabited
the right side of the Adriatic gulph,
including Dalmatia and Sclavonia ; a
hardy race of people. Their country
was over against Italy.

—*Those reapers, &c.*] Meaning the
people of Africa, who supplied Rome
with corn.

118. *The city.*] Rome.

—*Intent, &c.*] Vacantem—empty
of all other employment, and mind-
ing nothing else but the public diversions of the circus, and of the
theatres.

119. *How great rewards, &c.*] But
suppose you oppress the poor Africans,
what can you get by it.

120. *Marius.*] Priscus, who being
pro-consul of Africa, pillaged the
people of the province, for which he

was condemned and banished. See
Sat. i. 139.

—*Stripp'd.*] Discinxerit—lit. un-
girded ; a metaphorical expression,
alluding to the act of those who take
away the garments of others, and
who begin by loosening the girdle by
which they are fastened.

122. *The brave and miserable, &c.*]
Beware of provoking such by any un-
warrantable oppression ; they will
certainly find some way to revenge
themselves. Though you pillage them
of all their money and goods, yet remember they have arms left, with
which they can revenge their wrong.

—*Entirely.*] Omne quod usquam ;
lit. every thing which (is) any where.

126. *Leaf of a Sibyl.*] The Sibyls
were supposed to be inspired with
knowledge of future events, which
came to pass as they foretold. See
sat. iii. l. 3, and note.

Do not think, says Juvenal, that I
am here giving you a mere random
opinion of my own—no ; what 1 say
is as true as an oracle, as fixed as fate
itself, and will certainly come to pass ;
therefore regard it accordingly.

127. *A virtuous set, &c.*] Cohors
here signifies cohors prætoria, those
that accompanied the magistrate who
went into a province. See AINSW.
Cohors, No. 5.—*q. d.* If the persons

Rough Spain is to be avoided, the Gallic axis,
And the coast of Illyria: spare also those reapers
Who supply the city, intent upon the circus, and the
　　theatre.
But how great rewards of so dire a crime will you bring
　　from thence,
Since Marius has lately stripp'd the slender Africans? 120
First care is to be taken, lest great injury be done
To the brave and miserable; though you may take away
　　entirely every thing.
Of gold and silver, you will leave the shield and sword,
And darts, and helmet:—arms remain to the plunder'd.
What I have now proposed is not a mere opinion, but 125
Believe me to recite, to you a leaf of a Sibyl.

If you have a virtuous set of attendants; if no favourite
Sells your seat of judgment; if no crime be in your wife;
Nor through the districts, and through the towns, with
　　crooked
Talons, does she, a Celæno, contrive to go to seize money;
Then, you may reckon your lineage from Picus, and, if
　　high names　　　　　　　　　　　　　　　131
Delight you, you may place the whole Titanian battle,

of your retinue, who attend you as your officers, and ministers within your province, are virtuous and good. —*If no favourite, &c.*] Acersecomes was an epithet of Apollo, (Gr. ακιροτικομης, intonsus,) and was transferred to the smooth-faced boys, which great men kept among their attendants.

These favourites had great interest and influence with their masters, and people used to give them bribes to obtain their interference with the prefect when he sat in judgment, so as to incline him to favour their friends in his decisions.

128. *No crime be in your wife.*] It was too frequent for the governors of the provinces to be influenced by their wives in their determinations of causes.

129. *Districts.*] See AINSW. Conventus, No. 3. It being put here with oppida, seems to mean those districts into which the provinces were divided, like our counties, wherein the people were summoned by the magistrate to meet for the dispatch of

judicial business. In each of these the prefect held a court, something like our judges on the circuits, to try criminal and civil causes. So likewise in the cities, which were districts of themselves, like some of ours. This custom is very ancient, see 1 Sam. vii. 16. On these occasions the prefect's, or judge's wives, might attend, with no small advantage to herself, if she were inclined to extort money from the suitors, to influence her husband in their favour.

129–30. *Crooked talons, &c.*] Like an harpy, seizing on all she could get. Of Celæno, and the other harpies, read Æn. iii. l. 211–18, 245, 365, 703.

131. *Picus.*] The first king of the Aborigines, an ancient people of Italy, who incorporated themselves with the Romans. He was said to be the son of Saturn.

132. *Titanian battle.*] All the Titans, who were set in battle array against Jupiter, these were sons of Saturn also.

Inter majores, ipsumque Promethea ponas:
De quocunque voles proavum tibi sumito libro.
Quod si præcipitem rapit ambitus atque libido,   135
Si frangis virgas sociorum in sanguine, si te
Delectant hebetes lasso lictore secures :
Incipit ipsorum contra te stare parentum
Nobilitas, claramque facem præferre pudendis.
OMNE ANIMI VITIUM TANTO CONSPECTIUS IN SE   140
CRIMEN HABET, QUANTO MAJOR, QUI PECCAT, HABETUR.
Quo mihi te solitum falsas signare tabellas
In templis, quæ fecit avus ; statuamque parentis
Ante triumphalem ? quo, si nocturnus adulter
Tempora Santonico velas adoperta cucullo ?   145
  Præter majorum cineres, atque ossa volucri
Carpento rapitur pinguis Damasippus ; et ipse,
Ipse rotam stringit multo sufflamine Consul :
Nocte quidem : sed luna videt, sed sidera testes

---

133. *Prometheus himself.*] The son of Iapetus, · one of the Titans, and Clymene, whom the poets feigned to have been the first former of men out of clay, and then to have animated them by fire stolen from heaven. See sat. iv. 131,

134. *Whatever book, &c.*] i. e. From whatever history of great and famous men you please.—*q. d.* You are welcome to this if you are yourself a worthy man and a good magistrate.

136. *Break rods, &c.*] If you break the rods, which you prepare for the allies over which you preside, on their bloody backs—i. e. if you cruelly torment them with scourges.

137. *The lictor, &c.*] If you delight in putting the poor people to death, till the very axes are blunted by frequent use, and the executioner himself be tired out with the number of executions.

138. *The nobility, &c.*] So far from the nobility of your family's reflecting any honour upon you, it rises, and stands in judgment, as it were, against you, and condemns you for your degeneracy.

139. *A clear torch.*] Makes your foul deeds the more conspicuous, and exposes your shame in a clearer light,

140. *Every vice.*] Such as cruelty, avarice, and the like. · Pravitates animi, vitia recte dicuntur. Cic.

—*More conspicuous, &c.*] So far from deriving any sanction from high and noble birth, the vices of the great are the more blameable, and more evidently inexcusable in proportion to the greatness of their quality ; their crimes are the more notorious, their examples the more malignant. ·

142. *Wherefore, &c.*] Jactas is here understood—Quo mihi jactas te solitum, &c.—*q. d.* " It is of very " little consequence, that you, who " are, in the habit of forging wills, " should be boasting to me your no- " bility : to what end, intent, or pur- " pose, can you do it ?" Quo. here, has the sense of quorsum.

143. *In the temples,*] It was usual to sign, as a witness to a will, in the temples of the gods, to put men in mind that they were obliged by religion to be true and faithful. See sat. i. l. 54—5.

—*Your grandfather built.*] Fecit —lit. made. The piety of your ancestors reflects no honour upon you.

144. *The triumphal statue.*] Which being set up in the temple, is, as it were, a witness of your villainy.

—*A nightly adulterer.*] Taking advantage of the night to conceal your

And Prometheus himself, among your ancestors:
Take to yourself a great grandfather from whatever book
    you please.
But if ambition, and lust, hurry you headlong,   135
If you break rods in the blood of the allies, if thee,
Blunt axes delight, the lictor being tired,
The nobility of your ancestors themselves begins to stand
Against you, and to carry a clear torch before your shame-
    ful deeds.
EVERY VICE OF THE MIND HAS BY SO MUCH MORE CONSPI-
    CUOUS   140
BLAME, BY HOW MUCH HE THAT OFFENDS IS ACCOUNTED
    GREATER.
Wherefore to me boast yourself accustomed to sign false
    wills
In the temples, which your grandfather built, and before
The triumphal statue of your father? what, if a nightly
    adulterer,
You veil your cover'd temples with a Santonic hood?   145
  ' By the ashes of his ancestors, and their bones, in a swift
Chariot, fat Damasippus is whirled along, and he,
Himself, the consul, binds the wheel with many a drag.
By night indeed, but the moon sees, but the conscious stars

deeds of darkness. See Job xxiv. 13–17.

145. *Your temples.*] Your head and face, of which the temples are a part. Synec.

—*A Santonic hood.*] The Santones were a people of Aquitain, a part of France, from whom the Romans derived the use of hoods, or cowls, which covered the head and face.

146. *By the ashes, &c.*] The poet here inveighs against the low and depraved taste of the noblemen in Rome, whose passion it was to become charioteers. The name Damasippus (from Gr. δαμαω, to tame, and ἱππος, an horse) signifies an horse-tamer, and is applicable not merely to any single person, but to all of the same taste. Damasippus, says he, drives furiously by the ashes and bones of his great progenitors; so totally uninfluenced by their examples of true greatness, as to sink into the mean character of a coachman, or charioteer. The emperor Nero affected

this, and was followed in it by many by way of paying court to him; and indeed the poet here must be understood to glance at this.

148. *Binds the wheel, &c.*] The sufflamen was the drag put on the wheel of a carriage to stop or stay it, that it should not go too fast down hill, or run back when going up hill. The person who attended to put this on was some slave; but Damasippus, though consul, submits to this office himself. Multo sufflamine implies his often doing this.

149. *By night, &c.*] This indeed he does in the night, when he thinks nobody sees him; but the moon and stars are witnesses of the fact, which is so degrading to a man in his situation, and which would not happen had he a due regard to his own dignity. Testis signifies, lit. a witness. Hence, met. that is privy to a thing, conscious. Sat. iii. 49; and sat. xiii. 75.

Intendunt oculos. Finitum tempus honoris   150
Cum fuerit, clarâ Damasippus luce flagellum
Sumet, et occursum nusquam trepidabit amici
Jam senis, at virgâ prior innuet, atque maniplos
Solvet, et infundet jumentis hordea lassis.
Interea dum lanatas, torvumque juvencùm   155
More Numæ cædit Jóvis ante altaria, jurat
Hipponam, et facies olida ad præsepia pictas.
Sed cum pervigiles placet instaurare popinas,
Obvius assiduo Syrophœnix udus amomo
Currit, Idumææ Syrophœnix incola portæ,   160
Hospitis affectu Dominum, Regemque salutat,
Et cum venali Cyane, succincta lagenâ.
Defensor culpæ dicet mihi : fecimus et nos
Hæc juvenes. Esto ; desisti nempe, nec ultra
Fovisti errorem. Breve sit, quod turpiter audes.   165
Quædam cum primâ resecentur crimina barbâ.
Indulge veniam pueris : Damasippus ad illos
Thermarum calices, inscriptaque lintea vadit,

150. *The time of honour is finished.*] When he goes out of office at the end of the year.

151. *In the clear light, &c.*] In open day light he will appear as a charioteer.

153. *Now old.*] And therefore grave and sedate ; yet Damasippus will feel no shame at meeting him.

—*Make a sign, &c.*] Salute him with a dexterous crack of his whip. See sat. iii. 305–6.

154. *Loosen, &c.*] Will feed his horses himself, coachman like. Manipulum is an handful, armful, or bundle ; here we may suppose it to mean a truss of hay.

155. *Kills sheep.*] When he goes to offer sacrifices, according to the rites established by Numa, the successor of Romulus, at the altar of Jupiter.

156–7. *Swears by Hippona.*] Hippona (from ἵππος an horse) is the goddess he swears by, and in whose name he makes his vows. She was the goddess of horses and stables ; her image was placed in the middle of the stalls, and curiously bedecked with chaplets of fresh roses. By et facies pictas, we may suppose that there were other deities, of a like kind, painted on the walls of the stables.

158. *To renew the watchful taverns.*] To renew his visits, and repair to the taverns, where people sat up all night.

159. *A Syrophœnician.*] A name of Syria and Phœnicia, from whence the finest perfumed ointments came, as did also those who prepared them best.

—*Wet, &c.*] Greasy, by continually busying himself in his trade.

160. *Inhabitants of the Idumæan gate.*] The Idumæan gate at Rome was so called from Vespasian's and Titus's entry through it, when they triumphed over the Jews. Idumæa is a part of Syria, bordering on Judæa. This part of Rome, which was called the Idumæan gate, was probably much inhabited by these Syrian perfumers.

161. *With the affectation, &c.*]— The innkeepers at Rome were very lavish of their flatteries and civil speeches to people who came to their houses, in order to engage their custom. This perfumer affects the same, in order to bespeak the custom of Damasippus, and flatters him with the highest titles that he can think of.

Fix their eyes upon him : when the time of honour is
    finished,   150
Damasippus, in the clear light, the whip will
Take, and no where tremble at the meeting of a friend.
Now old, but will first make a sign, with his whip ; and
    trusses
Of hay will loosen, and pour in barley to his tired beasts.
Mean time while he kills sheep, and the fierce bullock, 155
After the manner of Numa, before the altars of Jove, he
    swears by
Hippona, and faces painted at the stinking mangers :
But when he pleases to renew the watchful taverns,
A Syrophœnician, wet with a constant perfume, runs to
Meet him, a Syrophœnician inhabitant of the Idumæan
    gate ;   160
With the affectation of an host, he salutes him lord and
    king ;
And nimble Cyane with a venal flagon.
A defender of his fault will say to me, "We also have done
    " these things
" When young men." "Be it so—but you left off, nor
    " farther
" Cherished your error.—Let that be short which you
    " shamefully adventure."   165
Some crimes should be cut off with the first beard.
Indulge favour to boys. Damasippus goes to those
Cups of the hot baths, and to the inscribed linen,

162. *Nimble Cyane.*] The woman of the house loses no time in setting a bottle of liquor before him. *Succinctus cursitat hospes.* Hor. lib. ii. sat. vi. l. 107. Succinctus—lit. girt, trussed, tucked up, for the greater expedition.

—*A venal flagon.*] Of wine, which was sold at the tavern.

163. *A defender, &c.*] Some person may perhaps say, by way of excuse.

165. *Let that be short,*] *i. e.* Stop short, and never persist in doing ill. " *Nec lusisse pudet sed non incidere ludo.*" Hor.

166. *Should be cut off.*] Left off when we come to manhood.

167. *Indulge favour.*] Make all proper allowances for the errors of youth.

—*Damasippus, &c.*] True, one would make every allowance for the follies of young men ; but Damasip-

pus is of an age to know and to do better. See l. 169—71.

168. *Cups of the hot baths.*] The Thermæ, or hot baths at Rome, were places, where some, after bathing, drank very hard. Hence Epigrammatogr. lib. xii. epigr. 71. cited by Grangius, in his note on this passage.

Frangendos calices, effundendumque
     Falernum.
Clamabat, biberet, qui modo lotus eques.
A sene sed postquam nummi venere
     trecenti,
Sobrius a Thermis nescit abire do-
     mum.

They also drank hot wine, while bathing, to make them perspire.

168. *The inscribed linen.*] Alluding to the brothels, over the doors of which the entertainment which the guests might expect was set forth on painted linen.

Maturus bello Armeniæ, Syriæque tuendis
Amnibus, et Rheno, atque Istro.   Præstare Neronem   170
Securum valet hæc ætas.   Mitte Ostia, Cæsar,
Mitte; sed in magnâ legatum quære popinâ.
Invenies aliquo cum percussore jacentem,
Permistum nautis, aut furibus, aut fugitivis,
Inter carnifices, et fabros sandapilarum,   175
Et resupinati cessantia tympana Galli.
Æqua ibi libertas, communia pocula, lectus
Non alius cuiquam, nec mensa remótior ulli.
Quid facias, talem sórtitus, Pontice, servum?
Nempe in Lucanos, aut Thusca ergastula mittas.   180
At vos, Trojugenæ, vobis ignoscitis, et quæ
Turpia cerdoni, Volesos Brutosque decebunt.
  Quid, si nunquam adeo fœdis, adeoque pudendis
Utimur exemplis, ut non pejora supersint?
Consumptis opibus vocem, Damasippe, locâsti   185

169. *Mature for the war, &c.*]—Damasippus is now grown up to manhood, and ripe for entering upon the service of his country.

—*Armenia.*] In the reign of Nero, Armenia excited new and dangerous tumults.

169-70. *Rivers of Syria, &c.*]—As the Euphrates, Tigris, and Orontes, which were to be well defended, to prevent the incursions of enemies into Syria.

170. *The Rhine and Ister.*] The former anciently divided Germany and France: the latter means the Danube, the largest river in Europe; as it passeth by Illyricum, it is called the Ister. On the banks of both these rivers the Romans had many conquered nations to keep in subjection, and many others to fear.

171. *This age is able.*] Persons, at the time of life to which Damasippus is arrived, are capable of entering into the armies, which are to protect both the emperor and the empire. By Neronem any emperor may be meant—perhaps Domitian. Sat. iv. 38.

—*Send Cæsar, &c.*] q. d. Have you occasion, O Cæsar, for an ambassador to dispatch on business of state to Ostia, or to the coasts of the Roman provinces? Ostia was a city built by

Ancus Martius, at the mouth of the river Tiber. Ostia-æ, sing. or Ostiaorum, plur.

172. *Seek your legate, &c.*] If you should choose to employ Damasippus, you must look for him in some tavern, and among the lowest and most profligate company.

175. *Makers of coffins.*] Sandapila was a bier, or coffin, for the poorer sort, especially for those who were executed.

176. *The ceasing drums, &c.*] The priests of Cybele, in their frantic processions, used to beat drums. Here is an account of one asleep on his back, perhaps dead drunk, with his drums by him quite silent. They were called Galli, from Gallus, a river in Phrygia, in which country Cybele was peculiarly worshipped.

177. *There is equal liberty, &c.*] All are here upon one footing; they drink out of the same cup.

—*Another couch, &c.*] The Romans, at their entertainments, lay upon couches, or beds; and people of distinction had their couches ornamented, and some were raised higher than others; but here all were accommodated alike.

178. *Table more remote, &c.*] No table set in a more or less honourable place; no sort of distinction made,

Mature for the war of Armenia, and for defending the
    rivers
Of Syria, and for the Rhine and Ister. To make Nero 170
Safe, this age is able. Send, Cæsar, send to Ostia,
But seek your legate in a great tavern.
You will find him lying by some cut-throat,
Mix'd with sailors, or thieves, or fugitives,
Among hangmen, and makers of coffins,   175
And the ceasing drums of a priest of Cybele lying on his
    back.
There is equal liberty, cups in common, not another couch
To any one, nor a table more remote to any.
What would you do, Ponticus, if you had such a slave?
You would surely send him among the Lucani, or the Tus-
    can workhouses.   180
But you, sons of Troy, forgive yourselves, and what things
Are base to a cobler, will become the Volesi or Bruti.
    What, if we never use so foul, and so shameful
Examples, that worse cannot remain?
Thy riches consumed, thy voice, Damasippus, thou hast
    hired to   185

or respect shewn, to one more than
another. They were all " Hail fel-
" low! well met!" as we say.
    179. *Such a slave, &c.*] If you had
a slave that passed his time in such a
manner, and in such rascally company; if such a one had fallen to your
lot, what would you do with him?
    180. *The Lucani.*] Lucania was a
country of Italy, belonging to Naples, where the slaves were punished
by being made to dig in fetters.
    —*Tuscan workhouses.*] Ergastula
—places of punishment for slaves,
where they were made to work in
chains. These were very frequent in
Tuscany.
    181. *Sons of Troy.*] A sneer on
the low-minded and profligate nobility, who were proud of deriving
their families from the ancient Trojans, who first settled in Italy. See
sat i. 86.
    —*Forgive yourselves.*] Easily find
out excuses for what you do.
    182. *Will become the Volesi or
Bruti.*] By these he means the nobles of Rome, the most ancient families being derived from Valerius

Volesus, who came and settled at
Rome, with Tatius king of the Sabines, on the league of amity with
Romulus. Brutus also was a name
highly reverenced, on account of the
noble acts of some who had borne it.
Junius Brutus was the first consul
after the expulsion of the kings; Domitius Junius Brutus was one of the
conspirators against Julius Cæsar;
these were the chiefs of a noble family in Rome, who bore the name
of Brutus.
    The poet here observes, that the
Roman nobility were got to such a
state of shameless profligacy, that
they gloried in actions and practices,
which a low mechanic would have
been ashamed of, and which would
have disgraced even a cobler.
    183. *If we never, &c.*] *q. d.* What
will you say, if after the examples
which I have produced, so infamous
and shameful, there should remain
yet worse?
    185. *Damasippus.*] See his charac-
ter, l. 147—180. At last he is supposed to have ruined himself, and to
go upon the stage.

X.

Sipario, clamosum ageres ut Phasma Catulli.
Laureolum Velox etiam bene Lentulus egit,
Judice me, dignus verâ cruce.   Nec tamen ipsi
Ignoscas populo: populi frons durior hujus,
Qui sedet, et spectat triscurria patriciorum :   190
Planipedes audit Fabios, ridere potest qui
Mamercorum alapas.   Quanti sua funera vendant,
Quid refert ? vendunt nullo cogente Nerone,
Nec dubitant celsi Prætoris vendere ludis.
Finge tamen gladios inde, atque hinc pulpita pone :   195
Quid satius ? mortem sic quisquam exhorruit, ut sit
Zelotypus Thymeles ; stupidi collega Corinthi ?
Res haud mira tamen, citharædo principe, mimus
Nobilis : hæc ultra, quid erit nisi ludus ? et illic
Dedecus urbis habes : nec mirmillonis in armis,   200

186. *The stage.*] Siparium, properly, is the curtain of a theatre: here, by synec. it denotes the theatre itself.

—*Phasma.*] Catullus wrote a play, entitled Phasma, or the Vision ; so called from Gr. φαινομαι, appareo. Probably the work of some scribbler of that name, full of noise and rant.

187. *Velox Lentulus.*] Another of these profligate noblemen.

—*Laureolus.*] The name of a tragedy, in which the hero Laureolus, for some horrid crime, is crucified.

188. *Worthy, &c.*] Richly deserving to be crucified in earnest, for condescending to so mean a thing as to turn actor upon a public stage.

—*I being judge.*] In my opinion ; in my judgment.

189. *The very people.*] Even the commonalty who attend at these exhibitions.

—*The front of this people, &c.*]— The spectators are still, if possible, more inexcusable, who can impudently sit and divert themselves with such a prostitution of nobility.

190. *Buffooneries.*] Triscurria, from tris (Gr. τρις) three times, and scurra, a buffoon ; the threefold buffooneries of persons acting so out of character.

—*Patricians.*] Noblemen of the highest rank.

191. *Barefooted Fabii*] Planipes—

an actor or mimic, that acted without shoes, or on the plain ground.

A fine piece of diversion, for the spectators to behold a man, descended from one of the first families, acting so low a part !

192. *Of the Mamerci.*] A great family in Rome, descended from Mamercus Æmilius, who, when dictator, subdued the rebels at Fidenæ.

A curious entertainment, truly, to see a descendant of this family suffering kicks, and slaps on the face, like a merry-andrew, on a public stage, for the diversion of the people !

192. *Sell their deaths, &c.*] i. e. Expose their persons to be put to death. *q. d.* No matter for what price these nobles run the hazard of their lives ; they do it voluntarily, therefore nobody will pity them if they be killed.   He now proceeds to satirize the noble gladiators.

193. *No Nero compelling, &c.*]— Alluding to the cruelty of Nero, who commanded four hundred senators, and six hundred knights, to fight in the amphitheatre ; these were excusable, for they could not help it ; but this was not the case with those the poet is here writing of, who, of their own accord, exposed their lives upon the stage for hire, like common gladiators ; which we may understand by vendunt.

194. *Nor doubt, &c.*] They make

The stage, that thou mightest act the noisy Phasma of
	Catullus.
Velox Lentulus also acted well Laureolus,
Worthy, I being judge, a real cross.   Nor yet can you
Excuse the very people: the front of this people is still
	harder,
Who sits, and beholds the buffooneries of patricians: 190
Hears barefoot Fabii—who can laugh at the slaps
Of the Mamerci.   At what price they may sell their deaths
What does it signify? they sell them, no Nero compelling,
Nor doubt to sell them to the shows of the haughty prætor.
But imagine the swords there, and put the stage here: 195
Which is best? has any one so feared death, that he should
	be
Jealous of Thymele; the colleague of stupid Corinthus?
Yet it is not surprising, when the prince is a harper, that
	the noble
Is a mimic: after these things, what will there be but a
	play? and there
You have the disgrace of the city: Gracchus, neither in
	the arms of a Mirmillo,	200

no scruple to engage in the shows of
gladiators given by the prætor, who
sat on high, exalted in a car, to direct and superintend the whole.   See
sat. x. l. 36.   They hire themselves,
as it were, for this purpose.
	195. *Imagine the swords, &c.*]—
Suppose you were to choose, put the
lists for sword-playing on one hand,
the stage on the other, which should
you think best; which would you
choose?
	196. *Has any one, &c.*] Has any
one known the fear of death so much,
as not to risk his life in a combat, rather than to play the fool as an actor.
	We are to understand the poet here
to say, that it is more shameful to
act upon the stage, than to fight as a
gladiator, though at the hazard of
life: for who would not detest to
play the part of the cuckold Latinus,
the jealous husband of Thymele, or
be a fellow-actor with that stupid fellow Corinthus, a low mimic and
buffoon.
	197. *Thymele.*] See sat. i. l. 34.
and note.
	198. *Prince a harper.*] No wonder

a nobleman, born under the reign of
Nero, who turned actor and harper
himself, should be influenced by, and
follow the example of the emperor.
	The poet is here shewing the mis-
chief which accrues from the evil example of princes.
	199. *After these things, &c.*] After
this, what can you expect, but that
it should become a general fashion,
and that nothing should be found, in
the polite world, but acting plays
and prize-fighting.   Ludus signifies
both.
	—*There.*] i. e. In that manner of
employment, so unworthy the nobility of Rome, you have Gracchus,
&c.   Some read Illud, agreeing with
dedecus—*q. d.* You have Gracchus,
that disgrace, &c.
	200. *The disgrace, &c.*] A severe
rebuke of Gracchus, a nobleman of
one of the greatest families in Rome,
who debased himself, to the scandal
of even the city itself, in fighting
upon the stage.   Juvenal censures
him for three enormities at once.
	1st. For his baseness, in such a
condescension.

Nec clypeo Gracchum pugnantem, aut falce supinâ,
(Damnat enim tales habitus, sed damnat et odit,)
Nec galeâ frontem abscondit : movet ecce tridentem,
Postquam libratâ pendentia retia dextrâ .
Nequicquam effudit, nudum ad spectacula vultum　　205
Erigit, et totâ fugit agnoscendus arenâ.
Credamus tunicæ, de faucibus aurea cum se
Porrigat, et longo jactetur spira galero.
Ergo ignominiam graviorem pertulit omni
Vulnere, cum Graccho jussus pugnare secutor.　　210
　　Libera si dentur populo suffragia, quis tam
Perditus, ut dubitet Senecam præferre Neroni ?
Cujus supplicio non debuit una parari
Simia, nec serpens unus, nec culeus unus.
Par Agamemnonidæ crimen ; sed causa facit rem　　215

2ndly. For his impudence, in not choosing an habit which might have disguised him.

3dly. For his cowardice in running away, and meanly shewing himself to the people to obtain their favour.

—*Mirmillo.*] There were two sorts of gladiators among the Romans, which had different names according to the arms and habit which they appeared in. One fought with a sword, or falchion, shaped like a scythe (falce) in his right hand, a target on his left arm, and an helmet on his head ; he was called Mirmillo, (from μυρμος, an ant, which is covered with scales like armour. See Aɪɴsw.) or Secutor : the other wore a short coat without sleeves, called tunica ; a hat on his head ; he carried in his right-hand a javelin, forked like a trident, called fuscina ; on his left arm a net, in which he endeavoured to catch his adversary, and from thence was called Retiarius.

Now Gracchus did not take the arms of the Mirmillo, which would have covered him from being so easily known, but took the habit of the Retiarius, and impudently exposed his person to the knowledge of the beholders.

203. *A trident.*] The fuscina. See note on l. 200.

204. *After the nets, &c.*] It was the play of the Retiarius to throw his net over the Mirmillo, and so, confining him, to have him in his power ; to this end he took the best aim he could, balancing the net as exactly as possible, that it might cover his mark. But Gracchus missed it, and then fled to escape his antagonist.

205. *The scaffolds.*] Spectacula— the scaffolds on which the spectators sat to behold the shows. Spectaculum sometimes signifies a beholder. Aɪɴsw. No. 4.

206. *Acknowledged, &c.*] Be known by the spectators, that, seeing who he was, they might not make the signal for his being put to death, as a bad and cowardly gladiator. See sat. iii. l. 36, note 2.

—*Arena.*] Literally signifies sand ; but, by metonymy, the part of the amphitheatre where the gladiators fought, because strewed with sand, to keep them from slipping, and to drink up the blood.

207. *Trust to his tunic.*] The Retiarius wore a sort of coat without sleeves, called tunica—hence Gracchus is called tunicatus. His was so rich and magnificent, as plainly to shew what he was. Some instead of credamus read cedamus, let us yield —i. e. to the evidence of his habit, to prove his rank.

—*Since, &c.*] Cum—here used as quandoquidem—forasmuch as—seeing that.

Nor fighting with the shield, or held-up scythe,
(For he condemns such habits, but he condemns and hates
  them,)
Nor hides his forehead with an helmet : behold he moves a
  trident,
After the nets, hanging from his balanced right-hand,
He has cast in vain, his countenance naked to the scaffolds
He erects, and flies to be acknowledged over the whole
  arena.   206
Let us trust to his tunic, since a golden wreath from his
  jaws
Stretches itself, and is tossed from his long cap.
Therefore the Secutor bore an heavier ignominy than any
Wound, being commanded to fight with Gracchus.   210
  If free suffrages were allowed the people, who is so
Lost, as that he should doubt to prefer Seneca to Nero ?
For whose punishment there ought not to be prepared
One ape, nor one serpent, nor one sack.
The crime of Orestes was equal ; but the cause makes the
  thing   215

—*A golden wreath.*] The spira was a band, or twisted lace, which was fastened to the hat, and tied under the chin, to keep it upon the head. This band, or lace, also, being of gold, plainly shewed that he was no common gladiator.

————" *See*
" *His coat and hat-band shew his*
" *quality.*"   STEPNEY."

208. *Stretches itself, &c.*] Being untied, hangs down on each side of his face—porrigat defaucibus—loosely from the hat, or cap, which, having an high crown, appeared of a considerable length from the base to the top—longo galero.

—*Is tossed.*]. Blown to and fro by the air, in his running from the Mirmillo.

209. *The Secutor.*] Or follower. The Mirmillo was so called from his following the Retiarius to kill him, after the latter had missed with his net, unless his life were begged.

—*An heavier ignominy, &c.*] The gladiator who fought with so inexperienced and cowardly a fugitive, got more dishonour in fighting with him, though he overcame him, than if he

had himself received a wound from a brave and experienced antagonist.

211. *If free suffrages, &c.*] If the people were allowed to give their votes freely. See sat. x. 77–81.

212. *Seneca to Nero.*] Lucius Seneca, uncle to Lucan the poet, and appointed tutor to Nero by Agrippina, who recalled him from banishment. He was an orator, poet, philosopher, and historian. He was put to death by Nero. *q. d.*—Who is so lost to all sense of virtue, who so abandoned, as even to doubt whether he should prefer Seneca to Nero ?

213. *For whose punishment.*] *i. e.* For Nero's.

213-14. *Nor one ape, &c.*] A parricide, by the Roman law, was sewn up in a sack, with a cock, a serpent, an ape, and a dog, and thrown into the sea.

The poet means, that Nero's many parricides deserved more than one death.

215. *Of Orestes.*] Agamemnonidæ, the son of Agamemnon and Clytemnestra.

—*Crime equal.*] He slew his mother, and therefore was a parricide as

Dissimilem : quippe ille Deis auctoribus ultor
Patris erat cæsi media inter pocula : sed nec
Electræ jugulo se polluit, aut Spartani
Sanguine conjugii : nullis aconita propinquis
Miscuit : in scena nunquam cantavit Orestes :   220
Troïca non scripsit. Quid enim Virginius armis
Debuit ulcisci magis, aut cum Vindice Galba ?
Quid Nero tam sævâ, crudâque tyrannide fecit ?
Hæc opera, atque hæ sunt generosi principis artes,
Gaudentis fœdo peregrina ad pulpita cantu   225
Prostitui, Graiæque apium meruisse coronæ.
Majorum effigies habeant insignia vocis,
Ante pedes Domiti longum tu pone Thyestæ
Syrma, vel Antigones, seu personam Menalippes,

well as Nero, who slew his mother Agrippina, by whose means he got the empire.

—*The cause makes, &c.*] The occasion and the motive from which Orestes acted were very different from that of Nero, and therefore make a great difference as to the act itself.

216. *Was the avenger, &c.*]— Orestes killed his mother Clytemnestra, because she, with her paramour, Ægysthus, had murdered his father Agamemnon; therefore Orestes might be looked upon as a minister of divine justice, to execute the vengeance of the gods, and to act, as it were, by their command.

217. *In the midst of his cups.*]— Homer—Odyss. δ. and λ.—is of Juvenal's opinion, that Agamemnon was slain at a banquet, when he little expected such treatment.

Homer, as well as Juvenal, justifies this revenge, as being undertaken by the advice of the gods.

218. *Throat of Electra.*] Orestes did not kill his sister Electra, as Nero did his brother Britannicus. Hor. lib. ii. sat. iii. l. 137–40.

219. *Spartan wedlock.*] He did not kill his wife Hermione, the daughter of Menelaus king of Sparta, as Nero murdered his wives Octavia, Antonia, and Poppæa.

—*Poison for none, &c.*] As Nero did for his brother Britannicus; and for his aunt Domitia.

220. *Never sang, &c.*] Orestes, (see sat. i. l. 5, note,) mad as he was, never sang upon the stage, as Nero did, who not only sang upon the theatre among the ordinary comedians, but took a journey to Greece, on purpose to try his skill among the most famous artists, from whom he bore away the garland, and returned to Rome in triumph, as if he had conquered a province.

221. *Never wrote Troïcs.*] Nero had also the vanity of being thought a good poet, and made verses on the destruction of Troy, called Troïca; and, it is reported, that he set Rome on fire, in order to realize the scene better. It is also said, that he placed himself, dressed in a theatrical habit, on an eminence in Rome, and sang a part of his Troïca to his harp, during the conflagration.

—*What ought Virginius, &c.*— Nero's monstrous frolicks and cruelties could not but make the people weary of his government. Virginius Rufus, his lieutenant-general in Gaul, by the assistance of Junius Vindex, (a nobleman of that country,) soon persuaded the armies under his command to fall from their allegiance, and solicited Sergius Galba, lieutenant-general in Spain, to do the like, by offering him the empire in favour of mankind, which he at last accepted, upon intimation that Nero had issued secret orders to dispatch him, and marched, with all the forces he could

Unlike, for he, the gods being commanders, was the
   avenger
Of a father slain in the midst of his cups: but he neither
Polluted himself with the throat of Electra, nor with the
   blood
Of Spartan wedlock: poison for none of his relations
Did he mix. Orestes never sang upon the stage :   220
Never wrote Troïcs: for what ought Virginius with his
   arms
Rather avenge, or Galba with Vindex ?
What did Nero in a tyranny so savage and bloody ?
These are the works, and these the arts of a noble prince,
Rejoicing, with shameless song, on foreign stages to be 225
Prostituted, and to have deserved the parsley of a Grecian
   crown.
" Let the statues of your ancestors have the tokens of your
   " voice,
" Before the feet of Domitius do thou place the long gar-
   " ment
  " Of Thyestes ; or of Antigone ; or the mask of Menalippe ;

gather, towards Rome. Nero, not being in a condition to oppose such troops, fell into despair, and endeavoured to make his escape; he put himself in disguise, and crept, with four attendants only, to a poor cottage, where, perceiving he was pursued, as a sacrifice to public vengeance, and fearing to fall into the hands of the people, with much ado he resolved to stab himself.

223. *What did Nero, &c.*] What, among all his acts of cruelty and tyranny, has he ever done worthy a prince? what has he achieved by them? or, indeed, what beside these can be said of him?

224. *These are the works, &c.*] If you ask me, says an answerer, I will tell you all that can be said of him ; *viz.* That it was his delight to prostitute the dignity of a prince, to the meanness of a common fidler, by exposing himself on the public stages of Greece, that, instead of glorying in real crowns of triumph, his ambition was to get a garland of parsley (the reward of the best fidler) in the Nemæan games, from the Grecian music-masters. These games were

celebrated to the memory of Archemorus, the young son of Lycurgus.

227. *" Let the statues," &c.*] As such were your exploits, O Nero, and you have no other trophies wherewith to ornament the statues of your ancestors, let the parsley-crown, which you won by singing, be placed before them. Insigne, plur. insignia, signifies all marks and tokens of honour, such as crowns, robes, &c.

228. *" Of Domitius."*] Thy grandfather and father, both of which were named Domitius. His father was Caius Domitius Ahenobarbus, consul, and afterwards governor of Transalpine Gaul ; he was slain in the war with Pompey.

229. *" Of Thyestes ; or of Antigone."*] *i. e.* The dress which you wore when you played in the tragedies so called. Syrma, a long garment which tragic players used.

—*" The mask of Menalippe."*] The mask which you wore when you acted the part of Menalippe, the sister of Antiope, queen of the Amazons, in the comedy of Euripides, written on her story. She was taken captive by Hercules, and given to Theseus to wife.

Et de marmoreo citharam suspende colosso.   230
  Quis, Catilina, tuis natalibus, atque Cethegi
Inveniet quicquam sublimius ? arma tamen vos
Nocturna, et flammas domibus templisque parâstis,
Ut Braccatorum pueri, Senonumque minores,
Ausi quod liceat tunicâ punire molestâ :   235
Sed vigilat consul, vexillaque vestra coërcet.
Hic novus Arpinas, ignobilis, et modo Romæ
Municipalis eques, galeatum ponit ubique
Præsidium attonitis, et in omni gente laborat.
Tantum igitur muros intra toga contulit illi   240
Nominis et tituli, quantum non Leucade, quantum
Thessaliæ campis Octavius abstulit udo
Cædibus assiduis gladio.   Sed Roma parentem,
Roma patrem patriæ Ciceronem libera dixit.

230. " *Suspend an harp,*" &c.]— Nero, according to Pliny, erected a colossal statue of Augustus, one hundred and ten feet high, (according to Suetonius, one hundred and twenty.) Suetonius, de Ner. ii. 10. says, that Nero honoured highly a harp that was given him by the judges, (in his contest with the Grecian musicians,) and commanded it to be carried to the statue of Augustus. This the poet alludes to in this place.

The apostrophe to Nero, in the above four lines, is conceived with much humour, and at the same time with due severity ; these are greatly heightened by the ironical use of the word insignia, l. 227.

231. *Catiline.*] The conspirator, whose plots and contrivances were found out and defeated by Cicero. He was so debauched and profligate, that his name is frequently used to denote the vilest of men. So Juvenal, sat. xiv. 41, 2.

——*Catilinam*
*Quocunque in populo videas, quo-
cunque sub axe.*
Yet he was well born.

232. *Cethegus.*] Caius, one of the conspirators with Catiline, a man of senatorial dignity.

232-3. *Nocturnal arms.*] Meditated the destruction of the people of Rome by night, and armed yourselves accordingly with torches, and other instruments of mischief.

234. *Sons of the Gauls.*] Bracca-

torum. The Gauls were called Braccati, from the breeches, or trowsers, which the people of Narbonne and Provence used to wear.

—*Senones.*] A people of the ancient race of the Celtæ, inhabiting the Lionnois in Gaul.

These people, under Brennus, their general, sacked and burnt Rome, and besieged the capitol, but, by the conduct and valour of the dictator Camillus, were defeated.

235. *A pitched coat.*] Tunica molesta. This was a coat, or garment, bedaubed and interwoven with pitch and other combustibles, and put on criminals, who were chained to a post, and thus burnt alive. See AINSW. *Molestus.* This instrument of torture was expressed by the phrase, tunica molesta.

The emperor Nero, after charging the Christians with setting Rome on fire, publicly tortured and slew them on the stages in the day-time, and at night put tunicæ molestæ on their bodies, and lighted them up, by way of torches, in the night-time. Comp. sat. i. l. 141. note 2.

236. *The consul.*] Cicero was then consul.

—*Restrains your banners.*] Under which many wicked and desperate men had enlisted : but the fury of their arms was restrained by the vigilance of the consul, who watched all their motions.

" And suspend an harp from a marble colossus."   230
Who, Catiline, will find out any thing more noble than
   your birth,
Or than that of Cethegus? but yet, nocturnal
Arms, and flames, for the houses and temples ye prepared,
As sons of the Gauls, or the posterity of the Senones,
Attempting what it would be right to punish with a pitched
   coat :   235
But the consul is vigilant, and restrains your banners.
This new man of Arpinum, ignoble, and lately at Rome
A municipal knight, puts every where an helmeted
Safeguard for the astonished people, and labours every
   where.
Therefore, the gown conferred on him, within the walls,
   more fame   240
And honour, than Octavius brought away from Leucas, or
   from
The fields of Thessaly, by his sword wet
With continual slaughters : but Rome, the parent,
Rome set free, called Cicero the father of his country.

237. *New man.*] The Romans gave this name to those who were the first dignified persons of their family, and who themselves were of obscure birth. Catiline, in derision, urged this name in contempt against Cicero.

—*Arpinum.*] An ancient town of the Volsci in Italy, famous for being the birth-place of Tully and Marius. Arpinas signifies one of Arpinum.

—*Ignoble.*] Of mean extraction.

238. *A municipal knight.*] Municipalis signified one who belonged to a town free of the city of Rome; this was the case with Tully, who was born at Arpinum, and had been, soon after his coming to Rome, admitted into the equestrian order. Catiline called him therefore municipaliseques, in contempt.

—*Helmeted.*] Armed. Synec. like galeatus, sat. i. 155; and caligatus, sat. iii. 310.

239. *Astonished people.*] Who were dreadfully terrified by the designs and attempts of the conspirators.

—*Labours every where.*] Bestirs himself in all quarters, for the security of the city.

I take—in omni gente—in this place, to mean something like ubique gentium, which signifies every where, in what part of the world soever.

And indeed Tully not only shewed his activity within the city, but he disposed guards and spies throughout all Italy, as well as among every tribe of the Roman people, finding out, by the Allobroges and others, the designs of the traitors.

240. *The gown.*] His robe of office; but here, by metonym. his prudence and wise counsels. Toga here is opposed to gladio, l. 243.

241. *Octavius.*] Cæsar, afterwards called Augustus.

—*Leucas.*] A promontory of Epirus, called also Leucate, near which Octavius Cæsar defeated Antony and Cleopatra, in a bloody naval battle.

242. *Fields of Thessaly, &c.*] Philippi, in Thessalia, where he defeated Brutus and Cassius.

244. *Rome set free.*] Delivered and set free from the dangers that threatened it, and restored to its laws and liberties, which for a while had been suspended by the public troubles.

—*Father of his country.*] This honourable title was given to Cicero, after the defeat of Catiline's conspiracy.

Y

Arpinas alius Volscorum in monte solebat   245
Poscere mercedes alieno lassus aratro;
Nodosam post hæc frangebat vertice vitem,
Si lentus pigrâ muniret castra dolabrâ:
Hic tamen et Cimbros, et summa pericula rerum
Excipit, et solus trepidantem protegit urbem.   250
Atque ideo postquam ad Cimbros, stragemque volabant,
Qui nunquam attigerant majora cadavera, corvi,
Nobilis ornatur lauro collega secundâ.
     Plebeiæ Deciorum animæ, plebeia fuerunt
Nomina: pro totis legionibus hi tamen, et pro   255
Omnibus auxiliis, atque omni plebe Latinâ
Sufficiunt Dîs infernis, Terræque parenti:
Pluris enim Decii, quam qui servantur ab illis.
Ancilla natus trabeam et diadema Quirini,
Et fasces meruit, regum ultimus ille bonorum.   260
Prodîtâ laxabant portarum claustra tyrannis

He was the first who bore it. It was afterwards given to some of the emperors; but much more from flattery, than because they deserved it.

245. *Another Arpinian.*] C. Marius, who also came from Arpinum, was a poor ploughman there, who hired himself out to plough the ground of others.

—*Of the Volsci.*] Arpinum was an ancient city in the country of the Volsci, now called Arpino, between Tuscany to the west, and Campania to the east.

247. *He broke a knotty vine, &c.*] The Roman centurions used to carry a piece of tough vine-branch in their hands, with which they corrected the soldiers when they did amiss. Marius was once a private soldier, and had had the centurion's stick broke upon his head, for being lazy at his work, when set to chop with an axe the wood used in fortifying the camp against the enemy.

249. *The Cimbri.*] The Teutones and Cimbri, neighbouring nations, joined their forces, and marched towards Rome, by which they struck a terror throughout Italy; but C. Marius, with Q. Catullus the proconsul, marched out against them, sustained their attack, and totally defeated them.

—*Dangers of affairs.*] When the

affairs of Italy, of Rome especially, seemed to be in the utmost danger from these powerful enemies.

250. *And alone, &c.*] Though Q. Catullus was with Marius in this victory, yet Marius was the commander in chief in the Cimbrian war, therefore the whole honour of the victory was ascribed to him. Comp. l. 253.

251. —*After—the crows, &c.*] And other birds of prey, which, after the battle, came to feed upon the slain. See Hom. Il. i. 5. 2. 393, et al. q. d. After the battle was ended. See sat. iv. l. 109.

252. *Greater carcases.*] The Cimbri were, in general, men of large stature.

253. *His noble colleague.*] Q. Catullus, who had been second in command, and was of noble birth.

—*Is adorned with the second laurel.*] Received only the second honours of the day.

254. *The Decii, &c.*] These, though originally of low extraction, yet gained immortal honours, by sacrificing their lives for their country; the father in the Latin war, the son in the Hetruscan, and the grandson in the war against Pyrrhus.

255. *Whole legions, &c.*] The Romans had a superstition, that if their general would consent to be devoted to death, or sacrificed to Jupiter

Another Arpinian, in the mountain of the Volsci, used 245
To demand wages, tired with the plough of another man ;
After this he broke a knotty vine with his head,
If, idle, he fortified the camp with a lazy axe.
Yet he both the Cimbri, and the greatest dangers of
   affairs,
Sustains, and alone protects the trembling city.   250
And so, after to the Cimbri, and to the slaughter, the
   crows
Flew, who had never touched greater carcases,
His noble colleague is adorned with the second laurel.
   The souls of the Decii were plebeian, their names
Plebeian : yet these, for whole legions, and for all   255
Our auxiliaries, and for all the Latin common people,
Suffice for the infernal Gods, and parent Earth :
For the Decii were of more value than those who were
   saved by them.
Born from a servant maid, the robe and diadem of Romulus,
And the fasces, that last of good kings deserved.   260
The youths of the consul himself were opening the fasten-
   ings

Mars, the Earth, and the infernal Gods, all the misfortunes of his party would be transferred on their enemies. This opinion was confirmed by several successful instances, particularly two, in the persons of the Decii, father and son. The first being consul with Manlius in the wars against the Latins, and perceiving the left wing, which he commanded, give back, called out to Valerius the high priest to perform on him the ceremony of consecration, (Livy, lib. viii.) and immediately spurred his horse into the thickest of the enemies, where he was killed, and the Romans gained the battle. His son afterwards died in the same manner in the war against the Gauls, with the like success.

257. Suffice.] i. e. To appease, and render them propitious to the Roman arms.

258. More value, &c.] Such men as these are to be more highly prized than all the army and people for whom they thus nobly sacrificed their lives.

259. Born from a servant maid.]— Servius Tullius, born of the captive Oriculana. But Livy supposes her

to have been wife to a prince of Corniculum,—(a town of the Sabines in Italy,) who was killed at the taking of the town, and his wife carried away captive by Tarquinius Priscus, and presented as a slave to his wife Tanaquil, in whose service she was delivered of this Tullius.

259. The robe, &c.] The ensigns of royalty are here put for the kingdom, or royalty itself ; so the fasces, for the highest offices in the state. See sat. iii. 118, note.

—Romulus.] Called Quirinus. See sat. iii. l. 67, note on " O Quirinus."

260. Last of good kings.] Livy says that, with him, justa ac legitima regna ceciderunt.

261. Youths of the consul, &c.— The two sons of L. Junius Brutus, Titus and Tiberius, who, after their father had driven Tarquin, and his whole race, out of Rome, and taken an oath of the Romans never more to suffer a king, entered into a conspiracy to restore the Tarquins ; the sum of which was, that the gates of the city should be left open in the night-time for the Tarquins to enter : to this purpose they sent letters, un-

Exulibus juvenes ipsius consulis, et quos
Magnum aliquid dubiâ pro libertate deceret,
Quod miraretur cum Coclite Mutius, et quæ
Imperii fines Tiberinum virgo natavit.   265
Occulta ad patres produxit crimina servus.
Matronis lugendus: at illos verbera justis
Afficiunt pœnis, et legum prima securis.
Malo pater tibi sit Thersites, dummodo tu sis
Æacidæ similis, Vulcaniaque arma capessas,   270
Quam te Thersitæ similem producat Achilles.
Et tamen, ut longe repetas, longeque revolvas
Nomen, ab infami gentem deducis asylo.
Majorum primus quisquis fuit ille tuorum,
Aut pastor fuit, aut illud, quod dicere nolo.   275

der their own hands, with promises to this effect.

—*The fastenings, &c.*] The bars of the city gates, which were to be betrayed to the Tarquins.

262. *Exiled tyrants.*] The Tarquins.

263. *Some great thing, &c.*] It would have been becoming these sons of the patriot Brutus to have stricken some great stroke, that might have tended to secure the public liberty; which, under the new government, after the expulsion of the kings, must have been in a doubtful and uncertain state; not as yet established.

264. *Mutius.*] Scævola, who, when Porsenna, king of Tuscany, had entered into an alliance with the Tarquins, to restore them by force, went into the enemy's camp with a resolution to kill their king Porsenna, but, instead of him, killed one of his officers; and, being brought before the king, and finding his error, burnt off his right hand, as a penalty for his mistake.

—*Cocles.*] Horatius, being to guard a bridge, which he perceived the enemy would soon be master of, he stood and resolutely opposed part of their army, while his own party repassed the bridge, and broke it down after them. He then threw himself, armed as he was, into the Tiber, and escaped into the city.

265. *Who swam, &c.*] Clelia, a Roman virgin, who was given to king Porsenna as an hostage, made her escape from the guards, and swam over the Tiber. King Porsenna was so stricken with these three instances of Roman bravery, that he withdrew his army, and courted their friendship.

266. *A slave.*] Vindicius, a slave who waited at table, overhearing part of the discourse among the conspirators, went strait to the consuls, and informed them of what he had heard. The ambassadors from the Tarquins were apprehended and searched; the letters above mentioned were found upon them, and the criminals seized.

—*Bewailed by matrons, &c.*] By the mothers of such of the conspirators as were put to death, as the sad cause of their destruction, by accusing them to the senate.

—*Produced.*] Produxit—brought out, discovered.

267. *But stripes, &c.*] The proof being evident against them, they suffered the punishment (which was newly introduced) of being tied naked to a stake, where they were first whipped by the lictors, then beheaded: and Brutus, by virtue of his office, was unhappily obliged to see this rigorous sentence executed on his own children. See Æn. vi. 817-23.

268. *First axe of the laws.*] i. e. The first time this sentence had been

Of the gates, betrayed to the exiled tyrants, and whom
Some great thing for doubtful liberty might have become,
Which Mutius, with Cocles, might admire, and the virgin
Who swam the Tiber, the bounds of our empire.   265
A slave, to be bewailed by matrons, produced their hidden
    crimes
To the fathers: but stripes affected them with just
Punishment, and the first axe of the laws.
I had rather thy father were Thersites, so thou art
Like Achilles, and take in hand the Vulcanian arms,   270
Than that Achilles should produce thee like Thersites.
And yet, however far you may fetch, and far revolve
Your name, you deduce your race from an infamous
    asylum.
Whoever he, the first of your ancestors, was,
Either he was a shepherd, or that which I am unwilling to
    say.   275

executed since the making of the
law.

269. *Thersites.*] An ugly buffoon
in the Grecian army before Troy.
See Hom. Il. b. l. 216–22.

270. *Achilles.*] Æacides-æ, or—is,
so called from his grandfather Æacus,
who was the father of Peleus, the
father of Achilles.

—*The Vulcanian arms.*] Or armour, that was made by Vulcan, at
the request of Thetis, the mother of
Achilles, which could be pierced by
no human force.

271. *Than that Achilles, &c.*]. The
poet here still maintains his argument, *viz.* that a virtuous person, of
low and mean birth, may be great
and respectable : whereas a vicious
and profligate person, though of the
noblest extraction, is detestable and
contemptible.

272. *However far, &c.*] Juvenal
here strikes at the root of all family-
pride among the Romans, by carrying them up to their original. Revolve, roll or trace back, for however
many generations.

273. *An infamous asylum.*] Romulus, in order to promote the peo-
pling of the city in its first infancy,
established an asylum, or sanctuary,

where all outlaws, vagabonds, and
criminals of all kinds, who could
make their escape thither, were sure
to be safe.

275. *Either he was a shepherd.*]—
As were Romulus and Remus, and,
their bringer up, Faustulus.

—*Unwilling to say.*] As the poet
does not speak his own meaning, it
may not be very easy to determine
it; but it is likely that he would insinuate, that none of the Romans had
much to brag of in point of family
grandeur, and that none of them
could tell but that they might have
come from some robber, or cut-throat,
among the first fugitives to Rome,
or even from something worse than
that, if worse could be : and indeed
Romulus himself, their founder, was
a parricide, for he is said to have
killed his brother Remus.

Thus Juvenal concludes this fine
Satire on family-pride, which he
takes every occasion to mortify, by
shewing, that what a man is in himself, not what his ancestors were, is
the great matter to be considered.

Worth makes the man, the want of
    it the fellow ;
The rest is all but leather or pru-
    nello.   POPE.

Satira Decima.

ARGUMENT.

The Poet's design in this Satire, which deservedly holds the first rank among all performances of the kind, is to represent the various wishes and desires of mankind, and to shew the folly of them. He mentions riches, honours, eloquence, fame for martial achievements, long life, and beauty, and gives instances of their having proved ruinous to the possessors of them. He concludes,

OMNIBUS in terris, quæ sunt a Gadibus usque
Auroram et Gangem, pauci dignoscere possunt
Vera bona, atque illis multum diversa, remotâ
Erroris nebulâ : quid enim ratione timemus,
Aut cupimus ? quid tam dextro pede concipis, ut te   5
Conatûs non pœniteat, votique peracti ?
Evertêre domos totas optantibus ipsis
Dî faciles.   Nocitura togâ, nocitura petuntur

* This satire has been always admired; Bishop Burnet goes so far, as to recommend it (together with Persius) to the serious perusal and practice of the divines in his diocese, as the best common places for their sermons, as the storehouses and magazines of moral virtues, from whence they may draw out, as they have occasion, all manner of assistance for the accomplishment of a virtuous life. The tenth Satire (says Crusius in his Lives of the Roman Poets) is inimitable for the excellence of its morality, and sublime sentiments.

Line 1. *Gades.*] An island without the streights of Gibraltar in the south part of Spain, divided from the continent by a small creek. Now called Cadiz, by corruption Cales.

2. *The East.*] Aurora, (quasi aurea hora, from the golden-coloured splendour of day-break,) metonym. the East.

—*Ganges.*] The greatest river in the East, dividing India into two parts.

3—4. *Cloud of error.*] That veil of darkness and ignorance which is over the human mind, and hides from it, as it were, the faculty of perceiving our real and best interests, as distinguished from those which are deceitful and imaginary.

4. *What, with reason.*] According to the rules of right and sober reason.

5. *So prosperously, &c.*] Tam dextro pede—on so prosperous a footing —with ever such hope and prospect of success, that you may not repent your endeavour (conatus) and pains to accomplish it, and of your desires and wishes being fully completed and answered ?—votique peracti.

Tenth Satire.*

ARGUMENT.

therefore, that we should leave it to the gods to make a choice for us, they knowing what is most for our good. All that we can safely ask is health of body and mind: possessed of these, we have enough to make us happy, and therefore it is not much matter what we want besides.

IN all lands, which are from Gades to
The East and the Ganges, few can distinguish
True good things, and those greatly different from them,
   the cloud
Of error removed: for what, with reason do we fear,
Or desire? what do you contrive so prosperously, that
   you   5
May not repent of your endeavour, and of your accom-
   plished wish?
The easy gods have overturned whole houses, themselves
Wishing it. Things hurtful by the gown, hurtful by war-
   fare,

The right and left were ominous—dexter-a-um, therefore, signifies lucky, favourable, fortunate, propitious—as lævus-a-um, unlucky, inconvenient, unseasonable.

Tam dextro pede is equivalent to tam fausto—secundo—prospero pede. I pede fausto—go on and prosper. HOR. lib. ii. epist. ii. l. 37. So VIRG. Æn. viii. l. 302.

Et nos et tua dexter adi pede sacra secundo.

"Approach us, and thy sacred "rites, with thy favourable pre- "sence."—

Pes—lit. a foot, that member of the body on which we stand—sometimes means the foundation of any thing—a plot for building;—so, in a moral sense, those conceptions and contrivances of the mind, which are the foundations of human action, on which men build for profit or happiness:—this seems to be its meaning here.

7. *The easy gods, &c.*] The gods, by yielding to the prayers and wishes of mankind, have often occasioned their ruin, by granting such things as in the end proved hurtful. So that, in truth, men, by wishing for what appeared to them desirable, have, in effect, themselves wished their own destruction.

8. *By the gown.*] Toga here being opposed to militia, may allude to the gown worn by the senators and magistrates of Rome; and so, by me-

Militiâ. Torrens dicendi copia multis,
Et sua mortifera est facundia. Viribus ille	10
Confisus periit, admirandisque lacertis.
Sed plures nimiâ congesta pecunia curâ
Strangulat, et cuncta exsuperans patrimonia census,
Quanto delphinis balæna Brittanica major.
Temporibus diris igitur, jussuque Neronis,	15
Longinum, et magnos Senecæ prædivitis hortos
Clausit, et egregias Lateranorum obsidet ædes
Tota cohors: rarus venit in cœnacula miles.
Pauca licet portes argenti vascula puri,
Nocte iter ingressus, gladium contumque timebis,	20
Et motæ ad lunam trepidabis arundinis umbram.
CANTABIT VACUUS CORAM LATRONE VIATOR.
Prima fere vota, et cunctis notissima templis,
Divitiæ ut crescant, ut opes; ut maxima toto
Nostra sit arca foro: sed nulla aconita bibuntur	25

ton. signify their civil officers in the government of the state.—*q. d.* Many have wished for a share in the government and administration of civil affairs, others for high rank and post of command in the army, each of which have been attended with damage to those who have eagerly sought after them.

9. *A fluent copiousness, &c.*] Many covet a great degree of eloquence; but how fatal has this proved to possessors of it! Witness Demosthenes and Cicero, who both came to violent deaths;—the former driven, by the malice of his enemies, to poison himself: the latter slain by order of M. Antony. See KEYSLER's Travels, vol. ii. p. 342, note.

10. *To his strength.*] Alluding to Milo, the famous wrestler, born at Croton, in Italy, who, presuming too much on his great strength, would try whether he could not rend asunder a tree which was cleft as it grew in the forest; it yielded at first to his violence, but it closed presently again, and, catching his hands, held him, till the wolves devoured him.

12. *Destroys.*] Lit. strangles. Met. ruins, destroys. Strangulo quasi stringo gulam.

The poet is here shewing, that, of all things which prove ruinous to the possessors, money, and especially an overgrown fortune, is one of the most fatal—and yet, with what care is this heaped together!

13. *Exceeding, &c.*] i. e. Beyond the rate of a common fortune.

14. *A British whale.*] A whale found in the British seas.

16. *Longinus.*] Cassius Longinus, put to death by Nero: his pretended crime was, that he had, in his chamber, an image of Cassius, one of Julius Cæsar's murderers, but that which really made him a delinquent was his great wealth, which the emperor seized.

16. *Seneca.*] Tutor to Nero—supposed to be one in Piso's conspiracy, but put to death for his great riches. Sylvanus the tribune, by order of Nero, surrounded Seneca's magnificent villa, near Rome, with a troop of soldiers, and then sent in a centurion to acquaint him with the emperor's orders, that he should put himself to death. On the receipt of this, he opened the veins of his arms and legs, then was put into a hot bath; but this not finishing him, he drank poison.

17. *Surrounded.*] Beset—encompassed.

—*Laterani.*] Plautius Lateranus had a sumptuous palace, in which he was beset by order of Nero, and

Are asked : a fluent copiousness of speech to many
And their own eloquence is deadly.—He, to his strength 10
Trusting, and to his wonderful arms, perished.
But money, heaped together with too much care, destroys
More, and an income exceeding all patrimonies,
As much as a British whale is greater than dolphins.
Therefore in direful times, and by the command of Nero,
A whole troop Longinus, and the large gardens of wealthy
    Seneca,   16
Surrounded, and besieged the stately buildings of the Late-
    rani—
The soldier seldom comes into a garret.
Though you should carry but few small vessels of pure silver,
Going on a journey by night, you will fear the sword and
    the pole,   -   20
And tremble at the shadow of a reed moved, by moon-
    light.
AN EMPTY TRAVELLER WILL SING BEFORE A ROBBER.
   Commonly the first things prayed for, and most known
    at all temples, '
Are, that riches may increase, and wealth ; that our chest
    may be
The greatest in the whole forum: but no poisons are
    drunk   25

killed so suddenly, by Thurius the tribune, that he had not a moment's time allowed him to take leave of his children and family. He had been designed consul.

18. *The soldier, &c.*] Cœnaculum signifies a place to sup in—an upper chamber—also a garret, a cockloft in the top of the house, commonly let to poor people; the inhabitants of which were too poor to run any risk of the emperor's sending soldiers to murder them for what they have.

19. *Though you should carry, &c.*] Though not so rich as to become an object of the emperor's avarice and cruelty, yet you cannot travel by night, with the paltry charge of a little silver plate, without fear of your life from robbers, who may either stab you with a sword, or knock you down with a bludgeon, in order to rob you.

20. *Pole.*] Contus signifies a long pole or staff—also a weapon, where-

with they used to fight beasts upon the stage. It is probable that the robbers about Rome armed themselves with these, as ours, about London, arm themselves with large sticks or bludgeons.

21. *Tremble, &c.*] They are alarmed with the least appearance of any thing moving near them, even the trembling and nodding of a bulrush, when its shadow appears by moonlight.

22. *Empty traveller, &c.*] Having nothing to lose, he has nothing to fear, and therefore has nothing to interrupt his jollity as he travels along; though in the presence of a robber.

23. *Temples.*] Where people go to make prayers to the gods, and to implore the fulfilment of their desires and wishes.

25. *The greatest, &c.*] The forum, or market-place, at Rome, was the place where much money-business was transacted, and where money-

Fictilibus: tunc illa time, cum pocula sumes
Gemmata, et lato Setinum ardebit in auro.
Jamne igitur laudas, quod de sapientibus alter
Ridebat, quoties a limine moverat unum
Protuleratque pedem : flebat contrarius alter ?   30
Sed facilis cuivis rigidi censura cachinni :
Mirandum est, unde ille oculis suffecerit humor,
Perpetuo risu pulmonem agitare solebat
Democritus, quanquam non essent urbibus illis
Prætexta, et trabeæ, fasces, lectica, tribunal.   35
Quid, si vidisset Prætorem in curribus altis
Extantem, et medio sublimem in pulvere circi,
In tunicâ Jovis, et pictæ Sarrana ferentem
Ex humeris aulæa togæ, magnæque coronæ
Tantum orbem, quanto cervix non sufficit ulla ?   40
Quippe tenet sudans hanc publicus, et sibi Consul

lenders and borrowers met together ; and he that was richest, and had most to lend, was sure to make the greatest sums by interest on his money, and perhaps was most respected. Hence the poet may be understood to mean, that it was the chief wish of most people to be richer than others. Or, he may here allude to the chests of money belonging to the senators, and other rich men, which were laid up for safety in some of the buildings about the forum, as the temple of Castor, and others. Comp. sat. xiv. l. 258-9.

—*No poisons, &c.*] The poorer sort of people might drink out of their coarse cups of earthen ware, without any fear of being poisoned for what they had.

26. *Them.*] Poisons.

27. *Set with gems.*] This was a mark of great riches.

—*Setine wine.*] So called from Setia, a city of Campania. It was a most delicious wine, preferred by Augustus, and the succeeding emperors, to all other. Glows with a fine red colour, and sparkles in the cup.

—*Wide gold.*] Large golden cups. Those who were rich enough to afford these things, might indeed reasonably fear being poisoned by somebody, in order to get their estates.

28. *Do you approve.*] Laudas—praise or commend his conduct ; for

while these philosophers lived, many accounted them mad.

—*One of the wise men, &c.*] Meaning Democritus of Abdera, who always laughed, because he believed our actions to be folly : whereas Heraclitus of Ephesus, the other of the wise men here alluded to, always wept, because he thought them to be misery.

29. *As oft as, &c.*] Whenever he went out of his house—as oft as he stepped over his threshold.

30. *The other.*] Heraclitus. See note on line 28.

31. *The censure, &c.*] It is easy enough to find matter for severe laughter. Rigidi here, as an epithet to laughter, seems to denote that sort of censorious sneer which condemns and censures, at the same time that it derides the follies of mankind.

32. *The wonder is, &c.*] How Heraclitus could find tears enough to express his grief at human wretchedness, guilt, and woe, the occasions of it are so frequent.

34. *In those cities.*] As there is at Rome. The poet here satirizes the ridiculous appendages and ensigns of office, which were so coveted and esteemed by the Romans, as if they could convey happiness to the wearers. He would also insinuate, that these things were made ridiculous by the conduct of the possessors of them.

From earthen ware: then fear them, when you take cups
Set with gems, and Setine wine shall sparkle in wide gold.
Nor therefore do you approve, that one of the wise men
Laughed, as oft as from the threshold he had moved, and
Brought forward one foot; the other contrary, wept?   30
But the censure of a severe laugh is easy to any one;
The wonder is whence that moisture could suffice for his
        eyes.
With perpetual laughter, Democritus used to agitate
His lungs, though there were not, in those cities,
Senatorial gowns, robes, rods, a litter, a tribunal.   35
What, if he had seen the prætor, in high chariots
Standing forth, and sublime in the midst of the dust of the
        circus,
In the coat of Jove, and bearing from his shoulders the
        Tyrian
Tapestry of an embroidered gown, and of a great crown
So large an orb, as no neck is sufficient for?   40
For a sweating officer holds this, and lest the consul should

33. *Senatorial gowns.*] Prætexta—
so called because they were faced and
bordered with purple—worn by the
patricians and senators.
—*Robes.*] Trabeæ—robes worn by
kings, consuls, and augurs.
—*Rods.*] Fasces—bundles of birch-
en rods carried before the Roman magistrates, with an axe bound up in
the middle of them, so as to appear
at the top. These were ensigns of
their official power to punish crimes,
either by scourging or death.
—*A litter.*] Lectica. See sat. i. 32,
note.
—*Tribunal.*] A seat in the forum,
built by Romulus, in the form of an
half-moon, where the judges sat, who
had jurisdiction over the highest offences: at the upper part was placed
the sella curulis, in which the prætor
sat.
36. *The prætor, &c.*] He describes
and derides the figure which the prætor
made, when presiding at the Circensian games.
—*In high chariots.*] In a triumphal
car, which was gilt, and drawn by
four white horses—perhaps, by the
plural curribus, we may understand
that he had several for different occasions.

37. *Dust of the circus.*] He stood,
by the height and sublimity of his
situation, fully exposed to the dust,
which the chariots and horses of the
racers raised.
38. *Coat of Jove.*] In a triumphal
habit; for those who triumphed wore
a tunic, or garment, which, at other
times, was kept in the temple of
Jupiter.
38-9. *The Tyrian tapestry, &c.*]—
Sarra, (from Heb. ‏צר‎,) a name of
Tyre, where hangings and tapestry
were made, as also where the fish was
caught, from whence the purple was
taken with which they were dyed.
This must be a very heavy material
for a gown, especially as it was also
embroidered with divers colours; and
such a garment must be very cum-
bersome to the wearer, as it hung
from his shoulders.
40. *So large an orb, &c.*] Add to
this, a great heavy crown, the circumference of which was so large
and thick, that no neck could be
strong enough to avoid bending under
it.
41. *A sweating officer.*] Publicus
signifies some official servant, in some
public office about the prætor on these
occasions, who sat by him in the cha-

Ne placeat, curru servus portatur eodem.
Da nunc et volucrem, sceptro quæ surgit eburno,
Illinc cornicines, hinc præcedentia longi
Agminis officia, et niveos ad fræna Quirites,　　　　　45
Defossa in loculis quos sportula fecit amicos.
Tunc quoque materiam risûs invenit ad omnes
Occursus hominum; cujus prudentia monstrat,
Summos posse viros, et magna exempla daturos,
Vervecum in patriâ, crassoque sub aëre nasci.　　　　50
Ridebat curas, necnon et gaudia vulgi,
Interdum et lachrymas; cum fortunæ ipse minaci
Mandaret laqueum, mediumque ostenderet unguem.
Ergo supervacua hæc aut perniciosa petuntur,
Propter quæ fas est genua incerare Deorum.　　　　55

riot, in order to assist in bearing up the crown, the weight of which made him sweat in holding it up.

41. *Lest the consul, &c.*] The ancients had an institution, that a slave should ride in the same chariot when a consul triumphed, and should admonish him to know himself, lest he should be too vain.

This was done with regard to the prætor at the Circensian games, who, as we have seen above, appeared like a victorious consul, with the habit and equipage of triumph—Juvenal seems to use the word consul, here, on that account.

43. *Add the bird, &c.*] Among other ensigns of triumph, the prætor, on the above occasion, held an ivory rod, or sceptre, in his hand, with the figure of an eagle, with wings expanded, as if rising for flight, on the top of it.

44. *The trumpeters*] Or blowers of the horn, or cornet. These, with the tubicines, which latter seem included here under the general name of cornicines, always attended the camp, and, on the return of the conqueror, preceded the triumphal chariot, sounding their instruments

—*The preceding offices, &c*] Officium signifies sometimes a solemn attendance on some public occasion, as on marriages, funerals, triumphs, &c. Here it denotes, that the prætor was attended, on this occasion, by a long train of his friends and dependents, who came to grace the solemnity, by marching in procession before his chariot.

45. *Snowy citizens, &c*] Many of the citizens, as was usual at triumphs, dressed in white robes, walking by the side of the horses, and holding the bridles.

46. *The sportula.*] The dole-basket. See sat. i. l. 81.

—*Buried in his coffers*] The meaning of this passage seems to be, that these citizens appeared, and gave their attendance, not from any real value for him, but for what they could get.

By defossa in loculis is meant the mere promise of a sportula; it shews the corruption of the Romans, who were willing to attend in his train, and shew every mark of flattery, through the hope of a reward, which was safe in his own pocket —*q. d.* All this formed a scene which would have made Democritus shake his sides with laughing. Comp. l. 33-4.

47. *Then also he*] Democritus in his time.

47-8. *At all meetings of men*]—Every time he met people as he walked about—or, in every company he met with.

48. *Whose prudence*] Wisdom, discernment of right and wrong.

50. *Of blockheads.*] Vervex literally signifies a wether-sheep, but was proverbially used for a stupid person; as we use the word sheepish, and sheepishness, in something like the same sense, to denote an awkward, stupid shyness.

Please himself, a slave is carryed in the same chariot.
Now add the bird which rises on the ivory sceptre,
There the trumpeters, here the preceding offices of a long
Train, and the snowy citizens at his bridles,   45
Whom the sportula, buried in his coffers, has made his
   friends.
Then also he found matter of laughter at all
Meetings of men; whose prudence shews,
That great men, and those about to give great examples,
May be born in the country of blockheads, and under
   thick air.   50
He derided the cares, and also the joys of the vulgar,
And sometimes their tears; when himself could present a
   halter.
To threatening Fortune, and shew his middle nail.
Therefore, these (are) unprofitable, or pernicious things,
   (which) are asked,
For which it is lawful to cover with wax the knees of the
   gods.   55

The poet therefore means, a country of stupid fellows. Plaut. Pers. act ii. has, Ain' vero vervecum caput?

50. *Thick air.*] Democritus was born at Abdera, a city of Thrace, where the air, which was foggy and thick, was supposed to make the inhabitants dull and stupid.

So Horace, speaking of Alexander the Great, as a critic of little or no discernment in literature, says, Bœötum in crasso jurares aere natum. Epist. i. lib. ii. l. 244. By which, as by many other testimonies, we find that the inhabitants of Bœotia were stigmatized also in the same manner. Hence Bœoticum ingenium was a phrase for dulness and stupidity.

52. *Present a halter, &c.*] Mandare laqueum alicui, was a phrase made use of to signify the utmost contempt and indifference, like sending a halter to a person, as if to bid him hang himself. Democritus is here represented in this light as continually laughing at the cares and joys of the general herd, and as himself treating with scorn the frowns of adverse fortune.

53. *His middle nail.*] i. e. His middle finger, and point at her in derision. To hold out the middle finger, the rest being contracted, and bent downwards, was an act of great contempt; like pointing at a person among us. This mark of contempt is very ancient. See Isa. lviii. 9.

54. *Therefore, &c.*] It follows, therefore, from the example of Democritus, who was happy without the things which people so anxiously seek after, and petition the gods for, that they are superfluous and unnecessary. It likewise follows, that they are injurious, because they expose people to the fears and dangers of adverse fortune; whereas Democritus, who had them not, could set the frowns of fortune at defiance, possessing a mind which carried him above worldly cares or fears.

55. *Lawful.*] Fas signifies that which is permitted, therefore lawful to do.

—*To cover with wax, &c.*] It was the manner of the ancients, when they made their vows to the gods, to write them on paper, (or waxen tables,) seal them up, and, with wax, fasten them to the knees of the images of the gods, or to the thighs, that being supposed the seat of mercy. When their desires were granted, they

Quosdam præcipitat subjecta potentia magnæ
Invidiæ ; mergit longa atque insignis honorum
Pagina ; descendunt statuæ, restemque sequuntur ;
Ipsas deinde rotas bigarum impacta securis .
Cædit, et immeritis franguntur crura caballis.   60
Jam strident ignes, jam follibus atque caminis
Ardet adoratum populo caput, et crepat ingens
Sejanus : deinde ex facie toto orbe secundâ
Fiunt urceoli, pelves, sartago, patellæ.
Pone domi lauros, duc in Capitolia magnum   65
Cretatumque bovem ; Sejanus ducitur unco
Spectandus : gaudent omnes : quæ labra ? quis illi
Vultus erat ? nunquam (si quid mihi credis) amavi
Hunc hominem : sed quo cecidit sub crimine ? quisnam
Delator ? quibus indiciis ? quo teste probavit ?   70
Nil horum : verbosa et grandis epistola venit

took away the paper, tore it, and offered to the gods what they had promised. The gods permit us to ask,
but the consequences of having our
petitions answered are often fatal.
Comp. l. 7,—8.

56. *Precipitates some.*] *viz.* Into
ruin and destruction.

57. *Catalogue, &c.*] Pagina, in its
proper and literal sense, signifies a
page of a book, but here alludes to a
plate, or table of brass, fixed before
the statues of eminent persons, and
containing all the titles and honours
of him whose statue it was.

—*Overwhelms.*] With ruin, by exposing them to the envy and malice
of those, in whose power and inclination it may be to disgrace and destroy them.

58. *Statues descend.*] Are pulled
down.

· *Follow the rope.*] With which the
populace (set on work by a notion of
doing what would please the emperor,
who had disgraced his prime-minis-
ter Sejanus) first pulled down all the
statues of Sejanus, of which there
were many set up in Rome, and then
dragged them with ropes about the
streets.

59. *The driven axe.*] Impacta—
driven—forced against. There were
some statues of Sejanus, by which
he was represented on horseback ;
others in a triumphal car, drawn by

two horses (comp. sat. viii. l. 3.) ; all
which were broken to pieces, the
very chariots and horses demolished,
and, if made of brass, carried to the
fire and melted.

60. *Undeserving horses, &c.*] Their
spite against Sejanus, who could alone
deserve their indignation, carried
them to such fury, as to demolish
even the most innocent appendages
to his state and dignity.

61. *The fires roar, &c.*] From the
force of the bellows, in the forges
prepared for melting the brass of the
statues.

—*Stoves.*] Or furnaces.

62. *The head adored, &c.*] Of Sejanus, once the darling of the people, who once worshipped him as a
god.

63. *Cracks.*] By the violence of the
flames.

—*Second face, &c.*] Sejanus was
so favoured by Tiberius, that he
raised him to the highest dignity next
to himself.

64. *Water-pots, &c.*] The meanest household utensils are made from
the brass, which once conferred the
highest honour on Sejanus, when
representing him in the form of
statues.

65. *Laurels, &c.*] Here the poet
shews the malicious triumph of envy.
It was customary to adorn the doors
of their houses with crowns, or gar-

Power, subject to great envy, precipitates some,
A long and famous catalogue of honours overwhelms,
Statues descend and they follow the rope ;
Then, the driven axe, the very wheels of two-horse cars
Demolishes, and the legs of the undeserving horses are
    broken.   60
Now the fires roar, now with bellows and stoves,
The head adored by the people burns,—and the great
    Sejanus
Cracks : then, from the second face in the whole world,
Are made water-pots, basons, a frying-pan, platters.
Place laurels at your house, lead to the capitol a large   65
White bull ; Sejanus is dragged by a hook
To be looked upon : all rejoice : " what lips ? what a
    " countenance
" He had ? I never (if you at all believe me) loved
" This man :—but under what crime did he fall ? who
    " was
" The informer ? from what discoveries ? by what witness
    " hath he proved it ?"   70
" Nothing of these : a verbose and great epistle came from

---

lands of laurel, on any public occasion of joy ; such was the fall of poor Sejanus to his enemies.

66. *A white bull.*] The beasts sacrificed to the celestial gods were white (cretatum, here, lit. chalked, whited) ; those to the infernal gods were black. This offering to Jupiter, in his temple on the capitol hill, must be supposed to have been by the way of thanksgiving for the fall of Sejanus. A lively mark of the hatred and prejudice which the people had conceived against him, on his disgrace ; as it follows—

—*Dragg'd by a hook.*] To the Scalæ Gemoniæ, and then thrown into the Tiber.

67. *To be look'd upon.*] As a spectacle of contempt to the whole city.

—*All rejoice.*] At his disgrace and misery the people triumph.

—" *What lips, &c.*] The poet here supposes a language to be holden, which is very natural for a prejudiced ignorant people to utter on such an occasion, as they saw him dragging along by the hands of the executioner, or perhaps as they viewed him lying dead on the bank of the Tiber, (comp.

l. 86.) before his body was thrown into it.

What a blubber-lipp'd, ill-looking fellow ! say they.

69. *What crime.*] What was charged against him (says one) that he should be brought to this.

70. *Informer.*] Delator—his accuser to the emperor.

—*What discoveries.*] Of the fact, and its circumstances ? and on what evidence hath he (i. e. the informer) proved the crime alleged against him ?

—" *Nothing of these.*"] Says the answerer—i. e. there was no regular form of conviction.

—*A great epistle, &c.*] It, some how or other, came to the ears of Tiberius, that his favourite Sejanus had a design upon the empire, on which he wrote a long pompous epistle to the senate, who had Sejanus seized, and sentenced him to be punished, as is mentioned above : viz. that he should be put to death, then have a hook fixed in him, be dragged through the streets of Rome to the Scalæ Gemoniæ, and thrown at last into the Tiber.

A Capreis—bene habet : nil plus interrogo ; sed quid
Turba Remi ? Sequitur fortunam, ut semper, et odit
Damnatos. Idem populus, si Nurscia Thusco
Favisset, si oppressa foret secura senectus   75
Principis, hâc ipsâ Sejanum diceret horâ
Augustum. Jampridem, ex quo suffragia nulli
Vendimus, effudit curas—nam qui dabat olim
Imperium, fasces, legiones, omnia, nunc se
Continet, atque duas tantum res anxius optat,   80
Panem et Circenses. Perituros audio multos :
Nil dubium : magna est fornacula : pallidulus mî
Brutidius meus ad Martis fuit obvius aram—
Quam timeo, victus ne pœnas exigat Ajax,

Tiberius was at that time at Capreæ, an island on the coast of Naples, about twenty-five miles south
of that city, indulging in all manner
of excess and debauchery.

The Scalæ Gemoniæ was a place
appointed either for torturing criminals, or for exposing their bodies after execution. Some derive the name
Gemoniæ from one Gemonius, who
was first executed there ; others from
gemere, to groan, because the place
rang with the groans and complaints
of those who were put to death. It
was on the hill Aventinus, and there
were several steps leading up to it,
whence the place was called Scalæ
Gemoniæ. The dead bodies of those
who died under the hands of the executioner were dragged thither by an
iron hook, and after they had been
some time exposed to public view,
were thrown into the Tiber. See
Ant. Univ. Hist. vol. xii. p. 214,
note F.

73. *Mob of Remus.*] i. e. The
people in general ; so called because
descended from Romulus and Remus.
How did they behave ? says the
querist.

—" *It follows fortune,*" &c.] It
is answered—The common people behaved as they always do, by changing with the fortune of the condemned, and treating them with the
utmost spite.

74. *Nurscia, &c.*] Sejanus was a
Tuscan, born at Volscinium, where
the goddess of Nurscia, the same as
Fortune, was worshipped. q. d. If
fortune had favoured Sejanus.

75. *Secure old age, &c.*] If Tiberius had thought himself secure from
any plot against him, and therefore
had taken no measures to prevent the
consequences of it.

76. *Oppress'd.*] By death, from the
hands of Sejanus. q. d. If the plot
of Sejanus had succeeded, and the
emperor had been dethroned.

—*Would, &c.*] That very populace who now treat the poor fallen
Sejanus so ill, would have made him
emperor, and have changed his name
to the imperial title of Augustus.

—*This very hour.*] Instead of his
being put to death, dragged by the
hook, and insulted by the populace,
they would, at that very hour, have
been heaping the highest honours
upon him. So precarious, fluctuating, and uncertain, is the favour of
the multitude !

77. *We sell, &c.*] The poorer sort
of plebeians used to sell their votes
to the candidates for public offices,
before Julius Cæsar took from them
the right of electing their magistrates. Since that time—

78. *It.*] The populace.

—*Done with cares.*] Effudit, literally, has poured out, as a person
empties a vessel by pouring out the
liquor. The poet means, that since
the right of electing their magistrates
was taken from them, and they could
no longer sell their votes, they had
parted with all their cares about the
state.

—*For it.*] That same populace.

—*Which once gave, &c.*] By their

" Capreæ :"—" It is very well, I ask no more : but what
   " did

" The mob of Remus ?"—" It follows fortune, as always,
   " and hates

" The condemned—The same people, if Nurscia had
   " favoured

" The Tuscan—if the secure old age of the prince had
   " been   75

" Oppressed, would, in this very hour, have called Sejanus,

" Augustus.   Long ago, ever since we sell our suffrages

" To none, it has done with cares ; for it, which once gave

" Authority, fasces, legions, all things, now itself

" Refrains, and anxious only wishes for two things,   80

" Bread and the Circenses."—" I hear many are about to
   " perish"—

" No doubt : the furnace is large : my friend Brutidius

" Met me, a little pale, at the altar of Mars"—

" How I fear lest Ajax conquered should exact punishment,

---

having the right of election, conferred public offices on whom they chose.

79. *Authority.*] Power, or government : this alludes to the great offices in the state, which were once elective by the people.

—*Fasces.*] Consuls and prætors, who had the fasces carried before them.

—*Legions.*] Military prefectures.

—*All things.*] All elective offices.

79–80. *Itself refrains.*] From concerns of state.

80. *Only wishes, &c.*] Now they care for nothing else, at least with any anxiety, but for bread to be distributed to them as usual, by the command of the emperor, to satisfy their hunger ; and the games in the circus to divert them : of these last the populace were very fond.

81. " *I hear many,*" *&c.*] Here begins a fresh discourse on the occasion and circumstances of the time.

I hear, says one of the standers by, that Sejanus is not the only one who is to suffer ; a good many more will be cut off, as well as he, about this plot. No doubt, says the other—

82. *The furnace is large.*] And made to hold more statues for melt-

ing than those of Sejanus. See l. 61.

82–3. *Brutidius met me.*] This was a rhetorician and famous historian, a great friend of Sejanus, and therefore was horridly frightened, lest it should be his turn next to be apprehended and put to death, as concerned in the conspiracy.

84. *Lest Ajax conquer'd, &c.*]— Alluding to the story of Ajax, who, being overcome in his dispute with Ulysses about the armour of Achilles, (see OVID. Met. lib. xiii.) went mad, fell upon man and beast, and afterwards destroyed himself.

These seem to be the words of Brutidius, expressing his fears of being suspected to have been concerned in the conspiracy with Sejanus ; and, in order to wipe off all imputation of the kind, not only from himself, but from the person he is speaking to, he advises, that no time should be lost, but that they should hasten to the place where the corpse of Sejanus was exposed, and do some act which might be construed into an abhorrence of Sejanus, and consequently into a zeal for the honour and service of the emperor.

" How I fear," says Brutidius, looking aghast, " lest the emperor,

Ut male defensus ! curramus præcipites, et,   85
Dum jacet in ripâ, calcemus Cæsaris hostem.
Sed videant servi, ne quis neget, et pavidum in jus
Cervice astrictâ dominum trahat.   Hi sermones
Tunc de Sejano : secreta hæc murmura vulgi.
Visne salutari sicut Sejanus ? habere   90
Tantundem, atque illi sellas donare curules ?
Illum exercitibus præponere ? tutor haberi
Principis Augustâ Caprearum in rupe sedentis
Cum grege Chaldæo ? vis certe pila, cohortes,
Egregios equites, et castra domestica—quidni   95
Hæc cupias ? et qui nolunt occidere quenquam,
Posse volunt.   Sed quæ præclara, et prospera tanti,
Cum rebus lætis par sit mensura malorum ?

"thinking his cause not cordially
"espoused, and that he was badly
"defended, should wreak his ven-
"geance on such as he suspects to
"have been too remiss, and, like the
"furious Ajax, when overcome, like
"another victus Ajax, destroy all
"that he takes to be his enemies, as
"Ajax destroyed the sheep and oxen
"when he run mad on his defeat,
"taking them for the Grecians, on
"whom he vowed revenge." Other
expositions are given to this place,
but I think this suits best with l.
82-3.

85. *Let us run, &c.*] As precipi-
tately, as fast as we can ; let us lose
no time to avoid the emperor's sus-
picion of our favouring Sejanus,
and wreaking his vengeance upon
us.

—*While he.*] Sejanus—i. e. his
corpse.

86. *Lies on the bank.*] i. e. Exposed on the bank, before it is thrown
into the river Tiber.

—*Trample, &c.*] Set our feet upon
his corpse, to shew our indignation
against this supposed enemy of Tiberius.

87. *Let the slaves see, &c.*] That
they may be witnesses for their masters, in case these should be accused
of not having done it, or of having
shewn the least respect to Sejanus,
and so be brought under the displeasure of the emperor, and hurried to
judgment.

88. *Shackled neck.*"] Those who

were dragged to punishment, had a
chain or halter fastened about the
neck : this was the condition of some
when brought to trial ; so, among us,
felons, and others accused of capital
offences, are usually brought to their
trial with gyves or fetters upon their
legs.

88–9. *The discourses, &c.*] Thus
do the people talk about poor Sejanus,
the remembrance of his greatness
being all passed and gone, and his
shameful sufferings looked upon with
the most ignominious contempt.

90. *Saluted, &c.*] You, who think
happiness to consist in the favour of
the prince, in great power, and high
preferment, what think you ? do you
now wish to occupy the place which
Sejanus once held, to have as much
respect paid you, to accumulate as
many riches, to have as many prefer-
ments and places of honour in your
gift ?

91. *Chief chairs, &c.*] Sellas
curules. The poet speaks in the plural number, as each of the great officers of Rome had a chair of state,
made of ivory, carved, and placed in
a chariot—curru—in which they were
wont to be carried to the senate ; so
the prætor had his sella curulis, in
which he was carried to the forum,
and there sat in judgment. See before, l. 35. n. No. 4. When an ædile
was a person of senatorial dignity, he
was called curulis, from the curule
chair in which he was carried.

Sellas curules, here, is used in a

" As defended badly!—let us run headlong, and, while
     " he   85
" Lies on the bank, trample on the enemy of Cæsar.
" But let the slaves see, lest any should deny it, and drag
     " into
" Law their fearful master with shackled neck :" these were
     the
Discourses then about Sejanus ; these the secret murmurs
     of the vulgar.
Will you be saluted as Sejanus? have   90
As much—and give to one chief chairs of state—
Set another at the head of armies? be accounted guardian
Of a prince, sitting in the august rock of Capreæ,
With a Chaldæan band? you certainly would have jave-
     lins, cohorts,
Choice horsemen, domestic tents. " Why should you not
" Desire these things?" Even those who would not kill
     any one   96
Would be able. But what renowned and prosperous things
     are of so much
Value, since to prosperity there may be an equal measure
     of evils?

---

metonymical sense. Like curule ebur, Hor. lib. i. epist. vi. L 53–4. to denote the chief offices in the state, which had all been in the disposal of the once-prosperous Sejanus. See the last n. ad fin.

92. *Guardian, &c.*] Who, in the absence of Tiberius, at his palace on the rock at Capreæ, (see note on l. 71–2, ad fin.) amidst a band of astrologers from Chaldæa, (who amused the prince with their pretended knowledge of the stars, and their government of human affairs,) governed all his affairs of state, and managed them, as a tutor or guardian manages the affairs of a youth under age. Thus high was Sejanus in the opinion and confidence of Tiberius? but do you envy him?

94. *Javelins.*] Pila were a kind of javelins with which the Roman foot were armed: therefore the poet is here to be understood as saying to the person with whom he is supposed to discourse, " You certainly wish to be an officer, and to have soldiers under your command."

—*Cohorts.*] A cohort was a tenth part of a legion.

95. *Domestic tents, &c.*] The castra domestica were composed of horse, who were the body-guards of the prince or prætor ; hence called also prætoriani. These seem to have been something like our life-guards.

—" *Why should you not,*" *&c.*]— What harm, say you, is there in such a desire?—" I don't desire this " for the sake of hurting or killing " any body."—" Aye, that may be, " but still, to know that such a thing " may be in your power, upon occa- " sion, gives you no small idea of " self-importance."

97. *What renowned, &c.*] But, to consider cooly of the matter, what is there so valuable in dignity and prosperity, since, amid the enjoyment of them, they are attended with an equal measure of uneasiness, and when a fatal reverse, even in the securest and happiest moments, may be impending? the evil, therefore, may be said, at least, to counterbalance the good.

Hujus, qui trahitur, prætextam sumere mavis,
An Fidenarum, Gabiorumque esse potestas,   100
Et de mensurâ jus dicere, vasa minora
Frangere pannosus vacuis Ædilis Ulubris?
Ergo quid optandum foret, ignorâsse fateris
Sejanum: nam qui nimios optabat honores,
Et nimias poscebat opes, numerosa parabat   105
Excelsæ turris tabulata, unde altior esset
Casus, et impulsæ præceps immane ruinæ.
    Quid Crassos, quid Pompeios evertit, et illum,
Ad sua qui domitos deduxit flagra Quirites?
Summus nempe locus, nullâ non arte petitus,   110
Magnaque numinibus vota exaudita malignis.
Ad generum Cereris sine cæde et vulnere pauci
Descendunt reges, et siccâ morte tyranni.
    Eloquium ac famam Demosthenis, aut Ciceronis
Incipit optare, et totis Quinquatribus optat,   115
Quisquis adhuc uno partam colit asse Minervam,

99. *Of this man, &c.*] Of Sejanus. Had you rather be invested with his dignity?

100. *The power.*] The magistrate of some little town, like Fidenæ, or Gabii. Called in Italy, Podestà. Something like what we should call a country justice.

102, *A ragged Ædile.*] Pannosus signifies patched or ragged. The Ædile, in the burghs of Italy, was an officer who had jurisdiction over weights and measures, and if these were bad, he had authority to break them. He was an officer of low rank, and though, like all magistrates, he wore a gown, yet this having been delivered down from his predecessors, was old and ragged, very unlike the fine robe of Sejanus, and other chief magistrates at Rome. See PERS. sat. i. l. 130, and note.

—*Empty Ulubræ.*] A small town of Campania, in Italy, very thinly inhabited. Comp. sat. iii. l. 2.

103. *Therefore, &c.*] In this, and the four following lines, the poet very finely applies what he has said, on the subject of Sejanus, to the main argument of this Satire; viz. that mortals are too short-sighted to see, and too ignorant to know, what is best for them, and therefore those things which are most coveted, often prove

the most destructive; and the higher we rise in the gratification of our wishes, the higher may we be raising the precipice from which we may fall.

107. *Enforced ruin.*] Impulsæ ruinæ, into which he was driven, as it were, by the envy and malice of those enemies, which his greatness, power, and prosperity, had created. Impulsæ, metaph. alluding to the violence with which a person is thrown, or pushed, from an high precipice. Immane—dreadful—immense—huge —great.

108. *The Crassi.*] M. Crassus making war upon the Parthians for the sake of plunder, Surena, general of the enemy, slew him, and cut off his head and his hand, which he carried into Armenia to his master.

—*The Pompeys.*] Pompey the Great, being routed at the battle of Pharsalia, fled into Egypt, where he was perfidiously slain. He left two sons, Cneius and Sextus; the first was defeated in a land battle in Spain, the other in a sea-fight on the coast of Sicily. We are not only to understand here Crassus and Pompey, but, by Crassos et Pompeios, plural, all such great men who have fallen by ill-fated ambition.

Had you rather take the robe of this man, who is dragged
Along, or be the power of Fidenæ, or Gabii,   100
And judge about a measure, and lesser vessels
Break, a ragged Ædile at empty Ulubræ ?—
Therefore, what was to be wished for, you will confess
    Sejanus
To have been ignorant; for he who desired too many
    honours,
And sought too much wealth, was preparing numerous 105
Stories of an high tower, from whence his fall might be
Higher, and the precipice of his enforced ruin be dreadful.
  What overthrew the Crassi, the Pompeys, and him
    who
Brought down the subdued Romans to his scourges?
Why truly, the chief place, sought by every art,   110
And great vows listened to by malignant gods.
To the son-in-law of Ceres, without slaughter and wound,
    few
Kings descend, and tyrants by a dry death.
  For 'the eloquence and fame of Demosthenes, or of
    Cicero,
He begins to wish, and does wish during the whole Quin-
    quatria,   115
Whoever reveres Minerva, hitherto gotten for three far-
    things,

109. *Brought down, &c.*] i. e. Julius Cæsar, who, after he had obtained the sovereignty, partly by arms and violence, partly by art and intrigue, was publicly assassinated in the senate-house, as a tyrant and enemy to the liberty of his country. His scourges—i. e. made them slaves, as it were, and subject to his will, liable to be treated in the most humiliating manner.

110. *Chief place.*] The ambition of reigning absolutely. The poet here shews the fatal source of misery to the aspiring and ambitious, namely, a restless desire after greatness, so as to leave no stone unturned to come at it—nulla non arte, &c.

111. *Great vows.*] i. e. Wishes and prayers for greatness, honours, riches, &c.

—*By malignant gods.*] Who, provoked by the unreasonable and foolish wishes of mortals, punish them, with

accepting their vows, and with granting their desires. Comp. l. 7-8.

112. *Son-in-law of Ceres.*] Pluto, the fabled god, and king of the infernal regions: he stole Proserpina, the daughter of Jupiter and Ceres, and carried her to his subterranean dominions.

The poet means here to say, that few of the great and successful ambitious die, without some violence committed upon them.

113. *A dry death.*] Without bloodshed.

115. *The whole, &c.*] Minerva was the goddess of learning and eloquence; her festival was celebrated for five days, hence called Quinquatria; during this the school-boys had holidays.

116. *Whoever reveres, &c.*] The poor school-boy, who has got as much learning as has cost him about three farthings; i. e. the merest young

Quem sequitur custos angustæ vernula capsæ :
Eloquio sed uterque perit orator : utrumque
Largus et exundans letho dedit ingenii fons :
Ingenio manus est et cervix cæsa ; nec unquam   120
Sanguine causidici maduerunt rostra pusilli.——
" O fortunatam natam, me consule, Romam !"
Antoni gladios potuit contemnere, si sic
Omnia dixisset : ridenda poëmata malo,
Quam te conspicuæ, divina Philippica, famæ.   125
Volveris a primâ quæ proxima.   Sævus et illum
Exitus eripuit, quem mirabantur Athenæ
Torrentem, et pleni moderantem fræna theatri.
Dis ille adversis genitus, fatoque sinistro,
Quem pater ardentis massæ fuligine lippus,   130
A carbone et forcipibus, gladiosque parante
Incude, et luteo Vulcano ad rhetora misit.
Bellorum exuviæ, truncis affixa trophæis

beginner at the lower end of the school.

117. *A little slave, &c.*] This is a natural image of little master going to school, with a servant-boy to carry his satchel of books after him, and heightens the ridiculous idea of his coveting the eloquence of the great orators.

118. *Each orator, &c.*] See note on l. 9. *i. e.* Both Demosthenes and Cicero. Demosthenes, to avoid the cruelty of Antipater, poisoned himself.

120. *Hand and neck, &c.*] Of Cicero, which were cut off by the emissaries of Antony, when they attacked and murdered him in his litter on the road. They, *i. c.* Tully's head and hand, were afterwards fixed up at the rostra, from whence he had spoken his Philippics, by order of Antony.

—*Cut off by genius.*] *i. e.* His capacity and powers of eloquence, which he used against Antony, brought this upon him.

121. *Rostra*] A place in the forum, where lawyers and orators harangued. See AINSW. *Rostra*, No. 2. No weak lawyer, or pleader, could ever make himself of consequence enough to be in danger of any design against his life, by what he was capable of saying in public.

122. *O fortunatam, &c.*] Mr. Dryden renders this line,

*Fortune fore-tun'd the dying notes
    of Rome,*
*Till I, thy consul sole, consol'd thy
    doom :*

and observes, that " the Latin of this " couplet is a verse of Tully's, (in " which he sets out the happiness of " his own consulship,) famous for " the vanity and ill poetry of it."

It is bad enough ; but Mr. Dryden has made it still worse, by adding more jingles to it. However, to attempt translating it is ridiculous, because it disappoints the purpose of the passage, which is to give a sample of Tully's bad poetry in his own words.

123. *If thus, &c.*] *q. d.* If Tully had never written or spoken better than this, he needed not to have dreaded any mischief to himself ; he might have defied the swords which Antony employed against him.

124. *Laughable poems*] Ridenda —ridiculous, that are only fit to be laughed at.

125. *Divine Philippic*] Meaning Cicero's second Philippic, which, of all the fourteen orations which he made against Antony, was the most cutting and severe, and this probably cost him his life.

Whom a little slave follows, the keeper of his narrow
    satchel:
But each orator perished by eloquence; each
A large and overflowing fountain of genius consigned to
    death.
The hand and neck was cut off by genius; nor ever   120
Were rosta wet with the blood of a weak lawyer.
" O fortunatam natam, me consule, Romam !"
He might have contemned the swords of Antony, if thus
He had said all things. I like better laughable poems,
Than thee, divine Phillippic of conspicuous fame,   125
Who art rolled up next from the first. Him also a cruel
Death snatched away; whom Athens admired,
Rapid, and moderating the reins of the full theatre.
He was begotten, the gods adverse, and fate unpropitious,
Whom his father, blear-eyed with the reek of a burning
    mass,   130
From coal and pincers, and from the anvil preparing
Swords, and from dirty Vulcan, sent to a rhetorician.
    The spoils of war, to maimed trophies a breast-plate

He called these orations Philippics,
as he tells Atticus, because in the
freedom and manner of his speech he
imitated the Philippics (Φιλιππικοι
λογοι) of Demosthenes, whose orations against Philip were so called.

126. *Roll'd up, &c.*] Volvens. The
books of the ancients were rolled up
in volumes of paper or parchment;
this famous Philippic stood second in
the volume. See sat. xiv. l. 102.

127. *Athens admired.*] Demosthenes. See note on l. 9.

128. *Rapid.*] Torrentem, his eloquence rapid and flowing, like the
torrent of a river.

—*Moderating*—] Or governing the
full assembly of his hearers as he
pleased, as a horse is governed and
managed by a rein; so Demosthenes
regulated and governed the minds of
his auditory.

129. *Gods adverse, &c.*] It was a
current notion among the ancients,
that where people were unfortunate
in their lives, the gods were displeased
at their birth, and always took a part
against them.

130. *His father.*] Demosthenes is
said to have been the son of a black-
smith at Athens.

—*Of a burning mass.*] Large
masses of iron, when red-hot out of
the forge, are very hurtful to the eyes
of the workmen, from their great
heat.

131. *Coal and pincers, &c.*] His
father at first thought of bringing up
his son Demosthenes to his own
trade; but he took him from this, and
put him to a rhetorician to be taught
eloquence.

132. *Dirty Vulcan*] Vulcan was
the fabled god of smiths, whose trade
is very filthy and dirty. Sat. xiii. l.
44–5.

133. *Maimed trophies.*] The trophy
was a monument erected in memory
of victory. The custom came from
the Greeks, who, when they had
routed their enemies, erected a tree,
with all the branches cut off, on
which they suspended the spoils of
armour which they had taken from
them, as well as other ensigns of victory · several of which the poet here
enumerates; but as nothing was entire, the poet calls them maimed
trophies.

Lorica, et fractâ de casside buccula pendens,
Et curtum temone jugum, victæque triremis   135
Aplustre, et summo,tristis captivus in arcu,
Humanis majora bonis creduntur : ad hæc se
Romanus, Graiusque ac Barbarus induperator
Erexit : causas discriminis atque laboris
Inde habuit. TANTO MAJOR FAMÆ SITIS EST, QUAM   140
VIRTUTIS : QUIS ENIM VIRTUTEM AMPLECTITUR IPSAM,
PRÆMIA SI TOLLAS ? patriam tamen obruit olim
Gloria paucorum, et laudis, titulique cupido
Hæsuri saxis cinerum custodibus : ad quæ
Discutienda valent sterilis mala robora ficûs,   145
Quandoquidem data sunt ipsis quoque fata sepulchris.
Expende Hannibalem : quot libras in duce summo
Invenies ? hic est, quem non capit Africa Mauro

134. *A beaver.*] Buccula, from bucca, the cheek, seems to have been that part of armour which was fastened to the helmet, and came down over the checks, and fastened under the chin.

135. *Beam*] Temo was the beam of the wain, or the draught-tree, whereon the yoke hung : by this the chariot was supported and conducted, while drawn by the yoke.

136. *A sad captive, &c.*] On the top of the triumphal arch, which was built upon these occasions, they made some wretched captive place himself, and there sit bemoaning his wretched fate, while the conquerors were exulting in their victory. So DRYDEN:
—*an arch of victory,*
On whose high convex sits a captive
foe,
And sighing casts a mournful look
below.

137. *To be greater, &c.*] Such is the folly of mankind, that these wretched trifles are looked upon not only as bearing the highest value, but as something more than human.

—*For these, &c.*] Commanders of all nations have exerted themselves, through every scene of danger and fatigue, in order to get at these ensigns of fame and victory. Erexit se —hath roused himself to mighty deeds.

139. *The Roman.*] By the Roman, perhaps, we may understand Julius

Cæsar, M. Antony, and others, who, while they were greedily following military glory, were preparing ruin for themselves, as well as many sad calamities to their country.

—*Greek.*] Here Miltiades and Themistocles, the two Athenian generals, may be alluded to, who, while they were catching at military fame, perished miserably.

138. *Barbarian.*] A name which the Greeks and Romans were fond of fixing on all but themselves.

Here may be meant Hannibal, the great Carthaginian general, who, while he vexed the Romans with continual wars, occasioned the overthrow of his country, and his own miserable death.

139. *Causes of danger, &c*] These things have been the grand motives of their exertions, in the very face of difficulty, and even of death.

140. *So much greater, &c.*] i. e. All would be great ; how few wish to be good !

142. *If you take away, &c*] Who is so disinterestedly virtuous, as to love and embrace virtue, merely for the sake of being and doing good ? indeed, who would be virtuous at all, unless the fame and reputation of being so brought something with them to gratify the pride and vanity of the human heart ? Virtue seldom walks forth, saith one, without vanity at her side.

Fixed, and a beaver hanging from a broken helmet,
A yoke deprived of its beam, the flag of a conquered   135
Three-oared vessel, and a sad captive at the top of an arch,
Are believed to be greater than human goods: for these
The Roman, Greek, and Barbarian commander hath
Exerted himself: the causes of danger and labour hath had
From thence.   So much greater is the thirst of fame than
Of Virtue: for WHO EMBRACES EVEN VIRTUE ITSELF,   141
IF YOU TAKE AWAY ITS REWARDS?—yet formerly the glory
    of a few
Has ruined a country, and the lust of praise, and of
A title to be fixed to the stones, the keepers of their ashes;
    which,
To throw down, the evil strength of a barren fig-tree is
    able,   145
Since fates are given also to sepulchres themselves.
Weigh Hannibal—how many pounds will you find in that
Great General? this is he, whom Africa, washed by the
    Moorish

—*The glory of a few.*] As Marius, Sylla, Pompey, Antony, &c.—*q. d.* Many instances have there been, where a few men, in search of fame, and of the gratification of their ambition, have been the destroyers of their country.

144. *A title, &c.*] An inscription to be put on their monuments, in which their remains were deposited; this has often proved a motive of ambition, and has urged men to the most dangerous, as well as mischievous exploits.

145. *Evil strength, &c.*] There was a sort of wild fig-tree, which grew about walls and other buildings, which, by spreading and running its roots under them, and shooting its branches into the joinings of them, in length of time weakened and destroyed them, as we often see done by ivy among us. See PERS. sat. i. l. 25. Evil here is to be understood in the sense of hurtful, mischievous.

A poor motive to fame, then, is a stone monument with a fine inscription, which, in length of time, it will be in the power of a wild fig-tree to demolish.

146. *Fates are given, &c.*] Even sepulchres themselves must yield to fate, and, consequently, the fame and glory, which they are meant to preserve, must perish with them; how vain then the pursuit, how vain the happiness, which has no other motive or foundation!

147. *Weigh Hannibal.*] Place him in the scale of human greatness; *i. e.* consider him well, as a great man.

Hannibal was a valiant and politic Carthaginian commander; he gave the Romans several signal overthrows, particularly at Cannæ, a village of Apulia, in the kingdom of Naples.

—*How many pounds, &c.*] Alas, how little is left of him! a few inconsiderable ashes! which may be contained within the compass of an urn, though, when living, Africa itself was too small for him! So DRYDEN:

Great Hannibal within the balance
    lay,
And tell how many pounds his ashes
    weigh;
Whom Afric was not able to con-
    tain, &c.

148. *Wash'd, &c.*] By the Moorish sea. The poet describes the situation of Africa, the third part of the globe then known. From Asia it is sepa-

2 B

Perfusa occano, Niloque admota tepenti.
Rursus ad Æthiopum populos, aliosque elephantos.   150
Additur imperiis Hispania : Pyrenæum
Transilit : opposuit natura Alpemque nivemque :
Diduxit scopulos, et montem rupit aceto.
Jam tenet Italiam, tamen ultra pergere tendit ;
Actum, inquit, nihil est, nisi Pœno milite portas   155
Frangimus, et mediâ vexillum pono Suburrâ.
O qualis facies, et quali digna tabellâ,
Cum Gœtula ducem portaret bellua luscum !
Exitus ergo quis est ? ô gloria ! vincitur idem
Nempe, et in exilium præceps fugit, atque ibi magnus   160
Mirandusque cliens sedet ad prætoria regis,
Donec Bithyno libeat vigilare tyranno.

rated by the Nile; on the west it is washed by the Atlantic ocean, which beats upon the shores of Ethiopia and Libya, joining to which were the people of Mauritania, or Moors, conquered by Hannibal.

149. *Warm Nile.*] Made so by the great heat of the sun, it lying under the torrid zone.

150. *Again.*] Rursus—*i. e.* insuper, moreover.

—*Other elephants*] Other countries where elephants are bred; meaning, here, Libya and Mauritania, which were conquered by Hannibal.

151. *Spain is added, &c.*] To the empires he had conquered he added Spain, yet was not content.

—*The Pyrenean.*] The Pyrenees, as they are now called, that immense range of high mountains which separate France from Spain.

152. *Nature opposed, &c.*] For nature, as Pliny says, raised up the high mountains of the Alps as a wall, to defend Italy from the incursions of the Barbarians. These are constantly covered with snow.

153. *Severed rocks, &c.*] By immense dint of labour and perseverance he cut a way in the rocks, sufficient for his men, horses, and elephants to pass.

—*With vinegar.*] Livy says, that, in order to open and enlarge the way above mentioned, large trees were felled, and piled round the rock, and set on fire ; the wind blowing hard, a fierce flame soon broke out, so that

the rock glowed like the coals with which it was heated. Then Hannibal caused a great quantity of vinegar to be poured upon the rock, which piercing into the veins of it, which were now cracked by the intense heat of the fire, calcined and softened it, so that he could the more easily cut the path through it.

Polybius says nothing of this vinegar, and therefore many reject this incident as fabulous.

Pliny mentions one extraordinary quality of vinegar, viz. its being able to break rocks and stones which have been heated by fire. But, admitting this, it seems difficult to conceive how Hannibal could procure a quantity of vinegar sufficient for such a purpose, in so mountainous and barren a country. See ANT. Univ. Hist. vol. XVII. p. 597, 8.

154. *Possesses Italy, &c.*] *i. e.* Arrives there, comes into Italy, which for sixteen years together he wasted and destroyed, beating the Roman troops wherever he met them; but he was not content with this, he determined to go further, and take Rome.

155. *Nothing is done, &c.*] This is the language of an ambitious mind, which esteemed all that had been done as nothing, unless Rome itself were conquered.

—*Punic army*] The Pœni (quasi Phœni a Phœnicibus unde orti) were a people of Africa, near Carthago; but being united to them, Pœni is

Sea, and adjoining to the warm Nile, does not contain :
Again, to the people of Ethiopa, and to other elephants,
Spain is added to his empires : the Pyrenean   151
He passes : nature opposed both Alps and snow :
He severed rocks, and rent the mountain with vinegar.
He now possesses Italy, yet endeavours to go farther :
" Nothing is done," says he, " unless, with the Punic army,
     " we break   -   155
" The gates, and I place a banner in the midst of Suburra."
O what a face ! and worthy of what a picture !
When the Getulian beast carried the one-eyed general !
Then what his exit ? O glory ! for this same man
Is subdued, and flies headlong into banishment, and there
     a great   160
And much to be admired client sits at the palace of the
     king,
Till it might please the Bithynian tyrant to awake.

used, per synec. for the Carthaginians in general.

156. *Suburra.*] One of the princi-pal streets in Rome. See before, sat. iii. 5, note.

157. *What a face !*] What a figure was he all this while ; how curious a picture would he have made, mount-ed on his elephant, and exhibiting his one-eyed countenance above the rest ?

When Hannibal came into Etruria (Tuscany) the river Arno was swelled to a great height, insomuch that it occasioned the loss of many of his men and beasts, particularly of the elephants, of which the only one re-maining was that on which Hannibal was mounted. Here, by the damps and fatigue, he lost one of his eyes.

158. *Getulian beast.*] i. e. The ele-phant. The Getulians were a people of Lybia, bordering on Mauritania, where many elephants were found.

159. *His exit.*] What was the end of all his exploits, as well as of him-self ?

—O glory !] Alas, what is it all !

160. *Is subdued, &c.*] He was at last routed by Scipio, and forced to fly for refuge to Prusias king of Bithynia.

161. *Client.*] Cliens signifies a re-tainer, a dependent, one who has put himself under the protection of a pa-tron, to whom he pays all honour and observance.

This great and wonderful man was thus reduced, after all his glorious deeds.

—Sits, &c.] Like a poor and mean dependent.

162. *Till it might please, &c.*]— The word tyrant is not always to be taken, as among us it usually is, in a bad sense. It was used in old time in a good sense for a king, or sove-reign.

—To awake.] When he came to prefer his petition for protection, he could gain no admission till the king's sleeping hours were over : Hannibal was now in too abject and mean a condition to demand an audience, or even to expect one, till the king was perfectly at leisure.

It is the custom of the eastern princes to sleep about the middle of the day (2 Sam. iv. 5.) when the heats are intense, and none dare disturb them. This was the occasion of the deaths of many in our time at Cal-cutta, where, when taken by the Su-bah Surajah Dowlah, a number of gentlemen were put into a place called the Black-hole, where the air was so confined, that it suffocated the great-est part of them : but they could not be released while their lives might have been saved ; for, being put there

Finem animæ, quæ res humanas miscuit olim,
Non gladii, non saxa dabant, non tela, sed ille
Cannarum vindex, et tanti sanguinis ultor,   165
Annulus. I, demens, et sævas curre per Alpes,
Ut pueris placeas, et declamatio fias.
Unus Pellæo juveni non sufficit orbis :
Æstuat infelix angusto limite mundi,
Ut Gyaræ clausus scopulis, parvâque Seripho.   170
Cum tamen a figulis munitam intraverat urbem,
Sarcophago contentus erat. MORS SOLA FATETUR
QUANTULA SINT HOMINUM CORPUSCULA. Creditur olim
Velificatus Athos, et quicquid Græcia mendax
Audet in historiâ ; constratum classibus îsdem,   175
Suppositumque rotis solidum mare : credimus altos
Defecisse amnes, epotaque flumina Medo
Prandente, et madidis cantat quæ Sostratus alis.

---

by order of the Subah, who alone could order their release, the officers of that prince only answered their cries for deliverance, by saying, that the Subah was lain down to sleep, and nobody dared to wake him.

. 163. *Disturbed human affairs.*]— Miscuit, disordered, put into confusion; a great part of the world, by his ambitious exploits and undertakings.

166. *A ring, &c.*] When he overthrew the Romans at Cannæ, he took above three bushels of gold rings from the dead bodies, which, says the poet, were fully revenged by his ring, which he always carried about him, and in which he concealed a dose of poison ; so that when the Romans sent to Prusias to deliver him up, Hannibal, seeing there were no hopes of safety, took the poison and died. Thus fell that great man, who had so often escaped the swords, and the darts, and stones hurled by the enemy, as well as the dangers of the horrid rocks and precipices of the Alps !

· 166. *Go madman.*] For such wert thou, and such are all who build their greatness and happiness on military fame.

167. *Please boys, &c.*] The boys in the schools used to be exercised in making and speaking declamations, the subjects of which were usually

taken from histories of famous men. A fine end, truly, of Hannibal's Alpine expedition, to become the subject of a school-boy's theme or declamation ! well worthy so much labour, fatigue, and danger !

168. *Pellæan youth.*] Alexander the Great, born at Pella, a city of Macedon, died of a fever, occasioned by drinking to excess at Babylon. He had lamented that, after having conquered almost all the East, all Greece, and, in short, the greatest part of the world, there were no more worlds for him to conquer. He died three hundred and twenty-three years before Christ, æt. thirty-three.

170. *Gyaras.*] One of the Cyclades (islands in the Ægean sea) whereto criminals were banished : it was full of rocks. See i. 60.

171. *The city.*] Babylon.

—*Brickmakers.*] This city was surrounded by a wall of brick, of an immense height and thickness. Ov. Met. iv. l. 58. Figulus signifies any worker in clay ; so a maker of bricks.

172. *Sarcophagus.*] A grave, tomb, or sepulchre. A σαρξ, flesh, and φαγειν, to eat, because bodies there consume and waste away.

—*Death only, &c.*] Death alone teaches us how vain and empty the pursuits of fame and earthly glory are ; and that, however the ambitious

The end of that life, which once disturbed human affairs,
Nor swords, nor stones, nor darts gave, but that
Redresser of Cannæ, and avenger of so much blood,   165
A ring.—Go, madman, and run over the savage Alps,
That you may please boys, and become a declamation.
    One world did not suffice the Pellæan youth:
He chafes unhappy in the narrow limit of the world,   169
As one shut up in the rocks of Gyaras, or small Seriphus,
Yet when he had entered the city fortified by brickmakers,
He was content with a Sarcophagus. DEATH ONLY DIS-
    COVERS
HOW LITTLE THE SMALL BODIES OF MEN ARE. It is
    believed, that, formerly,
Athos was sailed through, and whatever lying Greece
Adventures in history; the solid sea strowed with   175
Those very ships, and put under wheels: we believe deep
Rivers to have failed, and their waters drunk up when the
    Mede
Dined, and what things Sostratus sings with wet wings.

may swell with pride, yet, in a little while, a small urn will contain the hero, who, when living, thought the world not sufficient to gratify his ambition.

174. *Athos, &c.*] A mountain in Macedon, running like a peninsula into the Ægean sea. Xerxes is said to have digged through a part of it to make a passage for his fleet.

175. *Adventures in history.*] *i. e.* Dares to record in history. The Grecian historians were very fond of the marvellous, and, of course, were apt to introduce great improbabilities and falsehoods in their narrations.

175. *Strowed.*] Covered, paved, as it were; for Xerxes is said to have had twelve thousand ships with him in his expedition, with which he formed the bridge after mentioned.

176. *Those very ships.*] Which had sailed through the passage at mount Athos.

—*Put under wheels.*] He, in order to march his forces from Asia into Europe, made a bridge with his ships over the sea, which joined Abydus, a city of Asia, near the Hellespont, to Sestos, a city of the Thracian Chersonesus, which was opposite to Aby-

dus, and separated by an arm of the sea; this part is now known by the name of the Dardanelles. The sea being thus made passable by the help of the bridge, the army, chariots, horses, &c. went over, as if the sea had been solid under them; therefore the poet says, sepositum rotis solidum mare, the firm sea. Hol.

—*We believe.*] *i. e.* If we give credit to such historians.

177. *Rivers failed, &c.*] It is said that Xerxes' army was so numerous, as to drink up a river at once, whenever they made a meal. HERODOT. lib. ii.

—*The Mede.*] The Medes and Persians composed the army of Xerxes.

178. *Sostratus.*] A Greek poet, who wrote the Persian expedition into Greece.

—*Wet wings.*] The fancy of a poet may be compared to wings, for it is by this he takes his flight into the regions of invention. The fancy of Sostratus is here supposed to have been moistened with wine; in short, that no man who was not drunk, which is signified by madidus, could ever have committed such improbabilities to writing.

Ille tamen qualis rediit Salamine relictâ,
In Corum atque Eurum solitus sævire flagellis　　　180
Barbarus, Æolio nunquam hoc in carcere passos,
Ipsum compedibus qui vinxerat Ennosigæum?
Mitius id sane; quod non et stigmate dignum
Credidit: huic quisquam vellet servire deorum.
Sed qualis rediit? nempe unâ nave cruentis　　　185
Fluctibus, ac tardâ per densa cadavera prorâ.
Has toties optata exegit gloria pœnas.
　Da spatium vitæ, multos da, Jupiter, annos:
Hoc recto vultu, solum hoc et pallidus optas.
Sed quam continuis et quantis longa senectus　　　190
Plena malis! deformem, et tetrum ante omnia vultum,
Dissimilemque sui, deformem pro cute pellem,
Pendentesque genas, et tales aspice rugas,
Quales, umbriferos ubi pandit Tabraca saltus,

179. *What, &c.*] What manner of
man—qualis—how wretched, how
forlorn, how changed from what he
was! Comp. l. 185.
　—*That barbarian.*] Xerxes.
　Salamis being left.] When he left
and fled from Salamis, an island and
city in the Ægean sea, near which
Themistocles, the Athenian general,
overcame him in a sea-fight, and
forced him to fly.
　180. *Rage with whips, &c.*] When
he found the sea raging, and being
raised by those winds, to have destroyed his bridge, he was mad enough
to order the Hellespont to be scourged
with three hundred lashes. I don't
read any where, but in this passage of
Juvenal, of his whipping the winds.
　181. *Never, suffered, &c.*] The
poet here alludes to Æn. i. L 56—67.
where Æolus is represented as holding the winds in prison, and giving
them liberty to come forth as he
pleased.
　182. *Who bound Ennosigæus, &c.*]
Xerxes was also mad enough to cast
iron fetters into the sea, as if to bind
Neptune in chains; who was called
Ennosigæus, the earth-shaker, from
the notion that he presided over the
waters of the sea, which made their
way into the earth, and caused earth-
quakes. From Gr. εννοσις, concus-
sio, and γαια, terra. See GEL-

LIUS. See the Orphic hymn, quoted
in PARKH. Heb. Lex. under בהר
No. 1.
　183. *Rather mild, &c.*] The poet
ironically says, "that, to be sure, all
"this was very gentle in Xerxes, and
"that he did not carry the matter
"farther, must be considered as very
"gracious in a man who might have
"thought proper to have marked him
"as a slave." Stigma signifies a
brand or mark set on the forehead of
fugitive slaves, to which, no doubt,
this passage alludes.
　184. *Any of the gods.*] As well as
Neptune, would, doubtless, without
murmuring, have served so mild and
gracious a prince! Still speaking
ironically, in derision of the pride and
folly of Xerxes.
　185. *What manner, &c.*] After all
this extravagance of pride. See note
on l. 179.
　—*One vessel.*] Navis signifies any
vessel of the sea or river. The vessel
in which Xerxes made his escape,
after his defeat near Salamis, was a
poor fishing-boat.
　186. *Bloody waves.*] Made so by
the slaughter of such numbers of the
Persian army.
　—*Slow prow, &c.*] The sea was
so crowded with the floating carcases
of the slain, that the boat could hardly
make its way.

But what did that barbarian return, Salamis being left,
Who was wont to rage with whips, against the north-west
  and . 180
East wind, (which never suffered this in the Æolian
  prison,)
Who bound Ennosigæus himself with fetters?
That indeed was rather mild, that not worthy a mark also
He thought him.—Any of the gods would be willing to
  serve him.
But what manner of man returned he? Truly with one
  vessel in the 185
Bloody waves, and, with slow prow, through thick carcases,
Glory so often wished for exacted this punishment.
  Give length of life, give, O Jupiter, many years!
This with upright countenance, and this, pale, alone you
  wish.—
But with what continual, and with how great evils is old
  age 190
Full! See the countenance deformed, and hideous beyond
  every thing,
And unlike itself, an unsightly hide instead of a skin:
And pendent cheeks, and such wrinkles,
As, where Tabraca extends its shady forests,

187. *Glory, &c.*] This haughty prince, who had collected so vast a force together, in order to carry on the war with the Athenians, begun by his father Darius, and invading Greece with seven hundred thousand men of his own kingdoms, three hundred thousand auxiliaries, and with twelve thousand ships, after beating Leonidas and taking Sparta, is defeated by Themistocles, his army cut to pieces, his fleet destroyed, and himself forced to escape in a wretched fishing-boat. All this might be well called the just demand of vengeance against his pride, and mad thirst after glory.

188. *Give, &c.*] The poet now satirizes the folly of wishing for long life: he supposes one praying for it.

189. *Upright countenance, &c.*] i. e. Looking up to heaven—pale, with fear of death, or lest the petition should be refused.

But, perhaps, recto vultu may here be a phrase to express one in youth and health; and the following palli-dus may denote a state of old age and sickness: comp. l. 191.
  " *Both sick and healthful, old and young, conspire*
  " *In this one silly, mischievous desire.*" DRYDEN.
192. *Itself.*] Its former self.
  —*Unsightly hide.*] Here is a distinction between cutis and pellis, the former signifying the skin of a man, the other the hide of a beast; to the last of which, by an apt catachresis, the poet compares the coarse and rugged appearance of an old man's skin.
193. *Pendent cheeks.*] It is observable, that, in old persons, the cheeks, not only in the part of them which is immediately below the eyes, hang in purses downwards, but also in that part which, in youth, forms the roundness, and contributes so much to the beauty and comeliness of the face, hang downwards in a relaxed and pendent state.
194. *Tabraca, &c.*] Now called Tunis, on the Mediterranean, near

In vetulâ scalpit jam mater simia buccâ.   195
Plurima sunt juvenum discrimina, pulchrior ille
Hoc, atque ille alio : multum hic robustior illo :
Una senum facies, cum voce trementia membra,
Et jam læve caput, madidique infantia nasi.
Frangendus misero gingivâ panis inermi :   200
Usque adeo gravis uxori, gnatisque, sibique,
Ut captatori moveat fastidia Cosso.
Non eadem vini atque cibi, torpente palato,
Gaudia quid refert, sedeat quâ parte theatri,
Qui vix cornicines exaudiat, atque tubarum   205
Concentus ? clamore opus est, ut sentiat auris,
Quem dicat venisse puer, quot nunciet horas.
Præterea minimus gelido jam in corpore sanguis
Febre calet solâ : circumsilit agmine facto
Morborum omne genus, quorum si nomina quæras,   210
Promptius expediam, quot amaverit Hippia mœchos,
Quot Themison ægros autumno occiderit uno ;

which was a wood, wherein was a
vast quantity of apes.

195. *Her old cheek.*] Bucca properly signifies the cheek, or that part
of it which swells out on blowing ;
but here it seems (by synec.) to denote the whole face, every part of
which, in the animal he speaks of,
especially when old, is in a wrinkled
state.

Dryden has well preserved the humour of this simile :

Such wrinkles as a skilful hand
    would draw,
For an old grandam-ape, when,
    with à grace,
She sits at squat, and scrubs her
    leathern face.

196. *The differences, &c.*] The poet
is here to be understood as observing,
that, however, in the days of youth,
one is distinguishable from another
by different beauties of countenance,
and strength of body, old age renders all distinctions void ; and, in
short, one old man is too like another to admit of them, both with respect to countenance and bodily
strength.

199. *Smooth head.*] Bald with the
loss of hair.

—*Infancy, &c.*] A running and
drivelling nose, like a young child.

200. *Unarm'd gum.*] Having lost
all his teeth, he has nothing left but
his bare gums to mumble his food
withal.

202. *The flatterer Cossus.*] Capta-
tor signifies one who endeavoureth to
get or procure any thing, particularly
he who flattereth a man to be his heir.
This mean occupation was frequent
in Rome, and this Cossus seems to
have been famous for it ; yet old age,
like what the poet has been describing, is sufficient, says he, even to
disgust Cossus himself, so as to keep
him away from paying his court.

203. *The palate, &c.*] Every
thing now grows insipid ; all difference of meats and drinks is lost.
See this symptom of age mentioned
by Barzillai. 2 Sam. xix. 35.

205. *The cornets.*] Cornicen (from
cornu, an horn, and cano, to sing)
signifies a blower on the horn, or cornet, the sound of which was probably very loud and harsh, as was that
of the trumpets. If he be so deaf
that he cannot hear these, he cannot
expect to hear the singers, and the
soft instruments.

206. *Bawling, &c.*] His boy must
bawl as loud as he can into his ear,
when he would tell him who called to
visit him, or to let him know what

A mother-ape scratches in her old cheek.   195
The differences of youths are very many, one is handsomer
    than
This, and he than another: this far more robust than
    that:
The face of old men is one, the limbs trembling with the
    voice,
And now a smooth head, and the infancy of a wet nose.
Bread is to be broken by the wretch with an unarmed
    gum: 200
So very burthensome, to wife, and children, and himself,
That he would move the loathing of the flatterer Cossus.
The palate growing dull, the joys of wine and food are not
    the same:
What signifies it in what part of a theatre he may sit,
Who can hardly hear the cornets, and the sounding of
    the   205
Trumpets? There needs a bawling, that the ear may per-
    ceive
Whom his boy may say has come, how many hours he may
    bring word of.
Beside, the very little blood, now in his cold body,
Is only warm from fever: there leap around, formed into a
    troop,
All kind of diseases, the names of which were you to ask,
I could sooner unfold, how many adulterers Hippia has
    loved,   211
How many sick Themison has killed in one autumn;

o'clock it was. They had not watches and clocks as we have, but sun-dials and hour-glasses, which a boy was to watch, and acquaint the master how the time went.

    Horas quinque puer nondum tibi
        nuntiat, et tu
    Jam convita mihi, Cæciliane, venis.
            MART. lib. viii. ep. 67.

209. *Warm from fever.*] The blood is so cold, and circulates so slowly, that nothing can warm or quicken it but that hectic, feverish habit, which frequently is an attendant on the decays of of old age.

Gelidus tardante senecta
    Sangnis hebet, &c. Æn. v. l. 395-6.

—*Leap around, &c.*] Surround him on all sides, ready to rush upon

him, like wild beasts leaping on their prey.

—*Form'd into a troop.*] A whole troop of diseases, in array against him. Agmine facto. See VIRG. Æn. i. 86. from whence our poet borrows this expression. See sat. iii. 151, and note 2.

211. *Hippia.*] A woman famous for her debaucheries.

212. *Themison.*] A physician much commended by Pliny and Celsus, though here spoken of in no very favourable light. Perhaps Juvenal gives this name to some empiric, in derision.

—*Autumn.*] The autumn was usually a sickly time at Rome. See sat. iv. l. 55-6, and notes.

2 c

Quot Basilus socios, quot circumscripserit Hirrus
Percurram citius, quot villas possideat nunc,
Quo tondente, gravis juveni mihi barba sonabat.   215
Ille humero, hic lumbis, hic coxâ debilis, ambos
Perditit ille oculos, et luscis invidet : hujus
Pallida labra cibum capiunt digitis alienis.
Ipse ad conspectum cœnæ diducere rictum
Suetus, hiat tantum, ceu pullus hirundinis, ad quem   220
Ore volat pleno mater jejuna.   Sed omni
Membrorum damno major dementia, quæ nec
Nomina servorum, nec vultum agnoscit amici,
Cum quo præteritâ cœnavit nocte, nec illos,
Quos genuit, quos eduxit : nam codice sævo   225
Hæredes vetat esse suos ; bona tota feruntur
Ad Phialen : tantum artificis valet halitus oris,
Quod steterat multos in carcere fornicis annos.
Ut vigeant sensus animi, ducenda tamen sunt

213. *Allies, &c.*] When the Romans had conquered any people, they
reduced them into the form of a province, which, being subject to Rome,
was governed by a Roman prætor,
and the inhabitants were called socii,
allies, and, indeed, looked upon, in
all respects, as such, not daring to
refuse a confederacy with their conquerors. Basilus was one of these
prætors, who shamefully plundered
his province.

—*Hirrus.*] Some read Irus. Whoever this was, his character is here
noted, as a cheater and circumventer
of youth, committed to his care and
guardianship.

He that had the tuition of a ward
was called tutor. The word was called
Pupillus. The pupilli were orphans,
who had lost their parents, and thus
fell under the tuition of guardians,
who frequently, instead of protecting
them, plundered and cheated them
out of their patrimony.

215. *Who clipping.*] See sat. i. 23,
and notes.

Cinnamus was a barber at Rome,
who got a knight's estate, and growing very rich, had several villas, and
lived in a sumptuous manner ; but,
at last, he broke, and fled into Sicily. See MART. vii. epigr. 64.

216. *One is weak, &c.*] That host
of diseases, mentioned l. 209-10. are

here represented as making their attacks on different parts of the body.

218, *Of this.*] Hujus—i. e. hominis.

—*Take food, &c.*] So feeble and
childish that he cannot feed himself,
and is forced to be fed by another.

219. *He, at the sight, &c.*] As
soon as supper is served, he, as it
were mechanically, stretches open his
jaws ; but, unable to feed himself,
he only gapes, like a young swallow
in a nest, when it sees the old one
flying towards it with food in her
mouth. This natural image is beautifully expressed.

222-3. *Neither knows.*] i. e. Re-
collects ; his memory now failing.

223. *The names of servants.*] The
poet here brings his old man into the
last stage of superannuation, when the
understanding and memory fail,
which, as he says, is worse than all
the rest.

225. *Brought up.*] Though he has
not only begotten, but brought up his
children, so that they must have
lived much with him, yet they are
forgotten ; he makes a will, by which
he disinherits them, and leaves all
he has to some artful strumpet who
has got possession of him.

—*A cruel will.*] Codex, or caudex,
literally means the trunk, stem, or
body of a tree. Hence, by metonym-

How many of our allies Basilus, how many Hirrus has
    cheated.
Sooner run over how many country-houses he may now
    possess,
Who clipping, my beard, troublesome to me a youth,
    -sounded. 215
One is weak in his shoulder, another in his loins, another
    in his hip,
Another has lost both his eyes, and envies the blind of one.
The pale lips of this take food from another's fingers:
He, at the sight of a supper, accustomed to stretch open his
Jaw, -only gapes, like the young one of a swallow, to
    whom 220
The fasting dam flies with her mouth full. But, than all
    the loss
Of limbs, that want of understanding is greater, which
    neither
Knows the names of servants, nor the countenance of a
    friend,
With whom he supped the night before, nor those
Whom he hath begotten, whom brought up: for, by a
    cruel will, 225
He forbids them to be his heirs; all his goods are carried
To Phiale: so much avails the breath of an artful mouth,
Which has stood for many years in the prison of a brothel:
Though the senses of the mind may be strong, yet funerals
    of children

a table-book, made of several boards joined together, on which they used to write; hence any writing, as a deed, will, &c. See sat. vii. 110.

226. *Forbids them.*] He excludes them from inheriting his estate, *i. e.* he disinherits them.

—*Are carried.*] Are disposed of, conveyed by the will.

227. *To Phiale.*] See above, l. 225. note the first.

—*So much avails, &c.*] Such an old dotard as this, may be easily persuaded to any thing by an artful strumpet; so great an ascendancy does she acquire over him by her artful and insinuating tongue.

228. *Prison of a brothel.*] Fornix, lit. an arch or vault in houses; also, meton. a stew or brothel, because these were in vaults or wells under ground. AINSW. Hence, from the darkness or filthiness of their situation, as well as from the confinement of the wretched inhabitants therein, who stood ready for every comer, Juvenal represents Phiale as having stood in carcere fornicis, which is describing her as a common prostitute.

HOR. lib. i. sat. ii. 30. alluding to the filth of these dungeons, says,

    Contra alius nullam nisi olenti in
        fornice stantem.

Carcer signifies also a starting-place at the chariot-races; hence, by metonym. a beginning; in this sense it may mean the entrance of a brothel, where the harlots presented themselves to the view of the passers-by. Comp. sat. iii. l. 65. n. l.

229. *Tho' the senses, &c.*] i. e. Yet

Funera gnatorum, rogus aspiciendus amatæ   230
Conjugis, et fratris, plenæque sororibus urnæ.
Hæc data pœna diu viventibus ; ut renovatâ
Semper clade domûs, multis in luctibus, inque
Perpetuo mœrore, et nigrâ veste senescant.
Rex Pylius (magno si quicquam credis Homero)   235
Exemplum vitæ fuit a cornice secundæ :
Felix nimirum, qui tot per sæcula mortem
Distulit, atque suos jam dextrâ computat annos,
Quique novum toties mustum bibit : oro, parumper
Attendas, quantum de legibus ipse queratur   240
Fatorum, et nimio de stamine, cum videt aeris
Antilochi barbam ardentem : nam quærit ab omni,
Quisquis adest, socio, cur hæc in tempora duret ;
Quod facinus dignum tam longo admiserit ævo.
Hæc eadem Peleus, raptum cum luget Achillem,   245
Atque alius, cui fas Ithacum lugere natantem.

allow him to retain his senses in full vigour, what grievous scenes of distress has he to go through !
—*Children.*] So VIRG. Æn. vi. l. 308.

Impositisque rogis juvenes ante ora parentum.

230. *To be attended.*] Ducere funera is a phrase peculiarly adapted to the ceremony of funerals, and probably it is derived from a custom of the friends of the deceased walking in procession before the corpse. See i. 132. See GRANG. in loc. " Du-" cere—verbum sepulturæ. Albinov. " ad Liviam. Funera ducuntur Ro-" mana per oppida Drusi."
—*The pile.*] The funeral pile, on which the body was reduced to ashes.

231. *Urns fill'd, &c.*] *i. e,* With their bones and ashes, which it was customary to preserve in pots (after being gathered from the funeral pile) called urns.

232. *This pain, &c.*] This is the sad lot of long-lived people, as it must be their fate to out-live many of their friends.

232–3. *Slaughter of the family, &c.*] Some part or other of which is continually dropping off.

233. *Many sorrows, &c.*] *i. e.* Bewailings of the death of friends.

234. *Black habit.*] By this we find,

that the wearing of mourning for the loss of relations is very ancient, and that black was the colour which the ancients used on such occasions. See sat. iii. l. 201.

235. *Pylian king.*] Nestor, the king of Pylos, in Peloponnesus, who, according to Homer, is said to have lived three hundred years.

236. *Second from a crow.*] Cornix signifies a crow, or rook. This species of bird is fabled to live nine times the age of a man. Nestor (says the poet) stands second to this long-lived bird.

238. *With the right.*] The ancients used to count their numbers with their fingers ; all under one hundred was counted on the left hand, all above on the right.

239. *So often drank, &c.*] Mustum signifies new wine. The vintage, when this was made, was in the autumn ; so that the poet here means to observe that Nestor lived for many returns of this season.
—*Attend.*] The poet calls for attention to what he is going to prove, by various examples, namely, that happiness does not consist in long life.

240–1. *Laws of the fates.*] The ancients believed all things, even the gods themselves, to be governed by the fates. Old men, who were from

Are to be attended, the pile to be seen of a beloved   230
Wife, and of a brother, and urns filled with sisters.
This pain is given to long-livers, so that, the slaughter
Of the family being continually renewed, in many sorrows,
    and in
Perpetual grief, and in a black habit, they may grow old.
The Pylian king (if you at all believe the great Homer)
Was an example of life second from a crow :   236
Happy, no doubt, who through so many ages had deferred
Death, and now computes his years with the right hand,
And who so often drank new must : I pray, attend
A little—How much might he complain of the laws   240
Of the fates, and of too much thread, when he saw the
    beard of
Brave Antilochus burning : he demands of every friend
Which is present, why he should last till these times—
What crime he had committed worthy so long life.
The very same does Peleus, while he mourns Achilles
    snatched away,   245
And another, to whom it was permitted to lament the
    swimming Ithacus.

various causes afflicted, might be apt to complain of their destiny, and Nestor among the rest.

241. *Of too much thread.*] The fates were supposed to be three sisters, who had all some peculiar business assigned them by the poets, in relation to the lives of men. One held the distaff, another spun the thread, and the third cut it. *q. d.* How might he complain that the thread of his life was too long.

242. *Antilochus.*] The son of Nestor, slain, according to Homer, by Memnon, at the siege of Troy ; according to Ovid, by Hector. His beard burning, *i. e.* on the funeral pile. This mention of the beard implies, that he was now grown to man's estate.

—*He demands, &c.*] The poet here very naturally describes the workings and effects of grief, in the afflicted old man, who is now tempted to think, that his great age was granted him as a punishment for some greater crime than he could recollect to have committed, as he was permitted to live to see so sad an event as the death of his brave and

beloved son. He is therefore represented as inquiring of his friends what could be the cause of his being reserved for such an affliction.

245. *Peleus.*] The father of Achilles, slain by Paris, who shot him in the heel in the temple of Apollo, the only part where he was vulnerable. His father Peleus had to lament his untimely death.

246. *Another.*] Laertes, a prince of Ithaca, father of Ulysses. He, during his son's absence, and wanderings over the seas, wearied himself with daily labour in husbandry, and having no other attendant than an old maid-servant, who brought him food : during this period his constant petition to Jupiter was, that he might die.

—*Swimming Ithacus.*] Ulysses was called Ithacus, from Ithaca, a country of Ionia where he reigned. After the destruction of Troy, he suffered many toils and hardships, for ten years together, before his return home. The word natantem perhaps alludes to his shipwreck near the island of Calypso, where he was forced to swim to save his life ; or

Incolumi Trojâ Priamus venisset ad umbras
Assaraci magnis solennibus, Hectore funus
Portante, ac reliquis fratrum cervicibus, inter
Iliadum lachrymas, ut primos edere planctus   250
Cassandra inciperet, scissâque Polyxena pallâ,
Si foret extinctus diverso tempore, quo non
Cœperat audaces Paris ædificare carinas.
Longa dies igitur quid contulit? omnia vidit
Eversa, et flammis Asiam ferroque cadentem   255
Tunc miles tremulus positâ tulit arma tiarâ,
Et ruit ante aram summi Jovis, ut vetulus bos,
Qui domini cultris tenue et miserabile collum
Præbet, ab ingrato jam fastiditus aratro.
Exitus ille utcumque hominis: sed torva canino   260
Latravit rictu, quæ post hunc vixerat, uxor.
Festino ad nostros, et regem transeo Ponti,

perhaps it may allude, in general, to the length of time he passed in sailing on the sea.

247. *Troy being safe*] i. e. Had Troy stood, and remained in safety.

—*Priam.*] The last king of Troy, who lived to see the city besieged by the Greeks for ten years together, and at length taken.

247–8. *Shades of Assaracus, &c.*] Had joined his ancestor's ghosts, or shades, in the infernal regions: i. e. had died in peace, and had been buried with the splendid funeral rites belonging to his rank. See Virg. Æn. i. 288; and Ainsw. *Assaracus.*

248. *Hector carrying, &c.*] Among the ancients, the corpse of the parent was carried forth to the funeral pile by the sons of the deceased. If Troy had remained in quiet, Priam's son Hector had not been slain by Achilles, but had survived his father, and have, as the custom was, been one of his bearers to the funeral pile.

249. *The rest of the shoulders, &c.*] Reliquis cervicibus—for cervicibus reliquorum, &c. Hypallage. According to Homer, Priam had fifty sons and twelve daughters: the former of which would have assisted Hector in carrying their father's corpse. Pliny says, (lib. vii. c. 44.) Quintus Metellus Macedonicus, a quatuor filiis illatus est rogo.

Priam was slain in the siege by

Pyrrhus, the son of Achilles, and most of his children were destroyed. See Æn. ii. 501–54.

250. *As soon as, &c.*] This was the signal for the funeral procession to move forward towards the pile.

—*Cassandra, &c.*] She was the daughter of Priam and Hecuba. It was customary to hire women to mourn at burials, who went before the corpse to lament the dead; the chief of them who began the ceremony was called præfica, (a præficio, planctuum princeps. Ainsw.) This part must here most naturally have been taken by Cassandra, Priam's daughter, who would, doubtless, have put herself at the head of the mourning women. See 2 Chron. xxxv. 25.

After the taking of Troy, she fell to the share of Agamemnon. She was married to Chorœbus, and debauched by Ajax Oileus, in the temple of Minerva. See Æn. i. 44. and ii. l. 103–7.

251. *Polyxena, &c*] The daughter also of Priam, who gave her in marriage to Achilles; but he, coming into the temple of Apollo to perform the nuptial rites, was there treacherously slain by Paris. She was afterwards sacrificed at the tomb of Achilles. See before, l. 215. note.

—*Rent garment.*] Rending the garments, in token of grief, was very ancient.

Troy being safe, Priam had come to the shades
Of Assaracus with great solemnities, Hector carrying
The corpse, and the rest of the shoulders of his brethren,
    among
The tears of the Trojans, as soon as Cassandra should
    begin   250
To utter the first wailings, and Polyxena with a rent gar-
    ment,
Had he been extinct at another time, in which Paris
Had not begun to build the daring ships.
What therefore did long life advantage to him ? he saw all
    things
Overturned, and Asia falling by fire and sword.   255
Then, a trembling soldier, the diadem being laid aside, he
    bore arms,
And fell before the altar of high Jove, as an old ox,
Who, to the master's knife, offers his lean and miserable
Neck, now despised by the ungrateful plough.
However, that was the exit of a man : but his fierce wife,
Who outlived him, barked with a canine jaw.   261
I hasten to our own, and pass by the king of Pontus,

252. *Been extinct*] i. e. If he had died.

—*At another time, &c*] i. e. Before Paris prepared to sail into Greece, in order to ravish Helen from her husband Menelaus. Had this been the case, Priam would have been borne to the grave by his sons, and his funeral solemnized by the public lamentations of his daughters.

253. *Daring ships*] So called from the daring design they were employed in ; the execution of which occasioned the Trojan war, and the destruction of the country by the Greeks.

254. *What therefore, &c.*] The poet here applies this instance of old king Priam to his main argument against wishing to live to old age, seeing with how many sorrows it may be accompanied.

255. *Asia falling.*] See VIRG. Æn. iii. l. 1. By Asia is here meant the Lesser Asia, containing the Greater and Lesser Phrygia, the kingdom of Priam.

256. *Trembling soldier.*] Priam, now trembling, and almost worn out by age.

—*Diadem being laid aside*] Having laid aside all ensigns of royalty.

—*Bore arms*] In defence of his country. See Æn. ii. 207-558. where these parts of Priam's history are described.

257. *Fell before the altar.*] Of Jupiter Herceus, erected by Priam in an open court belonging to the palace : hither he fled for succour and protection, but was slain by Pyrrhus. Æn. ii. 501-2.

259. *Ungrateful plough*] Prosopopeia. The plough is here represented as ungrateful, as forgetting the labours of the old worn-out ox, and despising him as now useless. Some understand aratro for agricola —meton.

260. *Exit of a man.*] He died, however, like a man—this was not the case of his wife

—*Fierce wife, &c*] Hecuba, wife of Priam, who, after the sacking of Troy, railed so against the Greeks, that she is feigned to have been turned into a bitch. OVID Met. lib. xiii. l. 567-9.

262. *To our own*] To mention in-

Et Crœsum, quem vox justi facunda Solonis
Respicere ad longæ jussit spatia ultima vitæ.
Exilium et carcer, Minturnarumque paludes,   265
Et mendicatus victâ Carthagine panis,
Hinc causas habuêre.   Quid illo cive tulisset
Natura in terris, quid Roma beatius unquam,
Si circumducto captivorum agmine, et omni
Bellorum pompâ, animam exhalâsset opimam,   270
Cum de Teutonico vellet descendere curru?
Provida Pompeio dederat Campania febres
Optandas; sed multæ urbes, et publica vota
Vicerunt: igitur fortuna ipsius, et urbis
Servatum victo caput abstulit.   Hoc cruciatu   275
Lentulus, hâc pœnâ caruit, ceciditque Cethegus
Integer, et jacuit Catilina cadavere toto.
Formam optat modico pueris, majore puellis
Murmure, cum Veneris fanum videt anxia mater,

stances and examples among our own
people.

—*The king of Pontus.*] Mithridates, who maintained a long war
with the Romans, but was at last
routed by Pompey. He would have
shortened his days by poison, but had
so fortified himself by an antidote,
invented by him, and which still
bears his name, that none would operate upon him.

263. *Crœsus, whom, &c.*] Crœsus
was the last king of Lydia. so rich,
that Crœsi divitiæ was a proverbial
saying. He asked Solon (one of the
wise men of Greece, and lawgiver of
the Athenians) who was the happiest
man? The philosopher told him,
" no man could be said to be happy
" before death." This, afterwards,
Crœsus found to be true; for, being
taken prisoner by Cyrus, and ordered to be burned, he cried out, " So-
" lon! Solon! Solon!" Cyrus asked
the reason of this, and was told what
Solon had said; whereupon, considering it might be his own case, he
spared his life, and treated him with
much respect. Respicere—to consider—mind—regard.

265. *Marshes of Minturnæ.*]—
Caius Marius being overcome in the
civil war by Sylla, was forced to skulk
in the marshes of Minturnæ, a city
by the river Liris, where he was

found, taken, and imprisoned; he
then escaped into Africa, where he
lived in exile, and begged his bread
in the streets of Carthage, which had
been conquered by the Romans.

267. *Hence had their causes.*] All
these misfortunes were owing to Marius's living so long; he died in the
sixty-eighth year of his age.

—*Than that citizen.*] i. e. Than
Marius.

269-71. *If—when, &c.*] If when,
in his triumph after conquering the
Cimbri, he had numbers of captives
led around his triumphal car, and
amidst all the pomp and glory of victory, he had breathed out his mighty
soul, as he descended, after the triumph was over, from his chariot, he
had been the happiest man in nature,
or that Rome ever bred, and have
escaped the miseries which afterwards
befel him.

271. *Teutonic chariot.*] The Teutones were a people bordering on the
Cimbri, conquered by Marius; the
chariot in which Marius rode in his
triumph over these people, is therefore called Teutonic, as used on that
occasion.

272. *Provident Campania.*] When
first Pompey engaged in the civil war
against Cæsar, he had a violent fever
at Naples, and another at Capua, of
which he was like to have died; these

And Crœsus, whom the eloquent voice of just Solon
Commanded to look at the last period of a long life.
Banishment and a prison, and the marshes of Minturnæ,
And bread begged in conquered Carthage, 266.
Hence had their causes—what, than that citizen, had
Nature on the earth, or Rome ever borne, more happy,
If, the troop of captives being led around, and in all
The pomp of wars, he had breathed forth his great soul,
When he would descend from the Teutonic chariot ? 271
Provident Campania had given Pompey fevers
To be wished for; but many cities, and public vows
Overcame them; therefore his own fortune, and that of the
    city,
Took off his preserved head from him conquered; this tor-
    ment, 275
This punishment Lentulus was free from; and Cethegus
    fell
Entire, and Catiline lay with his whole carcase.
    With moderate murmur, the anxious mother desires
    beauty
For her boys—with greater for her girls, when she sees the
    temple of Venus,

seem to have been provided against the miseries which afterwards befel him.

273. *To be wished for.*] In order to take him out of life, while he was great and happy.

274. *Overcame them.*] The united wishes and prayers of so many cities and people, for his recovery, prevailed against the effects of his sickness, and saved his life.

—*His own fortune.*] Which reserved him to be slain in his flight to Egypt, after his defeat by Cæsar.

—*That of the city.*] Doomed to fall under the dominion of Pompey's enemy, after suffering so much by a civil war.

275. *Took off, &c.*] That life which had been preserved in a dangerous sickness (see note on l. 274.) was destroyed after his defeat, and his head severed from his body by Achillas and Salvius, sent for that purpose from Ptolemy, who intended it as a present to Cæsar.

Of Pompey's death, see ANT. Univ. Hist. vol. xiii. p. 217.

276. *Lentulus—Cethegus.*] These were in the conspiracy with Catiline, and being put into prison, by order of Cicero, then consul, were strangled, so that their bodies were not dismembered.

277. *Catiline, &c.*] The famous conspirator, whose designs were detected and frustrated by Cicero, died in battle, without the loss of any part of his body. See SALLUST. All these died young men, and thus were taken away from the miseries which those meet with who live to old age.

278. *Moderate murmur.*] The word murmur here implies that sort of muttering which they used at their prayers to the gods; this was louder, and more distinct, on some occasions than on others, according to the degree of fervency in the suppliant. Comp. PERS. sat. ii. 6–8.

—*Anxious mother, &c.*] The poet here represents another popular folly, in supposing a mother anxious for having handsome children, and praying for this at the shrine of Venus, the fabled goddess of beauty.

2 D

Usque ad delicias votorum : cur tamen, inquit,   280
Corripias ? pulchrâ gaudet Latona Dianâ.
Sed vetat optari faciem Lucretia, qualem
Ipsa habuit.   Cuperet Rutilæ Virginia gibbum
Accipere, atque suam Rutilæ dare.   Filius autem
Corporis egregii miseros trepidosque parentes   285
Semper habet.   RARA EST ADEO CONCORDIA FORMÆ
ATQUE PUDICITIÆ ! sanctos licet horrida mores
Tradiderit domus, ac veteres imitata Sabinas.
Præterea, castùm ingenium, vultumque modesto
Sanguine ferventem tribuat natura benignâ   290
Larga manu : (quid enim puero conferre potest plus
Custode, et curâ Natura potentior omni ?)
Sed casto quid forma nocet ? quid profuit olim
Hippolyto grave propositum ? quid Bellerophonti ?
Erubuit nempe hæc, ceu fastidita repulsâ :   295
Nec Sthenobœa minus quam Cressa excanduit, et se
Concussêre ambæ.   Mulier sævissima tunc est,

280. *Even to the delight, &c.*] So
that the highest and fondest of them
might be gratified ; delicias means
gratification ; she prays they might
be so handsome as fully to satisfy her
wishes.

281. *Blame me.*] A question supposed from the mother to the poet, on
his finding fault with her for what she
did.

—*Latona rejoices, &c.*] She defends
what she does by quoting an example.
Latona, daughter of Cœus, one of the
Titans, bore, to Jupiter, Apollo and
Diana at the same birth.

282–3. *Lucretia forbids, &c.*] The
poet answers the example brought for
asking beautiful children, by the instance of Lucretia, whose beauty
proved her undoing. She was a beautiful Roman lady, the daughter of Lu-
cretius, prefect of the city, and wife
of Tarquinius Collatinus, ravished by
Sextus Tarquinius, son of Tarquinius
Superbus, which she so resented, that
she sent for her father and husband,
and stabbed herself before them. The
people of Rome, on this, rose in arms,
expelled the Tarquins, and changed
the monarchy to a commonwealth.

283. *Virginia.*] A Roman virgin,
exceedingly beautiful, whom her own
father, to prevent her being exposed

to the lust of Appius, one of the De-
cemviri, stabbed in the middle of the
forum.

283–4. *Rutila.*] An ugly deformed
old woman, above seventy-seven years
old, as Pliny says, was in no danger
of such a death, and therefore happier in her deformity than Virginia
in her beauty ; so that the latter
might have gladly changed her person
for that of Rutila.

284. *But a son, &c.*] *i. e.* A son
with an accomplished and beautiful
person makes his parents unhappy,
and keeps them in perpetual fear, so
very rarely do beauty and modesty
meet together.

285. *Person.*] The word corporis,
which literally signifies the body, is
here used for the whole person of the
man, per synec.

287. *Homely house, &c.*] *i. e.*
Though the plain family, rough and
honest, should have furnished him
with the best morals, and brought
him up in all the plain and virtuous
simplicity of the old Sabines, transmitting modesty and chastity by their
own examples also.

289. *Glowing, &c.*] Easily blush-
ing at every species of indecency.

292. *More pow'rful, &c.*] *i. e.*
Who is more powerful than all out-

Even to the delight of her wishes. Yet, why, says she,
Should you blame me? Latona rejoices in fair Diana. 281
But Lucretia forbids a face to be wished for, such
As she had. Virginia would desire to accept the hump of
    Rutila,
And give her (shape) to Rutila. But a son, with a
Remarkable person, always has miserable and trembling
Parents—So RARE IS THE AGREEMENT OF BEAUTY   286
AND CHASTITY!—Though the homely house chaste morals
    should
Have transmitted, and imitated the old Sabines.
Beside, a chaste disposition, and a countenance glowing
With modest blood, let bounteous nature give him   290
With a kind hand, (for what more upon a boy can
Nature, more powerful than a guardian, and than all care,
    bestow?)
But how does beauty hurt the chaste? what, once on a time,
    did
A solemn resolution benefit Hippolytus? what Belle-
    rophon?
Truly this one reddened as if scorned by a repulse: 295
Nor was Sthenobœa less on fire than the Cretan, and both
Vexed themselves. A woman is then most cruel

ward restraints. q. d. Natural good
dispositions are more powerful preser-
vatives against vice, than all the
watchfulness and care of guardians
and parents.

293. *How does beauty, &c.*] Granting that beauty may be pernicious, in
instances like those above mentioned,
yet how can it injure the chaste and
virtuous?

294. *A solemn resolution, &c.*]—
This was the solemn resolve of Hippolytus, to refuse the love of his step-
mother Phædra, who, for this, accused him of tempting her to incest.
He fled away in a chariot by the sea
side, but the horses taking fright at
the sea-calves lying on the shore,
overturned the chariot, and killed
him.

—*Bellerophon.*] Sthenobœa (the
wife of Pœtus, king of the Argives)
falling in love with him, he refused
her; at which she was so incensed,
that she accused him to her husband;
this forced him upon desperate adventures, which he overcame. Sthe-

nobœa, hearing of his success, killed
herself.

295. *This one redden'd, &c.*] Phædra
reddened with anger and resentment,
as thinking herself despised.

296. *Sthenobœa, &c.*] See note on
l. 294.

—*The Cretan.*] Phædra was the
daughter of Minos, king of Crete.

—*Both.*] Phædra and Sthenobœa.

297. *Vexed themselves.*] Concussere.
The verb concutio literally signifies
to shake, jog, or stir; and, when
applied to the mind, to trouble, vex,
or disquiet. Here it intimates, that
these women shook, or stirred themselves, into a fit of rage and vexation.
It seems to be used metaphorically,
from the custom of the wrestlers and
boxers at the theatres, who, before
they engaged, gave themselves blows
on the breast, or sides, to excite anger and fury. Thus the lion is said
to shake his mane, and lash himself
with his tail, when he would be furious.

—*Most cruel, &c.*] A woman is

Cum stimulos odio pudor admovet... Elige quidnam
Suadendum esse putes, cui nubere Cæsaris uxor
Destinat: optimus hic, et formosissimus idem   300
Gentis patriciæ rapitur miser extinguendus
Messalinæ oculis: dudum sedet illa parato
Flammeolo; Tyriusque palam genialis in hortis
Sternitur, et ritu decies centena dabuntur
Antiquo: veniet cum signatoribus auspex.   305
Hæc tu secreta, et paucis commissa putabas?
Non nisi legitime vult nubere. Quid placeat, dic:
Nî parere velis, pereundum est ante lucernas:
Si scelus admittas, dabitur mora parvula, dum res
Nota urbi et populo, contingat principis aures: 310
Dedecus ille domûs sciet ultimus. Interea tu
Obsequere imperio, si tanti est vita dierum
Paucorum: quicquid melius, leviusque putaris,

---

then most savage and relentless,
when, on being disappointed, the fear
of shame adds spurs to her resentment, and her passion of love is
changed to hatred. See Gen. xxxix.
7-20.

Virgil represents Juno as stirred
up to her relentless hatred to Æneas,
and the Trojans, from several motives; among the rest, from the contempt which had been shewn her by
Paris, in his judgment against her at
mount Ida.

Necdum etiam causæ irarum, sævi-
que dolores,
Exciderant animo, manet alta mente
repostum
Judicium Paridis, spretæque in-
juria formæ, &c. &c.
        Æn. i. 29, 30, 31.
See also Æn. v. 5-7.

298. *Choose, &c.*] *i. e.* Think it
over, and determine, all things considered, what advice you would give.

299. *To him whom, &c.*] Silius is
meant here, a noble Roman, whom
the empress Messalina so doated upon,
that she made him put away his wife
Julia Syliana, and resolved to marry
him in the absence of her husband,
the emperor Claudius, who was gone
no farther than Ostia, a city near the
mouth of the Tiber.

302. *By the eyes, &c.*] By her having fixed her eyes upon him, so as to
become enamoured with him.

—*Long she sits, &c.*] The time

seems long to her, while waiting for
Silius.

302-3. *Prepared bridal veil.*]—
Which she had prepared for the ceremony.

303. *Openly, &c.*] She transacts
her matter openly, without fear or
shame; accordingly she omits nothing
of the marriage ceremony; she put
on the flame-coloured marriage veil;
the conjugal bed was sumptuously
adorned with purple, and prepared
in the Lucullan gardens, a place of
public resort. See note on l. 307.

304. *Ten times an hundred.*] She
had her portion ready, according to
ancient custom. On this instance it
amounted to the vast sum of one
thousand sestertia. See sat. i. l. 92.
note. This was supposed to be given
to the husband, in consideration of
the burdens of matrimony.

305. *Soothsayer—signers, &c.*]—
The soothsayer, who always attended
on such occasions. VALER. lib. ii.
says, that, among the ancients, nothing of consequence was undertaken,
either in private or public, without
consulting the auspices; hence a
soothsayer attended on marriages.—
Auspex—quasi avispex—because they
divined from the flight and other actions of birds.

The signatories were a sort of public notaries, who wrote and attested
wills, deeds, marriage-settlements,
&c. These also were present; for,

When shame adds goads to hatred.   Choose what
You think to be advised, to him whom Cæsar's wife
    destines
To marry: this the best and most beautiful too   300
Of a patrician family is hurried, a wretch, to be destroyed
By the eyes of Messalina: long she sits in her prepared
Bridal veil, and openly the Tyrian marriage-bed is strowed
In the gardens, and ten times an hundred will be given by
    ancient
Rite: the soothsayer, with the signers, will come.   305
Do you think these things secret, and committed to a
    few?
She will not marry unless lawfully,   Say—what like
    you?—
Unless you will obey, you must perish before candle-
    light.
If you commit the crime, a little delay will be given, till the
    thing,
Known to the city and to the people, reaches the prince's
    ears,   310
(He will last know the disgrace of his house.) In the
    mean while
Do thou obey the command, if the life of a few days is
Of such consequence; whatever you may think best and
    easiest,

before the marriage, they wrote down in tables, (tabulis,) by way of record, the form of the contract, to which they, with the witnesses, set their seals.

306. *These things secret, &c.*] That she does things privately, so that only a few chosen secret friends should know them? by no means.

307. *Unless lawfully.*] She determines to marry publicly, with all the usual forms and ceremonies; and this, says Tacitus, in the face of the senate, of the equestrian order, and of the whole people and soldiery. See ANT. Univ. Hist, vol. xiv. p. 344. note i.

—*Say, what like you?*] Quid placeat—what it may please you to do. Say, Silius, which part will you take in such a situation? what do you think best to do, under so fatal a dilemma?

308. *Unless, &c.*] If you refuse

this horrid woman's offer, she will have you murdered before night.

309. *If you commit the crime.*]—Of marrying the wife of another.

—*A little delay, &c.*] You will probably live for a few days; the public rumour will reach the prince's ears, though later than the ears of others, as he will probably be the last who hears the dishonour done to his family, few, perhaps, daring to break such a thing to him.

312. *The command.*] Of Messalina.

—*If the life of a few days, &c.*] If you think that living a few days more or less is of so much consequence, that you will sooner commit a crime of such magnitude to gain a short respite, than risk an earlier death, by avoiding the commission of it, then to be sure you must obey; but whichever way you determine—

Præbenda est gladio pulchra hæc et candida cervix.
Nil ergo optabunt homines? si consilium vis,　　315
PERMITTES IPSIS EXPENDERE NUMINIBUS, QUID
CONVENIAT NOBIS, REBUSQUE SIT UTILE NOSTRIS.
Nam pro jucundis aptissima quæque dabunt Dî.
CARIOR EST ILLIS HOMO, QUAM SIBI: nos animorum
Impulsu, et cæcâ magnâque cupidine ducti,　　　320
Conjugium petimus, partumque uxoris: at illis
Notum, qui pueri, qualisque futura sit uxor.
Ut tamen et poscas aliquid, voveasque sacellis
Exta, et candiduli divina tomacula porci;
ORANDUM EST, UT SIT MENS SANA IN CORPORE SANO. 325
Fortem posce animum, et mortis terrore carentem;
Qui spatium vitæ extremum inter munera ponat
Naturæ, qui ferre queat quoscunque labores;

314. *Neck, &c.*] This beautiful person of yours will be sacrificed, either to Messalina's resentment, if you do not comply, or to the emperor's, if you do. However, the marriage took place, and they pleased themselves in all festivity that day and night; afterwards Silius was seized by the emperor's command, and put to death; thus exhibiting a striking example of the sad consequences which often attend being remarkable for beauty. Messalina, soon after, was killed in the gardens of Lucullus, whither she had retired. See ANT. Univ. Hist. vol. xiv. p. 348-9.

315. *Shall men therefore, &c.*] If all you say be considered, the consequence seems to be, that it is wrong to wish, or pray, for any thing.
—*Have advice.*] If you will be advised what is best to do, I answer—

316. *Permit the gods, &c.*] Leave all to the gods; they know what is best for us, and what is most suitable to our circumstances and situations.

318. *Instead of pleasant things, &c.*] They can, though we cannot, foresee all consequences which will arise, and therefore, instead of bestowing what may be pleasing, they will give what is most proper, most suitable, and best adapted to our welfare; and this, because mortals are dearer to them than we are to ourselves. Comp. 1 Pet. v. 7.

319-20. *By the impulse, &c.*] We are impelled to wish for things, merely from the strong desire we have to possess them; and do not reflect, as we ought, on the blindness of our minds, which cannot see farther than present things, and therefore are led to judge amiss of what may be for our good in the end.

321. *Wedlock, and the bringing forth, &c.*] We pray for a wife, and that that wife may bring forth children; but the gods only can foresee how either the wife or children may turn out, consequently, whether the gratification of our wishes may be for our happiness.

323. *Ask something.*] In the former part of this fine passage the poet speaks of leaving all to the gods, in such an absolute and unreserved manner, as seemingly to exclude the exercise of prayer: as to outward things, such as power, riches, beauty, and the like, he certainly does, inasmuch as these matters ought to be left entirely to Providence, we not being able to judge about them; and, indeed, as he has shewn throughout the preceding part of this Satire, the having of these things may prove ruinous and destructive, therefore are not proper subjects either of desire or prayer: but now the poet finely shews, that there are subjects of prayer, which are not only desirable, but to be petitioned for, as conducive to our real good and happiness.

This fair and white neck is to be yielded to the sword.

    Shall men therefore wish for nothing? If you will have advice,   315

PERMIT THE GODS THEMSELVES TO CONSIDER WHAT
MAY SUIT US, AND BE USEFUL TO OUR AFFAIRS.

For, instead of pleasant things, the gods will give what-
    ever are fittest.

MAN IS DEARER TO THEM, THAN TO HIMSELF; we, led by
    the

Impulse of our minds, and by a blind, and great desire,

Ask wedlock, and the bringing forth of our wife: but to
    them.   321

Is known, what children, and what sort of a wife she may
    be.

However, that ye may ask something, and vow in chapels

Entrails, and the divine puddings of a whitish swine.

YOU MUST PRAY, THAT YOU MAY HAVE A SOUND MIND IN
    A SOUND BODY.   325

Ask a mind, strong, and without the fear of death;

Which puts the last stage of life among the gifts of

Nature; which can bear any troubles whatsoever;

—Vow in chapels.] Sacellum signi-fies a chapel, a little temple, or per-haps any place consecrated to divine worship. Here it may signify the sacred shrines of their gods, before which they offered their vows, prayers, and sacrifices.

324. *Entrails.*] The bowels, or in-wards, of animals, which were ex-ecta, (unde exta,) cut out, and offer-ed in sacrifice.

—Divine puddings, &c.] Toma-cula, or tomacla, from Gr. τιμνω, to cut, were puddings, or sausages, made of the liver and flesh of the animal, chopped and mixed together, and were called also farcimina, gut-puddings; and, like our sausages, were made by stuffing a gut taken from the animal with the above in-gredients. These accompanied the sacrifices, and were therefore called divine.

—Whitish swine.] This was of-fered to Diana, under the name of Lucina, in order to make her propi-tious to child-bearing women, as also on other occasions. See Hor. lib. iii. ode xxii.

325. *You must pray, &c*] As if the poet had said, "I by no means "object either to sacrifices or prayers "to the gods, provided what is asked "be reasonable and good, we cannot "be too earnest."

—A sound mind, &c.] *q. d.* Health of body and mind is the first of bless-ings here below: without a sound mind we can neither judge, deter-mine, or act aright; without bodily health there can be no enjoyment.

326. *A mind, strong, &c*] Forti-tude, by which, unmoved and undis-mayed, you can look upon death without terror.

327. *The last stage, &c.*] Ultimum spatium, in the chariot and horse-racing, signified the space between the last bound or mark, and the goal where the race ended. Hence, by an easy metaphor, it denotes the lat-ter part of life, when we are near our end, and are about to finish our course of life.

So the apostle, 2 Tim. iv. 7. says, τον δρομον· τετελεκα, I have finished my course.

327–8. *Gifts of nature*] The word

Nesciat irasci ; cupiat nihil ; et potiores
Herculis ærumnas credat, sævosque labores,　　　330
Et Venere, et cœnis, et plumis Sardanapali.
Monstro quod ipse tibi possis dare : SEMITA CERTE
TRANQUILLE PER VIRTUTEM PATET UNICA VITÆ.
Nullum numen habes, si sit prudentia : sed te
Nos facimus, Fortuna, deam, cœloque locamus.　　· 335

munus either signifies a gift, or a
duty or office If we take munera,
here, in the former sense, we must
understand the poet to mean, that
true fortitude, so far from fearing
death as an evil, looks on it as a gift
or blessing of nature. So Mr. DRY-
DEN :

*A soul that can securely death
defy,
And count it nature's privilege to
die.*

In the other sense, we must understand the poet to mean, that death
will be looked upon, by a wise and
firm mind, as an office, or duty,
which all are to fulfil, and therefore
to be submitted to as such, not with
fear and dismay, but with as much
willingness and complacency as any
other duty which nature has laid upon
us.

328. *Any troubles, &c*] Any misfortunes, without murmuring and re-
pining, much less sinking under
them.

329. *Knows not to be angry*] Can
so rule the tempers and passions of
the soul, as to control, on all occasions, those perturbations which arise
within, and produce a violence of
anger.

—*Covets nothing*] Being content
and submissive to the will of Providence, desires nothing but what it
has, neither coveting what others
have, or uneasy to obtain what we
ourselves have not.

330. *The toils of Hercules, &c.*]—
Alluding to what are usually called,
the twelve labours of Hercules.

331. *Than the lasciviousness, &c.*
Such a mind as has been ascribed
esteems the greatest sufferings and
labours, even such as Hercules un-
derwent, more eligible than all the
pleasures and enjoyments of sensuality.

—*Sardanapalus*] The last king of
Assyria, whose life was such a scene
of lasciviousness, luxury, and effeminacy, that he fell into the utmost
contempt in the eyes of his subjects,
who revolted ; and he, being overcome, made a pile, set it on fire, and
burnt himself, and his most valuable
moveables in it : " The only thing,"
says Justin, " he ever did like a
" man."

As the word venere, in this line,
is metonymically used for lewdness,
or lasciviousness, Venus being the
goddess of these, and cœnis for all
manner of gluttony and luxury, so
plumis may here be used to denote
softness and effeminacy of dress.

Plumæ, in one sense, is used
sometimes to denote plates, scales,
or spangles, wrought on the armour
or accoutrements of men or horses,
one whereof was laid upon another.
Garments also were adorned with
gold and purple plumage, feather-
work. AINSW. See Æn. xi. l. 770-1.

332. *What yourself may give, &c.*]
While others are disquieting themselves, and asking for the gratification
of their foolish and hurtful desires,
let me tell you the only way to solid
peace and comfort, and what it is
in your own power to bestow upon
yourself ; I mean, and it is most certainly true, that there is no other
way to happiness, but in the paths
of virtue. Comp Eccl. xii. 13-14.
The heathen thought that every man
was the author of his own virtue
and wisdom ; but there were some at
Rome, at that time, who could have
taught Juvenal, THAT EVERY GOOD
GIFT, AND EVERY PERFECT GIFT,
IS FROM ABOVE, AND COMETH
DOWN FROM THE FATHER OF
LIGHTS. Comp. Jer. x. 23.

HOR. lib. i. epist. xviii. l. 111-12,
says,

P

Knows not to be angry; covets nothing; and which
   thinks
The toils of Herculus, and his cruel labours, better   330
Than the lasciviousness, and luxury, and plumes of Sar-
   danapalus.
I shew what yourself may give to yourself: SURELY THE
   ONLY
PATH TO A QUIET LIFE LIES OPEN. THROUGH VIRTUE.
You have no deity, O Fortune, if there be prudence;
   but
Thee we make a goddess, and place in heaven.   335

*Sed satis est orare Jovem qui donat
  et aufert,
  Det vitam, det opes, æquum mi
  animum ipse parabo.*
CIC. Nat. Deorum. lib. iii. c.
xxxvi. declares it as a general opinion,
that mankind received from the gods
the outward conveniencies of life,
virtutem autem nemo unquam accep-
tam Deo retulit; " but virtue none
" ever yet thought they received
" from the Deity." And again,
" this is the persuasion of all, that
" fortune is to be had from the gods,
" wisdom from ourselves." Again,
" who ever thanked the gods for his
" being a good man? men pray to
" Jupiter, not that he would make
" them just, temperate, wise, but
" rich and prosperous " Thus
" they became vain in their imagi-
" nations, and their foolish heart
" was darkened; professing them-
" selves to be wise, they became
" fools." Rom. i. 21–2.

The Greeks had many temples dedicated to Fortune, under the name of
TYXH. Pindar makes her one of
the destinies, the daughter of Jupiter. Ancus Martius, king of the
Romans, first built a temple at Rome
to this deity. Servius Tullus also
built one at the capitol. Afterwards
the Romans consecrated temples to
her under various titles, as Fortuna
libera, redux, publica, equestris, &c.
See BROUGHTON, Bibl. Hist. Sacr.
tit. FORTUNE.

Horace's description of this goddess, and her great power, forms one
of the most beautiful of his odes.
See lib. i. ode xxxv.

*O Diva gratum quæ regis Antium,
Præsens, &c. &c.*]
336. *Place in heav'n.*] Give her a
place among the gods —q. d. As
things are, men are foolish enough to
erect temples to Fortune, make her
a goddess, worship her as such, and
attribute all their miscarriages and
troubles, not to their own neglect,
folly, and mismanagement, but to
the power and influence of this imaginary deity.

For the ideas which the Romans
entertained about the goddess Fortune, see sat. iii. 39–40.

I should observe, that some copies
read, l. 334.
   Nullum numen abest, &c.
   No deity is absent, &c.
As if it were said, that if there be
prudence, that is, if a man acts wisely
and prudently, all the gods are present with him, not one absents himself from him; or, prudence is all-
sufficient, and no other piety can be
wanting But the sense first above
given, on the reading nullum numen
habes, appears to be most consonant
to the intention of the two lines taken
together.

I know not how to end my observations on this Tenth Satire of Juvenal, without calling it the finest
piece, in point of composition, matter, and sentiment, which we have
derived from heathen antiquity. I
should call it imitably fine, had not
the late Dr. SAMUEL JOHNSON's
poem on " THE VANITY OF HUMAN
" WISHES," appeared; such a copy,
of such an original, is rarely to be
met with.

Satira Tredecima.

ARGUMENT.

The Poet writes this Satire to Calvinus, to comfort him under the loss of a large sum of money, with which he had entrusted one of his friends, and which he could not get again. Hence Juvenal takes occasion to speak of the

EXEMPLO quodcunque malo committitur, ipsi
Displicet authori. Prima est hæc ultio, quod se
Judice nemo nocens absolvitur; improba quamvis
Gratia fallacis prætoris vicerit urnam.
Quid sentire putas omnes. Calvine, recenti 5
De scelere, et fidei violatæ crimine? Sed nec
Tam tenuis census tibi contigit, ut mediocris
Jacturæ te mergat onus: nec rara videmus
Quæ pateris; casus multis hic cognitus, ac jam
Tritus, et e medio Fortunæ ductus acervo. 10
Ponamus nimios gemitus. Flagrantior æquo

Line 1. With bad example.] Every evil deed which tends to set a bad example to others.

—Displeases.] Gives him unpleasant sensations.

2. *First revenge.*] The vengeance which first seizes upon him arises from himself; his own conscience will condemn him, though he should have no other judge.

4. *Should have overcome the urn.*] Vicerit—*i. e.* should have defeated the urn's impartial decision, and have declared him innocent.—The prætor, who was the chief judge, had others appointed with him as assistants. The names of these were written upon little balls, and cast into an urn by the prætor: after they were shaken together, he drew out as many as the law required for the cause; after which the parties had power to reject such as they thought would be partial. The number of those excepted against

were filled up by the prætor's drawing other names out of the urn. Then the judges, which were thus appointed, took an oath to judge according to law; but, on many occasions, others were often substituted by the prætor. The cause being heard, the prætor gave to each of the judges three waxen tables. On one was the letter A, to signify the acquittal or absolution of the defendant. On another C, to imply his condemnation. On another N L, for non liquet, signified that a farther hearing was necessary: which delay of the cause was called ampliation. Then the judges, being called upon, cast the billet, expressing their opinion, into urn, according to which the prætor pronounced sentence. But if the prætor was a wicked judge, and inclined that partiality should get the better of justice, he might so manage matters, in all these many turns of

Thirteenth Satire.

ARGUMENT.

villainy of the times—shews that nothing can happen but by the permission of Providence—and that wicked men carry their own punishment about with them.

WHATEVER is committed with bad example, dis-
 pleases even
The author of it. This is the first revenge, that, himself
Being judge, no guilty person is absolved; altho' the wicked
Favour of the deceitful prætor should have overcome the urn.
What do you suppose all to think, Calvinus, of the recent
Wickedness, and crime of violated faith? But neither   6
Has so small an income come to your share, that the burden
Of a moderate loss should sink you: nor do we see rare
Those things which you suffer. This misfortune is known
 to many, and now
Trite, and drawn from the midst of Fortune's heap.   10
Let us lay aside too many sighs. More violent than what is just,

the business, that the defendant, however guilty, might appear to have the
urn in his favour. This our poet very properly calls, Improba gratia fallacis prætoris.

5. *What do you suppose.*] What,
think you, are the opinions of people
in general, of this injustice which you
lately suffered, and of the breach of
trust in your friend, of which you so
loudly complain?

—*Calvinus.*] Juvenal's friend, to
whom he addresses this Satire. And
here he comforts him by many con-
siderations: first, that he must have
all the world on his side; every body
must join with him in condemning
such a transaction.

7. *So small an income.*] Another
comfort is, that his circumstances are
such, that such a loss won't ruin him.
Census means a man's estate, or yearly revenue, as recorded in the Censor's
books.

—*The burden.*] A metaphor taken
from a ship's sinking by being over-
loaded.

8. *Rare, &c.*] His case was not singular, but very commonly happened
to many as well as to Calvinus: he
therefore must not look upon himself
as a sufferer beyond others.

—*Drawn from the midst, &c.*] Not
taken from the top, or summit, of
that heap of miseries, which Fortune
stores up for mankind, but from the
middle, as it were—not so small as
not to be felt, nor so severe as to over-
whelm you. He calls it onus mediocris jacturæ, l. 7, 8.

11. *Too many sighs.*] Immoderate
grief.

—*More violent.*] A man's concern
should never exceed the proper bounds.

Non debet dolor esse viri, nec vulnere major.
Tu quamvis levium minimam, exiguamque malorum
Particulam vix ferre potes, spumantibus ardens
Visceribus, sacrum tibi quod non reddat amicus   15
Depositum.   Stupet hæc, qui jam post terga reliquit
Sexaginta annos, Fonteio Consule natus?
An nihil in melius tot rerum proficis usu?
Magna quidem, sacris quæ dat præcepta libellis,
Victrix Fortunæ Sapientia.   Dicimus autem   20
Hos quoque felices, qui ferre incommoda vitæ,
Nec jactare jugum, vitâ didicere magistrâ. ·
  Quæ tam festa dies, ut cesset prodere furem,
Perfidiam, fraudes, atque omni ex crimine lucrum
Quæsitum, et partos gladio vel pyxide nummos?   25
RARI QUIPPE BONI : numero vix sunt totidem, quot
Thebarum portæ, vel divitis ostia Nili.
Nunc ætas agitur, pejoraque sæcula ferri

12. *Than his wound*] Should not rise higher than that which occasions it requires. Sorrow should be proportioned to suffering.

13. *Tho' you &c*] The poet here reproves the impatience and anger of his friend, who, instead of apportioning his grief to his loss, which was comparatively small, according to the preceding maxim, (l. 11, 12.) shewed a violence of grief and resentment on the occasion, which bespake him unable to bear, in any measure as he ought, a light injury or misfortune.

14. *Burning, &c.*] Your very bowels on fire with rage and indignation. We often find the intestines, such as the heart, liver, and bowels, or entrails, represented as the seat of moral feelings.

15. *Your friend, &c.*] The poet calls the money which Calvinus had intrusted his false friend with, and which he was afraid to lose, a sacred deposit, because delivered to him to keep, under the sacred confidence of friendship.

16. *Does he wonder.*] Does my friend Calvinus, now turned of sixty, and consequently well acquainted with the nature of mankind from many years experience, stand astonished at such a common transaction as this?

17. *Fonteius*] L. Fonteius Capito was consul with C. Vipsanius, in the reign of Nero.

18. *Of so many things*] Of so many things of a like kind, which your knowledge of the world must have brought to your observation—has all your experience of men and things been of no use or profit to you?

19. *Wisdom, indeed, &c.*] The volumes of philosophers, held sacred by the followers of them, contain rules for a contempt of fortune: and the wisdom by which they were indited, and which they teach, is the great principle which triumphs over the misfortunes we meet with. So SENECA, epist. 98. Valentior omni fortuna est animus sapientis. The books of moral philosophy abound in maxims of this kind.

22. *Nor to toss the yoke.*] A metaphor taken from oxen which are restive, and endeavour to get rid of the yoke by flinging and tossing their necks about.

The poet means, that much may be learned on the subject of triumphing over fortune from the sacred volumes of philosophy : but those are to be pronounced happy also, who, by the experience of life only, have learned to bear, with quietness, submission, and patience, any inconveniences, or misfortunes, which they may meet with.

The grief of a man ought not to be, nor greater than his
  wound.
Tho' you can hardly bear the least, and small particle
Of light misfortunes, burning with fretting
Bowels, because your friend may not return to you a sa-
  cred   15
Deposit. Does he wonder at these things, who already has
  left behind
His back sixty years, born when Fonteius was consul?
Do you profit nothing for the better by the experience of so
  many things?
Wisdom, indeed, which gives precepts in the sacred books,
Is the great conqueror of fortune. But we call   20
Those also happy, who, to bear the inconvenieces of life,
Nor to toss the yoke have learnt, life being their mistress.
What day so solemn, that it can cease to disclose a thief,
Perfidy, frauds, and gain sought from every crime,
And money gotten by the sword, or by poison?   25
For GOOD MEN ARE SCARCE: they are hardly as many in
  number
As the gates of Thebes, or the mouths of the rich Nile.
An age is now passing, and worse ages than the times of

---

*—Levius fit patientiâ
Quicquid corrigere est nefas.*
       HOR. lib. i. ode xxiv. ad fin.
Superanda omnis Fortuna ferendo
est. VIRG. Æn. v. l. 710. See Jer.
xxxi. 18.
—*Life being their mistress.*] Their
teacher or instructor; *i. e.* who are
instructed by what they meet with in
common life, and profit by daily experience.
       ———*To know* .
*That which before us lies in daily life
Is the prime wisdom.* MILTON.
23. *What day.*] Festa dies signifies
a day set apart for the observance of
some festival, on which some sacrifices or religious rites were performed;
a holiday, as we call it.
Festus also signifies happy, joyful.
Perhaps the poet means to say, what
day is so happy as not to produce some
mischief or other?
24. *Gain sought, &c.*] Every sort
of wickedness practised for the sake
of gain.
25. *Money gotten.*] Somebody or
other murdered for their money, either

more openly by the sword, or more
secretly by poison.
—*Poison.*] Pyxis signifies a little
box; but here, by meton. poison,
which used to be kept in such boxes,
by way of concealment and easiness
of conveyance.
27. *Thebes.*] A city of Bœotia, built
by Cadmus, the son of Agenor; it
was called Heptapylos, from having
seven gates. There was another Thebes
in Egppt, built by Busiris, king of
Egypt, which was called Heliopolis,
famous for an hundred gates. The
first is meant here.
—*Mouths of the rich Nile.*] Which
were seven. The Nile is called rich,
because it made Egypt fruitful by its
overflowing, thus enriching all the
country within its reach.
28. *An age, &c.*] *i. e.* The present
age in which we live, now passing on
in the course of time. The verb ago,
when applied to age or life, has this
signification: hence agere vitam, to
live. Si octogesimum agerent annum:
if they were eighty years old. CIC.
—*Worse ages.*] The word sæculum,

Temporibus: quorum sceleri non invenit ipsa
Nomen, et a nullo posuit natura metallo.   30
Nos hominum Divûmque fidem clamore ciemus,
Quanto Fæsidium laudat vocalis agentem
Sportula. Dic senior bullâ dignissime, nescis
Quas habeat Veneres aliena pecunia? nescis
Quem tua simplicitas risum vulgo moveat, cum   35
Exigis a quoquam ne pejeret, et putet ullis
Esse aliquod numen templis, aræque rubenti?
Quondam hoc indigenæ vivebant more, prius quam
Sumeret agrestem posito diademate falcem
Saturnus fugiens: tunc, cum virguncula Juno,   40
Et privatus adhuc Idæis Jupiter antris.
Nulla super nubes convivia Cœlicolarum,
Nec puer Iliacus, formosa nec Herculis uxor

like ætas, means an age; a period of an hundred years. Here the poet would represent the age in which he wrote as worse than any that had gone before.

28–9. *The times of iron.*] The last of the four ages into which the world was supposed to be divided, and which was worse than the three preceding. See Ov. Met. lib. i.

29. *Nature itself, &c.*] The wickedness of the present age is so great, that nothing in nature can furnish us with a proper name to call it by.

30. *Imposed, &c.*] Literally put it.—*q. d.* Nor has any name been affixed to it from any metal. The first age of the world was named Golden, from its resembling gold in purity; and after this came the Silver, the Brazen, the Iron Age; but now the age is so bad, that no metal can furnish it with a name which can properly describe the nature of it. Nomen ponere signifies to put or affix a name, *i. e.* to name. Nature herself can find no metal base enough to call it by.

31. *We invoke &c.*] Pro Deûm atque hominum fidem! was a usual exclamation on any thing wonderful or surprizing happening.—*q. d.* We can seem much amazed, and cry aloud against the vices of the age—we can call heaven and earth to witness our indignation.

32. *The vocal sportula.*] The dole-basket; the hope of sharing which opens the mouths of the people who

stand by Fæsidius while he is pleading at the bar, and makes them, with loud shouts, extol his eloquence: hence the poet calls it vocalis sportula. See an account of the sportula, sat. I. l. 81. Comp. x. l. 46.

HOR. lib. i. epist. xix. l. 37, 8.
Non ego ventosæ plebis suffragia venor
Impensis cœnarum, et tritæ munere vestis.

" *I never hunt th' inconstant peo-
   " ple's vote,*
" *With costly suppers, or a thread-
   " bare coat.*"   FRANCIS.

The name Fæsidius, or Fessidius, as some editions have it, may mean some vain pleader of the time, who courted the applause of the mob, by treating them with his sportula. Perhaps no particular person may be only meant, but such sort of people in general.

33. *Old man, worthy the bulla.*] The bulla was an ornament worn about the necks of Children, or at their breasts, made like an heart and hollow within; they wore it till seventeen years of age, and then hung it up to the household gods.—PERS. sat. v. l. 31. It was originally given as a mark of distinction to the children of those Sabine women who reconciled Romulus and Tatius.

The poet addresses himself to his old friend Calvinus, in a joking manner; as if he said, "Well old gen-
" tleman," (comp. l. 16, 17.) " wor-

Iron: for the wickedness of which, nature itself has not
Found a name, nor imposed it from any metal.   30
We invoke the faith of gods and men with clamour,
With as much as the vocal sportula praises Fæsidius
Pleading. Say, old man, worthy the bulla, know you not
What charms the money of another has? know you not
What a laugh your simplicity may stir up in the vulgar, when
You require from any not to forswear, and that he should
    think, that to any
Temples there is some deity, and to the reddening altar?
Formerly our natives lived in this manner, before
Saturn, flying, took the rustic sickle, his diadem
Laid down: then, when Juno was a little girl,   40
And Jupiter as yet private in the Idæan caves.
No feasts of the gods above the clouds,
Nor Iliacan boy, nor handsome wife of Hercules

" thy again to wear your childish
" baubles, are you, at sixty years
" old, such a child, as not to know"—
. 34. *What charms, &c.*] *i. e.* As to
be ignorant how great the temptation
is when a knave. has other people's
money in his power?
35. *What a laugh, &c.*] How the
whole town will laugh at your simplicity.
35—6. *When you require. &c.*] *q. d.*
If you expect that people will not forswear themselves, when perjury is so
common.
36. *Should think.*] *i. e.* And require
that they should think, &c.
37. *Some deity, &c.*] Should believe
that religion is not all a farce, but
that really there is not any of the
temples without some deity which
notices the actions and behaviour of
men, so as to punish perjury and
breach of faith.
—*The reddening altar.*] *i. e.* Red
with the blood of the sacrifices; or
with the fire upon it. *q. d.* How childish would you appear, and what a
laughter would be raised against you,
if you professed to expect either religion or morals in the present age?
38. *Natives.*] Indigenæ. The first
natives and inhabitants of Italy, our
homebred ancestors.
—*Lived in this manner.*] Avoiding
perjury and fraud, and believing the
presence of the gods in their temples,
and at their altars.

39. *Saturn flying.*] Saturn was expelled from Crete by his son Jupiter,
and fled into Italy, where he hid himself, which from thence was called
Latium, a latendo, and the people
Latins. See VIRG. Æn. viii. l. 319,
20. The poet means the Golden Age,
which the poets place during the reign
of Saturn.
—*Rustic sickle.*] Or scythe, which
Saturn is said to have invented, and
to have taught the people husbandry,
after his expulsion from his kingdom:
for during the Golden Age, the earth
brought forth every thing without cul-
ture. See OVID. Met. lib. fab. iii.
—*His diadem, &c.*] His kingdom
being seized by his son Jupiter—and
he being driven out of it.
40. *When Juno, &c.*] The daughter of Saturn, sister and wife to Jupiter—a little girl—*i. e.* before she was
grown up, and marriageable.
41. *Idæan caves.*] Jupiter, when
born, was carried to mount Ida, in
Crete, where he was concealed, and
bred up, lest his father Saturn should
devour him. See ANSW. *Saturnus.*
42. *No feasts, &c.*] No carousing,
as in after times there was supposed
to be. Comp. l. 45.
43. *Iliacan boy.*] Ganymede, the
son of Tros, king of Troy, or Illium,
whom Jupiter, in the form of an
eagle, snatched up from mount Ida,
and, displacing Hebe, made cup-
bearer at the feasts of the gods.

Ad cyathos: et jam siccato nectare, tergens
Brachia Vulcanus Liparææ nigra tabernâ. 45
Prandebat sibi quisque Deus, nec turba Deôrum
Talis, (ut est hodie,) contentaque sidera paucis:
Numinibus, miserum urgebant Atlanta minori
Pondere. Nondum aliquis sortitus triste profundi
Imperium, aut Siculâ torvus cum conjuge Pluto: 50
Nec rota, nec Furiæ, nec saxum, aut vulturis atri
Pœna: sed infernis hilares sine regibus umbræ.
Improbitas illo fuit admirabilis ævo.
Credebant hoc grande nefas, et morte piandum,
Si juvenis vetulo non assurrexerat; et si 55
Barbato cuicunque puer: licet ipse videret
Plura domi fraga, et majores glandis acervos.
Tam venerabile erat præcedere quatuor annis,
Primaque par adeo sacræ lanugo senectæ:
Nunc, si depositum non inficietur amicus, 60

43. *Wife of Hercules.*] Hebe, the daughter of Juno, and cup-bearer to Jupiter; she happened to make a slip at a banquet of the gods, so was turned out of her place, and Ganymede put into it: she was afterwards married to Hercules.

44. *The nectar, &c.*] Nectar, a pleasant liquor, feigned to be the drink of the gods. Siccato nectare, the nectar being all drunk up, the feast now over, Vulcan retired to his forge. Or Vulcan on account of his lameness did not arrive until the feast was over. Siccato nectare; although he had not even taken time to wash his hands. ELR. All this happened after the Golden Age, but not during the continuance of it.

45. *Wiping his arms,*] From the soot and dirt contracted in his filthy shop.

—*Liparææn.*] Near Sicily were several islands, called the Lipary Islands; in one of which, called Vulcania, Vulcan's forge was fabled to be. See VIRG. viii. 416, et seq. This was in the neighbourhood of mount Ætna. See sat. i. l. 8.

46. *Every god dined by himself.*] The poet here, and in the whole of this passage, seems to make very free with the theology of his country, and, indeed, to satirize the gods of Rome as freely as as he does the people.

—*Crowd of gods.*] The number of gods which the Romans worshipped might well be called turba deorum, for they amounted to above thirty thousand.

47. *This day.*] The Roman polytheism and idolatry went hand in hand with the wickedness of the times; they had a god for every vice, both natural and unnatural. The awful origin of all this, as well as its consequences, is set down by St. Paul, Rom. i. 21—32.

—*The stars.*] The heavens, per metonym.

48. *Urged miserable Atlas.*] A high hill in Mauritania, feigned by the poets to bear up the heavens. See sat viii. 32. note.

49. *Shared the same empire, &c.*] The world as yet was not divided by lot among the three sons of Saturn, by which Neptune shared the dominion of the sea—Jupiter heaven—and Pluto the infernal regions.

50. *His Sicilian wife.*] Proserpine, the daughter of Ceres, whom Pluto ravished out of Sicily, and made her his wife.

51. *A wheel.*] Alluding to the story of Ixion, the father of the Centaurs; Jupiter took him up into heaven, where he would have ravished Juno, but Jupiter formed a cloud in her shape, on which he begat the Centaurs. He was cast down to hell, for boasting that he had lain with Juno,

At the cups; and now the nectar being drunk up, Vulcan
Wiping his arms black with the Liparæan shop.   45
Every god dined by himself, nor was the crowd of gods
Such, (as it is at this day,) and the stars content with a few
Deities urged miserable Atlas with a less
Weight. Nobody as yet shared the sad empire
Of the deep; or fierce Pluto with his Sicilian wife.   50
Nor a wheel, nor furies, nor a stone, or the punishment of
      the black
Vulture: but the shades happy without infernal kings.
Improbity was in that age to be wondered at.
They believed this a great crime, andtobepunish'd by death,
If a youth had not risen up to an old man, and if   55
A boy to any who had a beard: tho' he might see
At home more strawberries, and greater heaps of acorn.
So venerable was it to precede by four years,
And the first down was so equal to sacred old age.
Now, if a friend should not deny a deposit,   60

where he was tied to a wheel, and
surrounded with serpents.
—*Furies.*] Of which there were
three. Alecto, Megæra, Tisiphone.
These were sisters, the daughters of
Acheron and Nox; they are described
with torches in their hands, and snakes
instead of hair, on their heads.

51. *A stone.*] Alluding to Sisyphus,
the son of Æolus; he greatly infested
Attica with his robberies, but being
slain by Theseus, he was sent to hell,
and condemned to roll a great stone
up an hill, which stone, when he
had got it to the top, rolled back
again, so that his labour was to be
constantly renewed.

51–2. *Black vulture.*] Prometheus
was chained to mount Caucasus for
stealing fire from heaven, where a
black vulture was continually preying
on his liver, which grew as fast as it
was devoured.

52. *But the shades.*] The ghosts of
the departed—were

—*Happy without infernal kings.*]
For there being, at that time, no
crimes, there wanted no laws nor
kings to enforce them; of course no
punishments.

53. *Improbity, &c.*] Villainy of
all kinds was scarcely known; any
crime would have been a wonder.

55. *If a youth, &c.*] In those days
of purity and innocence, the highest

subordination was maintained. It was
a capital crime for a young man even
to have sat down in the presence
of an old one, or if sitting, not to
have risen up on his approach. Comp.
Job xxix. 8.

So for a boy not to have done the
same in the presence of a youth, now
arrived at the age of puberty, which
was indicated by having a beard.

56. *Tho' he might see, &c.*] Strawberries, acorns, and such-like are
here supposed to be the first food of
mankind in the Golden Age. The
poet's meaning here is, that supe-
riority in age always challenged the
respect above mentioned, from the
younger to the elder, though the former might be richer, in the possessions
of those days, than the latter.

58. *So venerable, &c.*] So observant
were they of the deference paid to
age, that even a difference of four
years was to create respect, insomuch
that the first appearance of down upon
the chin was to be venerated by
younger persons, as the venerable
beard of old age was by those grown
to manhood; so there was an
equal and proportionate subordination
throughout.

60. *Now.*] In our day.

—*Should not deny.*] Either deny
that he received it, or should not refuse to deliver it.

2 F

Si reddat veterem cum totâ ærugine follem,
Prodigiosa fides, et Thuscis digna libellis:
Quæque coronatâ lustrari debeat agnâ.
Egregium sanctumque virum si cerno, bimembri
Hoc monstrum puero, vel mirandis sub aratro   ·35
Piscibus inventis, et fœtæ comparo mulæ;
Sollicitus tanquam lapides effuderit imber,
Examenque apium longâ consederit uvâ
Culmine delubri, tanquam in mare fluxerit amnis
Gurgitibus miris, et lactis vortice torrens.   70
Intercepta decem quereris sestertia fraude
Sacrilegâ? quid si bis centum perdidit alter
Hoc arcana modo? majorem tertius illâ
Summam, quam patulæ vix ceperat angulus arcæ?
Tam facile et pronum est Superos contemnere testes,   75

—A deposit.] Something committed to his trust.

61. *With all the rust.*] *i. e.* The coin, which has lain by so long as to have contracted a rust, not having been used. Meton.

62. *Prodigious faithfulness.*] Such a thing would be looked upon, in these times, as a prodigy of honesty.

A like sentiment occurs in TER. Phorm. act i. sc. ii. where Davus returns to Geta some money which he had borrowed.

DAV. *Accipe hem;*
Lectum est, convenict numerus;
   quantum debui.
GET. *Amo te, et non neglexisse*
   habeo gratiam.
DAV. *Præsertim ut nunc sunt*
   mores: adeo res redit,
Si quis quid reddit, magna ha-
   benda est gratia.

62. *Worthy the Tuscan books!*]— To be recorded there among other prodigies. It is said, that the art of soothsaying first came from the Tuscans, which consisted in foretelling future events from prodigies; these were recorded in books, and were consulted on occasion of any thing happening of the marvellous kind, as authorities for the determination of the auspices, or soothsayers, thereupon.

63. *Expiated, &c.*] When any prodigy happened, the custom of the Tuscans was to make an expiation by sacrifice, in order to avert the consequences of ill omens, which were gathered from prodigies. This the Romans followed.

—A crowned she-lamb.] They put garlands of flowers, or ribbands, on the heads of the victims. A she-lamb was the offering on such an occasion.

64. *An excellent.*] Egregium—ex toto grege lectum—*i. e.* as we say, one taken out of the common herd of mankind—choice—singular for great and good qualities.

65. *A boy of two parts.*] A monstrous birth, as prodigious as a child born with parts of two different species; hence the Centaurs were called bimembres.

—Wonderful fishes, &c.] A wondrous shoal of fish unexpectedly turned up in plowing the ground.

66. *A mule with foal.*] Which was never known to happen. Though Appian, lib. i. says, that, before the coming of Sylla, a mule brought forth in the city. This must be looked on as fabulous.

67. *Anxious.*] Solicitous for the event.

—As if a shower, &c.] As if the clouds rained showers of stones.

68. *A swarm, &c.*] It was accounted ominous if a swarm of bees settled on a house, or on a temple.

—Long bunch.] When bees swarm and settle any where, they all cling

If he should restore an old purse with all the rust ;
Prodigious faithfulness ! and worthy the Tuscan books !
And which ought to be expiated by a crowned she-
    lamb.
If I perceive an excellent and upright man, I compare
This monster to a boy of two parts, or to wonderful
    fishes   65
Found under a plough, or to a mule with foal.
Anxious as if a shower had poured forth stones,
And a swarm of bees had settled, in a long bunch,
On the top of a temple, as if a river had flowed into the
    sea
With wonderous gulfs, and rushing with a whirlpool of
    milk.   70
Do you complain that ten sestertiums are intercepted by
Impious fraud ? what if another has lost two hundred
    secret
Sestertiums in this manner? a third a larger sum than
    that,
Which the corner of his wide chest had scarce received ?
So easy and ready it is, to contemn the gods who are wit-
    nesses,   75

to one another, and hang down, a considerable length, in the form of a bunch of grapes. Hence VIRG. Georg. iv. 557–8.

    —*Jamque arbore summâ*
Confluere, et lentis uvam demittere
    ramis.

69. *A river, &c.*] All rivers run into the sea, and many with great violence; therefore the poet cannot mean that there is any wonder in this; but in flowing with unusual and portentous appearances, such as being mixed with blood, which Livy speaks of, lib. xxiv. c. 10. or the like.

70. *Rushing*] Torrens—violent, headlong, running in full stream, like the rushing of a land-flood, with dreadful violence, eddying in whirl-pools of milk. When we consider what has been said in the last seven lines, what an idea does it give us of the state of morals at Rome in the time of Juvenal !

71. *Ten sestertiums.*] About 80*l.* 11*s.* 7*d* of our money.

—*Intercepted.*] *i. e.* Prevented from coming to your hands.

72. *What if another, &c.*] The poet endeavours to comfort his friend under his loss, and to keep him from indulging too great a concern about it, by wishing him to consider that he is not so great a sufferer as many others perhaps might be by a like fraud

—*Secret, &c.*] Arcana—*q. d.* his centum sestertia arcana—*i. e.* delivered or lent secretly, when no witnesses were by, as had been the case of Juvenal's friend Calvinus.

74. *Which the corner, &c.*] Another, says he, may have lost so large a sum of money, as even to be greater than could be easily contained in a large chest, though stuffed at every corner, in which he had stowed it.

75. *So easy and ready, &c.*] So prone are men to despise the gods, who are witnesses to all their actions, that if they can but hide them from the eyes of men, they make themselves quite easy under the commission of the greatest frauds.

Si mortalis idem nemo sciat.   Aspice quantâ
Voce neget ; quæ sit ficti constantia vultûs.
Per solis radios, Tarpeiaque fulmina jurat,
Et Martis frameam, et Cirrhæi spicula vatis ;
Per calamos venatricis, pharetramque puellæ,   80
Perque tuum, pater Ægæi Neptune, tridentem :
Addit et Herculeos arcus, hastamque Minervæ,
Quicquid habent telorum armamentaria cœli.
Si vero et pater est, comedam, inquit, flebile gnati
Sinciput elixi, Pharioque madentis aceto.   85
    Sunt, in Fortùnæ qui casibus omnia ponunt,
Et nullo credunt mundum rectore moveri,
Naturâ volvente vices et lucis, et anni,
Atque ideo intrepidi quæcunque altaria tangunt.
    Est alius, metuens ne crimen pœna sequatur :   90

76. *Behold with how great, &c.*]—
This contempt of the gods is carried
so far, that men will not only defraud, but, with a loud unfaltering
voice, and the most unembarrassed
countenance, deny every thing that
is laid to their charge ; and this by
the grossest perjury.

77. *Feigned countenance.*] Putting
on, in his looks, a semblance of truth
and honesty.

78. *By the rays of the sun.*] This
was an usual oath. See Æn. iii. 599–
600. and note. Delph. edit.
   —*Tarpeian thunderbolts.*] *i. e.* The
thunder of Jupiter, who had a temple of the Tarpeian rock.

79. *Cyrrhæan prophet.*] Apollo,
who had an oracle at Delphos, near
Cirrha, a city of Phacis, where he
was worshipped.

80. *Virgin-huntress.*] Puellæ venatricis. Diana, the fabled goddess of
hunting ; she, out of chastity, avoided all company of men, retired into
the woods, and there exercised herself in hunting.

81. *Trident.*] Neptune's trident
was a sort of spear with three prongs
at the end, and denoted his being
king of the sea, which surrounded the
three then known parts of the world.
With this instrument he is usually
represented, and with this he was
supposed to govern the sea, and even
to shake the earth itself ; so that there
is no wonder that the superstitious
heathen should swear by it, as Nep-

tune was so considerable an object of
their veneration and worship. See
VIRG. Æn. i. 142–149. et al.
   —*Father of Ægeus.*] Ægeus was
the son of Neptune, the father of
Theseus. He reigned at Athens—
he threw himself into the Ægean sea,
which was so named after him.

82. *Herculean bows.*] Perhaps the
poet particularly here alludes to those
fatal bows and arrows of Hercules,
which he gave to Philoctetes, the son
of Pœas, king of Melibæa, a city of
Thessaly, at the foot of mount Ossa ;
and which weapons, unless Philoctetes had carried to Troy, it
was fated that the city could not
have been taken. See VIRG. Æn.
iii. 402. and note. Delph.

83. *Armories of heaven.*] Juvenal
held the Roman mythology in great
contempt ; he certainly means here
to deride the folly of imagining that
the gods had arsenals or repositories
of arms.

84. *A father, &c.*] Here is an allusion to the story of Thyestes, the
brother of Atreus, who, having committed adultery with the wife of
Atreus, Atreus in revenge killed and
dressed the child born of her, and
served him up to his brother at his
own table.

    The defrauder is represented as
perjuring himself by many oaths ;
and now he wishes, that the fate of
Thyestes may be his, that he may
have his son dressed and served up

If that same thing no mortal can know. Behold, with how
    great
A voice he denies it, what steadiness there is of feigned
    countenance.
By the rays of the sun, and the Tarpeian thunderbolts he
    swears;
And the javelin of Mars, and the darts of the Cyrrhæan
    prophet;
By the shafts, and the quiver of the virgin-huntress,   80
And by thy trident, O Neptune, father of Ægeus:
He adds also the Herculean bows, and the spear of Mi-
    nerva,
Whatever the armories of heaven have of weapons;
And truly if he be a father, I would eat, says he, a doleful
Part of the head of my boiled son, and wet with Pharian
    vinegar.   85
There are who place all things in the chances of Fortune,
And believe the world to be moved by no governor,
Nature turning about the changes both of the light and year,
And therefore intrepid they touch any altars whatsoever.
Another is fearing lest punishment may follow a crime:

to table for him to eat, if he be guilty
of the fraud which is laid to his charge.

85. *Part of the head.*] Sinciput
signifies the forepart, or, perhaps,
one half of the head, when divided
downwards. See AINSW. *Quasi se-
micaput*—or, a scindendo, from whence
sinciput.

—*Pharian vinegar.*] Pharos was
an island of Egypt, from whence
came the best vinegar, of which were
made sauces and seasonings for victuals of various kinds. The poet
does not add this without an ironical
fling at the luxury of his day.

86. *There are, &c.*] *i. e.* There
are some so atheistically inclined, as
to attribute all events to mere chance.

87. *The world to be moved, &c.*]—
Epicurus and his followers acknowledged that there were gods, but that
they took no care of human affairs,
nor interfered in the management of
the world. So HOR. sat. v. lib. i. l.
101-3.

    Deos didici securum agere ævum,
    Nec, si quid miri faciat natura,
    Deos id
    Tristes ex alto cæli demittere tecto.

88. *Nature, &c.*] A blind principle, which they call nature, bringing
about the revolutions of days and
years—(lucis et anni)—acting merely
mechanically, and without design.

89. *Intrepid they touch, &c.*]—
When a man would put another to
his solemn oath, he brought him to a
temple, and there made him swear,
laying his hand upon the altar. But
what constraint could this have on the
consciences of those who did not believe in the interference of the gods
—what altars could they be afraid to
touch, and to swear by in the most
solemn manner, if they thought that
perjury was not noticed?

90. *Another, &c.*] The poet, having before mentioned atheists, who
thought the world governed by mere
chance, or, though they might allow
that there were gods, yet that these
did not concern themselves in the ordering of human affairs, now comes
to another sort, who did really allow,
not only the existence, but also the
providence of the gods, and their attention to what passed among mortals, and yet such persons having a

Hic putat esse Deos, et pejerat, atque ita secum ;
Decernat quodcunque volet de corpore nostro
Isis, et irato feriat mea lumina sistro,
Dummodo vel cæcus teneam, quos abnego, nummos.
Et phthisis, et vomicæ putres, et dimidium crus   95
Sunt tanti ? pauper locupletem optare podagram
Ne dubitet Ladas, si non eget Anticyrâ, nec
Archigene : quid enim velocis gloria plantæ
Præstat, et esuriens Pisææ ramus olivæ ?
UT SIT MAGNA, TAMEN CERTE LENTA IRA DEORUM EST.
Si curant igitur cunctos punire nocentes,   101
Quando ad me venient ? sed et exorabile numen
Fortasse experiar : solet his ignoscere   Multi
Committunt eadem diverso crimina fato.
Ille crucem pretium sceleris tulit, hic diadema.   105

salvo, to console themselves under the commission of crimes, which he well describes in the following lines.

91. *Thus with himself.*] i. e. Thus argues with himself, allowing and fearing that he will be punished.

92. " *Let Isis,*" &c.] Isis was originally an Egyptian goddess ; but the Romans having adopted her among their deities, they built her a temple at Rome, where they worshipped her. She was supposed to be much concerned in inflicting diseases and maladies on mankind, and particularly on the perjured.

93. *Strike my eyes.*] Strike me blind.

—*Angry sistrum.*] The sistrum was a musical instrument ; it is variously described, but generally thought to be a sort of timbrel, of an oval, or a triangular form, with loose rings on the edges, which, being struck with a small iron rod, yielded a shrill sound. The Egyptians used it in battle instead of a trumpet. It was also used by the priests of Isis at her sacrifices, and the goddess herself was described as holding one in her right hand.

Her angry sistrum—per hypallagen—for the angry goddess with her sistrum.

94. *Keep the money,* &c.] Juvenal here describes one, who, having money intrusted to him, refuses to deliver it up when called upon, and who is daring enough, not only to deny his ever having received it, but to defy all punishment, and its consequences, so that he may but succeed in his perjury and fraud, and still keep the money in his possession.

95. *A phthisic.*] (From Gr. φθισις, a φθιω, to corrupt.) A consumption of the lungs.

—*Putrid sores.*] Vomicæ—imposthumes of a very malignant kind.

95. *Half a leg.*] The other half being amputated, on account of incurable sores, which threatened mortification.

96. *Of such consequence*] Tanti—of so much consequence—i. e. as to counterbalance the joy of possessing a large sum of money.

—*Ladas.*] The name of a famous runner, who won the prize at the Olympic games.

97. *The rich gout.*] So called, because it usually attacks the rich and luxurious.

—*If he does not want Anticyra.*]—i. e. If he be not mad. Anticyra, an island of the Archipelago, was famous for producing great quantities of the best hellebore, which the ancients esteemed good to purge the head in cases of madness. Whence naviga Anticyram, was so much as to say—you are mad. See HOR. lib. ii. sat. iii. l. 166.

98. *Archigenes.*] Some famous physician, remarkable, perhaps, for curing madness.

He thinks there are gods, and forswears, and thus with
 himself—   91
" Let Isis decree whatever she will concerning this body
" Of mine, and strike my eyes with her angry sistrum,
" So that, even blind, I may keep the money which I
 deny.
" Are a phthisic, or putrid sores, or half a leg 95
" Of such consequence ? let not poor Ladas doubt to wish
  " for
" The rich gout, if he does want Anticyra, nor
" Archigenes : for what does the glory of a swift foot
" Avail him, and the hungry branch of the Pisæan olive?"
" THOUGH THE ANGER OF THE GODS BE GREAT, YET CER-
 " TAINLY IT IS SLOW.   100
" If they take care therefore to punish all the guilty,
" When will they come to me?—But, perhaps too, the
 " deity
" Exorable I may experience : he useth to forgive these
 " things.
" Many commit the same crimes with a different fate.
" One has borne the cross as a reward of wickedness, ano-
 " ther a diadem."   105

—*The glory of a swift foot, &c.*]
What good does the applause got by
his swiftness do him ? it will not fill
his belly.

99. *Hungry branch of the Pisæan
olive.*] Pisa was a district of Elis, in
Peloponnesus, in which was Olympia, where the Olympian games were
celebrated : the victors in which were
crowned with chaplets made of olive
branches, hence called Pisæan.

The hungry branch—*i. e.* that will
afford no food to the gainers of it.—
See note on l. 93, ad fin.

The speaker here means, that to be
sick and rich, is better than to be
healthy and poor ; that the famous
Ladas, unless he were mad, would
sooner choose to be laid up with the
gout and be rich, than to enjoy all
the glory of the Olympic games and
be poor.

100. *Tho' the anger, &c*] Another
flatters himself, that, though punishment may be heavily inflicted some
time or other, yet the evil day may
be a great way off. See Eccl. viii.
11.

101. *If they take care, &c.*] q. d.
If they do observe the actions of men,
and attend to what they do, so as to
take order for the punishment of
guilt, wherever they find it, yet it
may be a great while before it comes
to my turn to be punished.

103. *Exorable, &c*] It may be I
shall escape all punishment ; for perhaps I may obtain forgiveness, and
find the Deity easy to be entreated.

—*He useth, &c*] t. e. Crimes
of this sort, which are not committed out of contempt of the Deity,
but merely to get a little money, he
usually forgives.

104. *Different fate.*] Another sub-
terfuge of a guilty conscience is, that
though, in some instances, wrong
doers are punished grievously, yet in
others they succeed so happily as to
obtain rewards ; so that the event of
wickedness is very different to different people.

105. *Borne the cross, &c.*] The
same species of wickedness that has
brought one man to the gallows, has
exalted another to a throne.

Sic animum diræ trepidum formidíne culpæ
Confirmant.   Tunc te sacra ad delubra vocantem
Præcedit, trahere imo ultro, ac vexare paratus.
Nam cùm magna malæ superest audacia causæ,
Creditur a multis fiducia: mimum agit ille,   110
Urbani qualem fugitivus scurra Catulli.
Tu miser exclamas, ut Stentora vincere possis,
Vel potius quantum Gradivus Homericus: audis,
Jupiter, hæc? nec labra moves, cum mittere vocem
Debueras, vel marmoreus, vel aheneus? aut cur   115
In carbone tuo chartâ pia thura solutâ
Ponimus, et sectum vituli jecur, albaque porci
Omenta? ut video, nullum discrimen habendum est
Effigies inter vestras, statuamque Bathylli.
Accipe, quæ contra valeat solatia ferre,   120
Et qui nec Cynicos, nec Stoïca dogmata legit

106–7. *Thus they confirm.*] By all
these specious and deceitful reason-
ings, they cheat themselves into the
commission of crimes, and endeavour to silence the remonstrances and
terrors of a guily conscience.

108. *He precedes, &c.*] Thus con-
fident, the wretch whom you summon to the temple, in order to swear
to his innocence, leads the way before you, as if in the utmost haste to
purge himself by oath.

—*Ready to draw, &c.*] He is ready
to drag you along by force, and to
harass and teaze you to get on faster,
in order to bring him to his oath.

109. *When great impudence, &c.*]
When a man is impudent enough,
however guilty, to set a good face
upon the matter, this is mistaken by
many for a sign of honest confidence,
arising from innocence.

110. *He acts the farce, &c.*] Alluding to a play written by one Lucius Catullus, called the Phasma, or
Vision, (see sat. viii. 185–6.) in which
there was a character of a buffoon,
who ran away from his master, after
having cheated him, and then vexed,
and even provoked him, that he
might be brought to swear himself
off, cheerfully proposing thus to be
perjured.   This play is lost by time,
so that nothing certain can be said
concerning this allusion; but what is
here said (after Holyday) seems probable.

111. *Witty Catullus.*] Some expound urbani, here, as the cognomen
of this Catullus.

112. *You miserable exclaim.*] You,
half mad with vexation at finding
yourself thus treated, and in amaze-
ment at the impudence of such a perjury, break forth aloud.

112. *Stentor.*] A Grecian mentioned by Homer, Il. ε l. 785–6. to have
a voice as loud as fifty people together.

113. *Homerican Gradivus.*] Homer says, Il. ε 860–2.) that when
Mars was wounded by Diomede, he
roared so loud that he frightened the
Grecians and Trojans, and made a
noise as loud as 10,000 men together.

In some such manner as this,
wouldst thou, my friend, Calvinus,
exclaim, and call out to Jupiter.

114. *Nor move your lips.*] Canst
thou be a silent hearer, O Jupiter, of
such perjuries as these? wilt thou not
so much as utter a word against such
things, when one should think thou
oughtest to threaten vengeance, wert
thou even made of marble or brass,
like thine images which are among
us?

115. *Or why.*] Where is the use—
to what purpose is it?

116–17. *From the loos'd paper.*]—
Some think that the offerers used to
bring their incense wrapped up in paper, and, coming to that altar, they

Thus the mind trembling with the fear of dire guilt
They confirm : then you, calling him to the sacred shrines,
He precedes, even ready of his own accord to draw you,
    and to teaze you.
For when great impudence remains to a bad cause,
It is believed confidence by many : he acts a farce,   110
Such as the fugitive buffoon of the witty Catullus.
You miserable exclaim, so as that you might overcome
    Stentor,
Or rather as much as the Homerican Gradivus : " Do you
    " hear,
" O Jupiter, those things ? nor move your lips, when you
    " ought
" To send forth your voice, whether you are of marble or
    " of brass ? or why,   115
" On thy coal, put we the pious frankincense from the
    " loosed
" Paper, and the cut liver of a calf, and of an hog
" The white caul ? as I see, there is no difference to be
    " reckoned,
" Between your images, and the statue of Bathyllus."
Hear, what consolations on the other hand one may bring,
And who neither hath read the Cynics, nor the Stoic doc-
    trines, differing   121

opened the paper, and poured the incense out of it upon the fire.

But others, by charta soluta (abl. absol.) understand a reference to the custom, mentioned sat. x. 55. (see note there,) of fastening pieces of paper, containing vows, upon the images of the gods, and taking them off when their prayers were granted, after which they offered what they had vowed.

117. " The cut liver," &c.] The liver cut out of a calf, and the caul which covered the inwards of an hog, were usual offerings.

119. " The statue of Bathyllus."] A fiddler and a player, whose statue was erected in the temple of Juno, at Samos, by the tyrant Polycrates. —q. d. At this rate, I do not see that there is any difference between thy images, O Jupiter, and those that may be erected in honour of a fiddler.

In this expostulatory exclamation to Jupiter, which the poet makes his friend utter with so much vehemence, there is very keen raillery against the folly and superstition that prevailed at Rome, which Juvenal held in the highest contempt. This almost reminds one of that fine sarcasm of the prophet Elijah—1 Kings xviii. 27.

120. Hear, &c.] The poet is now taking another ground to console his friend, by representing to him the frequency not only of the same, but of much greater injuries than what he has suffered ; and that he, in being ill used, is only sharing the common lot of mankind, from which he is not to think himself exempt.

120. Hear.] Accipe—auribus understood.

121. Neither hath read.] Never hath made these his study.

—The Cynics.]   followers of Diogenes.

—Stoic doctrines.] The doctrines of Zeno and his followers, who were

A Cynicis tunicâ distantia; non Epicurum
Suspicit exigui lætum plantaribus horti.
Curentur dubii medicis majoribus ægri,
Tu venam vel discipulo committe Philippi.   125
  Si nullum in terris tam detestabile factum
Ostendis, taceo; nec pugnis cædere pectus
Te veto, nec planâ faciem contundere palmâ;
Quandoquidem accepto claudenda est janua damno,
Et majore domûs gemitu, majore tumultu   130
Planguntur nummi, quam funera: nemo dolorem
Fingit in hoc casu, vestem diducere summàn
Contentus, vexare oculos humore coacto:
Ploratur lachrymis amissa pecunia veris.
Sed si cuncta vides simili forâ plena querelâ: 135
Si decies lectis diversâ parte tabellis,

called Stoics, from σroα, a porch, where they taught.

—*Differing, &c.*] The people differed from each other in their dress, the Cynics wearing no tunic (a sort of waistcoat) under their cloaks, as the Stoics did; but both agreed in teaching the contempt of money, and of the change of fortune.

122. *Epicurus.*] A philosopher of Athens, a temperate and sober man, who lived on bread and water and herbs: he placed man's chief happiness in the pleasure and tranquillity of the mind. He died of the stone at Athens, aged seventy-two. His scholars afterwards sadly perverted his doctrines, by making the pleasures of the body the chief good, and ran into those excesses which brought a great scandal on the sect. Suspicit—lit. looks up to.

124. *Dubious sick, &c.*] Those who are so ill, that their recovery is doubtful, should be committed to the care of very experienced and able physicians.

So, those who are afflicted with heavy misfortunes, stand in need of the most grave and learned advice.

125. *Commit your vein, &c.*] A person whose cause of illness is but slight, may trust himself in the hands of a young beginner.

So you, Calvinus, whose loss is but comparatively slight, have no need of Stoics, or Cynics, or of such a one as Epicurus, to console you; I

am sufficient for the purpose, though I do not read or study such great philosophers.

—*Philip.*] Some surgeon of no great credit or reputation; but even his apprentice might be trusted to advise bleeding, or not, in a slight disorder. So you may safely trust to my advice in your present circumstances, though I am no deep philosopher; a little common sense will serve the turn.

The whole of these two last lines is allegorical; the ideas are taken from bodily disorder, but are to be transferred to the mind.

126. *If you shew, &c.*] Could you shew no act in all the world so vile as this which has been done towards you, I would say no more—I would freely abandon you to your sorrows, as a most singularly unhappy man.

127. *Nor do I, &c.*] i. e. Go on, like a man frantic with grief—beat your breast—slap your face till it be black and blue.

129. *Since, &c.*] In a time of mourning for any great loss, it was usual to shut the doors and windows.

—*Loss being received.*] A loss of money incurred.—He is here rallying his friend Calvinus.—*q. d.* Inasmuch as the loss of money is looked upon as the most serious of all losses, doubtless you ought to bewail your misfortune, with every circumstance of the most unfeigned sorrow.

130. *Mourning of the house, &c.*]

From the Cynics by a tunic : nor admires Epicurus
Happy in the plants of a small garden.
The dubious sick may be taken care of by greater physi-
    cians,
Do you commit your vein even to the disciple of Philip.
If you shew no fact in all the earth so detestable,   126
I am silent : nor do I forbid you to beat your breast
With your fists, not to bruise your face with your open
    palm ; :
Since, loss being received, the gate is to be shut,
And with greater mourning of the house, with a greater
    tumult,   130
Money is bewailed than funerals : nobody feigns grief
In this case, content to sever the top of the garment,
To vex the eyes with constrained moisture :
Lost money is deplored with true tears.   134
But if you see all the courts filled with the like complaint,
If, tablets being read over ten times, by the different
    party,

i. e. Of the family—for, to be sure, the loss of money is a greater subject of grief, and more lamented than the deaths of relations.

131. *Nobody feigns, &c.*] The grief for loss of money is very sincere, however feigned it usually is at funerals.

132. *Content to sever, &c.*] Nobody contents himself with the mere outward show of grief—such as rending the upper edge of a garment, which was an usual sign of grief.

133. *Vex the eyes, &c.*] To rub the eyes, in order to squeeze out a few forced tears.

See TERENT. Eun. act. i. sc. i. where Parmeno is, describing the feigned grief of Phædria's mistress, and where this circumstence of dissimulation is finely touched :

Hæc verba unâ mehercle falsâ la-
   crumulâ.
Quam, oculos terendo misere, vix
   vi expresserit
Restinguet, &c.

So VIRG. Æn. ii. l. 196.

Captique dolis lachrymisque coacti.

134. *Lost money is deplored, &c.*] When we see a man deploring the loss of money, we may believe the sincerity of his tears.

The poet in this, and the preceding lines on this subject, finely satirizes the avarice and selfishness of mankind, as well as their hypocrisy, and all want of real feelings, where self is not immediately concerned.

135. *If you see, &c.*] *q. d.* However I might permit you to indulge in sorrow, if no instance of such fraud and villainy had happened to any body but yourself, yet if it be every day s experience, if the courts of justice are filled with complaints of the same kind, why should you give yourself up to grief, as singularly wretched, when what has happened to you is the frequent lot of others ?

136. *If tablets.*] *i. e.* Deeds or obligations written on tablets.

—*Read over, &c.*] *i. e.* Often read over in the hearing of witnesses, as well as of the parties.

—*By the different party.*] This expression is very obscure, and does not appear to me to have been satisfactorily elucidated by commentators.— Some read diversa in parte, and explain it to mean, that the deeds had been read over in different places— variis in locis, says the Delphin interpretation. However, after much consideration, I rather approve of

Vana supervacui dicunt chirographa ligni,
Arguit ipsorum quos litera, gemmaque princeps
Sardonyches, loculis quæ custoditur eburnis :
Ten', ô delicias, extra communia censes   140
Ponendum ? Quî tu gallinæ filius albæ,
Nos viles pulli nati infelicibus ovis ?
Rem pateris modicam, et mediocri bile ferendam,
Si flectas oculos majora ad crimina : Confer
Conductum latronem, incendia sulphure cœpta,   145
Atque dolo, primos cum janua colligit ignes :
Confer et hos, veteris qui tollunt grandia templi .
Pocula adorandæ rubiginis, et populorum
Dona, vel antiquo positas a rege coronas.
Hæc ibi si non sunt, minor extat sacrilegus, qui   150
Radat inaurati femur Herculis, et faciem ipsam

reading diversa parte, by the different
(i. e. the opposite) party. Pars means,
sometimes, a side or party in contention. AINSW. In this view, it
exaggerates the impudence and villainy of a man who denied his deed
or obligation, seeing that his adversary, the creditor, having frequently
read over the deed, could not be
mistaken as to its contents, any more
than the debtor, who had signified
and sealed it, as well as heard it read
over.

137. *They say.*] i. e. The fraudu-
lent debtors say, that the hand-writings contained in the bonds are false
and void.

Supervacuus means superfluous—
serving to no purpose or use.—Supervacui ligni, i. e. of the inscribed
wooden tablets, which are of no use,
though the obligation be written on
them.

q. d. Notwithstanding the hand-
writing appears against them, signed
and sealed by themselves, and that
before witnesses, yet they declare
that it is all false, a mere deceit, and
of no obligation whatsoever—they
plead, non est factum, as we say.

138. *Whom their own letter convicts.*] Whose own hand-writing
proves it to be their own deed.

—*A principal gem, &c.*] Their seal
cut upon a sardonyx of great value,
with which they sealed the deed.

139. *Which is kept, &c.*] Kept in
splendid cases of ivory, perhaps one

within another, for its greater security. By this circumstance, the poet
seems to hint, that the vile practice
which he mentions was by no means
confined to the lower sort of people,
but had made its way among the rich
and great.

140. *O sweet Sir,*] Delicias—hominis understood. An ironical apostrophe to his friend.

Deliciæ is often used to denote a
darling, a minion, in which a person delights : here delicias might be
rendered choice, favourite, i. e. of
fortune—as if exempted from the
common accidents of life—as if put
or placed out of their reach.

141. *How.*] Why—by what means
—how can you make it out ?
—*The offspring of a white hen.*]—
The colour of white was deemed
lucky. This expression appears to
have been proverbial in Juvenal's
time to denote a man that is born to
be happy and fortunate.

Some suppose the original of this
saying to be the story told by Suetonius in his life of Galba, where he
mentions an eagle, which soaring
over the head of Livia, a little after
her marriage with Augustus, let fall
into her lap a white hen, with a laurel branch in her mouth ; which hen,
being preserved, became so fruitful,
that the place where this happened
was called Villa ad Gallinus.

But the poet saying nothing of
fruitfulness, but of the colour only,

They say the hand-writings of the useless wood are vain,
Whom their own letter convicts, and a principal gem
Of a sardonyx, which is kept in ivory boxes.
Think you, O sweet Sir, that out of common things   140
You are to be put? How are you the offspring of a white hen,
We, vile chickens hatched from unfortunate eggs?
You suffer a moderate matter, and to be borne with mode-
        rate choler,
If you bend your eyes to greater crimes: compare
The hired thief, burnings begun with sulphur,   145
And by deceit, when the gate collects the first fires;
Compare also these, who take away the large cups
Of an old temple, of venerable rust, and the gifts
Of the people, or crowns placed by an ancient king.
If these are not there, there stands forth one less sacrilegi-
        ous, who   150
May scrape the thigh of a gilt Hercules, and the very
        face of

---

it is rather to be supposed that Eras-
mus is right in attributing this proverb to the notion which the Romans
had of a white colour, that it denoted
luck or happiness, as *dies albi*, and
albo lapillo notati, and the like.

142. *Unfortunate eggs.*] The infelicibus ovis, put here in opposition to
the white hen, seems to imply the
eggs of some birds of unhappy omen,
as crows, ravens, &c. figuratively to
denote those who are born to be unfortunate.

    *Sæpe sinistra cavâ prædixit ab ilice
    Cornix.*

        Virg. ecl. i. 18; and ix. 15.

143. *With moderate choler, &c.*] i.
e. Moderate wrath, anger, resentment, when you consider how much
greater injuries others suffer from
greater crimes.

144. *Compare.*] Consider in a comparative view.

145. *Hired thief.*] Or cut-throat,
who is hired for the horrid purpose
of assassination.

—*Burnings begun with sulphur.*]
Which is here put, by synec. for all
sort of cumbustible matter with
which incendiaries fire houses.

146. *By deceit.*] In a secret manner, by artfully laying the destructive
materials, so as not to be discovered

till too late to prevent the mischief.

—*Collects the first fires.*] So as to
prevent those who are in the house
from getting out, and those who are
without from getting in, to afford
any assistance. It is not improbable
that the poet here glances at the
monstrous act of Nero, who set
Rome on fire.

147. *Large cups, &c.*] Who are
guilty of sacrilege, in stealing the
sacred vessels which have been for
ages in some antique temple, and
which are venerable from the rust
which they have contracted by time.

148-9. *The gifts of the people.*]—
Rich and magnificent offerings, given
to some shrine by a whole people together, in honour of the god that
presided there.

149. *Crowns placed, &c.*] As by
Romulus and other kings, whose
crowns, in honour of their memory,
were hung up in the temples of the
gods.

150. *If these are not there.*] If it
so happen that there be no such valuable relics as these now mentioned,
yet some petty sacrilegious thief will
deface and rob the statues of the
gods.

151. *Scrape the thigh, &c.*] To get
a little gold from it.

Neptuni, qui bracteolam de Castore ducat.
An dubitet, solitus totum conflare Tonantem?
Confer et artifices, mercatoremque veneni.
Et deducendum corio bovis in mare, cum quo   155
Clauditur adversis innoxia simia fatis.
Hæc quota pars scelerum, quæ custos Gallicus urbis
Usque a Lucifero, donec lux occidat, audit?
Humani generis mores tibi nôsse volenti
Sufficit una domus; paucos consume dies, et   160
Dicere te miserum, postquam illinc veneris, aude.
Quis tumidum guttur miratur in Alpibus? aut quis
In Meroë crasso majorem infante mamillam?
Cærula quis stupuit Germani lumina, flavam
Cæsariem, et madido torquentem cornua cirro?   165
Nempe quod hæc illis natura est omnibus una.
Ad subitas Thracum volucres, nubemque sonoram

151-2. *Face of Neptune.*] Some image of Neptune, the beard whereof was of gold.

152. *Draw off the leaf-gold, &c.*] Peel it off, in order to steal it, from the image of Castor; there were great treasures in his temple. See sat. xiv. l. 260.

153. *Will he hesitate.*] At such comparatively small matters as these, who could steal a whole statue of Jupiter, and then melt it down; and who can make a practice of such a thing? A man who accustoms himself to greater crimes, cannot be supposed to hesitate about committing less.

154. *Contrivers, and the merchant of poison.*] Those who make and those who sell poisonous compositions, for the purposes of sorcery and witchcraft, or for killing persons in a secret and clandestine manner. See Hor. sat. ix. lib. i. 31; and epod. ix. l. 61.

155. *Launched into the sea, &c.*] Parricides were put into a sack made of an ox's hide, together with an ape, a cock, a serpent, and a dog, and thrown into the sea. See sat. viii. 214. The fate of these poor innocent animals is very cruel, they having done no wrong. Dedudecendum. Met. See Virg. G. i. 255.

157. *Keeper of the city.*] Rutilius Gallicus was appointed, under Domitian, præfectus urbis, who had cognizance of capital offences, and sat every day on criminal causes.— There is great force in the word *custos* here, it means a jailer, and denotes that Rome at this time resembled a prison, the chief magistrate of which was no better than a jailer.

158. *From the morning.*] Lucifero. The planet Venus, when seen at day-break, is called Lucifer—i. e. the bringer of light. See sat. viii. 12.

    Nascere, præque diem veniens age Lucifer almum.
           Virg. ecl. viii. l. 17.

    Lucifer ortus erat.
           Ov. Met. iv. 664.

It is not to be supposed that the præfectus urbis literally sat from morning to night every day, but that he was continually, as the phrase among us imports, hearing causes, in which the most atrocious crimes were discovered and punished.

160. *One house suffices, q. d.*] If you desire to be let into a true history of human wickedness, an attendance at the house of Gallicus alone will be sufficient for your purpose.

    —*Spend a few days, &c.*] Attend there for a few days, and when you come away, dare, if you can, to call yourself unhappy, after hearing what you have heard at the house of Gallicus. Domus is a very general word,

Neptune, who may draw off the leaf-gold from Castor.
Will he hesitate, who is used to melt a whole Thunderer?
Compare also the contrivers, and the merchant of poison,
And him to be launched into the sea in the hide of an ox,
With whom an harmless ape, by adverse fates, is shut
    up.   156
How small a part this of the crimes, which Gallicus, the
    keeper of the city,
Hears from the morning, until the light goes down?
To you who are willing to know the manners of the human
    race
One house suffices; spend a few days, and dare   160
To call yourself miserable, after you come from thence.
Who wonders at a swoln throat in the Alps? or who
In Meroë at a breast bigger than a fat infant?
Who has been amazed at the blue eyes of a German, his
    yellow
Hair, and twisting his curls with a wet lock?   165
Because indeed this one nature is to them all.
At the sudden birds of the Thracians, and the sonorous
    cloud,

and need not be restricted here to signify the private house of the judge, but may be understood of the court or place where he sat to hear causes.

162. *Swoln throat, &c.*] The inhabitants about the Alps have generally great swellings about their throats, occasioned, as some suppose, by drinking snow water. The French call these protuberances on the outside of the throat, goitres.

163. *Meroë.*] An island surrounded by the Nile. The women of this island are said to have breasts of an enormous size. Our poet is hardly to be understood literally.

164. *Blue eyes, &c.*] Tacit. de Mor. Germ. says, that the Germans have truces et cæruleos oculos, et comas rutilas—fierce and blue eyes, and red hair.

165. *Twisting his curls.*] Cornu—lit. an horn; but is used in many senses to express things that bear a resemblance to an horn—as here, the Germans twisted their hair in such a manner, as that the curls stood up and looked like horns.

—*A wet lock.*] Cirrus signifies a curled lock of hair. The Germans used to wet their locks with ointment of some kind, perhaps that they might the more easily take, and remain in, the shape in which the fashion was to put them; something like our use of pomatum; or the ointment which they used might be some perfume. Comp. Hor. lib. ii. ode vii. l. 7–8.

166. *Because, &c.*] Nobody would be surprised at seeing a German as above mentioned, and for this reason, because all the Germans do the same, it is the one universal fashion among them. Natura sometimes signifies, a way or method.

167. *Sudden birds, &c.*] A flight of cranes coming unexpectedly from Strymon, a river of Thrace.
    Strymoniæ grues.
See Virg. G. i. 120; Æn. x. 265.
—*Sonorous cloud.*] The cranes are birds of passage, and fly in great numbers when they change their climate, which they were supposed to do when the winter set in in Thrace; they made a great noise as they flew. See Æn. x. 265–6.

Pygmæus parvis currit bellator in armis :
Mox impar hosti, raptusque per aëra curvis
Unguibus a sævâ fertur grue : si videas hoc   170
Gentibus in nostris, risu quaterere : sed illic,
Quanquam eadem assidue spectentur prælia, ridet
Nemo, ubi tota cohors pede non est altior uno.
Nullane perjuri capitis, fraudisque nefandæ
Pœna erit ? abreptum crede hunc graviore catenâ   175
Protinus, et nostro (quid plus velit ira ?) necari
Arbitrio : manet illa tamen jactura, nec unquam
Depositum tibi sospes erit : sed corpore trunco
Invidiosa dabit minimus solatia sanguis :
At vindicta bonum vit' jucundius ipsâ.   180
Nempe hoc indocti, quorum præcordia nullis
Interdum, aut levibus videas flagrantia causis :
Quantulacunque adeo est occasio, sufficit iræ.
Chrysippus non dicet idem, nec mite Thaletis
Ingenium, dulcique senex vicinus Hymetto,   185

168. *Pygmæan warrior, &c.*] The Pygmies (from πυγμὴ, the fist, or a measure of space from the elbow to the hand, a cubit) were a race of people in Thrace, which were said to be only three inches high. AINSW. Juvenal says, a foot, l. 173. They were said always to be at war with the cranes.

—*Little arms.*] His diminutive weapons.

169. *The enemy.*] The cranes.

171. *In our nations, &c.*] In our part of the world, if an instance of this sort were to happen, it would appear highly ridiculous ; to see a little man fighting a crane, and then flown away with in the talons of the bird, would make you shake your sides with laughter, from the singularity of such a sight.

172. *The same battles, &c.*] In that part of the world, there being no singularity or novelty in the matter, though the same thing happens constantly, nobody is seen to laugh, however ridiculous it may be to see an army of people, not one of which is above a foot high.

The poet means to infer from all this, that it is the singularity and novelty of events which make them wondered at : hence his friend Calvinus is so amazed and grieved that he

should be defrauded, looking upon it as peculiar to him ; whereas, if he would look at what is going forward in the world, particularly in courts of civil and criminal judicature, he would see nothing to be surprised at, with respect to his own case, any more than he would be surprised, if he went among the Germans, to see blue eyes, and red hair, or locks curled and wetted with some ointment, seeing they all appear alike. Or if he were to go among the Pygmies, he would see nobody laugh at their battles with the cranes, which are constantly happening, and at the diminutive size of the Pygmy warriors, which is alike in all.

174. *"No punishment," &c.*] Well but, says Calvinus, though you observe that I am not to be surprised at what I have met with, because it is so frequent, is such a matter to be entirely unnoticed, and such an offender not to be punished ?

—*" A perjured head."*] A perjured person. Capitis, per synec. stands here for the whole man.

So HOR. lib. i. ode xxiv. l. 2.
          Tam chari capitis.

175. *" Wicked fraud."*] In taking my money to keep for me, and then denying that he ever had it.

—*" Suppose," &c.*] Juvenal answers,

The Pygmæan warrior runs in his little arms,
Soon unequal to the enemy, and seized, through the air,
    with crooked
Talons, he is carried by a cruel crane: if you could see this
In our nations, you would be shook with laughter: but
    there,   171
Though the same battles may be seen constantly, nobody
Laughs, when the whole cohort is not higher than one foot.
" Shall there be no punishment of a perjured head,
" And of wicked fraud ?" " Suppose this man dragged
    " away with   175
" A weightier chain immediately, and to be killed (what
    " would anger have more ?)
" At our will: yet that loss remains, nor will ever
" The deposit be safe to you:" " But from his maimed
    " body
" The least blood will give an enviable consolation.
" But revenge is a good more pleasant than life itself." 180
Truly this is of the unlearned, whose breasts you may see
Burning, sometimes from none, or from slight causes:
However small the occasion may be, it is sufficient for
    anger.
Chrysippus will not say the same, nor the mild disposition
Of Thales, and the old man neighbour to sweet Hymettus,

Suppose the man who has injured you hurried instantly away to prison, and loaded with fetters heavier than ordinary—graviore catena.

176. " Be kill'd," &c.] Be put to death by all the tortures we could invent—(and the most bitter anger could desire no more)—what then ?

177. " That loss"] i. e. Which you complain of.

—" Remains."] Is still the same.

178. " The deposit," &c.] The money which you deposited in his hands would not be the safer—i. e. at all the more secure.

179. " The least blood," &c.] True, replies Calvinus, but I should enjoy my revenge; the least drop of blood from his mangled body would give me such comfort as to be enviable; for revenge affords a pleasure sweeter than life itself.

181. Truly this, &c.] Truly, says Juvenal, ignorant and foolish people think so. q: d. This is the sentiment

of one who is void of all knowledge of true philosophy—indocti.

—Whose-breasts, &c.]. Præcordia signifies, literally, the parts about the heart, which is supposed to be the seat of the passions and affections; here it may stand for the passions themselves, which, says the poet, are set on fire, sometimes for no cause at all, sometimes from the most trivial causes, in silly people.

183. However small, &c.] Any trifling thing is sufficient to put them into a passion—but it is not so with the wise.

184. Chrysippus will not say, &c.] A famous Stoic philosopher, scholar to Zeno, who taught the government of the passions to be a chief good.

185. Thales.] A Milesian; one of the seven wise men of Greece He held that injuries were to be contemned, and was not himself easily provoked to anger.

—The old man.] Socrates.

Qui partem acceptæ sæva inter vinc'la cicutæ
Accusatori nollet dare. Plurima felix
Paulatim vitia, atque errores exuit omnes,
Prima docens rectùm Sapientia: quippe MINUTI
SEMPER ET INFIRMI EST ANIMI EXIGUIQUE VOLUPTAS 190
ULTIO. Continuo sic collige, quod vindictâ
Nemo magis gaudet, quam fœmina. Cur tamen hos tu
Evasisse putes, quos diri conscia facti
Mens habet attonitos, et surdo verbere cædit,
Occultum quatiente animo tortore flagellum? 195
Pœna autem vehemèns, ac multo sævior illis,
Quas et Cæditius gravis invenit aut Rhadamanthus,
Nocte dieque suum gestare in pectore testem.
    Spartano cuidam respondit Pythia vates,
Haud impunitum quondam fore, quod dubitaret 200
Depositum retinere, et fraudum jure tueri

185. *Neighbour to sweet Hymettus.*]
Hymettus, a mountain in Attica, famous for excellent honey, hence called dulcis Hymettus. See HOR. lib.
ii. ode vi. l. 14, 15. This mountain
was not far from Athens, where Socrates lived, and where he was put
to death.

186. *Who would not, &c.*] It was
a maxim of Socrates, that he who
did an injury was more to be pitied
than he who suffered it. He was accused of contemning the gods of
Athens, and for this, was condemned
to die, by drinking the juice of hemlock; which he did with circumstances
of calmness and fortitude as well as
of forgiveness of his accusers, that
brought tears from all that were present with him in the prison during the
sad scene.

An old scholiast has observed on
this passage, as indeed some others
have done, that one of his accusers,
Melitus, was cast into prison with
him; and asking Socrates to give
him some of the poison, that he might
drink it, Socrates refused it.

187. *Received hemlock.*] Which he
had received from the executioner,
and then held in his hand. For an
account of his death, see ANT. Univ.
Hist. vol. vi. p. 407, note z, translated from Plato.

—*Happy wisdom.*] The poet here
means the teachings of the moral

philosophers, some of which held,
that, even in torments, a wise man
was happy.

189. *First teaching what is right,
&c.*] To know what is right is first
necessary, in order to do it—this,
therefore, is the foundation of moral
philosophy, in order to strip the mind
of error, and the life of vicious actions.

Vitæ philosophia dux, virtutis inda-
gatrix, expultrixque vitiorum. CIC.
Tusc. v. ii.

"Philosophy is the guide of life,
"the searcher-out of virtue, the ex-
"peller of vice."

191. *Thus conclude.*] i. e. Conclude, without any farther reasoning,
that the above observation, viz. that
revenge is the pleasure of weak
minds, is true, because it is so often
found to be so in the weaker sex.

Persius uses the verb colligo in the
sense of conclude, or infer—mendose
colligis, you conclude falsely,

193. *To have escaped, &c.*] Though
no outward punishment should await
these evil-doers, and you may suppose them to have escaped quite free,
yet their very souls, conscious of
dreadful crimes, are all astonishment
—their guilty conscience smiting
them with silent, but severe, reproof.

195. *The conscience.*] i. e. Their
conscience, the executioner, shak-

Who would not, amidst cruel chains, give a part of	186
The received hemlock to his accuser. Happy wisdom,
By degrees puts off most vices, and all errors,
First teaching what is right: FOR REVENGE
IS ALWAYS THE PLEASURE OF A MINUTE, WEAK, AND
	LITTLE	190
MIND. Immediately thus conclude, because in revenge
Nobody rejoices more than a woman. But why should you
Think these to have escaped, whose mind, conscious of a
	dire
Fact, keeps them astonished, and smites with a dumb stripe,
Their conscience the tormentor shaking a secret whip?
But it is a vehement punishment, and much more cruel,
	than those	196
Which either severe Cæditius invented, or Rhadamanthus,
Night and day to carry their own witness in their breast.
	The Pythian prophetess answered a certain Spartan,
That in time to come he should not be unpunished, be-
	cause he doubted	200
To retain a deposit, and defend the fraud by swearing:

ing its secret scourge with terror over them.

A metaphor, taken from the whipping of criminals, whose terrors are excited at seeing the executioner's scourge lifted up and shaken over them.

Public whipping was a common punishment among the Romans for the lower sort of people. See HOR. epod. iv. l. 11.

196. *Vehement punishment, &c.*]—The poet here means, that the torments of a wounded conscience are less tolerable than those of bodily punishment. Comp. Prov. xviii. 14.

197. *Severe Cæditius.*] A very cruel judge in the days of Vitellius; or, according to some, in the days of Nero.

—*Rhadamantus.*] One of the judges of hell. See sat i. l. 10. note.

198. *Their own witness, &c.*] Continually bearing about with them the testimony of an evil conscience.

199. *Pythian prophetess.*] The priestess of Apollo, (called Pythius, from his slaying the serpent Python,) by whom Apollo gave answers at his oracle of Delphos.

The story alluded to is told by Herodotus, of one Glaucus, a Spartan, with whom a Milesian, in confidence of his honesty, had left a sum of money in trust. Glaucus afterwards denied having received the money, when it was demanded by the sons of the Milesian, and sent them away without it; yet he was not quite satisfied in himself, and went to the oracle, to know whether he should persist in denying it or not. He was answered, that if he foreswore the money, he might escape for a time; but for his vile intention, he and all his family should be destroyed. Upon this, Glaucus sent for the Milesians, and paid the whole sum. But what the oracle foretold came to pass, for he and all his kindred were afterwards extirpated.

200. *Time to come.*] Though he might escape from the present, yet, at a future time, he should not go without punishment.

—*Because he doubted.*] Could suffer himself even to entertain a doubt in such a case as this.

201. *A deposit*] Of money, committed to his trust.

—*By swearing.*] By perjury—jure jurando. Tmesis.

Jurando: quærebat enim quæ numinis esset
Mens; et an hoc illi facinus suaderet Apollo.
Reddidit ergo metu, non moribus; et tamen omnem
Vocem adyti dignam templo, veramque probavit,   205
Extinctus totâ pariter cum prole domoque,
Et quamvis longâ deductis gente propinquis.
Has patitur pœnas peccandi sola voluntas.
Nam SCELUS INTRA SE TACITUM QUI COGITAT ULLUM,
FACTI CRIMEN HABET: cedo, si conata peregit?   210
Perpetua anxietas: nec mensæ tempore cessat;
Faucibus ut morbo siccis, interque molares
Difficili crescente cibo.   Sed vina misellus
Exspuit: Albani veteris pretiosa senectus
Displicet: ostendas melius, densissima ruga   215
Cogitur in frontem, velut acri ducta Falerno.

202. *He asked, &c.*] In hopes that he might get such an answer as would quiet his mind, and determine him to keep the money.

203. *Would advise, &c.*] Would persuade him to the fact—*i. e.* to retain the deposit, &c.

204. *From fear, not, &c.*] More from a principle of fear of the consequences of keeping it, than an honest desire of doing right.

205. *The voice of the shrine.*]— Adytum signifies the most secret and sacred place of the temple, from whence the oracles were supposed to be delivered.

—*Worthy the temple, &c.*] It was reckoned highly for the reputation of the temple, when the things there foretold came to pass; on account of which, these oracles were usually delivered in equivocal terms, so that they might be supposed to tell truth, on whichever side the event turned out.

207. *Deduced from a long race.*]— Longa gente, from a long train of ancestors—all that were related to him, however distantly, were cut off.

208. *These punishments, &c.*] Thus was the mere intention of doing ill most justly punished.

210. *Hath the guilt, &c.*] Is as really guilty as if he had accomplished it. In this, and in many other passages, one would almost think Juvenal was acquainted with some-

thing above heathenism. Comp. Prov. xxiv. 8-9; and Matt. v. 28.

—" *Tell me,*" *&c.*] A question asked by Calvinus, on hearing what Juvenal had said before. Tell me, says Calvinus, if what you say be true, that the very design to do evil makes a person guilty of what he designed to do, what would be the case of his actually accomplishing what he intended, as my false friend has done?

211. " *Perpetual anxiety.*"] Juvenal answers the question, by setting forth, in very striking colours, the anguish of a wounded conscience. First, he would be under continual anxiety.

—" *The time of the table.*"] Even at his meals—his convivial hours.

212. " *With jaws dry,*" *&c.*] His mouth hot and parched, like one in a fever.

213. " *Difficult food increasing.*]— This circumstance is very natural— the uneasiness of this wretch's mind occasions the symptoms of a fever; one of which is a dryness in the mouth and throat, owing to the want of a due secretion of the saliva, by the glands appropriated for that purpose. The great use of this secretion, which we call saliva, or spittle, is in masticating and diluting the food, and making the first digestion thereof; also to lubricate the throat and œsophagus, or gullet, in order to facilitate deglutition; which, by these

For he asked what was the mind of the Deity,
And whether Apollo would advise this deed to him.
He therefore restored it from fear, not from morals, and
   yet all
The voice of the shrine, he proved worthy the temple, and
   true,   205
Being extinguished together with all his offspring, and
   family,
And with his relations, tho' deduced from a long race.
These punishments does the single will of offending
   suffer.
FOR HE WHO WITHIN HIMSELF DEVISES ANY SECRET WICK-
   EDNESS,
HATH THE GUILT OF THE FACT.—" Tell me, if he accom-
  " plish'd his attempts ?"   210
" Perpetual anxiety : nor does it cease at the time of the
  " table,
" With jaws dry as by disease, and between his grinders
" The difficult food increasing. But the wretch spits
  " out
" His wine: the precious old age of old Albanian   214
" Will displease : if you shew him better, the thickest
  " wrinkle
" Is gathered on his forehead, as drawn by sour Fa-
  " lernan.

means, in healthy persons, is attended with ease and pleasure.
But the direct contrary is the case,
where the mouth and throat are quite
dry, as in fevers—the food is chewed
with difficulty and disgust, and cannot be swallowed without uneasiness
and loathing, and may well be called
difficilis cibus in both these respects.
Wanting also the saliva to moisten
it, and make it into a sort of paste
for deglution, it breaks into pieces
between the teeth, and taking up
more room than when in one mass, it
fills the mouth as if it had increased
in quantity, and is attended with
a nausea, or loathing, which still increases the uneasiness of the sensation.

213-14. " Spits out his wine."]—
He cannot relish it, his mouth being
out of taste, and therefore spits it out
as something nauseous.

214. " Albanian."] This was reck-

oned the finest and best wine in all
Italy, especially when old. See HOR.
lib. iv. ode xi. l. 1–2.

215. " Shew him better."] If you
could set even better wine than this
before him, he could not relish it.

—" The thickest wrinkle," &c.]—
His forehead would contract into
wrinkles without end, as if they were
occasioned by his being offered sour
Falernan wine.

Densissima is here used, as in sat.
i. 105. to denote a vast number ; as
we say, a thick crowd, where vast
numbers of people are collected together.

Falernan wine was in high repute
among the Romans when it was of
the best sort ; but there was a kind
of coarse, sour wine, which came
from Falernus, a mountain of Campania, which, when drank, would
occasion sickness and vomiting.

Nocte brevem si forte indulsit cura soporem,
Et toto versata toro jam membra quiescunt,
Continuo templum, et violati numinis aras,
Et (quod præcipuis mentem sudoribus urget)   220
Te videt in somnis: tua sacra et major imago
Humanâ turbat pavidum, cogitque fateri.
Hi sunt qui trepidant, et ad omnia fulgura pallent,
Cum tonat; exanimes primo quoque murmure cœli:
Non quasi fortuitus, nec ventorum rabie, sed   225
Iratus cadat in terras, et vindicet ignis.
Illa nihil nocuit, curâ graviore timetur
Proxima tempestas; velut hoc dilata sereno.
Præterea lateris vigili cum febre dolorem
Si cœpêre pati, missum ad sua corpora morbum   230
Infesto credunt a numine: saxa Deorum

218. " *His limbs tumbled over,*" &c.] Tumbling and tossing from one side of the bed to the other, through the uneasiness of his mind. See sat. iii. 280, and note; and AINSW. *Verso,* No. 2.

219. " *The temple—the altars,*" &c.] He is haunted with dreadful dreams, and seems to see the temple in which, and the altar upon which, he perjured himself, and thus profaned and violated the majesty of the Deity.

220. " *What urges his mind,*" &c.] But that which occasions him more misery than all the rest (see AINSW. *Sudor;* and sat. i. 153.) is, that he fancies he beholds the man whom he has injured, appearing (as aggrandized by his fears) greater than a human form. The ancients had much superstition on the subject of apparitions, and always held them sacred; and (as fear magnifies its objects) they always were supposed to appear greater than the life. Hence Juvenal says, sacra et major imago. Comp. VIRG. Æn. ii. l. 772-3.

222. " *Compels him to confess,*"] i. e. The villainy which he has been guilty of—a confession of this is wrung from him by the terrors which he undergoes; he can no longer keep the secret within his breast.

223. " *All lightnings,*" &c.] The poet proceeds in his description of the miserable state of the wicked, and here represents them as filled with horror by thunder and lightning, and dreading the consequences.

224. " *First murmur,*" &c.]— They are almost dead with fear, on hearing the first rumbling in the sky.

225. " *Not as if,*" &c.] They do not look upon it as happening fortuitously, by mere chance or accident, without any direction or intervention of the gods, like the Epicureans.— See HOR. sat. v. lib. i. l. 101-3.

—" *Rage of winds.*"] Or from the violence of the winds, occasioning a collision of the clouds, and so producing the lightning, as the philosophers thought, who treated on the physical causes of lightning, as Pliny and Seneca.

226. " *Fire may fall,*" &c.] The wretch thinks that the flashes which he sees and dreads will not confine their fury to the skies, but, armed with divine vengeance, may fall upon the earth, and destroy the guilty.

227. " *That did no harm,*"] i. e. That last tempest did no mischief; it is now over and harmless: " So far is well," thinks the unhappy wretch.

—" *The next tempest,*" &c.]— Though they escape the first storm, yet they dread the next still more, imagining that they have only had a respite from punishment, and therefore that the next will certainly destroy them.

" In the night, if haply care hath indulged a short
   " sleep,
" And his limbs tumbled over the whole bed now are
   " quiet,
" Immediately the temple, and the altars of the violated
   " Deity,
" And (what urges his mind with especial pains)   220
" Thee he sees in his sleep : thy sacred image, and
   " bigger
" Than human, disturbs him fearful, and compels him to
   " confess."
" There are they who tremble, and turn pale at all light-
   " nings
" When it thunders : also lifeless at the first murmur of
   " the heavens :
" Not as if accidental, nor by rage of winds, but   225
" Fire may fall on the earth enraged, and may avenge."
" That did no harm"—" the next tempest is fear'd
" With heavier concern, as if deferred by this fair
   " weather.
" Moreover a pain of the side with a watchful fever,
" If they have begun to suffer, they believe the disease
   " sent   230
" To their bodies by some hostile deity : they think these
   " things

228. " *As if deferr'd*," &c.] As
if delayed by one fair day, on purpose, afterwards, to fall the heavier.
. This passage of Juvenal reminds
one of that wonderfully fine speech,
on a similar subject, which our great
and inimitable poet, Shakespeare, has
put into the mouth of king Lear,
when turned out by his cruel and ungrateful daughters, and, on a desolate
and barren heath, is in the midst of
a storm of thunder and lightning.
   LEAR.   " *Let the great gods*
. " *That keep this dreadful pother*
   " *o'er our heads,*
_ " *Find out their enemies now.*
   " *Tremble thou wretch*
   " *That hast within thee undivulged*
   " *crimes,*
   " *Unwhipt of justice: hide thee,*
   " *thou bloody hand ;*
   " *Thou perjur'd and thou simular*
   " *man of virtue*

   " *That art incestuous: Caitiff, to*
   " *pieces shake*
   " *That under covert and convenient*
   " *seeming*
   " *Hast practis'd on man's life!*
   " *Close pent-up guilts,*
   " *Rive your concealing continents,*
   " *and cry*
   " *These dreadful summoners grace!*"
   - LEAR, act III. sc. 1.
229. " *Pain of the side,*" &c.]—
The poet seems here to mean a pleurisy, or pleuritic fever, a painful and
dangerous distemper.
   —" *A watchful fever.*"] i. e. A fever which will not let them sleep, or
take their rest
   230. " *Begun to suffer,*" &c.]—
On the first attack of such a disorder,
they believe themselves doomed to
suffer the wrath of an offended Deity,
of which their illness seems to them
an earnest.

Hæc, et tela putant : pecudem spondere sacello
Balantem, et Laribus cristam promittere galli
Non audent.   Quid enim sperare nocentibus ægris
Concessum ? vel quæ non dignior hostia vitâ ?   235
Mobilis et varia est ferme natura malorum.
Cum scelus admittunt, superest constantia : quid fas,.
Atque nefas, tandem incipiunt sentire, peractis
Criminibus.   Tamen ad'mores natura recurrit
Damnatos, fixa et mutari nescia.   Nam quis   240
Peccandi finem posuit sibi ? quando recepit
Ejectum semel attritâ de fronte ruborem ?
Quisnam hominum est, quem tu contentum videris uno
Flagitio ? dabit in laqueum vestigia noster
Perfidus, et nigri patietur carceris uncum,   245
Aut maris Ægæi rupem, scopulosque frequentes

232. " *Stones and darts.*"] These were weapons of war among the ancients ; when they attacked a place, they threw, from engines for that purpose, huge stones to batter down the wall, and darts to annoy the besieged.

Here the poet uses the words in a metaphorical sense, to denote the apprehension of a sick criminal, who thinks himself, as it were, besieged by an offended Deity, who employs the pleurisy and fever, as his artillery, to destroy the guilty wretch.

—" *To engage a bleating sheep,*" &c.] Or lamb—pecus may signify either. It was usual for persons in danger, or in sickness, to engage by vow some offering to the gods, on their deliverance, or recovery ; but the guilty wretches here mentioned are supposed to be in a state of utter despair, so that they dare not so much as hope for recovery, and therefore have no courage to address any vows to the gods.

233. " *Comb of a cock,*" &c.]— So far from promising a cock to Æsculapius, they have not the courage to vow even a cock's comb, as a sacrifice to their household gods.

234. " *Allowed the guilty,*" &c.] Such guilty wretches can be allowed no hope whatever—their own consciences tell them as much.

235. " *Is not more worthy,*" &c.] *i. e.* Does not more deserve to live than they.

236. " *Fickle and changeable,*"]— *i. e.* Wavering and uncertain, at first ; before they commit crimes, they are irresolute, and doubting whether they shall or not, and often change their mind, which is in a fluctuating state.

237. " *Remains constancy.*"]— When they have once engaged in evil actions, they become resolute.

—" *What is right,*" &c.] After the crime is perpetrated, they begin to reflect on what they have done—they are forcibly stricken with the difference between right and wrong, insomuch that they feel, for a while, a remorse of conscience ; but notwithstanding this—

239. " *Nature recurs,*" &c.]— Their evil nature will return to its corrupt principles, and silence all remorse ; fixed and unchangeable in this respect, it may be said, Naturam expellas furca tamen usque recurret. Hor. lib. i. epist. x. l. 24.

241. " *Hath laid down to himself,*" &c.] What wicked man ever contented himself with one crime, or could say to his propensity to wickedness, " hitherto shalt thou come, " and no farther," when every crime he commits hardens him the more, and plunges him still deeper ?

—" *When recovered,*" &c.] No man ever yet recovered a sense of shame, who had once lost it.

242. " *Worn forehead,*" &c.]— Attritus signifies rubbed or worn

" The stones and darts of the gods: to engage a bleating
"   sheep
" To the little temple, and to promise the comb of a cock
"   to the Lares
" They dare not; for what is allowed the guilty sick
" To hope for? or what victim is not more worthy of life?
" The nature of wicked men is, for the most part, fickle,
"   and changeable;   236
" When they commit wickedness, there remains constancy:
"   what is right
" And what wrong, at length they begin to perceive, their
"   crimes
" Being finish'd: but nature recurs to its damned
" Morals, fix'd, and not knowing to be changed. For
"   who   240
" Hath laid down to himself an end of sinning? when re-
"   cover'd
" Modesty once cast off from his worn forehead?
" Who is there of men, whom you have seen content with
"   one
" Base action? our perfidious wretch will get his feet into
" A snare, and will suffer the hook of a dark prison, 245
" Or a rock of the Ægean sea, and the rocks abounding

away, as marble, or metals, where
an hard and polished surface remains;
so a wicked man, by frequent and
continual crimes, grows hardened a-
gainst all impressions of shame, of
which the forehead is often represented as the seat. See Jer. iii. 3.
latter part.

243. " Who is there," &c.] Who
ever contented himself with sinning
but once, and stopped at the first
fact?

244. " Our perfidious wretch,"
&c.] Noster perfidus, says Juvenal,
meaning the villain who had cheated
Calvinus, and then perjured himself.
As if the poet had said, Do not be so
uneasy, Calvinus, at the loss of your
money, or so anxious about reveng-
ing yourself upon the wretch who has
perjured you; have a little patience,
he will not stop here, he will go on
from bad to worse, till you will find
him sufficiently punished, and yourself amply avenged.

244-5. " Into a snare."] He will
do something or other which will

send him to gaol, and load him with
fetters. Or, he will walk into a snare
(Comp. Job xviii. 8–10.) and be entangled in his own devices.

245. " Suffer the hook," &c.] The
uncus was a drag, or hook, by which
the bodies of malefactors were dragged
about the streets after execution. See
sat. x. l. 66.

But, by this line, it should seem
as if some instrument of this sort
was made use of, either for torture,
or closer confinement in the dungeon.

246. " Rock of the Ægean sea."]
Or, if he should escape the gallows,
that he will be banished to some
rocky, barren island in the Ægean
sea, where he will lead a miserable
life. Perhaps the island Seriphos is
here meant.

—" The rocks frequent," &c.]—
The rocky islands of the Cyclades, to
which numbers were banished, and
frequently, either by the tyranny of
the emperor, or through their own
crimes, persons of high rank.

2 I

Exulibus magnis.　Pœnâ gaudebis amarâ
Nominis invisi : tandemque fatebere lætus
Nec surdum, nec Tiresiam quenquam esse Deorum.

247. " *You will rejoice*," &c.]— will not be mentioned, but with the
You, Calvinus, will at last triumph utmost detestation and abhorrence.
over the villain that has wronged you,　　—"*At length—confess.*"] However,
when you see the bitter sufferings in time past, you may have doubted
which await him, fall upon him. of it, you will in the end joyfully
248. " *His hated name.*"]　Which own—

" .With great exiles.. You will rejoice in the bitter punish-
    " ment
" Of his hated name, and, at length, glad will confess,
    " that no one of
" The gods is'either deaf, or a Tiresias."

248-9. " *That no one of the gods,*"   249. " *Tiresias.*"] A blind sooth-
&c.] Whose province it is to punish   sayer of Thebes, fabled to be stricken
crimes, is either deaf, so as not to   blind by Juno, for his decision in
hear such perjury, or blind, so as not   a dispute between her and her hus-
to see every circumstance of such a   band, in favour of the latter, who
transaction, and to punish it accord-   in requital gave him the gift of pro-
ingly.   Comp. l. 112-19.   phecy.

Satira Quartadecima.

ARGUMENT.

This Satire is levelled at the bad examples which parents set their children, and shews the serious consequences of such examples, in helping to contaminate the morals of the rising generation, as we are apt, by nature, rather to receive ill impressions than good, and are, besides,

PLURIMA sunt, Fuscine, et famâ digna sinistrâ,
Et nitidis maculam hæsuram figentia rebus,
Quæ monstrant ipsi pueris traduntque parentes.
Si damnosa senem juvat alea, ludit et hæres
Bullatus, parvoque eadem movet arma fritillo :   5
Nec de se melius cuiquam seperare propinquo
Concedet juvenis, qui radere tubera terræ,
Boletum condire, et eodem jure natantes
Mergere ficedulas didicit, nebulone parente,

Line 1. *Fuscinus.*]. A friend of Juvenal's, to whom this Satire is addressed.

—*Worthy of unfavourable report.*] Which deserve to be ill spoken of, to be esteemed scandalous.

The word sinistra here is metaphorical, taken from the Roman superstition, with regard to any thing of the ominous kind, which appeared on the left hand; they reckoned it unlucky and unfavourable. See sat. x. l. 129, where the word is applied, as here, in a metaphorical sense.

2. *Fixing a stain, &c.*] A metaphor, taken from the idea of clean and neat garments being soiled, or spotted, with filth thrown upon them, the marks of which are not easily got out. So these things of evil report fix a spot, or stain, on the most splendid character, rank, or fortune—all which, probably, the poet means by nitidis rebus.

3. *Which parents, &c.*] The things worthy of evil report, which are afterwards particularized, are matters which parents exhibit to their children by example, and deliver to them by precept. Comp. l. 9.

4. *If the destructive die pleases, &c.*] If the father be fond of playing at dice.

—*Wearing the bulla, &c.*] His son, when a mere child, will imitate his example.—For the bulla, see sat. xiii. l. 33. note.

5. *The same weapons, &c.*] Arma, literally, denotes all kind of warlike arms and armour, and, by met. all manner of tools and implements, for all arts, mysteries, occupations, and diversions. AINSW. The word is peculiarly proper to express dice, and other implements of gaming, wherewith the gamesters attack each other, each with an intent to ruin and destroy the opponent. See sat. i. 78. note.

Fourteenth Satire.

ARGUMENT.

more pliant in our younger than in our riper years.
From hence he descends to a Satire on avarice, which he
esteems to be of worse example than any other of the vices
which he mentions before; and concludes with limiting
our desires within reasonable bounds.

THERE are many things, Fuscinus, worthy of un-
    favourable report,
And fixing a stain which will stick upon splendid things,
Which parents themselves shew, and deliver to their chil-
    dren.
If the destructive die pleases the old man, the heir wearing
    the bulla
Will play too, and moves the same weapons in his little
    dice-box.   5
Nor does the youth allow any relation to hope better of him,
Who has learnt to peel the fungi of the earth,
To season a mushroom, and, swimming in the same sauce,
To immerse beccaficos, a prodigal parent,

---

5. *Little dice-box.*] Master, being
too young to play with a large dice-
box, not being able to shake and manage it, has a small one made for
him, that he may begin the science
as early as possible. See AINSW.
Fritillus.

6. *Nor does the youth allow, &c.*]
The poet, having mentioned the
bringing up children to be gamesters,
here proceeds to those who are early
initiated into the science of gluttony.
Such give very little room to their
family to hope that they will turn out
better than the former.

7. *To peel the fungi of the
earth,*] Tuber (from tumeo, to swell
or puff up) signifies what we call a
puff, which grows in the ground like

a mushroom—a toadstool. But I apprehend that any of the fungous productions of the earth may be signified
by tuber; and, in this place, we are
to understand, perhaps, truffles, or
some other food of the kind, which
were reckoned delicious.

—*To peel.*] Or scrape off the
coat, or skin, with which they are
covered.

8. *A mushroom.*] The boletus was
reckoned the best sort of mushroom.
See AINSW. *Condio.*

9. *Beccaficos.*] Ficedulas—little
birds which feed on figs, now called
beccaficos, or fig-peckers; they are
to this day esteemed a great dainty.

It was reckoned a piece of high
luxury to have these birds dressed,

Et canâ monstrante gulâ. Cum septimus annus.   10
Transierit puero, nondum omni dente renato,
Barbatos licet admoveas mille inde magistros,
Hinc totidem, cupiet lauto cœnare paratu
Semper, et a magnâ non degenerare culinâ.

Mitem animum, et mores, modicis erroribus'æquos   15
Præcipit, atque animas servorum, et corpora nostrâ
Materiâ constare putat, paribusque elementis?
An sævire docet Rutilus? qui gaudet acerbo
Plagarum strepitu, et nullam Sirena flagellis
Comparat, Antiphates trepidi laris, ac Polyphemus.   20
Tum felix, quoties aliquis tortore vocato
Uritur ardenti duo propter lintea ferro?
Quid suadet juveni lætus stridore catenæ,
Quem mire afficiunt inscripta ergastula, carcer

---

and served up to table, in the same sauce, or pickle, with fungi of various kinds.

9. *A prodigal parent.*] Nebulo signifies an unthrift, a vain prodigal; and is most probably used here in this sense. See AINSW. *Nebulo*, No. 2.

10. *A grey throat, &c.*] Gula is, literally, the throat or gullet; but, by met. may signify a glutton, who thinks of nothing but his gullet. So γαςρ, the belly, is used to denote a glutton; and the apostle's quotation from the Cretan poet, Tit. i. 12. γαςρες αργοι, instead of slow bellies, which is nonsense, should be rendered lazy gluttons, which is the undoubted sense of the phrase.

Cana gula here, then, may be rendered an hoary glutton—*i. e.* the old epicure, his father setting the example, and shewing him the arts of luxurious cookery.

10. *The seventh year, &c.*] When he is turned of seven years of age, a time when the second set of teeth, after shedding the first, is not completed, and a time of life the most flexible and docile.

12. *Tho' you should place, &c.*]— Though a thousand of the gravest and most learned tutors were placed on each side of him, so as to pour their instructions into both his ears at the same time, yet they would avail nothing at all towards reclaiming him.

—q. d. The boy having got such an early taste for gluttony, will never get rid of it, by any pains which can be taken with him for that purpose.

The philosophers and learned teachers wore beards; and were therefore called barbati. They thought it suited best with the gravity of their appearance. See HOR. lib. ii. sat. iii. l. 35. and note.

13. *He would desire, &c.*] He would never get rid of his inclination to gluttony.

13-14. *With a sumptuous preparation.*] With a number of the most delicious provisions, dressed most luxuriously, and served up in the most sumptuous manner.

14. *Not to degenerate, &c.*] Either in principle or practice, from the profuse luxury of his father's ample kitchen.

So true is that of HOR. Epist. lib. i. epist. ii. l. 68-9.
Quo semel imbuta est recens servabit odorem
Testa diu.

15. *Rutilus.*] The name of some master, who was of a very cruel disposition towards his servants.

—Kind to small errors.] Making allowance for, and excusing, small faults.

16. *And the souls of slaves, &c.*]— Does he think that the bodies of slaves consist of the same materials, and that their souls are made up of the

And a grey throat shewing him. When the seventh year
Has passed over the boy, all his teeth not as yet renewed,
Though you should place a thousand bearded masters
　　there,
Here as many, he would desire always to sup with a
Sumptuous preparation, and not to degenerate from a great
　　kitchen.
Does Rutilus teach a meek mind and manners, kind to
　　small errors,　　　　　　　　　　　　　　　　15
And the souls of slaves, and their bodies, does he think
To consist of our matter, and of equal elements?—
Or does he teach to be cruel, who delights in the bitter
Sound of stripes, and compares no Siren to whips,
The Antiphates and Polyphemus of his trembling house-
　　hold—　　　　　　　　　　　　　　　　　　20
Then happy, as often as any one, the tormentor being
　　called,
Is burnt with an hot iron on account of two napkins?
What can he who is glad at the noise of a chain advise to
　　a youth,
Whom branded slaves, a rustic prison, wonderfully

same elements as ours, who are their masters? Does he suppose them to be of the same flesh and blood, and to have reasonable souls as well as himself?

18. *Or does he teach to be cruel.*]—Instead of setting an example of meekness, gentleness, and forbearance, does he not teach his children to be savage and cruel, by the treatment which he gives his slaves?

18-19. *In the bitter sound of stripes.*] He takes a pleasure in hearing the sound of those bitter stripes, with which he punishes his slaves.

19. *Compares no Siren, &c*] The song of a Siren, would not, in his opinion, be so delightful to his ears, as the crack of the whips on his slaves' backs.

20. *The Antiphates and Polyphemus, &c.*] Antiphates was a king of a savage people near Formiæ, in Italy, who were eaters of man's flesh.

Polyphemus the Cyclops lived on the same diet. See VIRG. Æn. iii. 620. et seq.

Rutilus is here likened to these two monsters of cruelty, inasmuch as that he was the terror of his whole fa-

mily, which is the sense of laris in this place.

21. *Then happy*] It was a matter of joy to him.
—*As often as any one.*] i. e. Of his slaves.

22. *Is burnt, &c.*] Burnt with an hot iron on his flesh, for some petty theft, as of two towels or napkins. These the Romans wiped with after bathing.

23. *What can he advise, &c.*] What can a man, who is himself so barbarous, as to be affected with the highest pleasure at hearing the rattling of fetters, when put on the legs or bodies of his slaves—what can such a father persuade his son to, whom he has taught so ill by his example?

24. *Branded slaves—a rustic prison.*] Ergastulum—lit. signifies a workhouse, a house of correction, where they confined and punished their slaves, and made them work. Sometimes (as here it means a slave.) Inscriptus-a-um, signifies marked, branded; inscripta ergastula, branded slaves; comp. l. 22. note. *q d.* Whom the sight of slaves branded with hot irons, kept in a workhouse

Rusticus? Expectas, ut non sit adultera Largæ   25
Filia, quæ nunquam maternos dicere mœchos
Tam cito nec tanto poterit contexere cursu,
Ut non ter decies respiret? conscia matri
Virgo fuit: ceras nunc hâc dictante pusillas
Implet, et ad mœchum dat eisdem ferre ministris.   30
Sic natura jubet: velocius et citius nos
Corrumpunt vitiorum exempla domestica, magnis
Cùm subeunt animos authoribus.   Unus et alter
Forsitan hæc spernant juvenes, quibus arte benignâ,
Et meliore luto finxit præcordia Titan.   35
Sed reliquos fugienda patrum vestigia ducunt;
Et monstrata diu veteris trahit orbita culpæ.
Abstineas igitur damnandis: hujus enim vel
Una potens ratio est, ne crimina nostra sequantur
Ex nobis geniti; quoniam dociles imitandis   40
Turpibus et pravis omnes sumus; et Catilinam
Quocunque in populo videas, quocunque sub axe:

in the country, where they are in fetters, (l. 23.) and which is therefore to be looked on as a country-gaol, affects with wonderful delight. We may suppose the ergastula something like our bridewells.

25. *Larga.*] Some famous lady of that day; here put, for all such characters.

25. *Should not be, &c.*] When she has the constant bad example of her mother before her eyes.

26. *Who never, &c.*] Who could never repeat the names of all her mother's gallants, though she uttered them as fast as possibly she could, without often taking breath before she got to the end of the list, so great was the number.

28. *Privy, &c.*] She was a witness of all her mother's lewd proceedings, and was privy to them; which is the meaning of conscia in this place. See sat. iii. l. 49.

29. *Now.*] *i. e.* Now she is grown something bigger, she does as her mother did.

—*She dictating.*] The mother instructing, and dictating what she shall say.

—*Little tablets.*] Cera signifies wax, but as they wrote on thin wooden tablets smeared over with wax, ceras,

per met. means the tablets or letters themselves. See sat. i. l. 50.

Some understand by ceras pusillas, small tablets, as best adapted to the size of her hand, and more proper for her age, than large ones. As the boy (l. 5.) had a little dice-box to teach him gaming, so this girl begins with a little tablet, in order to initiate her into the science of intrigue. But, perhaps, by pusillas ceras the poet means what the French would call petits billets-doux.

30. *She fills.*] *i. e.* Fills with writing. The daughter employs the same messengers that her mother did, to carry her little love-letters.

31. *So nature commands, &c.*]— Thus nature orders it, and therefore it naturally happens, that examples of vice, set by those of our own family, corrupt the soonest.

32. *When they possess minds, &c.*] When they insinuate themselves into the mind, under the influence of those who have a right to exercise authority over us. See AINSW. *Auctor*, No. 6.

33. *One or two.*] Unus et alter—here and there one, as we say, may be found as exceptions, and who may reject, with due contempt, their parent's vices, but then they must

Delight ?—Do you expect that the daughter of Larga
    should not be   25
An adulteress, who never could say over her mother's
    gallants,
So quickly, nor could join them together with so much
    speed,
As that she must not take breath thirty times; privy to her
    mother
Was the virgin : now, she dictating, little tablets
She fills, and gives them to the same servants to carry to
    the gallant.   30
So nature commands ; more swiftly and speedily do domestic
Examples of vices corrupt us, when they possess minds
From those that have great influence. Perhaps one or two
Young men may despise these things, for whom, by a be-
    nign art
And with better clay, Titan has formed their breasts. 35
But the footsteps of their fathers which are to be avoided,
    lead the rest,
And the path of old wickedness, long shewn, draws them.
Abstain therefore from things which are to be condemned ;
    for of this at least
There is one powerful reason, lest those who are begotten
    by us
Should follow our crimes; for in imitating base and wicked
Things we are all docile ; and a Catiline   41
You may see among every people, in every clime :

be differently formed from the generality.

34. *By a benign art, &c.*] Prometheus, one of the Titans, was feigned,
by the poets, to have formed men of
clay, and put life into them by fire
stolen from heaven.

The poet here says, that, if one or
two young men are found who reject
their father's bad example, it must
be owing to the peculiar favour of
Prometheus, who, by a kind exertion
of his art, formed their bodies, and
particularly the parts about the heart
(præcordia) of better materials than
those which he employed in the for-
mation of others.

36. *Footsteps, &c.*] As for the common run of young men, they are led,
by the bad example of their fathers,
to tread in their fathers' steps, which
ought to be avoided.

37. *Path of old wickedness, &c.*]
And the beaten track of wickedness,
constantly before their eyes, draws
them into the same crimes.

38. *Abstain therefore, &c.*] Refrain
therefore from ill actions ; at least we
should do this, if not for our own
sakes, yet for the sake of our children, that they may not be led to follow our vicious examples, and to
commit the same crimes which they
have seen in us.

40. *In imitating, &c.*] Such is the
condition of human nature, that we
are all more prone to evil than to
good, and, for this reason, we are
easily taught to imitate the vices of
others.

41. *A Catiline, &c.*] See sat. viii.
231. Vicious characters are easily to
be met with, go where you may.

Sed nec Brutus erit, Bruti nec avunculus usquam.
Nil dictu fœdum, visuque hæc limina tangat,
Intra quæ puer est. Procul hinc, procul inde puellæ   45
Lenonum, et cantus pernoctantis parasiti.
Maxima debetur puero reverentia. Si quid
Turpe paras, ne tu pueri contempseris annos:
Sed peccaturo obsistat tibi filius infans.
Nam si quid dignum Censoris fecerit irâ,   50
(Quandoquidem similem tibi se non corpore tantum,
Nec vultu dederit, morum quoque filius,) et cum
Omnia deterius tuâ per vestigia peccet,
Corripies nimirum, et castigabis acerbo
Clamore, ac post hæc tabulas mutare parabis.   55
Unde tibi frontem, libertatemque parentis,
Cum facias pejora senex? vacuumque cerebro
Jampridem caput hoc ventosa cucurbita quærat?

43. *Brutus.*] M. Brutus, one of the most virtuous of the Romans, and the great assertor of public liberty.

—*Uncle of Brutus.*] Cato of Utica, who was the brother of Servilia, the mother of Brutus, a man of severe virtue.

So prone is human nature to evil, so inclined to follow bad example, that a virtuous character, like Brutus or Cato, is hardly to be found any where, while profligate and debauched characters, like Catiline, abound all the world over; this would not be so much the case, if parents were more careful about the examples which they set their children.

44. *Filthy.*] Indecent, obscene.

—*Should touch, &c.*] Should approach those doors, where there are children; lest they be corrupted. Therefore—

45. *Far from hence, &c.*] Hence far away, begone; a form of speech made use of at religious solemnities, in order to hinder the approach of the profane. So HORACE, lib. iii. ode i. l. 1. when he calls himself musarum sacerdos, says, Odi profanum vulgus et arceo.

VIRG. Æn. vi. 258-9. makes the Sibyl say:

—*Procul, O procul este profani*
—*Totoque absistite luco.*

45-6. *Girls of bawds.*] The common prostitutes, who are kept by common panders, or pimps, for lewd purposes.

46. *The nightly parasite.*] Pernoctans signifies tarrying, or sitting up all night. The parasites, who frequently attended at the table of great men, used to divert them with lewd and obscene songs, and for this purpose would sit up all night long.

47. *Greatest reverence, &c.*] People should keep the strictest guard over their words and actions, in the presence of boys; they cannot be under too much awe, nor shew too great a reverence for decency, when in their presence.

48. *You go about, &c.*] If you intend, or purpose, or set about, to do what is wrong, do not say, " There " is nobody here but my young son, " I don't mind him, and he is too " young to mind me."—Rather say, " My little boy is here, I will not " hurt his mind by making him a " witness of what I purposed to do, " therefore I will not do it before " him."

50. *Of the censor.*] The censor of good manners, or morum judex, was an officer of considerable power in Rome, before whom offenders against the peace and good manners were carried and censured. Sat. iv. l. 11.

q. d. Now, if, in after times, your son should be taken before the censor,

But neither will Brutus, nor uncle of Brutus, be any where.
Nothing filthy, to be said, or seen, should touch these
· thresholds.
Within which is a boy.   Far from hence, from thence the
    girls   45
Of bawds, and the songs of the nightly parasite :
The greatest reverence is due to a boy.   If any base thing
You go about, do not despise the years of a boy,
But let your infant son hinder you about to sin.
For if he shall do any thing worthy the anger of the
    censor,   50
(Since he, like to you not in body only, nor in countenance,
Will shew himself, the son also of your morals,) and when
He may offend the worse, by all your footsteps,
You will, forsooth, chide, and chastise with harsh
Clamour, and after these, will prepare to change your will.
Whence assume you the front, and liberty of a parent, 56
When, an old man, you can do worse things, and this
    head,
Void of brain, long since, the ventose cupping-glass may
    seek ?

for some crime cognizable and pu-
nishable by him.

, 52. *Shew himself, &c.*] (For he
will exhibit a likeness to his father,
not in person, or face only, but in his
moral behaviour and conduct , therefore, if you set him a bad example,
you must not wonder that he follows
it, and appears his father's own son
in mind as well as in body.)

53. *Offend the worse, &c.*] And it
is most probable, that following your
steps has made him do worse than he
otherwise would.

54. *You will, &c.*] You will call
him to a severe account.   Nimirum
here is to be understood like our English—forsooth.

—*And chastise, &c.*] You will be
very loud and bitter in your reproaches
of his bad conduct, and even have
thoughts of disinheriting him, by
changing your last will.

56. *Whence, &c.*] With what confidence can you assume the countenance and authority of a father, so
as freely to use the liberty of paren-
tal reproof? We may suppose sumas
to be understood in this line.

57. *When, &c.*] When you, at

an advanced age, do worse than the
youth with whom you are so angry.

—*This head, &c.*] When that
brainless head of yours may, for some
time, have wanted the cupping-glass
to set it right—*i. e.* when you have
for a long time been acting as if you
were mad.

58. *Ventose cupping-glass*] Cucurbita signifies a gourd, which, when
divided in half, and scooped hollow,
might, perhaps, among the ancients,
be used as a cupping instrument. In
after times they made their cupping
instruments of brass, or horn, (as
now they are made of glass,) and applied them to the head to relieve pains
there, but particularly to mad people The epithet ventosa, which signifies windy, full of wind, alludes to
the nature of their operation, which
is performed by rarifying the air which
is within them, by the application of
fire, on which the blood is forced
from the scarified skin into the cupping glass, by the pressure of the
outward air; so that the air may be
called the chief agent in this operation. The operation of cupping on
the head in phrensies is very ancient.

Hospite venturo, cessabit nemo tuorum:
Verre pavimentum, nitidas ostende columnas,　　　60
Arida cum totâ descendat aranea telâ:
Hic læve argentum, vasa aspera tergeat alter:
Vox domini fremit instantis, virgamque tenentis.
Ergo miser trepidas, ne stercore fœda canino
Atria displiceant oculis venientis amici?　　　65
Ne perfusa luto sit porticus: et tamen uno
Semodio scobis hæc emundet servulus unus:
Illud non agitas, ut sanctam filius omni
Aspiciat sine labe domum, vitioque carentem?
Gratum est, quod patriæ civem populoque dedisti,　　　70
Si facis, ut patriæ sit idoneus, utilis agris,
Utilis et bellorum, et pacis rebus agendis:
Plurimum enim intererit, quibus artibus, et quibus hunc tu

59. *A guest, &c.*] When you expect a friend to make you a visit, you set all hands to work, in order to prepare your house for his reception.

60. " *Sweep the pavement,* &c.] " Sweep" (say you to your servant) " the floors clean—wipe the dust " from all the pillars."

The Roman floors were either laid with stone, or made with a sort of mortar, or stucco, composed of shells reduced to powder, and mixed in a due consistency with water; this, when dry, was very hard and smooth. Hence, Britannicus observes, pavimentum was called ostraceum, or testaceum. These floors are common in Italy to this day,

The Romans were very fond of pillars in their buildings, particularly in their rooms of state and entertainment. See sat. vii. 182-3. The architraves, and other ornamental parts of pillars, are very apt to gather dust.

61. " *Dry spider,* &c.] The spiders, which have been there so long as to be dead and dried up, sweep them, and all their cobwebs, down.

62. " *Smooth silver.*"] The unwrought plate, which is polished and smooth.

—" *The rough vessels.*"] The wrought plate, which is rough and uneven, by reason of the embossed figures upon it, which stand out on its surface. See sat. i. 63.—So Æn. xi. 263,

Bina dabo argento perfecta atque aspera, signis
Pocula.——

63. *Holding a rod.*] To keep them all to their work, on pain of being scourged.

—*Blusters.*] He is very loud and earnest in his directions to get things in order.

64. *Therefore, &c.*] Canst thou, wretch that thou art, be so solicitous to prevent all displeasure to thy guest, by his seeing what may be offensive about thine house, either within or without, and, for this purpose, art thou so over anxious and earnest, when a very little trouble might suffice for this, and, at the same time, take no pains to prevent any moral filth or turpitude from being seen in your house by your own son? This is the substance of the poet's argument.

65. *Thy courts.*] Atrium signifies a court-yard, a court before an house, a hall, a place where they used to dine. Αιχsw. All these may be meant, in this place, by the plur. atria; for, to all these places their favourite dogs might have access, and, of course, might daub them.

66. *The porch, &c.*] A sort of gallery, with pillars, at the door (ad portam) of the house; or a place where they used to walk, and so liable to be dirty.

—*Servant boy.*] Servulus (dim of servus) a servant lad.

A guest being to come, none of your people will be
　　idle.

" Sweep the pavement, shew the columns clean, .　　60
" Let the dry spider descend with all her web :
" Let one wipe the smooth silver, another the rough
　　" vessels :"
The voice of the master, earnest, and holding a rod,
　　blusters.
Therefore, wretch, dost thou tremble, lest, foul with canine
　　dung,
Thy courts should displease the eyes of a coming friend ?
Lest the porch should be overspread with mud ? and yet
　　one servant boy,
With one half bushel of saw-dust, can cleanse these :
Dost thou not manage it, that thy son should see
Thine house, sacred without all spot, and having no
　　vice ?
It is acceptable, that you have given a citizen to your
　　country and people,　　　　　　　　　　　　　　　70
If you make him, that he may be meet for his country,
　　useful in the fields,
Useful in managing affairs both of war and peace :
For it will be of the greatest consequence, in what arts, and
　　with what morals　　　　　　　　　　　　　　　73

67. *Saw-dust &c.*] Scobs signifies any manner of powder, or dust, that cometh of sawing, filing, or boring. Probably the Romans sprinkled over the floors of their porticoes with saw-dust, as we do our kitchens and lower parts of the house with sand, to give them a clean appearance, and to hinder the dirt of people's shoes from sticking to the floor. See HOLYDAY, note 3, on this Satire, who observes, that Heliogabalus was said to strew his porticus, or gallery, with the dust of gold and silver.

68. *Manage it, &c.*] *viz.* To keep your house sacred to virtue and good example, and free from all vicious practices, that your son may not be corrupted by seeing them.

70. *Acceptable, &c.*] *i. e.* To the public, that, by begetting a son, you have added to the country a subject, and to Rome a citizen.

71. *If you make him, &c.*] If you

so educate and form him, that he may be an useful member of society.
　—*In the fields.*] Well skilled in agriculture.

72. *In managing affairs, &c.*] Capable of transacting the business of a soldier, or that of a lawyer or senator. The opposition of belli et pacis, like arma et togæ, in cedant arma togæ, seems to carry this meaning.
　So HOLYD.—the helmet or the gown.
　The old Romans were careful so to breed up their sons, that afterwards they might be useful to their country in peace or war, or ploughing the ground. J. DRYDEN, jun.

73. *In what arts, &c.*] So as to make him useful to the public.
　—*What morals, &c.*] So as to regulate his conduct, not only as to his private behaviour, but as to his demeanour in any public office which he may be called to,

Moribus instituas. Serpente ciconia pullos
Nutrit, et inventâ per devia rura lacertâ :   75
Illi eadem sumptis quærunt animalia pennis.
Vultur jumento, et canibus, crucibusque relictis,
Ad fœtus properat, partemque cadaveris affert.
Hinc est ergo cibus magni quoque vulturis, et se
Pascentis, propriâ cum jam facit arbore nidos.   80
Sed leporem, aut capream, famulæ Jovis, et generosæ
In saltu venantur aves : hinc præda cubili
Ponitur : inde autem, cum se matura levârit
Progenies stimulante fame, festinat ad illam,
Quam primum rupto prædam gustaverat ovo.   85
Ædificator erat Centronius et modo curvo
Littore Cajetæ, summâ nunc Tiburis arce,
Nunc Prænestinis in montibus, alta parabat
Culmina villarum, Græcis, longeque petitis
Marmoribus, vincens Fortunæ atque Herculis ædem ;   90
Ut spado vincebat Capitolia nostra Posides.
Dum sic ergo habitat Centronius, imminuit rem,
Fregit opes, nec parva tamen mensura relictæ

74. *A stork nourishes, &c.*] i. e. Feeds her young ones with snakes and lizards.

75. *Devious fields.*] Devius (ex de and via—quasi a recta via remotum) signifies out of the way, or road.

Devia rura may be understood of the remote parts of the country, where serpents and lizards are usually found.

76. *Take their wings.*] i. e. The young storks when able to fly and provide for themselves, will seek the same animals for food, with which they were fed by the old ones in the nest.

77. *Cattle, &c.*] Jumento, canibus, crucibus, are all ablatives absolute.

—*Having left crosses.*] i. e. The remains of the bodies of malefactors that were exposed on crosses, or gibbets, she brings part of the carcase to her nest—l. 78.

79. *Hence, &c.*] From thus being supplied with such sort of food by the old one, the young vulture, when she is grown up to be a great bird, feeds upon the same.

80. *When now, &c.*] She feeds herself and her young in the same

manner, whenever she has a nest of her own, in some tree which she appropriates for building in.

81. *Handmaids of Jove.*] Eagles. See HOR. lib. iv. ode iv. l. 1. et seq. where the eagle is called ministrum fulminis alitem, because supposed to carry Jove's thunder. See FRANCIS, note there.

81-2. *Noble birds, &c.*] Not only eagles, but the falcons of various kinds, hunt hares and kids, and having caught them, carry them to their nests to feed their young with.

83. *Thence, &c.*] i. e. From being fed with such sort of food when young.

—*The mature progeny.*] The young ones, when grown up, and full fledged.

84. *Raised itself, &c.*] Upon its wings, and takes its flight.

—*Hunger stimulating.*] When sharpened by hunger.

84-5. *Hastens to that prey.*] To the same sort of food.

85. *Which it had first tasted, &c.*] Which it had been used to from the time it was first hatched—rupto ovo, from the broken egg—from its very egg-shell, as we say.

You may train him up. With a serpent a stork nourishes
Her young, and with a lizard found in the devious fields ;
They, when they take their wings, seek the same animals.
The vulture cattle, and dogs, and crosses, being left,
Hastens to her young, and brings part of a dead body.
Hence is the food also of a great vulture, and of one feeding
Herself, when now she makes nests in her own tree.   80
But the hare or the kid, the handmaids of Jove, and the
        noble
Birds, hunt in the forest : hence prey is put
In their nest : but, thence, the mature progeny, when
It has raised itself, hunger stimulating, hastens to that
Prey, which it has first tasted the egg being broken.   85
        Centronius was a builder, and now on the crooked
Shore of Caieta, now on the highest summit of Tibur,
Now in the Praenestine mountains, was preparing the
        high
Tops of villas, with Grecian, and with marble sought
Afar off, exceeding the temple of Fortune and of Hercules:
As the eunuch Posides out-did our capitols.   91
While thus, therefore, Centronius dwells, he diminished
        his estate,
He impaired his wealth, nor yet was the measure of the re-
        maining

86. *Centronius*] A famous extravagant architect, who, with his son,
(who took after him,) built away all
his estate, and had so many palaces
at last, that he was too poor to live
in any of them.

87. *Caieta*] A sea-port in Campania, not far from Baiæ, built in
memory of Caieta, nurse to Æneas.
See Æn. vii. 1 1–4. The shore was
here remarkably sinuous and crooked.
—*Summit of Tibur.*] See sat. iii.
181. note.

88. *Praenestine mountains.*] On the
mountains near Præneste, a city of
Italy, about twenty miles from Rome.
—*Was preparing*] Planning and
building, thus preparing them for habitation.

88–9. *The high tops, &c.*] Magnificent and lofty country-houses.

89. *With Grecian, &c.*] Finished
in the most superb taste with Grecian
and other kinds of foreign marble.

90. *Temple of Fortune.*] There was
one at Rome built of the finest mar-

ble by Nero; but here is meant that
at Præneste.
—*Of Hercules.*] At Tibur, where
there was a very great library.

91. *Eunuch Posides, &c.*] A freedman and favourite of Claudius Cæsar,
who was possessed of immense
riches; he built on the shore at
Baiæ some baths which were very
magnificent, and called, after him,
Posidianæ.
—*Our capitols.*] Of which there
were several, besides that at Rome,
as at Capua, Pompeia, and other
places. But the poet means particularly the capitol at Rome, which,
after having been burnt, was rebuilt
and beautified most magnificently by
Domitian.

92. *While thus, &c.*] While he
thus builds and inhabits such expensive and magnificent houses, he out-
runs his income.

93. *Nor yet, &c.*] Nevertheless,
though he lessened his fortune, yet
there was no small part of it left.

Partis erat : totam hanc turbavit filius amens,
Dum meliore novas attollit marmore villas.   95
  Quidam sortiti metuentem Sabbata patrem,
Nil præter nubes, et cœli numen adorant ;
Nec distare putant humanâ carne suillam,
Quâ pater abstinuit ; mox et præputia ponunt :
Romanas autem soliti contemnere leges,   100
Judaïcum ediscunt, et servant, ac metuunt jus,
Tradidit arcano quodcunque volumine Moses :
Non monstrare vias, eadem nisi sacra colenti ;
Quæsitum ad fontem solos deducere verpos.
Sed pater in causâ, cui septima quæque fuit lux   105
Ignava, et partem vitæ non attigit ullam.

94. *His mad son, &c.*] His son,
who, from the example of his father,
had contracted a sort of madness for
expensive building, consumed the re-
maining part of his father's fortune,
when it came to him, after his
father's death.

95. *Raised up new villas, &c.*] Endeavouring to excel his father, and
to build at a still greater expence,
with more costly materials.

This instance of Centronius and his
son is here given as a proof of the
poet's argument, that children will
follow the vices and follies of parents,
and perhaps even exceed them (comp.
l. 53.) ; therefore parents should be
very careful of the example which
they set their children.

96. *Some chance, &c.*] Sortiti—*i.e.*
it falls to the lot of some.

—*Fears the sabbaths.*] Not only
reverences the seventh day, but the
other Jewish feasts, which were called
Sabbaths.

The poet having shewn, that children follow the example of their parents in vice and folly, here shews,
that in religious matters also children
are led by their parents' example.

97. *Beside the clouds.*] Because the
Jews did not worship images, but
looked toward heaven when they
prayed, they were charged with worshipping the clouds, the heathen having no notion but of worshipping
some visible object.

—*The Deity of heaven.*] Juvenal,
though he was wise enough to laugh
at his own country gods, yet had not

any notion of the ONE TRUE GOD,
which makes him ridicule the Jewish
worship.

However, I doubt much, whether,
by numen cœli, in this place, we are
not to suppose Juvenal as representing the Jews to worship the material
heaven, "the blue ætherial sky," (as
Mr. Addison phrases it in his translation of the 19th Psalm,) imagining
that they made a deity of it, as he
supposed they did of the clouds ; this
I think the rather, as it stands here
joined with nubes, and was likewise
a visible object. See TACIT. Hist. v.
initio.

As for the God of Heaven, he was
to Juvenal, as to the Athenians,
αγνωϛος θεος, (See Acts xvii. 23.)
utterly unknown ; and therefore the
poet could not mean him by numen
cœli. "After the wisdom of God, the
"world by wisdom knew not God."
I Cor. i. 21.

98. *Swine's flesh to be different
from human.*] They think it as abominable to eat the one, as the other.
Here he ignorantly ridicules their observance of that law, Lev. xi. 7,
&c.

99. *The father, &c.*] He treats it
as a matter of mere tradition, as if
the son only did it because his father
did it before him.

—*Soon they lay aside, &c.*] Here
he ridicules the rite of circumcision,
which was performed on the eighth
day after their birth, according to
Gen. xvii. 10. et seq.

100. *Used to despise, &c.*] It being

Part small : his mad son confounded all this, .
While he raised up new villas with better marble.　　95.
　Some chance to have a father who fears the Sabbaths,
They adore nothing beside the clouds, and the Deity of
　　heaven :
Nor do they think swine's flesh to be different from human,
From which the father abstained ; and soon they lay aside
　their foreskins :
But used to despise the Roman laws,　　-　　100
They learn, and keep, and fear the Jewish law,
Whatsoever Moses hath delivered in the secret volume :
Not to shew the ways, unless to one observing the same
　rites,
To lead the circumcised only to a sought-for fountain ;
But the father is in fault, to whom every seventh day was
Idle, and he did not meddle with any part of life.　　106

their wonted custom and practice to hold the laws of Rome, relative to the worship of the gods in particular, in the highest contempt. See Exod. xxii. 24.

101. *They learn.*] From their childhood. Ediscunt—learn by heart.
　—*And keep.*] Observe.
　—*And fear,*] And reverence.

102. *Whatsoever Moses, &c*] i. e. Whatsoever it be that Moses, &c. From this passage it appears, that Moses was known and acknowledged by the heathen, to be the lawgiver of the Jews.
　—*Secret volume*] By this is meant the Pentateuch, (so called from πιντι, five, and τευχος, a book or volume,) or five books of Moses. A copy of this was kept, as it is to this day, in every synagogue, locked up in a press, or chest (arca), and never exposed to sight, unless when brought out to be read at the time of worship in the synagogue, and then (as now) it was returned to its place, and again locked up. This is probably alluded to by Juvenal's epithet of arcano, from arca—as Romanus, from Roma. See AINSW. *Arcanus-a-um.* Volumine, from volvo, to roll, denotes that the book of the law was rolled, not folded up. See sat. x 126. note.

103. *Not to shew the ways, &c*]— They were forbidden certain connections with the heathen ; but when

the poet represents them so monstrously uncharitable, as not to shew a stranger the way to a place which he was inquiring after, unless he were a Jew, he may be supposed to speak from prejudice and misinformation. So in the next line—

104. *To lead, &c.*] He supposes, that if a man, who was not a Jew, were ever so thirsty, and asked the way to some spring to quench his thirst, they would sooner let him perish than direct him to it. But no such thing was taught by Moses. See Exod. xxii. 21 ; and ch. xxiii. 9.
　Verpos, like Horace's apella, is a word of contempt.

105. *The father, &c.*] Who, as the poet would be understood, set them the example.
　—*Every seventh day, &c.*] Throughout the year this was observed as a day of rest, the other sabbaths at their stated times. The poet ignorantly imputes this merely to an idle practice, which was handed down from father to son, not knowing the design and importance of the divine command.

106 *Meddle, &c.*] i. e. He refrained from all business, even such as related to the necessaries of common life. The Jews carried this to a superstitious height ; they even condemned works of necessity and charity, if done on the sabbath. See

Sponte tamen juvenes imitantur cætera: solam
Inviti quoque avaritiam exercere jubentur.
Fallit enim vitium specie virtutis, et umbrâ,
Cum sit triste habitu, vultuque et veste severum.   110
Nec dubie tanquam frugi laudatur avarus,
Tanquam parcus homo, et rerum tutela suarum
Certa magis, quam si fortunas servet easdem
Hesperidum serpens, aut Ponticus: adde quod hunc, de
Quo loquor, egregium populus putat, atque verendum 115
Artificem: quippe his crescunt patrimonia fabris.
Sed crescunt quocunque modo, majoraque fiunt
Incude assiduâ, semperque ardente camino.
Et pater ergo animi felices credit avaros,

John vii. 23. They also declared self-defence to be unlawful on the Sabbath-day. See Ant. Univ. Hist. vol. x. p. 272.

107. *Young men, &c.*] The poet now begins on the subject of avarice, in order to shew how this also is communicated from father to son; but here he makes a distinction. As to other vices, says he, youth want no force to be put upon them to incline them to imitation; whereas, this of avarice, being rather against their natural bent towards prodigality, requires some pains to be taken, in order to instil it into their minds.

—*The rest.*] The other vices which have been mentioned.

108. *Commanded, &c.*] They have much pains taken with them to force them, as it were, into it, against their natural inclinations.

109. *Vice deceives, &c.*] They are deceived at first, by being taught to look upon that as virtuous, from its appearance, which in truth, in its real nature and design, is vicious. Nothing is more common than for vice to be concealed under the garb of virtue, as in the instance which the poet is about to mention. In this sense it may be said—Decipimur specie recti. Hor. de Art. l. 25.

110. *Sad in habit, &c.*] The poet, in this line, in which he is describing vice, wearing the garb, and putting on the semblance, of wisdom and virtue, has probably in his eye the hypocrites, whom he so severely lashes at the beginning of the second Satire.

Habitu here means outward carriage, demeanour, manner. Sad—triste—grave, pensive, demure.

—*Severe in countenance, &c.*] A severity of countenance, and a negligence in dress, were supposed characteristic of wisdom and virtue, and were therefore in high esteem among the philosophers, and those who would be thought wiser and better than others. Hence, in order to deceive, these were assumed by vicious people. See Matt. vi. 16.

111. *Doubtfully praised, &c.*] Nobody doubts his sincerity, or that he is other than his appearance bespeaks him, *viz.* a frugal man, and careful of his affairs, which is certainly a laudable character.

Sic timidus se cautum vocat, sordidus parcum.   Sen.

113. *More certain. &c.*] At the same time he is acting from no better principle, than that of the most sordid avarice, and takes care to hoard up and secure his money-bags in such a manner, as that they are safer than if guarded by the dragon which watched the garden of the Hesperides, the daughters of Atlas, from whence, notwithstanding, Hercules stole the golden apples; or by the dragon, which guarded the golden fleece at Colchis, in Pontus, from whence, notwithstanding, it was stolen by Jason.

114. *Add.*] We may also add to this account of the character here spoken of, that he is in high estimation with the generality of people,

Young men, nevertheless, imitate the rest of their own
   accord ; only
Avarice they are commanded to exercise against their
   wills ;
For vice deceives under the appearance and shadow of
   virtue,
When it is sad in habit, and severe in countenance and
   dress.   110
Nor is the miser doubtfully praised as frugal,
As a thrifty man, and a safeguard of his own affairs,
More certain, than if, those same fortunes, the serpent
Of the Hesperides or of Pontus should keep. Add, that
This man, of whom I speak, the people think an excellent,
   and venerable   115
Artist, for to these workmen patrimonies increase :
But they increase by whatsoever means, and become greater
By the assiduous anvil, and the forge always burning.
And the father therefore believes the covetous happy of
   mind,

who always judge of a man by what he is worth.

> *At bona pars hominum, decepta cu-*
>   *pidine falsâ,*
> *Nil satis est, inquit, quia tanti*
>   *quantum habeas, sis.*
>   HOR. lib. i. sat. i. l. 61–2.

> " *Some self-deceiv'd, who think*
>   " *their lust of gold*
> " *Is but a love of fame, this maxim*
>   " *hold—*
> " *No fortune's large enough, since*
>   " *others rate*
> " *Our worth proportion'd to a large*
>   " *estate.*"   FRANCIS.

115. *The people think, &c.*] They reckon this man, who has been the fabricator of his own fortune to so large an amount, an excellent workman in his way, and to be highly reverenced.

116. *To these workmen, &c.*] Fabris here is metaphorical, and is applied to these fabricators of wealth for themselves, because those who coined or made money for the public were called fabri, or monetæ fabricatores. Faber usually denotes a smith —i. e. a workman in iron and other hard materials, a forger, a hammerer : so these misers, who were continually at work to increase their wealth,

might be said to forge and hammer out a fortune for themselves, and in this sense might be called fabri. To such as these, says the poet, riches increase.

117. *By whatsoever means*] They were not very scrupulous or nice, as to the means of increasing their store, whether by right or wrong.

118. *By the assiduous anvil, and the forge, &c.*] The poet still continues his metaphor. As smiths, by continually beating their iron on the anvil, and having the forge always heated, fabricate and complete a great deal of work ; so these misers are always forging and fashioning something or other to increase their wealth. Their incessant toil and labour may be compared to working at the anvil, and the burning desire of their minds to the lighted forge. Camino here is to be understood of the forge or furnace in which the iron is heated.

119. *The father therefore, &c.*]—Seeing these men abound in wealth, and not recollecting what pains it cost them, both of body and mind, to acquire it, thinking the rich are the only happy people, and that a poor man must be miserable.—

Qui miratur opes, qui nulla exempla beati   120
Pauperis esse putat ; juvenes hortatur, ut illam
Ire viam pergant, et eidem incumbere sectæ.
Sunt quædam vitiorum elementa : his protinus illos
Imbuit, et cogit minimas ediscere sordes.
Mox acquirendi docet insatiabile votum :   125
Servorum ventres modio castigat iniquo,
Ipse quoque esuriens : neque enim omnia sustinet unquam
Mucida cœrulei panis consumere frusta,
Hesternum solitus medio servare minutal
Septembri ; nec non differre in tempora cœnæ   130
Alterius, conchen æstivi cum parte lacerti
Signatam, vel dimidio putrique siluro,
Filaque sectivi numerata includere porri :

121. *Exhorts his young men.*] His
sons that are growing up.
122. *To go that way.*] To tread in
the steps of these money-getting
people.
—*Apply earnestly, &c.*] Incumbo
signifies to apply with earnestness
and diligence to any thing. The father here recommends it to his sons,
to apply themselves diligently to the
practices of these people, whom the
poet humourously styles a sect, as if
they were a sect of philosophers, to
which the word properly belongs.
Those who joined in following the
doctrines of Plato, were said to be
of the Platonic sect—so secta So-
cratica. Secta comes from sequor, to
follow.
123. *Certain elements, &c.*] Certain rudiments or beginnings. The
father does not all at once bid his sons
to be covetous, but insinuates into
their minds, by little and little, sordid principles. This he does as soon
as they are capable of receiving them,
which I take to be the meaning of
protinus here. Imbuo signifies to
season meat, or the like ; so, by metaph. to season the mind ; also to
furnish, or store.
124. *Compels them to learn, &c.*]
From his example, little paltry acts
of meanness and avarice—minimas
sordes.
125. *By-and-by.*] As they grow up,
he opens his grand plan to them ;
and as they have been taught to be
mean and stingy in lesser matters, he

now instructs them how to thrive, by
applying the same principles to the
science of getting money by low and
illiberal means.
—*Insatiable wish.*] A desire that
can never be satisfied—such is the in-
ordinate love of money. Amor ha-
bendi. VIRG. Æn viii. l. 327.
126. *He chastises, &c.*] The poet
in this, and in some of the following
lines, particularizes certain instances
of those minimæ sordes, which he
had hinted at, l. 124. and which the
father is supposed to set an example
of to his sons, in order to season and
prepare their minds for greater acts of
sordidness and avarice.
First, Juvenal takes notice of the
way in which the father treats his servants. He pinches their bellies, by
withholding from them their due allowance of food, by giving them
short measure, which is implied by
iniquo modio. The Romans mea-
sured out the food which they gave
their slaves ; this was so much a
month, and therefore called demen-
sum, from mensis—or rather, perhaps, from demetior—whence part.
demensus-a-um.
We find this word in TER. Phorm.
act i. sc. i. l. 9. where Davus is representing Geta, as having saved
something out of his allowance, as a
present for the bride of his master's
son.
Quod ille unciatim vix de demenso
sua,
Suum defraudans genium, compar-
sit miser.

Who admires wealth, who thinks that there-are no ex-
amples   120
Of an happy poor man; he exhorts his young men, that
they
May persist to go that way, and apply earnestly to the same
sect.
There are certain elements of vices; with these he immedi-
ately seasons
Them, and compels them to learn the most trifling stingi-
ness.
By-and-by he teaches an insatiable wish of acquiring: 125
He chastises the bellies of the servants with an unjust
measure,
He also hungering: for neither does he ever bear
To consume all the musty pieces of blue bread,
Who is used to keep the hash of yesterday in the midst of
September; also to defer, to the time of another supper,
The bean, sealed up with a part of a summer   131
Fish, or with half a stinking shad,
And to shut up the numbered threads of a sective leek.

Geta had saved of his corn, of which the slaves had so many measures every month, and turned it into money. Modium was a measure of about a peck and an half. AINSW.

127. *He also hung'ring.*] Half starving himself at the same time.

—*Neither does he, &c*] He does not suffer, or permit, all the pieces of bread, which are so stale as to be blue with mouldiness, and musty with being hoarded up, to be eaten up at once, but makes them serve again and again.

129. *The hash, &c.*] Minutal, a dish made with herbs and meat, and other things chopped together; from minuo, to diminish, or make a thing less.

—*Of yesterday*] Which had been dressed the day before, and now served up again. This he will still keep, though in the month of September, a time of year when, from the autumnal damps, victuals soon grow putrid. The blasts of the south-wind at that time were particularly insalubrious.

130. *Also to defer, &c.*] Who accustoms himself to keep for a second meal.

131. *The bean.*] Conchis.—See sat. iii. 281. note.

—*Sealed up.*] Put into some vessel, the cover or mouth of which was sealed up close with the master's seal, to prevent the servants getting at it. Or perhaps into some cupboard, the door of which had the master's seal upon it.

131–2. *Part of a summer fish.*]—Lacerti æstivi.—What fish the lacertus was, I do not any where find with certainty. Ainsworth calls it a kind of cheap fish usually salted.—This, mentioned here, is called a summer fish; I suppose, because caught in the summer time; and for this reason, no doubt, not very likely to keep long sweet.

132. *With half a stinking shad.*] See sat. iv. 32, and AINSW. Silurus. Lit. and with an half and putrid silurus.

133. *To shut up.*] Includere—i. e. to include in the same sealed vessel. The infinitive includere, like the servare, l. 129. and the non differe, l. 130. is governed by the solitus, l. 129.

—*Number'd threads, &c*] Sectivi porri. In sat. iii. 281–2. Juvenal

Invitatus ad hæc aliquis de ponte negaret.
Sed quo divitias hæc per tormenta coactas ?   135
Cum furor haud dubius, cum sit manifesta phrenesis,
Ut locuples moriaris, egenti vivere fato ?
Interea pleno cum turgit sacculus ore,
CRESCIT AMOR NUMMI, QUANTUM IPSA PECUNIA CRESCIT ;
Et minus hanc optat, qui non habet. Ergo paratur   140
Altera villa tibi, cum rus non sufficit unum,
Et proferre libet fines ; majorque videtur,
Et melior vicina seges : mercaris et hanc, et
Arbusta, et densâ montem qui canet olivâ :
Quorum si pretio dominus non vincitur ullo,   145
Nocte boves macri, lassoque famelica collo
Armenta ad viridis hujus mittentur aristas ;
Nec prius inde domum, quam tota novalia sævos

calls it sectile porrum. See there. There were two different species of the leek ; one sort was called sectum, sectile, and sectivum ; the other capitatum ; the former of which was reckoned the worst. See PLIN. lib. xix. c. 6.

From the bottom of a leek there are fibres which hang downwards, when the leek is taken out of the ground, which the poet here calls fila, or threads, which they resemble. He here humourously represents a person so sordidly avaricious, as to count the threads, or fibres, at the bottom of a leek, that if one of these should be missing he might find it out.

The epithets, sectivum and sectile, are given to that sort of leek, from its being usual to cut or shred it into small pieces when mixed with victuals of any kind. See AINSW. Sectivus.

134. *Invited from a bridge.*] See sat. iv. 114. The bridges about Rome were the usual places where beggars took their stand, in order to beg of the passengers.

The poet, to finish his description of the miser's hoard of victuals, here tells us, that if this wretch were to invite a common beggar to such provisions as he kept for himself and family, the beggar would refuse to come.

135. *But for what end, &c.*] Some verb must be understood here, as

habes, or possides, or the like—otherwise the accusative case is without a verb to govern it. We may then read the line—

To what purpose do you possess riches, gathered together by these torments—*i. e.* with so much punishment and uneasiness to yourself ? See sat. x. l. 12, 13.

136. *Undoubted madness, &c.*] So HOR. sat. iii. lib. ii. l. 82.

Danda est hellebori multo pars maxima avaris,
Nescio an Anticyram ratio illis destinet omnem.
Misers make whole Anticyra their own ;
Its hellebore reserved for them alone.
    FRANCIS.

For Anticyra, see above, JUV. sat. xiii. l. 97, note.

137. *A needy fate, &c.*] *i. e.* To share the fate of the poor ; to live as if destined to poverty and want, for the sake of being rich when you die, a time when your riches can avail you nothing, be they ever so great.

138. *When the bag swells, &c.*]— And all this, for which you are tormenting yourselves at this rate, you find no satisfaction or contentment in ; for when your bags are filled up to the very mouth, still you want more. The getting of money and the love of money increase together ; the more you have, the more you want.

Any one invited from a bridge to these, would refuse.
But for what end are riches gathered by these torments,
Since it is an undoubted madness, since it is a manifest
    phrensy,   136.
That you may die rich, to live with a needy fate?
In the mean time, when the bag swells with a full mouth,
THE LOVE OF MONEY INCREASES, AS MUCH AS MONEY IT-
    SELF INCREASES;
And he wishes for less, who has it not. Therefore is pre-
    pared   140
Another villa for you, when one country seat is not suffi-
    cient;
And it likes you to extend your borders; and greater ap-
    pears
And better your neighbour's corn: you buy also this, and
Groves of trees, and the mountain which is white with the
    thick olive: 144
With any price of which if the owner be not prevailed on,
By night the lean oxen, and the famished herds, with tired
Necks, will be sent to the green corn of this man.
Nor may they depart home from thence, before the whole
    crop

Crescit indulgens sibi dirus hydrops,
&c. See HOR. lib. ii. ode ii. and lib.
iii. ode xvi. l. 17, 18.
Crescentem sequitur cura pecuniam
. *Majorumque fames.*
140. *He wishes for it less, &c*] A
poor man looks no farther than for a
supply of his present wants; he never
thinks of any thing more.
—*Therefore.*] Because thou art
insatiable in thy desires.
—*Is prepared, &c.*] Not content
with one country-house, another is
purchased, and gotten ready, prepared
for thy reception, as one will not suffice.
142. *It likes you to extend, &c.*]—
You think the present limits of your
estate too confined, and therefore you
want to enlarge them.
143. *Neighbour's corn.*] Arista is
properly the beard of corn, and, by
synec. the whole ear; and so the corn
itself, as growing. You take it into
your head that your neighbour's corn
looks better than yours, therefore you
determine to purchase, and to possess
yourself of his estate.

144. *Groves of trees.*] Arbustum
signifies a copse or grove of trees,
pleasant for its shade.
—*Which is white, &c.*] The bloom
of the olive is of a white or light grey
colour. Densa here means a vast
quantity. See sat. i. 105, note.
145. *With any price of which, &c.*]
If you cannot tempt the owner to part
with them for any price which you
offer for the purchase, then you have
recourse to stratagem to make him
glad to get rid of them.
146. *By night the lean oxen, &c*]
In the night-time, when you are not
likely to be discovered, you turn your
oxen which are half-starved, and your
other herds of grazing beasts, which
are kept sharp for the purpose, into
your poor neighbour's corn.
146—7. *Tired necks*] That have
been yoked, and at work all day, and
therefore the more hungry.
147. *To the green corn, &c.*] In
order to eat it up.
148. *Nor may they depart home,*
&c] They are not suffered to stir
homeward, till they have eaten up the

In ventres abeant, ut credas falcibus actum.
Dicere vix possis, quam multi talia plorent,   150
Et quot venales injuria fecerit agros.
Sed qui sermones ? quam fœdæ buccina famæ ?
Quid nocet hoc ? inquit : tunicam mihi malo lupini,
Quam si me toto laudet vicinia pago
Exigui ruris paucissima farra secantem.   155
Scilicet et morbis et debilitate carebis,
Et luctum et curam effugies, et tempora vitæ
Longa tibi post hæc fato meliore dabuntur ;
Si tantum culti solus possederis agri,
Quantum sub Tatio populus Romanus arabat.   160
Mox etiam fractis ætate, ac Punica passis
Prælia, vel Pyrrhum immanem, gladiosque Molossos,
Tandem pro multis vix jugera bina dabantur

whole crop, as clean as if it had been reaped.

—*The whole crop.*] Tota novalia. Novale est, saith Pliny, quod alternis annis seritur—" Land sown every " other year," and therefore produces the more plentiful crops. Here, by met. novalia signifies the crops that grow on such land. See VIRG. Geor. i. l. 71.

151. *Injury, &c.*] Many have had reason to complain of such treatment, and have been forced to sell their land to avoid being ruined.

152. " *What speeches ?*"] What does the world say of you, says the poet, for such proceedings ?

—" *Trumpet of foul fame*"—] The poet is interrupted before he has finished, by the eager answer of the person to whom he is supposed to be speaking, and with whom he is expostulating.

153. " *What does this hurt ?*"]— Says the miser ; what harm can what the world says do ? See HOR. sat. i. l. 64—7.

—*Coat of a lupine.*] Lupinus signifies a kind of pulse, of a bitter and harsh taste, covered with a coat, husk, or shell. See VIRG. G. i. l. 75, 6. Isidorus says, that the best definition of lupinus is, απο της λυπης, quod vultum gustantis amaritudine contristet. Ainsworth thinks that lupinus signifies what we call hops ; and this seems likely, as we may gather

from the story in Athenæus, lib. ii. c. xiv. where he relates of Zeno the Stoic, that he was ill-tempered and harsh, till he had drunk a quantity of wine, and then he was pleasant and good-humoured. On Zeno's being asked the reason of this change of temper, he said, that " the same " thing happened to him as to lupi- " nes ; for lupines," says he, " be- " fore they are soaked in water, are " very bitter ; but when put into wa- " ter, and made soft by steeping, and " are well soaked, they are mild and " pleasant." Hops grow with coats, or laminæ, one over another. But whatever be the exact meaning of lupini, the meaning of this hasty an- swer of the miser's is as follows : " Do not talk to me of what speeches " are made about me, or what the " trumpet of fame may spread abroad, " to the disadvantage of my charac- " ter. I would not give a pin's head " for all they can say against me, if " I do but get rich : but I would not " give the husk of a lupine for the " praise of all the town, if my farm " be small, and afford but a poor " crop."

q. d. If I am rich, they cannot hurt me by their abuse ; but if poor, their praise will do me no good.

155. *The very scanty produce.*]— Paucissima farra. Far denotes all manner of corn. Paucissima need not be taken literally in the superlative

Is gone into their cruel bellies, so that you would believe it
　　done by sickles.
You can hardly say, how many may lament such things,
And how many fields injury has made to be set to sale. 150
" But what speeches ? how the trumpet of foul fame ?"—
" What does this hurt?" says he : " I had rather have the
　　" coat of a lupine,
" Than if the neighbourhood in the whole village should
　　praise me.
" Cutting the very scanty produce of a little farm." 155
I warrant you will want both disease and weakness,
And you will escape mourning and care ; and a long space
　　of life,
After these things, will be given you with a better fate ;
If you alone possessed as much cultivated ground,
As, under Tatius, the Roman people ploughed. 160
Afterwards even to those broken with age, and who had
　　suffered the Punic
Wars, or cruel Pyrrhus, and the Molossian swords,
At length hardly two acres were given for many

sense, but as intensive, and as meaning a very small, an exceeding scanty
crop of corn. See note on deneissima
lectica, sat. i. l.,106, n. 2. The comparative and superlative degrees are
often used by the Latin writers only
in an intensive sense.

156. *I warrant, &c.*] Here the
poet is speaking ironically, as if he
had said to the miser—To be sure,
Sir, people like you, who are above
the praise or dispraise of the world,
are doubtless exempted too from the
calamities which the rest of the world
suffer, such as sickness and infirmities. See sat. x. l. 216. You are also
out of the reach of affliction and sorrow. See sat. x. l. 231-4. Carebis—
you will be without—free from.

158. *After these things, &c.*] Add
to all this, that you must live longer
than others, and be attended with un-
common happiness—meliore fato—
with a more prosperous and more favourable destiny.

159. *If you alone possess'd, &c.*]—
Provided that you were so wealthy as
to possess, and be the sole owner of as
much arable land as the people of
Rome cultivated, when the empire
was in its infancy; under Romulus,

and Tatius the Sabine ; who, for the
sake of the ladies he brought with
him, was received into the city, and
consociated with Romulus in the government. However this might be
considered as small, to be divided
among all the people, yet, in the hands
of one man, it would be a vast
estate.

161. *Afterwards.*] In after times
—mox—some while after.

—*Broken, with age.*] Worn out
with age and the fatigues of war.
Gravis annis miles. Hor. sat. i. 5.

161-2. *Had suffered the Punic
wars.*] Had undergone the toils and
dangers of the three wars with the
Carthagenians, which almost exhausted the Romans.

162. *Cruel Pyrrhus.*] The king of
Epirus, who vexed the Romans with
perpetual wars, but, at last, was defeated and driven out of Italy.

—*Molossian swords.*] The Mo-
lossi were a people of Epirus, who
fought against the Romans in Pyrrhus's army.

163. *At length.*] i. e. After so
many toils and dangers.

—*Hardly two acres.*] Jugerum—
an acre, so called from jugum boum,

Vulneribus : merces ea sanguinis atque laboris
Nullis visa unquam meritis minor, aut ingratæ   165
Curta fides patriæ : saturabat glebula talis
Patrem ipsum, turbamque casæ, quâ fœta jacebat
Uxor, et infantes ludebant quatuor, unus
Vernula, tres domini : sed magnis fratribus horum
A scrobe vel sulco redeuntibus, altera cœna   170
Amplior, et grandes fumabant pultibus ollæ.
Nunc modus hic agri nostro non sufficit horto.
Inde fere scelerum causæ, nec plura venena
Miscuit, aut ferro grassatur sæpius ullum
Humanæ mentis vitium, quam sæva cupido   175
Indomiti censûs ; nam dives qui fieri vult,
Et cito vult fieri ; sed quæ reverentia legum ?
Quis metus, aut pudor est unquam properantis avari ?
Vivite contenti casulis et collibus istis,
O pueri, Marsus dicebat et Hernicus olim,   180
Vestinusque senex ; panem quæramus aratro,

being as much land as a yoke of oxen could plough in a day. Scarcely so much as two acres were given as a reward for many wounds in battle.

165. *Than no deserts, &c.*] And this portion of two acres, given to a soldier, as a reward for the blood which he had shed, and the toils he had undergone in the service of his country, was never found fault with as too little for his deserts, or as an instance of a breach of faith in his country towards him, by rewarding him less than he had reason to expect. Curtus means little, short, curtailed, imperfect, broken. Curta fides may be applied to express a man's coming short of his promise.

166. *Little glebe.*] Such a small piece of arable land.

166-7. *Satisfied the father.*] The poor soldier, who was the father of a numerous family.

167. *Rabble of his cottage.*] Consisting of his wife and many children, some small, others grown up.

167. *Big.*] i. e. Big, or great, with child.

169. *Bond-slave—three masters.*] One of the four children that were playing together was a little bond-slave born of a she slave. The three others were children of the wife, and therefore masters over the little slave, but all playing together, happy and content.

—*Great brothers.*] The elder children now big enough to go out to labour.

170. *Ditch or furrow, &c.*] Coming home from their day's work, at digging and ploughing.

171. *More ample.*] Their being grown up, and returning hungry from their labour, required a more copious meal, than the little ones who stayed at home.

—*Great pots.*] Pots proportionally large to the provision which was to be made.

—*Smoked with pottage.*] Boiling over the fire. Puls was a kind of pottage made of meal, water, honey, or cheese and eggs sodden together. AINSW.

172. *Measure of ground.*] viz. Two acres, which, in ancient days, was thought a sufficient reward for an old valiant defender of his country, after all his dangers, toils, and wounds, and which provided for, and made him and all his family happy, is not, as times go, thought big enough for a pleasure-garden.

173. *Thence, &c.*] From covetousness. Comp. l. 175.

Wounds. That reward of blood, and of toil,
Than no deserts ever seemed less, or the faith small   165
Of an ungrateful country. Such a little glebe satisfied
The father himself, and the rabble of his cottage, where
    big lay :
The wife, and four infants were playing, one a little
Bond-slave, three masters: but for the great brothers of
    these,
From the ditch or furrow returning, another supper   170
More ample, and great pots smoked with pottage.
Now this measure of ground is not sufficient for our garden.
Thence are commonly the cause of villainies, nor more
    poisons
Has any vice of the human mind mixed, or oftener
Attacked with the sword, than a cruel desire   175
Of an unbounded income ; for he who would be rich,
Would be so quickly too. But what reverence of the laws ?
What fear, or shame, is there ever of a hastening miser ?—
" Live contented with those little cottages and hills,
" O youths," said the Marsian and Hernician formerly. 180
And the old Vestinian, " let us seek bread by the plough,

—*Causes of villainies*, &c.] *i. e.* From this vile principle arise, as from their source, all manner of cruel and bad actions. See 1 Tim. vi. 10. former part.

—*More poisons*, &c.] Contrived more methods of destroying people in order to come at their property, either by poison or the sword. See James iv. 1–2.

175. *A cruel desire.*] Which thinks no act of cruelty too great, so that its end may be accomplished.

So VIRG. Æn. iii. 1. 56–7.

   *Quid non mortalia pectora cogis
   Auri sacra fames ?*

176. *Unbounded.*] Lit. untamed— *i. e.* that cannot be kept or restrained within any bounds. A metaphor taken from animals that are wild and untamed, which are ungovernable, and not to be restrained.

—*He who would be rich.*]— So the apostle, 1 Tim. vi. 9. οἱ βουλόμενοι πλουτεῖν.

177. *Would be so quickly.*] And therefore takes the shortest way to carve for himself, through every obstacle.

—*Reverence of the laws.*] The laws

which are made to restrain all acts of murder, and violence, and fraud, are put totally out of the question ; he treads them under his feet.

178. *Hastening miser.*] A covetous man who hastens to be rich has neither fear nor shame ; he dreads not what the laws can do to him, nor what the world will say of him. See Prov. xxviii. 22.

179. " *Live contented*," &c.] The poet here mentions what was the doctrine of ancient times, in the days of simplicity and frugality, by introducing the exhortation of some wise and thrifty father to his children.

180. " *O youths*," &c.] Such was the language formerly of the fathers among the Marsi, the Hernici, and the Vestini, to their children, in order to teach them contentment, frugality, and industry.

—*Marsian.*] The Marsi were a laborious people, about fifteen miles distant from Rome.

—*Hernician.*] The Hernici, a people of New Latium.

181. *Vestinian.*] The Vestini were a people of Latium, bordering on the Sabines.

Qui satis est mensis : laudant hoc numina ruris,
Quorum ope et auxilio, gratæ post munus aristæ,
Contingunt homini veteris fastidia quercûs.
Nil vetitum fecisse volet, quem non pudet alto   185
Per glaciem perone tegi ; qui summovet Euros
Pellibus inversis : peregrina, ignotaque nobis
Ad scelus atque nefas, quodcunque est, purpura ducit.
Hæc illi veteres præcepta minoribus : at nunc
Post finem autumni mediâ de nocte supinum   190
Clamosus juvenem pater excitat : accipe ceras,
Scribe, puer, vigila, causas age, perlege rubras
Majorum leges, aut vitem posce libello.
Sed caput intactum buxo, naresque pilosas
Annotet, et grandes miretur Lælius alas.   195
Dirue Maurorum attegias, castella Brigantûm,

181. *"Seek bread by the plough,"* &c.] Let us provide our own bread by our industry, as much as will suffice for our support.

182. *"Deities of the country."*]— The Romans had their rural gods, as Ceres, Bacchus, Flora, &c. which they particularly worshipped, as presiding over their lands, and as at first inventing the various parts of husbandry.

183. *"By whose help,"* &c.] He means particularly Bacchus, who first found out the use of wine, and Ceres, who found out corn and tillage.

184. *"Loathing,"* &c.] Since the invention of agriculture, and the production of corn, men disdain living upon acorns, as at first they did. See VIRG. G. i. l. 5–23; where may be seen an invocation to Bacchus and Ceres, and the other rural deities, as the inventors and patrons of agriculture.

185. *"Any thing forbidden,"* &c.] Those who are bred up in poverty and hardship, are unacquainted with the temptations to vice, to which those who are in high life are liable.

186. *"Thro' ice to be cover'd,"* &c.] Pero—a sort of high shoe, made of raw leather, worn by country people as a defence against snow and cold. AINSW.

187. *"Inverted, skins."*]-The skins of beasts with the wool or hair turned inwards next the body, to defend it

from the cold winds, and to keep the wearer warm.

Thus shod and thus clothed were the hardy rustics of old time: they lived in happy ignorance of vice and luxury, and of all offences to the laws.

— *"Purple,"* &c.] q. d. The Tyrian purple, with which the garments of the rich and great are dyed, is a foreign piece of luxury, and unknown to us. The introduction of this, as well as other articles of foreign luxury, is the forerunner of all manner of vice and wickedness : for when once people cast off a simplicity of dress and manners, and run into luxury and expence, they go all lengths to supply their vanity and extravagance. It cannot be said of any such—nil velitum fecisse volet. Quadcunque refers to scelus atque nefas— some copies read quæcunque, and refer it to purpura—q. d. this foreign purple whatsoever it is, &c.

189. *These precepts,* &c.] Such were the lessons which those rustic veterans taught their children, and delivered to the younger part of the community, for the benefit of posterity.

—*But now.*] i. e. As matters are now, fathers teach their children very different lessons.

190. *After the end of Antumn.*]— When the winter sets in, and the nights are long and cold.

—*From the middle of the night.*] As soon as midnight is turned.

"Which is enough for our tables: the deities of the
"country approve this,
"By whose help and assistance, after the gift of acceptable
"corn.
"There happen to man loathings of the old oak.
"He will not do any thing forbidden, who is not ashamed
"Through ice to be covered with an high shoe; who keeps
"off the east wind . 186
"With inverted skins. Purple, foreign, and unknown
"to us,
"Leads to wickedness and villainy, whatsoever it may be."
These precepts those ancients gave to their posterity: but
now,
After the end of Autumn, from the middle of the night,
the noisy 190
Father rouses the supine youth: "Take the waxen tablets,
"Write, boy, watch, plead causes, read over the red
"Laws of our forefathers, or ask for a vine by a petition.
"But your head untouched with box, and your hairy
"nostrils,
"Lælius may take notice of, and admire your huge arms.
"Destroy the tents of the Moors, the castles of the Bri-
"gantes, 196

190-1. *The noisy father.*] Bawling to wake his son, who is lying along on his back (supinum) in his bed fast asleep.

191. " *The waxen tablets.*"] See note on l. 30.

192. " *Write.*"] Pen something that you may get money by.

—" *Watch.*"] Sit up all night at study.

—" *Plead causes.*"] Turn advocate—be called to the bar.

—" *Read over,*" &c.] Study the law.

192-3. " *The red laws.*"] So called, because the titles and beginnings of the chapters were written in red letters. Hence the written law was called rubrica. See PERS. sat. v. l. 90.

193. " *Ask for a vine,*" &c.] For a centurion's post in the army—draw up a petition for this.

The centurion, or captain over an hundred men, carried, as an ensign of his office, a stick or batoon in his hand, made out of a vine branch; as our captains do spontoons, and our

serjeants halberds. See sat. viii. l. 247, note.—If a man were to advise another to petition for an halberd, it would be equivalent to advising him to petition to be made a serjeant. So here, the father advising his son to petition for a vine, i. e. vine-branch, is equivalent to his petitioning to be made a centurion

194. " *Untouched with box.*"]— Your rough and martial appearance, owing to your hair lying loose, and not being combed. The Romans made their combs of box-wood.

— " *Hairy nostrils.*"] Another mark of hardiness; for effeminate and delicate people plucked off all superfluous hairs.

195. " *Lælius.*"] Some great general in the army may notice these things, as bespeaking you fit for the army.

—" *Huge arms.*"] Probably rough with hair. See above, n. 2. on l. 194. Ala signifies the armpit, also the arm. See AINSW.

196. " *Destroy the tents of the*

Ut locupletem aquilam tibi sexagesimus annus
Afferat : aut longos castrorum ferre labores
Si piget, et trepido solvunt tibi cornua ventrem
Cum lituis audita, pares, quod vendere possis   200
Pluris dimidio, nec te fastidia mercis
Ullius subeant ablegandæ Tiberim ultra :
Nec credas ponendum aliquid discriminis inter
Unguenta, et corium : LUCRI BONUS EST ODOR EX RE
QUALIBET.   Illa tuo sententia semper in ore   205
Versetur, Dìs atque ipso Jove digna, poëtæ :
UNDE HABEAS QUÆRIT NEMO : SED OPORTET HABERE.
Hoc monstrant vetulæ pueris poscentibus assem :
Hoc discunt omnes ante Alpha et Beta puellæ.
Talibus instantem monitis quemcunque parentem   210
Sic possem affari : dic, ô vanissime, quis te
Festinare jubet ? meliorem præsto magistro

Moors."] Go and do some great ex-
ploit—distinguish yourself in an expedition against the people of Mauritania. Attegiæ (from ad and tegere,
to cover) signifies cottages, huts, ca-
bins, tents, and the like, in which
people shelter themselves from the
weather.
—" *Castles of the Brigantes.*"] Of
the inhabitants of Britain. The people of Lancashire, Yorkshire, and
other northern parts of England, were
called Brigantes ; they had strong
castles.
197. " *That a rich eagle,*" &c.]—
The Roman ensign was the figure of
an eagle, which was carried at the
head of every regiment. The care of
this standard was committed to the
eldest captain of the regiment, and
was a very rich post.
The father is here exhorting his son
to go into the army ; in order to
which, first, he is to petition for the
vine-rod, or centurion's post ; then
he exhorts him to go into service, and
distinguish himself against the enemy,
that, at sixty years old, he may be
the eldest captain, and enrich himself
by having the care of the standard,
which was very lucrative. Hence
Juvenal calls it *locupletem aquilam.*
198. " *Or if to bear,*" &c.] If you
dislike going into a military life.
199. " *The horns,*" &c.] If the
cornets and trumpets throw you into

a panic at the sound of them, so that
you are ready to befoul yourself when
you hear martial music.
200. " *You may purchase,*" &c.]
You may go into trade, and buy
goods which you may sell for half as
much more as they cost you.
201. " *Nor let the dislike,*" &c.]—
Do not be nice about what you deal
in, though ever so filthy, though
such as must be manufactured on the
other side of the Tiber.
202. " *Sent away beyond the Tiber.*"] Tanning, and other noisome
trades, were carried on on the other
side of the river, to preserve the city
sweet and healthy.
203. " *Do not believe,*" &c.] Do
not take it into your head that one
thing, which you may get money by,
is better than another. So as you do
but enrich yourself, let it be the same
thing to you, whether you deal in
perfumed ointments, or stinking
hides.
204. " *The smell of gain,*" &c.]—
He alludes to the answer made by
Vespasian to his son Titus, who was
against raising money by a tax on
urine.—Titus remonstrated with him
on the meanness of such an imposition ; but he, presenting to his son
the first money that accrued to him
from it, asked him whether the smell
offended him. ANT. Univ. History,
vol. xv. p. 26.

" That a rich eagle to thee the sixtieth year
" May bring: or if to bear the long labours of camps.
" It grieves you, and the horns heard with the trumpets
    " loosen
" Your belly, you may purchase, what you may sell   200
" For the half of more, nor let the dislike of any merchan-
    " dise,
" Which is to be sent away beyond the Tiber, possess you.
" Do not believe there is any difference to be put between
" Ointments and an hide.   THE SMELL OF GAIN IS SWEET
" FROM ANY THING WHATSOEVER.   Let that sentence of
    " the poet   205
" Be always in your mouth, worthy the gods, and of Jove
    " himself:
" NOBODY ASKS FROM WHENCE YOU HAVE, BUT IT BE-
    " HOVES YOU TO HAVE."
This, the old women shew to the boys asking three far-
    things:
This, all the girls learn before their Alpha and Beta.
Whatsoever parent is instant with such admonitions,   210
I might thus speak to: " Say, (O most vain man,) who
    " commands
" Thee to hasten? I warrant the scholar better than

205. " Sentence of the poet," &c.]
i. e. Of the poet Ennius, quoted l.
207.
206. " Be always in your mouth."]
Be always at your tongue's end, as
we say.
—" Worthy the gods," &c.] Juvenal very naturally represents this old
covetous fellow as highly extolling a
maxim so exactly suited to his sorded
principles.
See MOLIERE'S Avare, act iii. sc.
v. where the miser is so pleased with
a saying which suits his principles,
as to want it written in letters of
gold.
207. " Nobody asks," &c.]
T'have money is a necessary task,
From whence 'tis got the world
    will never ask.
            J. DRYDEN, jun.
And therefore only take care to be
rich, nobody will inquire how you
came so. The poet, in the next two
lines, humourously observes the early
implanting this doctrine in the minds
of children.

208. This, the old women, &c.]—
This maxim, old women, when their
children ask them for a trifle to buy
play-things, or some trash to eat, always take care to instil into their
minds; they take this opportunity
to preach up the value of money, and
the necessity of having it, no matter
how; nobody will trouble their head
about that.
The Roman AS was about three
farthings of our money.
209. This, all the girls, &c.] In
short, children of the other sex too
are taught this before their A B C.
No marvel then, that avarice is so
general and so ruling a principle.
210. Is instant.] Takes pains to
impress such maxims upon his children.
211. Thus speak to.] Thus address
myself to.
212. " To hasten."] Who bid thee
be in such a hurry to teach your son
such principles? why begin with him
so young, and take so much pains?
—— " I warrant."] So præsto

Discipulem : securus abi : -vincêris, ut Ajax
Præteriit Telamonem, ut Pelea vicit Achilles.
Parcendum est teneris ; nondum implevêre medullas·   215
Nativæ mala nequitiæ : cum pectere barbam
Cœperit, et longi mucronem admittere cultri;
Falsus erit testis, vendet perjuria summâ
Exiguâ, Cereris tangens aramque pedemque.
Elatam jam crede nurum, si limina vestra   220
Mortiferâ cum dote subit : quibus illa premetur
Per somnum digitis ? nam quæ terraque marique
Acquirenda putes, brevior via conferet illi :
Nullus enim magni sceleris labor.   Hæc ego nunquam
Mandavi, dices olim, nec talia suasi :   225
Mentis causa malæ tamen est, et origo penes te :
Nam quisquis magni censûs præcepit amorem,
Et lævo monitu pueros producit avaros ;

signifies here. See AINSW., *Præsto.*
No. 8.
—" *The scholar better,*" &c.] A
greater proficient than yourself in
avarice, and in every other vice, in
which you may instruct him.
213. " *Depart secure.*"] Make yourself quite secure and easy upon this
subject.
—" *As Ajax,*" &c.] Your son will
outdo you in avarice, as much as
Ajax surpassed his father Telamon,
or as Achilles surpassed his father
Peleus, in valour and warlike achievements.
215. " *You must spare,*" &c.]—
You must make allowance for the
tenderness of youth, and not hurry
your son on too fast ; have patience
with him, he will be bad enough by-
and-by.
—" *Their marrows,*" &c.] The
evil dispositions and propensities with
which they were born (mala nativæ
nequitiæ) have not had time to grow
to maturity, and to occupy their
whole minds, marrow fills the bones.
The marrow, which is placed within
the bones, like the bowels, which
are placed within the body, is often
figuratively, and by analogy, made
use of to signify the inward mind.
Tully says Fam. xv. 16. Mihi
hæres in medullis—I love you in my
heart. And again, Philip. i. 15. In
medullis populi Romani, ac visceribus

hærebant—they were very dear to the
Roman people.
217. " *To comb his beard.*"| i. e.
When he is grown up to maturity.
—" *To admit the point,*" &c.] The
edge of a razor—a periphrasis for
being shaved. See sat. i. 23. and sat.
x. 215.
218. " *Sell perjuries,*" &c.] He
will forswear himself for a very small
price.
219. " *Touching both the altar,*"
&c.] It was the custom among the
Romans, on occasions of solemn
oaths, to go to a temple, and when
they swore, to lay their hand upon
the altar of the god. Here, to make
his oath the more solemn, the miser's son is represented, not only as
laying his hand upon the altar of
Ceres, but also on the foot of her
image. See sat. iii. l. 133. and
note.
—" *Of Ceres.*"| The altar of
Ceres was reckoned the most sacred,
because, in the celebration of her
worship, nothing was to be admitted
that was not sacred and pure.
220. " *Your daughter-in-law.*"]—
Your son's wife—pronounce her dead,
if she comes within your doors with
a large fortune, for your son, her
husband, will murder her, in order to
get the sole possession of it.
—" *Carried forth.*"] i. e. To be
buried, or, as the manner then was,

" The master: depart secure: you will be outdone, as
  " Ajax
" Surpassed Telamon, as Achilles outdid Peleus:
" You must spare the tender ones: as yet their marrows
  " the evils   215
" Of native wickedness have not filled: when he has begun
" To comb his beard, and to admit the point of a long
  " knife,
" He will be a false witness, he will sell perjuries for a small
" Sum, touching both the altar and foot of Ceres."
" Already believe your daughter-in-law carried forth, if
  " your thresholds   220
" She enters with a deadly portion. By what fingers will
  " she be pressed
" In her sleep?—for, what things you may suppose to be
  " acquired
" By sea and land, a shorter way will confer upon him?
" For of great wickedness there is no labour. These things
  " I never
" Commanded, may you some time say, nor persuaded such
  " things,   225
" But the cause of a bad mind, nevertheless, and its origin,
  " is in you:
" For whoever has taught the love of a great income,
" And, by foolish admonition, produces covetous boys,

to be burned on the funeral pile. See
TER. Andria. act i. sc. i. l. 90.
221. " With a deadly portion."]—
Mortifera cum dote—i. e. which is
sure to occasion her death, by the
hands of her covetous husband.
—" By what fingers," &c.] How
eager will his fingers be to strangle
her in her sleep!
222. " For, what things," &c.]—
What you may suppose others to get
by traversing land and sea, in order
to trade and acquire riches, your son
will find a shorter way to come at,
by murdering his wife.
224. " There is no labour."]—
There is very little trouble in such a
business as this, it is soon done.
224-5. " I never commanded,"
&c.] The time may come, when,
seeing your son what I have been describing, you will be for exculpating
yourself, and you may say, " I ne-
" ver gave him any such orders;

" this was owing to no advice of
" mine."
226. " But the cause," &c.] The
poet answers—No, you might not
specifically order him to do such or
such an action, but the principle
from which he acts such horrid scenes
of barbarity and villainy, is owing to
the example which you have set him,
and originates from the counsel which
you have given him to enrich himself by all means, no matter how;
therefore all this is penes te—lies at
your door,
227. " Whoever has taught," &c.]
Whoever has given a son such precepts as you have given yours, in order to instil into him an unbounded
love of wealth.
228. " Foolish admonition," &c.]
So Lævus seems to be used, Æn. ii.
54; and Eclog. 1. 16. Si mens non
læva fuisset. See AINSW. Lævus,
No. 2. But perhaps it may mean

Et qui per fraudes patrimonia conduplicare
Dat libertatem, totas effundit habenas   230
Curriculo ; quem si revoces, subsistere nescit,
Et te contempto rapitur, metisque relictis.
Nemo satis credit tantum delinquere, quantum
Permittas : adeo indulgent sibi latius ipsi.
Cum dicis juveni, stultum, qui donet amico,   235
Qui paupertatem levet, attollatque propinqui ;
Et spoliare doces, et circumscribere, et omni
Crimine divitias acquirere, quarum amor in te est,
Quantus erat patriæ Deciorum in pectore, quantum
Dilexit Thebas, si Græcia vera, Menœceus,   240
In quarum sulcis legiones dentibus anguis
Cum clypeis nascuntur, et horrida bella capessunt
Continuo, tanquam et tubicen surrexerat una.
Ergo ignem, cujus scintillas ipse dedisti,
Flagrantem late, et rapientem cuncta videbis.   245
Nec tibi parcetur misero, trepidumque magistrum

unlucky, unfortunate, like sinistro. See this Satire, l. 1. and note.

Or lævo may be here understood, as we sometimes understand the word sinister, when we mean to say, that a man's designs are indirect, dishonest, unfair.

—" *Produces covetous boys.*"|— Brings up his children with covetous principles.

230. " *Gives liberty,*" &c.] i. e. So far from checking such dispositions, gives them full liberty to exercise themselves, pleased to see the thriftiness of a son, who is defrauding all mankind, that he may double his own property.

— " *Loosens all the reins,*" &c.] Gives full and ample loose to every kind of evil. A metaphor, taken from a charioteer, who by loosening the reins, by which he holds and guides the horses, too freely, they run away with the chariot, and when he wants to stop them he cannot.

231. " *Which if you would recall,*" &c.] It is in vain to think of stopping or recalling such a one, who knows no restraint.

232. " *You contemned.*"] Having forfeited the authority of a father, all you can say, to stop his career, is held in the utmost contempt.

—" *The bounds being left.*"] As the charioteer is run away with by his horses (see note above, l. 230.) beyond the bounds of the race ; so your son, who has had the reins thrown upon the neck of his vices, can neither be stopped, nor kept within any bounds whatsoever in his wickedness, but is hurried on, rapitur, by his passions, without any power of control.

233. " *Nobody thinks it enough,*" &c.] Nobody will ever draw a line, so as to stop just at a given point, and only sin as far as he is permitted, and no farther.

234. " *So much do they indulge.*" So prone are they to indulge their propensity to evil, in a more extensive manner.

235. " *When you say,*" &c.] When you tell your son, that giving money to help a distressed friend, or relation, is a folly.

236. " *Who may lighten,*" &c.]— Alleviate his distress, and raise up his state of poverty into a state of plenty and comfort.

237. " *You both teach him to rob.*"] By thus seeking to destroy the principles of humanity and charity within him, you teach him, indirectly at least, to rob, to plunder other people.

" And he who to double patrimonies by frauds,
" Gives liberty, loosens all the reins to the chariot,   230
" Which if you would recall, it knows not to stop,
" And, you contemned, and the bounds being left, it is
    " hurried on.
" Nobody thinks it enough to offend so much, as you may
" Permit, so much do they indulge themselves more widely,
" When you say to a youth, he is a fool who may give to
    " a friend,   235
" Who may lighten, and raise up the poverty of a relation;
" You both teach him to rob, and to cheat, and by every
    " crime
" To acquire riches, the love of which is in thee,
" As much as of their country was in the breast of the
    " Decii, as much
" As Menœceus loved Thebes, if Greece be true,   240
" In the furrows of which, legions from the teeth of a
    " snake
" With shields are born, and horrid wars undertake
" Immediately, as if a trumpeter too had risen with them.
" Therefore the fire, the sparks of which yourself have
    " given,
" You will see burning wide, and carrying off all things.
" Nor will he spare your miserable self, and the trembling
    " master   246

—" To cheat."] Circumscribere—
to over-reach and circumvent, that
he may enrich himself.
—" By every crime," &c.] To
scruple no villainy which can enrich
him.
239. " The Decii."] The father,
son, and grandson, who for the love
they bare their country, devoted
themselves to death for its service.
See sat. viii. 254. note.
240. " Menœcius."] The son of
Creon, king of Thebes, who, that he
might preserve his country, when
Thebes was besieged by the Argives,
devoted himself to death ; the oracle
having declared, that Thebes would
be safe, if the last of the race of
Cadmus would willingly suffer death.
—" If Greece be true."] If the
Grecian accounts speak truth.
241. " In the furrows of which,"
&c.] He alludes to the story of Cadmus, who having slain a large ser-

pent, took the teeth, and sowing
them in the ground, there sprang up
from each an armed man : these presently fell to fighting, till all were
slain except five, who escaped with
their lives. See OVID, Met. lib. iii.
fab. i. See AINSW. Cadmus.
243. " Trumpeter too had risen."]
To set them together by the ears. See
above, l. 199. note. The Romans
had cornets and trumpets to give the
signal for battle.
244. " The fire," &c.] The principles which you first communicated
to the mind of your son, you will see
breaking out into action, violating all
law and justice, and destroying all he
has to do with ; like a fire that first
is kindled from little sparks, then
spreads far and wide, till it devours
and consumes every thing in its
way.
246. " Nor will he spare," &c.]—
He will not even spare you that are

In caveâ magno fremitu leo tollet alumnus.
Nota Mathematicis genesis tua : sed grave tardas
Expectare colos : morieris stamine nondum
Abrupto : jam nunc obstas, et vota moraris ;　250
Jam torquet juvenem longa et cervina senectus.
Ocyus Archigenem quære, atque eme quod Mithridates
Composuit, si vis aliam decerpere ficum,
Atque alias tractare rosas : medicamen habendum est
Sorbere ante cibum quod debeat aut pater aut rex.　255
Monstro voluptatem egregiam, cui nulla theatra,
Nulla æquare queas Prætoris pulpita lauti,
Si spectes, quanto capitis discrimine constent
Incrementa domûs, æratâ multus in arcâ
Fiscus, et ad vigilem ponendi Castora nummi,　260
Ex quo Mars ultor galeam quoque perdidit, et res

his own wretched father, or scruple to take you off (i. e. murder you) to possess himself of your property.

247. " *The young lion*," &c.] Alluding to the story of a tame lion, which, in the time of Domitian, tore his keeper, that had brought him up, to pieces.

Laserat ingrato leo perfidus ore magistrum.
MARTIAL, Spectac. ep. x.

248. " *Your nativity*," &c.] But, say you, the astrologers, who cast nativities, and who by their art can tell how long people are to live, have settled your nativity, and calculated that your life will be long.

—" *But it is grievous.*"] But, says Juvenal, it is a very irksome thing to your son.

249. " *To expect slow distaffs.*"]— To be waiting while the fates are slowly spinning out your thread of long life. See sat. iii. 27. note ; and sat. x. 241. note.

—" *You'll die*," &c.] You will be taken off by a premature death, not by the course of nature, like those who live till their thread of life is cut by their destinies. See the references in the last note above.

250. " *You even now hinder*," &c.] You already stand in your son's way, and delay the accomplishment of his daily wishes for your death, that he may possess what you have.

251. " *Stag-like old age.*"] The

ancients had a notion that stags, as well as ravens, were very long-lived.

CIC. Tuscul. iii. 69. says, that Theophrastus, the Peripatetic philosopher, when he was dying, accused nature for giving long life to ravens and stags, which was of no signification ; but to men, to whom it was of great importance, a short life. See sat. x. l. 236.

—" *Torments the youth.*"] Gives the young man, your son, daily uneasiness and vexation, and will, most likely, put him upon some means to get rid of you ; therefore take the best precautions you can.

252. " *Archigenes.*"] Some famous physician ; see sat. xiii. 98. to procure for him some antidote against poison.

253. " *If you are willing*," &c.]— If you wish to live to another autumn—the time when figs are ripe.

254. " *Other roses.*"] And to gather the roses of another spring.

—" *A medicine is to be had*," &c.] You must get such an antidote against poison, as tyrants, who fear their subjects, and as fathers, who dread their children, always ought to swallow before they eat, in order to secure them from being poisoned at their meals ; the tyrant, by some of his oppressed and discontented subjects—the father, by a son who wants to get his estate.

" The young lion in his cage, with great roaring, will take
      " off."
" Your nativity is known to astrologers."—" But it is
      " grievous
" To expect slow distaffs: you will die, your thread not yet
" Broken off: you even now hinder, and delay his wishes,
" Now a long and stag-like old age torments the youth.
" Seek Archigenes quickly, and buy what Mithridates 252
" Composed, if you are willing to pluck another fig,
" And to handle other roses: a medicine is to be had,
" Which either a father, or a king, ought to sup up before
      " meat."   255
I shew an extraordinary pleasure, to which no theatres,
No stages of the sumptuous prætor, you can equal,
If you behold, in how great danger of life may consist
The increase of an house, much treasure in a brazen
Chest, and money to be placed at watchful Castor,   260
Since Mars, the avenger, also lost his helmet, and his own

256. *I shew, &c.*] The poet is now about to expose the folly of avarice, inasmuch as the gratification of it is attended with cares, anxieties, and dangers, which its votaries incur, and for which they are truly ridiculous. Now, says he, monstro voluptatem egregiam—I will exhibit an highly laughable scene, beyond all theatrical entertainments, &c.

256. *No theatres.*] Nothing upon the stage is half so ridiculous.

257. *No stages of the sumptuous prætor.*] It was the office of the prætor to preside, and have the direction at the public games. See sat. x. l. 36—41; notes.

The pulpitum was the higher part of the stage, where poets recited their verses in public.

It also signifies a scaffold, or raised place, on which the actors exhibited plays.

The prætor is here called lautus—sumptuous, noble, splendid, from the fine garments which he wore on those occasions, as well as from the great expence which he put himself to, in treating the people with magnificent exhibitions of plays and other sports.

258. *If you behold, &c.*] If you only observe what hazards and perils, even of their lives, those involve themselves in, who are increasing and hoarding up wealth—so far from security, danger and riches frequently accompany each other, and the means of increasing wealth may consist in the exposing life itself to danger.

259. *Increase of an house.*] The enlargement and increase of family-property.

—*In a brazen chest.*] See sat. xiii. l. 74; and Hor. sat. i. lib. l. l. 67. The Romans locked up their money in chests.

260. *Placed at watchful Castor.*] i.e. At the temple of Castor. They used to lay up their chests of treasure in the temples, as places of safety, being committed to the care of the gods, who were supposed to watch over them. Sat. x. 25. note, and fin.

261. *Since Mars, &c.*] The wealthy used to send their chests of money to the temple of Mars; but some thieves having broken into it, and stolen the treasures, even stripping the helmet from the head of Mar's image, they now sent their treasures to the temple of Castor, where there was a constant guard; hence the poet says, vigelem Castora.

—*The avenger.*] When Augustus returned from his Asiatic expedition, which he accounted the most glorious of his whole reign, he caused a

Non potuit servare suas : ergo omnia Floræ
Et Cereris licet, et Cybeles aulæa relinquas,
Tanto majores humana negotia ludi.
Au magis oblectant animum jactata petauro　　　265
Corpora, quique solent rectum descendere funem,
Quam tu, Coryciâ semper qui puppe moraris,
Atque habitas, Coro semper tollendus et Austro,
Perditus, ac vilis sacci mercator olentis ?
Qui gaudes pingue antiquæ de littore Cretæ　　　270
Passum, et municipes Jovis advexisse lagenas ?
Hic tamen ancipiti figens vestigia plantâ
Victum illâ mercede parat, brumamque famemque
Illa reste cavet : tu propter mille talenta,
Et centum villas tamerarius. Aspice portus,　　　275

temple to be built in the capitol to Mars the Avenger. See ANT. Univ. Hist. vol. xiii. p. 507–8, and note *f.*

261–2. *His own affairs, &c.*] The poet takes an opportunity here, as usual, to laugh at the gods of his country. See sat xiii. 39–52.

263. *The scenes.*] Aulæa were hangings, curtains, and other ornaments of the theatres; here, by synec. put for the theatres themselves.

You may leave, says the poet, the public theatres; you will not want the sports and plays which are exhibited at the feasts of Flora, Ceres, or Cybele, to divert you.

264. *By so much, &c.*] You may be better entertained, and meet with more diversion, in observing the ridiculous business of mankind.

265. *Bodies thrown from a machine, &c.*] The petaurum (from πιτᾶυρον, pertica, a perch, a long staff or pole) was a machine, or engine, made of wood, hung up in an high place, out of which the petauristæ (the persons who exhibited such feats) were thrown into the air, and from thence flew to the ground. AINSW.

Others say, that the petaurus was a wooden circle, or hoop, through which the petauristæ threw themselves, so as to light with their feet upon the ground.

Holyday gives a plate of the petaurum, which is taken from Hieron. Mercurialis, whom he calls an excellent Italian antiquary, and represents

the petaurus like a swing, in which a person sits, and is drawn up by people who pull ropes, which go over a pole at top, placed horizontally, and thus raise the petaurista into the air, where probably he swang backwards and forwards, exhibiting feats of activity, and then threw himself to the ground upon his feet. See more on this subject, Delph. edit. in notis.

Whatever the petaurus might be, as to its form, it appears, from this passage of Juvenal, to have afforded an amusement to the spectators, something like our tumbling, vaulting, and the like.

266. *To descend a strait rope, &c.*] First climbing up, and then sliding down. Or if we take rectum here in the sense of tensum, stretched, we may suppose this a periphrasis for rope-dancing.

After all, taking the two lines together, I should doubt whether the poet does not mean rope-dancing in both, and whether the petaurum, according to the definition given by Ainsworth, signifies, here, any thing else than the long pole which is used by rope-dancers, in order to balance them as they dance, and throw their bodies into various attitudes on the rope. Comp. l. 272–4.

267. *Than thou.*] q. d. Art not thou as much an object of laughter— full as ridiculous ?

— *Who always abidest.*] Who livest

Affairs he could not keep. Therefore you may leave
All the scenes of Flora, and of Ceres, and of Cybele,
By so much are human businesses greater sports.
Do bodies thrown from a machine more delight　　265
The mind, and those who are used to descend a strait-
　　rope,
Than thou, who always abidest in a Corycian ship,
And dwellest, always to be lifted up by the north-west
　　wind, and the south,
Wretched, the vile merchant of a stinking sack?
Who rejoicest, from the shore of ancient Crete, to have
　　brought　　270
Thick sweet wine, and bottles the countrymen of Jove.
He nevertheless fixing his steps, with doubtful foot,
Procures a living by that recompence; and winter and
　　hunger
By that rope he avoids: you on account of a thousand
　　talents,
And an hundred villas are rash. Behold the ports,　　275

on shipboard, and are tossed up and down by every gale of wind.

—*A Coryciaa ship.*] i. e. Trading to Corycium, a promontory in Crete, where Jupiter was born.

269. *Wretched.*] Perditus signifies desperate, past being reclaimed, lost to all sense of what is right.

—*A stinking sack.*] Olentis is capable of two senses, and may be understood either to signify that he dealt in filthy stinking goods, which were made up into bales, and packed in bags; or that he dealt in perfumes, which he brought from abroad; but by the epithet vilis, I should rather think the former.

271. *Thick sweet wine.*] Passum was a sweet wine made of withered grapes dried in the sun. Uva passa, a sort of grape hung up in the sun to wither, and afterwards scalded in a lixivium, to be preserved dry, or to make a sweet wine of. AINSW. The poet calls it pingue, from its thickness and lusciousness.

—*The countrymen of Jove.*] Made in Crete, where Jove was born. See sat. iv. l. 31.

272. *He nevertheless, &c.*] The ropedancer above mentioned, l. 265-6.

272. *Fixing his steps.*] Upon the narrow surface of the rope.

—*With doubtful foot.*] There being great danger of falling. Planta signifies the sole of the foot.

273. *By that recompence.*] Which he receives from the spectators for what he does.

—*Winter and hunger.*] Cold and hunger. See HOR. lib. i. sat. ii. l. 6.

274. *He avoids.*] Cavet—takes care to provide against.

—*You on account, &c.*] The poor rope-dancer ventures his limbs to supply his necessary wants; you rashly expose yourself to much greater dangers, to get more than you want.

—*A thousand talents*] Amounting to about 187,500l. of our money. See HOLYDAY, note 9, on this Satire.

275. *An hundred villas.*] Or country-houses, when one would satisfy any reasonable mind.

—*Are rash.*] Rashly run yourself into all the dangers of the sea.

—*Behold the ports.*] What numbers of ships are there fitting for sea.

Et plenum magnis trabibus mare : plus hominum est jam
In pelago : veniet classis, quocunque vocârit
Spes lucri ; nec Carpathium, Gætulaque tantum
Æquora transiliet : sed longe Calpe relictâ,
Audiet Herculeo stridentem gurgite solem.———   280
Grande operæ pretium est, ut tenso folle reverti
Inde domum possis, tumidâque superbus alutâ,
Oceani monstra, et juvenes vidisse marinos.
Non unus mentes agitat furor : ille sororis
In manibus vultu Eumenidum terretur et igni.   285
Hic bove percusso mugire Agamemnona credit,
Aut Ithacum : parcat tunicis licet atque lacernis,
Curatoris eget, qui navem mercibus implet
Ad summum latus, et tabulâ distinguitur undâ ;
Cum sit causa mali tanti, et discriminis hujus,   290

276. *Large ships.*] The sea covered with ships. Trabs signifies a beam, any larger piece of timber. With these ships were built : but here, by meton. is meant the ships themselves. See Virg. Æn. iii. 191.—cava trabe currimus æquor.

—*The majority, &c.*] Plus hominum—the greater part of the people.—*q. d.* There are more people now at sea than on land. This hyperbole (for we cannot take the words literally) is to be understood to express the multitudes who were venturing their lives at sea for gain. So with us, when any thing grows general, or gets into fashion. we say—every body follows it—all the world does it.

277. *The fleet will come.*] No matter how distant or perilous the voyage may be, in whatever part of the world money is to be gotten, the hope of gain will induce, not merely, here and there, a single ship, but a whole fleet at once to go in search of it.

278. *Carpathian and Getulian seas.*] The Carpathian sea lay between Rhodes and Egypt, and was so called from the island Carpathus.

By the Gætulian, we are to understand what now is called the Straits of Gibraltar.

279. *Calpe being far left, &c.*]— Calpe, a mountain or high rock on the Spanish coast (hod. Gibraltar,)

and Abyla (now Ceuta) on the African coast, were called the pillars of Hercules. These pillars were generally believed, in Juvenal's time, to be the farthest west.

280. *The sun hissing.*] Alluding to the notion of the sun's arising out of the ocean in the east, and setting in the ocean in the west.

—*Herculean gulph.*] i. e. The Atlantic ocean, which, at the Straits, was called the Herculean gulph, because there Hercules is supposed to have finished his navigation, and on the two now opposite shores of Spain and Africa, which then united, (as is said,) to have built his pillars ; (see note above, l. 279.) If they sailed beyond these, they fancied they could, when the sun set, hear him hiss in the sea, like red-hot iron put into water. This was the notion of Posidonius the philosopher, and others.

281. *It is a great reward of labour.*] Grande operæ pretium—a labour exceedingly worth the while ! Ironice.

—*A stretched purse.*] Filled full of money.

282. *A swelled bag.*] Aluta signifies tanned or tawed leather ; and, by metonym, any thing made thereof, as shoes, scrips, or bags of any kind —here it means a money-bag.

—*Swelled.*] Distended—puffed out —with money.

And the sea full with large ships—the majority of mankind
　are now,
On the sea: the fleet will come wherever the hope of gain
Shall call; nor the Carpathian and Gætulian seas only
Will it pass over, but, Calpe being far left,
Will hear the sun hissing in the Herculean gulph.　　280
It is a great reward of labour, that with a stretched purse,
You may return home from thence, and proud with a
　swelled bag,
To have seen monsters of the ocean, and marine youths.
Not one madness agitates minds: he, in the hands of his sister,
Is affrighted with the countenance, and fire of the Eume-
　nides.　　285
This man, an ox being stricken, believes Agamemnon to
　roar,
Or Ithacus. Though he should spare his coats and cloaks,
He wants a keeper, who fills with merchandise a ship
To the topmast edge, and by a plank is divided from the
　water;
When the cause of so great evil, and of this danger,　　290

283. *Monsters, &c.*] Whales, or other large creatures of the deep.
—*Marine youths.*] Tritons, which were supposed to be half men, half fish. Mermaids also may be here meant, which are described with the bodies of young women, the rest like fishes.

　Desinat in piscem mulier formosa superne.
　　　　　Hor. de Art. Poet. l. 4.

284. *Not one madness, &c.*] i. e. Madness does not always shew itself in the same shape; men are mad in different ways, and on different subjects.
—*He, in the hands of his sister, &c.*] Alluding to the story of Orestes, who, after he had slain his mother, was tormented by furies: his sister Electra embracing him, endeavoured to comfort him; but he said to her, "Let me alone, thou art one of the furies; you only embrace me, that you may cast me into Tartarus." Eurip. in Orest.

285. *Eumenides.*] The three furies; the daughters of Acheron and Nox—Alecto, Tisiphone, and Megæra.—They were called Eumenides, by antiphrasis, from ευμενης, kind, bene-

volent. They are described with snakes on their heads, and with lighted torches in their hands.

286. *This man, an ox being stricken, &c.*] Ajax, on the armour of Achilles being adjudged to Ulysses, (see Ov. Met. lib. xiii.) ran mad, and destroyed a flock of sheep, thinking he was destroying the Greeks. He slew two oxen, taking one for Agamemnon, the other for Ulysses. See Sophoc. Ajax Mastigophorus.

287. *Ithacus.*] Ulysses, king of Ithaca. See sat. x. 246.
—*Spare his coats, &c.*] Though he should not be so furiously mad, as to tear his clothes off his back.

288. *Wants a keeper.*] Curatoris eget—stands in need of somebody to take care of him.
—*Who fills, &c.*] Who, for the hopes of gain, loads a ship so deep, that there is nothing left of her above the water, but the uppermost part, or edges of her sides.

289. *A plank, &c.*] Has nothing between him and the fathomless deep but a thin plank.

290. *When the cause, &c.*] The only motive to all this.

2 o

Concisum argentum in titulos faciesque minutas.
Occurrunt nubes et fulgura: solvite funem,
Frumenti dominus clamat, piperisque coëmptor;
Nil color hic cœli, nil fascia nigra minatur:
Æstivum tonat: infelix, ac forsitan ipsâ   295
Nocte cadet fractis trabibus, fluctuque premetur
Obrutus, et zonam lævâ morsuve tenebit.
Sed, cujus votis modo non suffecerat aurum,
Quod Tagus, et rutilâ volvit Pactolus arenâ,
Frigida sufficient velantes inguina panni,   300
Exiguusque cibus: mersâ rate naufragus assem,
Dum petit, et pictâ se tempestate tuetur.
Tantis parta malis, curâ majore metuque
Servantur: misera est magni custodia census.
Dispositis prædives hamis vigilare cohortem   305

291. *Silver battered, &c.*] A periphrasis for money. The silver of which it was made was first cut into pieces, then stamped with the name and titles of the reigning emperor, and also with a likeness of his face. See Matt. xxii. 20–1.

292. *Clouds and lightnings occur:*] The weather appears cloudy, and looks as if there would be a storm of thunder and lightning; but this does not discourage the adventurer from leaving the port.

—"*Loose the cable.*"] Says he— "unmoor the ship, and prepare for "sailing."

Funem may signify either the cable with which the vessel was fastened on shore, or the cable belonging to the anchor, by which she was fastened in the water.

293. *Cries the owner, &c.*] The owner of the freight calls out aloud.

—*The buyer-up of pepper.*] Juvenal does not simply say, emptor, the buyer, but coemptor, the buyer-up; as if he meant to describe a monopolizer, who buys up the whole of a commodity, in order to sell it on his own terms.

294. "*This colour of the heaven.*"] This dark complexion of the sky.

—"*This black cloud.*"] Fascia signifies a swathe or band. A thick cloud was called Fascia, because it seemed to swathe or bind up the sun, and hinder its light; but, perhaps, rather from its being an assemblage

of many clouds collected and bound, as it were, together.

295. "*It is summer thunder.*"]— Nothing but a mere thunder shower, which will soon be over, and which in summer time is very common, without any storm following.

—*Unhappy wretch.*] Who is blinded by his avarice, so as to consider no consequences.

296. *Beams being broken.*] Shipwrecked by the ensuing tempest, he will fall into the sea, the timbers of his ship broken to pieces.

297. *His girdle, &c.*] Some think that the ancients carried their money tied to their girdles, from whence Plautus calls a cut-purse, sector zonarius. But I should rather think that they carried their money in their girdles, which were made hollow for that purpose. See Hor. epist. ii. l. 40. Suet. Vitell. c. 16. says, Zona se aureorum plena circumdedit.

—*Left hand.*] While he swims with his right.

—*Or with his bite.*] *i. e.* With his teeth, that he may have both hands at liberty to swim with.

298. *But for him, &c.*] Whose wishes were boundless, and whose desires after wealth were insatiable.

299. *Tagus.*] A river of Portugal. See Ov. Met. ii. 251.

—*Pactolus.*] A river in Lydia, called also Chrysorrhoas. Both these rivers were said to have golden sands. See Hor. epod. xv. 20.

Is silver battered into titles, and small faces.
Clouds and lightnings occur: " Loose the cable"—
(Cries the owner of the wheat, and the buyer-up of pep-
    per—)
" Nothing this colour of the heaven, nothing this black
    " cloud threatens :
" It is summer-thunder."—Unhappy wretch! and perhaps
    that very   295
Night he will fall, the beams being broken, and be pressed
    down by a wave,
Overwhelmed, and will hold his girdle with his left hand,
    or with his bite.
But for him, for whose wishes a while ago the gold had not
    sufficed,
Which Tagus, and Pactolus rolls in its shining sand,
Rags covering his cold thighs will suffice,   300
And a little food; while, his ship being sunk, shipwrecked, he
Asks a penny, and supports himself by a painted tempest.
Things gotten with so many evils, with greater care and fear
Are kept—miserable is the custody of great wealth.
Wealthy Licinus commands his troop of servants, with 305

Rolls.] Or throws up, by the
course of its waters over the sands,
so that it is found at low water. This
is said to be the case of some waters
in Africa, which flow down precipices
with great impetuosity, and leave
gold-dust, which they have washed
from the earth in their passage, in
the gullies and channels which they
make in their way.

300. _Rags covering, &c._] This
very wretch, who could not before
have been satisfied with all the gold
of the Tagus and Pactolus, is now,
having been shipwrecked and ruined
by the loss of his all, very content, if
he can but get rags to cover his na-
kedness from the inclemency of the
weather.

301. _A little food._] Bestowed upon
him in charity, or purchased with the
few pence he gets by begging.

301-2. _He asks a penny._] Who before wanted a thousand talents, more
than he had, to content him. See l.
274.

302. _A painted tempest._] Persons
who had lost their property by shipwreck used to have their misfortune

painted on a board, and hung at their
breasts, to move compassion in the
passers by; as we often see sailors
and others begging in the streets,
with an account of their misfortunes
written on paper or parchment, and
pinned on their breasts. Tuetur means
he defends or supports himself in this
manner.

303. _With so many evils._] But
suppose all this be avoided, and the
man comes home rich and prosperous, still he is not happy; he must
be harassed with continual care, anxiety, and dread, in order to keep what
he has gotten, and these may give
him more uneasiness than any thing
else has given him in the pursuit of
his wealth.

304. _Miserable is the custody, &c._]
The constant watchfulness, the incessant guard, that are to be kept over
heaps of wealth, added to the constant dread of being plundered, may
be truly said to make the owner lead
a miserable life. This is well described by Horace, sat. l. l. 76-9.

305. _Licinus._] The name of some
very rich man. It stands here for

Servorum noctu Licinus jubet, attonitus pro
Electro, signisque suis, Phrygiâque columnâ,
Atque ebore, et latâ testudine : dolia nudi
Non ardent Cynici : si fregeris, altera fiet
Cras domus ; aut eadem plumbo commissa manebit.   310
Sensit Alexander, testâ cum vidit in illâ
Magnum habitatorem, quanto felicior hic, qui
Nil cuperet, quam qui totum sibi posceret orbem,
Passurus gestis æquanda pericula rebus.
Nullum numen habes, si sit prudentia : sed te,   315
Nos facimus, Fortuna, Deam.   Mensura tamen quæ
Sufficiat censûs, si quis me consulat, edam.
In quantum sitis atque fames et frigora poscunt :
Quantum, Epicure, tibi parvis suffecit in hortis :
Quantum Socratici ceperunt ante Penates.   320

any such. Wealthy—prædives, very rich, beyond others wealthy.

306. *Buckets set in order.*] Hama signifies a water-bucket made of leather. AINSW. *Dispositis,* properly disposed, so as to be ready in case of fire.

—*Affrighted.*] Half distracted, as it were, with apprehension.

307. *His amber.*] Lest he should lose his fine cups and other vessels made of amber. Electrum also signifies a mixture of gold and silver, whereof one fifth part was silver.— AINSW.

—*His statues.*] Signum denotes a graven, painted, or molten image, a figure of any thing.

—*Phrygian column.*] His fine ornamented pillars, made of marble brought out of Phyrgia, a country of the Lesser Asia.

308. *For his ivory.*] His furniture made or inlaid with ivory.

—*Broad tortoise-shell.*] His couches, and other moveables, richly inlaid and ornamented with large and valuable pieces of tortoise-shell.

—*The casks, &c.*] Dolia, the plural put for the singular, per synec. The cask of Diogenes, the Cynic philosopher, is here meant, which was not made of wood, as has been commonly supposed, but of clay baked, and so in no danger of fire. Dolium signifies any great vessel, as a tun, pipe, or hogshead. In these dolia the ancients used to keep their wine,

Hence TER. Heaut. act iii. sc. i. l. 51. Relevi omnia dolia—which some translators have rendered; "I have "pierced every cask." But, however that may be agreeable to our idiom, piercing an earthen vessel, which the dolium was, is not to be supposed. Lino signified the securing the mouth, or bung hole, of any vessel with pitch, rosin, or wax, to prevent the air's getting in, to the prejudice of what might be contained in it : and as this was never omitted, when any vessel was filled with wine, hence it is used for putting wine into casks.

HOR. Od. lib. i. ode xx. l. 1-3.
   Vile potabis modicis Sabinum
   Cantharis, Græca quod ego ipse
      testa
   Conditum LEVI.
Relino-evi signifies, consequently, to remove the rosin, or pitch, upon opening the vessel for use.

309. *Break them.*] Should you dash them all to pieces, so as not to be repaired, such another habitation is very easily provided.

310. *Solder'd with lead.*] Any fracture or chink may easily be stopped, by fixing some lead over it, or pouring some melted lead into the crack, which would fill it up.

311. *Alexander.*] Alexander the Great might easily perceive how much happier, and more content, Diogenes was in his poverty, than he who coveted empire so much as not

Buckets set in order, to watch by night, affrighted for
His amber, and for his statues, and his Phrygian column,
And for his ivory, and broad tortoise-shell. The casks of
   the naked
Cynic do not burn : should you break them, another house
Will be made to-morrow, or the same will remain soldered
   with lead.   310
Alexander perceived, when he saw, in that cask,
The great inhabitant, how much happier this man was, who
Desired nothing, than he, who required the whole world,
About to suffer dangers to be equalled to things done.
Thou hast no divinity, O Fortune, if there be prudence :
   but thee   315
We make a goddess. Nevertheless the measure of an estate
Which may suffice, if any should consult me, I will declare.
As much as thirst and hunger, and cold require ;
As much, Epicurus, as sufficed thee in thy little garden ;
As much as the Socratic Penates had taken before.   320

to be content with one world. This
alludes to the story of Alexander's
coming to Corinth, where he found
Diogenes, and not being saluted by
him, Alexander went up to him, and
asked him, " if he could do any
" thing for him ?". " Yes," said
Diogenes, " stand from between me
" and the sun."

   —*In that cask.*] Testa. This shews
that the vessel, or hogshead, which
Diogenes lived in, was not made of
wood.

   312. *The great inhabitant.*] Diogenes, the chief of the Cynics, very
properly so styled, from *κυων, κυνος,*
a dog, from the snarling surliness of
their manners; of this we have a
specimen in the answer of Diogenes
to Alexander above-mentioned.

   314. *About to suffer, &c.*] i. e. To
expose himself to, and to undergo
dangers, proportionate to his attempts
to accomplish his vast designs, and
equal to all the glory which he might
acquire.

   315. *No divinity, &c.*] See sat. x.
l. 365–6, and notes.

   316. *The measure, &c.*] If I were
asked what I thought a competency
sufficient to furnish the comfortable
necessaries of life, I would answer as
follows:—

   318. *As much, &c.*] That which
will suffice—as much as is required
for food and raiment. So St. Paul,
1 Tim. vi. 8.

Necis quo valeat nummus; quam
   præbeat usum ?
Panis ematur, olus, vini sextarius ;
   adde
Queis humana sibi doleat natura ne-
   gatis.
                 HOR. sat. i. l. 73–5.
" *Would you the real use of riches*
   " *know ?*
" *Bread, herbs, and wine are all*
   " *they can bestow.*
" *Or add what nature's deepest*
   " *wants supplies,*
" *These, and no more, thy mass*
   " *of money buys.*"
                    FRANCIS.
So POPE, in his use of riches, Eth.
ep. iii. l. 81–2.
" *What riches give us let us first*
   " *inquire,*
" *Meat, fire, and clothes—what*
   " *more ? meat, clothes, and*
   " *fire.*"

   319. *Little garden.*] See sat. xiii.
122–3. hortis, plur. per synec. pro
horto, sing.

   320. *Socratic penates, &c.*] i. e. As
much as Socrates required and took
for the maintenance of his household,

NUNQUAM ALIUD NATURA, ALIUD SAPIENTIA DICIT.
Acribus exemplis videor te claudere ; misce
Ergo aliquid nostris de moribus ; effice summam,
Bis septem ordinibus quam lex dignatur Othonis.
Hæc quoque si rugam trahit, extenditque labellum,   325
Sume duos Equites, fac tertia quadringenta :
Si nondum implevi gremium, si panditur ultra ;
Nec Crœsi fortuna unquam, nec Persica regna
Sufficient animo, nec divitiæ Narcissi,
Indulsit Cæsar cui Claudius omnia, cujus   330
Paruit imperiis, uxorem occidere jussus.

Here, by meton. called Penates, from the household gods which were in his house.

—*Before.*] i. e. In earlier times, before Epicurus. Socrates died four hundred years before Christ ; Epicurus two hundred and seventy-one.

321. *Nature never says, &c.*] i. e. Nature and wisdom always agree in teaching the same lesson. By nature, here, we must understand that simple principle which leads only to the desire of the necessary comforts of life.

If we go farther, the term nature may extend to the appetite and passions, which, in their desires and pursuits, suit but ill with the dictates of wisdom.

POPE, Eth. epist. iii. l. 25, 6.
" *What nature wants*" *(a phrase I must distrust)*
" *Extends to luxury, extends to " lust,*" *&c.*

322. *I seem to confine, &c.*] By saying this, I may seem, perhaps, too

severe, and to circumscribe your desires in too narrow a compass, by mentioning such rigid examples of persons, of what you may think sour dispositions.

323. *Our manners.*] That I may not be thought too scanty in my allowance, I will permit you to mingle something of our more modern way of thinking and living.

—*Make the sum, &c.*] Suppose you make up, together with what I have mentioned as sufficient, a sum equal to a knight's estate, which, by a law of Roscius Otho the tribune, called the Roscian law, was to amount to four hundred sestertia revenue per annum, about 3,125l. of our money.

324. *Twice seven ranks, &c.*] Fourteen ranks or rows of seats in the theatre were assigned to the equestrian order. See HOR. ep. iv. l. 15, 16 ; and JUV. sat. iii. l. 144, 5, and notes.

325. *If this also draws, &c.*] If

NATURE NEVER SAYS ONE THING, WISDOM ANOTHER.
I seem to confine you by sour examples; mix
Therefore something from our manners, make the sum
What the law thinks worthy the twice seven ranks of Otho.
If this also draws a wrinkle, and extends your lip,　　325
Take two knights, make the third four hundred.
If as yet I have not filled your bosom, if it be opened
　　farther,
Neither the fortune of Crœsus, nor the Persian kingdoms,
Will ever suffice your mind, nor the riches of Narcissus,
To whom Claudius Cæsar indulged every thing, whose 330
Commands he obeyed, being ordered to kill his wife.

this contracts your brow into a frown, and makes you pout out your lips, as in disdain or displeasure—as we say, hang the lip—*i. e.* if this, as well as the examples before mentioned, of Socrates and Epicurus, displeases you.

326. *Take two knights.*] Possess an estate sufficient for two of the equestrian order. See above, L. 323, note 2.

—*Make the third four hundred.*] Even add a third knight's estate, have three times four hundred sestertia.

327. *Filled your bosom, &c.*] A metaphor alluding to the garments of the ancients, which were loose, and which they held open before to receive what was given to them. Comp. Isa. lxv. 6, 7. Luke vi. 38.

The poet means, If I have not yet satisfied your desires by what I allow you: if I have not thrown enough into your lap, as we say. See sat. vii. 215, and note.

—*Opened farther.*] The metaphor is still continued—*q. d.* If your desires are still extended beyond this.

328. *Fortune of Crœsus.*] The rich king of Lydia. See sat. x. 263.

—*Persian kingdoms.*] The kings of Persia, particularly Darius and Xerxes, were famed for their magnificence and riches.

329. *Suffice your mind.*] Will be sufficient to gratify your desires.

—*Riches of Narcissus.*] A freedman and favourite of Claudius Cæsar, who had such an ascendancy over the emperor, as to prevail on him to put Messalina to death, after her paramour Silius. See sat. x. l. 298—314. Claudius would have pardoned her adultery, but, at the instigation of Narcissus, he had her killed in the gardens of Lucullus. By the favour of the emperor, Narcissus was possessed of immense wealth.

AULI

PERSII FLACCI

SATIRÆ.

THE

SATIRES

OF

AULUS FLACCUS PERSIUS.

2 p

PREFACE.

AULUS PERSIUS FLACCUS was born at Volaterræ, in Etruria (now Tuscany), about the twentieth
year of the emperor Tiberius, that is to say, about two
years after the death of Christ. Flaccus, his father, was
a Roman knight, whom he lost when he was but six
years of age. His mother, Fulvia Sisennia, afterwards
married one Fusius, a Roman knight, and within a few
years buried him also. Our poet studied, till the age of
twelve years, at Volaterræ; he then came to Rome, where
he put himself under the instruction of Remmius Palæmon, a grammarian, and Virginius Flaccus, a rhetorician;
to each of which he paid the highest attention. At
sixteen he made a friendship with Annæus Cornutus, (by
country an African, by profession a Stoic philosopher,)
from whom he got an insight into the Stoic philosophy.
By means of Cornutus he became acquainted with
Annæus Lucanus, who so admired the writings of Persius,
that on hearing him read his verses, he could scarcely
refrain from crying out publicly, that " they were abso-
" lute poems."

He was a young man of gentle manners, of great modesty, and of remarkable sobriety and frugality: dutiful
and affectionate towards his mother, loving and kind to
his sisters; a most strenuous friend and defender of virtue—an irreconcileable enemy to vice in all its shapes, as
may appear from his Satires, which came from his masterly pen in an early time of life, when dissipation,
lewdness, and extravagance were cultivated and followed
by so many of his age, and when, instead of making them

his associates, he made them the objects of his severest animadversion.

He died of a disorder in his stomach about the thirtieth year of his age, and left behind him a large fortune; the bulk of which he bequeathed to his mother and sisters; leaving an handsome legacy to his friend and instructor Cornutus, together with his study of books: Cornutus only accepted the books, and gave the money, which had been left him, to the surviving sisters of Persius.

Some have supposed, that Persius studied obscurity in his Satires, and that to this we owe the difficulty of unravelling his meaning; that he did this, that he might with the greater safety attack and expose the vicious of his day, and particularly the emperor Nero, at whom some of his keenest shafts were aimed: however this may be, I have endeavoured to avail myself of the explanations which the learned have given, in order to facilitate the forming of my own judgment, which, whether coincident with theirs or not, I have freely set down in the following notes, in order that my readers may the more easily form theirs.

As to the comparisons which have been made between Horace, Persius, and Juvenal, (the former of which is so often imitated by Persius,) I would refer the reader to Mr. Dryden's Dedication to the Earl of Dorset, which is prefixed to the translation of *Juvenal and Persius*, by himself and others, and where this matter is very fully considered. For my own part, I think it best to allow each his particular merit, and to avoid the invidious and disagreeable task of making comparisons, where each is so excellent, and wherein prejudice and fancy too often supersede true taste and sound judgment.

However the comparative merit of Persius may be determined, his positive excellence can hardly escape the readers of his Satires, or incline them to differ from Quintilian, who says of him, *Inst. Orator.* lib. x. cap. 1.

" *Multum et veræ gloriæ, quamvis uno libro Persius*
" *meruit.*"

Martial seems of this opinion, lib. iv. epig. xxviii. l.
7, 8.

> " Sæpius in libro memoratur Persius uno,
> " Quam levis in tota Marsus Amazonide."

On which the Scholiast observes, by way of note,
" *Gratior est parvus liber Satirarum Persii, quam in-*
" *gens volumen Marsi, quo bellum Herculis scripsit*
" *contra Amazonas.*"

Nor were the Satires of Persius in small esteem, even
among some of the most learned of the early Christian
writers—such as Cassiodore, Lactantius, Eusebius, St.
Jerom, and St. Austin. This is observed by Holyday,
who concludes his preface to his translation with these
remarkable words, " Reader, be courteous to thyself,
" and let not the example of an heathen condemn thee,
" but improve thee."

PROLOGUS

AD

Satiram Primam.

ARGUMENT.

" *The design of the author was to conceal his name and quality.—He lived in the dangerous times of Nero, and aims particularly at him in most of his Satires: for which reason, though he was of equestrian dignity, and of a plentiful fortune, he would appear, in this Prologue,*

NEC fonte labra prolui Caballino:
Nec in bicipiti somniasse Parnasso
Memini; ut repente sic poeta prodirem.
Heliconidasque, pallidamque Pirenen
Illis remitto, quorum imagines lambunt   5
Hederæ sequaces. Ipse semipaganus

Line I. *Caballine fountain.*] A fountain near Helicon, a hill in Bœotia, sacred to the Muses and Apollo, which the horse Pegasus is said to have opened with his hoof: therefore sometimes called Hippocrene, from the Gr. ἵππος, an horse, and κρήνη, a fountain.

The poet in derision calls it caballinus, from caballus, which is a name for a sorry horse, a jade, a pack-horse, and the like.

The poets feigned, that drinking of this sacred fountain inspired, as it were, poetic fancy, imagination, and abilities. Thus VIRG. Æn. vii. 641; and Æn. x. 163.

Pandite nunc Helicona, Deæ, cantusque movete.

Persius means to ridicule this notion.

2. *Have dreamed, &c.*] Parnassus is a mountain of Phocis, in Achaia; in which is the Castalian spring, and

temple of Apollo. It was a notion, that whosoever ascended this hill, and staid there for any time, immediately became a poet. It hath two tops, Cyrrha and Nisa, or, as others, Helicon and Cytheron, or Thithorea and Hyampeus according to Herodotus, the former sacred to Apollo and the Muses, the latter to Bacchus.—Hence our poet says—bicipiti Parnasso.

He is supposed to allude to the poet Ennius, who is said to have dreamed that he was on mount Parnassus, and that the soul of Homer entered into him.

3. *Suddenly.*] *i. e.* All on a sudden —without any pains or study—by immediate inspiration, as it were.

4. *Heliconides.*] The Muses, so called from Helicon. See l. 1, note.

—*Pirene.*] Pirene was another fountain near Corinth, sacred to the

Stöss

PROLOGUE

TO

First Satire.

ARGUMENT.

but a beggarly poet, who writes for bread. After this
he breaks into the business of the first Satire, which is
chiefly to decry the poetry then in fashion, and the im-
pudence of those who were endeavouring to pass their
stuff upon the world."   DRYDEN.

I HAVE neither moistened my lips with the Caballine
   fountain,
Nor to have dreamed in two-headed Parnassus,
Do I remember, that thus I should suddenly come forth a
   poet,
Both the Heliconides, and pale Pirene,
I leave to those, whose images the pliant ivy-boughs   5
Touch softly. I, half a clown,

Muses; so called from Pirene, the
daughter of Achelous, who is fabled
to have wept forth from her eyes the
fountain called by her name. The
epithet pale may refer to the complexion of Pirene pale with grief:
or, as some think, is to be understood
figuratively, to denote the paleness
of those poets who studied and la-
boured hard to make their verses.
See sat. i. l. 121, and note.

5. *Those, whose images, &c.*] The
poet feigns himself to be an untu-
tored rustic, and to write merely
from his own rude genius, without
those assistances which others have
derived from the Muses and the sacred fountains: these, says he, I
leave to such great men as have their
images set up in the temple of the
Muses, and crowned with ivy, in
token of honour.

Me doctarum hederæ præmia fron-
  tium
Diis miscent superis.
        HOR. ode i. lib. i. l. 29-30.
  —*The pliant ivy.*] The ivy bends,
and intwines whatever it is planted
against, and may be said to follow
the form and bent thereof; hence the
epithet sequaces. So, when gathered
and made into chaplets, it follows exactly the circular form of the head on
which it is placed, easily bending and
intwining it. Some think that sequaces here intimates its following distinguished poets as their reward.

6. *Touch softly.*] Lambo properly
signifies to lick with the tongue—
hence, to touch gently or softly. Lambunt is peculiarly applicable, as ivy is
in the shape of a tongue.

  —*I, half a clown.*] See above, note
on l. 5.

Ad sacra vatum carmen affero nostrum.
  Quis expedivit psittaco suum χαῖρε?
Picasque docuit verba nostra conari?
Magister artis, ingeniîque largitor   10
—Venter, negatas artifex sequi voces.
  Quod si dolosi spes refulserit nummi,
Corvos poetas, et poetrias picas,
Cantare credas Pegaseium melos.

7. *Consecrated repositories, &c.*] *i. e.*
The temple of Apollo and the Muses
built by Augustus on mount Palatine,
where the works of the poets were
kept and recited. See Juv. sat. i. l.
1, note.

8. *Who has expedited, &c.*] Expedivit—lit. hastened—*q. d.* Who has
made a parrot so ready at speaking
the word χαῖρε. This, like salve,
ave, or the like, was a salutation
among the ancients at meeting or parting; this they taught their parrots,
or magpies, who used to utter them,
as ours are frequently taught to speak
some similar common word. See
Mart. lib. xiv. ep. 73–6.

9. *Taught magpies, &c.*] The mag-
pie, as we daily see, is another bird
which is often taught to speak.

11. *The belly.*] *i. c.* Hunger,
which is the teacher of this, as of

many other arts—the giver of genius
and capacity—skilful and cunning to
follow after the most difficult attain-
ments from which it can hope for relief to its cravings.

—*Cunning.*] Artifex-icis. adj. See
Ainsw.

—*Denied words.*] This hunger is a
great artist in this way, of teaching
birds to utter human language, which
naturally is denied them.

The birds are, in a manner, starved
into this kind of erudition, the masters of them keeping them very sharp,
and rewarding them with a bit of
food, when they shew a compliance
with their endeavours, from time to
time. On this principle we have, in
our day, seen wonderful things, quite
foreign to the nature of the animals,
taught to horses, dogs, and even tu
swine.

Bring my verse to the consecrated repositories of the poets.
   Who has expedited to a parrot his χαίρε ?
And taught magpies to attempt our words ?
A master of art, and a liberal bestower of genius,   10
The belly, cunning to follow denied words.
   But if the hope of deceitful money should glitter,
Raven-poets, and magpie-poetesses,
You may imagine to sing Pegaseian melody.

The poet means, that as parrots and magpies are starved into learning to speak, which by nature is denied them, so the scribblers, which he here intends to satirize, are driven into writing verses, by their poverty and necessity, without any natural genius or talents whatsoever.

12. *If the hope, &c.*] These poor poets, who are without all natural genius, and would therefore never think of writing; yet, such is their poverty, that if they can once encourage themselves to hope for a little money by writing, they will instantly set about it.

— *Deceitful money.*] Money may, on many accounts, deserve the epithet here given it. But in this place particularly it is so called, from its deceiving these scribblers into doing what they are not fit for, and by attempting of which they expose themselves to the utmost contempt and derision.

13. *Raven-poets, &c.*] Once let the gilded bait come in view, you will hear such a recital of poetry, as would make you think that ravens and magpies were turned poets and poetesses, and had been taught to recite their performances.

14. *Pegaseian melody.*] They would do this with so much effrontery, that instead of the wretched stuff which they produced, you would think they were reciting something really poetical and sublime, as if they had drunk of Hippocrene itself, (see above, note on l. 1.) or had mounted and soared aloft on the winged Pegasus.

Satira Prima.

ARGUMENT.

This Satire opens in form of a dialogue between Persius and a friend.—We may suppose Persius to be just seated in his study, and beginning to vent his indignation in satire An acquaintance comes in, and, on hearing the first line, dissuades the poet from an undertaking so dangerous; advising him, if he must write, to accommodate his vein to the taste of the times, and to write like other people.

Persius acknowledges, that this would be the means of gaining applause; but adds, that the approbation of such patrons as this compliance would recommend him to was a thing not to be desired.

PERSIUS. MONITOR.

P. O CURAS hominum ! ô quantum est in rebus inane!
M. Quis leget hæc ? *P.* Min' tu istud ais? *M.* Nemo, Hercule. *P.* Nemo ?
M. Vel duo, vel nemo ; turpe et miserabile. *P.* Quare ?
Ne mihi Polydamas et Troiades Labeonem
Prætulerint ? nugæ !—Non, si quid turbida Roma   5

Line 1. O the cares, &c.] Persius is supposed to be reading this line, the first of the Satire which he had composed, when his friend is entering and overhears it. Comp. Eccl. i. 2–14.

2. Who will read these?] Says his friend to him—*i. e.* Who, as the present taste at Rome is, will trouble themselves to read a work which begins with such serious reflections ? Your very first line will disgust them —they like nothing but trifles.

—Do you say that, &c.] Do you say that to me and my writings ?

—Nobody.] Yes I do, and aver that you will not have a single reader ; nay, I will swear it by Hercules—an usual oath among the Romans.

—Nobody?] Says Persius—Do you literally mean what you say ?

3. Perhaps two, &c.] It may be, replies the friend, that here and there a few readers may be found ; but I rather think that even this will not be the case ; I grant this to be very hard, after the pains which you have bestowed, and very shameful.

—Wherefore?] Wherefore do you call it a miserable, or a shameful thing, not to have my writings read ? Are you afraid that I should be uneasy at seeing my performances thrown aside, and those of a vile scribbler preferred ?

4. Polydamas and the Troiads, &c.] The poet dares not speak out, there-

First Satire.

ARGUMENT.

After this, he exposes the wretched taste which then pre-
vailed in Rome, both in verse and prose, and shews what
sad stuff the nobles wrote themselves, and encouraged in
others. He laments that he dares not speak out, as
Lucilius and Horace did—but it is no very difficult
matter to perceive that he frequently aims at the emperor
Nero.
He concludes, with a contempt of all blockheads, and says,
that the only readers, whose applause he courts, must be
men of virtue and sense.

PERSIUS. MONITOR.

P. O THE cares of men! O how much vanity is there
    in things !—
M. Who will read these? P. Do you say that to me?
    M. Nobody, truly. P. Nobody?
M. Perhaps two, perhaps nobody; it is a shameful and la-
    mentable thing. P. Wherefore?
Lest Polydamas and the Troiads should prefer Labeo
To me?—trifles!—do not, if turbid Rome should dis-
    parage   5

fore designs Nero and the Romans, under the feigned name of Polyda-mas and the Trojans, in allusion to Hector's fearing the reproaches of Polydamas (the son-in-law of Priam, and who is said to have betrayed Troy to the Greeks) and of the Tro-jan men and women, if he retired within the walls of Troy. See Il. χ. 1. 100–5.

—*Labeo.*] A wretched poet, who made a miserable translation of Ho-mer's Iliad. He was a court-poet, and a minion of Nero.

5. *Trifles.*] So far from its being the miserable thing which you ima-gine, I look on it as ridiculous and trifling, nor do I trouble my head about it.

—*If turbid Rome, &c.*] Metaph. from waters, which, by being dis-turbed, are mud, thick, turbid, as we say.

If the people of Rome, says the poet, turbid, *i. e.* muddy, not clear in their judgment, having their minds vexed and disturbed too with what is written against them, disparage any work, and speak lightly of it, through anger and prejudice, I desire you will not agree with them in what they say, or accede to their opinion. The word

Elevet, accedas : examenve improbum in istâ
Castiges trutinâ : ne te quæsiveris extra.
Nam Romæ quis non—? Ah, si fas dicere ! Sed fas
Tunc, cum ad canitiem, et nostrum istud vivere triste,
Aspexi, et nucibus facimus quæcunque relictis :   10
Cum sapimus patruos—tunc, tunc ignoscite. *M.* Nolo.
P. Quid faciam ? nam sum petulanti splene cachinno.
M. Scribimus inclusi, numeros ille, hic pede liber,

elevet is metaphorical, and alludes to scales, where that which is lightest is raised up, and signifies undervaluing, disparaging, or, as we say, making light of any thing.

6. *Nor correct, &c.*] Examen properly signifies the tongue, needle, or beam of a balance, which always inclines toward the side where the weight preponderates—where this does not act truly, and in due proportion, it shews that the balance is false ; how false it is, and, of course, how it may be properly judged of and corrected, may be seen, by weighing the same thing in a true scale, or by a true balance ; this will exactly discover the deficiency.

The poet, alluding to this, advises his friend not to attempt correcting one false balance by another ; he means, that, if any thing should be amiss, which the people in general find fault with, yet it is not to be weighed or considered according to their opinion, which, like a false balance, is erroneous ; much less to be corrected by their standard of judgment.

7. *Seek not thyself, &c.*] i. e. Judge for yourself, by your own conscience and opinion, not by what other people say. The more exact meaning of this stoical maxim seems to be—You can judge of yourself better by what passes within you, than by the opinions of others ; so, go not out of yourself, in order to draw just and true conclusions concerning yourself. The Stoics maintained, that a wise man should not make other people's opinions, but his own reason, his rule of action.

The conscience is the test of ev'ry mind ;
Seek not thyself, without thyself, to find.   DRYDEN.

The poet seems to urge this sentiment upon his friend, in order to guard him against such an attention to popular opinion, as might lead him to assent to it, contrary to his own opinion, judgment, and conscience. In this view it answers to what he has before said :

——*Non, si quid turbida Roma*
Elevet, accedas.   l. 5, 6.

8. *Who does not ?*] i. e. Who does not leave his own judgment and conscience out of the question, and suffer himself to be led away by popular opinion ? This is an aposiopesis : but I think the nam refers us to the preceding sentence to make out the sense. This view of it furnishes a farther argument against trusting the opinions of others, since even they do not judge for themselves.

——*Ah ! if I might say !*] i. e. Alas ! if I were but at liberty to speak out plainly.

——*But I may, &c.*] Persius lived in the reign of Nero, a dangerous period for the writers of satire ; he was therefore, as he hints in the preceding line, afraid to speak out : but yet he will not quite refrain ; the objects of satire were too many, and too gross, for him to be silent, and therefore he determines to attack them.

9. *When I have beheld greyness.*] When I have turned my eyes on the grey hairs of old age.

——*Our grave way of life.*] Vivere, here, for vita, a Græcism—these often occur in Persius.

When I behold, says the poet, the gravity and austerity with which we appear to live.

10. *Whatever we do, &c.*] The manner in which people employ themselves, as soon as they have left their playthings, and are become men.

Any thing, agree with it, nor correct a false balance
By that scale; seek not thyself out of thyself,
For at Rome who does not—? Ah, if I might say!—But I
    may
Then, when I have beheld greyness, and that our grave
    way of life,
And whatever we do after our playthings are left;   10
When we have the relish of uncles—then, then forgive.
    M. I will not.
P. What shall I do? for I am a great laugher with a
    petulant spleen.
M. We write shut up.   One numbers, another prose,

Nuces, lit. nuts—and tali, little square stones, or bones with four sides—were the usual playthings of children. The nuces were little balls of ivory, or round stones. See FRAN-CIS' Hor. lib. ii. sat. iii. l. 172. Hence nucibus relictis signifies ceasing to be children. See HOR. lib. ii. sat. iii. l. 171-2.

11. *Relish of uncles, &c.*] Patruus is a father's brother, on whom sometimes the care of children devolved on the loss of their father. The father's brother, thus having the authority of a father, without the tenderness and affection of a father, was apt to be very rigid and severe; this was so much the case, as almost to become proverbial; hence patruus signified a severe, rigid reprover. See AINSW. Hence HOR. lib. ii. sat. iii. l. 87-8.

    —*Sive ego prave,*
 Seu recte hoc volui, ne sis, patruus
   mihi.

Comp. lib. iii. ode xii. l. 3, where we find,
 Metuentes patruæ verbera linguæ.
See also the note there, in edit. Delph.

The poet's meaning seems to be as follows:
"When I consider the vanity and folly in which we Romans (he speaks in the first person, as if he meant to include himself, to avoid offence) are employed, from our first becoming men to our old age, and, at the same time, that pretended and assumed gravity and severity which we put on, insomuch that we have the relish, or savour of morose uncle-guardians in our reproofs of others, and in our

carriage towards them, though we are in truth as vain and foolish as those whom we reprove, then, then I think I may be forgiven if I write and publish my satires, when the times so evidently stand in need of reproof."

11. *I will not.*] Says the friend—All you say does not convince me that you should publish your satires.

12. *What shall I do?*] Says Persius—How can I contain myself? how can I control my natural temper and disposition?

—*A great laugher.*] Cachinno-onis, from Cachinnus, a loud laughing, a laughter in derision or scorn. AINSW.

—*A petulant spleen.*] The spleen, or milt, was looked upon by the ancients to be the organ of laughter.— See CHAMBERS, tit. Spleen. Also the receptacle of the atrabilious, or melancholic humour. Hence when people are low-spirited or melancholy, they are said to be splenetic; so when they are disgusted and out of humour. Thus SWIFT, in his City Shower:
  "Saunt'ring in coffee-house is Dul-
  "man seen,
  "Rails on the climate and com-
  "plains of spleen."

Our poet gives his friend to understand, that he can't take his advice to suppress his Satires; for that his spleen, which is of the petulant kind, and his natural disposition to laugh at the follies of men, make it impossible for him to resist the temptation of publishing.

13. *We write shut up.*] Persius

Grande aliquid—*P.* Quod pulmo animæ prælargus anhelet.
Scilicet hæc populo, pexusque togâque recenti,   15
Et natalitiâ tandem cum sardonyche albus,
Sede leges celsâ, liquido cum plasmate guttur
Mobile collueris, patranti fractus ocello.
Tun', vetule, auriculis alienis colligis escas ?

having expressed his turn for satire, from his natural disposition, and having asked his friend what he should do, were he to be silent, and lay by his intention of writing—the friend gives him to understand, that he may indulge his desire for writing, without writing satires—" Do as others " do, who indulge their genius for " writing on popular and inoffensive " subjects, some in verse, others in " prose, shut up in their studies, for " their greater quiet and privacy, " where they compose something in " a grand and lofty style."—" Aye," says Persius, interrupting him, " so " grand, as to require a very large " portion of breath to last through " their periods and sentences, which " are too bombast and long-winded " to be read by ordinary lungs."— The speaker uses the first person plural—scribimus inclusi—we—nous autres (as the French say). By this mode of speech, the pointedness and personality of what is said are much lessened ; consequently the prejudice and offence with which a more direct charge on the persons meant would have been received.

Hor. lib. ii. epist. i. l. 117.
Scribimus indocti, doctique poemata passim.
" But ev'ry desperate blockhead " dares to write,
" Verse is the trade of every living " wight."   Francis.

13. *One numbers.*] *i. e.* One pens verses.

—*Another prose.*] Pede liber—a periphrasis for prose-writing, which is free from the shackles of feet and numbers, by which writers in verse are confined.

14. *Something grand.*] The speaker is going on with his advice, and in his enforcing it from the examples of the writers of his day ; but at the words grande aliquid, Persius interrupts.

him, as though not able to bear such an epithet as grande, when applied to the bombast and fustian which were daily coming forth in order to catch the applause of the vulgar. In this Persius has, no doubt, a stroke at Nero's writings, some samples of which we meet with in a subsequent part of this Satire, l. 90–2, and l. 96–9.

—*Which lungs, &c.*] See note on l. 14. The word anhelet is well applied here. Anhelo signifies to breathe short and with difficulty—to pant, as if out of breath—also to labour in doing a thing—and well denotes the situation of one who has to read aloud the poems and performances in question.

—*Large of air.*] Capable of containing a very large portion of air.

15. *Doubtless these to the people, &c.*] Persius, as we shall find, by using the second person singular, l. 17, leges, and collueris, l. 18, is not to be understood as confining what he says to the person with whom he is discoursing, but means covertly to attack and expose all the poetasters at Rome, who shut themselves up to compose turgid and bombast poems and declamations, to recite in public, in order to get the applause of their ignorant and tasteless hearers.

The Monitor had said—scribimus, l. 13; hence the poet addresses him particularly ; but, no doubt, means to carry his satire to all the vain scribblers of the time, and especially to those who exposed themselves in the ridiculous manner after described; not without a view to the emperor Nero, who was vain of his poetry, and used to recite his poems in public. See my note on l. 131, ad fin. and comp. Juv. viii. 220–30, and notes there.

I would observe, that in the arrangement of the dialogue, v. 13–14,

Something grand—*P.* Which lungs, large of air, may
   breathe.
Doubtless these to the people, combed, and with a new
   gown,   15
White, and lastly with a birth-day sardonyx,
You will read, in a high seat, when with the liquid gargle
   you have washed
Your moveable throat, and effeminate with a lascivious eye:
   Dost thou, O old man, collect food for the ears of others?

I have followed Mr. Brewster, whose ingenious version of Persius is well worthy the reader's attention.

According to the usual arrangement, whereby scribimus indocti, &c. is given to Persius, he receives no answer to his question, quid faciam, l. 12, but abruptly introduces a new subject; whereas, according to the above method, the Monitor very naturally begins an answer, which introduces the chief subject of this Satire, and the poet as naturally interrupts, at the words grande aliquid, l. 14, in order to pursue it; which he does by describing the vanity and folly of these scribblers, some of whom, at an advanced time of life, when they ought to be wiser, are writing trifling and lascivious poems, and reading them to the people in public; this, with every disgraceful circumstance of dress and manner.

15. *Comb'd*] Or crisped, curled, and set in an effeminate style.

—*A new gown.*] Made, and put on, on the occasion.

16. *White.*] Albus. This cannot agree with toga, therefore some refer it to the man himself, as supposing him to look white, or pale, with fear and anxiety, for the success of his poem, and make it equivalent to pallidus. Hor. epod. vii. l. 15, says, albus pallor; and albus, in one sense of it, signifies pale or wan. Ainsw.

But I do not see why we may not read albus toga recenti, to denote the person's being clad in a new white garment—lit. white with a new gown.

His hair being first kemb'd and
   smooth, and then bedight
In a fair comely garment fresh and
   white.   Holyday.

The Romans wore white garments, as a piece of finery, on certain festival occasions, as on a birth day, and the like. So Ovid:

Scilicet expectas solitum tibi moris
   honorem,
Pendent ex humeris vestis ut alba
   meis.

—*A birth-day sardonyx.*] This species of precious stone, set in a ring, and worn on the finger, was reckoned a piece of finery, which the Romans were very ambitious of displaying. See Juv. sat. vii. l. 142, 3.

By a birth-day sardonyx, the poet probably means a present that had been made to the man, on his birth-day, of this ring, which he wore on this occasion. It was usual to send presents to a person on his birth-day.

17. *You will read.*] i. e. Rehearse aloud.

—*In a high seat.*] When authors read their works publicly, they had a sort of desk, or pulpit, raised above the auditory, by which means they could be better seen and heard.

—*Liquid gargle, &c.*] Plasma, a gargle, or medicine to prevent or take away hoarseness, and to clear the voice.

18. *Moveable throat.*] Mobilis—i. e. pliant, tractable, easily contracting or dilating, according to the sounds which are to be formed.

—*A lascivious eye.*] Suiting the lewdness of his look to the obscenity of his subject. See Ainsw. *Fractus*, No. 4, and *Patrans*, ib.

19. *Dost thou, O old man, &c.*]—Persius, in this apostrophe, inveighs against these lascivious old fellows, who wrote such poems as are before mentioned.

Auriculis ! quibus et dicas cute perditus, Ohe.   20
   " Quo didicisse, nisi hoc fermentum, et quæ semel intus
" Innata est, rupto jecore exierit caprificus ?"
   En pallor, seniumque ! O mores, usque adeone
Scire tuum nihil est, nisi te scire hoc sciat alter !
   " At pulchrum est, digito monstrari, et dicier, Hic est.
" Ten' cirratorum centum dictata fuisse,   26

Dost thou, who art old enough to be wiser, put together such obscene and filthy stuff, in order to become food for the ears of your libidinous hearers ?

20. *For ears, &c.*] He repeats the word auriculis, in order to make his reproof the more striking.

—*To which even thou, &c.*] The poet's imitations of Horace, in all his Satires, are very evident; in none more than in this line. There can be little doubt that Persius had in his eye that passage of HORACE, lib. ii. sat. v. l. 96–8.

Importunus amat laudari ? donec
    ohe jam !
Ad cœlum manibus sublatis dixerit,
    urge, et
Crescentem tumidis infla sermonibus
    utrem.

      ——*Should lust*
Of empty glory be the blockhead's
    gust,
Indulge his eager appetite, and puff
The glowing bladder with inspiring
    stuff ;
Till he, with hands uplifted to the
    skies,
Enough ! enough ! in glutted rap-
    ture cries.   FRANCIS.
Thus Persius represents the reciter of the obscene verses to be so flattered, as to be ready to burst with the vanity created within him ; so that he is forced to stop the fulsome applause and compliments of his hearers, with crying, " Enough ! for-" bear ! I can endure no more !"
      —*Ohe*
    Jam satis est !
HOR. sat. v. lib. i. l. 12, 13.
Cute perditus has perhaps a reference to the fable of the proud frog, who swelled till she burst. See HOR. sat. iii. lib. ii. l. 314–19.

21. " *Unless this ferment.*"] The old man answers—To what purpose,

then, is all my study and pains to excel in this kind of writing, unless they appear thus, and shew themselves in their effects on myself and hearers ? In vain would you mix leaven with the dough of which bread is made, unless it ferments and lightens the mass ; so all my science would be vain, if it lay dormant and quiet within me, and did not shew itself visibly to others, by being productive of such compositions which raise such a ferment in the minds of my hearers. Fermentum here is metaphorical.

—" *And what once, &c.*"] In order to understand this line, we are to observe, that the caprificus was a sort of wild fig-tree, which grew about walls and other buildings ; and by shooting its branches into the joints of them, burst a passage through them, and, in time, weakened and destroyed them. See JUV. sat. x. l. 145, note.

The apologist farther illustrates his meaning, by comparing his natural, as well as acquired talents, to the caprificus—these having once taken root within, will burst forth, through the inmost recesses of the mind, to the observation of all, as the caprificus does through the clefts of rocks, or stone-quarries, or stone-walls : and, " unless this were the case, " what good would these inbred ta-" lents do me ?" The ancients reckoned the liver as the seat of the concupiscible and irascible passions. See JUV. sat. i. l. 35, note. Here Persius uses the word jecore for the inward mental part, which contained the genius and talents of the poet, and was to be broken through by the energy of their exertions.

23. *Lo, paleness and old-age !*]— These words are by some supposed to be the end of the apologist's speech,

For ears, to which even thou, in skin destroyed, mayest
    say—" Enough."   20
  " For what purpose to have learnt, unless this ferment,
    " and what once
" Is within innate, the wild fig-tree, should come forth from
    " the bursten liver ?"
  Lo, paleness and old-age! O manners! is your know-
    ing, then,
Altogether nothing, unless another should know that you
    know it ?
  " But it is pleasant to be shewn with the finger, and to
    " be said—This is he."   25
" For thee to have been the exercises of an hundred curl-
    " pates,

---

as if he had said—See how pale I am
with study and application; and that
in my old age, a time of life when
others retire from labour—and shall
I meet with no reward for all this ?

  Others suppose the words to be the
reply of Persius, and a continuation
of his reproof. " Lo, paleness of
" countenance and old-age! and yet
" thou dost not cease from such vain
" toils! See Juv. vii. 96-7.

  —*O manners !*] Like that of Tully
O tempora! O mores! Catal. i.

q. d. What are we come to ! what
can we say of the manners of the
times, when an old fellow can write
such obscenity, and can find hearers
to approve his repetition of it!

  24. *Altogether nothing, unless, &c.*]
Persius here imitates a passage of Lucilius.

        ——*Id me*
Nolo scire mihi cujus sum conscin'
    solus,
Ne damnum faciam. Scire est nes-
    cire, nisi id me
Scire alius sciret.

  What, says Persius, is all your
science, then, nothing worth, unless
you tell all the world of it ? have you
no pleasure or satisfaction in what
you know, without you exert a principle of vain glory, by cultivating the
applause of others ? Is this the end of
your study and application ? Scire
tuum—*i. e.* scientia tua. Græcism.
Comp. istud vivere, l. 9.

  25. " *Shewn with the finger.*"]—
Here is an ironical prolepsis—the

poet anticipates some of the pleas of
these writers for their proceedings.
It is a pleasant thing, perhaps, you
may say, to be so famous for one's
writings, as to be pointed at as one
goes along by the passers-by, and to
hear them say, " That's he"—" that's
the famous poet."

  Horace disgraces one of his finest
odes, by mentioning, with pleasure,
such a piece of vanity—

Quod monstror digito prætereuntium
Romanæ fidicen lyræ.

        Ode iii. lib. iv. l. 22-3.

  CICERO, Tusc. v. 36, mentions it
as an instance of great weakness in
Demosthenes, in that he professed
himself much pleased with hearing a
poor girl, who was carrying water,
say to another, as he passed by,
" There, that is the famous Demos-
" thenes."—" Quid hoc levius ?" says
Tully—" At quantus orator ?—Sed
" apud alios loqui videlicet didicerat,
" non multum ipse secum."

  26. *The exercises, &c.*] Dictata.
Precepts or instructions of any kind—
particularly; and most frequently,
lessons which the master pronounceth
to his scholars; school-boys' exercises. AINSW. The poet continues his
banter—

  Is it nothing, think you, to have
your verses taught to the children of
the nobles at school; to have an
hundred such boys getting them by
heart, and repeating them as their
lessons, or writing themes on passages
of your works ? The poet, here, has

" Pro nihiló pendas ?"—Ecce, inter pocula, quærunt
Romulidæ saturi, quid dîa poemata narrent !
Hic aliquis, cui circum humeros hyacinthina læna est,
(Rancidulum quiddam balbâ de nare locutus,)　　30
Phyllidas, Hypsipylas, vatum et plorabile si quid,
Eliquat ; et tenero supplantat verba palato,
Assensêre viri—Nunc non cinis ille poetæ.
Felix ? nunc levior cippus non imprimit ossa ?
Laudant convivæ—Nunc non e manibus illis,　　35
Nunc non e tumulo, fortunatâque favillâ,
Nascentur violæ ? Rides, ait, et nimis uncis

a cut at the emperor Nero, who
ordered his poems to be taught in the
schools for youth.

—*Curl-pates.*] *i. e.* The young nobility, so called, from having their
hair dressed and curled in a particular manner.

27–8. *Satiated Romans, &c.*] He
calls the Roman nobility, Romulidæ,
dim. from Romulus their great pro-
genitor ; and he means hereby to insinuate, sarcastically, their declension
and defection from the sober and virtuous manners of their ancestors.—
Comp. Juv. sat. i. l. 86, note.

Here we see them at table, gorman-
dizing, and satiated with eating and
drinking ; then calling for somebody
to repeat passages from the writings
of poets for their entertainment, or
perhaps that they might inquire into
the merit of them.

28. *Divine poems.*] Dia, from Gr.
διος, divinus. The science of poetry
was reckoned divine ; but the poet's
use of the epithet, in this place, is
ironical, meaning to satirize those
productions which these Romulidæ
saturi were so pleased with. Quid
narrent—*i. e.* what they may contain
and set forth.

29. *Here.*] *i. e.* Upon this occasion.
—*Some one, &c.*] Some noble and
delicate person, dressed in a violet-
coloured garment, which was a sign
of effeminacy, and greatly in fashion
among such of the Roman nobility
who were the beaux of the time.

30. *Something rankish, &c.*] *i. e.*
Repeated something of the obscene
or filthy kind, though with a bad
voice, uttered through his nose by
way of preface to what follows.

31. *Phyllides.*] Phyllis, the dagh-
ter of Lycurgus, who fell in love with
Demophoon, the son of Theseus, on
his return from Troy, and entertained
him at bed and board. He, after
some time, going from her, promised
to return again ; but not performing
his promise, she hanged herself upon
an almond-tree.

—*Hypsipylæ.*] Hypsipyle was the
daughter of Thoas, and queen of
Lemnos, who, when all the women in
the island slew their male kindred,
preserved her father ; for which pious
deed she was banished. She entertained Jason in his way to Colchos,
and had twins by him.

The poet mentions the names of
these women in the plural number ;
by which we may understand, that
he means any women of such sort of
character, who have suffered by their
amours in some disastrous way or
other, and have been made subjects
of verse. Eliquo signifies to melt
down, or make liquid. Hence, to
sing, or speak softly and effeminately.
Ainsw.

—*Some lamentable matter, &c.*]—
Some mournful love-tale, either invented or related by the poets.

32. *Slurs his words, &c.*] He does
not utter the words in a plain, manly
manner, but minces and trips them
up, as it were, in their way through
his palate, to make them sound the
more apposite to the tender subject.
He alludes to Nero's reading tragedies
in the public Theatre. Sueton. Nero.
c. 10.

A metaphor, from wrestlers, who,
when they trip up their antagonists,
are said—supplantare.

" Dost thou esteem. as nothing?" Lo, among their cups,
  the satiated
Romans inquire, what divine poems may relate.
Here, some one, who has round his shoulders a hyacinthine
  cloak,
(Having spoken something rankish from a snuffling nos-
  tril,)   30
If he hath gently sung Phyllises, Hypsipylæ, and some la-
  mentable matter
Of the poets, and slurs his words with a tender palate,
The men have applauded: now are not the ashes of that poet
Happy? now does not a lighter hillock mark his bones?
The guests praise: now will there not from those manes,
Now will there not from the tomb, and the fortunate ember,
Violets spring up?—You laugh, says he, and too much
  indulge

————*His refining throat
Fritters, and melts, and minces
ev'ry note.*
          BREWSTER.
*His dainty palate tripping forth his
words.*   HOLYDAY.
33. *The men have assented.*] The
poet uses the word viri, here, as a
mark of censure—that those who
were called men, should be delighted
with such verses, so repeated.
  They all assented to the approbation
given by some of the company.
  —*Ashes of that poet, &c.*] Cinis
ille poetæ—i. e. cinis illius poetæ.
Hypallage. It was the custom to
burn the bodies of the dead, and to
gather up their ashes, and put them
into urns, in order to preserve them.
  To be sure, the very ashes of a
poet, thus approved by a set of drunken people, must be happy! Iron.
  34. *Lighter hillock.*] Cippus is a
grave-stone, or monument; also a
little hill of earth, such as is raised
over graves.
  This line alludes to the usual superstitious wish, which the Romans expressed for a deceased friend—Sit tibi
terra levis—may the earth be light
upon thee! The cippus marked the
grave.
  35. *The guests praise.*] Now they
all break forth into the highest commendation.
  —*Manes.*] Signifies the spirit, or

ghost, of one departed—sometimes
what we call the remains, or dead
body.
  Sepulchra diruta, nudati manes,
Liv. and this seems the sense of it
here.
  36. *From the tomb.*] Tumulus signifies an hillock, or heap of earth;
also a tomb, grave, or sepulchre.
AINSW.
  —*Fortunate ember.*] Favilla (from
φαυω, to shine) a hot ember; the
white ashes wherein the fire is raked
up.
  Here it means the embers of the
funeral pile, some of which were
mixed with the bones in the urn.
  37. *Violets spring up.*] It was usual
among the Greeks and Romans,
when they would extol a living person, to speak of flowers springing up
under his footsteps; and of the favoured dead, to speak of sweet-smell-
ing flowers growing over their graves.
Perhaps this idea was first derived
from the custom of strewing flowers
in the way of eminent persons as
they walked along, and of strewing
flowers over the graves of the departed.
  It is easy to see that Persius is
jeering the person to whom he is
speaking, when he mentions the
above circumstances of honour and
happiness, attending the writers of
such verses, as are repeated to; and

Naribus indulges : an erit qui velle recuset
Os populi meruisse ? et cedro digna locutus,
Linquere nec scombros metuentia carmina, nec thus ?　　40
　Quisque es, ô modo quem ex adverso dicere feci,
Non ego, cum scribo, si forte quid aptius exit,
(Quando hæc rara avis est,) si quid tamen aptius exit,
Laudari metuam : neque enim mihi cornea fibra est.
Sed recti fiuemque extremumque esse recuso.　　　　45
Euge tuum et Belle. Nam Belle hoc excute totum :
Quid non intus habet ? Non hic est Ilias Accî,
Ebria veratro ? Non si qua elegidia crudi
Dictarunt proceres ? Non quicquid denique lectis
Scribitur in citreis ?—Calidum scis ponere sumen ;　　50

approved by, a set of drunken libertines at a feast.

Juvenal, on another occasion, has
collected all the above ideas, as the
gift of the gods to the good and worthy. Sat. vii. l. 207–8.

—*You laugh, says he, &c.*] The
defender of such writings is not a
little hurt with the ironical sneer of
Persius. O, says the galled poet, you
are laughing all this while ; you are
too severe upon us.

38. *Hooked nostrils.*] Uncis naribus
indulges—a phrase for indulging
scorn and sneering ; taken from the
wrinkled and distorted shape assumed
by the nose on such occasions. Thus
Hor. lib. i. sat. vi. l. 5, where he is
observing, that " Mæcenas does not,
" as too many are apt to do, look
" with scorn and contempt on people
" of obscure birth," expresses himself in this manner :

　　　　　　　　　　　Nec——
*Ut plerique solent, naso suspendis
　adunco
Ignotos.*

The ideas of scorn and contempt
are often expressed among us by turning up the nose.

—*Will there be, &c.*] *i. e.* Is such
a person to be found, who is so lost
to all desire of praise, continues the
apologist, as to have no concern at all
to merit the approbation and countenance of the public ?

39. *Worthy of cedar, &c.*]—*i. e.*
Worthy to be preserved. Cedar was
looked upon as an incorruptible wood,
which never decayed. From the ce-

dar they extracted a juice, which being put on books, and other things,
kept them from moths, worms, and
even decay itself.

40. *To leave verses, &c.*] *i. e.* In no
danger of being used as waste paper,
either by fishmongers, to wrap or
pack their fish in when they sell it, or
by perfumers, for their frankincense
or other perfumes. See Hor. lib.
ii. epist. i. l. 266, &c. here imitated
by Persius.

41. *Whoever thou art, &c.*] The
poet here, after having severely satirized a desire of false praise, and
empty commendation of what really
deserves no praise at all, now allows,
that praise, where properly bestowed,
is not to be despised.

—*Made to speak, &c.*] *i. e.* Whom
I have been setting up as a supposed
adversary, or opponent, in this dispute. Whosoever thou art, that
findest what I have been saying applicable to thyself, let me confess to
thee, that—

42. *I, when I write, &c.*] *i. e.*
When I compose verses—if by chance
any thing well adapted to the subject, and well expressed, flows from
my pen, (since I confess this happens
but seldom, and therefore gives me
the greater satisfaction,) I should not
fear commendation.

44. *Inwards so horny.*] Fibra, the
inwards or entrails—here, by met.
the inward man, the moral sense.
Horny—hard—insensible like horn.
See Juv. sat. i. l. 29.

q. d. I am not so callous, so insen-

Your hooked nostrils. Will there be, who can refuse to be
    willing
To have deserved the countenance of the people? and,
    ' having spoken things worthy of cedar,
To leave verses fearing neither little fishes, nor frankincense?
. Whoever thou art, O thou, whom I just now made to
    speak on the adverse part,   41
I, when I write, if haply something more apt comes forth,
(Since this is a rare bird,) yet if something more apt comes
    forth,
Would not fear to be praised; nor indeed are my inwards
    so horny.
But to be the end and extreme of right I deny   45
Your " Well done !" and your " O fine !" for examine this
    whole " O fine,"
What has it not within? Is not the Iliad of Accius here,
Drunk with hellebore? are they not here, if crude nobles
    have dictated
Any little elegies? Is there not, lastly, whatever is written
In citron beds?—You know how to place a hot sow's-udder;

sible, or unfeeling, as not to be
pleased, as well as touched, with deserved praise.

48. *But to be the end, &c.*] But
that the eulogies of fools and sots
should be the end and aim of writing,
I deny; or indeed, that merely to
gain applause should be the view and
end of even doing right, I cannot allow.

49. *Your " Well done ! O fine !"*]
Euge !—belle ! like our Well done !
fine ! bravo ! which were acclamations of applause. See Juv. sat. vii.
l. 44, note.

46. *Examine this whole " O fine !"*]
Sift, canvass well this mark of applause which you are so fond of—lit.
shake out—met. from shaking out
the contents of a sack ; we say sift.

47. *What has it not within? &c.*]
What is there so absurd, that you
will not find it applied to as the object of it? in short, what is not contained within it?

—*The Iliad of Accius.*] Accius Labeo, who made a wretched translation
of Homer's Iliad. See note above, l.
4. Is not even this contained within
the compass of your favourite terms
of applause?

48. *Drunk with Hellebore.*] The
ancients made use of Hellebore, not
only when they were disordered in
the head, but also when in health,
in order to quicken the apprehension.
This the poet humourously supposes
Accius to have done, but in such a
quantity as to stupify his senses.

—*Are they not here, if crude nobles,
&c.*] Are not the flimsy and silly little
elegies and sonnets, which our raw
and unexperienced nobles write and
repeat, all subjects of your favourite
Belle ? Is not this constantly bestowed
upon them ?

49. *Is there not, lastly, &c.*] The
citron wood was reckoned very valuable and precious ; of this the nobles
had their beds and couches made, on
which they used to lie, or sit, when
they wrote. Lastly, says Persius,
all the trash which issues forth from
the citron couches of the great is contained within the compass of this
mark of applause; therefore your
making it your end and aim is but
very little worth your while ; it is so
unworthily bestowed, as to be no sort
of criterion of excellence and desert.

50. *How to place, &c.*] The poet

Scis comitem horridulum tritâ donare lacernâ;
Et verum, inquis, amo; verum mihi dicite de me.
　Qui pote? Vis dicam?—Nugaris, cum tibi, calve,
Pinguis aqualiculis propenso sesquipede extet.
　O Jane, a tergo quem nulla ciconia pinsit,　　　　　　55
Nec manus auriculas imitata est mobilis albas;
Nec linguæ, quantum sitiat canis Appula, tantum!
Vos, O patricius sanguis, quos vivere fas est
Occipiti cœco, posticæ occurrite sannæ!
　"Quis populi sermo est?"—Quis enim, nisi carmina
　　molli　　　　　　　　　　　　　　　　　　　　　60
Nunc demum numero fluere, ut per læve severos
Effundat junctura ungues? Scit tendere versum,

still continues to satirize empty applause, by shewing that it may be gained by the lowest and most abject means.

He therefore attacks those who bribe for it. You know how, says he, to place on your table a dainty dish.

51. *You know to present, &c.*]— You know the effect of giving an old shabby coat to one of your poor dependents. Comp. Hor. epist. xix. lib. ii. l. 37–8.

52. *"I love truth," &c.*] Then, when you have given a good dinner to some, and still meaner presents to others, in order to purchase their applause, you ask them their opinion, desiring them to speak the truth.

53. *How is it possible?*] i. e. That they should speak the truth, when they are afraid of offending you if they did? You have obliged them, and they fear to disoblige you, which, if they speak their real thoughts, they would most probably do.

　—*Would you have me say it?*]— Says Persius, who am no dependent of yours, or under any obligation to disguise my sentiments.

　—*You trifle, &c.*] I tell you plainly, and without disguise, that you are an old trifler, to pretend to wit or poetry, with that great belly of yours, that hangs down at least a foot and an half below your middle, and bespeaks a genius for gluttony, but for nothing else. Perhaps the poet hints at the Greek proverb.

Παχεια γαςηρ λεπτον ⊌ τικτει νοον.

" *A fat belly produceth not a subtle* " *mind.*"

55. *O Janus!*] Janus was the first king of Italy, who gave refuge to Saturn, when he fled from his son Jupiter from Crete. From his name the first month of the year is called January. He was pictured with two faces, one before and one behind, as regarding the time past and future.

q. d. Thou art happy, O Janus, inasmuch as, being able to see both before and behind, thou art in no danger of being ignorant of what passeth behind thy back, and, therefore, of enduring the flouts and jeers, which our nobles receive behind their backs, from those who flatter them to their faces.

　— *Whom no stork pecks, &c.*] There were three methods of scoff and ridicule: one was holding out the finger, and crooking it a little to imitate the bill of storks; they held it towards him who was the object of derision, moving it backwards and forwards, like the pecking of the stork. See AINSW.

56. *The moveable hand, &c.*] Another mode of derision was, putting the thumbs up to the temples, and moving them in such manner as to imitate asses' ears, which, in the inside, are usually white.

57. *Nor so much of the tongue, &c.*] A third method was to loll out the tongue, like a dog when thirsty.

　Apula was the hottest part of Italy, of course the dogs most thirsty, and

You know to present a shabby client with a worn garment;
And "I love truth (say you); tell me the truth concern-
    " ing me."
    How is it possible?—Would you have me say it? you
    trifle, when, O bald head,
Your fat paunch stands forth with a hanging-down foot and
    an half.
    O Janus! whom no stork pecks behind your back,   55
Nor has the moveable hand imitated white ears,
Nor so much of the tongue, as an Apulian bitch when
    athirst.
Ye, O patrician blood, whose condition it is to live with
The hinder part of the head blind, prevent flouts behind
    your backs!
    What is the speech of the people?—What forsooth, un-
    · less that the verses   60
Now at last flow with soft measure, so that, across the
    polish, the joining
May pour forth severe nails. He knows how to extend a
    verse,

most apt to loll out their tongues the farthest.

None of all this could happen to Janus without his seeing it.

58. *O patrician blood, &c.*] Ye sons of senators, ye nobles of Rome, whose fortune it is to be born without eyes at the back of your heads, and who therefore cannot be apprized of what passes behind your backs,

59. *Prevent flouts, &c.*] By avoiding all occasions of them; by not writing verses, for which your flatterers will commend you to your face, and laugh at you behind your backs.

60. *[What is the speech, &c.]*— Persius here seems to go back to the de me, l. 52; all between which, and this l. 60, is to be understood as a parenthesis, very properly introduced in the course of the subject.

Now, says the great man to his flatterer, after having treated him with a good dinner (l. 50), what does the world say of me and my writings?

—*What forsooth.*] i. e. What should they say, what can they say, unless to commend?

61. *Now at last, &c.*] That after all the pains you have taken, you

have at last produced a charming work—the verses flow in soft and gentle numbers.

—*Across the polish, &c.*] 'Your verses are so highly finished, that they will stand the test of the severest and nicest critics.

Metaph. taken from polishers of marble, who run their nail over the surface, in order to try if there be any unevenness; and if the nail passes freely, without any stop or hindrance whatsoever, even over where there are joinings, then the work is completely finished. (Comp. Hor. de Art. Poet. l. 294.) The surface being perfectly smooth, was said effundere unguem, it passing as smoothly as water poured forth over it.

62. *How to extend a verse.*] This period is also metaphorical, and alludes to the practice of carpenters and others, who work by line and rule, and who, when they would draw a straight line, shut one eye, the better to confine the visual rays to a single point. So, says the flatterer, this poet of ours draws forth his verses to their proper length, and makes them as exact as if he worked by line and rule.

312 PERSII SATIRÆ.

Non secus ac si oculo rubricam dirigat uno.
Sive opus in mores, in luxum, in prandia regum,
Dicere res grandes nostro dat Musa poetæ, 65
  Ecce, modo, heroas sensus afferre videmus
Nugari solitos Græce; nec ponere lucum
Artifices; nec rus saturum laudare, ubi corbes,
Et focus, et porci, et fumosa Palilia fœno :
Unde Remus, sulcoque terens dentalia, Quinti, 70
Quem trepida ante boves dictatorem induit uxor ;
Et tua aratra domum lictor tulit.—Euge, poeta!
  Est nunc, Brisæi quem venosus liber Accî,
Sunt quos Pacuviusque, et verrucosa moretur

63. *The rubric.*] Rubrica, a sort of ruddle, or red chalk, with which carpenters draw their lines on their work.

64. *On manners.*] Whatever the subject may be—whether he writes comedy, and ridicules the humours of the times.

—*On luxury.*] Or if he write satire, and lash the luxury of the great.

—*Or the dinners of kings.*] Or writes tragedy, and chooses for his subject the sad feasts of tyrants. Perhaps Persius here alludes to the story of Thyestes, the son of Pelops, and brother of Atreus, with whose wife he had committed adultery; to revenge which, Atreus dressed the child born of her, and served him up to his brother at his own table. On this Seneca wrote a tragedy.

65. *The Muse gives our poet, &c.*] In short, be what may the subject, a Muse is ever at hand, to inspire our poet with the most sublime and lofty poetry.

Such is the account which the great man receives of himself from his flatterer, as an answer to his question, l. 60, "What does the world " say of me ?"

66. *Behold now we see, &c.*] Our poet proceeds to satirize other writers of his time, who, allured with the hopes of being flattered, attempted the sublime heights of epic writing, though utterly unfit for the undertaking.

—*Heroic thoughts, &c.*] Heroas sensus. Sensus signifies not only sense, meaning, understanding, but also thought.

Heroas, from herous-a-um, heroic, stands here for heroos, masc.—i. e. heroicos. Heroi sensus is to be understood of sublime matters for poetry, such as heroic or epic subjects.

Now-a-days, saith Persius, we see certain writers attempting and bringing out heroic poems, who used to be writing trifles in Greek, such as little epigrams, or the like. Some copies, instead of videmus, read docemus, as if the poet attacked schoolmasters, and other instructors of children, for teaching boys to write in heroics, at a time when they are not fit for it: but as it is not the purpose of these papers to enter into controversy with editors and commentators, I take videmus, as it stands in the Delphin edition, Farnaby, and Marshall.

67. *Nor to describe a grove, &c.*] They are so unskilled, and such bad artists even in the lighter style of composition, that they know not how to describe, as they ought, the most trite and common subjects, such as a grove, fields, &c. Pono-ere, literally signifies to put or place: but it also signifies to paint, draw, or portray, and so to describe. See Hor. lib. iv. ode viii. l. 8.

Hic saxo, liquidis ille coloribus
Solers nunc hominem ponere, nunc
  deum.

68. *Nor to praise a fertile country.*] So as to set forth its beauties.

—*Where are baskets, &c.*] Instead of describing the great and leading features of a fine plentiful country, they dwell upon the most trivial circumstances :

Not otherwise than if he should direct the rubric with one
   eye;
Whether the work is on manners, on luxury, or the dinners
   of kings,
The Muse gives our poet to say great things.   65
   Behold now we see those bring heroic thoughts,
Who used to trifle in Greek, nor to describe a grove
Skilful; nor to praise a fertile country, where are baskets,
And a fire-hearth, and swine, and the feasts of Pales smoky
   with hay:
From whence Remus, and thou, O Quintius, wearing
   coulters in a furrow,   70
Whom thy trembling wife clothed dictator before the oxen,
And thy ploughs the lictor carried home. Well done, O poet!
   There is now, whom the veiny book of Brisæan Accius;
There are those whom both Pacuvius, and rugged Antiopa

---

*——His lay
Recounts its chimnies, panniers,
hogs and hay.*
         - BREWSTER.
69. *Feasts of Pales, &c.*] Pales
was the goddess of shepherds, who
kept feasts in honour of her, in order
to procure the safe parturition of their
cattle. The reason of the epithet
fumosa is, that during the feast of
Pales the rustics lighted fires with
hay, straw, or stubble, over which
they leaped, by way of purifying
themselves. These feasts of Pales
were sure to be introduced by these
jejune poets.
70. *From whence Remus.*]. Another circumstance which they introduce is a description of the birth-
place of Remus and Romulus.
  —*Thou, O Quintius, &c*] Cincin-
natus, who was called from the
plough to be made dictator of Rome
——he too is introduced on the occasion.
71. *Thy trembling wife, &c.*] They
tell us, how his wife Racilia was
frightened at the sight of the messengers from Rome, and how she helped
him on with his dictator's robe, as he
stood by the oxen which were in the
plough; and how one of the Roman
officers, who had attended the em-
bassy to call him to the dictatorship,
carried his plough home upon his
shoulders.

72. *Well done, O poet!*] Iron.—
Finely done, to be sure, to introduce
such weighty matters as these into
thy poem! thou art in a fair way to
gain the highest applause!
  Persius, in this passage, glances at
some poetaster of his time, who, in a
poem on the pleasures of a country
life, had been very particular and tedious upon the circumstances here recited. See Casaubon
73. *There is now, &c.*] The poet
now proceeds to censure those who
affected antiquated and obsolete
words and phrases, and who professed to admire the style of antiquated authors.
  —*The veiny book.*] Venosus—metaph. from old men, whose veins stand
out and look turgid, owing to the
shrinking of the flesh, through old
age. Venosus liber hence signifies a
book of some old and antiquated author—a very old book.
  —*Brisæan Accius.*] Brisas was a
town in Thrace, where Bacchus was
worshipped with all the mad rites
used at his feasts; hence he was
called Brisæus. Persius gives this
name to Accius, on account of the
wild and strange bombast which was
in his writings.
74. *Pacuvius*] An ancient tragic
poet of Brundusium, who wrote the
tragedy of Antiopa, the wife of Ly-
cus, king of Thebes, who was repu-

Antiopa, " ærumnis cor luctificabile fulta."   75
    Hos pueris monitus, patres infundere lippos
Cum videas, quærisne unde hæc sartago loquendi
Venerit in linguas? unde istud dedecus, in quo
Trossulus exultat tibi per subsellia lævis?
Nilne pudet, capiti non posse pericula cano   80
Pellere, quin tepidum hoc optes audire, *Decenter?*
    Fur es, ait Pedio: Pedius quid? crimina rasis
Librat in antithetis: doctas posuisse figuras
Laudatur: *bellum hoc*—hoc bellum? An, Romule, ceves?
Men' moveat quippe, et, cantet si naufragus, assem   85

diated by her husband, on account of her intrigue with Jupiter. The poet says, verrucosa Antiopa, to express the roughness and ruggedness of the style in which this tragedy was written. Verrucosus, full of warts, tumps, or hillocks — so uneven, rugged.

75. *Might detain.*] Moretur—i. e. might detain their attention.

—*Having propp'd, &c.*] This strange fustian expression is probably to be found in the tragedy. The poet appears to cite it, as a sample of the style in which the play is written.

There are those, says Persius, who, now-a-days, can spend their time in reading these authors.

76. *Blear-eyed fathers, &c.*] In old men the eyes are apt to be weak, moist, and to distil corrosive matter. When you see such advising their children to study the old barbarous Latin poets, and to be fond of the obsolete words—

77. *Do you seek, &c.*] Are you at a loss to know whence this jargon, of obsolete and modern words, as heard in our common speech?

Sartago literally signifies a frying-pan; and the poet, perhaps, calls the mixture or jargon of old words and new, sartago loquendi, in allusion to the mixture of ingredients, of which they made their fried cakes, as bran, fat, honey, seeds, cheese, and the like.

Some think that he alludes to the crackling, bouncing, and hissing noise of the frying-pan, with these ingredients in it, over the fire; this seems to relate to the manner of utterance, more than to what was uttered. See AINSW. *Sartago,* No. 2.

78. *Whence that disgrace.*] That style of writing, and of speaking, so disgraceful to the purity and smoothness of the Latin language.

79. *Smooth Trossulus, &c.*] The Roman knights were called Trossuli, from Trossulus, a city of Tuscany, which they took without the assistance of any infantry. Here the poet joins it with the epithet lævis, soft, effeminate; therefore Trossulus, here, appears to signify a beau, a coxcomb, a petit-maitre. See AINSW. *Trossulus;* and Cassaubon in loc.

—*Thro' the benches.*] Subsellia— the seats at the theatre, or at the public recitals of poetry, and other compositions. These fine gentlemen were so pleased with the introduction of obsolete words and phrases, that they could hardly keep their places; they spread a general applause thro' all the benches where they sat, and leaped up with ecstacy in their seats, charmed with such a poet.

80. *Does it nothing shame you, &c.*] Persius now proceeds to censure the vanity of the orators, who paid more regard to the commendations of their auditors; than to the issue of the most important causes, even where life or fame was at stake.

Are you not ashamed says Persius, ought you not to blush at your vanity and folly, that, if accused of some capital crime, instead of using plain arguments to defend your life from the danger which awaits it, and to make that your end and aim, you are endeavouring so to speak, as to catch the applause of your judges, and of the auditory, and make it your chief wish to hear them say—" Well, the

Might detain, having propped her mournful heart with
   sorrows.   75
When you see blear-eyed fathers pour these admonitions
   into
Their children, do you seek whence this bombast manner
   of speaking
Came on their tongues? Whence that disgrace, in which
The smooth Trossulus exults to thee through the benches?
Does it nothing shame you, not to be able to drive away
   dangers from   80
Your grey head, but you must wish to hear this luke-
   warm—Decently?
Thou art a thief (says one to Pedius)—What Pedius?
   his crimes
He weighs in polished antitheses; to have laid down
   learned figures
He is praised: this is fine!—this is fine! O Romulus, do
   you wag the tail?
For if a shipwrecked mariner sings, could he move me, and
   a penny   85

"man speaks decently:" a poor lukewarm expression at best.

82. *Pedius.*] Pedius Blesus was accused, in the time of Nero, by the Cyrenians, of having robbed and plundered the temple of Æsculapius. He was condemned, and put out of the senate.

Hence the poet uses the name of Pedius here, as denoting any supposed person accused of theft.

"Thou art a thief," says some accuser, laying a robbery to his charge.

—*What Pedius?*] i. e. What says Pedius, or what doth he, on such an accusation?

83, *He weighs in polished antithesis.*] He opposes to his accusation curious figures of speech, affected phrases, sentences, and periods, in order to catch applause, instead of producing weighty, pertinent, and plain arguments for his defence. He puts, as it were, his accusation in one scale, and his affected periods in the other, and thus weighs one against the other. Antithesis (from αντι, contra, and τιϑημι, pono) is a rhetorical flourish, when contraries are opposed to each other. Here, by sy-

nec. it stands for all the affected flowers of speech.

84. *He is praised.*] The judges and auditory are highly delighted with the learned figures of speech which he has laid before them in his oration.

—*This is fine!*] Say his hearers—finely spoken! finely said!

—*This is fine!*] Answers Persius, with indignation at the absurdity of such ill-timed applause, of such affected and ill-timed flourishes.

—*O Romulus, &c.*] Can any Roman shew himself thus degenerate from his great and virtuous ancestor Romulus, as to fawn and flatter on such an occasion, and be like a dog that wags his tail when he would curry favour? Ceveo signifies to wag, or move the tail, as dogs do when they fawn upon one. Hence, metaph. it is used to express fawning and flattery.

Persius uses the word Romule, as Juv. sat. iii. l. 67, uses Quirine. See the note there.

85. *If a shipwreck'd mariner sings, &c.*] If a poor sailor, that had been cast away, should meet me in the

Protulerim? cantas, cum fractâ te in trabe pictum
Ex humero portes? Verum, nec nocte paratum
Plorabit, qui me volet incurvasse querelâ.
M. Sed numeris decor est, et junctura addita crudis.
P. Claudere sic versum didicit: Berecynthius Attin,   90
Et qui cœruleum dirimebat Nerea delphin:
Sic costam longo subduximus Apennino.
M. Arma virum, nonne hoc spumosum, et cortice pingui?
P. Ut ramale vetus prægrandi subere coctum.
M. Quidnam igitur tenerum, et laxâ cervice legendum?

street, and ask an alms, at the same time appearing very jolly and merry, would this be the way to move my compassion; to make me pull some money out of my pocket and give it him?

86. *Do you sing, &c.*] It was the custom for persons that had been shipwrecked, and had escaped with their lives, to have themselves, together with the scene of their misfortune and danger, painted on a board, which they hung by a string from their shoulders upon their breast, that the passers-by might be moved with compassion at the sight, and relieve them with alms. These tables were afterwards hung up in the temples, and dedicated to some god, as Neptune, Juno, &c. hence they were called votivæ tabulæ. See HOR. lib. i. ode v. ad fin.

The poet here allegorizes the case of Pedius. Do you sing, when you are carrying your miserable self painted on a board, and represented as suffering the calamity of shipwreck, in order to move compassion.—*i. e.* Are you studying and making fine flourishing speeches, filled with affected tropes and figures, at a time when you are accused of such a crime as theft, and are standing in the dangerous situation of an arraigned robber? Is this the way to move compassion towards you?

87. *A true, &c.*] There wants ploratum, dolorem, or some such word, after verum—plorare verum dolorem, like vivere vitam, for instance.

—*Not prepared by night.*] Not conned, studied, or invented beforehand; over night, as we say.

88. *Bend me by his complaint.*] i. e.

Make me bow or yield to the feelings of commisseration for his sufferings.

The poet means, that the complainant who would move his pity, must speak the true and native language of real grief from the heart, not accost him with an artful studied speech, as if he had conned it over beforehand.

Si vis me flere, dolendum est
Primum ipsi tibi.
HOR. de Art. Poet. l. 102–3.

So Pedius, however he might get the applause of his hearers, by his figurative eloquence and flowery language, when on his trial, could never excite pity for his situation.

89. *But there is beauty, &c.*] Well, but however the flights which you have been mentioning, says the poetaster, and the studied and flowery style, may be unsuitable in declamation, especially on such occasions, yet surely they have a peculiar beauty in our verses, which would be quite raw, and appear crude and undigested without them.

—*And composition added, &c.*]—Junctura is literally a coupling, or joining together; hence a composition, or joining words in a particular form, as in verse.

Notum si callida verbum
Reddiderit junctura novum.
HOR. de Art. Poet. l. 47–8.

The poetaster would fain contend for the great improvement made in writing verses by the modern studied composition, and the introduction of figurative writing.

90. *Thus hath he learnt to conclude a verse.*] The didicit here, without a nominative case, is rather abrupt and

Should I bring forth ? do you sing, when yourself painted
    on a broken plank
You carry from your shoulder ? A true (misfortune), not
    prepared by night,
{ He shall deplore, who would bend me by his complaint.
   M. But there is beauty and composition added to crude
    numbers.
P. Thus hath he learnt to conclude a verse : " Berecyn-
    " thian Attin,   90
" And the dolphin which divided cærulean Nereus—
" Thus we removed a rib from the long Apennine."
   M. " Arms and the man"—is not this frothy, and with
    a fat bark ?
P. As an old bough dried with a very large bark.
   M. What then is tender, and to be read with a loose
    neck ?   95

obscure, but the poet affects to be so ;
he does not venture to name the person meant, though his quoting some
verses of Nero, as instances of the
great improvements which had been
made in the composition of verse,
plainly shews his design, which was
to ridicule the emperor, whose affected, jingling, and turgid style,
was highly applauded by his flatterers.

— " *Berecynthian Attin.*"] This
and the next verse rhyme in the
original.

91. " *And the dolphin,*" &c.] Alluding to ths story of Arion, who was
carried safe to land, when thrown
overboard, on the back of a dolphin.
Nereus, a sea god, is here affect-
edly put for the sea itself.

92. " *Thus we removed,*" &c.]—
There is a jingle in this verse between
the longo in the middle, and Apennino
at the end. The writer of these three
quoted lines changes Atys or Attis
into Attin, to make it rhyme with
Delphin.

Atys, or Attis, the subject of this
poem, was a handsome youth of
Phyrgia, beloved by Cybele, who
from Berecynthus, a mountain of
Asia Minor, where she was worshipped, was called Berecynthia : hence
the writer of the poem affects to call
Atys Berecynthius.

— " *Thus we removed a rib,*" &c.]

The end of this verse is spondaic,
which Nero much affected in his heroics. He calls Hannibal's opening
a way for his army over the Alps,
removing a rib from the Apenine
mountains—a strange, affected phrase.

93. " *Arms and the man,* &c.]—
Arma virumque—Æn. 1. l. 1. Well,
replies the poetaster, if you find fault
with what you have quoted, I suppose you will find fault with Virgil's
arma virumque cano, and perhaps
with his whole Æneid, as frothy, turgid, and, like a tree with a thick
bark, appearing great, but having
little of value within.

94. *As an old bough,* &c.] Ramale
is a dead bough cut from a tree.
Persius answers, Yes, Virgil is like
an old bough with a thick bark ; but
then we must understand, such a
bough as has been cut from the tree,
and whose bark has been dried for
many years by the sun, so that all its
gross particles are exhaled and gone,
and nothing but what is solid remains.
Suber signifies the cork tree, which
is remarkable for its thick bark—
therefore put here for the bark ; syn.
—thus cortex, the bark, is sometimes
put for the tree, which is remarkably
light. HOR. ode ix. lib iii. 1 22.

95. *What then is tender,* &c.]—
Well, says the opponent to Persius,
let us have done with heroics, and

P. " Torva Mimalloneis implerunt cornua bombis ;   96
" Et raptum vitulo caput ablatura superbo
" Bassaris ; et lyncem Mænas flexura corymbis,
" Evion ingeminat : reparabilis adsonat echo."
Hæc fierent, si virtutis vena ulla paterni   100
Viverit in nobis ? Summâ delumbe salivâ
Hoc natat in labris ; et in udo est Mænas et Attin ;
Nec pluteum cædit, nec demorsos sapit ungues.
    M. Sed quid opus teneras mordaci radere vero
Auriculas ? Vide sis, ne majorum tibi forte   105
Limina frigescant. Sonat hic de nare canina

'tell me what you allow to be good of the tender kind of writing.

—*With a loose neck.*] With a head reclined, in a languishing, soft, and tender manner. This is humourously put in opposition to the attitudes made use of in reading the bombast and fustian heroics of these poetasters, who stood with the neck stretched as high as they could, and straining their throats, to give force and loudness to their utterance.

96. " *They fill'd their fierce horns,*" &c.] Giving a fierce and warlike sound. Some render torva here writhed, twisted, or crooked, quasi torta.

Persius deriding the querist, quotes four more lines, which are supposed to have been written by Nero, and which exhibit a specimen of one of the most absurd rhapsodies that ever was penned.

—" *Mimallonean blosts.*"] The Mimallones were priestesses of Bacchus ; they were so called from Mimas, a mountain of Ionia, sacred to Bacchus.

Bombus signifies a hoarse sound or blast, as of a trumpet or horn.

97. " *Bassaris.*"] Agave, or any other of the priestesses ; called Bassaris, from Bassarus, a name of Bacchus.

Having given the alarm, Agave and the rest of the Mimallones cut off the head of Pentheus (the son of Agave and Echion), and tore him to pieces, because he would drink no wine, and slighted the feasts of Bacchus. Pentheus is thought to be meant here by the superbo vitulo.

98. " *Mænas.*"] These priestesses of Bacchus were also called Mænades (from Gr. μαινεσθαι, insanire.)

—" *To guide a lynx.*"] These were beasts of the leopard or tyger kind, and represented as drawing the chariot of Bacchus. The word flexura here, like flectere, VIRG. Geo. ii. 357, means to guide.—So again, Æn. i. 156. flectit equos—" he guides or " manages his horses." Thus the priestesses of Bacchus might be said flectere, to guide or manage lynxes with bands or rods of ivy. This was sacred to Bacchus, because, returning conqueror from India, he was crowned with ivy.

99. " *Redoubles Evion.*"] Ingemino signifies to redouble—to repeat often. Evios, or Evius, a name of Bacchus, on which the Bacchantes used to call (Evoi, Gr.) till they wrought themselves into a fury like madness. See Juv. sat. vii. l. 62, and note.

—" *The reparable echo,*" &c.] So called from repeating, and so repairing the sounds, which would otherwise be lost.

100. *Would these be made.*] i. e. Would such verses as these be made, but more especially would they be commended.

—*If any vein,* &c.] If there were the least trace of the manly wisdom of our ancestors among us ?

101. *This feeble stuff.*] Delumbis —weak, feeble, broken-backed, as it were.

102. *Swims in the lips.*] The poet, by this phrase, seems to mean, that the flatterers of Nero had these lines always at their tongue's end, (as we

P: " They filled their fierce horns with Mimallonean blasts,"
" And Bassaris, about to take away the head snatched from
    " the proud
" Calf, and Mænas, about to guide a lynx with ivy,"
" Redoubles Evion : the reparable echo sounds to it."
    Would these be made, if any vein of our paternal manli-
        ness   ·   ➝   100
Lived in us ? This feeble stuff, on the topmost spittle,
Swims in the lips, and in the wet is Mænas and Attys.
Nor does he beat his desk, nor taste his gnawn nails.
    M. But where is the need to grate tender ears with
        biting truth ?
See to it, lest haply the thresholds of the great   105
Should grow cold to you : here from the nostril sounds the
    canine letter—

say) and were spitting them out, *i. e.*
repeating and quoting them continually.

—*And in the wet.*] In udo esse,
and in summa saliva natare, seem to
imply the same thing ; *viz.* that these
poems of Atys and Mænas were always in people's mouths, mixed with
their spittle, as it were.

103. *Nor does he beat his desk, &c.*]
The penman of such verses as these
is at very little pains about them. He
knows nothing of those difficulties,
which, at times, pains-taking poets
are under, so as to make them smite
the desk which they write upon, and
gnaw their nails to the quick with
vexation.

See HOR. lib. ii. sat. iii. l. 7-8.
    *Culpantur frustra calami, frus-
        traque laborat.*
    Iratis natus paries Dis atque poetis.
And again, lib. i. sat. x. l. 70-1.
        ——*In versu faciendo*
    *Sæpe caput scaberet, vivos et roderet
        ungues.*

104. *Where's the need, &c.*] We
are to recollect, that this Satire opens
with a dialogue between Persius and
his friend, that the latter persuades
Persius against publishing ; that Persius says, he is naturally of a satiri-
cal turn of mind, and does not know
how to refrain, (l. 12.) and then
launches forth into the severest censure on the writers of his day. His
friend perceiving that what he first

said against publishing would not
have its effect, still farther dissuades
him, by hinting at the danger he ran
of getting the ill-will of the great.

    " Where is the necessity, (says his
" friend,) supposing all you say to
" be true, yet where is the necessity
" to hurt the ears of those who have
" been used to hear nothing but flat-
" tery, and therefore must be very
" tender and susceptible of the acut-
" est feelings of uneasiness and dis-
" pleasure, on hearing such bitter and
" stinging truths as you deliver."

105. *See to it.*] Vide sis (*i. e.* si
vis)—take care, if you please.

    —*Lest haply the thresholds, &c.*]—
Lest it fall out, that you should so
offend some of the great folks, as to
meet with a cool reception at their
houses.

    So HOR. sat. i. lib. ii. l. 60-3.
        ——*O puer, ut sis.*
    *Vitalis metuo, et majorum ne quis
        amicus*
    Frigore te feriat.

106. *Here.*] *i. e.* In these Satires
of yours, there is a disagreeable sound,
like the snarling of a dog, very unpleasant to the ears of such people.

    —*From the nostril sounds the
canine letter.*] R is called the dog's
letter, because the vibration of the
tongue in pronouncing it resembles
the snarling of a dog. See Alchy-
mist, act ii. sc. vi.

Litera—*P.* Per me, equidem, sint omnia protinus alba;
Nil moror. Euge, omnes, omnes bene miræ eritis res.
Hoc juvat; hic, inquis, veto quisquam faxit oletum;
Pinge duos angues: Pueri, sacer est locus, extra　　110
Meite: discedo. Secuit Lucilius urbem,
Te, Lupe, te Muti; et genuinum fregit in illis.
Omne vafer vitium ridenti Flaccus amico
Tangit; et admissus circum præcordia ludit,
Callidus excusso populum suspendere naso.　　　115
Men' mutire nefas? Nec clam, nec cum scrobe? *M.* Nus-
　　quam.
P. Hic tamen infodiam: "Vidi, vidi ipse, libelle:
" Auriculas asini quis non habet?"—Hoc ego opertum,

107. *For my part, truly, &c.*]—
Well, answers Persius, if this be the
case, I will have nothing to do with
them; all they do and say shall be
perfectly right, for me, from henceforward. The ancients put black for
what was bad, and white for what
was good, according to that of Pythagoras:

Το μεν λευκον της Αγαθου φυσεως,
　το δε μελαν κακου.

*White is of the nature of good—
　black of evil.*

108. *I hinder not.*] I shall say nothing to prevent its being thought so.
Or, nil moror may be rendered, I do
not care about it. Comp. Hor. sat.
iv. lib. i. l. 13.

—*O brave! &c.*] Well done!
every thing, good people, that ye say
and do shall be admirable. Iron.
This wretched verse is supposed to be
written as a banter on the bad poets.

109. *This pleases.*] Surely this
concession pleases you, my friend.

—*Here say you, I forbid, &c.*]—
Metaph. It was unlawful to do their
occasions, or to make water, in any
sacred place; and it was customary
to paint two snakes on the walls or
doors of such places, in order to mark
them out to the people. The poet is
ironically comparing the persons and
writings of the great (glancing, no
doubt, at Nero) to such sacred places;
and as these were forbidden to be defiled with urine and excrement, so he
understands his friend to say, that
neither the persons or writings of the

emperor and of the nobles were to be
defiled with the abuse and reproofs of
satirists. See Juv. sat. i. 117.

110. *Paint two snakes.*] These
were representatives of the deity or
genius of the sacred place, and painted there as signals to deter people,
children especially, who were most
apt to make free with such places,
from the forbidden defilement. Mark
out, says Persius, these sacred characters to me, that I may avoid defiling them. Iron.

111. *I depart.*] Says Persius, I am
gone—I shall not tarry a moment on
forbidden ground, nor drop my Satires
there.

—*Lucilius cut the city.*] Lucilius,
whose works are not come down to
us, was almost the father of the Roman satire. He was a very severe
writer; hence our poet's saying, secuit uroem, he cut up, slashed as with
a sword, the city, i. e. the people of
Rome, from the highest to the lowest.
So Juv. sat. i. l. 151.

*Ense velut stricto quoties Lucilius
　ardens.*
Infremuit, &c.
Comp. Hor. sat. iv. lib. i. l. 1—12.

Persius seems to bethink himself.
He has just said, I depart—i. e. I
shall not meddle with the great people—" But why should I depart? Lu-
" cilius could lash all sorts of people,
" and why should not I?"

112. *Thee, Lupus, thee, Mutius.*]
Pub. Rutilius Lupus, the consul, and
Titus Mutius Albutius, a very pow-
erful man—q. d. Lucilius not only

P. For my part, truly, let every thing be henceforward
  white.
I hinder not. O brave! all things, ye shall all be very
  wonderful.
This pleases.—Here, say you, I forbid that any should
  commit nuisance;
Paint two snakes; boys, the place is sacred:—without   110
Make water—I depart.—Lucilius cut the city,
Thee, Lupus, thee, Mūtius; and he brake his jaw-tooth
  upon them.
Sly Horace touches every vice, his friend laughing:
And admitted round the heart, plays
Cunning to hang up the people with an unwrinkled nose.
Is it unlawful for me to mutter? neither secretly, nor with
  a ditch? *M.* No where.   116
P. Nevertheless I will dig here. "I have seen, I myself
  "have seen, O little book:—
"Who has not the ears of an ass?" I this hidden thing,

satirized the great, but did it by
name.

—Brake his jaw-tooth, &c.] Metaph. from grinding food between the
jaw-teeth, to express the severity with
which he treated them, grinding
them to pieces as it were; brake his
very teeth upon them.

113. *Sly Horace touches, &c.*] Horace, though he spared not vice, even
in his friends, yet he was shrewd
enough to touch it in such a manner
as to please even while he chas-
tised.

114. *And admitted, &c.*] He insinuated himself into the affections,
and seemed in sport, having the
happy art of improving, without
the least appearance of severity or
sneering.

115. *Cunning to hang up, &c.*]—
Suspendere, to hang them or hold
them up to view, as the subjects of
his satires.

Excusso naso here stands in opposition to naribus uncis, supr. l. 58,
see note there, and to the naso adunco
of Horace; and means the unwrinkled
and smooth appearance of the nose
when in good humour, and so,
good-humour itself: Quasi—rugis excusso.

116. *To mutter, &c.*] If others, in

their different ways, could openly satirize, may not I have the liberty of
even muttering, secretly with myself,
or among a few select friends privately.

—Nor with a ditch.] Alluding to
the story of Midas's barber, who,
when he saw the asses ears which
Apollo had placed on the head of
Midas, not daring to tell it to others,
he dug a ditch or furrow in the
earth, and there vented his wish to
speak of it, by whispering what he
had seen.

117. *Nevertheless I will dig here,
&c.*] Though I cannot speak out, yet
I will use my book as the barber did
the ditch; I will secretly commit to
it what I have seen. Infodiam relates to the manner of writing with
the point of an iron bodkin, which
was called a style, on tablets of wood
smeared with wax, so that the writer
might be said to dig or plough the
wax as he made the letters.

—'O little book.'] Here, with indignation, the poet relates, as it were,
to his book (as the barber did to his
ditch) what he had seen; namely, the
absurdity and folly of the modern
taste for poetry, in Nero, in the nobles, and in all their flatterers.

118. *'The ears of an ass.'*] Allud-

Hoc ridere meum, tam nil, nullâ tibi vendo
Iliade.——Audaci quicunque afflate Cratino,   120
Iratum Eupolidem prægrandi cum sene palles,
Aspice et hæc. Si forte aliquid decoctius audis,
Inde vaporatâ lector mihi ferveat aure.
Non hic, qui in crepidas Graiorum ludere gestit
Sordidus, et lusco qui possit dicere, Lusce :   125
Sese aliquem credens, Italo quod honore supinus,
Fregerit heminas Aretî ædilis iniquas.

ing still to the story of Midas, who, finding fault with the judgment of the country deities, when they adjudged the prize to Apollo, in his contention with Pan, had asses' ears fixed on him by Apollo.

Who, says the poet, does not judge of poetry as ill as Midas judged of music? One would think they had all asses' ears given them for their folly. SUET. in Vit. Persii, says, that this line originally stood for mida rex habet, which Cornutus, his friend and instructor, advised him to change to quis non habet? lest it should be thought to point too plainly at Nero.

—*I this hidden thing.*] This secret joke of mine.

119. *This laugh of mine.*] Hoc ridere, for hunc risum, a Græcism; meaning his Satires, in which he derides the objects of them. See l. 9, and note.

119. *Such a nothing.*] So insignificant and worthless in thine opinion, my friend, (comp. l. 2, 3.) and perhaps in the eyes of others, that they would not think them worth reading, as you told me.

—*I sell to thee, &c.*] Nero, as well as Labeo, had written a poem on the destruction of Troy; to these the poet may be supposed to allude, when he says he would not sell his Satires —his nothing, as others esteemed them—for any Iliad : perhaps the word nulla may be understood as extending to Homer himself.

120. *O thou whosoever, &c.*] Afflate—hast read so much of Cratinus, as to be influenced and inspired with his spirit. Cratinus was a Greek comic poet, who, with a peculiar boldness and energy, satirized the

evil manners of his time. The poet is about to describe what sort of readers he chooses for his Satires, and those whom he does not choose.

121. *Art pale.*] With reading and studying hast contracted that paleness of countenance, which is incident to studious people. See JUV. sat. vii. l. 97 ; and Pers. sat. v. l. 62.

—*Angry Eupolis.*] This was another comic poet, who, incensed at the vices of the Athenians, lashed them in the severest manner. He is said to have been thrown into the sea by Alcibiades, for some verses written against him.

—*With the very great old man.*] The poet here meant is Aristophanes, who lived to a very great age. He was of a vehement spirit, had a genius turned to raillery, wit free and elevated, and courage not to fear the person when vice was to be reproved. He wrote thirty-four comedies, whereof eleven only remain.

HOR. lib. i. sat. iv. l. 1, mentions all these three poets together.

Persius gives him the epithet of prægrandi; either on account of his age, for he lived till he was fourscore, or on account of the great eminence of his writings, for he was the prince of the old comedy, as Menander was of the new; but so as we must join, says Ainsworth, Eupolis and Cratinus with the former, Diphilus and Polemon with the latter.

122. *These too behold.*] Look also on these Satires of mine.

—*If haply any thing more refined, &c.*] The poet speaks modestly of his own writings, si forte, (see before l. 41, 2.) if it should so happen, that thou shouldest meet with any thing

This laugh of mine, such a nothing, I sell to thee for no
Iliad. O thou whosoever art inspired by bold Cratinus,
Art pale over angry Eupolis, with the very great old man,
These too behold : if haply any thing more refined you
    - hear,   122
Let the reader glow towards me with an ear evaporated
    from thence.
Not he, who delights to sport on the slippers of the
    Grecians,
Sordid, and who can say to the blinkard, thou blinkard :
Thinking himself somebody; because, lifted up with Ita-
    -lian honour,   126
An ædile he may have broken false measures at Aretium.

more clear, well digested, pure, refined than ordinary. Metaph. taken
from liquors, which, by being often
boiled, lose much of their quantity,
but gain more strength and clearness.
It is said of Virgil, that he would
make fifty verses in a morning, or
more, and in the evening correct and
purge them till they were reduced to
about ten.

123. *Let the reader glow, &c.*] If,
says Persius, there be any thing in my
writings better than ordinary, let the
reader, who has formed his taste on
the writings of the poets above mentioned, glow with a fervour of delight
towards the author. This I take to
be the meaning of the line, which literally is—

Let the reader glow towards me
with an ear evaporated (*i. e.* purified
from the false taste of the present
times) from thence (*i. e.* from, or by,
reading and studying the writings of
Cratinus, &c.)—such' I wish to be
my readers. Vaporo signifies to send
out vapours, to evaporate: thus the
metaphor is continued through both
the lines.

124. *Not he, who delights, &c.*]—
Persius now marks out those who
were not to be chosen for his readers.

The first class of men which he
objects to are those who can laugh
at the persons and habits of philosophers; this bespeaks a despicable,
mean, and sordid mind.

—*Slippers of the Grecians.*] Crepidas Graiorum, a peculiar sort of slippers, or shoes, worn by philosophers

—here put by synec. for the whole
dress; but it is most likely, that Persius here means the philosophers
themselves, and all their wise sayings
and institutes; these were originally
derived from Greece.

125. *Sordid.*] See note, No. 1, above,
at l. 124, ad fin.

—*Say to be blinkard, &c.*] Luscus
is he that has lost an eye, a one-eyed
man.

Persius means those who can up-
braid and deride the natural infirmities or misfortunes of others, by way
of wit :

Can mock the blind : and has the
    wit to cry—
(Prodigious wit!)—" Why, friend,
    " you want an eye."
                           BREWSTER.

126. *Thinking himself somebody.*]
A person of great consequence.

—*Lifted up, &c.*] Puffed up with
self-importance, because bearing an
office in some country-district of Italy,
and therefore flippant of his abuse, by
way of being witty, l. 124-5.

127. *An ædile, &c.*] An inferior
kind of country-magistrate, who had
jurisdiction over weights and measures, and had authority to break and
destroy those which were false. JUV.
sat. x. l 102.

—*Aretium.*] A city of Tuscany,
famous for making earthen-ware, but,
perhaps, put here for any country
town.

So heminas, half sextaries, little
measures holding about three quarters of a pint, are put for mea-

Nec, qui abaco numeros, et secto in pulvere metas,
Scit risisse vafer ; multum gaudere paratus,
Si Cynico barbam petulans Nonaria vellat.   130
His, mane, edictum ; post prandia, Callirhoën, do.

sures in general. Comp. Juv. sat. x. 101–2. -

128. *Nor who, arch, &c.*] Another class of people, which Persius would exclude from the number of his readers, are those who laugh at and despise all science whatsoever.

Abacus signifies a bench, slate, or table, used for accounts by arithmeticians, and for figures by mathematicians—here put for arithmetic. and mathematics.

129. *Bounds in divided dust.*] The geometricians made their demonstrations upon dust, or sanded floors, to the end that their lines might be easily changed and struck out again—here geometry is meant.

130. *Petulant Nonaria, &c.*] Who think it an high joke, if they see an impudent strumpet meet a grave Cynic in the street, and pull him by the beard ; which was the greatest affront that could be offered. Comp. Hor. sat. iii. lib. i. l. 133, 4.

The ninth hour, or our three o'clock in the afternoon, was the time when the harlots made their first appearance ; hence they were called Nonariæ. Perhaps our poet may allude, in this line, to the story of Diogenes, (mentioned by Athen. lib. xiii.) who was in love with Lais, the famous courtezan, and had his beard plucked by her.

131. *In the morning, an edict.*] To such people as these I assign employments suitable to their talents and characters. It has been usually thought, that edictum here means the prætor's edict, and that by Callirhoë

Nor who, arch, knows to laugh at the numbers of an ac-
countable,
And bounds in divided dust; prepared to rejoice much,
If petulant Nonaria should pluck a Cynic's beard.   130
I give to these, in the morning, an edict; after dinner,
Callirhoë.

is meant some harlot of that name; and therefore this line is to be understood, as if Persius meant that these illiterate fellows should attend the forum in the morning, and the brothel in the evening: but the former seems too serious an employ for men such as he is speaking of.

Marcilius, therefore, more reasonably, takes edictum (consonant to the phrases edictum ludorum, edictum muneris gladiatorii, &c.) to signify a programma, a kind of play-bill, which was stuck up, as ours are, in the morning; and Callirhoë to be the title of some wretched play, written on the story of that famous parricide (who slew her father because he would not consent to her marriage) by some of the writers at which this Satire is

levelled, and which was announced to be performed in the evening.

q. d. Instead of wishing such to read my Satires, I consign these pretty gentlemen to the study of the play-bills in the morning, and to an attendance on the play in the evening. Thus this Satire concludes, in conformity with the preceding part of it, with lashing bad writers and their admirers.

Marcilius contends, that this line is to be referred to Nero, against whom, as a poet, this Satire is principally, though covertly, levelled—who, by ordering bills to be distributed, called the people together, in order to hear him sing over his poems on Callirhoë.

Satira Secunda.

—

ARGUMENT.

It being customary among the Romans for one friend to send a present to another on his birth-day—Persius, on the birth-day of his friend Macrinus, presents him with this Satire, which seems (like Juv. Sat. x.) to be founded un Plato's dialogue on prayer, called The Second Alcibiades.

The Poet takes occasion to expose the folly and impiety of those, who, thinking the gods to be like themselves, imagined that they were to be bribed into compliance with their prayers by sumptuous presents; whereas, in truth, the gods regard not these, but regard only the pure intention of an honest heart.

AD PLOTIUM MACRINUM.

HUNC, Macrine, diem numera meliore lapillo,
Qui tibi labentes apponit candidus annos.
Funde merum genio : non tu prece poscis emaci,
(Quæ, nisi seductis, nequeas committere divis :)
At bona pars procerum tacitâ libabit acerrâ.　　　　5

Line 1. Macrinus.] Who this Macrinus was does not sufficiently appear; he was a learned man, and a friend of Persius, who here salutes him on his birth-day.

—Better stone.] The ancients reckoned happy days with white pebbles, and unhappy days with black ones, and at the end of the year cast up the reckoning, by which they could see how many happy, and how many unhappy days had past.

The poet here bids his friend distinguish his birth-day among the happiest of his days, with a better, a whiter stone than ordinary.

2. Which.] i. e. Which day—
—White.] i. e. Happy, good, propitious.

—Adds to thee sliding years.] Sets one more complete year to the score, and begins another.
—Sliding years.]
*Eheu fugaces, Posthume, Posthume,
Labuntur anni.*

HOR. ode xiv. lib. ii.
Years that glide swiftly, and almost imperceptibly away.

3. Pour out wine to your genius.] The genius was a tutelar god, which they believed to preside at their birth, whom they worshipped every year on their birth-day, by making a libation of wine. They did not slay any beast in sacrifice to their genius on that day, because they would not take away life on the day on which they received it. They supposed a genius

Second Satire.

ARGUMENT.

In the course of this Satire, which seems to have given occasion to the Tenth Satire of Juvenal, Persius mentions the impious and hurtful requests which men make, as well as the bad means which they employ to have their wishes fulfilled.

The whole of this Satire is very grave, weighty, and instructive; and, like that of Juvenal, contains sentiments, more like a Christian than an heathen.

Bishop Burnet says, that "this Satire may well pass for "one of the best lectures in divinity."

TO PLOTIUS MACRINUS.

THIS day, Macrinus, number with a better stone,
Which, white, adds to thee sliding years.
Pour out wine to your genius. You do not ask with mercenary prayer,
Which you cannot commit unless to remote gods :
But a good part of our nobles will offer with tacit censer. 5

not only to preside at their birth, but to attend and protect them constantly through their life; therefore, on other days, they sacrificed beasts to their genii.——Hence Hor. lib. iii. ode xvii. l. 14-16.

——*Cras genium mero*
Curabis, et porco bimestri,
Cum famulis operum solutis.

The libation of wine on their birthday was attended also with strewing flowers. The former was an emblem of cheerfulness and festivity; the latter, from their soon fading, of the frailty and shortness of human life.

Hor. epist. i. lib. ii. l. 143-4.

Tellurem porco, Sylvanum lacte piabant,
Floribus et vino genium, memorem brevis ævi.

3. *Mercenary prayer.*] Emaci, from emo, to buy—i. e. with a prayer, with which, as with a bribe, or reward, you were to purchase what you pray for.

4. *Which you cannot commit, &c.*] Which you must offer to the gods in secret, and as if the gods were taken aside, that nobody but themselves should hear what you say to them.

Committere, here, has the sense of —to intrust, to impart.

5. *A good part.*] A great many, a large portion.

So Hor. lib. i. sat. i. l. 61. Bona pars hominum; a good many, as we say.

—*Tacit censer.*] Acerra properly signifies the vessel, or pan, in which the incense is burnt in sacrifice; they

Haud cuivis promptum est, murmurque humilesque su-
    surros
Tollere de templis, et aperto vivere voto.
' Mens bona, fama, fides ; hæc clare, et ut audiat hospes.
Illa sibi introrsum, et sub linguâ immurmurat, ' O si
' Ebullît patrui præclarum funus !—et, O si   10
' Sub rastro crepet argenti mihi seria, dextro
' Hercule !—Pupillumve utinam, quem proximus hæres
' Impello, expungam ! namque est scabiosus, et acri
' Bile tumet—Nerio jam tertia ducitur uxor.'
  Hæc sancte ut poscas, Tiberino in gurgite mergis   15
Mane caput, bis, terque ; et noctem flumine purgas.
  Heus age, responde ; minimum est quod scire laboro :

said their prayers as the smoke of the incense ascended ; but these nobles spake so low, as not to be heard by others, so that the incense seemed silently to ascend, unaccompanied with any words of prayer. This seems to be the meaning of tacita libabit ascerra. In short, their petitions were of such a nature, that they cared not to utter them loud enough for other people to hear them ; they themselves were ashamed of them.

_ 6. *It is not easy, &c.*] As times go, people are not very ready to utter their wishes and prayers publicly, and to remove from the temples of the gods those inward murmurs and low whispers in which their impious petitions are delivered.

7. *And to live, &c.*] i. e. To make it their practice to utter their vows and prayers openly, in the sight and hearing of all.

8. ' *A good mind, reputation,' &c.*] These things, which are laudable and commendable, and to be desired by virtuous people, these they will ask for with a clear and audible voice, so that any stander-by may hear them perfectly.

9. *Those, &c.*] i. e. Those things that follow (which are impious and scandalous) and which he does not care should be heard by others, he mutters inwardly.

—*Under his tongue.*] Keeps them within his mouth, fearing to let them pass his lips.

10. ' *The pompous funeral.'*] One prays for the death of a rich uncle.

—' *Bubble up.'*] i. e. Appears in all its pomp. Ebullit, for ebullierit—metaph. from water when boiling up, which swells, as it were, and runs over.

11. ' *A pot of silver,' &c.*] Another prays that he may find a vessel of hidden treasure, as he is raking his field. See Hor. lib. ii. sat. vi. l. 10.

—' *Hercules, &c.*] He was supposed to preside over hidden treasures.

12. *Or my ward, &c.*] If it were not to be his lot to have his avarice gratified by finding hidden treasure, yet, says this covetous suppliant— " I have a rich orphan under my " care, to whom I am heir at law, O " that I could but put him out of the " way !" Expungam—blot him out.

13. ' *Impel.'*] A metaph. taken from one wave driving on another, and succeeding in its place.

—' *He is scabby.' &c.*] Here is an instance of the petitioner's hypocrisy —he pretends not to wish his pupil's death, that he might inherit his estate, but out of compassion to an unhealthy young man ; pretends to wish him dead, that he may be released from his sufferings, from his scrophulous disorders.

14. ' *A third wife,' &c.*] Another prays for the death of his wife, that he may be possessed of all she has, and that he may get a fresh fortune by marrying again. He thinks it very hard that he cannot get rid of one, when Nerius, the usurer, has been

It is not easy to every one, their murmur, and low whispers
To remove from the temples, and to live with open prayer.
' A good mind, reputation, fidelity ;' these clearly, that a
    stranger may hear.
Those inwardly to himself and under his tongue he mut-
    ters—' O if
' The pompous funeral of my uncle might bubble up ? O if
' Under my rake a pot of silver might chink, Hercules
    ' being propitious   11
' To me ! or my ward, whom I the next heir
' Impel, I wish I could expunge ! for he is a scabby, and
    ' with sharp
' Bile he swells. A third wife is already married by
    ' Nerius.'
   That you may ask these things holily, in the river Tiber
    you dip   15
Your head in the morning two or three times, and purge
    the night with the stream.
   Consider, mind, answer, (it is a small thing which I
    labour to know,)

so lucky as to bury two, and is now possessed of a third. On the death of the wife, her fortune went to the husband; even what the father had settled out of his estate, if his daughter survived him.

15. *That you may ask, &c.*] That the gods may be propitious, and give a favourable answer to your prayers, you leave no rite or ceremony unobserved, to sanctify your person, and render yourself acceptable.

—*In the river Tiber, &c.*] It was a custom among the ancients, when they had vows or prayers to make, or to go about any thing of the religious or sacred kind, to purify themselves by washing in running water.

Attrectare nefas, donec me flumine vivo
Abluero—
          See Æn. ii. l. 719, 20.

Hence the Romans washed in the river Tiber—sometimes the head, sometimes the hands, sometimes the whole body.

—*You dip.*] Or put under water. Those who were to sacrifice to the infernal gods only sprinkled themselves with water; but the sacrificers to the heavenly deities plunged themselves

into the river, and put their heads under water.

16. *In the morning.*] At the rising of the sun; the time when they observed this solemnity in honour of the cœlestial gods: their ablutions in honour of the Dii Manes, and infernal gods, were performed at the setting of the sun.

—*Two or three times.*] The number three was looked upon as sacred in religious matters.

Terna tibi hæc primum triplici diversa colore
Licia circumdo, terque hæc altaria circum
Effigiem duco: numero Deus impare gaudet.
VIRG. ecl. viii. l. 73-5; and note there, 75. Delph. See G. i. 345.

—*Purge the night, &c.*] After nocturnal pollution they washed.— Comp. Deut. xxiii. 10, 11. The ancients thought themselves polluted by the night itself, as well as by bad dreams in the night, and therefore purified themselves by washing their hands and heads every morning; which custom the Turks observe to this day.

17. *Consider, mind, &c.*] The poet,

2 U

De Jove quid sentis ?—Estne ut præponere cures
Hunc Cuiquam !—Cuinam ? vis Staio ? an, scilicet, hæres?
Quis potior judex ? puerisve quis aptior orbis ?　　　　20
Hoc igitur, quo tu Jovis aurem impellere tentas,
Dic agedum Staio.　Proh Jupiter ! O bone, clamet,
Jupiter !—At sese non clamet Jupiter ipse ?
Ignovisse putas, quia. cum tonat, ocyus ilex
Sulfure discutitur sacro, quam tuque domusque ?　　　　25
An, quia non fibris ovium, Ergennâque jubente,
Triste jaces lucis, evitandumque bidental,
Idcirco stolidam præbet tibi vellere barbam
Jupiter ? Aut quidnam est, quâ tu mercede deorum
Emeris auriculas ? pulmone, et lactibus unctis ?　　　　30
-Ecce avia, aut metuens divûm matertera, cunis
Exemit puerum, frontemque, atque uda labella,

having stated the impiety of these
worshippers, now remonstrates with
them on their insult offered to the
gods.　See AINSW. *Heus*, No. 3.
. " Come," says he, "let me ask
" you a short question."
　18. *What think you of Jove ?*]—
What are your notions, what your
conceptions of the god which you
pray to, and profess to honour ?
—*Is he, that you would care, &c.*]
Do you think him preferable to any
mortal man ?
　19, *To whom*—] Do you prefer
him ?
　—*Will you to Staius ?*] Will you
prefer him to Staius?
　—*Do you doubt, &c.*] Do you hesitate in determining ? which is the
best judge, or the best guardian of
orphans, Jupiter or Staius ? From this
it appears that this Statius was some
notorious wretch, who had behaved ill
in both these capacities.
　22. *Say it to Staius.*] As you must
allow Staius not comparable to Jupiter, but, on the contrary, a very vile
and wicked man, I would have you,
that you may judge the better of the
nature of your petitions, propose to
Staius what you have proposed to
Jupiter—how would Staius receive
it ?
　—*O Jupiter ! &c. would he cry.*]
Even Staius, bad as he is, would be
shocked and astonished, and call on
Jupiter for vengeance on your head.

　23. *And may not Jupiter, &c.*]—
Think you that Jupiter then may not,
with the highest justice, as well as
indignation, call on himself for vengeance on you ?
　24. *To have forgiven.*] Do you
suppose that Jupiter is reconciled to
your treatment of him, because you
and yours are visited with no marks
of divine vengeance ?
　26. *Bowels of sheep.*] Offered in
sacrifice by way of expiation.
　—*Ergenna.*] Ergenna was the
name of some famous soothsayer,
whose office it was to divine, by inspecting the entrails of the sacrifices.
　27. *A sad bidental.*] When any
person was struck dead by lightning,
immediately the priest came and buried the body, enclosed the place, and
erecting there an altar, sacrificed two
two-year old sheep (bidentes)—hence
the word bidental is applied by authors, indifferently, to the sacrifice,
to the place, or (as here) to the
person.
　—*In the groves.*] Or woods, where
the oak was rent with lightning, and
where you remained unhurt. Comp.
l. 24—5.
　28. *Jupiter offer you, &c.*] Because
you have hitherto escaped, do you
imagine that you are at full liberty to
insult Jupiter as you please, and this
with impunity, and even with the
divine permission and approbation ?

What think you of Jove? is he, that you would care to
    prefer
Him to any one? to whom? will you to Staius? what!—
    do you doubt?
Who is the better judge? who the fittest for orphan chil-
    dren?   20
This, therefore, with which you try to persuade the ear of
    Jove,
Come, say it to Staius: O Jupiter! O good Jupiter! would
    he cry:
And may not Jupiter cry out upon himself?
Do you think him to have forgiven, because, when he
    thunders, the oak sooner
Is thrown down, by the sacred sulphur, than both you, and
    your house?   25
Or because, with the bowels of sheep, Ergenna commanding,
You do not lie a sad, and to-be-avoided bidental, in the
    groves,
Therefore does Jupiter offer you his foolish beard to pluck?
Or what is it? with what reward hast thou bought the ears
Of the gods? with lungs, and with greasy entrails?   30
Lo! a grandmother, or an aunt fearing the gods, from
    the cradle
Takes a boy, and his forehead and his wet lips,

Plucking or pulling a person by the beard was one of the highest marks of contempt and insult that could be offered—see sat. i. l. 129, note; for the beard was cherished and respected as a mark of gravity and wisdom—see Juv. sat. xiv. 12, note.

29. *Or what is it!*] i. e. What hast thou done, that thou art in such high favour with the gods?

—*With what reward, &c.*] With what bribe hast thou purchased the divine attention?

30. *With lungs.*] Contemptuously put here, per. meton. for any of the larger intestines of beasts offered in sacrifice.

—*And with greasy entrails.*] Lactes signifies the small guts, through which the meat passeth first out of the stomach; perhaps so called from the lacteals, or small vessels, the mouths of which open into them to receive the chyle, which is of a white or milky colour. The poet says,

unctis lactibus, because they are surrounded with fat.

The poet mentions these too in a sneering way, as if he had said, "What! do you think that you have "corrupted the gods with lungs and "guts?"

31. *Lo! a grandmother, &c.*[The poet now proceeds to expose the folly of those prayers which old women make for children.

—*An aunt.*] Matertera—quasi mater altera—the mother's sister, the aunt on the mother's side, as amita is on the father's side.

—*Fearing the gods.*] Metuens divûm—superstitious; for all superstition proceeds from fear and terror; it is therefore that superstitious people are called in Greek δεισιδαιμονες, from δειδω, to fear, and δαιμων, a dæmon, a god. See Acts xvii. 22.

32. *His forehead, &c.*] Persius here ridicules the foolish and superstitious rites which women observed on these occasions.

Infami digito, et lustralibus ante salivis
Expiat; urentes oculos inhibere perita.
Tunc manibus quatit, et spem macram, supplice voto, 35
Nunc Licinî in campos, nunc Crassi mittit in ædes.
' Hunc optent generum rex et regina! puellæ.
' Hunc rapiant! quicquid calcaverit hic, rosâ fiat!'
Ast ego nutrici non mando vota: negato,
Jupiter, hæc illi, quamvis te albata rogarit. 40
Poscis opem nervis, corpusque fidele senectæ:
Esto, age: sed grandes patinæ, tucetaque crassa
Annuere his superos vetuere, Jovemque morantur.
Rem struere exoptas, cæso bove; Mercuriumque

First, after having taken the infant out of the cradle, they, before they began their prayers, wetted the middle finger with spittle, with which they anointed the forehead and lips of the child, by way of expiation, and preservative against magic.

32. *Wet lips.*] i. e. Of the child, which are usually wet with drivel from the mouth.

33. *Infamous finger.*] The middle finger, called infamis, from its being made use of in a way of scorn to point at infamous people. See JUV. sat. x. l. 53, and note.

—*Purifying spittle.*] They thought fasting spittle to contain great virtue against fascination, or an evil eye; therefore with that, mixed with dust, they rubbed the forehead and lips by way of preservative. Thus in Petronius—" Mox turbatum sputo pulverem, anus medio sustulit digito, frontemque repugnantis signat."

—*She beforehand.*] i. e. Before she begins her prayers for the child.

34. *Expiates.*] See above, note on l. 32, ad fin.

Skilled to inhibit, &c.] Skilful to hinder the fascination of bewitching eyes. Uro signifies, lit. to burn; also to injure or destroy. VIRG. G. ii. l. 196. One sort of witchcraft was supposed to operate by the influence of the eye. VIRG. ecl. iii. 103.

35. *Then shakes him, &c.*] Lifts him up, and dandles him to and fro, as if to present him to the gods.

—*Her slender hope.*] The little tender infant.

—*With suppliant wish.*] Or prayer.

Having finished her superstitious rites of lustration, she now offers her wishes and prayers for the infant.

36. *She now sends, &c.*] Mittit is a law term, and taken from the prætor's putting a person in possession of an estate which was recovered at law. Here it denotes the old woman's wishing, and, in desire, putting the child in possession of great riches, having her eye on the possessions of Crassus and Licinius, the former of which (says Plutarch) purchased so many houses, that, at one time or other, the greatest part of Rome came into his hands. Licinius was a young slave of so saving a temper, that he let out the offals of his meat for interest, and kept a register of debtors. Afterwards he was made a collector in Gaul, where he acquired (as Persius elsewhere expresses it, quantum non milvus oberret) " more lands than a " kite could fly over."

37. ' *King and queen wish,' &c.*]—May he be so opulent as that even crowned heads may covet an alliance with him as a son-in-law.

37–8. ' *Girls seize him.'*] May he be so beautiful and comely, the girls may all fall in love with him, and contend who shall first seize him for her own.

38. ' *Shall have trodden upon,' &c.*] This foolish, extravagant hyperbole well represents the vanity and folly of these old women, in their wishes for the children.

39. *But to a nurse, &c.*] For my part, says Persius, I shall never leave it to my nurse to pray for my child.

With infamous finger, and with purifying spittle, she
    beforehand
Expiates, skilled to inhibit destructive eyes.
Then shakes him in her hands, and her slender hope, with
    suppliant wish,   35
She now sends into the fields of Licinius, now into the
    houses of Crassus.
' May a king and queen wish this boy their son-in-law;
    ' may the girls
' Seize him; whatever he shall have trodden upon, may it
    ' become a rose !'
But to a nurse I do not commit prayers : deny,
O Jupiter, these to her, though clothed in white she should
    ask.   40
You ask strength for your nerves, and a body faithful to
    old age :
Be it so—go on : but great dishes, and fat sausages,
Have forbidden the gods to assent to these, and hinder
    Jove.
You wish heartily to raise a fortune, an ox being slain,
    and Mercury

39-40. *Deny, O Jupiter, &c.*] If
she should ever pray thus for a child
of mine, I beseech thee, O Jupiter,
to deny such petitions as these, however solemnly she may offer them.

40. *Tho' cloth'd in white.*] Though
arrayed in sacrificial garments. The
ancients, when they sacrificed and
offered to the gods, were clothed with
white garments, as emblems of innocence and purity.

41. *You ask strength, &c.*] Another prays for strength of nerves, and
that his body may not fail him when
he comes to be old.

42. *Be it so—go on.*] I see no harm
in this, says Persius; you ask nothing but what may be reasonably desired, therefore I don't find fault with
your praying for these things—go on
with your petitions.

—*Great dishes.*] But while you are
praying for strength of body, and for
an healthy old age, you are destroying your health, and laying in for a
diseased old age, by your gluttony
and luxury.

—*Sausages.*] Tuceta, a kind of
meat made of pork or beef chopped,
or other stuff, mingled with suet.

43. *Have forbidden, &c.*] While
you are praying one way, and living
another, you yourself hinder the gods
from granting your wishes.

—*Hinder Jove.*] Prevent his giving you health and strength, by your
own destroying both.

The poet here ridicules those in-
consistent people, who pray for health
and strength of body, and yet live
in such a manner as to impair both.
nothing but a youth of temperance
is likely to ensure an old age of
health. This is finely touched by the
masterly pen of our Shakespeare :

  Tho' I look old, yet I am strong
    and lusty :
  For in my youth I never did apply
  Hot and rebellious liquors in my
    blood ;
  Nor did not with unbashful fore-
    head woo
  The means of weakness and debility ;
  Therefore my age is as a lusty
    winter,
  Frosty, but kindly——
    As you like it, act ii. sc. iii.

44. *You wish, &c.*] Another is endeavouring to advance his fortune by
offering costly sacrifices, little think-

Arcessis fibrâ : ' da fortunare penates !   45
' Da pecus, et gregibus fœtum !'—Quo, pessime, pacto,
Tot tibi cum in flammis junicum omenta liquescant ?
Et tamen hic extis, et opimo vincere farto
Intendit: ' jam crescit ager, jam crescit ovile :
' Jam dabitur, jam jam :' donec deceptus, et exspes,   50
Nequicquam fundo suspiret nummus in imo.
Si tibi crateras argenti, incusaque pingui
Auro dona feram, sudes; et pectore lævo
Excutias guttas : lætari prætrepidum cor.
Hinc illud subiit, auro sacras quod ovato   55
Perducis facies.   Nam, fratres inter ahenos,
Somnia pituitâ qui purgatissima mittunt,
Præcipui sunto ; sitque illis aurea barba.

---

ing that these are diminishing what he wants to augment.

—*Ox being slain.*] i. e. In sacrifice—in order to render the god propitious; but you don't recollect that by this you have an ox the less.

—*Mercury.*] The god of gain.

45. *You invite.*] Arcessis—send for, as it were—invite to favour you.

—*With inwards.*] Extis, the entrails of beasts offered in sacrifice.

—" *The household gods,*" &c.] " Grant, O Mercury," say you, " that " my domestic affairs may prosper." See AINSW. *Penates.*

46. " *Give cattle,*" &c.] Grant me a number of cattle, and let all my flocks be fruitful, and increase !

46. *Wretch, by what means ?*]—How, thou silliest of men, can this be ?

47. *When the cauls of so many,* &c.] When you are every day preventing all this, by sacrificing your female beasts before they are old enough to breed, and thus, in a two-fold manner, destroying your stock ?

—*The cauls.*] Omentum is the caul or fat that covers the inwards.

—*Melt in flames.*] Being put on the fire on the altar.

—*For you.*] In hopes to obtain what you want.

48. *Yet this man,* &c.] Thinks he shall overcome the gods with the multitude of sacrifices which he offers—this is his intention.

—*With bowels.*] The inwards of beasts offered in sacrifice.

—*A rich pudding.*] They offered a sort of pudding, or cake, made of bran, wine, and honey.

49. " *Now the field increases.*"] Says he, fancying his land is better for what he has been doing.

—" *Now the sheep-fold.*] " Now " methinks my sheep breed better."

50. " *Now it shall be given,*" &c.] " Methinks I already see my wishes " fulfilled—every thing will be given " me that I asked for."

—" *Now presently.*"] " I shall not " be able to wait much longer."

—*Till deceived and hopeless.*] Till, at length, he finds his error, and that, by hoping to increase his fortune by the multitude of his sacrifices, he has only just so far diminished it—he has nothing left but one poor solitary sesterce at the bottom of his purse, or chest ; which, finding itself deceived, and hopeless of any accession to it, sighs, as it were, in vain, for the loss of its companions, which have been so foolishly spent and thrown away.

The Roman nummus, when mentioned as a piece of money, was the same with the sestertius, about one penny three farthings. The prosopopeia here is very humourous.

52. *If to thee cups,* &c.] Men are apt to think the gods like themselves, pleased with rich and costly gifts—to such the poet now speaks.

If, saith Persius, I should make you a present of a fine piece of silver plate, or of some costly vessel of the finest gold—

You invite with inwards—" grant the household gods to
 " make me prosperous !   45,
" Give cattle, and offspring to my flocks !"—Wretch, by
  what means,
When the cauls of so many young heifers can melt for you
  in flames?
And yet this man to prevail with bowels, and with a rich
  pudding
Intends; " Now the field increases, now the sheep-fold—
" Now it shall be given, now presently :" till deceived, and
  hopeless,   50
In vain the nummus will sigh in the lowest bottom.
  If to thee cups of silver, and gifts wrought with rich gold
I should bring, you would sweat, and from your left breast
Shake out drops—your over-trembling heart would rejoice.
Hence that takes place, that with gold carried in triumph
  you   55
Overlay the sacred faces. For, among the brazen brothers,
Let those who send dreams most purged from phlegm,
Be the chief, and let them have a golden beard.

53. *You would sweat.*] You would
be so pleased and overjoyed, that you
would break into a sweat with agitation.
 —*Left breast.*] They supposed the
heart to lie on the left side.
 54. *Shake out drops.*] i. e. You
would weep, or shed tears. Lachrymas excutere, to force tears. TER.
Heaut. act i. sc. i. l. 115. Tears of
joy would drop, as it were, from your
very heart. Lachrymor præ gaudio.
TER. Some understand Lævo here in
the sense of foolish, silly ; as in
VIRG. ecl. i. 16. Casaub.
 —*Your over-trembling heart, &c.*]
Palpitating with unusual motion, from
the suddenness and emotion of your
surprise and joy, would be delighted.
 55. *That takes place.*] The notion
or sentiment takes place in your
mind, that, because you are so overjoyed at receiving a rich and sumptuous present of silver or gold, therefore the gods must be so too—judging of them by yourself.
 —*Gold carried in triumph, &c.*]
Hence, with the gold taken as a spoil
from an enemy, and adorning the
triumph of the conqueror, by being

carried with him in his ovation, you
overlay the images of the gods—thus
complimenting the gods with what
has been taken from your fellow mortals by rapine and plunder.
 56. *The brazen brothers.*] There
stood in the porch of the Palatine
Apollo fifty brazen statues of the fifty
sons of Ægyptus, the brother of Danaus, who, having fifty sons, married
them to the fifty daughters of Danaus,
and, by their father's order, they all
slew their husbands in the night of
their marriage, except Hypermnes-
tra, who saved Lynceus. See HOR.
lib. iii. ode xi. l. 30, &c.
 These were believed to have great
power of giving answers to their inquirers, in dreams of the night, relative to cures of disorders.
 57. *Most purged, &c.*] Most clear
and true, as most defecated and uninfluenced by the gross humours of
the body.
 58. *Be the chief.*] Let these be had
in honour above the rest—q. d. Bestow most on those from whom you
expect most.
 —*A golden beard.*] This alludes to
the image of Æsculapius, in the temple of Epidaurum, which was sup-

Aurum vasa Numæ, Saturniaque impulit æra :
Vestalesque urnas, et Tuscum fictile mutat.   60
O curvæ in terras animæ, et cœlestium inanes !
Quid juvat hoc, templis nostros immittere mores,
Et bona diis ex hac scelerata ducere pulpa ?
Hæc sibi corrupto Casiam dissolvit olivo ;
Et Calabrum coxit, vitiato murice, vellus.   65
Hæc baccam conchæ rasisse ; et stringere venas
Ferventis massæ, crudo de pulvere, jussit.
Peccat et hæc, peccat : vitio tamen utitur. At vos
Dicite, pontifices, in sacris quid facit aurum ?)
Nempe hoc, quod Veneri donatæ a virgine pupæ.   70
Quin damus id superis, de magna quod dare lance

posed to reveal remedies for disorders in dreams. This image had a golden beard, which Dionysius the tyrant of Syracuse took away, saying jestingly, that, "as the father of Æsculapius, "Apollo, had no beard, it was not "right for the son to have one."

This communicating, through dreams, such remedies as were adapted to the cure of the several disorders of the inquirers, was at first accounted the province of Apollo and Æsculapius only ; but, on the breaking out of Egyptian superstition, Isis and Osiris were allowed to have the same power, as were also the fifty sons of Ægyptus, here called the brazen brothers, from their statues of brass.

59. Driven away, &c.] Has quite expelled from the temples the plain and simple vessels made use of in the days of Numa, the first founder of our religious rites.

—The Saturnian brass.] The brazen vessels which were in use when Saturn reigned in Italy.

60. Changes the vestal urns.] The pitchers, pots, and other vessels, which the vestal virgins used in celebrating the rites of Vesta, and which were anciently of earthen-ware, are now changed into gold.

60. The Tuscan earthen-ware.]—Aretium, a city of Tusdany, was famous for earthen-ware, from whence it was carried to Rome, and to other parts of Italy. This was now grown quite out of use. Comp. Juv. sat. iii. l. 157.

The poet means to say, that people, now-a-days, had banished all the simple vessels of the ancient and primitive worship, and now, imagining the gods were as fond of gold as they were, thought to succeed in their petitions, by lavishing gold on their images. Comp. Isa. xlvi. 6.

61. O souls bowed, &c.] This apostrophe, and what follows to the end, contain sentiments worthy the pen of a Christian.

62. What doth this avail.] What profiteth it.

—To place our manners, &c.] Immittere,—to admit, or suffer to enter. Our manners—i. e. our ways of thinking, our principles of action—who, because we so highly value, and are so easily influenced by rich gifts, think the gods will be so too. See Ainsw. Immitto, No. 3, and 7.

63. And to esteem, &c.] To prescribe, infer, or reckon what is good in their sight, and acceptable to them.

—Out of this wicked pulp.] From the dictates of this corrupted and depraved flesh of ours. Flesh here, as often in Scripture, means the fleshly, carnal mind, influenced by, and under the dominion of, the bodily appetites —των σαρκικων επιθυμιων, 1 Pet. ii. 11. "That which is born of the "flesh is flesh." John iii. 6.

Pulpa literally means the pulp, the fleshy part of any meat—a piece of flesh without bone. Ainsw.

64. This.] This same flesh—

—Dissolves for itself Cassia.] Cas-

Gold has driven away the vessels of Numa, and the
　　Saturnian brass,
And changes the vestal urns, and the Tuscan earthen-
　　ware.　　　　　　　　　　　　　　　　　60
O souls bowed to the earth—and void of heavenly things!
What doth this avail, to place our manners in the temples,
And to esteem things good to the gods out of this wicked
　　pulp?
This dissolves for itself Cassia in corrupted oil,
And hath boiled the Calabrian fleece in vitiated purple.
This has commanded to scrape the pearl of a shell, and to
　　draw the veins　　　　　　　　　　　　　　66
Of the fervent mass from the crude dust.
This also sins, it sins: yet uses vice. But ye,
O ye priests, say what gold does in sacred things?
Truly this, which dolls given by a virgin to Venus.　　70
　　But let us give that to the gods, which, to give from a
　　　great dish,

sia, a sweet shrub, bearing spice like
cinnamon, here put for the spice ; of
this and other aromatics mingled with
oil, which was hereby corrupted from
its simplicity, they made perfumes,
with which they anointed themselves.

65. *Hath boiled, &c.*] To give the
wool a purple dye, in order to make
it into splendid and sumptuous garments.

The best and finest wool came
from Calabria. The murex was a
shell-fish, of the blood of which the
purple dye was made. The best were
found about Tyre. See VIRG. Æn.
iv. 262. HOR. epod. xii. 21.—Vitiated—*i. e.* corrupted to the purposes
of luxury.

66. *To scrape, &c.*] This same
pulp, or carnal mind, first taught
men to extract pearls from the shell
of the pearl-oyster, in order to adorn
themselves.

—*And to draw, &c.*] Stringere—
to bring into a body or lump (AINSW.)
the veins of gold and silver, by melting down the crude ore. Ferventis
massæ—the mass of gold or silver
ore heated to fusion in a furnace, and
thus separating them from the dross
and earthly particles.

The poet is shewing that the same
depraved and corrupt principle, which
leads men to imagine the gods to be

like themselves; and to be pleased
with gold and silver because men are,
is the inventor and contriver of all
manner of luxury and sensual gratifications.

68. *This also sins, &c.*] This evil
corrupted flesh is the parent of all sin,
both in principle and practice. Comp.
Rom. vii. 18–24.

—*Yet uses vice.*] Makes some use
of vice, by way of getting some emolument from it, some profit or pleasure.

69. *O ye priests, &c.*] But tell
me, ye ministers of the gods, who
may be presumed to know better than
others, what pleasure, profit, or emolument, is there to the gods, from all
the gold with which the temples are
furnished and decorated?

70. *Truly this, &c.*] The poet answers for them—" Just as much as
" there is to Venus, when girls offer
" dolls to her." Pupa, a puppet, a
baby, or doll, such as girls played with
while little, and, being grown big,
and going to be married, offered to
Venus, hoping, by this, to obtain her
favour, and to be made mothers of
real children. The boys offered their
bullæ to their household gods. JUV.
sat. xiii. 33, note.

71. *But let us give, &c.*] The poet
is now about to shew with what sacri-

2 x

Non possit magni Messalæ lippa propago :
Compositum jus, fasque animi ; sanctosque recessus
Mentis, et incoctum generoso pectus honesto.
Hæc cedo, ut admoveam templis, et farre litabo.   75

fices the gods will be pleased, and
consequently what should be offered.
—*A great dish.*] The lanx—lit. a
deep dish—signifies a large censer,
appropriated to the rich ; but sometimes they made use of the ascerra
(v. 5.) a small censer appropriated to
the poor.

72. *The blear-eyed race, &c.*] Val.
Corv. Messala took his name from
Messana, a city of Sicily, which was
besieged and taken by him ; he was
the head of the illustrious family of
the Messalæ. The poet here aims at
a descendant of his, who degenerated
from the family, and so devoted him-

self to gluttony, drunkenness, and
luxury of all kinds, that, in his old
age, his eyelids turned inside out.

Let us offer to the gods, says Persius, that which such as the Messalæ
have not to offer, however large their
censers may be, or however great the
quantities of the incense put within
them.

73. *What is just and right.*] Jus
is properly that which is agreeable to
the laws of man—fas, that which is
agreeable to the divine laws.

— *Disposed.*] Settled, fashioned,
set in order or composed, fitted, set
together, within the soul. It is very

The blear-eyed race of great Messala could not—
What is just and right disposed within the soul, and the
    sacred recesses
Of the mind, and a breast imbued with generous honesty—
    These give me, that I may bring to the temples, and I
      will sacrifice with meal.   75

difficult to give the full idea of compositum in this place by any single
word in our language.

73-4. *The sacred recesses of the
mind.*] The inward thoughts and
affections — what St. Paul calls
τα κρυπτα των ανθρωπων. Rom.
ii. 16. Prov. xxiii. 26.

74. *A breast imbued, &c.*] Incoctum—metaph. taken from wool, which
is boiled, and so thoroughly tinged
with the dye. It signifies that which
is infused; not barely dipped, as it
were, so as to be lightly tinged, but
thoroughly soaked, so as to imbibe
the colour. See VIRG. G. iii. 307.

75. *That I may bring to the temples.*] Let me be possessed of these,
that I may with these approach the
gods, and then a little cake of meal
will be a sufficient offering. Comp.
VIRG. Æn. v. l. 745; and HOR. lib.
iii. ode xxiii. l. 17, &c.

Lito not only signifies to sacrifice,
but, by that sacrifice, to obtain what
is sought for.

    *Tum Jupiter faciat ut semper
    Sacrificem, nec unquam liteni*
              PLAUT. in Persa.

Satira Tertia.

ARGUMENT.

Persius in this Satire, in the person of a Stoic preceptor, upbraids the young men with sloth, and with neglect of the study of philosophy. He shews the sad consequences which will attend them throughout life, if they do not apply themselves early to the knowledge of virtue.

NEMPE hæc assidue? Jam clarum mane fenestras
Intrat, et angustas extendit lumine rimas.
Stertimus, indomitum quod despumare Falernum
Sufficiat, quintâ dum linea tangitur umbrâ.
En, quid agis? siccas insana canicula messes   5

Line 1. " *What—these things con-*
" *stantly ?*"] The poet here introduces a philosopher, rousing the pupils under his care from their sloth,
and chiding them for lying so late in
bed. " What," says he, " is this to
" be every day's practice."
  —" *Already the clear morning,*"
&c.] *q. d.* You ought to be up and at
your studies by break of day; but
here you are lounging in bed at full
day-light, which is now shining in at
the windows of your bed-room.'.
  2. " *Extends with light, &c.*]—
Makes them appear wider, say some.
But Casaubon treats this as a foolish
interpretation. He says, that this is
an " Hypallage. Not that the chinks
" are extended, or dilated, quod qui-
" dem inepte scribunt, but the light
" is extended, the sun transmitting
" its rays through the chinks of the
" lattices."
  Dr. Sheridan says—" this image
" (angustas extendit lumine rimas)
" very beautifully expresses the widen-
" ing of a chink by the admission of
" light." But I do not understand
how the light can be said to widen a
chink, if we take the word widen in

its usual sense, of making any thing
wider than it was. Perhaps we may
understand the verb extendit, here,
as extending to view—*i. e.* making
visible the interstices of the lattices,
which, in the dark, are imperceptible
to the sight, but when the morning
enters become apparent. It should
seem, from this passage, that the fenestræ of the Romans were lattice
windows.
  But the best way is to abide by experience, which is in favour of the
first explanation; for when the bright
sun shines through any chink or
crack, there is a dazzling which makes
the chink or crack appear wider than
it really is. Of the first glass windows, see Jortin, Rem. vol. iv. p.
196.
  3. " *We snore.*"] Stertimus—*i. e.*
stertitis. The poet represents the
philosopher speaking in the first person, but it is to be understood in
the second—" We students," says he,
as if he included himself, but meaning, no doubt, those to whom he
spake. Comp. sat. i. l. 13.
  —" *To digest untamed,*" *&c.*] Instead of rising to study, we (*i. e.* ye

Third Satire.

ARGUMENT.

The title of this Satire, in some ancient manuscripts, was, " The Reproach of Idleness ;" though in others it is inscribed, " Against the Luxury and Vices of the Rich ;"— in both of which the poet pursues his intention, but principally in the former.

" WHAT—these things constantly ? Already the clear
 " morning enters
" The windows, and extends with light the narrow chinks.
" We snore, what to digest untamed Falernan
" Might suffice : the line is already touched with the fifth
 " shadow.
" Lo ! what do you ? the mad dog-star the dry harvests 5

young men) are sleeping, as long as would suffice to get rid of the fumes of wine, and make a man sober, though he went to bed ever so drunk.

—" To digest."] Despumare— metaph. taken from a new wine, or any other fermenting liquor, which rises in froth or scum : the taking off this scum or froth was the way to make the liquor clear, and to quiet its working. Thus the Falernan, which was apt, when too much was drunk of it, to ferment in the stomach, was quieted and digested by sleep. The epithet indomitum refers to this fermenting quality of the wine.

Perhaps the master here alludes to the irregularities of these students, who, instead of going to bed at a reasonable hour and sober, sat up late drinking, and went to bed with their stomachs full of Falernan wine.

4. " The line is already touched," &c.] Hypallage ; for quinta linea jam tangitur umbra, i. e. the fifth line,

the line or stroke which marks the fifth hour, is touched with the shadow of the gnomon on the sun-dial.

The ancient Romans divided the natural day into twelve parts. Sun-rising was called the first hour ; the third after sun-rising answers to our nine o'clock ; the sixth hour was noon ; the ninth answers to our three o'clock P. M. and the twelfth was the setting of the sun, which we call six o'clock P. M. The fifth hour, then, among the Romans, answers to our eleven o'clock A. M. The students slept till eleven—near half the day.

5. " Lo ! what do you ?"] What are you at—why don't you get up ?

—" The mad dog-star."] Cani-cula—a constellation, which was supposed to arise in the midst of summer, when the sun entered Leo ; with us the dog-days. This is reckoned the hottest time in the year ; and the ancients had a notion, that the influence of the dog-star occa-

Jamdudum coquit, et patulâ pecus omne sub ulmo est.
Unus ait comitum, 'Verumne? Itane? Ocius adsit
' Huc aliquis.   Nemon'? Turgescit vitrea bilis:
Finditur, Arcadiæ pecuaria rudere credas.
Jam liber, et bicolor positis membrana capillis,   10
Inque manus chartæ, nodosaque venit arundo.
Tum queritur, crassus calamo quod pendeat humor;
Nigra quod infusâ vanescat sepia lymphâ:
Dilutas, queritur, geminet quod fistula guttas.
O miser, inque dies ultra miser ! huccine rerum   15
Venimus? at cur non potius, teneroque columbo
Et similis regum pueris, pappare minutum

sioned many disorders among the human species, but especially madness in dogs.

Jam Procyon furit,
Et stella vesani Leonis,
Sole dies referente siccos.
   HOR. ode xxix. lib. iii. l. 18-20.
   Rabiosi tempora signi.
      HOR. sat. vi. lib. i. l. 126.
   The dog-star rages.   POPE.

6. " *Long since is ripening.*"]— They supposed that the intense heat, at that time of the year, was occasioned by the dog-star, which rose with the sun, and forwarded the ripening of the corn.   The poets followed this vulgar error, which sprang from the rising of the dog-star when the sun entered into Leo; but this star is not the cause of greater heat, which is, in truth, only the effect of the particular situation of the sun at that season.

—" *All the flock,*" &c.]
Jam pastor umbras cum grege languido
Rivumque fessus quærit, et horridi
Dumeta Silvani——
   HOR. ode xxix. lib. iii. l. 21-3.
   Nunc etiam pecudes umbras et frigora captant.
      VIRG. ecl. ii. 8.

7. *Fellow students.*] This seems to be the meaning of comites in this place.

—" *Quick,*" &c.] Let some of the servants come immediately, and bring my clothes, that I may get up.

8. " *Is there nobody,*" &c.] = Does nobody hear me call?

—*Vitreous bile swells.*] He falls

into a violent passion at nobody's answering.

Horace speaks of splendida bilis, clear bile—*i. e.* furious—in opposition to the atra bilis, black bile, which produces melancholy. This is probably the meaning of vitrea, glassy, in this place.

9. " *I am split.*"] Says the youth, with calling so loud for somebody to come to me—

—" *That you'd believe,*" &c.] You may well say you are ready to split, for you make such a noise, that one would think that all the asses in Arcadia were braying together, answers the philosopher. Eclipsis. Arcadia, a midland country of Peloponnesus, very good for pasture, and famous for a large breed of asses. See JUV. sat. vii. l. 160, note.

10. *Now a book.*] At last he gets out of bed, dresses himself, and takes up a book.

—*Two-coloured parchment.*] The students used to write their notes on parchment: the inside, on which they wrote, was white: the other side, being the outer side of the skin, on which the wool or hair grew, was of a yellow cast. See JUV. sat. vii. l. 23, note.

—*The hairs,* &c.] The hairs, or wool, which grew on the skin, were scraped off, and the parchment smoothed, by rubbing it with a pumice-stone.

11. *Paper.*] Charta signifies any material to write upon. The ancients made it of various things, as leaves, bark of trees, &c. and the Egyptians

" Long since is ripening, and all the flock is under the
" " spreading elm."
' Says one of the fellow-students—" Is it true? Is it so?
" " Quick let somebody
" Come hither—Is there nobody?"—vitreous bile swells.
" I am split;"—" that you would believe the cattle of
" " Arcadia to bray."
   Now a book, and two-coloured parchment, the hairs
    being laid aside,   10
And there comes into his hand paper, and a knotty reed.
Then he complains that a thick moisture hangs from the pen:
That the black cuttle-fish vanishes with water infused :
He complains that the pipe doubles the diluted drops.
  " O wretch ! and every day more a wretch ! to this pass.
" Are we come? but why do not you rather, like the ten-
    " der dove,   16.
" And like the children of nobles, require to eat pap,

of the flag of the river Nile, which was called Papyrus—hence the word paper. Charta Pergamena, i. e. apud Pergamum inventa (PLIN. Ep. xiii. 12.) signifies the parchment or vellum which they wrote upon, and which was sometimes indifferently called charta, or membrana. Comp. Hor. sat. x. lib. i, l. 14 ; and sat. iii. lib. ii. l. 2.

But chartæ here seems to mean paper of some sort, different from the membrana; l. 10.

The lazy student now takes pen, ink, and paper, in order to write.

—*A knotty reed.*] A pen made of a reed, which was hollow, like a pipe, and grew full of knots, at intervals, on the stalk.

12. *He complains, &c.*] That his ink is so thick that it hangs to the nib of his pen.

13. *Cuttle-fish, &c.*] This fish discharges a black liquor, which the ancients used as ink.

—*Vanishes with water, &c.*] He first complained that his ink was too thick ; on pouring water into it, to make it thinner, he now complains that it is too thin, and the water has caused all the blackness to vanish away.

14. *The pipe.*] i. e. The pen made of the reed.

—*Doubles the diluted drops.*] Now the ink is so diluted, that it comes too fast from the pen, and blots his paper. All these are so many excuses for his unwillingness to write.

15. " *O wretch !*" &c.] The philosopher, hearing his lazy pupil contrive so many trivial excuses for idleness, exclaims—" O wretch, O " wretched young man, who art likely " to be more wretched every day you " live !"

16. "'*Are we come,*" &c.] Are all my hopes of you, as well as those of your parents, who put you under my care, come to this !

—" *Why do you not rather.*"]— Than occasion all this expence and trouble about your education.

— " *The tender dove.*"] These birds were remarkably tender when young—the old ones feed them with the half-digested food of their own stomachs.

17. " *Children of nobles.*"] And of other great men, which are delicately nursed.

—" *Require to eat pap.*"] Pappare is to eat pap as children. Minutus-a-um, signifies any thing lessened, or made smaller. Here it denotes meat put into a mother's or nurse's mouth, there chewed small, and then given to the child—as the dove to her young. Comp. the last note on l. 16.

Poscis ; et iratus mammæ, lallare recusas ?
-' An tali studeam calamo ?' Cui verba ? Quid istas
Succinis ambages ? Tibi luditur : effluis amens.　　- 20
Contemnêre.　Sonat vitium percussa, maligne.
Respondet, viridi non cocta fidelia limo.
Udum et molle lutum es ; (nunc, nunc properandus, et acri
Fingendus sine fine rotâ.) Sed rure paterno
Est tibi far modicum ; purum, et sine labe, salinum.　　25
Quid metuas ? cultrixque foci secura patella est.
Hoc satis ? An deceat pulmonem rumpere ventis,

18. " *Angry at the nurse.*"] The
word mammæ here refers to the mother or nurse, which the children
call mamma, as they called the father
tata.

This well describes the pettish-
ness of an humoured and spoiled
child, which, because it has not immediately what it wants, flies into a
passion with its nurse when she attempts to sing it to sleep, and will
not suffer her to do it.　See AINSW.
Lallo.

The philosopher sharply reproves
his idle pupil.　Rather, says he, than
come to school, you should have
stayed in the nursery, and have
shewed your childish perverseness
there rather than here.

19. " *Can I study with such a*
pen ?"] The youth still persists in his
frivolous excuses, totally unimpress-
ed by all that his master has said—
" blame the pen, don't blame me—
" can any mortal write with such a
" pen ?"

—" *Whom dost thou deceive ?*"]—
I should suppose, that cui verba is
here elliptical, and that das, or existi-
mas dare, is to be understood.　Verba
dare is to cheat or deceive ; and here
the philosopher is representing his
pupil, who is framing trivial excuses
for his unwillingness to study, as a
self-deceiver—tibi luditur; saith he,
in the next line.

19-20. " *Those shifts.*"] Ambages
—shifts, prevaricating, shuffling excuses.

20. " *Repeat.*"] Succinis.—The
verb succino signifies to sing after
another, to follow one another in singing or saying—here properly used,
as expressing the repetition of his
foolish excuses, which followed one

another, or which he might be said to
repeat one after the other.

—" *'Tis you are beguiled.*"]　Luditur here is used impersonally ; as
concurritur, HOR. sat. i. lib. i. l. 7.

—" *Thoughtless you run out.*"]—
Amens—foolish, silly, out of one's
wits (from a priv. and mens)—so,
unthinking, without thought.　You
run out—effluis—metaph. from a bad
vessel, out of which the liquor leaks.
You, foolish and unthinking as you
are, are wasting your time and opportunity of improvement, little
thinking, that, like the liquor from a
leaky vessel, they are insensibly passing away from you—your very life is
gliding away, and you heed it not.

21. " *You'll be despised.*"] By all
sober, thinking people.

—" *A pot,*" &c.] Any vessel, made
of clay that is not well tempered—
viridi limo, which is apt to chap and
crack in the fire—non cocta, not
baked as it ought to be—will answer
badly, when sounded by the finger,
and will proclaim, by its cracked and
imperfect sound, its defects.

Thus will it be with you, none
will ever converse with you, or put
you to the proof, but you will soon
make them sensible of your deficiency in wisdom and learning, and be
the object of their contempt.

23. " *Wet and soft clay.*"]　The
poet still continues the metaphor.

As wet and soft clay will take its
impression, or be moulded into any
shape, so may you ; you are young,
your understanding flexible, and im-
pressible by instruction—

—*idoneus arti*
Cuilibet : argillâ quidvis imitaberis
udâ.
HOR. epist. ii. lib. ii. l. 7-8.

" And angry at the nurse, refuse her to sing lullaby."—
  " Can I study with such a pen ?" " Whom dost thou
  " deceive ? Why those
" Shifts do you repeat ? 'Tis you are beguiled : thoughtless
  " you run out.   20
" You will be despised. A pot, the clay being green, not
  " baked, answers
" Badly, being struck, its sounds its fault.
" You are wet and soft clay ; now, now you are to be
  " hastened,
" And to be formed incessantly with a brisk wheel. But
  " in your paternal estate
" You have a moderate quantity of corn, and a salt-cellar
  " pure and without spot.   25
" What can you fear ? and you have a dish a secure wor-
  " shipper of the hearth."—
" Is this enough ? Or may it become you to break your
  " lungs with wind,

—" Hasten'd."] Now, now you are young, you are to lose no time, but immediately to be begun with.

24. " Formed incessantly," &c.] The metaphor still continues. As the wheel of the potter turns, without stopping, till the piece of work is finished, so ought it to be with you ; you ought to be taught incessantly, till your mind is formed to what it is intended, and this with strict discipline, here meant by acri rota.

24. " Paternal estate," &c.] But perhaps you will say, " Where is the " occasion for all this ? I am a man " of fortune, and have a sufficient " income to live in independency ; " therefore why all this trouble about " learning."

25. " Moderate quantity." &c.]— Far signifies all manner of corn which the land produces ; here, by metonym. the land itself—far modicum, a moderate estate, a competency.

—" A salt-cellar without spot."] The ancients had a superstition about salt, and always placed the salt-cellar first on the table, which was thought to consecrate it : if the salt was forgotten, it was looked on as a bad omen. The salt-cellar was of silver, and descended from father to son.

See Hor. ode xvi. lib. ii. l. 13, 14. But here the salinum, per synec. seems to stand for all the plate which this young man is supposed to have inherited from his father, which he calls purum and sine labe, either from the pureness of the silver, or from the care and neatness with which it was kept, or from the honest and fair means by which the father had obtained that and all the rest of his possessions.

26. " What can you fear ?"] Say you who are possessed of so much property ?

—" You have a dish," &c.] Patella—a sort of deep dish, with broad brims, used to put portions of meat in that were given as sacrifice.

Before eating, they cut off some part of the meat, which was first put into a pan, then into the fire, as an offering to the Lares, which stood on the hearth, and were supposed the guardians of both house and land, and to secure both from harm : hence the poet says—cultrix secura.

q. d. You have not only a competent estate in lands and goods, but daily worship the guardian gods, who will therefore protect both, what need you fear ?

27. " Is this enough ?"] To make you happy.

Stemmate quod Tusco ramum millesime ducis ;
Censoremve tuum vel quod trabeate salutas ?
Ad populum phaleras : ego te intus, et in cute, novi. 30
Non pudet ad morem discincti vivere Nattæ ?
Sed stupet hic vitio ; et fibris increvit opimum
Pingue : caret culpâ : nescit quid perdat : et alto
Demèrsus, summâ rursus non bullit in undâ.
  Magne pater divûm, sævos punire tyrannos 35
Haud aliâ ratione velis, cum dira libido
Moverit ingenium, ferventi tincta veneno :
' Virtutem videant, intabescantque relictâ.'
Anne magis Siculi gemuerunt æra juvenci ;

27. *" May it become you."*] Having
reason, as you may think, to boast
of your pedigree, can you think 'it
meet—
  —*" To break your lungs,"* &c.]
To swell up with pride, till you are
ready to burst, like a man that draws
too much air at once into his lungs.
  28. *" A thousandth, derive,"* &c.]
Millesime, for tu millesimus, antipto-
sis ; like trabeate, for tu trabeatus,
in the next line—because you can
prove yourself a branch of some
Tuscan family, a thousand off from
the common stock. The Tuscans
were accounted of most ancient nobility. Horace observes this, in most
of his compliments to Mæcenas, who
was derived from the old kings of
Tuscany. See ode i. lib. i. l. 1, et al.
freq.
  29. *" Censor,"* &c.] The Roman
knights, attired in the robe called
trabea, were summoned to appear before the censor (see AINSW. *Censor*),
and to salute him in passing by, as
their names were called over. They
led their horses in their hand.
  Are you to boast, says the philosopher to his pupil, because the censor is your relation (tuum), and that
when you pass in procession before
him, with your knight's robe on, you
may claim kindred with him ?
  30. *" Trappings to the people—"*]
q. d. These are for the ignorant vulgar to admire. The ornaments of
your dress you may exhibit to the
mob ; they will be pleased with such
gewgaws, and respect you accordingly.

The word phaleræ-arum, signifies
trappings, or ornaments for horses ;
also a sort of ornament worn by the
knights : but these no more ennobled
the man, than those did the horse.
  —*" I know you intimately,"* &c.]
Inside and out, as we say ; therefore
you cannot deceive me.
  31. *" Does it not shame you,"* &c.]
Do you feel no shame at your way of
life, you that are boasting of your
birth, fortune, and quality, and yet
leading the life of a low profligate
mechanic ?
  Natta signifies one of a sorry,
mean occupation, a dirty mechanic.
But here the poet means somebody
of this name, or at least who deserves it by his profligate and worthless character. See HOR. sat. vi. lib.
i. l. 124 ; and JUV. sat. viii. l. 95.
  32. *" He is stupified with vice."*]
He has not all his faculties clear, and
capable of discernment, as you have,
therefore is more excusable than you
are. By your contracted habits of
vice he has stupified himself.
  —*" Fat hath increased,"* &c.]—
Pingue, for pinguedo. These words
are, I conceive, to be taken in a moral
sense ; and by fibris, the inwards or
entrails, is to be understood the mind
and understanding, the judgment
and conscience, the inward man,
which, like a body overwhelmed with
fat, are rendered torpid, dull, and
stupid, so as to have no sense and
feeling of the nature of evil remain-
ing. See Ps. cxix. 70, former part.
  33. *" He is not to blame."*] i. e.

" Because you, a thousandth, derive a branch from a Tus-
" can stock ;
" Or because robed you salute the censor (as) yours ?—
" Trappings to the people—I know you intimately and
" thoroughly.　　　　　　　　　　　　　　　　30
" Does it not shame you to live after the manner of disso-
" lute Natta ?
" But he is stupified with vice, rich fat hath increased in his
" Inwards) he is not to blame : he knows not what he may
" lose, and with the deep
" Overwhelmed, he does not bubble again at the top of the
" water."

Great father of gods ! will not to punish cruel　　　35
Tyrants by any other way, when fell desire
Shall stir their disposition, imbued with fervent poison :
Let them see virtue, and let them pine away, it being left.
Did the brass of the Sicilian bullock groan more,

Comparatively. See Juv. sat. ii. l. 15-19.

—" He knows not," &c.] He is insensible of the sad consequences of vice, such as the loss of reputation, and of the comforts of a virtuous life. He has neither judgment to guide him, nor conscience to reprove him.

34. " Overwhelmed."] Sunk into the very depths of vice, like one sunk to the bottom of the sea.

—" Bubble again," &c.] i. e. He does not emerge, rise up again. Metaph. from divers, who plunge to the bottom of the water, and, when they rise again, make a bubbling at the surface as they approach the top. Therefore, O young man, beware of imitating, by thine idleness and mis-spending of time, this wretched man, lest thou shouldst bring thyself into the same deplorable state.

36. By any other way.] Than by giving them a sight of the charms of that virtue, which they have forsaken, and to which they cannot attain. Hand velis—i. e. noli.

—When dire lust, &c.] When they find their evil passions exciting them, to acts of tyranny. See AINSW. Libido, No. 1, 2.

37. Imbued with fervent poison.] Tincta—imbued, full of, abounding (met.) with the inflaming venom of cruelty, which may be called the poison of the mind, baleful and fatal as poison in its destructive influence.

38. Let them see virtue.] Si virtus humanis oculis conspiceretur, miros amores excitaret sui. SENEC.—This would be the case with the good and virtuous ; but it would have a contrary effect towards such as are here mentioned ; it would fill them with horror and dismay, and inflict such remorse and stings of conscience, as to prove the greatest torment which they could endure.

—Let them pine away.] For the loss of that which they have forsaken and despised, as well as from the despair of ever retrieving it.

—It being left.] i. e. Virtute relicta. Abl. absol.

39. The Sicilian bullock, &c.] Alluding to the story of Phalaris's brazen bull. Perillus, an Athenian artificer, made a figure of a bull in brass, and gave it to Phalaris, tyrant of Syracuse, as an engine of torment : the bull was hollow ; a man put into it, and set over a large fire, would, as the brass heated and tormented him, make a noise which might be supposed to imitate the roaring of a bull. The tyrant accepted the present, and ordered the experiment to be first tried on the inventor himself.

Et magis, auratis pendens laquearibus, ensis 40
Purpureas subter cervices terruit, ' imus,
' Imus præcipites,' quam si sibi dicat ; et intus
Palleat infelix, quod proxima nesciat uxor ?
    Sæpe oculos, memini, tangebam parvus olivo,
Grandia si nollem morituri verba Catonis 45
Discere, non sano multum laudanda magistro ;
Quæ pater adductis sudans audiret amicis :
Jure ; etenim id summum, quid dexter senio ferret,
Scire erat in voto ; damnosa canicula quantum
Raderet ;(angustæ collo non fallier orcæ ;) 50

40. *The sword hanging, &c.*] Damocles, the flatterer of Dionysius, the Sicilian tyrant, having greatly extolled the happiness of monarchs, was ordered, that he might be convinced of his mistake, to be attired, as a king, in royal apparel ; to be seated at a table spread with the choicest viands, but withal, to have a naked sword hung over his head, suspended by a single hair, with the point downwards ; which so terrified Damocles, that he could neither taste of the dainties, nor take any pleasure in his magnificent attendance.

41. *Purple neck, &c.*] i. e. Damocles, who was placed under the point of the suspended sword, and magnificently arrayed in royal purple garments. Meton. Purpureas cervices, for purpuream cervicem—synec.

41-2. *" I go, I go," &c.*] A person within the bull of Phalaris would not utter more dreadful groans ; nor would one seated like Damocles, under the sharp point of a sword, suspended over his head by a single horse-hair, feel more uneasy, than the man who is desperate with guilt, so as to give himself over for lost, and to have nothing else to say than, " I am going, I am plunging head- " long into destruction, nothing can " save me."

42-3. *Within unhappy.*] Having an hell, as it were, in his conscience.

43. *Turn pale.*] Palleo literally signifies to be pale—as this often arises from fear and dread, palleo is used to denote fearing, to stand in fear of, per meton. So Hor. lib. iii. ode xxvii. l. 27, 8.

—*Mediasque fraudes*
Palluit audax.
In the above passage of Horace, palleo, though a verb neuter, is used actively, as here by Persius ; likewise before, sat i. l. 121, where palles is used metonymically for hard studying, which occasions paleness of countenance.

—*Nearest wife, &c.*] His conscience tormented with the guilt of crimes, which he dares not reveal to the nearest friend that he has, not even to the wife of his bosom, who is nearest of all.

44. *Besmear'd my eyes, &c.*] The philosopher here relates some of his boyish pranks. I used, says he, when I was a little boy, and had not a mind to learn my lesson, to put oil into my eyes, to make them look bleary, that my master might suppose they really were so, and excuse me my task.

45-6. *Great words of dying Cato.*] Cato of Utica is here meant, who killed himself, that he might not fall into the hands of Julius Cæsar, after the defeat of Pompey. His supposed last deliberation with himself before his death, whether he should stab himself, or fall into the hands of Cæsar, was given as a theme for the boys to write on ; then they were to get the declamation, which they composed, by heart, and repeat it by way of exercising them in eloquence.

46. *Much to be praised.*] It was the custom for the parents and their friends to attend on these exercises of their children, which the master was sure to commend very highly,

Or the sword hanging from the golden ceiling, did it   40
More affright the purple neck underneath ; " I go,
" I go headlong," (than if any one should say to himself,)
     and, within
Unhappy, should turn pale at what his nearest wife must
     be ignorant of ?
     I remember, that I, a little boy, often besmeared my eyes
     with oil,
If I was unwilling to learn the great words of dying   45
Cato, much to be praised by my insane master ;
Which my father would hear sweating, with the friends he
     brought :
With reason ; for it was the height of my wish to know
     what
The lucky sice would bring, how much the mischievous
     ace
Would scrape off—not to be deceived by the neck of the
     narrow jar—   50

by way of flattering the parents with a notion of the progress and abilities of their children, not without some view, that the parents should compliment the master on the pains which he had taken with his scholars.

—*Insane.*] This does not mean that the master was mad, but that, in commending and praising such puerile performances, and the vehemence with which he did it, he did not act like one that was quite in his right senses.

47. *Sweating.*] i. e. With the eagerness and agitation of his mind, that I might acquit myself well before him and the friends which he might bring to hear me declaim. See above, note on l. 46, No. 1.

48. *With reason, &c.*] Jure—not without cause.—q. d. My father might well sweat with anxiety ; for instead of studying how to acquit myself with credit on these occasions, it was the height of my ambition to know the chances of the dice, play at chuck, and whip a top, better than any other boy.

49. *Lucky sice, &c.*] Dexter, lucky, fortunate—from dexter, the right hand, which was supposed the lucky side, as sinister, the left, was accounted unlucky.

The sice—the six—the highest number on the dice, which won.

—*Mischievous ace, &c.*] The ace was the unluckiest throw on the dice, and lost all. See AINSW. *Canicula.* No, 5.

It was the summit of his wish to be able to calculate the chances of the dice ; as, what he should win by throwing a six, and what he should lose if he threw an ace. How much a sice, ferret, might bring, i. e. add, contribute to his winnings — how much the ace, raderet, might scrape off, i. e. diminish, or take away from them. Metaph. from diminishing a thing, or lessening its bulk by scraping it.

50. *Neck of the narrow jar.*] Orca signifies a jar, or like earthen vessel, which had a long narrow neck : the boys used to fix the bottom in the ground, and try to chuck, from a little distance, nuts, or almonds, into the mouth ; those which they chucked in were their own, and those which missed the mouth, and fell on the ground, they lost.

I made it my study, says he, to understand the game of the orca, and to chuck so dexterously as not to miss the mouth, however narrow the neck might be.

Neu quis callidior buxum torquere flagello.
Haud tibi inexpertum, curvos deprendere mores ;
Quæque docet sapiens, braccatis illita Medis,
Porticus : insomnis quibus et detonsa juventus
Invigilat, siliquis et grandi pasta polentâ.   55
Et tibi, quæ Samios deduxit litera ramos,
Surgentem dextro monstravit limite callem.
Stèrtis adhuc ? laxumque caput, compage solutâ,
Oscitat hesternum, dissutis undique malis ?
Est aliquid quo tendis, et in quod dirigis arcum ?   60
An passim sequeris corvos testâque lutoque,
Securus quo pes ferat, atque ex tempore vivis ?
Helleborum frustra, cum jam cutis ægra tumebit,

51. *The top.*] Buxus—lit. the box-tree, box-wood. As the children's tops were made of this, therefore, per meton. it is used to denote a top, as well as any thing else made of box-wood. Consistently with his plan, he was determined to excel, even in whipping a top.

52. *Unexperienced, &c.*] The philosopher makes use of what he has been saying, by way of remonstrance with his pupil. You, says he, are not a child as I was then, therefore it does not become you to invent excuses to avoid your studies, in order to follow childish amusements—you know better, you have been taught the precepts of wisdom and moral philoso-phy, and know by experience the dif-ference between right and wrong.

—*Crooked morals.*] Morals which deviate from the straight rule of right. Metaph. from the things that are bent, bowed, crooked, and out of a straight line.

53. *Wise portico.*] Meton. the place where wisdom is taught, put for the teachers. The Stoics were so called, from ϛοα, a portico, in Athens, spacious, and finely embellished, where they used to meet and dispute.

53. *Daub'd over, &c.*] On the walls of the portico were painted the battles of the Medes and Persians with the Athenians, who, with their kings Xerxes and Darius, were defeated by Miltiades, Leonidas, and Themisto-cles, Athenian generals, at Marathon, Thermopylæ, and on the coast of Sa-lamis.

—*Trowser'd Medes.*] The bracca was a peculiar dress of the Medes, which, like trowsers, reached from the loins to the ancles.

54. *Which.*] i. e. The things taught by the Stoics.

—*Sleepless youth.*] The young men who follow the strict discipline of the Stoics, and allow themselves but little sleep, watching over their studies night and day.

—*Shorn.*] After the manner of the Stoics, who did not suffer their hair to grow long.

55. *Bean-pods.*] Siliqua is the husk, pod, or shell of a bean, pea, or the like ; also the pulse therein : put here to denote the most simple and frugal diet.

—*A great pudding.*] Polenta—barley-flour, dried at the fire and fried, after soaking in water all night.—Aιχσω. This made a sort of fried pudding, or cake, and was a kind of coarse food.

56. *And to thee, the letter, &c.*] The two horns, or branches, as Per-sius calls them, of the letter Y, were chosen, by Pythagoras, to de-monstrate the two different paths of virtue and vice, the right branch leading to the former, the left to the latter : it was therefore called his letter : and Persius calls the two branches, into which the Y divides itself, Samios, from Samos, an island in the Ionian sea, where Pythagoras was born, who hence was called the Samian philosopher, and the Y the Samian letter.

Nor that any one should whirl more skilfully the top with a
    scourge.
  It is not a thing unexperienced to you, to discover
    crooked morals,
And the things which the wise portico, daubed over with
    the trowsered Medes,
Teaches, which the sleepless and shorn youth
Watch over, fed with bean-pods and a great pudding : 55
And to thee, the letter, which hath severed the Samian
    branches,
Hath shewn the path rising with the right-hand limit.
Do you still snore? and does your lax head, with loosened
    (joining)
Yawn from what happened yesterday, with cheeks unsewed
    in all parts?
Is there any thing whither you tend? and to what do you
    direct your bow?   60
Or do you follow crows up and down with a potsherd and
    mud,
Careless whither your foot may carry you; and do you live
    from the time?
  In vain hellebore, when now the sickly skin shall swell,

57. *Shewn the path raising. &c.*] i. e.
He had been well instructed in the
doctrine of Pythagoras, concerning
the way to virtue.
  *Litera Pythagoræ discrimine secta
    bicorni,*
  *Humanæ vitæ speciem præferre
    videtur.*   MART.
  58. *Do you still snore?*] Thou,
who hast been taught better things,
from the principles and practices of
the Stoics and Pythagoreans, art
thou sleeping till almost noon? See
l. 4.
  —*Your lax head, &c.*] In sleep,
the muscles which raise the head, and
keep it upright, are all relaxed, so,
that the head will nod, and drop, as if
it had nothing to confine it in its
place : this is often seen in people who
sleep as they sit.
  59. *Yawn, &c.*] From the sleepi-
ness and fatigue occasioned by yesterday's debauch are you yawning as
if your jaws were ripped asunder?
Dissutis—metaph. from the parting,
or gaping, of things sewed together,
when unstitched, or ripped asunder.

Mala signifies either the cheek, or
jaw-bone.
  Oscitat hesternum. Græcism. q. d.
Yawn forth yesterday's debauch.
  *Oscitando evaporat, et edormit, hes-
    ternam crapulam.*   MART.
  60. *Is there any thing, &c.*] Have
you any pursuit, end, or point in
view?
  —*Direct your bow.*] What do you
aim at? Metaph. taken from an
archer's aiming at a mark.
  61. *Follow crows, &c.*] Or do you
ramble about, you not why, nor whither, like idle boys, that follow crows
to pelt them with potsherds and mud,
in order to take them? (as we should
say, to lay salt upon their tails.) A
proverbial expression to denote vain,
unprofitable, and foolish pursuits.
  62. *Live from the time.*] Ex tempore—without any fixed or premedi-
tated plan, and looking no farther
than just the present moment.
  63. *In vain hellebore, &c.*] The
herb hellepore was accounted a great
cleanser of noxious humours, therefore administered in dropsies.

(Poscentes videas.) Venienti occurrite morbo ;
Et quid opus Cratero magnos promittere montes ?   65
Discite, ô miseri ! et causas cognoscite rerum :
Quid sumus : et quidnam victuri gignimur : ordo
Quis datus : et metæ qua mollis flexus, et undæ.
Quis modus argento : quid fas optare : quid asper
Utile nummus habet : patriæ, carisque propinquis,   70
Quantum elargiri deceat : quem te Deus esse
Jussit ; et humanâ quâ parte locatus es in re—
Disce : nec invideas, quod multa fidelia putet
In locuplete penu, defensis pinguibus Umbris ;

When the skin is swoln with a dropsy, it is too late to begin with remedies, in very many cases.

64. *Prevent, &c.*] The wisest way. is to prevent the disorder by avoiding the causes of it, or by checking its first approaches, Occurrite—meet it in its way to attack you.

Principiis obsta : sero medicina paratur.

Cum mala per longas invaluére moras.   OVID.

65. *What need is there, &c.*] What need have you to let the distemper get such a head, as that you may be offering mountains of gold for a cure. Craterus was the physician of Augustus—put here for any famous and skilful practitioner.

The poet here, is speaking figuratively, and means, that what he says of the distempers of the body should be applied to those of the mind ; of which all he says is equally true.

The first approaches of vice are to be watched against, and their progress prevented ; otherwise, if disregarded till advanced into habits, they may be too obstinate for cure. Comp. l. 32-4.

66. *Learn, &c.*] Here the philosopher applies what he has been saying, by way of reproof and remonstrance, in a way of inference. Learn then, says he, ye miserable youths, who are giving way to sloth, idleness, and neglect of your studies—learn, before it be too late, the causes, the final causes of things, which are the great objects of moral philosophy, which teacheth us the causes and purposes for which all things were made.

67. *What we are.*] Both as to body and soul ; how frail and transitory as to the one, how noble and exalted as to the other.

—What we are engender'd, &c.]— To what end and purpose we are begotten, in order to live in this world, and what life we are to lead.

67–8. *What order is given.*] In what rank or degree of life we are placed.

68. *By what way the turning, &c.*] Metaph. to denote the wise, well-ordered, and well-directed management, and right conduct of our affairs ; as charioteers in the circus used all their care and management in turning the meta, or goal, so as to avoid touching it too nearly. To touch it with the inward wheel of the chariot, yet so as but to touch it, was the choice art of the charioteer : this they called stringere metam ; as to escape the danger in the performance of it they called evitare metam.

Metaque fervidis Evitata rotis.   HOR. ode i. If they performed not this very dextrously, they were in danger of having the chariot and themselves dashed to pieces.

—And of the water.] Another metaphor to the same purpose, alluding to the naumachia, or ship-races, wherein there were likewise placed metæ ; and the chief art was, when they came to the meta, to tack their ship so dextrously, as to sail as near as possible round it, yet so as to avoid running against it. See Æn. v. 129-31.

It was one part of moral philosophy, to teach the attainment of the best end, by the safest, easiest, and

Q

You may see people asking for. Prevent the coming dis-
ease ;
And what need is there to promise great mountains to
    Craterus ?   65
Learn, O miserable creatures, and know the causes of
    things,
What we are, and what we are engendered to live : what
    order
Is given, and by what way the turning of the goal, and of
    the water, may be easy :
What measure to money—what it is right to wish—what
    rough
Money has that is useful. To our country, and to dear
    relations,   70
How much it may become to give ; whom the Deity com-
    manded
Thee to be, and in what part thou art placed in the human
    system—
Learn :—nor be envious, that many a jar stinks
In a rich store, the fat Umbrians being defended,

---

best means, avoiding all difficulties and dangers as much as possible.

69. *What measure to money.*]— What limits or bounds to put to our desires after it, so as to avoid covetousness.

—*What it is right to wish.*] Or pray for. See sat. ii. per tot.

69–70. *Rough money, &c.*] The true use of money, for this alone can make it useful. Asper nummus is coined gold or silver ; so called from the roughness which is raised on the surface by the figures or letters stamped on it.

Not only money, but all wrought or chased silver or gold, is signified by the epithet asper.

Vasa aspera. Juv. sat. xiv. l. 62. *Cymbiaque argento perfecta atque aspera signis.* Æn. v. l. 267.

70. *Our country, &c.*] What we owe, and, consequently, what it becomes us to pay, to our country, our relations, and friends, &c.

71. *Whom the deity commanded, &c.*] Quem—what manner of person it is the will of heaven you should be in your station.

72. *In what part placed, &c.*] Locatus, Metaph. from the placing peo-

ple according to their rank on the benches at the theatres ; or from soldiers, who are placed in particular stations as centinels, &c. which they must not forsake, but by leave, or order, of the commander. Thus the Stoics taught that every man was placed, or stationed, in some destined part of the human system (humana re), which he must not quit at his own will and pleasure, but solely by the permission or command of the Deity.

73. *Learn.*] Get a thorough, practical knowledge of the above-mentioned important particulars, and then you need not envy any body.

—*A jar stinks, &c.*] Nor envy any great lawyer the presents which are made him, of such quantities of provisions, that they grow stale and putrid before he can consume them. Penus-i, or -us, signifies a store of provisions. Ainsw.

74. *Fat Umbrians.*] The Umbrian and the Marsian were the most plentiful of all the provinces in Italy.

—*Being defended.*] Ably and strenuously, in some great cause, in which they were defendants—they sent presents of provisions to their

Et piper, et pernæ, Marsi monumenta clientis :　　75
Mænaque quod primâ nondum defecerit orcâ. —
Hic aliquis de gente hircosâ centurionum
Dicat ; " Quod sapio, satis est mihi : non ego curo
" Esse quod Arcesilas, ærumnosique Solones,
" Obstipo capite, et figentes lumine terram ;　　80
" Murmura cum secum, et rabiosa silentia rodunt,
" Atque exporrecto trutinantur verba labello,
" Ægroti veteris meditantes somnia : *gigni*
" *De nihilo nihilum, in nihilum nil posse reverti.*

counsel, and this in such quantities, that they could not use them while they were good.

75. *And pepper, &c.*] And that there is pepper, &c. in the lawyer's store. The poet means to ridicule such vile presents, as after him Juvenal did. See Juv. sat. vii. 119—21.

—*Monuments, &c.*] Monumentum or monimentum (from moneo) a memorial of any person or thing. The poet calls these presents of the Marsians, monuments, or memorials of them, because they were the produce of their country, and bespake from whence they came as presents, to refresh their counsel's memory concerning his Marsian clients, who were, perhaps, plaintiffs in the cause against the Umbri.

76. *Because the pilchard, &c.*] Because a second jar of pickled herrings, or pilchards, was sent, before the first that had been sent was all used.

What fish the mæna was is not certain, but something, we may suppose, of the herring, pilchard, or anchovy kind, which was pickled, and put up in jars.

The Stoics were no friends to the lawyers ; not that they condemned the profession itself, but because it induced men to sell their voices, in order to gratify their covetous desire of gain, which, by the way, could not be very considerable, if it consisted only in such fees as are above mentioned. Comp. Juv. sat. vii. 106—21.

However, Persius makes his philosopher, in his discourse to his pupils, take an opportunity of ridiculing the lawyers, with no little contempt and severity, by telling the young men,

that, if possessed of all the valuable principles of moral philosophy, they need not envy the fees of the lawyers, which, by the way, he represents in the most ridiculous and contemptible light.

77. *Here some one, &c.*] The poet here represents the philosopher as anticipating some objections which might be made to his doctrines, on the subject of studying philosophy, which he does, by way of answering them ; and thus he satirizes the neglect and contempt of philosophy by the Roman people, and shews the fallacy and absurdity of their arguments against it.

—*Stinking centurions.*] Hircosus, from hircus, a goat, signifies stinking, rammish, smelling like a goat.

The centurions, and the lower part of the Roman soldiery, were very slovenly, seldom pulled off their clothes, and wore their beards, which they neglected ; so that, by the nastiness of their persons, they smelt rank like goats.

Persius makes one of these the spokesman, by which he means, doubtless, to reflect on the opponents, as if none could be of their party but such a low, dirty, ignorant fellow as this.

78. " *What I know,*" &c.] The foundation of all contempt of knowledge is self-sufficiency.

I know enough to answer my purpose, says the centurion ; I don't want to be wiser.

79. " *Arcesilas.*"] An Æolian by birth, and scholar to Polemon ; afterwards he came to Athens, and joined himself to Crantor, and became the founder of an academy. He

And pepper, and gammons of bacon, the monuments of a
 Marsian client,   75
And because the pilchard has not yet failed from the first
 jar.
 Here some one, of the rank race of centurions,
May say; " What I know is enough for me. I do not care
" To be what Arcesilas was, and the wretched Solons,
" With the head awry, and fixing the eyes on the ground,
" When murmurs with themselves, and mad silence they
 " are gnawing,   81
" And words are weighed with a stretched-out lip,
" Meditating the dreams of an old sick man—that *nothing*
 " can
" *Be produced from nothing, nothing can be returned into*
 " *nothing.*

opposed Zeno's opinions, and held, that nothing could be certainly known.

- Persius, probably, who was a Stoic, means here to give him a rub, by supposing this ignorant centurion to mention him as a great man.

—" *Wretched Solons.*"] Solon was one of the wise men of Greece, and the great lawgiver at Athens.

I would not give a farthing, says the centurion, to be such a philosopher as Arcesilas, or as wise as Solon, who was always making himself miserable with labour and study, or indeed as any such people as Solon was—(Solones.)

80. " *Head awry.*"] An action which the philosophers much used, as having the appearance of modesty and subjection. See Hor. sat. v. lib. ii. l. 92.

80. " *Fixing the eyes on the ground.*"] As in deep thought. Figentes lumine terram. Hypallage—for figentes lumina in terram.

81. " *Murmurs with themselves.*"] Persons in deep meditation are apt sometimes to be muttering to themselves.

—" *Mad silence,* &c.] They observed a silence, which, being attended with reclining the head, fixing their eyes on the ground, and only now and then interrupted by a muttering between the teeth, as if they were gnawing or eating their words,

made those who saw them take them for madmen, for they appeared like melancholy mad. Perhaps rabiosa silentia may allude to the notion of mad-dogs, who are supposed never to bark.

82. " *Words are weighed,*" &c.] Trutinantur—metaph. from weighing in scales: so these philosophers appear to be balancing, *i. e.* deeply considering, their words, with the lip pouted out; an action frequently seen in deep thought.

83. " *Meditating the dreams,*" &c.] Sick men's dreams are proverbial for thoughts which are rambling and incoherent; as such the centurion represents the thoughts and researches of these philosophers: of this he gives an instance—

83-4. " *Nothing can be produced,*" &c.] q. d. Ex nihilo nil fit. This was looked on as an axiom among many of the ancient philosophers, and so taken for granted, that the centurion is here supposed to deride those, who took the pains to get at it by study, as much as we should do a man who should labour hard to find out that two and two make four.

But we are taught, that God made the world out of matter, which had no existence till he created it, contrary to the blind and atheistical notion of the eternity of the world, or of the world's being God, as the Stoics and others taught.

" Hoc est, quod palles ! cur quis non prandeat, hoc est !"
His populus ridet ; multumque torosa juventus   86
Ingeminat tremulos, naso crispante, cachinnos.)
Inspice ; nescio quid trepidat mihi pectus, et ægris
Faucibus exsuperat gravis halitus ; inspice sodes,
Qui dicit medico ; jussus requiescere, postquam   90
Tertia compositas vidit nox currere venas,
De majore domo, modice sitente lagenâ,)
Lenia loturo sibi Surrentina rogavit.
" Heus, bone, tu palles." Nihil est.   " Videas tamen istud,
" Quicquid id est : surgit tacite tibi lutea pellis."   95
At tu deterius palles ; ne sis mihi tutor ;
Jampridem hunc sepeli : tu restas ? " Perge, tacebo."

85. *Is this what you study ?"*]—Palles—lit. art pale. See note on sat. i. l. 121.
—*" Should not dine."*] Is it for this that you philosophers half-starve yourselves with fasting, that your heads may be clear.
Mente uti recte non possumus multo cibo et potione completi. Cic. Tusc. Quæst. 5. Quis for aliquis—lit. some one.

86. *The people laugh at this.*] At these words the people, who are the supposed hearers of this centurion, burst into a horse-laugh.
—*The brawny youth, &c.*] The stout, brawny young fellows, the soldiers who stood around, were highly delighted with the centurion's jokes upon the philosophers, and with repeated loud laughter proclaimed their highest approbation.

87. *Tremulous loud laughs.*] Cachinnus signifies a loud laugh, particularly in derision or scorn—tremulos denotes the trembling or shaking of the voice in laughter, as ha ! ha ! ha !
—*Wrinkling nose.*] In laughter the nose is drawn up in wrinkles. See sat. i. l. 38, note.

88. *" Inspect," &c.*] The philosopher having ended the supposed speech of the centurion against the study of philosophy, now relates a story, by way of answer, in order to shew, that a man who rejects and ridicules the principles of philosophy, which are to heal the disorders of the mind, acts as fatal a part, as he who, with a fatal distemper in his body.

should reject and ridicule the advice of a physician, even act against it, and thus at last destroy himself. The qui, l. 90, is a relative without an antecedent, but may be supplied thus—
Let us suppose a man, who finding himself ill, says to a physician, " Pray " doctor, feel my pulse, observe my " case, examine what is the matter " with me."—Inspice.
—*" I know not why," &c.*] I don't know how or what it is, but I find an unusual fluttering of my heart.
89. *" Heavy breath abounds."*] I feel an heaviness and oppression of breath, a difficulty of breathing ; which seems here meant, as quickness of pulse and difficulty of breathing are usual symptoms of feverish complaints, especially of the inflammatory kind ; also a fetid smell of the breath, which gravis also denotes.
—*" Inspect, I pray you."*] Feeling himself ill, and not knowing how it may end, he is very earnest for the physician's advice, and again urges his request.
So would it be with regard to philosophy ; if men felt, as they ought, the disorders of their mind, and dreaded the consequences, they would not despise philosophy, which is the great healer of the distempered mind, but apply to it as earnestly as this sick man to the physician.
90. *Order'd to rest.*] Being ordered by the physician to go to bed, and keep himself quiet.
90-1. *After a third night.*] The

" Is this what you study? Is it this why one should not
    " dine ?"   85
    The people laugh at this, and much the brawny youth
Redoubles the tremulous loud laughs with wrinkling nose.
    " Inspect: I know not why my breast trembles, and from
    " my sick
" Jaws heavy breath abounds: inspect, I pray you"—
Who says to a physician;—being ordered to rest—after 90
A third night hath seen his veins to run composed,
From a greater house, in a flagon moderately thirsting,
He has asked for himself, about to bathe, mild Surrentine.
" Ho! good man, you are pale." " It is nothing." " But
    " have an eye to it,
" Whatever it is : your yellow-skin silently rises."—   95
" But you are pale—worse than I—do not be a tutor to me,
" I have long since buried him, do you remain ?"—" Go on
    " —I will be silent."

patient, after about three days observance of the doctor's prescription,
finds his fever gone, the symptoms
vanished, and his pulse quite composed and calm. As soon as he finds
this, he forgets his physician; and his
danger, and falls to eating and drinking again as usual.

92. *Greater house.*] He sends to
some rich friend, or neighbour, for
some surrentine wine ; which was a
small wine, not apt to affect the head,
as Pliny observes :

Surrentina vina caput non tenent.
                    PLIN. xxiii. c. 1.
therefore, drunk in a small quantity,
might not have been hurtful ; especially as this kind of wine was very
old, and therefore very soft and mild,
before it was drunk.

—*A flagon moderately thirsting.*]
Persons who thirst but little, drink
but little ; this idea seems to be used
here, metaphorically, to denote a flagon that did not require much to fill
it—i. e. a moderate sized flagon, but
yet holding enough to hurt a man re-
covering from sickness, if drunk all
at one meal, and particularly before
bathing, as seems to be the case here.

93. *About to bathe.*] Intending to
bathe, which, after much eating and
drinking, was reckoned very unwholesome. Comp. JUV. sat. i. l.
128-30.

94. " *Ho! good man,*", &c.] Away,
after an hearty meal, with his belly
full of wine and victuals. (l. 98.) he
goes to the baths, where his physician
happening to meet him, accosts him
with a friendly concern, and mentions
to him some symptoms, which appeared as if he had a dropsy.

—" *You are pale.*"] Says the physician ; you look ill.

—"*It is nothing.*"] O, says the
spark, I am very well—nothing ails
me.

—" *Have an eye,*" &c.] Says the
physician—be it what it may that
may occasion such a paleness, I
would have you take care of it in
time.

95. " *Yellow skin,*" &c.] Lutea
pellis—the skin of a yellow cast, like
the yellow-jaundice, which often precedes a dropsy.

—" *Silently rises.*"] Tacite—insensibly, by little and little, though you
may not perceive it—quasi sensim,
rises, swells.

96. " *You are pale,*" &c.] Says the
spark, in a huff, to the physician ;
you are paler than I am—pray look
to yourself.

—" *Don't be a tutor.*"] " Do not
" give yourself airs, as if you were
" my guardian, and had authority
" over me."

97. " *I have long since,*" &c.] " It

Turgidus hic epulis, atque albo ventre lavatur ;
Gutture sulphureas lente exhalante mephites.
Sed tremor inter vina subit, calidumque triental   100
Excutit e manibus : dentes crepuere retecti ;
Uncta cadunt laxis tunc pulmentaria labris :
Hinc tuba, candelæ. Tandemque beatulus alto
Compositus lecto, crassisque lutatus amomis,
In portam rigidos calces extendit. At illum   105
Hesterni capite induto subiere Quirites.

Tange, miser, venas ; et pone in pectore dextram :
Nil calet hic. Summosque pedes attinge, manusque :
Non frigent———visa est si forte pecunia, sive

" is a great while since I buried my
" tutor."

97. " *Do you remain ?*"] " Do you
" presume to take his place ?"

" *Go on—I'll be silent.*"] " O pray,"
replies the physician, " go on your
" own way—I shall say no more."

98. *Turgid with dainties.*] Having
his stomach and bowels full of meat
and drink.

—*A white belly.*] When the liver,
or spleen, is distempered, as in the
dropsy, and the chyle is not turned
into blood, it circulates in the veins
and small vessels of the skin, and
gives the whole body a white or pallid
appearance. Thus Hor. lib. ii. ode ii.

Crescit indulgens sibi dirus hydrops,
Nec sitim pellit, nisi causa morbi
Fugerit venis, et aquosus albo
Corpore languor.

—*Is bathed.*] '*i. e.* He persists in
going into the bath in this manner,
notwithstanding the warning which
had been given him.

99. *His throat slowly exhaling, &c.*]
The fumes of the meat and drink
ascend out of the stomach into the
throat, from whence they leisurely
discharge themselves in filthy steams.
Mephitis signifies a stink, particularly
a damp, or strong sulphurous smell
arising from corrupted water. See
Æn. vii. l. 84. Mephitis was a name
of Juno, because she was supposed to
preside over stinking exhalations.

100. *A trembling comes on, &c.*]
The riotous and gluttonous used to
bathe after supper, and in the going
in, and in the bath itself, they drank
large draughts of hot wine, to produce sweat. Hence Juv. sat. viii. l.

168. thermarum calices. As also after
bathing they sometimes drank very
hard. See my note on Juv. ubi supr.

—*Triental.*] A little vessel, which
was a third part of a larger, and held
about a gill ; this he has in his hand
full of warm wine, but it is shook out
of his hand by the trembling with
which he is seized.

101. *His uncovered teeth, &c.*] His
face being convulsed, the lips are
drawn asunder, and discover his teeth,
which grind or gnash—this is frequent
in convulsion-fits.

102. *Greasy soups, &c.*] Pulmen-
tarium, chopped meat, with pottage
or broth—Ainsw. which undigested
meat, vomited up, resembles. He
was seized with a violent vomiting,
and brought up all the dainties which
he had filled his stomach with before
he went into the bath.

—*From his loose lips.*] Hippocrat.
in Prognostic. says, that, when the
lips appear loose and hanging down,
it is a deadly sign.

103. *Hence the trumpet.*] Of this
intemperance he dies. The funerals
of the rich were attended with trumpets and lights—the poor had only
tibiæ, small pipes which played on the
occasion.

—*This happy fellow.*] Beatulus—
dim. from beatus, happy. Iron.

103-4. *On an high bed, &c.*] Laid
on an high bier. Compositus here
seems to express what we mean by
laying out a corpse.

104. *Daubed over, &c.*] After
washing the corpse with water, they
anointed it with perfumed ointment,
of which the amomum, an aromatic

He, turgid with dainties, and with a white belly is bathed,
His throat slowly exhaling sulphureous stenches:
But a trembling comes on whilst at his wine, and the warm
   (triental) *tuvy*   100
He shakes out of his hands ; his uncovered teeth crashed,
Then the greasy soups fall from his loose lips :
Hence the trumpet, the candles : and, at last, this happy
   fellow, on an high
Bed laid, and daubed over with thick ointments,
Extends his rigid heels towards the door : but him   105
The hesternal Romans, with covered head, sustained.
   " Touch, wretch, my veins, and put your right hand on
   " my breast :
" Nothing is hot here : and touch the extremes of my feet
   " and hands :
" They are not cold."—" If haply money be seen, or

---

shrub, which grew in Armenia, furnished the chief ingredient. The amomum was used in embalming. Hence momy or mummy. See AINSW.

105. *His rigid heels, &c.*] The Romans always carried the dead heels foremost, noting thereby their last and final departure from their house. Rigid—*i. e.* stiff with death.

106. *Hesternal Romans.*] See JUV. sat. iii. 6C, note. When a person of consequence died, all the slaves which he had made free in his life-time attended the funeral; some bore the corpse, (subiere—put themselves under the bier,) others walked in procession. These, being freedmen, were reckoned among the Roman citizens ; but they were looked on in a mean light, and were contemptuously called hesterni, Romans of yesterday—*i. e.* citizens whose dignity was of very short standing. Thus the first gentleman or nobleman of his family was called *novus homo.* So we, in contradistinction to families which are old, and have been long dignified, say, of some family lately ennobled, that it is a family of yesterday.

106. *Covered head.*] Wearing the pileus, or cap, which was the signal of liberty. Servum ad pileum vocare, signified to give a slave his liberty, which they did among the Romans, by first shaving his head, and then putting a cap upon it. AINSW.

107. " *Touch, wretch, my veins.*] It is very evident, from the four last lines, that the case, which the philosopher has put, is to be taken in an allegorical sense; and that, by the conduct of the wretched libertine, who rejected his physician's advice, and proceeded in his absurd courses, till he fixed a disorder upon him which brought him to the grave, he meant to represent the conduct of those who despised the philosophers, those physicians of the mind, and set at nought the precepts which they taught, till, by a continuance in their vices, their case became desperate, and ended in their destruction.

However, the opponent is supposed to understand what the philosopher said, in his story of the libertine, in a mere literal and gross sense, and is therefore represented as saying. " What's all this to the purpose ? " What is this to me ? I am not sick " —I don't want a physician—try, " feel my pulse."

—" *On my breast.*"] To feel the regular pulsation of my heart.

108. " *Nothing is hot here.*"]— There is no sign of any feverish heat.

—" *Touch the extremes,*" *&c.*]— You will find there the natural heat ; no coldness as in the feet and hands of a dying man.

109. " *If haply money be seen.*"]

.Candida vicini subrisit molle puella ;   ·110
.Cor tibi rite salit ? Positum est algente catino
Durum olus ; et populi cribro decussa farina :
Tentemus fauces.   Tenero latet ulcus in ore
Putre, quod haud deceat plebeiâ radere betâ.

    Alges, cum excussit membris timor albus aristas :   .115
Nunc, face suppositâ, fervescit sanguis, et irâ -
Scintillant oculi : dicisque, facisque, quod ipse
Non sani esse hominis, non sanus juret Orestes.

Here the philosopher explains him-self, and seems to say, " I grant that your bodily health is good, but how is your mind ? does not this labour under the diseases of covetousness, fleshly lust, intemperance, fear, and anger ? As a proof of this, let me ask you, if a large sum of money comes in view, or your neighbour's handsome daughter should smile upon you, does your heart move calmly as it ought, do you feel no desire of pos-sessing either ?"

    111. " *There is placed*," *&c.*]—What think you of a vile dish of hard, half-boiled cabbage, or coleworts, and coarse bread, such as the common people eat. Farina is lit. meal or flour; here, by meton. the bread it-self which is made of it. Shaken through the sieve of the people—*i. e.* of the poorer sort, who used coarse sieves, which let more of the bran and husks through, and therefore their bread was coarser than that of the gentry.

    113. *Try your jaws.*] Whether they can devour such coarse fare, or whether you would not find yourself as unable to chew, or swallow it, as if you had a sore and putrid ulcer lurking in your mouth, too tender for such coarse food, and which it would not be at all fitting to injure, by scratching, or rubbing against it with vulgar food.

    114. *Beet.*] Beta—some sort of

hard, coarse, and unsavoury herb. AINSW. Put here, by meton. for any kind of ordinary harsh food.

    If you found this to be the case, you may be certain that you have a luxurious appetite.

    115. *When white fear, &c.*] You said that you had no cold in the ex-tremes of your feet and hands—but how is it with you when you shudder with fear ? The Stoics were great ad-vocates for apathy, or freedom from all passions, fear among the rest. White fear, so called from the pale-ness of countenance that attends it.

    —*Rous'd the bristles.*] Arista signi-fies an ear of corn, or the beard of corn. Sometimes, by catachresis, an hair or bristle, which is often said to stand an end when people are in a fright.

    116. *Now with a torch, &c.*] He now charges him with the disease of violent anger, the blood set on fire, as if a burning torch were applied, and eyes sparkling and flashing fire as it were. In this situation, says he, you say and do things, that even Orestes himself, mad as he was, would swear were the words and actions of a per-son out of his senses. So that, though you may think you are well, because you find no feverish heat in your body, yet you are troubled with a fever of the mind every time you are angry. Therefore in this, as well as with regard to the diseases of covet-

" The fair girl of your neighbour smile gently,　　110
" Does your heart leap aright ?—there is placed in a cold
　　" dish
" An hard cabbage, and flour shaken through the sieve of
　-　" the people :
" Let us try your jaws : a putrid ulcer lies hid in your
　　" tender mouth,
" Which it would be hardly becoming to scratch with a
　　" plebeian beet.
　" You are cold, when white fear has roused the bristles
　　　" on your limbs :　　　　　　　　　　　　　　115
" Now, with a torch put under, your blood grows hot, and
　　　" with anger
" Your eyes sparkle, and you do and say, what, Orestes
　　" himself
" Not in his sound mind, would swear was not the part of
　　　" a man in his right senses."

ousness, lust, luxury, and fear, which are all within you, you as much stand in need of a physician for your mind, as the poor wretch whom I have been speaking of, stood in need of a physician for his body ; nor did he act more oppositely to the dictates of sound reason by despising his physician, and rejecting his remedies for his bodily complaints, than you do, by despising the philosophers, and rejecting their precepts, which are the only remedies for the disorders of the mind.

Thus the philosopher is supposed to conclude his discourse with his opponent, leaving an useful lesson on the minds of his idle and lazy pupils, who neglected their studies to indulge in sloth and luxury, not considering the fatal distempers of their minds, which, if neglected, must end in their destruction.

117. *Orestes.*] Was the son of Agamemnon and Clytemnestra. He slew his own mother, and Ægysthus, her adulterer, who had murdered his father. He killed Pyrrhus, the son of Achilles, in the temple of Apollo for marrying Hermione, who had been promised to him by her father Menelaus. Apollo sent furies to haunt him for the profanation of his temple, and forced him to expiate his crimes at the altar of Diana Taurica. See HOR. sat. iii. lib. ii. l. 133, et seq. in which satire Horace, with a degree of humour and raillery peculiar to himself, exposes the doctrine of the Stoic philosophers, which was, that all mankind were madmen and fools, except those of their own sect ; this he, with infinite humour and address, turns upon themselves, and naturally concludes, upon their own premises, that they were greater fools than the rest of the world.

The Stoics were a proud, harsh, severe, and sour sect, in many particulars not very different from the Cynics. The reader may find an instructive account of their principles, doctrines, and practices, as well as an edifying use made of them, in that masterly performance of Dr. Leland, entitled, "The Advantage and Ne- " cessity of the Christian Revelation," vol. ii. p. 140–223.

Satira Quinta.

ARGUMENT.

This Satire is justly esteemed the best of the six.—It con-
sists of three parts : in the first of which the Poet highly
praises Annæus Cornutus, who had been his preceptor,
and recommends other young men to his care.—In the
second part, he blames the idleness and sloth of young
men, and exhorts them to follow after the liberty and

PERSIUS. VATIBUS hic mos est, centum sibi poscere
    voces,
Centum ora, et linguas optare in carmina centum :
Fabula seu mœsto ponatur hianda tragœdo,
Vulnera seu Parthi ducentis ab inguine ferrum.
    CORNUTUS. Quorsum hæc ? aut quantas robusti carminis
    offas   5
Ingeris, ut par sit centeno gutture niti ?
Grande locuturi, nebulas Helicone legunto :
Si quibus aut Progues, aut si quibus olla Thyestæ

Line 1. *A custom, &c.*] Of epic
poets, and sometimes of orators, to
adopt this idea.
    HOM. Il. ii. for instance :
ὖδ μοι δεκα μεν γλωσσαι, δεκα δε
ϛοματα ειεν.
    So VIRG. Geor. ii. l. 43 ; and Æn.
vi. l. 625.
    Non mihi si centum linguæ sint,
    oraque centum.
    And, Quint. ad. fin. Decl. vi. Uni-
versorum vatum, scriptorumque ora
consentiant, vincet tamen res ista
mille linguas, &c.
    — *An hundred voices.*] Alluding
perhaps to the responses of the Sibyl
—VIRG. Æn. vi. l. 43-4.
    ———*Aditus centum, ostia centum,*
Unde ruunt totidem voces responsa
Sibyllæ.
    2. *For verses.*] *i. e.* That, when
they compose their verses, their style

and language might be amplified and
extended, adequately to the greatness
and variety of their subjects.
    3. *Whether a fable.*] The subject
or story on which they write is called
the fable.
    —*Bawled out, &c.*] *i. e.* Whether
they write tragedy, to be acted on the
stage.
    4. *Or the wounds of a Parthian,*
&c.] Or write an epic poem on the
wars of the Romans with the Parthians, in which the latter were overcome.
    Aut labentis equo describere vulnera
    Parthi.
        HOR. sat. i. lib. ii. l. 15.
    5. CORNUTUS. *Wherefore these*
things ?] Quorsum—to what end,
purpose, or intent, do you mention
these things, as if you were wishing
them for yourself?

Fifth Satire.

ARGUMENT.

; enfranchisement of the mind.—Thirdly, he shews wherein true liberty consists, and asserts that doctrine of the Stoics, that "a wise man only is free;" and that a slavery to vice is the most miserable of all.
The Satire begins in the form of a dialogue between Persius and Cornutus.

PERSIUS. THIS is a custom with poets, to ask for themselves an hundred voices,
And to wish for an hundred mouths, and an hundred tongues for their verses :
Whether a fable be proposed to be bawled out by the sad tragedian ;
Or the wounds of a Parthian drawing the sword from his groin.
CORNUTUS. Wherefore these things ? or how great pieces of robust verse   5
Dost thou thrust in, that it should be meet to strive with an hundred throats ?
Let those who are about to speak something great, gather clouds in Helicon,
If to any either the pot of Progne, or if to any that of Thyestes

---

—*How great pieces, &c.*] Metaph. from a person who puts large lumps or pieces of meat into his mouth, big enough to require a number of throats to swallow them.

q. d. What great and huge heroics art thou setting about, which thou canst think equal to such a wish, in order to enable thee to do them justice ?

7. *Gather clouds in Helicon.*] Let them go to mount Helicon, (see ante, the Prologue, l. 1, note,) and there gather up the mists which hang over the sacred top, and which teem, no doubt, with poetical rapture.

8. *The pot of Progne, &c.*] i. e. If any shall have his imagination warmed with the feasts of Progne and Thyestes, so as to write upon them.

Progne was the wife of Tereus, king of Thrace : Tereus fell in love with Philomela, sister to Progne, ravished her, and cut out her tongue. In revenge Progne killed Itys, her own son by Tereus, and served him up at a feast to be eaten by his father.

—*Thyestes*]. Atreus, king of My-

Fervebit, sæpe insulso cœnanda Glyconi.
Tu neque anhelanti, coquitur dum massa camino,   10
Folle premis ventos: nec, clauso murmure raucus,
Nescio quid tecum grave cornicaris inepte :
Nec scloppo tumidas intendis rumpere buccas.
Verba togæ sequeris, juncturâ callidus acri,
Ore teres modico, pallentes radere mores   15
Doctus, et ingenuo culpam defigere ludo.
Hinc trahe quæ dicas : mensasque relinque Mycenis
Cum capite et pedibus ; plebeiaque prandia nôris.
PERS. Non equidem hoc studeo, bullatis ut mihi nugis

cenæ, banished his brother Thyestes, for defiling his wife, Ærope : after-wards, recalling him, invited him to a banquet, ordered the children he had by her to be dressed and set before him on a table.

9. *Often to be supped on by foolish Glycon.*] He was some wretched tragedian of those times, who acted the parts of Tereus and Thyestes, and, accordingly, represented both of them as eating their children.

10. *Thou neither, while the mass, &c.*] Metaph. from smiths beating iron in furnaces, where the fire is kept up to a great heat by the blowing with bellows, in order to render the iron ductile, and easily formed into what shape they please.

q. d. You, says Cornutus, are not forging in your brain hard and difficult subjects, and blowing up your imagination, to form them into sublime poems. See Hor. lib. i. art. iv. l. 19–21.

11. *Nor hoarse, &c.*] Nor do you foolishly prate, like the hoarse croaking of a crow, with an inward kind of murmer to yourself, as if you were muttering something you think very grand and noble. See sat. iii. l. 81, and note.

13. *Tumid cheeks, &c.*] Scloppus is a sound made with puffing the cheeks, and then forcing the air out suddenly by striking them together with the hands.

q. d. Nor do you, when you repeat your verses, appear as if you were making a noise like that of cheeks puffed up almost to bursting, and then suddenly stricken together, like the swelling and bombast method of elo-

cution used by the fustian poets of our day.

Cornutus praises Persius in a threefold view. 1st. As not heating his imagination with high and difficult subjects. 2dly. As not affecting to be meditating and murmuring within himself, as if he would be thought to be producing some great performance. 3dly. As in the repetition of his verses avoiding all bombastic utterance.

14. *Words of the gown.*] Toga is often used to signify peace—Cedant arma togæ. Cic.—for, in time of peace, the Romans wore only the toga, or gown ; in time of war, the toga was thrown aside for the sagum, or soldier's cloak.

Cornutus here means to say, that Persius did not write of wars and bloodshed, but confined himself to subjects of common life, such as passed daily among the people, and made use of plain words suited to his matter.

—*Cunning in sharp composition.*] Acute and ingenious in a neat composition of verse. Metaph. from those who work in marble, who so exactly join their pieces together, and polish them so neatly, that the joints can't be perceived. See sat. i. l. 61, note.

15. *Smooth with moderate language.*] Teres signifies smooth, even ; also accurate, exact. Modico ore—with a moderate, modest language, or style of writing, neither rising above, nor sinking below the subject, nor flying out into that extravagance of expression, so much then in vogue. See sat. i. l. 95–99.

—*To lash.*] Radere, lit. signifies

Shall be hot, often to be supped on by foolish Glycon.
Thou neither, while the mass is heated in the furnace,   10
Pressest the wind with breathing bellows ; nor hoarse, with
   close murmur,
Foolishly croakest I know not what weighty matter with
   thyself :
Nor intendest to break thy tumid cheeks with a puff.
You follow the words of the gown, cunning in sharp com-
   position,
Smooth with moderate language, to lash vicious manners
Skilled, and to mark a crime with ingenuous sport.   16
Hence draw what you may say : and leave the tables at
   Mycenæ,
With the head and feet, and know plebeian dinners.
    PERS. I do not indeed desire this, that with empty
    trifles my

to scratch, or scrape up, or rub
against; here, by meton. to lash or
chastise. When a satirist does this
effectually, the guilty turn pale at his
reproof: for paleness is the effect of
fear ; and fear, of conscious guilt.—
Hence Hor. epist. 1. lib. i. l. 60, 1.
    ——*Hic murus aheneus esto,*
Nil conscire sibi, nullâ pallescere
   culpâ.
    —*Vicious manners.*] Pallentes
mores—lit. manners turning pale—
the effect for the cause. Meton. See
the last note.
    16. *Mark a crime with ingenuous
sport*] Defigere—metaph. from fixing a dagger, or critical mark, against
any word or sentence, either to be
corrected as faulty, or struck out as
superfluous. This the Greeks called
χεντειν, ςιζειν, compungere, confo-
dere, or the like.
   So Persius is said to stigmatize, or
mark down, a crime with ingenuous
sport—i. e. with well-bred raillery,
in order to its correction; to fix a
mark against it.
   Qu—If this be not going rather too
far with regard to Persius, who seems
not much inclined to politeness, with
respect to those whom he satirizes,
but rather treats them with severity
and roughness ?
   Horace indeed deserved such an
account to be given of him. Comp.
sat. i. l. 113-15.

John Hanvil, a monk of St. Alban's, about the year 1190, thus
writes on the different merits of Horace and Persius :
   *Persius in pelago Flacci decurrit,
    et audet*
   *Mendteasse stylum Satiræ, serraque
    cruentus*
   *Rodit, et ignorat polientem pectora
    limam.*
   17. *Hence draw, &c.*] From hence,
i. e. from the vices of mankind, select the subjects of your writings.
   —*Leave the tables, &c.*] Leave the
tragical banquet of Thyestes at Mycenæ for others to write on—trouble
not yourself about such subjects.
   18. *With the head and feet.*]—
Atreus reserved the heads, feet, and
hands of the children ; which after
supper he shewed to his brother Thyestes, that he might know whose flesh
he had been feasting upon.
   —*Know plebeian dinners.*] Acquaint yourself only with the enormities that pass in common life—nôris
—quasi, fac noscas—let these be your
food for satire.
   19. *I do not indeed desire this.*]—
Persius here answers his preceptor
Cornutus, and tells him, that he does
not want an hundred tongues and
voices, in order to be writing vain and
highflown poems ; but that he might
duly express Cornutus's worth, and
his sense of it.

Pagina turgescat, dare pondus idonea fumo.   20
Secreti loquimur: tibi nunc, hortante camœnâ,
Excutienda damus præcordia: quantaque nostræ
Pars tua sit, Cornute, animæ, tibi, dulcis amice,
Ostendisse juvat. Pulsa, dignoscere cautus
Quid solidum crepet, et pictæ tectoria linguæ.   25
His ego centenas ausim deposcere voces,
Ut, quantum mihi te sinuoso in pectore fixi,
Voce traham purâ: totumque hoc verba resignent,
Quod latet arcanâ non enarrabile fibrâ.
   Cum primum pavido custos mihi purpura cessit,   30
Bullaque succinctis Laribus donata pependit;
Cum blandi comites; totâque impune Suburrâ
Permisit sparsisse oculos jam candidus umbo;

Studeo signifies, literally, to study, but also to apply the mind to, to care for a thing, to mind, to desire it.

—*Empty trifles.*] Bullatis (from *bulla*, a bubble of water) *nugis*—by met. swelling lines, lofty words, without sense, empty expressions.—AINSW.

20. *Fit to give weight [to smoke.*] i. e. Fit for nothing else but to give an air of consequence and importance to trifles, which, in reality, have no more substance in them than smoke. Nugis addere pondus. HOR. Epist. lib. i. epist. xix. l. 42.

21. *Secret we speak.*] You and I, Cornutus, are not now speaking to the multitude, but to each other in private, and therefore I will disclose the sentiments of my heart.

—*The Muse exhorting.*] My Muse prompting and leading me to an ample disclosure of my thoughts, and to reveal how great a share you have in my affections—to do this is a pleasure to myself.

25. *What may sound solid.*] Try and examine me, knock at my breast; if you wish to know whether I am sincere or not, hear how that sounds. Metaphor, from striking earthen vessels with the knuckle, in order to try, by the sound, whether they were solid or cracked. See sat. iii. l. 21, 2, and note.

—*The coverings, &c.*] Tectorium —the plaster, parget, or rough-cast of a wall, which conceals it: hence dissimulation, flattery, which cover

the real sentiments of the heart. See Matt. xxiii. 27.

—*Painted tongue.*] Pictæ linguæ —i. e. a tongue adorned and garnished with dissimulation—varnished over with falsehood.

26. *For these things.*] i. e. Properly to disclose my friendship and gratitude to you, by drawing forth and uttering what I feel for you, whom I have fixed within the most intimate recesses of my breast. See AINSW. *Sinuosus*, No. 4. This sense of the word seems metaphorical, and to be taken from what hath many turnings and windings, and so difficult to find or trace out.

28. *With pure voice.*] With the utmost sincerity, pure from all guile.

—*Words may unseal.*] Resigno is to open what is sealed, to unseal; hence, met. to discover and declare.

29. *Not to be told.*] Not fully to be expressed.

—*In my secret inwards.*] In the secret recesses of my heart and mind. Comp. sat. i. l. 44.

30. *The guardian purple.*] The habit worn by younger noblemen was edged about with a border of purple; an ornament which had the repute of being sacred, and was therefore assigned to children as a sort of preservative. Hence Persius calls it custos purpura.

—*Fearful.*] Which protected me when a child, and when I was under the fear and awe of a severe master.

—*Yielded.*] Resigned its charge,

Page should swell, fit to give weight to smoke.   20.
Secret we speak: to you now, the Muse exhorting,
I give my heart to be searched, and how great a part
Of my soul, Cornutus, is yours, to you, my gentle friend,
It pleases me to have shewn: knock, careful to discern
What may sound solid, and the coverings of a painted
    tongue.   25
For these things I would dare to require an hundred voices,
That, how much I have fixed you, in my inmost breast,
I may draw forth with pure voice; and all this, words may
    unseal,
Which lies hid, not to be told, in my secret inwards.

    When first to fearful me the guardian purple yielded,
And the bulla presented to the girt Lares hung up;   31
When kind companions, and, with impunity, in the whole
    Suburra
Now the white shield permitted me to have thrown about
    my eyes,

and gave place to the toga virilis, or manly gown. About the age of sixteen or seventeen they laid aside the the prætexta, and put on the togá virilis, and were ranked with men.

31. *And the bulla.*] This was another ornament worn by children; it was worn hanging from the neck, or about the breast, and was made in the shape of an heart, and hollow within. This they left off with the prætexta, and consecrated to the household gods, and hung up in honour to them. See ANT. Univ. Hist. vol. xi. p. 289, note *s*.

31. *The girt Lares*] The images of the Lares, or household gods, were described in a sort of military habit, which hung on the left shoulder, with a lappet fetched under the other arm, brought over the breast, and tied in a knot. The idea of this dress was first taken from the Gabini, and called Cinctus Gabinus. See AINSW. *Gabinus;* and VIRG. Æn. vii. 612. and Servius's note there.

32. *Kind companions*] A set of young fellows, who were my companions, and ready to join in any scheme of debauchery with me. I cannot think that comites here is to be understood of " his schoolmasters, " or pedagogues, who now no longer

" treated him with severity." He was now a man, and had done with these. Of such a one HORACE says,

*Imberbis juvenis, tandem custode
    remoto, &c.*
    De Art. Poet l. 161–5.
And see KENNETT, Antiq. p. 311, edit 5. 1713.

—*In the whole Suburra.*] This was a famous and populous street in Rome, where were numbers of brothels, the harlots from which walked out by night, to the great mischief of young men. Here, says Persius, I could ramble as I pleased, and fix my eyes where I pleased, and had nobody to call me to account, or punish me for it. JUV. sat. iii. l. 5.

33. *The white shield, &c.*] When the young men put on the toga virilis, they were presented with a white shield; that is to say, a shield with no engraving, device, or writing upon it, but quite blank. This shield was a token that they were now grown up, and fit for war. Its being blank, signified their not having yet achieved any warlike action worthy to be described, or recorded, upon it by a device.

So VIRG. Æn. ix. l. 548.
*Ense levis nudo, parmáque inglorius
    albá.*

Cumque iter ambiguum est, et, vitæ nescius, error
Diducit trepidas ramosa in compita mentes;   35
Me tibi supposui : teneros tu sucipis annos,
Socratico, Cornute, sinu.   Tunc fallere solers,
Apposita intortos extendit regula mores ;
Et premitur ratione animus, vincique laborat,
Artificemque tuo ducit sub pollice vultum.   40
Tecum etenim longos memini consumere soles ;
Et tecum primas epulis decerpere noctes.
Unum opus, et requiem pariter disponimus ambo :
Atque verecundâ laxamus seria mensâ.
    Non equidem hoc dubites, amborum fœdere certo   45
Consentire dies, et ab uno sidere duci.

When this shield was a passport to me, says Persius, to go where I pleased, without being molested by my old masters.

34. *When the journey is doubtful.*] When the mind of a young man is doubting what road of life to take, like a traveller who comes to where two ways meet, and can hardly determine which to pursue.

· *—And error.*] So apt to beset young minds, and so easily to mislead them.

—Ignorant of life.] Of the best purposes and ends of life, and wholly unknowing and ignorant of the world. .

35. *Parts asunder trembling minds.*] Divides the young and inexperienced minds of young men, fearing and trembling between the choice of good and evil, now on this side, now on that.

35. *Branching cross-ways.*] Compitum is a place where two or more ways meet.   The poet here alludes to the Pythagorean letter Y.   See sat. iii. l. 56. note.

36. *I put myself under you.*] Under your care and instruction.

—You undertake, &c.] You admitted me under your discipline, in order to season my mind with the moral philosophy of the Stoics : you not only received me as a pupil, but took me to your bosom with the affection of a parent. .

Antisthenes, the master of Diogenes, was a disciple of Socrates ; Diogenes taught Crates the Theban,

who taught Zeno the founder of the Stoic school ; so that the Stoic dogmas might be said to be derived, originally, from Socrates, as from the fountainhead.

37. *Dextrous to deceive, &c.*] The application of your doctrine to my morals, which were depraved, and warped from the strict rule of right, first discovered this to me, and then corrected it ; but this you did with so much skill and address, that I grew almost insensibly reformed : so gradually were the severities of your discipline discovered to me, that I was happily cheated, as it were, into reformation ; whereas, had you at first acquainted me with the whole at once, I probably had rejected it, not only as displeasing, but as unattainable by one who thought as I then did.

38. *Applied rule.*] Metaph. from mechanics, who, by a rule applied to the side of any thing, discover its being warped from a straight line, and set it right.

—Rectifies.] Lit. extends. Metaph. from straitening a twisted or entangled cord, by extending or stretching it out. Intortos, lit. twisted, entangled.

39. *My mind is pressed by reason, &c.*] My mind and all its faculties were so overpowered by the conviction of reason, that it strove to coincide with what I heard from you, and to be conquered by your wisdom.

—Labours, &c.] The word laborat denotes the difficulties which lie

And when the journey is doubtful, and error, ignorant of
    life,
Parts asunder trembling minds into the branching cross-
    ways,   35
I put myself under you : you undertake my tender years,
Cornutus, with Socratic bosom. Then, dextrous to de-
    ceive,
The applied rule rectifies my depraved morals,
And my mind is pressed by reason, and labours to be
    overcome,
And draws, under your thumb, an artificial countenance.
For I remember to consume with you long suns,   41
And with you to pluck the first nights from feasts.
One work and rest we both dispose together,
And relax serious things with a modest table.
Do not indeed doubt this, that, in a certain agreement,
The days of both consent, and are derived from one star. 46

in the way of your minds to yield to
instruction, and to subdue and correct their vicious habits and inclinations.

40. *And draws, &c.*] Metaph.
from an artist, who draws forth, or
forms, figures with his fingers, out of
wax or clay. Ducere is a word peculiar to the making of statues in marble
also.

Vivos ducent de marmore vultus.
               Æn. vi. 848.

—*An artificial countenance.*] Artificem, hypallage, for artifici pollice.
The sense is—My mind, by thee
gently and wisely wrought upon, put
on that form and appearance which
you wished it should. The like
thought occurs, Juv. sat. vii. l. 237.

*Exigite ut mores teneros ceu pollice
    ducat,*
Ut si quis cerâ vultum facit—.

41. *Consume long suns.*] To have
passed many long days—soles, for
dies. Meton.

    ——*Sæpe ego longos*
*Cantando puerum memini me con-
    dere soles.*
             VIRG. ecl. ix. l. 51–2.

42. *To pluck the first nights, &c.*]
Decerpere—metaph. from plucking
fruit. The first nights—the first part
or beginning of nights ; we plucked,
i. e. we took away from the hours of
feasting.—*q. d.* Instead of supping at

an early hour, and being long at table, we spent the first part of the
evening in philosophical converse,
thus abridging the time of feasting
for the sake of improvement.

    ——*Of the night*
*Have borrow'd the first hours,
    feasting with thee*
On the choice dainties of philosophy.
               HOLYDAY.

43. *One work and rest, &c.*] We,
both of us, disposed and divided our
hours of study, and our hours of rest
and refreshment, in a like manner together.

44. *And relax serious things.*] Relaxed our minds from study.

—*A modest table.*] With innocent
mirth, as we sat at table, and with
frugal meals.

45. *Do not doubt this, &c.*] Beyond a doubt, this strict union of our
minds must be derived from an agreement in the time of our nativity, being born both under the same star.

So HOR. lib. ii. ode xvii. l. 21–2.

*Utrumque nostrum incredibili modo
Consentit astrum.*

The ancients thought that the
minds of men were greatly influenced
by the planet which presided at their
birth ; and that those who were born
under the same planet, had the same
dispositions and inclinations.

Nostra vel æquali suspendit tempora Librû
Parca tenax veri ; seu nata fidelibus hora
Dividit in Geminos concordia fata duorum ;
Saturnumque gravem nostro Jove frangimus una.   50
Nescio quod certe est, quod me tibi temperat, astrum.
   Mille hominum species, et rerum discolor usus :
Velle suum, cuique est ; nec voto vivitur uno.
Mercibus hic Italis mutat, sub sole recenti,
Rugosum piper, et pallentis grana cumini :   55
Hic, satur, irriguo mavult turgescere somno ;
Hic campo indulget : hunc alea decoquit : ille
In Venerem putret.   Sed cum lapidosa chiragra
Fregerit articulos, veteris ramalia fagi ;
Tunc crassos transisse dies, lucemque palustrem,   60

47. *Fate, tenacious of truth.*] Un-
erring fate, as we say.
   —*Suspended our times.*] Metaph.
from hanging things on the beam of
a balance, in order to weigh them.
   Fate weighed, with equal balance,
our times, when Libra had the ascendancy.
   48. *With equal Libra.*] A constellation into which the sun enters about
the twentieth of September, described
by a pair of scales, the emblem of
equity and justice.
   Felix æquatæ genitus sub pondere
   Libræ.   MANIL. lib. v.
   Seu Libra, seu me Scorpius aspicit
   Formidolosus, pars violentior
   Natalis horæ, &c.
   HOR lib. ii. ode xvii. l. 17-22.
   —*Framed for the faithful*] The
particular hour which presides over
the faithfulness of friendship.
   49. *Divides to the Twins, &c.*] The
Gemini, another constellation represented by two twin-children, under
which whosoever were born, were
supposed by the astrologers to consent, very exactly, in their affections
and pursuits.
   Magnus erit Geminis amor et con-
   cordia duplex.
            MANIL. lib. ii.
   50. *Break, &c.*] Frangere and tem-
perare were used by the astrologers,
when the malignant aspect of one star
was corrected, and its influence prevented, by the power of some other
propitious and benign planet.
   Hence that astrological axiom—

Quicquid ligat Saturnus, solvit Jupiter.
   The planet Saturn was reckoned to
have a malign aspect ; the planet Jupiter a mild and favourable one, and
to counteract the former.
   ——*Te Jovis impio*
   Tutela Saturno, refulgens
   Eripuit.
   HOR. ode xvii. lib. ii. l. 22-4.
   51. *I know not, &c.*] I will not
take upon me to be certain what star
it was ; but that it proceeds from the
influence of some friendly star or
other, which presided at our natal
hour, that we are one in heart and
sentiment, I am very clear.
   Tempero literally signifies to temper, mix or mingle together.
   52. *There are a thousand species,*
&c.] i. e. Different kinds of men, as
to their dispositions and pursuits.
   —*Different use, &c.*] Discolor—
literally, of a different colour. Their
use of what they possess differs as
much as one colour from another ;
some, (as it follows in the next lines,)
from avarice, trade to increase their
store ; others, through luxury and
extravagance, squander it away.
   53. *Has his will.*] Velle, i. e. voluntas, a Græcism. Vivitur, impers.
See sat. iii. 20, note.
   54. *The recent sun.*] In the east,
where the sun first appears.
   55. *Changes, &c.*] Sails to the
East Indies, where he barters the produce of Italy for the produce of the
East.

Fate, tenacious of truth, either suspended our times
With equal Libra; or the hour, framed for the faithful,
Divides to the Twins the concordant fates of both;
And we together break grievous Saturn with our Jupiter.
I know not what star it is certainly which tempers me with
    you.   51
    There are a thousand species of men, and a different use
  of things:
Every one has his will, nor do they live with one wish.
This man, for Italian merchandizes under-the recent sun,
Changes the wrinkled pepper, and grains of pale cumin:
Another, sated, had rather swell up with moist sleep: 56
Another indulges in the field; another the die consumes;
    another
Is rotten for Venus: but when the stony gout
Has broken his joints, the branches of the old beech,
Then, that their gross days have passed away, and the
    gloomy light,   60

—*Wrinkled pepper.*] When the pepper is gathered, and dried in the sun, the coat or outside shrivels up into wrinkles.

.—*Pale cumin.*] The seed of an herb, which being infused into wine, or other liquor, causes a paleness in those who drink it: it comes from Ethiopia. Probably it stands here for any Oriental aromatics.

Hor. epist. xix. lib. i. l. 17, 18, speaks of his imitators:

——*Quod si*
Pallerem casu, biberent exsangue
    cuminum.

56. *Sated.*] Satur—that has his belly full—glutted with eating and drinking.

—*Swell up.*] With fat.

—*Moist sleep*] Irriguus signifies wet, moist, watered; also, that watereth. Here, metaph. from watering plants, by which they increase and grow. So sleep is to those who eat much, and sleep much; it makes them grow, and increase in bulk.

57. *Indulges in the field.*] In the sports and exercises of the Campus Martius. Or perhaps field-sports may be understood. Comp. Hor. ode i. l. 3–6, and l. 25–8.

—*The die consumes.*] Is ruined by gaming. Decoquit—metaph. from boiling away liquors over a fire. So

the gamester, by continual play, consumes his substance.

58. *For Venus.*] i. e. Ruins his health—is in a manner rotten—by continual acts of lewdness and debauchery. Putris means also wanton, lascivious.

Omnes in Damalim putres deponent oculos.

Hor. lib. i. ode xxxvi. l. 17, 18.

—*The stony gout*] So called from its breeding chalk-stones in the joints, when long afflicted with it.

59. *Broken his joints.*] Destroyed the use of them as much as if they had been broken, and are so to all appearance.

—*The branches, &c.*] Ramalia—seared or dead boughs cut from a tree, which may be looked upon, from their withered and useless appearance, as very strong emblems of a gouty man's limbs, the joints of which are useless, and the flesh withered away—(see sat. i. 9 l.)—so that they appear like the dead branches of an old decayed beech-tree.

60. *Gross days.*] Crassos—the days which they have spent in gross sensuality, as well as in thick mental darkness and error.

—*Gloomy light*] Palustrem—metaph. from the fogs which arise in marshes and fenny places, which ob-

Et sibi jam seri vitam ingemuêre relictam.
  At te nocturnis juvat impallescere chartis,
Cultor enim juvenum, purgatas inseris aures
Fruge Cleantheâ. Petite hinc, juveneseque senesque,
Finem animo certum, miserisque viatica canis.   65
  ' Cras hoc fiet.' Idem cras fiet. ' Quid ! quasi magnum
' Nempe diem donas ?' Sed cum lux altera venit,
Jam cras hesternum consumpsimus : ecce aliud cras
Egerit hos annos, et semper paulum erit ultra :
Nam quamvis prope te, quamvis temone sub uno,   70
Vertentem sese frustra sectabere canthum,
Cum rota posterior curras, et in axe secundo.

scure the light, and involve those who live in it, or near them, in unwholesome mists. Such is the situation of those whose way of life is not only attended with ignorance and error, but with injury to their health, and with ruin of their comfort.

61. *Late bewailed.*] Too late for remedy.

—*The life now left, &c.*] They not only bemoan themselves, at the recollection of their past mispent life, but the portion of life which now remains, being embittered by remorse, pain, and disease, becomes a grief and burthen.

62. *Grow pale, &c.*] Your delight, O Cornutus, is to pass the time, when others sleep, in hard study, which brings a paleness on your countenance. See sat. i. l. 121 ; and sat. iii. l. 85.

63. *A cultivator of youths.*] Cultor —metaph. from colo, to till or cultivate the ground.

q. d. As the husbandman tills or cultivates the ground, and prepares it to receive seed, and to bring forth fruit—so do you, Cornutus, prepare youthful minds to receive and bring forth wisdom.

—*You sow their purged ears.*] The metaphor is still carried on ; as the husbandman casts the seed into the ground which he has prepared and cleaned, by tillage, from weeds—so do you sow the doctrines of moral philosophy, which were taught by Cleanthes, the disciple and successor of Zeno, in the ears of your pupils, after having purged away those errors,

falsehoods, and prejudices, with which they were at first possessed, by your wise and well-applied instruction. You first teach them to avoid vice and error, and then to embrace and follow truth and virtue.

Virtus est vitium fugere, et sapientia prima
Stultitiâ caruisse.

Hor. lib. i. epist. i. l. 41, 2.

64. *Hence seek, &c.*] Persius here invites both young and old to seek for wisdom from the Stoic philosophy, as taught by his friend and preceptor Cornutus : that, thereby, they might find some certain and fixed end, to which their views might be directed, and no longer fluctuate in the uncertainty of error.

Certum voto pete finem.

Hor. Epist. lib. i. ep. ii. l. 56.

65. *Stores, &c.*] Viatica, literally are stores, provisions, things necessary for a journey ; as money, victuals, &c.

The poet here advises their learning philosophy, that their minds might be furnished with what would suffice to support them through the journey of life, and more particularly through the latter part of it, when under the miseries and infirmities of old age.

66. " *To-morrow*," &c.] Persius here introduces some idle young man, as if saying—" To be sure you advise very rightly, but give me a lit-" tle time—to-morrow (*q. d.* some " time hence) I will apply myself to " the studies which you recommend."

—" *The same will be done to-mor-*

And they have late bewailed the life now left to them.
  But it delights you to grow pale with nightly papers,
For a cultivator of youths, you sow their purged ears
With Cleanthean corn. Hence seek, ye young and old,
A certain end to the mind, and stores for miserable grey
    hairs.   65
" To-morrow this shall be done"—" the same will be
  " done, to-morrow?"—" what !
" As a great thing truly do you give a day ?"—" but when
  " another day comes,
" We have already spent yesterday's to-morrow. Behold
  " another to-morrow
" Has spent these years, and will always be a little beyond:
" For although near you, although under one beam,   70
" You will in vain follow the felly turning itself,
" When you, the hinder wheel, do run, and on the second
    " axle."

row."] When to-morrow comes, answers Persius, the same thing will be done; that is, you will want to defer it for a day more.

66. " What !" &c.] What ! replies the procrastinator, will not you allow me another day before I begin ? —what ! do you make such a mighty matter of giving me a day, as if that were of so great consequence ?

68. " Yesterday's to-morrow."]— But, rejoins Persius, when another day comes, remember that yesterday, which was the morrow of the day before it, and which you wished to be allowed you, is passed and gone.

—" Behold, another to-morrow."] This day, which is the morrow of yesterday, is now arrived, and is, with all the past morrows, exhausting and consuming these years of ours; and thus the time you ask for will always be put off, and stand a little beyond the morrow you fix upon.

70. " Altho' near you," &c.] The poet, in allusion to the hind-wheel of a carriage, which is near to, and follows the fore-wheel, but never can overtake it, gives the young man to understand, that, though to-day is nearly connected with to-morrow, in point of time, yet it cannot overtake it, the morrow will always keep on from day to day, and it can never be overtaken—thus shewing, that procrastinated time will always fly on, keep out of his reach, however near he may be to it, all his resolutions to overtake it will be in vain.

—" Under one beam."] Temo signifies the beam of the wain, or the draught-tree, whereon the yoke hangeth. Sometimes, by synec. the whole carriage.—q. d. Our days may be considered as the wheels by which our lives roll on; each day, as well as another, is joined to the space allotted us, like wheels to the same chariot.

71. " The felly."] Canthus properly signifies the iron wherewith the wheel is bound, or shod, on the outward circle, called the felly—here, by synec. the wheel itself.

72. " The second axle."] Axis— the axle-tree on which the wheel is fixed, and about which it turns—the second, i. e. the hinder.—q. d. You will, like the hinder wheel of a carriage, which can never overtake the fore-wheel, be still following the time before you, but will never overtake it; therefore defer not till to-morrow, what you should do to-day. The whole of the metaphor, l. 70-2, is very fine, and well expressed. See Hor. lib. ii. ode xviii. l. 15, 16.

I must confess that I cannot dismiss this part of my task, without mentioning that beautiful description of the slipping away of time, unper-

Libertate opus est : non hâc, quâ, ut quisque Velinâ
Publius emeruit, scabiosum tesserulâ far
Possidet. Heu steriles veri, quibus una Quiritem   75
Vertigo facit !—Hic Dama est, non tressis agaso ;
Vappa, et lippus, et in tenui farragine mendax :
Verterit hunc dominus, momento turbinis exit
Marcus Dama.——Papæ ! Marco spondente, recusas
Credere tu nummos ?—Marco sub judice palles ?   80
—Marcus dixit : ita est.—Assigna, Marce, tabellas.—

ceived and unimproved, which we find
in Shakespeare :

" *To-morrow, and to-morrow, and*
" *to-morrow,*
" *Creeps in this petty pace from day*
" *to day,*
" *To the last syllable of recorded*
" *time :*
" *And all our yesterdays have light-*
" *ed fools*
" *The way to dusty death.*"——'

Macb. act v. sc. 5. edit. *Stockdale.*
73. *There is need of liberty.*] The
poet now advances to a discussion of
that paradox of the Stoics—that "only
" the wise are free ;"—and that those,
who would follow after, and attain to
true liberty, must be released from
the mental shackles of vice and error.
His treatment of the subject is exquisitely fine, and worthy our serious
attention.

—*Not this.*] Not merely outward
liberty, or liberty of the body, such
as is conferred on slaves at their manumission.

—*By which.*] See l. 74, note 2.
—*Every Publius.*] The slaves had
no prænomen ; but when they had
their freedom given them, they assumed one—so, for instance, a slave
that was called Licinius, would add
the name of his master to his own,
and call himself, if his master's name
were Publius, Publius Licinius—they
also added the name of the tribe into
which they were received and en-
rolled ; suppose the Velinan, then
the freed-man would style himself
Publius Licinius Velina—thus he was
distinguished from slaves.

74. *Been discharged.*] *i. e.* From
slavery—made free. Emeruit—metaph. from soldiers, who for some
meritorious service were sent home,
and discharged from going to war.—

Also from gladiators, who for their
valour and dexterity at the theatre
obtained their dismission from their
perilous occupation, and were donati
rude, presented with a rod, or wand,
in token of their discharge and release. Hor. epist. i. lib. i. l. 2.
These were styled Emeriti.

So slaves were often made free, on
account of their past services, as having deserved this favour—this is signified by emeruit here.

—*Mouldy corn, &c.*] Those who
are thus admitted to freedom, and en-
rolled in one of the tribes, were entitled to all public doles and donations, on producing a little ticket or
tally, which was given them on their
manumission. The corn laid up in
the public magazines was not of the
best sort, and was frequently damaged
with keeping.

The name of the person and of the
tribe, which he belonged to, was inscribed on the ticket, by which he was
known to be a citizen. See Juv. sat.
vii. l. 174, note.

75. *Alas ! ye barren, &c.*] The
poet speaks with commisseration, of
their ignorance, and total barrenness,
with respect to truth and real wisdom,
who could imagine that a man should
be called free, because he was emancipated from bodily slavery.

—*One turn.*] Vertigo (from ver-
tere, to turn). This was one of the
ceremonies of making a slave free :
he was carried before the prætor, who
turned him round upon his heel, and
said—Hunc esse liberum volo.

So Plautus, Menæchm. Liber esto,
ito quo voles. Thus he became Quiris, a Roman citizen. See Juv. sat.
iii. l. 60, note.

76. *Here is Dama.*] For instance,

There is need of liberty: not this, by which every Pub-
lius in the Velinan tribe,
As soon as he has been discharged, mouldy corn with his
    tally
Possesses. Alas! ye barren of truth—among whom one
    turn   75
Makes a Roman! here is Dama, a groom not worth three
    farthings;
A scoundrel, and blear-eyed, and a liar in a little corn:
If his master turn him—in the movement of a top, he comes
    forth
Marcus Dama. Wonderful! Marcus being security, re-
    fuse you
To lend money? Are you pale under judge Marcus?   80
Marcus said it—it is so.—Sign, Marcus, the tablets.

says the poet, here is the slave
Dama.

—A groom not worth, &c.] Agaso,
an horse-keeper, a groom that looks
after his master's horses, from ago and
asinus. Non tressis (qu. tres asses)
a poor, paltry fellow, worth hardly
three farthings if one were to purchase him. They bought their slaves.

77. *A scoundrel.*] Vappa signifies
wine that is palled, that has lost its
strength, therefore called vapid.—
Hence a stupid, senseless fellow; or
a scoundrel, a good-for-nothing fellow.

—Blear-eyed.] Perhaps from debauchery and drunkenness. See sat.
ii. l. 72, note.

—A liar in a little corn.] That will
cheat his master, and defraud his
horses of their slender allowance, and
then lie to conceal his petty knavery.
Farrago is a mixture of several grains
—Mesceline.

78. *If his master, &c.*] Let his
master but turn him upon his heel.
See note above, l. 75.

—Movement of a top.] In one turn
of a top, which is very swift when it
is spinning—i. e. as we say, in the
twinkling of an eye. This allusion to
the turning of a top, very humourously agrees with the veterit.

—He comes forth, &c.] He that
went before the prætor plain Dama,
now comes out from him with a noble prænomen, and calls himself
Marcus Dama.

79. *Wonderful!*] What a surprising change! or papæ may introduce
the following irony, where a person
is supposed to hesitate about lending
money, for which Marcus offers to
become surety. Papæ—How strange!
that you should scruple it, when so
respectable a person as Marcus offers
his bond, and engages for the payment!

80. *Are you pale?*] Do you fear
lest you should not have justice done
you, where so worthy a person is advanced to the magistracy?

81. *Marcus said it, &c.*] Marcus
gives his testimony, and who can
contradict so just and upright a witness—what he says must be true.

—Sign, Marcus, the tablets.]—
The poet here repeats the word Marcus, and drops the word Dama, as if
he would ludicrously insinuate, that
however great a rogue Dama was,
yet to be sure Marcus was a very different kind of person. He supposes
him called upon to sign his name, as
witness to somebody's will, which he
could not do when a slave, for their
testimony was not received.

—The tablets.] Thin planks of
wood, smeared over with wax, on
which they wrote wills, deeds, &c.
Here the will or deed itself.

The poet, in the preceding irony,
carries on his grand point, which was
to deride the common notion of liberty, or of a change being wrought,
with regard to the respectability of

Hæc mera libertas! Hoc nobis pilea donant!
 ' An quisquam est alius liber, nisi ducere vitam
 ' Cui licet, ut voluit? licet, ut volo, vivere: non sum
 ' Liberior Bruto?' Mendose colligis, inquit   85
Stoicus hic, aurem mordaci lotus aceto:
Hoc reliquum accipio; licet illud, et, ut volo, tolle.
 ' Vindictâ postquam meus a prætore recessi,
 ' Cur mihi non liceat, jussit quodcunque voluntas;
 ' Excepto, si quid Masuri rubrica vetavit?'   90
Disce; sed ira cadat naso, rugosaque sanna,
Dum veteres avias tibi de pulmone revello.
Non prætoris erat, stultis dare tenuia rerum

those who were still, however emancipated from bodily slavery, slaves
under ignorance, vice, and error.

82. *Mere liberty.*] Mera—bare,
naked liberty (says the Stoic)—*i. e.*
in the bare, outward, literal sense of
the word; but it is to be understood
no farther.

—*This caps give us.*] The slaves
went bare-headed, with their hair
growing long, and hanging down;
but when they were manumitted,
their heads were shaved, and a cap,
the ensign of liberty, put on their
heads in the temple of Feronia, the
goddess of liberty. See sat. iii. l. 106.

83. " *Any other free,*" &c.] Here
the poet introduces Dama as replying
—" Aye, you may deride my notions
" of liberty; but pray who is free if
" I am not? Is there any other free-
" dom but to be able to live as one
" pleases? But I may live as I please
" —therefore am I not free?" by this
syllogism thinking to prove hispoint.

85. " *More free than Brutus.*"]—
M. Junius Brutus, the great asserter
and restorer of liberty, by the expulsion of the Tarquins, &c. who sacrificed his own sons in the cause of
freedom, and changed the form of the
government into a commonwealth.

—" *You conclude falsely.*"] Your
argument is bad; the assumption
which you make, that " you live as
" you please," is not true, therefore
the conclusion which you gather or
collect from it is false, namely, " that
" you are free." See AINSW. *Colligo,*
No. 6.

85—6. *Says a Stoic.*] *i. e.* Methinks
I hear some Stoic say.

86. *Washed his ear,* &c.] At l.
63. we find purgatas aures, where
see the note; here, lotus aurem, meaning also the same as before, only under a different image, differently expressed. By vinegar, here, we are
to understand the sharp and severe
doctrines of the Stoic philosophy,
which has cleansed his mind from all
such false ideas of liberty, and made
his ear quick in the discernment of
truth and falsehood.

87. " *I accept,*" &c.] Your definition of liberty in your first proposition is true; I grant that " all who
" may live as they please are free;"
but I deny your minor, or second
proposition, *viz.* " that you live as
" you please;" therefore your conclusion, *viz.* " that you are free,"
is also wrong.

That—" *I may,*" *and* " *as I will.*"]
i. e. Take away your minor proposition, and I admit what remains—hoc
reliquum accipio—*viz.* all that is contained in the first proposition—that
" all who may live as they please are
" free:" this is certainly a good definition of liberty: but this is not your
case.

88. " *From the prætor.*"] Before
whom I was carried, in order to receive my freedom.

—" *My own.*"] Meus—*i. e.* my
own master; being made free, and
emancipated from the commands of
another, replies Dama, not at all understanding what the Stoic meant by
liberty.

—" *By the wand.*"] Vindicta. The
prætor laid a wand upon the slave's

This is mere liberty—this caps give us.
" Is there any other free, unless he who may live
" As he likes ?—I may live as I like : am not I   84
" More free than Brutus ?"—" You conclude falsely," says
A Stoic here, having washed his ear with sharp vinegar :
" I accept this which is left, take away that—" I may,"
    and " as I will."
    " After I withdrew from the prætor, my own by-the
    "wand,
" Why might I not do whatever my will commanded,
" Except if the rubric of Masurius forbad any thing ?"   90
    " Learn : but let anger fall from your nose, and the
    " wrinkling sneer, *sneer*
" While I pluck from your breast your old wives' tales.
    " It was not of the prætor to give the delicate manage-
    " ment of things

head, and said, " I will that this man "become free," and then delivered the wand out of his own hand into the lictor's ; (see post, l. 175.) This wand was called vindicta, as vindicating, or maintaining liberty. See Hor. lib. ii. sat. vii. l. 76.

90. "*Rubric.*"] The text of the Roman laws was written in red letters, which was called the Rubric. DRYDEN. According to others, the titles and beginnings of the different statutes were only written in red, and therefore to be understood by rubrica. See AINSW. See JUV. sat. xiv. l. 192, 3, note.

—"*Masurius.*"] An eminent and learned lawyer, in the reign of Tiberius, who made a digest of the Roman laws.

q. d. When I received my freedom from the prætor, surely I was at liberty to do as I would, except, indeed, breaking the law ; I do not say that I might do this.

91. "*Learn.*"] The Stoic here begins his argument, in order to refute what Dama was supposed to say in support of his notion of liberty.
Now listen to me, says the Stoic, that you may learn what true liberty is, and in what it consists.

—"*Let anger fall,*" &c.] Cease from your anger at me, for ridiculing your notion of liberty.
It is to be remarked, that the an-

cients represented the nose as denoting laughter, sat. i. 115. Contempt, sat. i. 37. Anger, as here. So we find the nose, or nostrils, denoting anger frequently in the Hebrew Bible. See the learned and accurate Mr. PARKHURST, Heb. and Eng. Lex. אף, No. 5.

—"*Wrinkling sneer.*"] Comp. sat. i. 37, 8. and note.

92. "*From your breast,*" &c.]—Pulmo, literally, signifies the lungs ; but here denotes the whole contents of the breast in a moral sense. " Put away anger and sneering at what I say, while I pluck up those foolish notions of liberty, which are implanted and rooted within your mind, and with which you are as pleased and satisfied, as a child is with an old woman's tale." Avia is literally a grandame, or grandmother : hence old women's tales. AINSW. *Fabellæ aniles.* Hor. lib. ii. sat. vi. l. 77, 8. Γεαωδεις μυθους. 1 Tim. iv. 7.

93. " *It was not of,*" &c.] It was not in the power of the prætor.
—" *The delicate management of things,* &c.] Though the prætor might confer civil liberty upon you at your manumission, and though you may know how to direct yourself, so as to avoid offending against the letter of the law—yet, you could receive from the prætor none of that wisdom and discernment, by which alone you can

3 c

Officia; atque usum rapidæ permittere vitæ—
Sambucam citius caloni aptaveris alto.   95
Stat contra ratio, et secretam garrit in aurem,
Ne liceat facere id, quod quis vitiabit agendo.
Publica lex hominum, naturaque continet hoc fas,
Ut teneat vetitos inscitia debilis actus.
Diluis helleborum, certo compescere puncto   100
Nescius examen? vetat hoc natura medendi.
Navem si poscat sibi peronatus arator,
Luciferi rudis; exclamet Melicerta, perisse
Frontem de rebus.—Tibi recto vivere talo
Ars dedit? et veri speciem dignoscere calles,   105
Ne qua subærato mendosum tinniat auro?

distinguish aright, as touching those more minute and delicate actions which concern you in the more nice duties of life, and which are to be attained by philosophy alone. I take this to be meant by tenuia officia rerum—lit. small offices, or duties of things or affairs.

94. " *To fools.*"] The Stoics held, that " all fools were slaves,"—and that " nobody was free except the " wise." A man must therefore be wise before he is free; but the prætor could not make you wise, therefore he could not make you free.

—" *To permit the use.*"] It was not in the prætor's power to commit to such that prudence and wisdom, by which they can alone be enabled to make a right use of this fleeting life, and of all things belonging to it.

95. " *Sooner fit,*" &c.] Sambuca was some musical instrument, as an harp, dulcimer, or the like; but what it exactly was we cannot tell.

—" *A tall footman.*"] Alto caloni. Calo, a soldier's boy, or any meaner sort of servant. Ainsw. Horace seems to use it in the latter sense, lib. i. sat. vi. l. 103; and perhaps it is so to be understood here.

You might sooner think of putting a harp, or some delicate musical instrument, into the hands of a great overgrown booby of a servant, and expect him to play on it, than to commit the nice and refined duties of life to fools, and expect them either to understand or practise them. Asinus ad Lyram. Prov.

96. " *Reason stands against it.*"] Reason itself opposes such an idea.

—" *Whispers into the secret ear.*"] Secretly whispers into the ear. Hypallage—Comp. supr. l. 40, and note.

97. " *Let it not be lawful.*"] Ne, before the potential, has the sense of the imperative mood. So Hor. ode xxxiii. lib. i. l. 1. Ne doleas; and ode xl. l. Ne quæsieres. Here, ne liceat is likewise imperative, and signifies that the voice of reason secretly whispers in the ear this admonition, " Let it not be permitted, that any " should undertake what they are not " fit for, but would spoil in doing it." Or ne liceat may be understood, here, as non licet.

98. " *The public law of men.*"]— The common rule, among mankind, as well as nature, may be said to contain thus much of what is right and just.

99. " *That weak ignorance,*" &c.] That an ignorance of what we undertake, which must render us inadequate to the right performance of it, should restrain us from attempting acts, which, by the voice of human, as well as of natural law, are so clearly forbidden to us. Comp. l. 96, 7.

100. " *Do you dilute hellebore.*"]— He here illustrates his argument by examples.

Suppose, says he, you were to attempt to mix a dose of hellebore, not knowing how to apportion exactly the quantity.

100–1. " *To a certain point.*"]— Metaph. Examen signifies the tongue,

" To fools, and to permit the use of rapid life—
" You would sooner fit a dulcimer to a tall footman. 95
" Reason stands against it, and whispers into the secret ear,"
" Let it not be lawful to do that, which one will spoil in
" doing :"
" The public law of men, and nature, contains this right,
" That weak ignorance should forbear forbidden acts.
" Do you dilute hellebore, not knowing how to confine,
" to a 100
" Certain point, the balance ? the nature of healing forbids
" this.
" If the high-shoed ploughman should require a ship for
" Himself, ignorant of Lucifer, Melicerta exclaims, that
" shame
" Has perished from things.—To live with an upright
" ancle
" Has art given you ?—Are you skilful to distinguish the
" appearance of truth, 105
" Lest any should tinkle false with gold having brass un-
" der it ?
" And what things are to be followed, and, in like manner,
" what avoided ?

or beam of a balance, by the inclination of which we judge of proporti-
onal weights.

101. " The nature of healing forbids this."] All medical skill, in the
very nature of it, must place this
among the vetitos actus, which weak
ignorance is not to attempt. See l. 99.

102. " High-shoed ploughman."]
Peronatus. The pero was an high
shoe worn by rustics, as a defence
against snow and cold. See Juv. sat.
xiv. l. 186.

103. " Ignorant of Lucifer."]—
Knowing nothing of the stars. Lucifer, or the day-star, is here put (by
synec.) for all the stars, from which
mariners take their observations to
steer by.

—" Melicerta exclaims," &c.] Also
called Portunus, or Portumnus, because supposed to preside over ports.
See his story, Ov. Met. lib. iv. fab.
xiii. Melicerta, the sea-god, would
exclaim, that all modesty was banished from among those who undertook the management and direction

of human affairs, when he saw so
impudent an attempt.

—" Shame."] Frontem, lit. the
forehead, or countenance, the seat
of shame—here, by met. shame or
modesty itself.

104. " Upright ancle."] Metaph.
from persons having their legs and
ancles straight, and walking upright-
ly ; which is often used, to denote
going on through life with an honest
and virtuous conduct. This occurs
frequently in Scripture as Ps. xv. 2.
lxxxiv. 11. Prov. x. 9. et al.

105. " Has art," &c.] That is philosophy, which is the art of living
well—has this enabled you to do this ?

106. " Lest any," &c.] Ne qua-
i. e. ne aliqua species veri. Have
you learnt to distinguish between the
appearance and reality of truth and
virtue, lest you should be deceived,
as people are who take bad money for
good, when, instead of answering to
the appearance of the outside, which
is fair, they find, upon sounding it,
that it is brass underneath, instead of
being all gold.

Quæque sequenda forent, quæque evitanda vicissim;
Illa prius cretâ, mox hæc carbone notasti?
Es modicus voti? presso lare? dulcis amicis?
Jam nunc astringas, jam nunc granaria laxes?   110
Inque luto fixum, possis transcendere nummum,
Nec glutto sorbere salivam mercurialem?
  Hæc mea sunt, teneo, cum vere dixeris; esto
Liberque ac sapiens, prætoribus ac Jove dextro.
  Sin tu, cum fueris nostræ paulo ante farinæ,   115
Pelliculam veterem retines; et, fronte politus,
Astutam vapido servas sub pectore vulpem:
Quæ dederam supra repeto, funemque reduco.
Nil tibi concessit ratio: digitum exere, peccas:
Et quid tam parvum est? sed nullo thure litabis,   120

108. "*Mark'd those with chalk,*" &c.] The ancients used to denote things good and prosperous with a white mark, and things bad and unlucky with a black one. In allusion to this, the Stoic is supposed to ask the question in the preceding line, which is, not only whether his opponent has been taught to distinguish the appearances of good and evil, but whether he has particularly noted down what a wise man ought to follow, and what he ought to avoid. See Hor. lib. ii. sat. iii. l. 246. Mendosum tinniat, for mendose: Græcism.

109. "*Moderate, &c.*"] Are your desires confined within the bounds of moderation?

—"*A confined household.*"] Your household-establishment frugal, and not expensive—contracted within a little compass; or perhaps by presso lare, may be signified a small house.

—"*Kind to your friends.*"] Dulcis —obliging, sweet, agreeable. See Hor. lib. i. sat. iv. l. 135.

110. "*Sometimes fasten,*" &c.]— Judging rightly when it is a time to withhold, and when to give. Here perhaps is an allusion to the public granaries, or magazines of corn at Rome, which, at a time of dearth and want, was dealt out in doles to the citizens, on producing their tickets, but, at other seasons, locked up. Jam nunc—lit. just now—i. e. just at a proper time.

111. "*Can you pass by money,*" &c.] Alluding to a practice among the boys at Rome, who used to fasten a piece of counterfeit money to the ground, or stick it in the mud, with a string tied to it; and if any miserly fellow coming by, and imagining it to be real, stooped to pick it up, they snatched it away, and laughed at him.
In triviis fixum qui se demittit ob assem.
Hor. lib. i. epist. xvi. l. 64.

112. "*Mercurial spittle.*"] Mercury was the god of gain; hence a desire of gain is called saliva mercurialis. Metaph. from gluttons, who, at beholding some dainty dish, have their spittle increased in such a manner, that if they did not swallow it, it would run out of the mouth. This we call, the mouth watering. Can you see money without your mouth watering at it? i. e. without being greatly delighted, and coveting it?

113. "*These.*"] All these good qualities.

114. "*Prætors and Jupiter propitious.*"] I then allow you to be free in the sight of God and man—i. e. not only with respect to the liberty of the body, which you received from the prætor, but with respect to freedom of the mind, of which Jupiter alone is the author.

115. "*But 'if you.*"] Now he comes to the other side of the question—

—"*Since you.*"] Since you, but a little before your manumission, were just like what we were till taught by

" Have you first marked those with chalk, then, these with
" a coal ? . . . .
" Are you moderate in your wish—with a confined house-
" hold—kind to your friends ?—. . . . . . .
" Can you sometimes fasten, and sometimes open your
" granaries ? 110
" And can you pass by money fixed in mud, ...
" Nor swallow with your gullet mercurial spittle ? . . .
" When you can truly say, these are mine, I possess
" them—be thou . . . .
" Free and wise, the prætors and Jupiter propitious. . . .
" But if you, since you were a little before of our meal,
" Retain your old skin, and, polished in front, 　 116
" Keep a cunning fox under your vapid breast : . . . .
" What I had above given I demand again, and bring
" back the rope.
" Reason has granted you nothing : put forth your finger,
" you sin :
" And what is so small ? but you will obtain, by no in-
" cense, 　　　　　　　　　　　　　　　120

philosophy—i. e. naturally full of ignorance and error.
　—" Of our meal."] Metaph. taken
from loaves of bread, which are all-
alike, and taste alike, if made of the
same flour—so mankind, having the
same nature, are all corrupt.
　116. " Retain your old skin."]—
Metaph. taken from snakes, which
cast off their old skin, and have a
new one every year.—q. d. If you retain your old depraved manners and
conduct (see l. 76, 7.) and have not
changed and cast them off.
　—" Polished in front."] Appearing with a countenance seemingly
open and ingenuous. Necquicquam
pelle decorus.
　117. " Keep a cunning fox," &c.]
Entertain wily, cunning, and deceitful principles within—
　—" Your vapid breast,"] Within
your rotten heart. See L. 77, note.
Nunquam te fallant animi sub vulpe
　latentes. . . . .
　　　　　Hor. Ars Poet. 437.
　118. " What I had above given."]
i. e. What I just now granted ; viz.
that you are free and wise.
　—" I demand again."] I recall.

　—" And bring back the rope."]
Metaph. from leading beasts with a
rope, which sometimes they lengthened, and gave the animal a good
deal of liberty ; but, if restive and
mischievous, they shortened it to
confine him. Thus the Stoic, who
lengthened his allowance so far as to
pronounce the man wise and free,
supposing him to answer the description which he gives of those who are
so, now, on finding the contrary,
draws back what he had said, and
reduces the man to his old narrow
bounds of bodily freedom only.
　119. " Reason has granted you nothing."] Whatever the prætor may
have done, wisdom has done nothing
for you.
　—" Put forth your finger, you
sin."] The Stoics held, that there
was no medium between wisdom and
folly, that a man was either perfectly
wise, or perfectly foolish ; therefore,
that the most trivial and indifferent
thing, if done by the latter, could not
be done aright, not even the putting
forth of a finger.
　120. " What is so small ?"] " What
" can be so trivial as this ?" yet, tri-

Hæreat in stultis brevis ut semuncia recti,
Hæc miscere nefas : nec, cum sis cætera fossor,
Tres tantum ad numeros satyri moveare Bathylli.
' Liber ego.' Unde datum hoc sumis, tot subdite rebus ?
An dominum ignoras, nisi quem vindicta relaxat ?   125
I, puer, et strigiles Crispini ad balnea defer;
Si increpuit, cessas, nugator ?—Servitium acre—
Te nihil impellit ; nec quicquam extrinsecus intrat,
Quod nervos agitet——Sed si intus, et in jecore ægro
Nascantur domini, qui tu impunitior exis   130
Atque hic, quem ad strigiles scutica et metus egit herilis ?
Mane piger stertis. Surge, inquit Avaritia : ' eja

vial as it is, it can only be done by the wise and free, as it ought, as every other action, of what nature or kind soever.

—" Will obtain."] Rito signifies not only to sacrifice, but to obtain that for which the sacrifice is offered. See sat. ii. l. 75, and note.

121. " Half ounce of right," &c.] In short, the Stoics held, that not a grain of what was right could reside within any but the wise and free, in their sense of the words ; or, in truth, in any but their own sect—all the rest of the world they accounted fools and mad, and that though they were to offer incense, in ever so great a quantity, to the gods, yet they could never obtain a single fixed principle of what was right.

122. " To mix these, &c.] i. e. Wisdom and folly ; there must be either all one, or all the other. See above, note on l. 119. It is impossible they should be mixed in the same person.

—" A digger."] Fossor—a ditcher, delver, and the like—q. d. A mere clown.

q. d. When, in every thing else—cætera, i. e. quoad cætera, Græcism—you are as clumsy and aukward as a common clown, it is impossible that you should dance, even three steps, like the famous dancer Bathyllus. Perhaps the poet, by fossor, alludes to the slaves, who were set to dig with fetters on their legs.

123. " The satyr Bathyllus."] He was a famous dancer in the time of Nero, and, for his great agility and nimble movements, was surnamed

the Satyr. Saltantes Satyros. VIRG. ecl. v. 73.

The Stoic concludes this part of his argument with averring, that those who are not wise and free, as in every thing else they are, are unable to do what is right, so neither can they, in the most trivial or indifferent action ; any more than an aukward clown could dance like Bathyllus for three steps together.

124. " I am free."] " Aye, it is " all very well," says Dama : " but " I do insist upon it, that I am free, " notwithstanding all you say."

—" Whence take you this," &c.]— Datum is a technical term—when any thing is yielded, agreed, and granted as true, it is called a datum. " Now," answers the Stoic, " whence " had you that datum, for so it ap- " pears to you, that you are free, " because you have had your freedom " given you by the prætor's wand, " you, who are put under (subdite) " the power and dominion of so much " error and folly ?" Comp. sat. iii. l. 28, and note.

125. " Are you ignorant," &c.]— " Know you not any other master " than he who exercised an outward " authority over you till you were " released from him by the prætor's " wand ?" See before, l. 88, note.

126. " Go, slave, and carry," &c.] I grant you that you have nothing to fear from your late master. If he were, in a loud and surly manner, to bawl out—" Here, slave, carry these " scrapers," &c. and scold you for the least delay—

127-8. " Sharp servitude," &c.]—

" That a small, half ounce of right should be fixed in fools:
" To mix these is impossibility : nor, when as to other things
  " you are a digger,
" Can you be moved to three measures only of the satyr
  " Bathyllus."
" I am free."—" Whence take you this for granted, sub-
  " jected by so many things
" Are you ignorant of a master, unless he whom the wand
  " relaxes 125
" Go, slave, and carry the scrapers to the baths of Cris-
  " pinus,"
" If he has sounded forth—" do you loiter, trifler ?" Sharp
" Servitude impels thee nothing, nor does any thing enter
  " from without
" Which may agitate your nerves. But if within, and in a
  " sick liver
" Masters are produced, how go you forth more un-
  " punished, 130
" Than he, whom the scourge, and fear of his master, has
  " driven to the scrapers?
" In the morning, slothful, you snore: " Rise," says
  " Avarice,

However, sharp and severe bodily servitude may be, yet you have nothing
to do with it; it cannot enforce any
such orders upon you.

[' 128. " Nor does any thing enter,"
&c.] Nor can any thing, as threats,
or menaces, of being punished, for not
obeying, enter into your mind, so as
to make you uneasy; all this I grant
—in this sense you are free.

129. " But if within"] If vice
and folly, generated within your disordered heart, are your masters, and
rule over you, so as to compel your
obedience to their commands.

Jecore ægro. See Juv. sat. i. 35,
and note.—The ancients looked on
the liver as the seat of the concupiscible and irascible affections, and
therefore jecore ægro may be understood, metonymically, to denote the
diseased or disordered affections, for
vice is the sickness or disease of the
mind.

130. " How go you forth," &c.]—
How can you be said to be less liable
to punishment, from the slavery and
misery of your mind, than the poor

slave, is, in a bodily sense, when compelled to obey his master, from the
terror of bodily punishment. The
only difference between you is, he
serves his master, you your vices.

[131. " The scrapers."] Strigiles.
These were the instruments which
the Greeks and Romans made use of
to scrape their bodies after bathing,
and were carried to the baths by their
slaves. Driven to the scrapers—i. e.
has forced to carry the scrapers to the
baths, when ordered.

[132. " Slothful, you snore."] The
poet proceeds to illustrate and confirm
his argument (in which he has been
contending for the " slavery of all
" but the wise," according to the
Stoic doctrine) by instancing the power of sloth, avarice, and luxury, over
the human mind, in its corrupted
state.

He introduces a dialogue between
Dama and Avarice. Avarice is supposed to find Dama snoring a-bed, in
the morning, in the luxurious ease of
his so highly-prized freedom.

—" Rise," says Avarice.] This

' Surge.'—Negas. Instat, ' surge,' inquit. Non queo.
    ' Surge.'
Et quid agam ? ' rogitas ? Saperdas advehe Ponto,
' Castoreum, stuppas, hebenum, thus, lubrica Coa.   135
' Tolle recens, primus. piper e sitiente camelo,
' Verte aliquid ; jura.' Sed Jupiter audiet. ' Eheu,
' Baro ! regustatum digito terebrare salinum,
' Contentus perages, si vivere cum Jove tendis.'
    Jam pueris pellem succinctus, et œnophorum aptas : 140
Ocius ad navem : nihil obstat quin trabe vastâ
Ægæum rapias, nisi solers Luxuria ante

word, " Rise," is repeated four times. Thus Vice ceases not from its importunity ; and the answers of Dama, " I will not"—" I cannot."— " what shall I do if I rise ?"—are a lively representation of the power of idleness and sloth, when indulged. This is finely described, Prov. vi. 9, 10. xxii. 13. xxvi. 13, 14.

134. " Fish from Pontus."] Saperdas—a sort of fish which came from Pontus, or the Black sea.

135. " Castor."] Castoreum.— This signifies either beavers' skins, or what we call castor—i. e. the medicinal part of the animal ; both of which were articles of traffic.

—" Flax."] Stuppa, or stupa— the coarse part of flax, tow, hards, oakum to calk ships with. AINSW.

—" Ebony."] A black wood, well known amongst us—the tree whereof bears neither leaves nor fruit. AINSW.

—" Slippery Coan wines."] From the island Co, or Coos, in the Ægean sea. They were soft, and of a laxative quality ; hence called lubrica.

136. " Take first the recent pepper."] Be sure be at the market first, that you may not only have the first choice, but return to a better sale, by coming home before the other merchants.

Hor. lib. i. epist. vi. l. 32, 3.
    ——Cave ne portus occupet alter :
    Ne Cybiratica, ne Bithyna negotia perdas.

—" Thirsting camel."] The eastern people loaded their pepper and other spices on the backs of camels. These animals are said to endure thirst, in their journeys over the deserts, for

many days together ; wherefore, in a part of the world where water is very scarce, they are peculiarly useful.

137. " Turn something."] Trade, barter—i. e. as we say, turn the penny.

—" Swear."] Do not mind a little perjury upon occasion, either with respect to the goodness of your wares, or concerning the first cost, and what you can afford to sell them at.

—" Jupiter will hear."] Dama is supposed to raise a scruple of conscience.

137-8. " Alas ! simpleton."] Baro, or varo—a servant that waited upon the common soldiers, who was usually very stupid and ignorant—hence a blockhead, a dolt, a foolish fellow.

138. " To bore with your fingers,"] &c.] If you aim at living (i. e. living in amity) with Jupiter, you must not think of trading to increase your fortune, but must be content to live in a poor, mean way. The poorer sort of people lived upon bread, with a little salt. Persius supposes the Stoic to tell Dama; that if he would not perjure himself, in order to get money by trade, he must be content to put his finger, and endeavour to scrape up a little salt from the bottom of his own poor salt-cellar ; where there were only a few grains left, from his having done this often, in order to give a relish to his palate, by licking his fingers, after they had rubbed the bottom of the salt-cellar, as if he meant to bore it through. This is proverbial, to express very great poverty. Salem lingere signified to live in the utmost poverty—to fare poorly.

PLAUT. Curcull. act iv. sc. the last.

" Rise."—You refuse—he urges—" Rise," says he.—" I
 " cannot."—" Rise."
" And what shall I do?" " Do you ask?—bring fish from
 " Pontus,
" Castor, flax, ebony, frankincense, and slippery Coan
 " wines :   135
" Take first the recent pepper from the thirsting camel :
" Turn something; swear."—" But Jupiter will hear."—
 " Alas !
" Simpleton, to bore with your finger the re-tasted salt-
 " cellar,
" Content you will pass your time, if you aim to live with
 " Jove.
" Now, ready, you fit the skin to the slaves, and a wine-
 " vessel :   140
" Quick to the ship : nothing hinders, but in a large ship
" You may hurry over the Ægean : unless sly Luxury
 " should

Hic hodie apud me nunquam delinges salem; that is as much as to say—" you shall not eat a morsel."

140. " *Now ready*."] Succinctus —literally, girt, trussed up. The ancients wore long loose garments, which, when they prepared to travel, they girded, or trussed up, about their loins, that they might walk the more freely. See Hor. lib. ii. sat. vi. 107. Hence, being ready, prepared; also nimble, expeditious. See Exod. xi. 11, former part. 1 Kings xviii. 46. Luke xii. 35.

— " *Fit the skin*," &c.] They had wallets, or knapsacks, made of skins, in which they packed their clothes, and other necessaries, when they travelled either by land or sea. You put your knapsack, and your cask of wine for the voyage, on the backs of your slaves, to carry on board.

141. " *Quick to the ship*."] You lose no time, you hurry to get on board.

— " *Nothing hinders*."] Nothing stands in your way, to prevent the immediate execution of your plan, or to discourage you—unless—See l. 142, note 2.

— " *A large ship*."] Trabs is a beam, or any great piece of timber,

of which ships are built; here, by meton. the ship itself. See Juv. sat. xiv l. 276. Virg. Æn. iii. 191.

142. " *The Ægean*."] A part of the Mediterranean sea, near Greece, dividing Europe from Asia. It is now called the Archipelago, and, by the Turks, the White sea. Its name is supposed to be derived from αιγος, Dor fluctus, from its turbulent waves. From this dangerous sea are made two adages, viz. Ægeum scaphula transmittere—to cross the Ægean sea in a little boat—i. e. to undertake a weighty business with small abilities; and Ægeum navigare—to undertake an hazardous enterprise. See Ainsw. Hence our Stoic mentions this sea in particular, to shew the power of avarice over the mind that is enslaved by it, and that no dangers will deter from its pursuits—Nihil obstat, says he.

— " *Sly luxury*."] Solers—shrewd, wily, cunning.
We have seen the victory of Avarice over Sloth, now Luxury is introduced, as putting in its claim for the mastery.
Thus, says the Stoic, will Avarice lord it over you, and drag you in her chains over the dangerous Ægean for lucre's sake, unless, being beforehand

3 D

Seductum moneat ; ' Quo deinde, insane, ruis? Quo?
' Quid tibi vis ? calido sub pectore mascula bilis
' Intumuit, quam non extinxerit urna cicutæ.   145
' Tun' mare transilias? Tibi, tortâ cannabe fulto,
' Cœna sit in transtro ? Veientanumque rubellum
' Exhalet, vapidâ læsum pice, sessiles obba?
' Quid petis ? ut nummi, quos hic quincunce modesto
' Nutrieras, pergant avidos sudare deunces?   150
' Indulge genio : carpamus dulcia ; nostrum est
' Quod vivis : cinis, et manes, et fabula fies.

seduced and enthralled by Luxury, you should listen to her admonitions. Ante---*i. e.* before you put in practice what Avarice has advised.

143. " *Whither thence,*" &c.]--- Whither from that warm and comfortable bed of yours, on which you so delightfully repose yourself, are you running headlong (ruis), like a madman as you are ? See l. 132.

144. " *Manly bile,*" &c.] Masculus---male ; hence manly, stout, hardy, than which nothing is more opposite to luxury. Your warm breast---*i. e.* hated and inflamed with the ardent dèsire which now possesses you to face the danger of the seas ; for this an hardy rage is risen up, (intumuit) swells within you, says Luxury, and prompts you to this dangerous resolution.

145. " *Urn of hemlock.*"] An urn was a measure of about four gallons. Cicuta---an herb like our hemlock, the juice of which was of an extremely cold nature, so as to be a deadly poison, when taken in a certain quantity. Also a sort of hellebore, administered medicinally, in madness, or frenzies, to cool the brain. See AINSW. *Cicuta,* No. 1, 2.

Quæ poterunt unquam satis expurgare cicutæ.

HOR. epist. ii. lib. ii. 53.

146. " *Can you cross the sea ?*"]--- Can you be so forgetful of the blandishments of ease and luxury, as to subject yourself to the dangers and inconveniencies of a sea-voyage ?

---" *A supper,*" &c.] Instead of an elegant and well spread table, can you bear to eat your supper upon a rough plank ; and instead of an easy

couch, to be supported by a coil of cable, by way of a seat ?

147. " *Red Veientan wine.*"] A coarse, bad wine, such as seamen carried with them among their sea-stores. See HOR. lib. ii. sat. iii. l. 143.

148. " *The broad-bottomed jug.*"] Obba---a bowl or jug with a great belly and broad bottom, that sitteth, as it were---sessilis. This sort of jug, or bowl, was peculiarly useful at sea, because not easily thrown down by the motion of the ship.

---" *Exhale.*"] Cast forth the fumes of.

---" *Injured by nasty pitch.*"]--- Smelling and tasting of the pitch with which every thing on board a ship is daubed---this, perhaps, was the case with the obba : or the pitch may be meant, with which the vessel which held the wine was stopped, and which being of a coarse sort, might give a disagreeable taste to the liquor.

149. " *What seek you?*"] What errand are you going upon ? Is it to make better interest of your money, than you can make by staying at home ?

---" *Modest five per cent.*"] This, as among us, was not reckoned usurious, but modest---*i. e.* moderate, legal interest.

150. " *Nourished.*"] Metaph. from nourishing, nursing, fostering a child, making it thrive and grow ; hence applied to money, as increasing it by care.

---*To sweat.*"] Metaph. from the effect of toil and labour---these must attend those who endeavour to make extraordinary interest of their money, by trading to foreign countries.

" Admonish you before seduced."—" Whither thence,
　" madman, do you rush?
" Whither? what would you have? under your warm
　" breast manly bile
" Has swelled up, which an urn of hemlock could not have
　" extinguished.　　　　　　　　　　　　　　　145
" Can you cross the sea? to thee shall there be a supper on
　" a bench,
" Propped with twisted hemp? and red Veïentan wine!
" Shall the broad-bottomed jug exhale, injured by nasty
　" pitch?
" What seek you? that money, which here with modest
　" five per cent.
" You had nourished, should go on to sweat greedy cent.
　" per cent.?　　　　　　　　　　　　　　　　150
" Indulge your genius—let us pluck sweets—It is mine
" That you live: you will become ashes, and a ghost, and
　" a fable.

150. " Greedy."] Mataph. from an
immoderate desire of food. Those
who strive to make exhorbitant interest of their money, may well be
called greedy of gain; and hence the
epithet greedy is applied to the gain
itself.
——" Cent per cent."] Deunx—
a pound lacking an ounce. A duo-
decim, una dempta uncia. Eleven
ounces—eleven parts of any thing
divided into twelve: so that deunces
here signifies eleven pounds gained
by every twelve, which is gaining very
near cent. per cent. as we say.
151. " Indulge your genius."]—
Here genio means natural inclination.
Indulgere genio, to make much of
himself. AINSW.
——" Pluck sweets."] Metaph. from
plucking fruits or flowers. HOR. lib.
i. ode xi. l. 8.
　Carpe diem.
q. d. Let us seize on and enjoy the
sweets of life.
This sentiment is finely expressed
in the apocryphal book of Wisdom,
ch. ii. 6. et seq.
Luxury has been dissuading Dama
from attempting his voyage, by representing the dangers and inconveniencies which must attend it: now
she invites him to stay, that he may

not lose the pleasures of ease and
luxury, which the shortness of life
affords him but a little time for the
enjoyment of.
151-2. " Mine that you live."] i. e.
It is owing to me, says Luxury, that
you enjoy the pleasures and sweets of
life, without which, to live is not life.
—Βιος βιυ δεομενος ουκ εστι βιος
says the Greek proverb. Among us
—" May we live all the days of our
" life," is a common convivial expression.
Horace, on another occasion, says
to the muse Melpomene,
　Quod spiro et placeo, si placeo,
　　tuum est.
　　　Lib. iv. ode iii. l. 24.
152. " Become ashes."] You will
soon die, and be carried to the funeral
pile, where you will be burnt to ashes.
—" A ghost."] Manes—a spirit
separated from the body.
—" A fable."] Fabula, (from for
-faris, to speak or talk,) a subject of
discourse. Persius, here, some think
to allude to Horace's fabulæque
manes—i. e. manes de quibus multæ
sunt fabulæ—the manes who are much
talked of. Lib. i. ode iv. l. 16.
But as the Stoic is here speaking as
an Epicurean, who believes body and
soul to die together, I should rather

' Vive memor lethi: fugit hora: hoc quod loquor
' inde est.'

En quid agis? duplici in diversum scinderis hamo.
Hunccine, an hunc, sequeris? subeas alternus oportet, 155
Ancipiti obsequio, dominos; alternus oberres.
Nec tu, cum obstiteris semel, instantique negaris
Parere imperio, 'rupi jam vincula,' dicas.
Nam et luctata canis nodum abripit: attamen illi,
Cum fugit, a collo trahitur pars longa catenæ. 160
Dave, cito, hoc credas jubeo, finire dolores
Præteritos meditor: (crudum Chærestratus unguem
Abradens, ait hæc.) An siccis dedecus obstem

---

think that fabula here means an invented story, a groundless tale---for
such they looked upon the doctrine of
a future state. See Wisd. ii. 1–9.

  "A nothing but an old wife's
  tale." DRYDEN.
Soon wilt thou glide a ghost for
  gossips' chat. BREWSTER.
153. "Live mindful of death."]—
q. d. Memento Mori.

  Dum licet in rebus jucundis vive
  beatus;
  Vive memor quam sis ævi brevis.
  HOR. lib. ii. sat. vi. l. 96, 7.
  —" The hour flies."]
  Currit enim ferox atas.
  HOR. lib. ii. ode v. l. 13, 14.
  Sed fugit interea, fugit irrepara-
  bile tempus.
VIRG. Georg. iii. l. 284. Comp. Æn.
x. 4 7, 8.

---" This, which I speak, is from
thence."] The time in which I am
now speaking is taken from thence---
i. e. from the flying hour. See HOR.
lib. i. ode xi. l. 7.

  Dum loquimur fugerit invida
  Ætas.

The late Lord Hervey, in a poetical epistle to a friend, applies this
very beautifully:

  "Even now, while I write, time
  " steals on our youth,
  " And a moment's cut off from our
  " friendship and truth."

The whole of Luxury's argument
amounts to---" Let us eat and drink,
" for to-morrow we die." Isai. xxii.
13. 1 Cor. xv. 32.

154. ("Lo, what do you?"] The
Stoic now turns his discourse, imme-

diately, as from himself, to Dama,
whom he has represented as beset by
Avarice and Luxury, and at a loss
which to obey. Now, says he, what
can you do, under these different solicitations?

---" You are divided," &c.] Metaph. from angling, with two hooks
fixed to the line, and differently
baited, so that the fish are doubtful
which to take.

155. "This do you follow," &c.]
Hunc---dominum understood. Which
master will you follow---Avarice or
Luxury.

---" By turns it behoves," &c.]---
The truth is, that you will sometimes
go under, or yield to, the dominion
of the one, sometimes of the other,
alternately--ancipiti obsequio---doubt-
ing which you shall serve most.---
Alternus-a-um. See AINSW.

156. " Wander."] Oberres---he
like one that is at a loss, and wanders
up and down; you will wander in
your determinations which to serve,
at times, their commands being contrary to each other. Avarice bids you
get more---Luxury bids you enjoy
what you have.

157. " Withstood," &c.] Perhaps
for once, or so, you may refuse to
obey their most importunate solicitations and commands; but do not,
from this, conclude, that you are free
from their service. It is not a single
instance, but a whole tenor of resistance to vice, which constitutes freedom. Instanti---earnest, urgent.

159. " A dog," &c.] A dog may
struggle till he breaks his chain, but

" LIVE MINDFUL OF DEATH ; THE HOUR FLIES : this,
   " which I speak, is from thence."
" Lo, what do you ? you are divided different ways with
   " a double hook.
" This do you follow, or this ? By turns it behoves that
   " you go under,   155
With doubtful obsequiousness, your masters : by turns,
   " you may wander.
" Nor can you, when once you have withstood, and have
   " refused to obey
" An instant command, say ' I now have broken my
   " ' bonds.'
" For also a dog, having struggled, breaks the knot : but
   " to him,
" When he flies, a long part of the chain is drawn by his
   " neck.   160
" Davus, quickly (I command that this you believe) to
   " finish griefs
" Past I meditate : (Chærestratus, his raw nail
" Gnawing, says these words) shall I, a disgrace, oppose
   " my sober

then runs away with a long piece of it hanging to him at his neck, by which he is not only incommoded in his flight, but easily laid hold of, and brought back to his confinement. Canis—here feminine—lit. a bitch.

So will it be with you; you may break loose; for a while, from the bondage and service of vice, but those inbred principles of evil, which you will carry about you, will hinder your total escape, and make it easy for the solicitations of your old masters to reduce you again into bondage to them. Therefore, while there remains any vice and folly within you, you will be a slave, however you may call yourself free.

161. " Davus," &c.] The Stoic, in confirmation of his main argument, to prove that " all but the " wise are slaves," having instanced sloth, avarice, and luxury, as lording it over the minds of men, now proceeds to shew that the passion of love is another of those claims by which the mind is bound.

He introduces a scene in the Eunuch of Menander, from which Terence took his Eunuch, where the lover is called Chærestratus (in Terence, Phædria) communicating to his servant Davus (in Terence, Parmeno) his intention of leaving his mistress Chrysis (in Terence, Thais).

" Davus," says Chærestratrus— " (and I insist on your believing me " to be in earnest), I am thinking to " give up my mistress, and to do this " shortly—cito—and thus to put an " end to all the plague and uneasiness " which she has cost me."

162-3. " His raw nail gnawing," &c.] Biting his nail to the quick; a very common action with people in deep and anxious thought.

163. " Shall I, a disgrace."] q. d. Shall I, who have made myself a disgrace to my family by keeping this woman—

—" Oppose."] Act contrary to the wishes and advice of my sober relations ?

Siccus signifies sober, in opposition to uvidus, soaked, mellow with liquor. HOR. ode iv. 5. 38-40.
   Dicimus integro
   Sicci mane die, dicimus uvidi
   Cum Sol oceano subest.
Hence sicci means sober, orderly

Cognatis ? An rem patriam, rumore sinistro,
Limen ad obscœnum, frangam, dum Chrysidis udas   165
Ebrius ante fores, extinctâ cum face, canto ?
  Euge, puer, sapias : diis depellentibus agnam
Percute. Sed censen' plorabit, Dave, relicta ?
Nugaris : soleâ, puer, objurgabere rubrâ,
Ne trepidare velis, atque arctos rodere casses.   170
Nunc ferus, et violens : at si vocet, haud mora dicas,
' Quidnam igitur faciam ? ne nunc, cum accersat, et ultrò
' Supplicet, accedam ?' Si totus, et integer, illinc

people in general, in contradistinction to rakes and libertines.

164. " *Paternal estate,*" &c.]—Spend and diminish my patrimony, at the expence of my reputation.

165. " *An obscene threshold.*"] At the house of an harlot. Synec. limen for domum.

—" *Wet doors,*" &c.] The doors wet with the dew of the night.—" Shall I serenade her at midnight, " when I am drunken, and have put " out the torch with which my ser- " vant is lighting me home, for fear " of being seen and known by the " passers by ?"

167. " *Well done,*" &c.] " Well " done, my young master," says Da- vus, " I hope you will come to your " senses at last."

—" *Repelling gods,*" &c.] It was usual to offer a thank-offering to the gods, on a deliverance from any dan- ger: hence Davus bids his master sa- crifice a lamb—diis depellentibus— to the gods, whose office it was to re- pel and keep off evil. Perhaps Cas- tor and Pollux are here meant, as they were reckoned peculiarly to avert mischief. See Delph. note. Horace sacrificed a lamb to Faunus, the god of the fields and woods, for his escape from the falling tree. Lib. ii. ode xvii. ad fin. Averruncus. Deus qui mala avertit. Ainsw.

168. " *Think you Davus,*" &c.] Here the young man wavers in his resolution, and shews that he is still a slave to his passion for Chrysis—he cannot bear the thought of making her uneasy.

169. " *You trifle.*"] Answers Da- vus. Is this the way in which you are to put an end to all the plague

and uneasiness of this amour, to be thus irresolute, and unable to bear the thought of her tears for the loss of you ? Alas ! how you trifle with your- self !

—" *You will be chidden,*" &c.]— O foolish youth, when once Chrysis finds out that you are so fond of her, that you cannot bear to grieve her by forsaking her, she will make her ad- vantage of it ; she will let you see her imperiousness, and will not only scold, but beat you.

—" *Red slipper.*"] Solea—a kind of pantofle, or slipper, covering only the sole of the foot, and fastened with laces. It was a fashion among the fine ladies to have these of a red or purple colour, as well as to make use of them for the chastisement of their humble admirers.

Thraso is represented by Terence (Eun. act v. sc. vii.) as intending, after his quarrel with the courtezan Thais, to surrender himself to her at discre- tion, and to do whatever she com- manded. The parasited GNATHO says—Qid est ?

THRASO. *Quî minus quam Hercules*
servivit Omphale ?
GN. *Exemplum placet :*
Utinam tibi commitigari videam
sandalio caput.

From this answer of Gnatho, it seems likely that there was represent- ed, on the Athenian stage, some comedy on the loves of Hercules and Omphale, in which that hero was seen spinning of wool, and his mis- tress sitting by, and beating him with her sandal, or slipper, when he did wrong. To this our poet may pro- bably allude. See the ingenious Mr.

" Relations? Shall I my paternal estate, with an ill report,
" Spend at an obscene threshold, while, before the wet
" doors ·   165
" Of Chrysis, drunken I, sing with an extinguished
" torch?"—
" Well done, boy, be wise; to the repelling gods a lamb
" Smite:"—" But think you, Davus, she will weep, being
" left?"
" You trifle—you will, boy, be chidden with a red
" slipper,
" Lest you should have a mind to struggle, and bite the
" tight toils :   170
" Now fierce and violent: but, if she should call, without
" delay you would say—
" What therefore shall I do? now, when she can send for
" me, and willingly
" Supplicate, shall I not go?"—" If whole and entire from
" thence

COLMAN's translation of this passage, and the note.
170. " To struggle."] i. e. That you may not again attempt your liberty. Metaph. from the fluttering of birds when caught on lime-twigs, who flutter their wings to free themselves, by which they are the more limed, and rendered more unable to escape. MARSHALL.
Sic aves dum viscum trepidantes excutiunt, plumis omnibus illinunt. SENECA, de Ira.
Trepido does not always signify trembling through fear, but, sometimes to hasten, to bustle, to keep a clutter.
Dum trepidant alæ.
VIRG. Æn. iv. 121; and ix. 114.
So struggling to get free from a haughty mistress :
Ac veluti primo Taurus detractat aratro,
Mox venit assueto mollis ad arva jugo.
Sic primo juvenes trepidant in amore feroces;
Dehinc domiti posthâc æquâ et iniqua ferunt. PROPERT. lib. ii.
—" And bite," &c.] Metaph. from wild beasts taken in nets, or toils, who endeavour to free themselves by biting them asunder.

In short, Chrysis will so use you, if you again put yourself in her power, that you will not dare to attempt a second time to escape her.
171. " Fierce and violent."] Now you are not with her you can bluster stoutly.
—" Call."] i. e. Invite you to come to her—
—" Without delay," &c.] You would instantly change your note, and say—
172. " What therefore, &c.] These are almost the words of Phædria, in TER. Eun. act i. sc. i. l. 1, 2.
Quid igitur fâtiam? non eam, ne nunc quidem
Cum accersor ultro?
HORACE also has imitated this passage :
Nec nunc cum me vocet altro
Accedam. Lib. ii. Sat. iii. 263.
173. " Whole and entire," &c.]—If when you left her, you had been entirely heart whole, and had shaken off the yoke of lust and passion, you would not—nec, nunc, not even now—return to her, even though she has sent to entreat you to do it; but, from your thought of yielding to her intreaties, I see very plainly that, notwithstanding all your deliberations about leaving her, you are still a slave to her.

Exieras, nec nunc. Hic, hic, quem quærimus, hic est :
Non in festucâ, lictor quam jactat ineptus. 175
Jus habet ille sui, palpe quem ducit hiantem
Cretata Ambitio ? Vigila, et cicer ingere large
Rixanti populo, nostra ut Floralia possint
Aprici meminisse senes ! quid pulchrius ?—At cum
Herodis venêre dies, unctâque fenestrâ 180

174. " *Whom we seek.*"] The man who can so far emancipate himself from his passion, as to free himself from its dominion, so as no longer to be a slave to it, which Chærestratus would have proved himself, if he could have kept his resolution against all solicitations to break it; this is the man I mean, says the Stoic, this is the man I allow to be free.

175. " *Not in the wand,*" &c.]— The better to explain this place, as well as l. 88 of this Satire, it may not be amiss to mention, particularly, the ceremony of manumission.

" The slave was brought before the consul, and, in after-times, before the prætor, by his master, who, laying his hand upon his servant's head, said to the prætor—Hunc hominem liberum esse volo, and, with that, let him go out of his hand, which they termed—e manu emittere, whence manumission : then the prætor, laying a rod upon his head, called vindictâ, said—Dico eum liberum esse more Quiritum ; and turned him round on his heel. See L. 75, 6. After this, the lictor, taking the rod out of the prætor's hand, struck the servant several blows upon the head, face, and back, (which part of the ceremony Persius refers to in this line,) and nothing now remained but Pileo donare, to present him with a cap in token of liberty, and to have his name entered in the common roll of freemen, with the reason of his obtaining that favour." See before, l. 88. See KENNET, Antiq. p. 100.

—" *The foolish lictor.*"] Ineptus, here, is either used in contempt of the lictor, who was a sort of beadle, that carried the fasces before the prætor, and usually, perhaps, an ignorant, illiterate fellow ; or it may be used in the sense of unapt, unfit, improper—i. e. to convey true liberty

on the slave, whom he struck with the rod, in that part of the ceremony which fell to his share.

—" *Shakes.*"] Jacto—is to shake or move ; to move to and fro, as in the action of striking often ; also to brag or boast.

176. " *Right of himself.*"] The poet now instances, in the vice of ambition, another chain which binds the enslaved mind, and which hinders that freedom for which our Stoic is contending.

Can he call himself his own master—meus, l. 88 ; or say that he is sui juris—i. e. that he can dispose of himself as he pleases, as having a sovereign right over his own person.

—" *Whom gaping.*"] Hiantem—gaping after, coveting greatly, like a creature gaping for food.

—" *With its lure.*"] Palpum-i. lit. a gentle, soft stroking with the hand ; hence obtrudere, palpum alicui—to wheedle, flatter, or coax. ΛΙΝΣΩ.

176-7. " *Chalked ambition.*"] This expression alludes to the white garments worn by candidates for offices ; in these they went about to ask the people's votes, and from these white garments, which to make still whiter they rubbed over with chalk, they were called candidati.

177. " *Ambition.*"] Literally signifies a going about, from ambio : hence a suing or canvassing for favour—hence that desire of honour and promotion, which is called ambition.

—" *Watch.*"] Says Ambition ; always be upon the look out ; lose no opportunity to make yousself popular.

—" *Heap vetches largely.*"] Those who aspired to public offices, endeavoured to gain the votes of the people by donations and largesses. These kinds of public bribes consisted in

" You had come forth, not now."—" This, this, this is he,
  " whom we seek,
" Not in the wand which the foolish lictor shakes.   175
  " Has he the right of himself, whom gaping, with its
    " lure, chalked
" Ambition leads? Watch: and heap vetches largely on
    " the
" Quarrelling people, that our feasts of Flora sunny old
    " men
" May remember : what more glorious? but when
" The days of Herod have come, and in the greasy
    " window   180

pease, beans, lupines or vetches, given away among the people. The Romans ran to such extravagance on these occasions, that several of the richest entirely ruined themselves. Julius Cæsar employed in such largesses near a million and an half more than his estate was worth.

In cicere atque faba bona tu perdasque lupinis,
Latus tu in circo spatiêre, aut æneus ut stes—

Hor. lib. ii. sat. iii. l. 182, 3.
178. " *Quarrelling people.*"] Quarrelling about their shares in the largesses and donations ; or, as we see at our elections, about the interests of the different candidates, whom they severally espoused.

—" *Our feasts,*" &c.] That the feasts which we gave, marked by our great liberality, may never be forgotten, to the latest old age of those who attended them.

—" *Feasts of Flora.*"| Flora was a noted courtezan in Rome, who having gotten a large sum of money by prostitution, made the Roman people her heir ; but they, being ashamed of her profession, made her the goddess of flowers.

In honour of her, feasts were held, and games exhibited, which were provided by the Ædile, who, on this occasion, was very liberal in his donations to the people, in hopes of gaining their votes for an higher place in the magistracy. The Floralia were held on the 28th of April.

—" *Sunny old men.*"] Aprici senes —old men who loved to bask in the sun, the warmth of which was very

acceptable to their cold habit of body, which old age brought on ; their delight was to bask on a sunny bank, and talk over old times.

In the well-known, beautiful ballad of Darby and Joan, the poet has made use of this idea, as one description of the amusement of old age—

Together they totter about,
Or sit in the sun at the door—&c.

179. " *What more glorious?*"]— Than thus to recommend ourselves to the people, gain their favour, and leave a lasting memory of our munificence? Iron.

180. " *The days of Herod,*" &c.] Another chain in which the human mind is holden in superstition ; to this all but the wise are slaves. He instances this in those Romans who had addicted themselves to many of the Jewish rites and superstitions, for such their whole religion appeared to the heathen. See Juv. sat. xiv. l. 96–106. We find, by Matt. xiv. 6. and Mark vi. 21. that the king's birth-day was an high festival, observed at Herod's court ; and, by this passage of Persius, it appears to have been celebrated by the Jews at Rome also, particularly by the Herodians, who constituted a society in honour of Herod, after the manner of the Sodalitia at Rome. See BROUGHTON, Bibliotheca—tit. Herodians.

—" *Greasy window.*"] They stuck up candles, or lamps, in their windows, in token of a rejoicing-day— they lighted them early in the day, and by their flaring and guttering they made the frames of the windows on which they stood all over grease.

3 E

Dispositæ, pinguem nebulam vomuêre lucernæ,
Portantes violas; rubrumque amplexa catinum,
Cauda natat thynni, tumet alba fidelia vino ;
Labra moves tacitus, recutitaque sabbata palles:
Tunc nigri lemures, ovoque pericula rupto: 185
Hinc grandes Galli, et cum sistro lusca sacerdos,
Incussêre deos inflantes corpora, si non·
Prædictum, ter mane, capút gustaveris alli.
Dixeris hæc inter varicosos centuriones,

181. " *Fat cloud.*"] *i. e.* Of smoke
---An exact description of the smoke
of a candle, or lamp, which is im-
pregnated with particles of the fat,
or grease, from which it ascends ; as
may be seen on ceilings, or other
places, on which this smoke has
alighted, and which when they are
attempted to be cleared, are found to
be soiled with a mixture of soot and
grease.

Vomuere is a 'word well adapted to
express the discharge of the thick and
filthy smoke from the wicks. So
Vino. Æn. v. 682.

Stupa vomens tardum fumum.
The tow discharging tardy, languid
smoke.

182. " *Bearing violets.*"] They
adorned their lamps with wreaths of
violets, and other flowers, on these
occasions.

--" *Embraced a red dish.*"] Hypallage, for the dish embracing the
tail of the fish. Thynnus, a large
coarse fish ; the poet mentions only
the tail of it, which was the worst
part—this he does, probably, by way
of derision of the Jews' festal-din-
ner. The dish, of red earthen-ware.

183. " *Swims.*"] In sauce.

--" *White pitcher.*"] An earthen
vessel, a white crock of earth.

: --" *Swells.*"] Is filled up to the
brim—or tumet may imply, that the
wine was bad and in a fermenting state,
frothing up above the brim. Every
circumstance of the entertainment
seems to be mentioned with a thorough air of contempt, and to denote
the poverty of the Jews.

184. " *Silent you move your lips.*"]
You join in the solemnity, you attend
at their proseuchæ, and like them,
mutter prayers inwardly, only moving your lips. See sat. ii. l. 6.

--" *And fear.*"] Pallidus is used by

our poet elsewhere to denote hard
study, which occasions paleness. See
sat. i. l. 121 ; and sat iii. 85. Here it
is used to denote that superstitious
fear, which occasions, from yielding
to it, a pale and wan appearance in
the countenance.

--" *Circumcised sabbaths.*"] Re-
cutita sabbata. Hypall. for sabbata
recutitorum—the sabbaths of the circumcised. Palles sabbata, here, is
equivalent to metuentem sabbata.—
Juv. sat. xiv. l. 96.—*q. d.* By degrees you will enter into all the Jewish
superstition.

The word sabbata, in the plural,
may here denote, not only the sab-
bath-days, but all the Jewish holidays, which were days of rest from
labour; among others, the festival
which they had instituted in honour
of Herod's birth-day.

185. " *Then black hobgoblins.*"]—
The mind enslaved by superstition,
falls from one degree of it into another.

Lemures—ghosts, spirits that walk
by night, hobgoblins ; quasi Remures
from Remus, whose spirit was supposed to haunt his brother. Ainsw.
Nocturnos lemures. Hor. ep. ii. lib. ii.
l: 209. They are only supposed to
appear by night—hence called black.

--" *Dangers from a broken egg.*"]
The ancients had a superstition about
egg-shells : they thought, that if an
egg-shell were cracked, or had an
hole bored through at the bottom of
it, they were subject to the power of
sorcery.

This is contrary to the superstition
of those, who, in the days when
witches were believed in, always broke
the bottom of an egg-shell, and
crossed it, after having eaten the egg,
lest some witch should make use of it
in bewitching them, or sailing over

" The candles disposed, have vomited a fat cloud,
" Bearing violets; and, having embraced a red dish,
" The tail of a tunny-fish swims, the white pitcher swells
    " with wine; ˖
" Silent you move your lips, and fear circumcised sabbaths :
" Then black hobgoblins, and dangers from a broken egg :
" Hence huge priests of Cybele, and a one-eyed priestess
    " with a sistrum, ˖   186
" Have inculcated gods inflating bodies, if you have not
" Tasted, three times in the morning, an appointed head
    " of garlick. ˖
    " If you say these things among the veiny centurions,

the sea in it, if it were whole. See DRYDEN's note.

For an instance of national superstition, as ridiculous as any that can be imagined, I would refer the reader to the solemn public statute of 1 Jac. I c. 12. against witchcraft, now repealed by 9 Geo. II. c. 5.

116. " *Hence.*"] *i. e.* From this superstitious principle in the minds of men, they are led from one degree of credulity to another : of this advantage has been taken by the priests of Cybele, and of Isis, to fill them with groundless terror.

186. " *Huge priests of Cybele.*"] See these described at large. They were called Galli, from Gallus, a river of Phrygia, the drinking of which made people furious. So OVID, Fast. iv.

Inter ait, viridem Cybelen altasque
    Celenas,
Amnis it insaniâ nomine Gallus
    aquâ.
Qui bibit inde furit, &c.

Persius calls them grandes—Juvenal says, ingens semivir, &c. They were usually of great stature, owing, as has been said, to their castration, which increased their bulk. Their strange, mad gestures, and their extraordinary appearance, as well as their loud and wild vociferation, had great effect upon weak and superstitious minds.

—" *One-eyed priestess with a sistrum.*"] The superstition of the Ægyptian goddess Isis had been transferred to Rome, where she had a temple. She was represented with a sis-

trum, a sort of brazen or iron timbrel, with loose rings on the edges in her hand. Σειρον, from σειω, to shake—its noise proceeding from its being shaken violently, and struck with the hand, or with an iron rod.

The priestess of Isis, when celebrating the wild rites of Isis, carried a sistrum in her hand, in imitation of the goddess, and had great influence over the minds of the superstitious.

The poet calls her one-eyed—perhaps this was her situation, and that she pretended to have lost an eye by a blow from the sistrum of Isis; for it seems that this was the way which the goddess took to avenge herself on those who offended her.

Decernat quodcumque volet de cor- ˖ *pore nostro*
Isis, et irato feriat mea lumina *-sistro.'*

JUV. sat. xiii. l. 92, 3. See the note there, on l 93.

187. " *Have inculcated, &c.*]— These vile impostors, when once the mind is enslaved so far by superstition as to receive their impositions, will inculcate their absurd and wild notions as so many truths—they will persuade you, that the gods which they serve will send dropsies, and other swellings of the body, unless you use some amulet or charm to prevent it ; such as eating a head, or clove, of garlick, for three mornings successively.

188. " *Appointed.*"] *i. e.* Ordered —prescribed—as a preservative.

189. " *If you say these things,*" &c.] If you were to discourse, as

Continuo crassum ridet Pulfenius ingens,　　**190**
Et centum Græcos curto centusse licebit.

I have done, in the hearing of one of our rough centurions (comp. sat. iii. l. 77.) in order to prove the slavery of all men to vice and folly, except the wise, he would set up a loud horse-laugh at you.

189. " *Veiny.*"] Varicosus, having large veins—perhaps from the robustness of his make.

190, " *Huge Pulfenius.*"] The name of some remarkable tall and lusty soldier of that day—put here for any such sort of person.

—" *Rudely laughs.*"] Crassum ridet, for crasse ridet. Græcism.

191. " *And cheapens.*"] Liceor eri, dep. to cheapen a thing, to bid money for it, to offer the price.

" *Greeks.*"] i. e. Philosophers, most of which first came from Greece,

" Immediately huge Pulfenius rudely laughs,   190
" And cheapens an hundred Greeks at a clipped centussis."

—" *A clipped centussis.*"] Centussis, a rate of Roman money, amounting to about six shillings and threepence of our money.

—" *Clipped.*"] Curtailed, battered —short of its nominal value, like bad money among us.

q. d. If Pulfenius, the centurion, were to hear what I have said on the subject of liberty, he would only laugh at it, but, if he were asked what he would give for an hundred philosophers, he would not offer a good six and three-penny piece for them all. However, though you may be of the same mind, Dama, yet what I have said is not the less true, nor are philosophers the less valuable in the eyes of all the wise and good.

Satira Sexta.

ARGUMENT.

Persius addresses this epistolary Satire to his friend Cæsius Bassus, a lyric poet. They both seem, as was usual with the studious among the Romans, in the beginning of winter, to have retired from Rome to their respective country-houses; Persius to his, at the port of Luna, in Liguria; Bassus to his, in the territories of the Sabines.
The Poet first inquires after his friend's manner of life

AD CÆSIUM BASSUM.

ADMOVIT jam bruma foco te, Basse, Sabino?
Jamne lyra, et tetrico vivunt tibi pectine chordæ?
Mire opifex, numeris veterum primordia rerum,
Atque marem strepitum fidis intendisse Latinæ;
Mox juvenes agitare jocos; et, pollice honesto,   5

Line 1. *Sabine fire-hearth.*] The ancient Sabines were a people between the Umbrians and Latins, but, after the rape of the Sabine women, incorporated into one people with the Latins, by agreement between Tatius and Romulus. This part of Italy still retained its name; and here Bassus had a country-house, to which he retired at the beginning of winter, for the more quiet and convenient opportunity of study. This was not far from Rome.

—*Fire-hearth.*] So focus literally signifies, quod foveat ignem—AINSW. but it is sometimes used for the whole house, by synec. and, perhaps, is so to be understood here. Sometimes, by meton. for the fire.

2. *Does now the lyre.*] The lyre was a stringed instrument, which gave a soft and gentle sound when touched with fingers; but when struck with a quill, which, when so used,

was called pecten, gave a louder and harsher sound.

The language here is figurative— the lyre stands for lyric, or the softer and gentler kind of poetry; and the strings or chords, being struck tetrico pectine, with the rough or harsh quill, denote the sharper and severer style of verse. The poet inquires whether Bassus, in his retirement, was writing lyric verses, and whether he was also employing himself in graver or severer kinds of composition.

—*Live to thee.*] When an instrument lies by, and is not played on, it may be said to be dead, and when taken up and played on, the strings may be said to be alive, from their motion and sound.

3. *Admirable artist!*] Opifex—lit. a workman: it also means an inventor, deviser, and framer.

Sixth Satire.

ARGUMENT.

*and studies, then informs him of his own, and where he
now is. He describes himself in his retirement, as quite
undisquieted with regard to care or passions; and, with
respect to his expences, neither profuse nor parsimoni-
ous. He then treats on the true use of riches; and
shews the folly of those who live sordidly themselves for
the sake of leaving their riches to others.*

TO CÆSIUS BASSUS.

HAS winter already moved thee, Bassus, to thy Sabine
 fire-hearth?
Does now the lyre, and do the strings, live to thee with a
 rough quill?
Admirable artist! in numbers the beginnings of things
To have displayed, and the manly sound of the Latin lute;
Then to agitate young jokes, and with an honest thumb 5

—In numbers.] *i. e.* In verses—in
metre.

—The beginnings.] Primordia—
the first beginnings—the history of
the earliest beginnings of things. So
Ovid, Met. lib. i. l. 3, 4.

*—Primâque ab origine mundi
Ad mea perpetuum deducite tempora
 carmen.*

Some understand the poet to mean,
that Bassus had written a treatise in
verse, concerning the original beginning or rise of old and antiquated
words, reading, after many copies,
veterum primordia vocum—and that
Bassus was not only a good poet, but
a learned antiquary. But rerum affords the easiest and most natural
sense—Malim igitur cum Casaubono
et aliis quibusdam, Θεογονιαν et
μυθιστοριαν intelligere. See Delph.
note.

4. *Displayed.*] Intendisse—lit. to
have stretched. The sound is given
from instruments by the tension of
the strings.

 —Manly sound of the Latin lute.]
i. e. To have written Latin lyric
verses in a noble, manly strain.

Among the Greeks they reckon nine
famous lyric poets: but two among
the Romans; viz. Horace and Cæsius
Bassus.

Horace calls himself, Romanæ fidicen lyræ. Ode iii. lib. iv. l. 23.

To be reckoned this was his great
ambition, as appears, ode i. lib. i. ad
fin. where he says to Mæcenas,

*Quod si me lyricis vatibus inseres,
Sublimi feriam sidera vertice.*

5. *Then to agitate young jokes.*]—
Then, in light and lively strains, to
describe the amours and frolics of
young men.

Egregios lusisse senes!—Mihi nunc Ligus ora
Intepet, hybernatque meum mare; qua latus ingens
Dant scopuli, et multâ littus se valle receptat.
' Lunaï portum est operæ cognoscere, cives:'
Cor jubet hoc Enni; postquam destertuit esse.   10
Mæonides, quintus pavone ex Pythagoreo.
  Hic ego securus vulgi, et quid præparet auster
Infelix pecori: securus et angulus ille
Vicini nostro quia pinguior: et si adeó omnes
Ditescant orti pejoribus, usque recusem   15
Curvus ob id minui senio, aut cœnare sine uncto;
Et signum in vapidâ naso tetigisse lagenâ.

5. *Honest thumb.*] Meton. with truth and faithfulness, representing the actions and worthy deeds of older men, who have distinguished themselves in a more advanced time of life.

6. *Ligurian.*] i. e. Being now removed from Rome into Liguria.— Ligus ora, for Ligustica ora.

6—7. *Coast grows warm.*] Either from its situation near mountains, which kept off the cold blasts of wind, or from the circumstance next mentioned, the agitation of the sea, which causes a warmth in the water.

TULLY, Nat. Deor. lib. ii. says— " Seas agitated by the wind grow so " warm, as easily to make us under- " stand, that in those large bodies of " water there is heat included: for " that heat which we perceive, is not " to be accounted merely external " and adventitious, but excited by the " agitation which is in the innermost " parts of the water; this also hap- " pens to our bodies, when by motion " they grow warm."

7. *My sea is rough.*] That is, the sea near Volaterra, a city of Tuscany, where Persius was born, and near which he now was.

—*Large side, &c.*] The rocks running out far into the sea, present an extensive side to the water, by which the waves are stopped, and a quiet bay formed.

8. *The shore draws itself in, &c.*] The shore retires, and forms a large circular valley between the mountains; which is another reason of the warmth of my situation; my house which is situated in that valley being sheltered from the wintry storms.

9. " *Port of Luna.*"] So called from the shape of the bay in which it was situate, which, from the circular form of the shore, was like an half-moon —Lunaï, per diærism, for Lunæ.

—" *It is worth while,*" &c.] This line is from Ennius, who began his annals of the Roman people with—
  Est operæ pretium, O cives, cog-
    noscere portum.
  Lunæ.

10. *The heart of Ennius, &c.*] He was an ancient poet, born at Rudiæ, a town of Calabria: he wrote annals of the Roman people; also satires, comedies, and tragedies; but nothing of his is come to us entire. He died 169 years before Christ.

Cor means, literally the heart; and, by meton. the mind, wisdom, judgment. Perhaps the poet means to say, that Ennius, when in his right mind and sober senses, recommended the port of Luna to his countrymen, after he came out of his vagaries after mentioned.

—*Dreaming, &c.*] See prologue to sat. i. l. 2, and note. Mæonides was a name given to Homer, on account of his supposed birth at Smyrna, in the country of Mæonia, i. e. Lydia.

11. *Fifth from the Pythagorean peacock.*] Some are for supposing Quintus, here, to be understood as a prænomen of Ennius:—but it should rather seem, as if Persius were here laughing at the extravagant idea of the Pythagorean doctrine of transmigration, which Ennius for a while had received, and who is said to have dreamt that the soul of a peacock had transmigrated, first into Euphorbus,

To have played remarkable old men. : To me now the Li-
    gurian coast
Grows warm, and my sea is rough, where a large side
The rocks give, and the shore draws itself in with much
    valley.
" The port of Luna it is worth while to know, O citizens:"
The heart of Ennius commands this, after he ceased dream-
    ing that he was   10
Mæonides, the fifth from the Pythagorean peacock.
    Here [am] I, careless of the vulgar, and what the south,
Unfortunate to the cattle, may prepare : and unconcerned
    because that corner
Is more fruitful than mine that's next to it : and if all,
Sprung from worse, should grow ever so rich, I should al-
    ways refuse,   15
On that account, to be diminished crooked with old age, or
    to sup without a dainty,
And to have touched with my nose the seal in the vapid
    cask.

then into Homer, then into Pythagoras, and then into Ennius; so that
he stood fifth from the peacock. See
DRYD. Trans. and note on this place.
    This is an evident banter on the
Pythagorean notion of the metempsy-
chosis.
    12. *Here am I, &c.*] In this com-
fortable retreat of the port of Luna, I
trouble not my head about what people say of me.
    —*What the south, &c.*] The south
wind, when it blew with any long
continuance, was reckoned very unwholesome, particularly to cattle. So
VIRG. Geor. i. l. 444.
    *Arboribusque, satisque, Notus, pe-
    corique sinister.*
    The poet seems to say, that he was
without care or anxiety in his retreat.
The modern Italians call this wind
Sirocco, or Scilocco, which blows
from the south-east.
    13. *That corner, &c.*] Horace sat.
vi. lib. ii. l. 8, 9.
    ——*O si angulus ille.*
    *Proximus accedat, qui nunc denor-
    mat agellum.*
Persius took his angulus ille from
this passage of Horace.
    14. *And if all, &c.*] If ever so
many of my inferiors, however lowly

and meanly born, should grow so
rich, adeo ditescant, as to have their
possessions exceed mine—
    15. *I should always refuse, &c.*]
I should not make myself uneasy, so
as to fret upon that account, and to
bring on old age before my time, as
if bowed under a weight of years.
    16. *Sup without a dainty.*] Unctus,
literally, is anointed, greasy, and applied to describe a dainty rich meal,
good cheer. Hence unctissimæ cœnæ.
See AINSW. *Unctus.*
    I will not live the worse ; envy
shall not spoil my appetite ; I will not
abate a single dish at my table, in order to save up what would make me
as rich as my neighbour.
    17. *And to have touched with my
nose, &c.*] I shall not bottle up dregs
of musty wine, and then examine the
seal, which I have put on the mouth
of the vessel, as closely as if I meant
to run my nose into the pitch which
has received its impression, to try
whether any of my servants have
opened it.
    q. d. I shall neither fret myself
into old age before my time with envy,
nor turn niggard, in order to save
money, that I may equal my richer
neighbours.

Discrepet his alius. Geminos, Horoscope, varo
Producis genio. - Solis natalibus, est qui
Tingat olus siccum muriâ, vafer, in callice emptâ,   20
Ipse sacrum irrorans patinæ piper. Hic bona dente
Grandia magnanimus peragit puer.—Utar ego, utar:
Nec rhombos, ideo, libertis ponere lautus;
Nec tenuem solers turdarum nôsse salivam.
    Messe tenus propriâ vive; et granaria (fas est)   25
Emole; quid metuas? occa, et seges altera in herbâ est.
   ' At vocat officium.   Trabe ruptâ, Bruttia saxa
' Prendit amicus inops: remque omnem, surdaque vota,

18. *Another may differ, &c.*] However such may be my way of thinking, yet as there are
    Mille hominum species, et rerum
      discolor usus.—See sat. v. 52.
it is certain that others may differ
from me in sentiments, with regard
to these matters.
    —*O Horoscope.*] Horoscopus here
signifies the star that had the ascend-
ant, and presided at one's nativity.
    q. d. Whatever astrologers may
say, two persons, even twins, born
under the same horoscope, are frequently seen to be produced with a
different genius, or natural inclination.
    19. *There is, who, &c.*] Of these
twins, one of them shall be covetous
and close, the other prodigal.
    One of them will grudge himself
almost the common comforts of life.
    — *On his birth-day.*] This was
usually observed as a time of feasting,
and making entertainments for their
friends.
    20. *Wily.*] Vafer—cunning, crafty.
    —*Dip his dry herbs.*] Olus-eris—
any garden herbs for food—probably
what we call a sallad. Hor. lib. ii.
sat. ii. l. 55, &c.
    Instead of pouring oil, or other
good dressing, over the whole, he, in
order to have no waste, craftily contrived to dress no more than he ate,
by dipping the herbs, as he took them
up to eat, into a small cup of pickle:
of this he had no store by him, but
bought a little for the occasion.
    Muria was a kind of sauce, or
pickle, made of the liquor of the
tunny-fish,—a very vile and cheap
sauce.

21. *Himself sprinkling, &c.*] He
would not trust this to a servant, for
fear of his sprinkling too much, therefore did it himself.
    —*Sacred pepper.*] Which he sets
as much store by as if it were sacred.
Hor. lib. i. sat. l. l. 71, 2.
      Tanquam parcere sacris
       Cogeris.
And lib. ii. sat. iii. l. 110.
      Metuensque velut contingere sa-
       crum.
    — *This.*] *i. e.* The other twin,
quite of a contrary disposition.
    —*A magnanimous boy.*] Yet not
grown to manhood, but having early
a noble disposition. Iron.
    22. *His tooth.*] By the indulgence
of his luxurious appetite—meton.—
devours all he has.
    —*Dispatches a great estate.*] *i. e.*
Makes an end of a large estate, by
spending it profusely upon his gluttony and luxury.
    —*I will use, &c.*] For my part,
says Persius, I will use what I have;
I say use, not abuse it, either by avarice on the one hand, or by prodigality
on the other.
    23. *Not therefore splendid, &c.*]—
Not so sumptuous and costly, as to
treat my freedmen, when they come
to see me, with turbot for dinner—
ideo, *i. e.* merely because I would
appear splendid.
    24. *Nor wise to know, &c.*] Nor
yet indulge myself in gluttony, or
cultivate a fine delicate palate, so as to
be able to distinguish the small difference between one thrush and another.
    These birds, which we commonly
translate thrushes, were in great repute as dainties. Some pretended to

Another may differ in these things: twins, O Horoscope,
    with a various
Genius you produce. There is, who, only on his birth-day,
Wily can dip his dry herbs in a cup with bought pickle,
Himself sprinkling on the dish sacred pepper. This a
    magnanimous boy   -   21
With his tooth dispatches a great estate.—I will use, I will
    use:
Not therefore splendid to put turbots to my freedmen,
Nor wise to know the small state of thrushes.
    Live up to your own harvest: and your granaries (it is
    right)   25
Grind out. What can you fear?—Harrow—and another
    crop is in the blade.
    " But duty calls.   With broken ship, the Bruttian rocks
" A poor friend takes hold of, and all his substance, and
    " his unheard vows

so nice a taste, as to be able to distinguish whether the bird they were eating was of the male or female kind, the juices of the latter being reckoned most relishing.

I will use what I have, says Persius, but then it shall be in a rational moderate way; not running into needless extravagance, for fear of being reckoned covetous, or setting up for a connoisseur in eating, for fear of not being respected as a man of a delicate taste.

25. *Your own harvest.*] Equal your expences to your income.

26. *Grind out.*] Do not hoard, but live on what you have—use it all. Fast est—*q. d.* You may do it, and ought to do it.

—*What can you fear?*] You have nothing to be afraid of; the next harvest will replace what you spend.—Comp. Matt. vi. 34.

—*Harrow.*] Occo is to harrow, to break the clods in a ploughed field, that the ground may lie even, and cover the grain. Here, by synec. it stands for all the operations of husbandry.—*q. d.* Plough, sow, harrow your land, and you may expect another crop. Herba is the blade of any corn, which, when first it appears, is green, and looks like grass. " First " the blade, then the ear, then the " full corn in the ear." Mark iv, 28.

Persius was for Horace's auream mediocritatem (ode x. lib. ii. l. 5–8.) neither for hoarding out of avarice, nor for exceeding out of profuseness.

27. " *But duty calls.*"] Aye, says a miser, all this is very well; but I may be called upon to serve a friend, and how can I be prepared for this if I spend my whole annual income?

—" *With broken ship.*"] Methinks, says the miser, who is supposing a case of a distressed friend—methinks I see him, ship-wrecked, and cast away on the Bruttian rocks, and seizing hold on a point of the rock to save himself. See Æneid, vi. 360.

Prensantemque uncis manibus capita aspera montis.

Brutium, or Bruttium, was a promontory of Italy, near Rhegium, hod. Reggio, not far from Sicily; nigh to which there were dangerous rocks.

28. " *His unheard vows.*"] Surdus means not only deaf, but also that which is not heard. It was usual for persons in distress at sea to make vows to some god, in order for their deliverance, that they would, if preserved, make such or such offerings on their arriving safe on shore. But, alas! the poor man's freight, and all the vows that he made, were all gone together to the bottom of the Ionian sea. The sea between Sicily and Crete was anciently so called.

' Condidit Ionio : jacet ipse in littore, et una
' Ingentes de puppe dei ; jamque obvia mergis,   30
' Costa ratis laceræ.'—Nunc, et de cespite vivo,
Frange aliquid ; largire inopi ; ne pictus oberret
Cæruleâ in tabulâ.   ' Sed cœnam funeris hæres
'Negliget, iratus quod rem curtaveris : urnæ
' Ossa inodora dabit : seu spirent cinnama surdum,   35
' Seu ceraso peccent Casiæ, nescire paratus.
' Tune bona incolumis minuas ?—Sed Bestius urget

30. " *The great gods from the
stern.*"] The ancients had large figures
of deities, which were fixed at the
stern of the ship, and were regarded
as tutelar gods.   Aurato fulgebat
Apolline puppis. VIRG. Æn. x. 171.
The violence of the waves is supposed to have broken these off from
the vessel, and thrown them on shore,
whither also the man is supposed to
have swum, and where he now lay.
—" *Sea-gulls.*"] Mergus is the
name of several sea-birds, from their
swimming and diving in the sea.—
Ainsworth says it particularly means
the cormorant.
   The ribs of the ship were now torn
open, and exposed to the birds of prey
which haunted the sea, who might
devour the dead bodies, or any provisions which were left on board.
   31. *The live turf, &c.*] *q. d.* Now,
upon such an occasion as this (which,
however, is not so likely to happen to
an individual of your acquaintance,
as in the prospect of it, to be a pretence for not freely and hospitably
spending the whole annual produce
of your land) you may relieve your
ruined friend by a sale of part of your
land, supposing that you have none
of the fruits of it left to help him
with.   Sell a piece of your land already sown, on which the blade is
now springing up, and give the money to your friend who has lost his
all ; that is, do not stay till you have
reaped, but help him immediately as
his wants require.
   Cespes is a turf, a sod, or clod of
earth, with the grass or other produce, as corn, &c. growing upon it ;
hence called vivus, living.
   So HOR. lib. i. ode xix. l. 13.
Hic vivum mihi cespitem, &c.

And lib. iii. ode viii. l. 3, 4.
———*Positusque carbo in
Cespite vivo.*
   Here cespite vivo is to be understood of the land itself, with the corn
growing upon it.   The image is taken
from the idea of a man's taking up a
sod, breaking off a piece of it, and
giving it to another.
   32–3. *Lest painted, &c.*] See sat. i.
l. 86, note.
   The table, or plank, on which the
story of the distress was painted, represented the sea, and therefore appeared of a sea-green colour.   Hence
Persius says—Cærulea tabula.
   33. " *Your funeral supper,*" &c.]
Prolepsis.   Persius, who well knew
the workings of avarice within the
human mind, and how many excuses
it would be making, in order to avoid
the force of what he has been saying,
here anticipates an objection, which
might be made to what he last said,
about selling part of one's estate, in
order to relieve a ship-wrecked friend.
   But perhaps you will say, that if
you sell part of your land, and thus
diminish the inheritance, your heir
will be offended, and resent his having less than he expected, by not af-
fording you a decent funeral.
   Horace says, epist. ii. lib. ii. l.
191–2.
   ———*Nec metuam quid de me ju-
dicet hæres.*
   Quod non plura datis invenerat—
   It was usual at the funerals of rich
people to make sumptuous entertainments, the splendour of which depended on the heir of the deceased,
at whose expence they were given.
These cœnæ ferales, or cœnæ funeris,
were three-fold.   1st. A banquet was
put on the funeral pile, and burnt

" He has buried in the Ionian : himself lies on the shore,
    " and together [with him]
" The great gods from the stern : and now obvious to the
    " sea-gulls   30
" Are the sides of the torn ship."—Now even from the live
    turf
Break something ; bestow it on the poor man, lest he should
    wander about
Painted in a cærulean table.   " But your funeral supper,
    " your heir
" Will neglect, angry that you have diminished your sub-
    " stance : To the urn
" He will give my unperfumed bones : whether cinnamons
    " may breathe insipidly,   35
" Or Casias offend with cherry-gum, prepared to be ig-
    " norant.
" Safe can you diminish your goods ?"—But Bestius urges

---

with the corpse. See Æneid, vi. 222-5. 2dly. A grand supper was given to the friends and relations of the family. CIC. de Leg. lib. ii. 3dly. A dish of provisions was deposited at the sepulchre. This last was supposed to appease their manes.

35. " *My unperfumed bones.*"]— After the bodies of the rich were burnt on the funeral pile, the ashes containing their bones were usually gathered together, and put into an urn with sweet spices.

—" *Whether cinnamons,*" &c.]— Persius here names cinnamon and Casia, the latter of which he supposes to be sophisticated, for the sake of cheapness, with cherry-gum, or gum from the cherry-tree. The cinnamon, if true and genuine, is a fine aromatic ; but the expression, spirent surdum, breathe insipidly—(surdum, Græcism, for surde—or, perhaps, odorem may be understood)—looks as if the cinnamon, as well as the Casia, were supposed to be adulterated, and mixed with some ingredient which spoiled its odour. The heir is supposed to lay out as little as he well could on the deceased.

36. " *Prepared to be ignorant.*"] i. e. Determined beforehand not to trouble his head about the matter— the worse the spices, the less the cost.

37. " *Safe diminish,*" &c.] Therefore can you, while alive and well, having no sickness or loss of your own—all which are meant by incolumis—subtract from your estate, and thus disoblige your heir ? Some suppose these to be the words of the heir, remonstrating against the old man's spending his money, and so diminishing the patrimony which he was to leave behind him : but I rather suppose the poet to be continuing the prolepsis which begins l. 33 ; and it is a natural question, which may be imagined to arise out of what the miser has been supposed to offer against being kind and generous to a distressed friend. The poet before supposes him to urge his fear of disobliging his heir, if he diminished his estate—Then, continues Persius, tune bona incolumis minuas ?—*q. d.* Can you then, on pain and peril of having your heir neglect your funeral, and shew the utmost contempt to your remains, think (while alive and well— incolumis—having no sickness, or loss of your own) of subtracting from your estate for the sake of other people ? this you will urge as an unanswerable objection to what I propose you should do for the sake of an unfortunate friend—by this you plainly shew, that you are more concerned for what may happen to you after you are

' Doctores Graios : ita fit, postquam sapere urbi,
' Cum pipere et palmis, venit nostrum hoc, maris expers,
' Fœnisecæ crasso vitiarunt unguine pultes.'   40
     Hæc cinere ulterior metuas ? At tu, meus hæres
Quisquis eris, paulum a turbâ seductior, audi ·
     O bone, num ignoras ? missa est a Cæsare laurus,
Insignem ob cladem Germanæ pubis ; et aris
Frigidus excutitur cinis : ac jam postibus arma,   45

dead, than for your friends while you are alive.

37. *But Bestius, &c.*] The name of some covetous fellow, a legacy hunter, who is represented very angry that philosophers have taught generosity, by which the sums which they expect may be lessened during the testator's life, and that from Greece has also been derived the custom of expensive funerals, which affect the estate after the testator's death.

37–8. *Urges the Grecian teachers.*] *i. e.* Rails, inveighs against the philosophers, who brought philosophy first from Greece, and taught a liberal bestowing of our goods on the necessities of others.

39. *" Pepper and dates," &c.*]— Pepper, dates, and philosophy, were all imported together from Asia. This is said in the same strain of contempt as Juvenal's

Advectus Romam, quo pruna et coctona vento.   Sat. iii. l. 83.

—*" This our wisdom."*] Nostrum sapere, Gr. for nostra sapientia—like vivere triste, for tristis vita, sat. i. l. 9.

—*" Void of manliness."*] A poor effeminate thing, void of that noble plainness and hardiness of our ancestors, who never thought of leading so lazy and indolent a life as the philosophers, or of laying out extravagant sums in spices, and burning aromatics on funeral piles, or putting costly spices into urns.

The poet uses marem strepitum for a strong manly sound, l. 4. of this Satire. This, among other senses given of this difficult phrase—maris expers—seems mostly adopted by commentators. But as Persius evidently applies the words—maris expers—from Hor. lib. ii. sat. viii. l. 15, it may perhaps be supposed that

he meant they should be understood in a like sense.

Fundanius is giving Horace an account of a great entertainment which he had been at, and, among other particulars, mentions the wines :

   —*Procedit fuscus Hydaspes*
Cæcuba vina ferens ; Alcon, Chium
     maris expers.

   —" *Black Hydaspes stalks*
" *With right Cæcubian, and the*
     wine of Greece—
" *Of foreign growth which never*
     crossed the seas."
                FRANCIS.

To this Mr. Francis subjoins the following note.

" Chium maris expers."] " It was " customary to mix sea-water with " the strong wines of Greece ; but " Fundanius, when he says that the " wine which Alcon carried had not " a drop of water in it, would have " us understand, that this wine had " never crossed the seas, and that it " was an Italian wine, which Nasi- " dienus (the master of the feast) re- " commended for Chian." LAMB.

This seems to be a good interpretation of Horace's maris expers, and, therefore, as analagous thereto, we may understand it, in this passage of Persius, in a like sense—to denote that the philosophy, which Bestius calls nostrum hoc sapere, " this same " wisdom of ours," and which came from Greece originally, is now no longer to be looked upon as foreign, but as the growth of Italy, seeing that that, and the luxurious manners which came from the same quarter, have taken place of the ancient simplicity and frugality of our forefathers. " And so it comes to pass " (ita fit, l. 38.) that we are to give " away our substance to others, and " that a vast expence is to attend our

The Grecian teachers : " So it is, after to the city, . .
" With pepper and dates, came this our wisdom void of
'   " manliness,
" The mowers have vitiated their pudding with thick oil."
    " Do you fear these things beyond your ashes ?—But
- " thou, my heir,   41
" Whoever thou shalt be, a little more retired from the
    " crowd, hear.
    " O good man, are you ignorant ? A laurel is sent from
        " Cæsar
" On account of the famous slaughter of the German youth,
        " and from the altars
" The cold ashes are shaken off; and now, to the posts,
    " arms,   45

" funerals, and that even a common
" rustic cannot eat his pudding with-
" out a rich sauce." But see Casaubon in loc.
    40. " The mowers," &c.] The
common rustics have been corrupted
with Grecian luxury, and now
    The ploughman truly could no longer
        eat,
    Without rich oils to spoil their
        wholesome meat.
Bestius is very right in saying, that
the philosophy which the Stoics taught
at Rome came from Greece ; but he
would not have railed at the philosophers, if they had not taught principles entirely opposite to his selfishness and avarice ; nor would he have
found fault with the introduction of
what made funerals expensive, had
he not carried his thoughts of parsimony beyond the grave, and dreaded
the expence he must be put to in
burying those whom he expected to
be heir to ; and even the luxury which
had been imported from Greece would
not have troubled him, but as it cost
money to gratify it.
    40. " Their puddings."] Puls -tis
—a kind of meat which the ancients
used, made of meal, water, honey,
or cheese and eggs ; a sort of hasty-
pudding—here put for any rustic,
homely fare. The words vitiarunt
well intimates the meaning of the
selfish Bestius, which was to express
his enmity to every thing that looked
like expence.
    41. " Beyond your ashes."] Be-

yond the grave, as we say—Do you.
miserable wretch, concern yourself
about what your heir says of you, or
in what manner your funeral is conducted ?
    —" But thou, my heir," &c.]—
Persius here, coincidently with the
subject he is now entering upon, represents, in a supposed conversation
in private with the person who might
be his heir, the right a man has to
spend his fortune as he pleases, without standing in awe of those who
come after him : and first, to be liberal and munificent on all public occasions of rejoicing ; next, to live handsomely and comfortably, and not
starve himself that his successor may
live in luxury.
    42. " Retired from the crowd."]—
Secretam garrit in aurem. sat. v. l.
96. Step aside a little, if you please,
that I might deal the more freely
with you, and listen to me.
    43. " O good man."] q. d. Hark
ye, my good friend, and heir that is
to be—
    —" Are you ignorant ?"] Have
you not heard the news ?
    —" A laurel is sent," &c.] Caius
Caligula affected to triumph over the
Germans, whom he never conquered,
as he did over the Britons ; and sent
letters to Rome, wrapt about with
laurels, to the senate, and to the empress Cæsonia his wife.
    45. " The cold ashes."] The ashes
which were to be swept off the altars
were either those that were left there

Jam chlamydas regum, jam lutea gausapa captis,
Essedaque ingentesque locat Cæsonia Rhenos.
Diis igitur, genioque ducis, centum paria, ob res
Egregie gestas, induco. Quis vetat? aude.
Væ, nisi connives—Oleum artocreasque popello   50.
Largior: an prohibes? dic clare. Non adeo, inquis,

after the last sacrifice for victory, or might, perhaps, mean the ashes which were left on the altars since some former defeat of the Romans by the Germans; after which overthrow the altars had been neglected. DRYDEN.

45. *"And now."*] i. e. On the receipt of this good news.

—*"To the posts, arms."*] Persius here enumerates the preparations for a triumph; such as fixing to the doors or columns of the temple the arms taken from the enemy. Thus VIRG. Æn. vii. 183–6.

Multaque præterea sacris in postibus arma,
Captivi pendent currus, curvæque secures,
Et cristæ capitum, et portarum ingentia claustra,
Spiculaque, clypeique, ereptaque rostra carinis.

And HOR. lib. iv. ode xv. l. 6–8.

Et signa postes restituit Jovi,
Derepta Parthorum superbis
Postibus.

46. *" Garments of kings."*]—Chlamys signifies an habit worn by kings and other commanders in war.

—*Ipse agmine Pallas*
In medio, chlamyde, et pictis conspectus in armis.

Æn. viii. l. 587, 8.

46. *" Sorry mantles on the captives."*] When captives were to be led in triumph, they put on them clothing of the coarsest sort, made of a dark frize, in token of their abject state.

47. *" And chariots."*] Essedum is a Gallic word—a sort of chaise or chariot used by the Gauls and Britons; also by the Germans.

Belgica vel molli melius feret esseda collo.

VIRG. G. iii. l. 204.

The Belge were originally Germans, but, passing the Rhine, settled themselves in Gaul, of which they

occupied what is now called the Netherlands.

—*"Huge Germans."*] Rhenos, so called because they inhabited the banks of the Rhine; they were men of great stature.

—*"Cæsonia."*] Wife to Caius Caligula, who afterwards, in the reign of Claudius, was proposed to be married to him, after he had executed the empress Messalina for adultery, but he would not have her. See her character—ANT. Univ. Hist. vol. xiv. p. 297.

48. *" To the gods, therefore."*]—By way of thanksgiving.

—*"The genius of the general."*] Of the emperor Caligula—see sat. ii. l. 3, note—who protected and prospered him.

—*"An hundred pair."*] i. e. Of gladiators. These were beyond the purse of any private man to give; therefore this must be looked upon as a threatening to his heir, that he would do as he pleased with his estate.

On public occasions of triumph, all manner of costly shows and games were exhibited, in honour of the gods, to whose auspices the victory was supposed to be owing: also in honour of the conqueror; therefore Persius adds—ob res egregie gestas.

49. *" I produce."*] Induco signifies to introduce—to bring in—to bring forth, or produce. AINSW.

—*"Who forbids."*] Who puts a negative on my intention?

—*"Dare."*] Will you, who are to be my heir, contradict this? do if you dare.

50. *" Woe! unless you connive."*] Conniveo is to wink with the eyes. Met. to wink at a matter, to take no notice, to make as if he did not see it.

Woe be to you, says Persius, if you offer to take notice, or to object

" Now the garments of kings, now sorry mantles on the
    " captives,
" And chariots, and huge Germans, Cæsonia places.
" To the gods, therefore, and to the genius of the general,
    " an hundred pair,
" On account of things eminently achieved, I produce:
    " Who forbids?—Dare—
" Woe! unless you connive—Oil and pasties to the people
" I bestow: do you hinder?—speak plainly."—" Your field
    " hard by,   51

to what I purpose doing on this occasion.

'—" Oil and pasties to the people."]
Moreover I intend to bestow a dole
upon the common people—popello
in order to enable them to celebrate
the victory. Oil was a favourite sauce
for their victuals. See l. 40, and
note.

Artocrea (from ἄρτος, bread, and
κρέας, flesh) a pie, or pasty of flesh.
Ainsw.

51. " Do you hinder?"] Says he
to his supposed heir; do you find
fault with this bounty of mine, would
you prevent it?

—" Speak plainly."] Come, speak
out.

—" Your field hard by," &c.] Perhaps you will say, that my estate
near Rome, though its vicinity to the
city makes it the more valuable,
yet is not fertile enough to afford all
this.

Exossatus, cleared of the stones,
called the bones of the earth. Ov.
Met. l. 193. to which Persius perhaps
alludes. Here it is supposed to mean
cleared of the stones—i. e. cultivated
to such a degree, as to be rich and
fertile enough to produce what would
be answerable to such an expence.

The above is the leading sense
given by some of the best commentators to this difficult passage; but I
cannot say that it satisfies me. I see
no authority, from any thing that
precedes or follows, to construe juxta
—nigh the city, and hence make juxta
equivalent to suburbanus: nor is the
taking est from juxta, and trans-
ferring it to exossatus or ager, as
done above, the natural method of
the syntax.

I would therefore place the words
in their natural order in which they
are to be construed—Non adeo, inquis, juxta est exossatus ager. The
Delph. interpret. says, Non ita, ais,
prope est ager sine ossibus.

Exosso-are—is to take out the
bones of an animal; to bone it, as
we say. Congrum istum maximum
in aqua sinito ludere paulisper, ubi
ego venero, exossabitur. Ter. Adelph.
Ager is a field, land, ground—hence,
a manor with the demesnes, an estate
in land. Hence, by Metaph. exossatus ager may mean, here, an estate
that has been weakened, diminished
by extravagance of great expence,
having what gave it its value and
consequence taken out of it.

In this view I think we may suppose the poet as representing his heir's
answer to be—

" An estate that has been exhaust-
" ed and weakened—exossatus, boned
" as it were, by such expence as you
" propose, is not so near—non adeo
" juxta est—i. e. so near my heart,
" so much an object of my concern,
" as to make it worth my while to
" interfere about it, or attempt to
" hinder this last expence of your
" dole to the mob, when the first of
" the hundred pair of gladiators, l.
" 48, will bone it—i. e. diminish
" its substance and value, sufficiently
" to render me very unconcerned as
" to being your heir." We often use
the word near, to express what concerns us.

This appears to me to be the most
eligible construction of the words, as
well as most naturally to introduce
what follows.

Exossatus ager juxta est. Age, si mihi nulla
Jam reliqua ex amitis; patruelis nulla; proneptis
Nulla manet; patrui sterilis matertera vixit;
Deque aviâ nihilum superest: accedo Bovillas,   55
Clivumque ad Virbî; præsto est mihi Manius hæres.
' Progenies terræ'—Quære ex me, quis mihi quartus
Sit pater; haud prompte, dicam tamen. Adde etiam unum,
Unum etiam: terræ est jam filius: et mihi ritu
Manius hic generis, prope major avunculus exit.   60
Qui prior es, cur me in decursu lampada poscas?
Sum tibi Mercurius: venio deus huc ego, ut ille
Pingitur. An renuis? vin' tu gaudere relictis?
' Deest aliquid summæ.' Minui mihi: sed tibi totum est,

52. " *Go to*—"] Says Persius—
very well, take your own way—think
as you please, I am not in the least
fear of finding an heir, though I
should not have a relation left in the
world.

53. " *My aunts.*"] Amita is the
aunt by the father's side—the father's
sister.

—" *Cousin-german.*"] Patruelis—
a father's brother's son or daughter.

—" *Niece's daughter.*"] So proneptis signifies.

54. " *The aunt of my uncle.*"]—
Matertera—matris soror—an aunt by
the mother's side.

—" *Lived barren.*"] Had no children.

55. " *Grandmother.*"] Avia, the
wife of the avus, or grandfather.

Persius means, that if he had no
relation, either near or distant, be
should find an heir who would be glad
of his estate.

—" *I go to Bovillæ.*"] A town in
the Appian way, about eleven miles
from Rome, so called from an ox
which broke loose from an altar, and
was there taken: it was near Aricia,
a noted place for beggars, the high-
way being very public.

*Dignus Aricinus qui mendicaret ad
axes.* See JUV. sat. iv. l. 115.

56. " *The hill of Virbius.*"] An
hill about four miles from Rome; so
called from Hippolytus, who was
named Virbius, and worshipped there,
on account of his living 'twice—inter
viros bis. See Æn. vii. 761-77. This
hill, too, was always filled with beg-

gars, who took their stands by the
road-side.

—" *Manius is ready.*" &c.] Manius is the name of some beggar, and
so put for any; the first which he
met with would immediately be glad
to be his heir. Præsto—ready at hand.

57. " *An offspring of earth*"—]
What, says the other, would you take
such a low base-born fellow as that,
whose family nobody knows any thing
about, a mere son of earth, to be your
heir?

—" *Inquire of me,*" &c.] As for
that, replies Persius, if you were to
ask me who was my great grandfather's father, who stood in the
fourth degree from my father, I could
not very readily inform you. But go
a step higher, add one, and then add
then add another, I could give you no
account at all; I then must come to
a son of earth, nobody knows who,
but somebody that, like the rest of
mankind, sprung from the earth.

Empedocles, and some other philosophers, held that mankind originally
sprang from the earth.

59-60. " *By the course of kindred,*" &c.] Perhaps, in this way of
reckoning, as the earth is our common mother, Manius may appear to
be my relation, my great uncle for
ought I know, or not very far from
it; for as children of one common
parent, we must be related.

61. " *You who are before,*" &c.]
This line is allegorical, and alludes to
a festival at Athens, instituted in honour of Vulcan, or of Prometheus,

" Say you, is not so fertile"—" Go to, if none to me
" Now were left of my aunts, no cousin-german, no niece's
" daughter
" Remains; the aunt of my uncle has lived barren,
" And nothing remains from my grandmother: I go to
" Bovillæ,   55
" And to the hill of Virbius; Manius is ready at hand to
" be my heir"—
" An offspring of earth"—" Inquire of me, who my fourth
" father
" May be, I should nevertheless not readily say. Add
" also one,
" Again one; he is now a son of earth: and to me, by the
" course
" Of kindred, this Manius comes forth almost my great
" uncle.   60
" You who are before, why do you require from me the
" torch in the race?
" I am to thee Mercury: I a god come hither, as he
" Is painted. Do you refuse?—Will you rejoice in what
" is left?
" There is wanting something of the sum:" " I have di-
" minished it for myself,

where a race was run by young men
with lighted torches in their hands,
and they strove who could arrive first
at the end of the race without extin-
guishing his torch. If the foremost
in the race tired as he was running,
he gave up the race, and delivered his
torch to the second; the second, if
he tired, delivered it to the third,
and so on, till the race was over.—
The victory was his who carried the
torch lighted to the end of the race.

Now, says Persius, to his presump-
tive heir, who appears to be more advanced in life, why do you, who are
before me in the race of life, i. e. are
older than I am, want what I have
before the course is over, i. e. before
I die, since, in the course of nature,
the oldest may die first? I ought
therefore to expect your estate instead of your expecting mine. It is
the first in the torch-race that, if he
fails, gives the torch to the second,
not the second to the first. See
AINSW. Lampas, ad fin.

62. " I am to thee Mercury."] Do

not look on me as thy nearest kinsman, on thyself as my certain heir,
and on my estate as what ought to
come to you by right; but rather
look on me as the god Mercury, who
is the bestower of unlooked-for and
fortuitous gain.

62-3. " As he is painted."] Mercury, as the god of fortuitous gain,
was painted with a bag of money in
his hand. Hercules was the god of
hidden treasures. See sat. ii. 11, and
note. Mercury presided over open
gain and traffic, and all unexpected
advantages arising therefrom.

63. " Do you refuse?"] Are not
you willing to look upon me in this
light, and to accept what I may leave,
as merely adventitious?

——— An magis excors
Rejectâ predâ, quam præsens Mer-
      curius fert?
      HOR. lib. ii. sat. iii. l. 67, 8.
—" Will you rejoice in what is
left?"] Will you thankfully and joyfully take what I leave?
   64. " There is wanting something,"

Quicquid id est. Ubi sit, fuge quærere, quod mihi quon-
   dam   65
Legârat Tadius, neu dicta repone paterna :
' Fœnoris accedat merces ; hinc exime sumptus.'
' Quid reliquum est ?' reliquum ? Nunc, nunc impensius
   unge,
Unge, puer, caules. Mihi, festâ luce, coquatur
Urtica, et fissâ fumosum sinciput aure.   70
   ' Vende animam lucro ; mercare ; atque excute soler'
' Omne latus mundi : ne sit præstantior alter
' Cappadocas rigidâ pingues plausisse catastâ.
' Rem duplica.' ' Feci.—Jam triplex ; jam mihi quarto,

&c.] But methinks you grumble, and find fault that a part of the estate has been spent.

—" Diminished it for myself."]— Well, suppose my estate to be less than it was, I, that had the right so to do, spent the part of it that is gone upon myself and my own concerns.

65. " But you have the whole," &c.] But you have all at my decease, whatever that all may be ; you could have no right to any part while I was alive ; so that you have no right to complain, when what I leave comes whole and entire to you.

—" Avoid to ask," &c.] Do not offer to inquire what I have done with the legacy which my friend Tadius left me, or to bring me to an account concerning that, or any thing else.

66. " Paternal sayings."] Nor think of laying down to me, as a rule, the lesson that old covetous fathers inculcate to their sons, whom they wish to make as sordid as themselves. Perhaps repone may here be rightly translated retort (comp. Juv. sat. I. l. 1, and note).—q. d. Do not cast this in my teeth.

67. " Let the gains of usury," &c.] q. d. " Put your money out to usury, " and live upon the interest which " you make, reserving the principal " entire :" let me hear none of this, says Persius, as if I were bound to live on the interest of what I have, that the principal may come to you.

68. " What is the residue ?"]— Well, but though I may not call you

to an account about your expences, yet let me ask you how much, after all, may be left for me to inherit.

—" The residue !"] Says Persius, with indignation ; since you can ask such a question, as if you meant to bind me down to leave you a certain sum, you shall have nothing, I will spend away as fast as I can.

—" Now, now more expensively," &c.] " Here," says Persius, " slave, " bring me oil, pour it more pro- " fusely over my dish of pot-herbs. " Now I see that your avarice leads " you to be more concerned about " what I am to leave, than you are " about my comfort while I live, or " for my friendship and regard, I " will even spend away faster than " ever."

70. " A nettle."] Shall I, even upon feast-days when even the poor live better, content myself with having a nettle cooked for my dinner ? i. e. any vile worthless weed.

—" And a smoky hog's cheek."]— An old rusty hog's cheek, with an hole made in the ear by the string which passed through it to hang it up the chimney.

Sinciput—the fore-part, or perhaps one half of the head ; also a hog's cheek. See Juv. sat. xiii. l. 85, and note.

Here it is put for any vile and cheap eatable.

71. " Sell your life for gain."]— Persius having pretty largely set forth how he should treat his supposed heir, who presumed to interfere with his manner of living, or with the dis-

" But you have the whole, whatever that is : avoid to ask
  " where that is which.   65
" Tadius formerly left me, nor lay down paternal say-
  " ings—
" Let the gains of usury accede; hence take out your ex-
  " pence."
" What is the residue ?"—" the residue !—Now—now—
  " more expensively anoint,
" Anoint, boy, the pot-herbs. Shall there be for me on a
  " festival-day boiled
" A nettle, and a smoky hog's cheek with a cracked ear. 70
  " Sell your life for gain ; buy, and, cunning, search
" Every side of the world : let not another exceed you
" In applauding fat Cappadocians in a rigid cage.
" Double your estate :—" I have done it :—Now three-
  " fold, now to me the fourth time,

posal of his fortune while alive ; and
all this in answer to what the miser
had said, on not daring to sell any
part of his estate in order to relieve
his shipwrecked friend, for fear his
heir should resent it after his decease
(see l. 33–7.) now concludes the Satire
with some ironical advice to the miser, in which he shews that the demands of avarice are insatiable.

  If, after all I have said, you still
persist in laying up riches, and hoarding for those who are to come after
you, even take your course, and see
what will be the end of it ; or rather
you will see no end of it, for neither
you, nor your heir, will ever be satisfied. However, sell your life and all
the comforts of it—i. e. expose it to
every difficulty and danger : in short,
take all occasions to make money, let
the risk be what it may. See sat. v.
l. 133–6. Epitrope.

  71. " Buy."] Purchase whatever
will turn to profit.
  —" Cunning."] Shrewd, dextrous,
in your dealings.
  71–2. " Search every side of the
world."] Sail to every part of the
world, that you may find new articles
of merchandize.
  72. " Let not another exceed," &c.]
Make yourself thorough master of the
slave-trade, that you may know how
to bring slaves to market, and to
commend and set them off to the

best advantage. Plausisse—literally,
to have clapped with the hand. It
was customary for the mangones, or
those who dealt in slaves, to put them
into a sort of cage, called catasta, in
the forum, or market-place, where the
buyers might see them : to whom
the owners commended them for their
health, strength, and fitness for the
business for which they wanted them ;
also they clapped or slapped their
bodies with their hands, to shew the
hardness and firmness of their flesh.
The slaves had fetters on ; therefore
the poet says—rigid catasta. They
had arts to pamper them, to make
them look sleek and fat ; they also
painted them to set them off, as to
their complexion and countenance :
hence the slave-dealers were called
mangones. See AINSW. Mango.
  73. " Fat Cappadocians."] Cap-
padocia was a large country in the
Lesser Asia, famous for horses, mules,
and slaves. It has been before observed, that the slaves, when imported for sale, were pampered to
make them appear sleek and fat—
or perhaps we may understand, by
pingues, here, that the Cappadocians
were naturally more plump and lusty
than others.
  74. " Double your estate."] i. e.
By the interest which you make.
  —" I have done it."] That, says
the miser, I have already done.

' Jam decies redit in rugam. Depunge ubi sistam,   75
' Inventus, Chrysippe, tui finitor acervi !'

75. " *Ten times it returns into a
fold.*"] *i. e.* It is now tenfold. Metaph. from garments, which, the
fuller they are, the more folds they
make : hence duplex, from duo, two,
and plico, to fold—triplex, from tres,
and plico, &c. So the verbs, du-
plico, to double, to make two-fold—
triplico, &c. Ruga, Gr. ρυτις a ρυω
—i. e. ιρυω, traho, quod ruga cus-
tim aut vestem in plicas contrahat.
See Ainsw.

—" *Mark down.*" &c.] Depunge
—metaph. from marking points on a
balance, at which the needle, or beam,
stopping, gave the exact weight.

The miser, finding his desires increase, as his riches increase, knows
not where to stop :

   *Crescit amor nummi quantum ipsa
    pecunia crescit.*

         Juv. sat. xiv. l. 139.

76. " *O Chrysippus,*" &c.] A
Stoic philosopher, a disciple of Zeno,
or, according to others, of Cleanthes.
He was the inventor of the argument,
or vicious syllogism, called sorites,
from Gr. σωρος, an heap, it consist-

ing of a great number of propositions
heaped one upon the other, so that
there was hardly any end to be found
—A proper emblem of covetous desire, which is continually increasing.

Persius calls Chrysippus, inventus
finitor, the only finisher, that was
found, of his own heap—because he
investigated the method of putting
an end to the propositions, or questions, in that mode of argument,
and wrote four books on the subject.

This the poet may be supposed to
be deriding in this place, as in truth
an impossible thing, Chrysippus himself having devised no better expe-
dient, than to state only a certain
number of propositions, and then to
be silent. But this would not do, he
might be forced on, ad infinitum, by
a question on what he said last. See
Cic. Acad. Qu. lib. ii. 29.

Marshall reads this line :

" *Inventor, Chrysippe, tui, et fini-
    tor acervi.*"

" Sic legas meo periculo," says he,
" sensu multo concinniore."

O Chrysippus ! thou that couldst

" Now ten times it returns into a fold; mark down where I
      " shall stop,   75
" O Chrysippus, the found finisher of your own heap."

Invent, and set bounds to thy increasing sorites, teach me to set bounds to my increasing avarice. Iron. The miser is supposed to be wearied out with the insatiableness of his avaricious desires, and longs to see an end put to them—but in vain.

Having now finished my work, which, like the sorites of Chrysippus, has, from the variety and redundancy of the matter, been so long increasing under my hands, much beyond what I at first expected, I should hope that the Reader, so far from blaming the length of the performance, will approve the particularity, and even minuteness, of the observations, which I have made on the preceding Satires of Juvenal and Persius, as on all hands they are allowed to be the most difficult of the Latin writers; therefore mere cursory remarks, here and there scattered on particular passages, would assist the Reader but little, in giving him a complete and consistent view of the whole; to this end every separate part should be explained, that it may be well understood and properly arranged within the mind: this, I trust, will stand as an apology for the length of these papers, which, wherever they may find their way, will be attended with the Editor's best wishes, that they may carry those solid and weighty instructions to the mind, which it is the business of our two Satirists to recommend—Delectando pariterque monendo.

However Persius may be deemed inferior to Juvenal as-a-poet, yet he is his equal as a moralist; and as to the honesty and sincerity with which he wrote—" There is a spirit of sin-" cerity," says Mr. Dryden, " in all " he says—in this he is equal to Ju-" venal, who was as honest and " serious as Persius, and more he " could not be."

I have observed, in several parts of the foregoing notes on Persius, his imitations of Horace—The reader may see the whole of these accurately collected, and observed upon—CASAUB. Persiana Horatii Imitatio, at the end of his Commentaries on the Satires.

$\dfrac{1}{D}$

415224

L.C - D.

6802 - 57

Pitts.

Lightning Source UK Ltd.
Milton Keynes UK
UKHW021934160519
342790UK00003B/579/P